Introduction to Child Development

Joseph T. Lawton
University of Wisconsin at Madison

wcb

Wm. C. Brown Company Publishers
Dubuque, Iowa

wcb group

Wm. C. Brown
Chairman of the Board

Mark C. Falb
Executive Vice President

wcb

Wm. C. Brown Company Publishers

College Division

Lawrence E. Cremer
President

Raymond C. Deveaux
Vice President, Product Development

David Wm. Smith
Vice President, Marketing

David A. Corona
Assistant Vice President, Production Development and Design

Marcia H. Stout
Marketing Manager

Janis M. Machala
Director of Marketing Research

William A. Moss
Production Editorial Manager

Marilyn A. Phelps
Manager of Design

Book Team

James L. Romig
Senior Editor

Susan J. Soley
Associate Developmental Editor

Joyce S. Oberhausen
Production Editor

Anthony L. Saizon
Designer

Michael F. Meyer
Design Layout Assistant

Mary M. Heller
Visual Research Editor

Copyright 1982 by Wm. C. Brown Company Publishers

Library of Congress Catalog Card Number: 81-69389

ISBN: 0-697-06642-8

Printed in the United States of America

Cover photo by Bob Coyle

Photo credits:
Part 1 © Julie O'Neil
Part 2 © Chuck Isaacs
Part 3 © Julie O'Neil
Part 4 © Richard L. Good
Part 5 © Paul Conklin
Part 6 © Peter Karas

*To Sarah, my mother, for her love
and support in my childhood; to
Pauline, my wife, for her love and
support; and to our children, Sarah,
John, Gerard, Matthew, and Andrew.*

Contents

Birth and Infancy 2 43

Adolescence 5 521

Preface

The purpose of *Child Development and Learning* is twofold. First, it provides a thorough, up-to-date commentary on physical, intellectual, and social development from conception through adolescence, including historical and contemporary viewpoints of major theoreticians in these areas. Each chapter combines discussions of theory, research, and application to show, as far as possible, important relationships among the establishment of theory, the basic and applied research associated with theory, and the possible applications of information from research to the real-world problems of rearing children. We now know more than ever before about such important aspects of child development and learning as early attachment of infants to care givers, intervention programs for infants who fail to thrive, the effects of impoverished environments, the effects of day care; and how children grow up in different cultures. We are not so convinced as we were a decade ago that children from middle- and upper middle-class environments are doing as well as they might. Although great advances have been made in our understanding of child development, information in certain areas is still quite limited, and expert opinions differ on many important issues. For this reason, whenever necessary and appropriate, discussion is provided on such controversial issues as the nature and implications of early attachment, the effects of early deprivation, "stage" development, the importance of educational programs, and identity crises of adolescence.

Second, this book discusses various viewpoints on the process of *learning* and identifies important relationships between development and learning. The discussion of learning has been highlighted in chapters 7 and 10. However, references to learning—the distinction that can be made between learning and development and important relationships between the two—are made throughout most of the chapters of this book. Unfortunately, I believe, it has been traditional in child development texts to focus on *development* without sufficient recognition of the various aspects of learning. Yet the relationship between development and learning has long been a controversial issue. Some theorists have treated development and learning as being synonymous; others have described development in terms of learning; still others have clearly distinguished between the two while, at the same time, pointing to important relationships between them. In paying particular attention to learning, one cannot avoid mentioning *instruction*. In my opinion, the importance of instruction should also be highlighted since researchers have given much attention in recent years to the question of whether children's development can be improved in important ways by careful instructional programs or whether children's potential for solving problems can only be fully realized through careful instruction as a necessary complement to the advantages gained from development.

Students can use this book at many levels. My main intention is to present the major theories of child development and learning by describing major ideas and concepts in detail. For the student coming to the subject for the first time, this book should be a helpful introduction because of its broad sampling of research and writing. The book should also appeal to more advanced students because of its comparisons of research findings and presentations of different viewpoints on major issues.

The basic organizational structure of the book is chronological. It covers the phases of development and learning from conception, birth, and infancy on through the preschool years, middle (or elementary school) years, and adolescence. Major topics on physical, intellectual, and social development and the processes of learning and instruction are traced through each of these four phases. The text includes such topics as the cognitive structuralist's view of intellectual and moral development; the behaviorist's view of cumulative learning; the implication of imitation for social development; the influence of peers, parents, and teachers on children's behavior; and the development of such aspects of personality as aggression, self-concept, and sex role. Concepts first met in the opening chapters will have become "old friends" by the time the reader reaches the final chapters. The relationships among development, learning, and instruction are carried through each part of the text, and special attention is given to instruction and learning in the preschool and middle years.

The first part of Chapter 1, "The Science of Child Development," introduces general ideas about child development and learning from various viewpoints, which are treated in detail in subsequent chapters. Reading carefully through this first chapter will give you a general understanding of the major concepts that you can progressively fill in with finer details as you continue through the book. The second part of Chapter 1 describes how research is organized in a scientific manner. This should provide you with an understanding of how scientific the study of children's behavior has become over the past one hundred years and help you realize that the most carefully organized research has limitations in the "basic" information it provides. We need to treat the results of experiments tentatively—taking care not to jump to conclusions about how and why children behave in certain ways—to compare information from various sources, and to keep in mind that there is still much to be learned about child development and learning.

In the last chapter, abnormal development is discussed. Many children have physical and mental handicaps that need careful diagnosis and treatment. If you intend to be a practitioner working with children in families, schools, or hospitals, you will undoubtedly meet many children with various types of handicaps. These may include such physical defects as visual or hearing impairment, or spina bifida, or such mental handicaps as Downs syndrome, autism, or schizophrenia. It is no longer unusual to meet such children integrated into groups of normal children since it has become the practice in recent years to encourage families, whenever possible, to take care of their disabled children in the home and "mainstream" them with normal children in school rather than send them to special institutions.

Learning Aids

A number of learning aids have also been included in *Child Development and Learning.* Chapter 1, for example, contains a list of ten questions about each theory of development and learning. These questions are accompanied by examples of how you can use them. It is important to refer to these questions while reading through the text because they serve as reminders of important issues. The questions are summarized in Table 1.3 for easy reference. Also at the end of Part 1 you will find two other tables that will be useful for reference as you read through various sections of the text. Table 1.1 lists the major theories of child development and learning, the theorists who best represent each theory, and a brief description of key concepts in each theory. Table 1.2 provides a summary comparison of changes in children's behavior as they are described by the theorists mentioned in Table 1.1. Information in Table 1.2 is organized according to three questions: "What kind of change?" "What influences change?" and "What gets changed?" Other tables with detailed, summarized information appear throughout the text as aids to the study of particular phases of child development and learning. These tables are also intended for repeated use, to help guide the initial learning of concepts and to summarize and organize comprehensive segments of information.

At the beginning of each chapter is a list of *key concepts* around which the chapter content is organized. Watch for explanations of these concepts as you read the chapter, and use the list as a memory aid.

Insets are another learning aid used in each chapter. They include detailed discussions of specific issues or related research.

Each chapter ends with a detailed *summary* of the main points of the chapter, which you can use as a study guide and an aid to review. Following the summary you will find a list of *questions for review,* a section that also includes suggestions for practical assignments. Following the review questions is a list of *suggested readings* that will guide you to a more in-depth study of topics.

At the end of the book is a detailed *glossary* of key terms. The glossary is followed by a *reference section* and separate author and subject *indexes.* These, too, may be used as study guides and reference aids when you are following up on particular topics or issues or looking for certain information.

Supplementary Aids

The study guide for *Introduction to Child Development* has been carefully designed to provide a useful study and review aid. The study guide is organized to correspond to the chapter in the text. Each chapter in the study guide begins with a list of learning objectives and key terms. This is followed by a programmed review, a series of sentence-completion exercises with correct answers presented to the right of each exercise. A self-test, composed of three multiple-choice examinations, provides important practice for objective test items that may be used on tests in class. Also a short series of thought questions are given to assist in preparation for essay tests.

An instructor's manual is also available for instructors using *Child Development and Learning*. This manual summarizes the main points of each chapter and includes an extensive list of test questions.

Using the Text in Various Ways

This book has been written for use in a one-semester course. However, it can also be used for shorter courses. For example, a course in "Development in Infancy and Early Childhood" can be organized around chapters 2–6 and 8. A course in "Intellectual and Social Development" can be organized around chapters 4–6, 8, 9, and 11–13. And a course in "Intellectual Development and Learning" can be organized around chapters 4, 6, 7, 9, 10, and 12.

Acknowledgments

I would like to express my thanks to the people who helped in various ways with the production of this book. The following reviewers provided constructive criticism, suggestions for revision, references and "applause" where they thought it was due, all of which I found both helpful and encouraging: Gene H. Brody, University of Georgia; Diane C. Draper, Iowa State University; James M. Gingles, Washington State University; Marilyn Milligan, Santa Rosa Junior College; Steven J. Pollock, Moorpark College; Maria Nieves Toms, St. Petersburg Junior College; Mary Knox Weir, Long Beach City College; Carol Witherell, University of Santa Clara; and Ruth L. Wynn, Syracuse University.

Special thanks are due to Diane Draper, University of Wisconsin, who provided detailed critiques and suggestions for revision for most of the chapters. Margaret Stevenson, University of Wisconsin, read every chapter of the second draft, and her suggestions for revision and pointers for additional, useful information were most helpful at that stage of the development of the text. She also used a selection of chapters in her course on child development. In providing an indication of how this book would be received by students taking an introductory course in child development, feedback in the shape of chapter reviews by a number of students proved to be very valuable. Tom Mancuso completed a very professional first editing of the second draft of each chapter and helped immeasurably with Chapter 1. I value not only his editing skills but the direction and support he gave me in our frequent phone discussions.

A special thanks is due to Marjorie Pfeifer who typed two drafts of the entire book and kept me on schedule. I am also grateful to my other typists, Alice Hanselman and Teri Romig, who prepared final versions of a number of chapters in a concerted effort to meet deadlines for turnover of the manuscript. Jim Romig and Susan Soley of Wm. C. Brown Company Publishers also deserve a special mention. Jim's advice on chapter reorganization was invaluable. Susan's efforts in helping me pull together and organize manuscript materials is greatly appreciated.

I am very grateful to my wife Pauline for her continuing encouragement as I wrote this book, and to my children for their keen interest and their "quiet" support. I forgive them for *sharing* the multitude of pencils we used up between us.

An Introduction

The Science of Child Development

1

The scientific approach has one characteristic that no other method of attaining knowledge has: self-correction. Even if a hypothesis seems to be supported in an experiment, the scientist will test alternative hypotheses that, if supported, may cast doubts on the first hypothesis. The important relationship between the scientific approach and theory is this; there is nothing more practical than a good theory in guiding the scientist. But the ultimate aim of the scientific approach is the establishment of general laws—or theory, if you will.

Adapted from Kerlinger, F. N., *Foundations of Behavioral Research*, 1964.

Everyone is familiar with the phenomenon of change. As we watch ourselves grow up and our parents age, we realize that our bodies change all our lives. Getting taller, stronger, and more coordinated are physical changes happening continuously during growth. Our interests change, too. Having a bike of our own or a radio may be most important when we are 10; but when we are 15 or 16, it is often boyfriends or girlfriends that are most important. Being in college and preparing for a particular career that suits our interests may take up most of our time and energy. Our emotional interests change in this way as we get older and discover more about who we are as individuals. In school we consciously concern ourselves with changing and improving our intellectual abilities, although we may forget while we are struggling with algebra that elementary multiplication used to be just as hard to learn. If we look around ourselves, we can also see our relationships changing. We find ourselves less and less dependent on our parents; and the issues we discuss and work out with them change accordingly—from staying up past 8 P.M. to what portion of our education we will pay for. Over the years our relationships with friends become more important, and our social lives begin to give us the security and encouragement our family life used to give us. Perhaps we notice from observations we share with friends in conversation that we all go through very similar changes—physical, intellectual, emotional, and social.

There are, in fact, patterns to the changes we experience. The more closely we look at these changes and their patterns, the more we can learn about our human nature, about how to rear children with the most benefit to them, and about how to teach them most effectively. In the process of careful observation, we can also learn something about the sources of change. Some changes such as physical development are inevitable because they are part of the process of growing older. For example, changes in the physical appearance and functioning of the body that occur at puberty come from the process of maturing—**maturation**. Other changes attributed to maturation include an increased ability to concentrate for long periods of time and improvements in the ability to consider other persons' points of view. Some changes seem to come about by the various experiences children have and the environments they grow up in. If, for example, parents give a child security and stimulation, that experience critically influences a child's intellectual and emotional growth. Lack of such experiences can retard a child's growth. To a degree, growing up in Manhattan will give one child different social skills and interests from another child who is growing up in Columbus, Ohio. We can learn, if we look closely enough, what role individual differences, in addition to the effects of maturation and environment, play in the changes children go through. One child may have a talent for music; another may find learning by intuition easier than learning by logic; another child may be learning in English when that child's first language is Spanish. In the end, looking at and studying the duration and variations of child development can teach us a great deal about the idea of development itself.

As people grow older they develop physically, intellectually, socially, and emotionally. (Photos by David A. Corona)

The Science of Child Development   **5**

In this chapter we will look at the pattern of changes we call development, the role science has in giving us our understanding of development, and the major theories that constitute our current understanding of what child development is. We will then go on to discuss the relationship between development and learning, and the relationship between family and development. Finally, we will introduce the basic procedures of research into child development.

Concept of Development

We have already said that development concerns change, that there are different areas of change (physical, intellectual, emotional, and social), and that there are different sources of change (maturation, experience, the environment, and individuality). Could we be more exact and come to a definition of development—in particular, child development?

We can start by examining the word *development*, which we see often enough. In photography to develop means to make the image visible by a chemical treatment. In music to develop means to unfold a theme by working out its various possibilities in rhythm and sound. In both cases there is the sense of something's fulfilling its possibilities. Even contractors who develop land or body builders who develop their muscles share the basic meaning of development: to evolve the possibilities.

To continue to define child development we will have to say more than we have so far about the patterns of change we observe in ourselves, our partners, our friends. We know people our age tend to share the same interests, have similar learning experiences, and even have similar physical concerns. Each age tends to have its own dominant issues and experiences and, for the most part, they get more complex over time. That is part of the pattern of change. No doubt we have observed that most people go through the same sequence of basic interests and experiences as they move through life from infancy (0–3 years) to preschool age (3–5 years) to middle childhood (5–11/12 years) to adolescence (12–18/19 years) to adulthood (20 years to old age). Those changes that fall into a fixed or one-way sequence of stages are a kind of universal path everyone follows. *Child development* is the universal sequence or pattern of physical, intellectual, emotional, and social changes occurring as a person passes from birth to adulthood, evolving the possibilities provided by maturation, experience, the environment, and individuality.

Child development is not concerned with the universal changes that occur in adulthood and old age. Those changes continue the pattern of changes we have discovered during "childhood" because the pattern goes on through the life span. For the sake of efficiency, however, we arbitrarily stop our discussion of child development with adolescence, which is the convention in psychology. Also, by definition child development is not concerned directly with abnormal development, that is, with changes so extreme or rare that they are not part of the universal path. Dwarfism, genius, or children raised without human contact are not a central part of the study of child development although they tell us a lot about normal development by their contrast.

In this text you will have the chance to examine each phase of child development. Four of the parts that follow cover the four chronological phases: Part 2, "Birth and Infancy"; Part 3, "The Preschool Years"; Part 4, "The Middle Years"; and Part 5, "Adolescence." In each of these parts separate chapters discuss development in terms of four areas of change—physical, intellectual, social, and personality development. Emotional changes, such an important part of our life, are discussed as part of personality development. Although we may choose to study each area of change individually, we know that in real life they are interdependent and in interaction with one another. We also know that, although these changes are shared by human beings, each individual experiences them in a unique way. Other chapters of the text are concerned with the important issues of learning and instruction and their relationship with development. Part 6, the final chapter of the text, is devoted to abnormal development.

Role of Science

Our understanding of child development is derived from close, careful observation of children's behavior, from the first moments of infancy to the close of adolescence. By observation, we are choosing a certain way of *learning* and knowing about our subject. We are choosing a way of knowing general truths by examining systematically all the particulars of what we observe—in other words, we are choosing science.

There are many other ways of knowing. Knowing how to skate backwards without thinking about it is kinesthetic knowledge. Knowing what an abstract painting means is artistic knowledge. Knowing a friend is emotional or intuitive knowledge. Knowing religious truths is knowledge by faith. All of these ways of knowing are subjective; they come from within, from personal judgments or impressions. We know from our experience that subjective knowledge is very valuable. The value of science, however, is that it can be objective. By using science, we can arrive at generalizations about the outside (observable) world that turn out to be true time after time and that people commonly accept. This is the role that science plays in the study of child development.

Science works cumulatively through discovery and verification. Using *scientific research*, a researcher (1) formulates a specific question to investigate, (2) collects relevant information on the question, (3) proposes a tentative answer based on the results of collected observations, and (4) then tests the answer with further observation to check its veracity. When successive research leads to the same answer, the answer becomes a generalization with the status of an axiom. Other researchers run their own tests to verify the results obtained in previous investigations, which provides an important double check on the veracity of results from research. In some cases researchers, satisfied with the accuracy of answers from observation and testing, relate the results of current research with those from past research. In this way large systems or assemblies of results are constructed into theories. Gradually, proven answers built on top of one another create a knowledge that is reasonably exact, logical, and comprehensive, although it will always need updating with the latest discoveries from research. Careful research on children's behavior conducted over lengthy periods of time has provided us with theories that both describe development and offer some explanation of how it occurs.

Major Theories of Development

The science of child development is approximately 100 years old. Many discoveries have been made and many are still being made. As the process of discovery and cumulative understanding goes on, different theories cover different areas of study, some theories overlap, and some disagree in places. In this section we will examine the earliest theories of child development and then go on to the current major theories. Afterwards we will compare the theories and discuss how to learn from both what they hold in common and what they hold in dispute.

Early Theories

Two theories that inspired quite different ideas about development were those of Locke (1632–1704) and Rousseau (1712–1778). Locke described the child's mind as being like a blank sheet of paper, a *tabula rasa*. What the child comes to know, and what will determine the child's behavior, results from learning and experience, but what the child comes to know is first of all out there in the environment. In other words, the environment "writes on the sheet of paper, determining what the child experiences and how the child will act."

Rousseau did not hold that the child's mind was waiting to be shaped by the environment. He believed that children think and feel differently from adults. From Rousseau's point of view, development is governed by "nature's plan," occurring partly from within (**maturation**) and partly as a result of the child's interactions with the environment. He argued that children should be free to explore their environment, develop their own capabilities, and learn in their own ways.

Rousseau described four stages of development: infancy, childhood, late childhood, and adolescence. He believed that these stages unfold in an unvarying sequence controlled by age and growth. According to nature's plan, various aspects of development "flower" during critical periods. Parents, in tune with nature, will be permissive in the sense that they will concentrate on providing opportunities for desirable development. According to Rousseau, the best child-rearing practice is to encourage learning by discovery. He said, "Let him [the child] know nothing because you have told him, but because he has learned it for himself" (Rousseau, 1948, p. 131).

Whereas Locke emphasized the influence of the external environment on development, Rousseau believed that there was an internal growth factor controlling the rate of development. Locke placed responsibility for the child's learning and development primarily on the shoulders of adults plus the effects of environmental stimuli. Adults are to direct the child in what, how, and when to learn. On the other hand, Rousseau insisted that children be left free to pursue their own learning; that adults should set some limits and encourage the child, but they should not attempt to determine what and how the child is to learn. These original opposing views still exist today in various forms and degrees in modern theories of development.

Modern Theories

The principles of Locke's theory can be found, in a more advanced form, in present-day environmentalist theories. These theories of people such as Skinner (1904–) and Gagné (1916–) are known as *environmentalist* because of the importance they attribute, just as Locke's theory did, to what the child learns from the environment as being crucial for development. The principles of Rousseau are represented in *cognitive-structuralist* theories such as those of Piaget (1896–1980) and Kohlberg (1927–). The term **cognitive structuralist** comes from the fact that these theorists believe that a child in the process of knowing (cognition) not only takes in but also interprets and organizes experiences of the environment into structures of knowledge and then stores these structures in memory to be referred to in understanding the world. In addition to the environmentalist and cognitive-structuralist schools, there is a third school of thinking in the contemporary study of child development. The theories of this school are called *psychoanalytical* or *psychodynamic* because they emphasize the influence of emotions on the child's learning and thinking—how the origins and dynamics of feelings affect knowledge and behavior. (In Greek mythology the young woman Psyche personified the Soul and her name came to represent a person's soul, both mind and emotions.) Freud (1856–1939) and Erikson (1902–) have presented psychoanalytical theories of child development.

This text explores these three major perspectives of development—the environmentalist, cognitive structuralist, and psychoanalytic, each represented by a number of theorists. We will briefly examine the themes of each of the three perspectives to give you a general picture of the psychology of child development before going into the details. Now is a good time to become familiar with Table 1.1 and Table 1.2 at the end of Part 1. Although these tables present more information than you need right now, you will find them useful to refer to periodically throughout the study of this text.

The environmentalist view.   An important environmentalist assumption is that all development and learning result from **stimulation** from the environment. The emphasis is upon a continuous process of learning whereby the child learns the structure and organization of the environment. The child's behavior changes to reflect the environment; thus the environment can be said to shape gradually the child's behavior (Skinner, 1953). What is the process of learning from this viewpoint, and how does it occur?

Environmentalists believe that a child's thoughts and feelings develop through **association,** that is, through one experience being linked in memory to another. For example, a young child may link in memory the suspense and happiness of opening Christmas presents with the scent of pine from the Christmas tree. Years later, hiking adventures in the pine woods may be attractive to the child partly because the scent of pine trees suggests suspense and happiness. Environmentalists also believe that all kinds of behavior such as writing, riding a bicycle,

and counting develop through practice. In other words repetition of behavior is important for learning. Learning can also occur through **imitation**. A child learns to behave in ways similar to the ways people familiar to him or her behave, especially parents. Finally, environmentalists believe that a child will learn behavior that brings praise or reward by **positive reinforcement** and refrain from behavior that results in **punishment**. Bandura, an environmentalist who believes that much of social learning can be attributed to imitation, has this to say about the relationship of imitation to reward:

Imitation is likely to bring the rewards the child is seeking. Through the repeated association of imitative behavior with reward, the child becomes motivated to behave like the parent. In other words, imitative behavior becomes rewarding in itself (Bandura & Walters, 1959, pp. 253–254).

The cognitive-structuralist view. Cognitive structuralists such as Piaget hold that human beings interact with the environment to construct knowledge of themselves and the world they live in (Langer, 1969, p. 87). This is a more active, more participatory view of development than that of the environmentalists. Cognitive structuralists believe—again, in disagreement with the environmentalists—that association as well as imitation, repetition, and reward are insufficient to explain some of the complex behavior that children acquire. They believe that knowledge and knowing depend on an active attempt to make sense out of experiences with objects and events in the environment. For example, when a child sees some colored plastic shapes of different sizes and arranges them into groups according to color, shape, and size, two things occur. First, the child recognizes that the objects have different colors, shapes, and sizes. Such knowledge can be learned from instruction. A parent may have told the child the names for different colors, shapes, and sizes while pointing at all kinds of objects. Words such as *red, round,* and *big* have been invented by our culture, and the cognitive structuralists would agree that they can be taught directly to the child (it is possible, by the way, for a child to recognize differences in the properties of objects without necessarily having words to signify them). Second, and more importantly, the child arranges the objects into groups according to properties that they have and some of them share. Knowing how to organize the objects in this way exists in the child's mind—not in the environment. In the opinion of cognitive structuralists, it is better that the child actively construct such knowledge through self-exploration and discovery.

According to the cognitive-structuralist view, therefore, a child derives from experiences of the environment structured ways of knowing that are useful in interpreting and organizing further experiences and that also act as a vehicle for storing information in memory. These structured ways of knowing, then, become an intermediate step in acquiring new knowledge. For example, an infant may experience the game of "peekaboo" with a parent hiding behind various objects, such as hands, a towel at bath time, or a pillow, and then reappearing. The parent may encourage the infant to take the part of the person who is hiding. This first experience is likely to be a simple imitation of the parent's hiding behind hands. But if the peekaboo situations are varied, the infant can construct an understanding of "hiding" from them and use this knowledge to eventually play the game with other people by using many ways of hiding. Cognitive structuralists believe that this happens because the child has created a structure for the action of hiding from the various experiences of hiding and can refer to this structure despite changing circumstances in the environment.

Cognitive structuralists maintain that a child has a biological tendency to adapt to the environment. They believe, as Rousseau did, that development prodded by age and growth occurs in a sequence of stages, each different from the rest but unfolding from previous stages. They hold that the cognitive structures that the child uses vary with the stage of development and that, therefore, change is discontinuous, not continuous as environmentalists believe. For example, at first an infant reflexively grasps at any object that touches its hand. At this stage an innate reflex is the only cognitive structure the child can use. When the infant is older, it uses the capabilities of a different stage; it may combine reaching and grasping in one action in order to possess a ball. At this stage the structure is more complicated; it now includes organization and intention. Out of the knowledge constructed at the first stage, the child reconstructs new, more comprehensive structures during subsequent stages of development (Piaget, 1967).

Lawrence Kohlberg. Moral reasoning develops in stages influenced by the child's level of intellectual development. (Photo from Wide World Photos)

Sigmund Freud. Father of the psychoanalytical theory of development. (Photo from United Press International)

Very briefly, it should be added that cognitive structuralists believe that moral reasoning also develops in stages (e.g., Kohlberg, 1963) and that it is influenced by the child's level of intellectual development.

The psychoanalytical view. The psychoanalytical view maintains that children (and adults, too) are basically irrational rather than rational. These theorists believe that biological, social, emotional, and sexual issues and behavior play a more important part in personality and development than do intellectual issues and behavior. In analyzing development they give importance *both* to environment and to stages of growth. This is clear from their conception of development as a process of learning to coordinate the inner world of desires with the outer world of reality. Inner and outer worlds are given equal importance. "Inner laws" provide the potential to interact with the environment, and the developmental process results from this interaction in separate stages of growth. Each stage has its own concerns and unfolds from the previous one. However, in all cases interaction with the environment has a transforming effect on personality. If development proceeds along the most advantageous path, unconscious instincts are transformed by conscious rational efforts into behavior that fulfills desires.

At first the infant is self-absorbed in instincts such as sucking, grasping, and eliminating body wastes. How parents react to these needs and how they help the child achieve and meet them will greatly influence the child's understandings, expectations, and approach to the external world. For example, a 1-year-old infant driven by irrational, instinctive appetites might try to use temper tantrums to control its environment and to fulfill its desires. If the parents respond by giving in to each tantrum in order to keep their child pacified at all times, the child will learn that outbursts of anger are an effective means to fulfill desire and that desire can be fulfilled almost all the time. If, on the other hand, the parents do not respond to tantrums and instead guide the child to more realistic methods of fulfilling desire, such as the child's expressing more clearly what he or she wants and facing more realistically what is necessary to achieve it, then the child will learn that taking time to know and express clearly what he or she wants is an effective means of fulfilling desire. At other ages other issues will come up; instead of self-gratification and control, the issues may be initiative versus guilt. Different psychoanalytical theorists describe the stages somewhat differently, but the belief in stages and the importance of environment are held in common.

Comparing Theories

It can be expected that each of us will react somewhat differently to the various views of child development. Because of differences in previous training and experience, one person might be very dissatisfied with a theory that another person finds attractive. Some people find it difficult to explain why they find themselves believing more in one theory than in another, and there will be those who are attracted to particular aspects of a number of theories. To help you compare the theories presented in this text, here are ten questions to ask about each theory. (They are based on questions suggested by Thomas, 1979, p. 29.)[1]

Question 1: What is the range of development described by the theory? In other words, what ages from conception (or birth) does it cover?
Piaget, for example, describes development as occurring between infancy and the end of adolescence or early adulthood. In contrast, Skinner, in his theory (an environmentalist view) describes development as a process that continues from birth through old age.

Question 2: How is development described?
Piaget describes development principally in terms of structured ways of acquiring knowledge through interaction with the environment, ways controlled by maturation. Environmentalists describe development in terms of cumulative rather than structured processes of learning knowledge from the environment. They do not describe development as limited by maturation.

Question 3: According to the theory, how are the changes of development expected to occur?
Piaget tells us, as Rousseau did, that development occurs in "stages." Structures of knowledge a child has at one stage of development, such as infancy, are different from those that develop during subsequent stages. However, each successive stage of development emerges out of the preceding stage. The sequence

1. *Source:* Thomas, R. M. *Comparing Theories of Child Development.* Copyright © 1979 by Wadsworth Publishing Company, Inc., Belmont, California. Reprinted by permission of Wadsworth Publishing Company.

of stages is invariant—a child cannot skip a stage. Freud's psychoanalytical theory is also built around the idea that development occurs in an invariant sequence of stages controlled by maturation. On the other hand environmentalists such as Skinner believe that the changes of development (described as learning) are cumulative and continuous, without stages to make them discontinuous. Much of what a child knows at 10, for example, is similar to (although more advanced than) what he or she knew at 3 or 5 years of age.

Question 4: According to the theory, what factors influence the course of development?
The cognitive-structuralist view is that maturation controls the pace of development, and the child's interaction with the environment determines the quality and extent of development. For example, a child cannot learn to ride a bicycle until he or she has reached a certain stage of physical coordination. In addition a child who lives in a deprived environment may never develop socially or intellectually beyond a certain stage. Erikson's psychoanalytical view of development agrees with the cognitive-structuralist view about one factor: the stage sequence of social development unfolds according to certain "inner laws" (maturation). But Erikson's view differs also. He places more emphasis on another factor, the instructional role of the environment (culture) in ensuring that the child learn to behave in socially appropriate ways. Skinner says that the course of development is primarily in the hands of the environment and that it can be shaped by such factors as reward, punishment, and carefully sequenced instruction.

Question 5: To what extent does heredity contribute to development and to what extent does environment contribute to development?
The environmentalist view is that heredity plays less of a role in development than environmental factors such as instruction. Freud, a psychoanalyst, places an emphasis on instinctual, inherited ways of behaving that continue to play a role in development even when children's behavior becomes modified by the influence of the external world.

Question 6: Which areas of development (physical, intellectual, social, and emotional) does the theory describe?
Environmentalist theories cover all areas of development because they tend to see no distinction in how different areas develop. The way in which a child learns a skill such as reading is very much the same as the way in which the child learns social behavior such as cooperation or sharing. Piaget's cognitive-structuralist theory refers primarily to intellectual development, physical knowledge (knowledge about the physical properties of objects), and, to a lesser degree, social knowledge (for example, moral reasoning), but it does not actually describe physical development. Erikson's psychoanalytical theory covers social and emotional development. Although Erickson insists that social and intellectual development are integrated, he does not describe intellectual development. Neither Piaget nor Erikson discusses in any detail the interaction of the areas each covers, although other theorists have attempted to do so.

Question 7: Does the theory account for individual differences in development?

Most theories account for individual differences such as inherited intelligence, cultural upbringing, and experiences that they claim affect development to a greater or lesser degree. In his theory of development Piaget, for example, makes the assumption that within a narrow range of individual differences children develop in much the same way. The pace at which individuals pass through the sequence of stages of development may differ, but the eventual outcome is about the same for all of them. Environmentalists account for differences in the rate, quality, and extent of development in terms of individual differences in experience and the differential effects of diverse environments. From this point of view we can expect a greater range in the quality and extent of individual development.

Question 8: Does the theory describe development and learning as synonymous or does it distinguish between development and learning?

Environmentalists consider development and learning to be synonymous because all behavior is learned from the environment. Cognitive structuralists distinguish between development (resulting from active or participatory interaction with the environment and controlled by maturation) and learning (knowledge provided by the environment). For these theorists development almost always facilitates learning. Only in those instances when a child has almost completed developmentally a new way of knowing is it expected that an organized learning experience will, as it were, tip the balance in the right direction. There are also theorists who believe that there should frequently be an important interaction between development (as a natural and spontaneous occurring process) and learning (as an environmentally controlled and structured process). Indeed, some go so far as to say that learning can significantly influence the course of development and, even more extremely, that without careful instruction and related learning, a child is not likely to achieve much of the potential for development.

Question 9: What special terminology does the theory use?

All theories tend to have their own special terminology. This creates something of a problem when we are learning about theories of development and learning. We need to familiarize ourselves with the terminology of a theory so that we will better understand the theory and eventually realize that although different theories use different terminology, they are sometimes describing very similar features of development. Environmentalists use the term *association* to describe how one piece of knowledge is linked to another in memory. Piaget uses the terms **assimilation** and **accommodation** to describe how a child organizes structures of knowledge. Ausubel (a learning theorist with both cognitive-structuralist and environmentalist views) also uses the term *assimilation* to describe the process whereby a child learns to relate new knowledge to previously learned knowledge. Piaget, Freud, Erikson, and Ausubel all use the term *stage* to describe a sequence of development. There are both differences and similarities in the way they use this term. Each of the theories has special terms, printed in italics and explained in detail in the chapters of this text. You can also find important special terms in figures and in an alphabetized list of special terms in a glossary at the end of the text.

Question 10: Does the theory distinguish between normal and abnormal development?

Freud and Erikson are both careful to distinguish normal, healthy development from abnormal development. Most theories, however, describe normal development without any reference to abnormal development. Because of this absence of any reference to abnormal development in the theories mentioned in this text, Part 6 deals specifically with this subject.

As you can see from the sample of answers to the ten questions, a comparison of theories makes much clearer the concerns and limits of each theory. As you read more about the theories presented in the rest of this text, you will find it worthwhile to refer occasionally to this set of questions in order to clarify and organize what you are learning. To make it easier for you to use these questions later, they are summarized in Table 1.3 at the end of Part 1.

Relationship Between Development and Learning

In one of the questions we used to compare theories of development—question 8—we asked: Does the theory distinguish between development and learning? We are going to examine this particular question in greater depth because it will help you to understand more clearly the orientation of this text and, at the same time, it will give you a chance to investigate for yourself the extent of the similarities and differences between development and learning.

Some of the theories mentioned so far make no distinction between development and learning because they presume that changes are entirely the result of either one or the other. For the cognitive structuralist the emphasis is on development. This view holds that as the child both matures and interacts with the environment he or she develops special skills to make sense out of diverse experiences. For example, the infant begins to understand the world by interacting with objects and events; by touching and moving objects; by being fed at regular intervals and acquiring expectations that the person who provides food can be trusted; by sensing such properties of objects as roughness, smoothness, hardness, and softness, and of people as warmth, comfort, and security. Because of maturing abilities, the older child makes sense out of the myriad objects in the environment by, for example, arranging together those that share some property—some animals are cats, some objects are round, tricycles can be used for riding, mothers are women but not all women are mothers. Classifying objects makes it easier to think about them—their appearance, function, and use. In this description you will notice that the emergence of such changes result from maturation and experience interacting with the environment. In this way the child develops intellectually, socially, and emotionally. Sometimes the process of interacting with the environment is called learning, but the meaning of "learning" for these theorists is virtually the same as development. Even when the child is guided in interacting with the environment by parents, teachers, and other adults, this view emphasizes the importance of the construction of knowledge by the child—not by the adult to "give" to the child to be learned. It is assumed that the child is disposed to develop in this fashion, though it is also considered important to provide encouragement, guidance, and an environment that will help the child achieve normal development.

Skinner and other environmentalists believe that changes result from a process of cumulative learning. In other words, change is influenced primarily by the environment, that what the child may come to know already exists in the environment. For example, there have evolved ways of arranging objects in the world to better understand their physical and functional properties and how we can use them to our advantage. The responsibility of a culture is to instruct its children about knowledge that already exists about which children may learn and understand. This condition does not preclude invention, but history persuades us that few people in a culture are inventors. Looking back over your own education, you will realize that in our Western society it is considered very important to teach children, beginning at an early age, skills in language, number, writing, science, music, art, and literature—culture. Therefore, according to this view it is important for the child to learn knowledge that already exists in the environment. Environmentalists would say that a child's behavior is changed through having an appropriate behavior rewarded, by associating some new knowledge with something already known, or by imitating someone else's behavior. Learning is a life-long process—each child's knowledge is the sum of what he or she has learned over a period of time. Learning is considered the measure of a child's development. It is expected that children will learn in different ways depending on individual experiences, differences in the environment they grow up in, temperament, and the fact that not all children appear to possess the same capabilities for learning. As you can see, theorists who see change in behavior exclusively one way fall into these two extreme positions of being either cognitive structuralists or environmentalists. These positions resemble the poles that separated the early theorists Locke and Rousseau.

Some theorists, however, attribute change not to one or the other but to both development and learning. Ausubel (1963), Bruner (Bruner, Olver, & Greenfield, 1966), and Montessori (1964) clearly distinguish between development and learning. Each of them describes development in cognitive-structuralist terms (with Ausubel and Bruner being influenced by Piaget's thinking). For example, they suggest that a period of time must elapse and certain physical changes occur before an infant begins to walk; infants first make cooing noises and then make

babbling noises before they begin to talk; most adolescents solve all the problems 7- or 8-year-olds can solve, but not many young children solve some of the problems most adolescents can solve. And each of the three theorists presents learning as a process separate from—though related to—development. Each acknowledges that to a certain extent learning is restrained by the child's level of development. All three also agree that learning can influence the course of development. Bruner puts it this way, "Experience has shown that it is worth the effort to provide the growing child with problems that tempt him into the next stages of development" (Bruner, 1960, p. 39).

Each theorist has a unique view of how learning occurs, and yet all agree that the child is helped in learning about the world by the way in which the world is already structured. For example, a very young child soon learns that there are some animals called cats, some called dogs, and, in fact, that there are many kinds of animals, with each group of animals looking alike in some way and sharing a name. To a certain extent a child learns about animals from personal experiences and his or her own readiness to learn. To some extent, however, a child is helped by adults who answer all those "What is it?" questions, who explain and question in return, and who help a young child in various instructional ways to better understand the world. Guidance and help from parents and teachers offer a child an interaction with the environment and a learning from the environment, which in turn augments development significantly. In this example we have considered intellectual development, but Ausubel, Bruner, and Montessori find the same important interaction between learning and development in the other areas of development.

Because of the importance these three theorists give to learning, they believe it is the responsibility of parents and teachers to instruct children in the values of the culture in which they live and to teach the skills of thinking and reasoning. Parents and teachers provide ideas about how to organize learning. Although each theorist recognizes the importance of the child's own autonomous learning, they all insist that whatever the child's potential for learning happens to be it can only be realized and influenced with careful guidance and instruction from trained teachers; "tools" created by the culture such as language; and the organization and transmission of knowledge through books, TV, and other media.

As you can see, the environment is important in all three views of the relationship between development and learning. A child cannot develop without an environment to interact with, and the quality of interactions is at least partly determined by the richness of the environment; nor can learning occur without some direction from the environment; nor can there be a combination of development and learning without the environment as a common ally.

Relationship Between Family and Development

In recent years there has been increasing research in the role that the family plays in child development. In order to give you a brief overview of this area, we will describe in general the ways in which families influence children's development.

Even before a baby is born its physical well-being depends to a large extent on the mother's physical condition: whether she is well or suffering from some disease; whether she drinks alcohol, smokes, or takes drugs; and how old she is. The age of the father at the time of a baby's conception can also have an effect on physical development. It appears that there are changes in the structure of the genes of both parents as they age; some of these changes may lead to physical and mental abnormalities in the baby.

Parents prepare for a baby long before the birth. They have expectations for the baby's sex, physical appearance, and future development; and they also have expectations of the role they will play as parents. After the birth of the baby parents also have expectations for how the baby will behave. Parents respond differently to babies depending on whether the babies are active or passive, responsive or unresponsive, and boys or girls. Particular interest has been given in recent research to possible differences in the ways mothers and fathers rear their children. It has been observed, for example, that fathers develop a distinctive way of playing with their newborn irrespective of whether the baby is a boy or a girl. Fathers tend to spend much time in rough and tumble play; mothers stress playing with toys with their infants. It has also been observed that mothers and fathers are equally competent in providing care for their infants—although it is also true that many fathers still apparently believe that it is the mother who should provide care.

Not only do parents give care to their babies, babies soon learn to respond to parents. Relationships become reciprocal, and a baby can have a most important effect on parents' behavior. The quality of these interactions will have a crucial effect on an infant's physical, intellectual, and social development. For example, a baby whose parents provide affection will develop a secure attachment to the parents, which is important for normal development. High levels of intellectual and social competencies will almost certainly develop in infants who have many opportunities to interact with parents in such activities as mutual gazing at one another, cooing and babbling at and with parents, parents talking to infants and infants later talking with parents, and often engaging in stimulating, playful activities. Such interactions between infants and parents are important for the development of a child's positive self-image and self-control over an aggressive desire to explore the environment and strive for autonomy.

Parents adopt different styles of *parenting* that have different effects on children's personality development. For example, parents may be consistently loving, provide firm control over their children's behavior by reasonable rules, share decisions about social behavior, and indicate reasonable expectations about their children's achievements; or parents can be distant in their relationships with their children, inconsistent in their expectations about behavior, and use physical punishment. The first style of parenting is much more likely to produce a child who has a good self-image and who is confident, determined, and a high achiever. In general, infants and older children learn to see themselves as parents see them.

During the preschool years in particular the family has a strong influence on children's social development. At least from the learning theorists' point of view, much of children's social behavior can be attributed to their imitation of parents. Imitation is more strongly reinforced by parents who are affectionate and caring and who exert strong control over their children's behavior. During these years parents can also function as teachers. A great deal of interest has been shown over the past several years in the role of the parent as educator. This is especially true with respect to the special education provided preschool children from deprived environments. For example, when parents of children in special educational programs are trained to help in their children's education, there is more improvement in intellectual and social behavior than when this job is left solely to professional teachers.

These are just some of the ways in which parents influence their children physically, socially, emotionally, and intellectually and in which parents are influenced by their children. In later chapters we will discuss these and other aspects of family influences on child development in greater detail.

Research into Child Development

Theories of child development emerge from researchers' observation of children. Although observation of children has been going on for thousands of years, it is only during the past 100 years that a systematic (that is, organized and regularized) approach for studying children has emerged. This study of child development and behavior is based on a number of important scientific principles. We described some of these principles earlier when we introduced the role of science. We described science as a way of knowing abstract general truths by examining systematically concrete particulars. We should add here that scientific examination involves taking precise measurements of all types of factors (size, time, and so on) and also classifying information (grouping information according to some common trait). We also pointed out the objective and cumulative nature of scientific discoveries and outlined the basic steps of the scientific method. In this section we will describe the process of research more thoroughly in order to give you a clear idea of how the information you are reading in this book came to be.

Whether in a laboratory or not, all research follows the scientific method in order to obtain objective, verifiable results. Researchers investigate or perform experiments in order to discover and interpret facts, build or update a theory, or apply a theory in some practical way. The general goal of scientific research into child development is to create a description of development that is reliable enough to predict, in general, how children develop.

Formulating a Specific Question to Investigate

A researcher usually begins with an area of interest and then narrows it down to something specific to investigate. Jerome Kagan (1972) was curious about the intellectual development of infants. He narrowed this area of interest toward a main idea. From his observation of infants, he began to suspect that the amount of visual attention infants give to objects affects their intellectual development—more time spent looking at objects seemed to evoke greater understanding of objects. Here was the main idea. If Kagan could establish this idea and determine what features of objects attract infants to look at objects, then parents could aid infants' intellectual development by providing them with visually stimulating objects. All of this, however, could not be investigated at the same time. Kagan narrowed down the idea still further to this question: What arrangement of objects will infants spend more time looking at?

Collecting Relevant Information on the Question

The next step is to review the scientific literature by looking up the topic in reference works or by having a computerized search made of research journals. An investigator wants to find out what results other investigators have obtained (if any) about the aspect of development to be studied and its related areas.

After this review of past research, the researcher must collect relevant information through observation. This step involves the **organization** of the process of observation in order to ensure that the information is relevant to the question. The researcher can organize by basic research designs. The investigator considers the pros and cons of each one in light of the research objectives and also time and money constraints. Four basic designs are clinical, interview, experimental, and correlational.

Clinical design.   Using this design, the investigator combines careful observations of children's behavior with individualized questioning. However, questions are not standardized. Although the questioning of each child might be aimed at eliciting similar information, the questions may be worded quite differently and be associated with different objects and events. Piaget used this method. **Clinical research** can provide important descriptive information about children's behavior. However, results obtained by this method will eventually require further support from other types of research.

Interview design.   No doubt you are familiar with the concept of a poll. A *poll* uses questions to establish people's beliefs, opinions, attitudes, and so on regarding some preferences; for example, a presidential candidate, how to bring up children, a good washing detergent, a favorite TV show.

Interview research uses more in-depth questioning to find out, for example, what types of parenting behaviors parents use, what they believe about their children, or their attitudes toward child rearing (e.g., Sears, Maccoby, & Levin, 1957). Questions used in polls and surveys are standardized. That is, each person is asked the same set of questions, worded in precisely the same way. This method provides an in-depth, broad picture. As an initial way of obtaining information, the method can prove very useful.

Experimental design.   The Kagan study of an infant's perception of objects is an example of **experimental research**. Studies using this method change the child's environment in some way, and the effects of this change on the child's behavior are then measured. "Basic" experimental research is more controlled than "applied" experimental research. In the first case the investigator carefully sets up a "laboratory" environment in which only selected factors are carefully manipulated and, as far as possible, all other factors that might also influence the behavior being observed are excluded. You will remember that Kagan was interested in what arrangement of objects infants will spend more time looking at. He imagined that changes in the arrangement of objects infants look at might increase the amount of time they spend looking at them. Infants were first shown

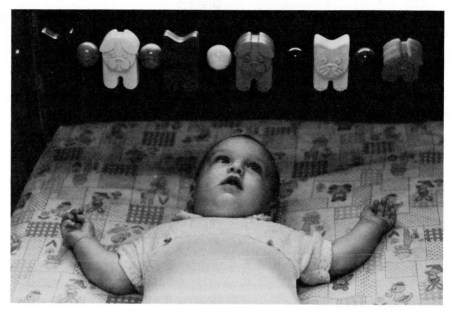

an arrangement of three colored geometric shapes in a "mobile" for 12 half-minute viewings. Their span of attention, as measured by the amount of time spent looking at the mobile, was recorded. Some of the infants' mothers were provided with mobiles, others were not. At home, for 30 minutes a day for three weeks, some infants saw the same arrangement of shapes they had originally viewed; others saw mobiles that differed from the original either slightly, moderately, or greatly. In this way the arrangement of shapes in the mobile was manipulated.

After three weeks Kagan again showed the infants the original arrangement of objects in the mobile, measured the span of attention, and recorded the changes in attention between the first and second viewing. He discovered that infants who had seen the moderately changed mobile at home paid the most attention.

When Kagan showed the infants the test mobile for the first and second viewings, the laboratory setting was very controlled. When the mothers of the infants showed them mobiles at home, the "laboratory setting" of the home could not be so carefully controlled. For example, some mothers may have provided encouragement and rewards to their babies, others may not have.

Applied experimental research uses the child's natural environment. Although in these settings a number of uncontrolled factors might influence the child's behavior to some extent, there are advantages to be gained from this type of research. In many training studies, for example, the investigator might hope to apply the results to the organization of school programs. It is better to use a natural classroom setting than an artificial laboratory setting. Whether the investigator chooses a basic or applied research setting will depend in large measure on the objectives of the research. The important feature of experimental studies is that they impose a condition on subjects by the manipulation of particular factors that are expected to produce some change in children's behavior. Therefore, in experimental research possible cause-and-effects relationships are examined.

Correlational design.   In a **correlational research** study by Scarr and Salapatek (1970), one of the questions asked was, "Is there any relationship between the development of infant's fears and locomotion?" Infants were between 2- and 23-months-old, and their fear of falling over a "cliff," of strangers, of separation from mother, of a jack-in-the-box, of a mechanical dog, of masks, and of a loud noise was measured according to whether they showed *no* fear, were sober and cautious, or fretted, cried, or fled to mother. Their stage of locomotion, from lying or sitting in one place to walking, was also measured. No attempt was made to manipulate the environment to cause a change in behavior. Each fear score was correlated with the locomotion score. It was found, for example, that less experience with creeping was related to greater fear of the cliff, the jack-in-the-box, and loud noise. Less experience with walking was related to greater fear of the cliff, jack-in-the-box, dog, and masks. From the results of this study it cannot be said that less experience with creeping or walking causes fear—only that it is related to fear.

A *correlation* is a relationship or correspondence between two factors such as stage of locomotion and fear of strangers. Correlations describe patterns of relationships, not cause-and-effect relationships.

A *positive* correlation means that two factors are changing in the same direction. For example, as the child's experience of walking increases, so does his or her lack of fear increase. The opposite is also true. A *negative* correlation means that two factors are changing in opposite directions. Although it was not the case, Scarr and Salapatek might have found that as experience of walking increased, lack of fear decreased (children became more afraid).

The actual degree or strength of a relationship between two factors can be measured. A perfect, positive correlation receives a score of $+1.0$. For the examples described above, a maximum score in "experience with walking" related to a maximum score on the fear scale (indicating complete lack of fear) would result in a correlation of $+1.0$; a maximum score in experience with walking related to a minimum score on the fear scale (indicating greatest evidence of

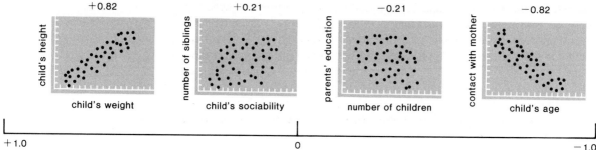

Figure 1.1 Correlation graphs. Examples of four scatter-diagrams illustrating hypothetical correlations between two variables in each case. The dots in each scatter-diagram total to the number of subjects tested or observed. The correlation between children's height and weight is positive, indicating that increases in height generally correspond to increases in weight. The correlation between contact with mother and children's age is negative, indicating that high values on one variable (say, contact with mother) are related to low values on the other variable (children's age). (Source: Adapted from Vasta, R. *An Introduction to Research Methods: Studying Children.* W. H. Freeman and Co. Copyright © 1979. W. H. Freeman and Company. Reprinted with permission.)

fear) would result in a correlation score of −1.0. A relationship can decrease from +1.0 through no relationship 0.0 to a negative relationship −1.0 (or vice versa). Strong and weak positive and negative correlations are illustrated in Figure 1.1.

Variables.   The design should clearly identify the factors to be investigated—more often referred to as **variables.** Variables are of two types, independent and dependent. An *independent variable* is considered to be the cause of a *dependent variable*, the presumed effect. In experimental research the investigator varies or manipulates the independent variables. In the Kagan study the independent variable was the arrangement of objects since the objects in the mobile could be altered to produce different arrangements. In correlational research it is the change of or varying together of two or more variables that is measured. It is important to remember that any measure of change (a correlation score) does not imply that changes in one variable caused the changes in another variable.

Sample.   When investigating relationships between variables, the investigator will have in mind a large group of persons (subjects) to which the questions refer. The entire group of subjects is called a **population**. Usually, the investigator cannot deal with all the subjects in a population. A group of subjects, representative of the population, is carefully selected. This smaller group of subjects is called a **sample**. One method used to select a representative sample of a population is to pick at random from the population the number of subjects required.

In the Kagan study a sample of 4-month-old infants was chosen from a population of infants. Although it was *not* the case, if Kagan had decided that the sample should include infant boys and girls from high and low socioeconomic social groups, then he would have selected equal numbers of boy and girl infants from both high and low socioeconomic groups to ensure that each of these independent variables was controlled in order not to bias the results. What do the results from a study's sample tell us about the population? If one group of 4-month-old infants views objects in a particular way, can we suppose *all* infants aged 4 months will do likewise? The investigator never makes this claim. What can be claimed if the sample is reasonably representative is that it is not unlikely that 4-month-old infants, generally, will view objects in ways very similar to those in the sample. Follow-up studies with samples from the same population may be drawn in different areas to check the generalizability of results. (These are called *replication* studies. They should follow the organization and implementation of the original study as carefully as possible.) Since it is unlikely that any individual study can include all the variables considered to be important, a series of related studies might be conducted by one or more investigators in order to include multiple variables.

Treatment groups.   For some experiments investigators might wish to test the effects of changes in independent variables or the effects of training. Each change in an independent variable will require a separate group of subjects (keeping groups *matched* according to the dependent variable, or variables). The Kagan study (1972, p. 76) had five **treatment groups**. They were:

Treatment group	Age	Treatment
E1	4 months	original arrangement of shapes
E2	4 months	arrangement slightly changed
E3	4 months	arrangement moderately changed
E4	4 months	arrangement greatly changed
Control	4 months	*no* mobile

Children in a control group are in all respects just like the children in the experimental groups, but they do not receive the experimental treatment. The importance of the **control group** is to ensure that one or more of the treatments did result in a change in behavior.

Proposing a hypothesis.   At the outset of a research project the researcher proposes a **research hypothesis** (which can be in the form of a question) that states a relationship between two or more factors (variables). For example, with respect to Kagan's study, our hypothesis might be stated as infants who are shown arrangements of objects that are moderately changed (discrepant) from an arrangement previously viewed will pay more attention to the original arrangement at a second viewing (adapted from Kagan, 1972, p. 76). An alternative to stating a hypothesis in this way is to ask a question such as, "Do *moderate* changes in objects result in infants' paying more attention to looking at them?" The hypothesis or question should clearly identify the variables to be tested.

Testing the Hypothesis

There are two basic ways of obtaining information in order to test a hypothesis and check its veracity. *Data*, factual information used as evidence, can be collected through longitudinal study or cross-sectional study.

The longitudinal study.   By its very name, the **longitudinal study** method suggests studying children across a long period of time. The length of time can actually vary from a few weeks to a number of years. In the Scarr and Salapatek study of the development of patterns of fear (1970), 34 infants from the original sample of 91 infants were tested after a 2-month interval from their first visit, to examine the stability of fear over time. Scores from the first and second times of testing were correlated, and the results showed a strong relationship of levels of fear at these two times of testing. In this study it can be safely assumed that infants who were initially afraid of a particular stimulus remained fearful of that stimulus two months later.

A longitudinal study has both advantages and disadvantages. The strongest point in favor of this approach is that the same children can be studied over a period of time. Changes in behavior can be assessed at different times, which should provide some indication of development that can certainly be attributed to the same children. However, it is not unusual to lose children from a longitudinal study. Some children may be sick for a few weeks, families may move away from the area, or lose interest and withdraw their children from the study. It then becomes a question of whether the remainder of the sample following dropouts is similar to the beginning sample. If it is not, we cannot have much confidence in the longitudinal results from what, in effect, has become a different sample. Another disadvantage is that longitudinal studies are time consuming and usually expensive.

The cross-sectional study. Measurement of the effects of a single variable or a number of independent variables on some dependent variable can be made by comparing samples of subjects who are similar according to one characteristic but who differ in other respects. This is called a **cross-sectional study**. For example, Kagan and Klein (1977) investigated the stage and rate of children's physical and intellectual development in Guatemalan and United States cultures. They selected groups of children of different ages and tested them—all at one time. This type of study could also be called cross-cultural. By including children of differing ages, Kagan was attempting to estimate physical and behavioral changes across time, and by including children from different cultures, how universal development appeared to be.

The advantages of this approach are that data can be collected over a short period of time, thus reducing the possibility of children's dropping out, and the cost of the research. What are the disadvantages? For example, if different groups of children aged 2, 5, 7, 10, and 15 years are tested at one time in order to provide a measure of intellectual behavior at different stages of development, it can only be assumed that the younger children will behave like the older children when they achieve that age. It is not quite the same thing as following 2-year-old children, testing them at ages 2, 5, 7, 10, and 15, and we cannot be so sure about the results from cross-sectional testing compared to those from longitudinal testing.

The cross-sectional/longitudinal study. Both cross-sectional and longitudinal (especially short-term longitudinal) approaches can be usefully combined. Suppose you wanted to find out to what extent locomotion experience affects 10- to 20-month-old infants' fear of various objects over a period of time. Infants do a lot of crawling between the ages of 10 and 15 months, and many walk confidently alone from about the age of 15 months. You might decide to provide lots of various crawling and walking experiences, but you do not wish to spend the time following a group of infants for 10 months. Instead you decide to select two experimental groups, one with infants aged 10 months, the other with infants aged 15 months. You also select control groups for each starting age. At the first time of testing, you measure locomotion and level of fear for the 10- and 15-month-old infants. Five months later you test the 10-month-olds now aged 15 months, and the 15-month-olds now aged 20 months. In the 5 months between times of testing, the experimental children get special crawling and walking experiences, but the control children do not. The length of time taken to complete the study has been reduced by 5 months.

Ethics of Research

When using children in experiments, researchers must abide by certain ethical principles to guide their research so that no harm comes to the children. Consider the following example of an intervention study by White and Held (1966) to facilitate infants' competencies by providing an enriched environment. The enriched environment was enjoyed by infants in the experimental group. For a period of time, infants in the control group were not provided the enriched environment enjoyed by the experimental infants. Is the withholding of experiences considered important in moving developmentally delayed children in the direction of normal development justified? This is a complicated question. We must avoid turning it into a "catch-22" situation. For example, research sometimes may be harmful to children, but if research is not conducted, we may never discover the best environments for children to grow up in. The question has been raised (e.g., Bandura & McDonald, 1963), "Does aggression on TV or in films produce aggressive behavior in children?" In one study children who had been shown a live or filmed adult model behaving aggressively toward a doll were later observed imitating the model's behavior. The possible effects of observed aggression or violence on children's behavior, however, is still a burning question. It is considered important to conduct such studies. However, whatever the research project, every means should be taken to reduce risk to children. Investigators who come into contact with children during a study should make the children's well-being their first priority.

Various agencies and committees have suggested guidelines for conducting research. A set of ethical principles drawn up by the American Psychological Association Committee on Ethical Standards in Psychological Research is outlined in Inset 1.1.

This set of principles clearly states the investigator's responsibilities toward participants in a research project. With young children, parents also have a responsibility in deciding whether their children should participate. It is up to the investigator to ensure that parents are informed about the research and the ways in which their children will be involved.

Before research with children can be conducted, it is necessary for the investigator to gain permission both from parents (or guardians) and a research proposal evaluation committee. These committees carefully study what will happen to the children included in the research. They require the investigator to show that within reason children will not be placed at risk physically, mentally, socially, or morally. A copy of a letter asking parents' permission for their children to be a part of a study must also be sent to these committees. Parents, of course, have a right to refuse such requests, or to withdraw their children from a research project at any time.

In 1972 the American Psychological Association's Board of Directors appointed an Ad Hoc Committee on Ethical Standards in Psychological Research to formulate a set of ethical principles as a guide for researchers. Principles developed by this committee were as follows.

The Ethical Principles

The decision to undertake research should rest upon a considered judgment by the individual psychologist about how best to contribute to psychological science and to human welfare. The responsible psychologist weighs alternative directions in which personal energies and resources might be invested. Having made the decision to conduct research, psychologists must carry out their investigations with respect for the people who participate and with concern for their dignity and welfare. The Principles that follow make explicit the investigator's ethical responsibilities toward participants over the course of research, from the initial decision to pursue a study to the steps necessary to protect the confidentiality of research data. These Principles should be interpreted in terms of the context provided in the complete document offered as a supplement to these Principles.

1. In planning a study the investigator has the personal responsibility to make a careful evaluation of its ethical acceptability, taking into account these Principles for research with human beings. To the extent that this appraisal, weighing scientific and humane values, suggests a deviation from any Principle, the investigator incurs an increasingly serious obligation to seek ethical advice and to observe more stringent safeguards to protect the rights of the human research participant.

2. Responsibility for the establishment and maintenance of acceptable ethical practice in research always remains with the individual investigator. The investigator is also responsible for the ethical treatment of research participants by collaborators, assistants, students, and employees, all of whom, however, incur parallel obligations.

3. Ethical practice requires the investigator to inform the participant of all features of the research that reasonably might be expected to influence willingness to participate and to explain all other aspects of the research about which the participant inquires. Failure to make full disclosure gives added emphasis to the investigator's responsibility to protect the welfare and dignity of the research participant.

4. Openness and honesty are essential characteristics of the relationship between investigator and research participant. When the methodological requirements of a study necessitate concealment or deception, the investigator is required to ensure the participant's understanding of the reasons for this action and to restore the quality of the relationship with the investigator.

5. Ethical research practice requires the investigator to respect the individual's freedom to decline to participate in research or to discontinue participation at any time. The obligation to protect this freedom requires special vigilance when the investigator is in a position of power over the participant. The decision to limit this freedom increases the investigator's responsibility to protect the participant's dignity and welfare.

6. Ethically acceptable research begins with the establishment of a clear and fair agreement between the investigator and the research participant that clarifies the responsibilities of each. The investigator has the obligation to honor all promises and commitments included in that agreement.

7. The ethical investigator protects participants from physical and mental discomfort, harm, and danger. If the risk of such consequences exists, the investigator is required to inform the participant of that fact, secure consent before proceeding, and take all possible measures to minimize distress. A research procedure may not be used if it is likely to cause serious and lasting harm to participants.

8. After the data are collected, ethical practice requires the investigator to provide the participant with a full clarification of the nature of the study and to remove any misconceptions that may have arisen. Where scientific or humane values justify delaying or withholding information, the investigator acquires a special responsibility to assure that there are no damaging consequences for the participant.

9. Where research procedures may result in undesirable consequences for the participant, the investigator has the responsibility to detect and remove or correct these consequences, including, where relevant, long-term aftereffects.

10. Information obtained about the research participants during the course of an investigation is confidential. When the possibility exists that others may obtain access to such information, ethical research practice requires that this possibility, together with the plans for protecting confidentiality, be explained to the participants as a part of the procedure for obtaining informed consent.

Source: American Psychological Association, *Ethical Principles in the Conduct of Research with Human Participants.* 1973. Reprinted by permission.

Epilogue

We are tempted by the very act of living to guess at how development occurs. Bruner has suggested that any account of development must refer to natural ways of thinking and behaving that seem ordinary and intuitive, to thinking and reasoning that is more precise and formal, and to the nature of culture in which a human being grows.

In our world we face many issues that encourage us to learn more about development. We need, for example, to know more about the natural ways in which attachment occurs during infancy because it appears so important for later normal development. We are surely concerned about how a child's development is affected by living in a deprived environment, by being physically and mentally abused by his or her parents, by being mentally retarded or, for that matter, exceptionally bright, by being born with some physical handicap. More children now than at any previous time are leaving home at age 2 years or younger to attend day-care or preschool. We need to learn what the special needs of these children are. There are many questions people ask about the effects of instruction on the quality of children's thinking and reasoning. The more we learn about the effects of instruction, the more we can aid teachers in improving instruction. And there is greater recognition now of the cultures of minority groups. We need to learn more about the importance of the development of cultural differences.

Even though we now have a better understanding of human development, many important questions are still to be answered. Their importance lies in the fact that our knowledge of development is still quite limited, that we are seeking to alleviate restraints on development, and that we are trying to improve the chances that each child will achieve more completely the potential for development.

How can such objectives be achieved? We must look to the science of child development. As you read the chapters of this book you will come across descriptions of a wide variety of investigations into particular aspects of children's development. They are all examples of carefully conducted research. Some of them can be praised as excellent, reliable research. Yet some of them can be criticized for some weakness in design, for the fact that some important variable was overlooked, or for limitations in the tests used to measure children's behavior or changes in behavior. But this is only to be expected and does not detract from the usefulness of research itself. We should keep in mind that our understanding of development is itself developing, "inched" along by the results of research, and that our methods of research are also in a process of development. We will continue our search because as human beings we are constantly amazed at ourselves, at the complexities of conception, the act of birth, and the child's growth and development toward adulthood. It is in a spirit of lively curiosity and in seeking to expand your understanding of child development that you should read the rest of this book.

Summary

The concept of child development includes physical, intellectual, emotional, social, and moral development. It is easier to chart physical development than any other human characteristic.

Facts about children's development acquired from observing, testing, and recording their behavior are used to construct theories of development. Theories describe and partly explain development and how it changes over time. Theories also lead to the construction of hypotheses about development.

Our understanding of child development comes from the careful work of countless specialists who have both constructed and carefully tested theories about children's behavior. It is only by means of scientific methods of research that theories can be constructed and tested.

Early theorists proposed either that children develop as a result of maturation and interactions with the environment or that the environment completely determines the nature and course of development. From the early theories have emerged three principal views of child development: environmentalist, cognitive structuralist, and psychoanalytic. Environmentalists believe that development is *continuous*. By means of repetition and practice children get better at behaviors that are *reinforced*. Improvement is cumulative, and changes in development are said to be *quantitative*. Cognitive structuralists believe that development is *discontinuous*. Behavior in general develops in an invariant sequence of stages. Behavior at one stage is qualitatively different from that at another. It is necessary to pass through each stage successively, with new behavior at each higher stage incorporating that of lower stages. Psychoanalytic theory sometimes provides a cognitive-structural perspective, at other times an environmentalist view, depending on which period of development is being explained.

Most theorists are not satisfied that any particular theory adequately describes development. This has resulted in the construction of a number of different theories. In order to better understand each theory and the possible relationships among theories, we can ask of each theory a common set of questions that relate to important, general aspects of development.

A number of psychologists have presented theories that clearly distinguish between development and learning but at the same time suggest important relationships between the two. Each acknowledges that to some extent learning is restrained by level of development, but they also suggest that learning can influence the quality and course of development. An important element in a child's development and learning for all these theorists is the "educator," parent or professional teacher. The theorists agree that the child will benefit best from learning that is carefully organized by an expert, although they have different opinions about the teacher's particular role in planning instruction and in choosing a method of instruction.

An important influence on child development is the family. Long before the baby is born, the physical state of the mother can have an effect on the baby. The age of both parents is also an important factor since the structure of the genes that go into forming a baby change as parents grow older, and some changes may lead to abnormal development. The way parents choose to rear their children, the ways children influence their parents' behavior, and the environment the child grows up in all have important influences on development.

Research on child development and learning follows a scientific method. Research begins with a specific question or questions about development or learning that seem(s) worth investigating. The researcher then selects a method for collecting data that will help provide an answer. Four basic designs for research are clinical, interview, experimental, and correlational. The researcher also needs to decide whether a study will be longitudinal, cross-sectional, or a combination of both.

Before beginning a research project the investigator should complete a review of related research, clearly state the hypothesis or research question to be addressed, identify the dependent and independent variables, select a sample of subjects, and if necessary arrange the subjects into treatment groups.

Ethical considerations are a part of organizing research on child development. The investigator must keep in mind the well-being of children who will be subjects in an experiment. Permission to conduct research usually must be obtained from a special committee that reviews research proposals. Careful note is taken of possible risks to children. Parents' permission to include their children in a research project must also be obtained, and parents must be told that they have the option to withdraw their children at any time during the course of an experiment.

Research has resulted in a better understanding of child development, but there is much about this subject that we still do not fully understand. Methods of research are being improved all the time, and we can look forward to a deepening of our knowledge of development and related benefits to children from future research.

Questions for Review

1. Why is the scientific study of children's behavior so important to our understanding of child development?

2. Describe the main features of the three basic theories of child development: psychoanalytic, environmentalist, and cognitive structuralist.

3. Certain environmentalists such as Skinner describe development in terms of learning. What is the process of learning from this viewpoint, and how is it distinguishable from the idea of development as used by cognitive-structuralist theorists such as Piaget?

4. What are the similarities and differences among the theories of Ausubel, Bruner, and Montessori regarding (a) development and (b) learning?

5. What are the relationships among development and learning mentioned by Ausubel, Bruner, and Montessori?

6. Imagine you are an investigator about to organize a research project. Make a checklist of all the important steps you would need to take in conducting your research.

7. Briefly describe the types of research designs and data collection strategies available to an investigator.

8. What are the advantages and disadvantages of longitudinal, cross-sectional, and longitudinal/cross-sectional data collection strategies?

9. Why is it so important to have ethical principles for conducting research?

Suggestions for Further Reading

Adler, M. *A parent's manual: Answers to questions on child development and child rearing.* Springfield, Ill.: Charles C Thomas, 1971. This manual covers topics on psychological, intellectual, and physical development. Includes chapters on general behavior, discipline, and how the family influences development.

Aries, P. *Centuries of childhood.* New York: Knopf, 1962. Describes changing attitudes toward child development and the child within the family from early to modern times.

Bronfenbrenner, U., ed. *Influences on human development.* Hinsdale, IL: Dryden, 1972. Covers a wide variety of topics including early deprivation and the effects of TV on children. Of special interest are the examples of research methods.

Cohen, S., & Cominskey, T. J., eds. *Child development: Contemporary perspectives.* Itasca, IL: F. E. Peacock Publishers, 1977. Includes sections on the roots of development, intelligence, attachment, aggression, and community influences.

Kessen, W. ed. *The child.* New York: Wiley, 1965. A collection of articles by specialists on childhood covering the period from the eighteenth to the twentieth century.

Vasta, R. *Studying children: An introduction to research methods.* San Francisco: W. H. Freeman, 1979. An introductory text dealing with the fundamentals of research in developmental psychology. Provides examples of research from infancy through adolescence.

Table 1.1 Major Theorists of Child Development and Learning

Theory	Theorist	Description of Development and Learning
		Learning
		Development is considered to be synonymous with learning and, depending on the theorist, is attributed to:
Environmentalist	*Pavlov*	1. *Classical conditioning*—stimulus-response learning.
	Skinner	2. *Operant conditioning*—appropriate behavior is reinforced.
	Gagné	3. *Learning hierarchies*—learning proceeds from a relatively simple level of *signal* and *stimulus-response* learning (conditioning) to a complex level of applying principles to the solving of problems
	Bandura	4. *Imitation*—social behavior is learned through the imitation of strong models such as parents.
		Development
	Piaget	*Stage theory* of cognitive development.
	Kohlberg	*Stage theory* of the development of moral reasoning.
		Development and Learning
Cognitive	*Bruner*	Development of enactive (by action) iconic (by image) and symbolic (by abstract sign such as language) ways of *representing* objects and events in the environment. The *cyclic* learning of concepts and strategies for solving problems.
Structuralist	*Montessori*	*Sensitive periods* of development and learning in a *prepared environment*.
	Ausubel	*Stage theory* of cognitive development associated with the learning of *subject matter*. Learning should be organized so as to proceed from the general to the specific.
	Bowlby and Ainsworth	*Parent-child attachment* and its importance for social and cognitive development.
Psychoanalytic	*Freud*	*Psychosexual* personality and social development. Stresses biological factors such as "seeking physical gratification" as determinants of development.
	Erikson	*Psychosocial* personality and social development. Stresses the influence of culture and society on development.

Table 1.2 A Comparison of Changes in Development from Three Major Theoretical Perspectives

Theoretical Perspectives	What Kind of Change?	What Influences Change?	What Gets Changed?
Environmentalist *Skinner* *Bandura*	*Quantitative*—a continuous accumulation of knowledge of objects and events in the environment and of ways of processing information	1. Reflex actions in infancy. 2. Environment strongly influences the process of learning and what is learned.	1. Knowledge of objects and events. 2. Processes of learning and problem-solving skills. 3. Social behavior—which more and more tends to conform to social norms and is shaped through imitation of social models.
Cognitive Structuralist *Piaget* *Kohlberg*	*Qualitative*—a discontinuous process of developing intellectual and social skills. Intellectual and moral reasoning developed at one stage is *different* from but *related* to that which develops at subsequent stages.	*Interaction* between the child and the environment. Changes in thinking and reasoning through interactions is mainly controlled by *maturation*. However, the child will benefit from help given by parents, other adults, and peers.	*Principally,* the child's *ability to reason* about objects and events in the environment which leads to a knowledge of (1) ways of reasoning, (2) the physical world, and (3) the social world.
Bruner *Montessori* *Ausubel*	*Partly qualitative and partly quantitative*—To a certain extent, ways of thinking and reasoning will *differ* as the child grows older. But the older child may also use more efficiently knowledge and ways of thinking and reasoning learned at an earlier age.	Development is partly controlled by maturation but also in large measure by environmental influences such as instruction.	1. The child's ability to think and reason (both qualitatively and quantitatively). 2. The child's ability to represent objects and events—which become increasingly abstract. 3. Subject-matter knowledge and skills for processing information. These changes apply as much to personality and social development as to intellectual development.
Bowlby and Ainsworth	*Mainly qualitative*—Social development is expected to develop in a sequence of stages.	1. Loving, caring parent-child interactions that provide a secure *attachment*. 2. Styles of parenting that influence normal social development.	The child's ability to deal with the social world. At first this depends on a *strong attachment* to parents. This initial attachment forms the basis for later social development. The quality of the parent-child attachment is also expected to influence changes in intellectual development.

Continued

Table 1.2 Continued

Theoretical Perspectives	What Kind of Change?	What Influences Change?	What Gets Changed?
Psychoanalytic *Freud*	*Qualitative*-with some quantitative change. For example, social skills are learned from the child's unique environment and are improved upon over time.	1. Pleasure seeking related to physical desires. 2. Obtaining gratification by behaving in socially desirable ways. 3. Development of an understanding of an *imposed* set of social norms and values.	1. Ways of seeking pleasure. 2. Gratification of physical desires are superceded by changes in social behavior that is acceptable. 3. An understanding of the need for social norms and values for the sake of the well-being of society and behavior that reflects this understanding.
Erikson	*Qualitative*—with some quantitative change. For example, social rules, regulations, attitudes, and values are organized in such a way as to invite a succession of social interactions and to encourage a proper rate and sequence of unfolding.	1. Pleasure seeking not only related to the gratification of physical needs but also to interacting with other persons. 2. Child–parent interactions. 3. Resolution of conflict between such opposing psychosocial forces as "basic trust versus mistrust" and "initiative versus guilt".	1. Ways of seeking pleasure through social interactions. 2. Learning to control relationships with adults and peers. 3. Achieving a sense of identity associated with an ability to behave autonomously with confidence and a desire for achievement.

Table 1.3 Ten Questions about Theories of Development

1. What is the range of development described by the theory?

2. How is development described?

3. According to the theory, how are the changes of development expected to occur?

4. According to the theory, what factors influence the course of development?

5. To what extent do heredity and environment contribute to development?

6. Which areas of development (physical, intellectual, social, and emotional) does the theory describe?

7. Does the theory account for individual differences in development?

8. Does the theory describe development and learning as synonymous or does it distinguish between development and learning?

9. What special terminology does the theory use?

10. Does the theory distinguish between normal and abnormal development?

Source: Thomas, R. M. *Comparing Theories of Child Development*. Copyright © 1979 by Wadsworth Publishing Company, Inc., Belmont California 94002. Reprinted by permission of the publisher.

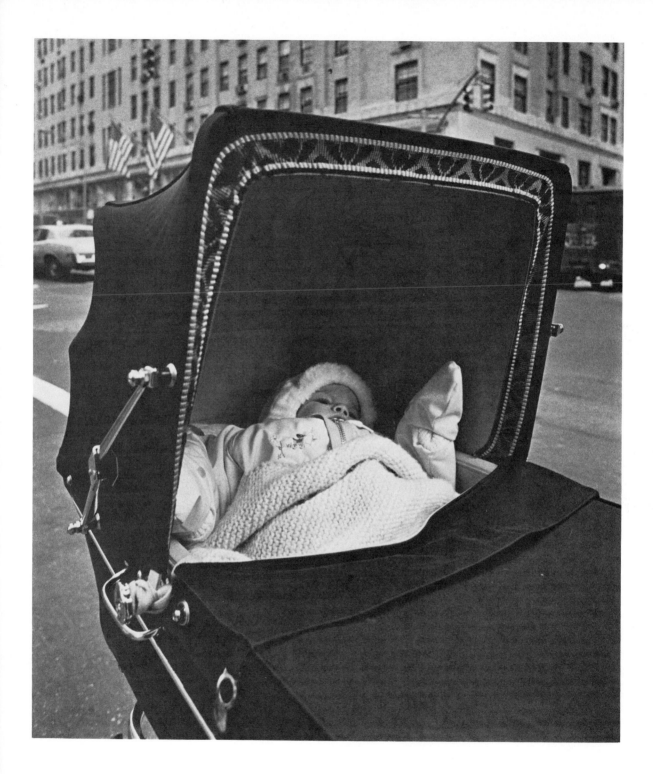

Birth and Infancy

Conception to Birth

2

I am not yet born; O hear me.
I am not yet born; console me.
I fear that the human race may with
tall walls wall me,
with strong drugs dope me, with wise
lies lure me.
I am not yet born; provide me
With water to dandle me, grass to
grow for me, trees to talk
to me, sky to sing to me, birds and a
white light
In the back of my mind to guide me

Macneice, Louis. "Prayer before Birth." In
The Collected Poems of Louis Macneice.
London: Faber and Faber Ltd.

The children in this large early-nineteenth-century family share physical similarities they have inherited from their parents. We can see that each child also has unique physical characteristics. Other factors, such as the way parents rear their children and a family's social and economic status, also affect children's development. (Photo by James L. Shaffer)

Before their baby is born parents begin to wonder what the baby will be like. Will it be a boy or a girl? Will it look like Mom or Dad? Will it be a normal, healthy baby? Everyone wonders at one time or another how these factors are decided. Is it just a fifty-fifty chance that a baby is a boy or a girl? Even if gender is determined by change, some things must not be; some things must, in fact, be predetermined. Otherwise, children would not look like their parents and healthy babies would not outnumber unhealthy ones.

Heredity is the biological mechanism that transmits characteristics of parents to their offspring. Some characteristics such as eye color are passed on directly. The baby receives genes from both parents that carry instructions regarding traits. For example, if both parents pass on instructions for brown eyes, their baby will have brown eyes. There are other direct influences on the embryo and fetus during those hidden months in the mother's uterus. The state of the mother that results from her diet; the control of her weight; her age; whether she smokes, drinks alcohol, or takes drugs; and whether she suffers from any disease or illness can have important influences on embryonic and fetal development. Other factors such as the age of the mother and father and the mother's previous childbearing history can have a direct impact on *prenatal development.* There are also indirect, environmental influences on prenatal development such as the culture the mother lives in, whether she enjoys the benefits of affluence or lives in poverty, and her level of education. We will discuss the mechanism of heredity, how it works through human reproduction, and what traits are due to heredity. We will also investigate the part the environment plays in determining traits.

For several months after conception the unborn baby will grow and develop from a fertilized egg until all parts are fashioned and formed inside the mother. Before birth the child will have slept, wakened, kicked, moved around, and sucked its thumb. How does a fertilized egg grow into a new human being? What controls the color of the hair and eyes, the forming of the hands, and those tiny protruberances that become fingers? How is it possible for newborn babies to be so humanly the same and yet so different from one another?

This chapter deals first with conception and the first nine months of life, moves on to consider various aspects of prenatal health, the genetic heritage, the "nature versus nurture" controversy, and closes with a discussion of the benefits of genetic counseling.

Human Reproduction

There can be no more fascinating subject than the story of how a human baby develops out of the meeting and fusing of a male sperm and female egg. Intercourse, under certain conditions, initiates the process of reproduction that requires the fertilization of a female egg by a single male sperm. How are the male sperm and female eggs produced and what is the schedule of events that leads to successful fertilization?

Male and Female Reproductive Organs

The male reproductive organs are illustrated in Figure 2.1. They consist of *testes* suspended outside the body in a skin sac called the *scrotom*. Each of the two testes is composed of coiled tubules known as *seminiferous ducts*. In the male, from puberty to old age, sperm are being constantly produced in the testes. Each sperm is about 0.06 mm long and looks like a tadpole with a head and a long tail, which is used for propulsion. At the climax of sexual stimulation sperm move from each epididymis (where they are stored following production in the tubules), through the sperm ducts (called the *vas deferens*) to the *seminal vesicle* where they combine with a whitish lubricating fluid called *semen*. This fluid is rich in sugar, which provides fuel for the sperm on its journey to meet the ovum. Secretions are also added from the *prostate gland* to stimulate the sperm. As the seminal fluid is being ejected from the penis, it picks up a slightly alkaline substance secreted from glands in the *urethra*. This substance helps neutralize any acidic urine present in the vagina, which can be lethal for the sperm.

In the female the reproductive organs develop within the body (see Figure 2.2). They consist of two *ovaries* within which the *ova* (eggs) develop. At birth a baby girl will have at least 150,000 ova in the two ovaries. Of this large number,

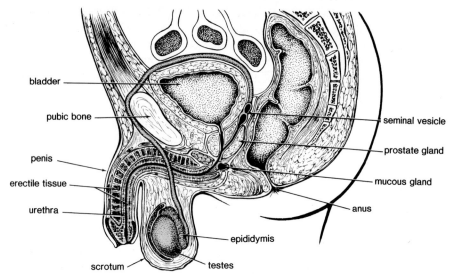

Figure 2.1 Male reproductive organs.

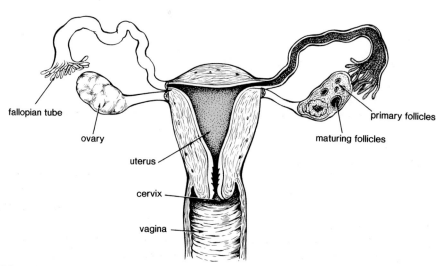

Figure 2.2 Female reproductive organs.

the female successfully ovulates between 300 and 400 during the reproductive years, which begin at puberty (Daniel, Harlow, & Ludwig, 1977, p. 88). Each egg is contained in a sac of surrounding cells called a *follicle*. About midway through the 28-day menstrual cycle, hormones trigger the growth of an immature ovum in one of the ovaries, the follicle ruptures, and the mature ovum begins its journey through the **fallopian tube** toward the **uterus** (see Figure 2.2).

Conception

When a man is sexually excited, blood flows quickly into the erectile tissue of the penis, which stiffens and can then be inserted into a woman's vagina. As the woman becomes sexually excited, her vagina becomes lubricated, ready to receive the penis and make its insertion and movement easy.

During the man's orgasm, achieved by thrusts of the penis in the vagina, rhythmic muscular contractions force sperm, in their surrounding secretion of seminal fluid, from the penis into the vagina and up toward the cervix, the mouth of the uterus. At this time more than 50 million sperm are ejected. About 75 percent of these sperm are normal and more than half of these are able to move. Of those able to move, more than half actually do move forward (Kaiser, 1977, p. 241). These sperm must travel by swimming almost 5 to 8 inches, depending on the placement of the sperm at ejaculation, up along one of the fallopian tubes. Of the sperm that enter the uterus only a few hundred make it to the vicinity of the ovum. It is known that a number of sperm can make contact with an ovum and actually penetrate the outer layer of the protective, gelatinous membrane surrounding the ovum. However, as soon as one sperm penetrates the ovum, a reaction occurs in the surrounding membrane making it impervious to other sperm (Kaiser, 1977, p. 242).

Conception occurs when a male sperm meets and enters a female ovum to create a fertilized cell called a **zygote.** This is the first in a series of four stages of prenatal development, which takes about nine months and ends with the birth of the baby. The other three stages of prenatal development are the *germinal, embryonic,* and *fetal stages.* Germinal and embryonic development occur in the first *trimester* (3-month period) of pregnancy. The fetal stage covers two further trimesters. The second trimester (4–6 months) sees the development of the major body systems, while the third trimester (7–9 months) is primarily a period of further growth of these developed systems.

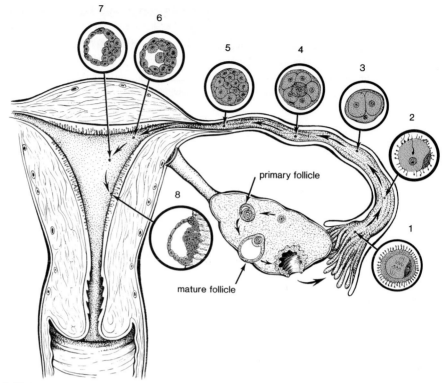

1. Mature ovum is released from ovary and enters fallopian tube.
2. Cells of corona have loosened; a sperm has entered the ovum; fertilization has occurred.
3. First cleavage of fertilized ovum.
4. Further cleavage—24 hours since fertilization.
5. By 48 hours, many cells.
6. 72–84 hours, ovum enters uterus; central cavity begins to form in ovum.
7. 120 hours, distinct cell mass on one side of ovum.
8. Implantation into wall of uterus; ovum is covered; trophoblast burrows into wall of uterus; by 9 days, germ disk and amnion are well formed.

Figure 2.3 Events of fertilization. (Source: Danforth, D. N. (ed.). *Obstretics and Gynecology*, 3rd ed. Copyright 1977 by Harper & Row. Reprinted by permission.)

The Germinal Stage

The events of ovulation, fertilization of the ovum, and the sequence that follows to implantation of the zygote into the wall of the uterus are illustrated in Figure 2.3.

During the first week the zygote moves freely in secretions from the oviduct down the fallopian tube into the uterine cavity. Rapid cell division is occurring, and by the time the zygote reaches the uterus, it has become a hollow sphere

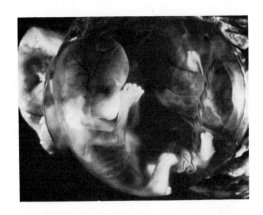

called a **blastocyst.** On one side is a large group of cells (an *embryonic disk*) that will form the **embryo.** The single layer of cells around the outside of the sphere (a **trophoblast**) will become the **placenta,** *umbilical cord,* and *amniotic sac.*

About the seventh day after fertilization the blastocyst attaches itself to the wall of the uterus. The trophoblast then produces tiny threads that penetrate the lining of the uterine wall. In this way the blastocyst burrows into a safe place under the surface. Once this has occurred, the developing mass of cells is called an **embryo.**

At about two weeks the embryonic disk is double-layered. The upper, outer layer called the **ectoderm** soon develops into skin, hair, nails, teeth, and the nervous system. The lower, outer layer called the **endoderm** becomes the digestive system, the respiratory system, the liver, pancreas, and salivary glands. Between these two outer layers lies the **mesoderm,** which develops into muscles and tissues. Scattered among these three layers are cells called **mesenchymes,** which become the heart, blood vessels, bones, and cartilage.

Well established by now, the baby-to-be is only a small disk about the size of a pinhead.

It does not look like very much, but during its third week the embryo will . . . develop . . . to a rounded little body with head, trunk, and umbilical cord (Nilsson, Furuhjelm, Ingelman-Sundberg, and Wirsen, 1977).

The Embryonic Stage

During this stage of from 2 to 8 weeks there is rapid growth of the major body systems. The first organs to develop are the most necessary, the brain and heart. In its *amniotic sac,* a protective, fluid-filled membrane, the embryo's blunt head hangs forward over a bulging heart. The "plump baby" is just over one-half inch long, with the lower body tapering to a tail-like projection. From the lower abdomen comes the umbilical cord, which safely moors the embryo to the placenta.

The *placenta* is a food- and waste-disposal unit. It is a layer of cells separating the embryo's developing systems from the mother's blood system. Through it oxygen flows into the embryo and carbon dioxide flows out of the embryo; nourishment is brought in and waste products are released. The placenta is an endocrine gland that secretes hormones. An important hormone is chorionic gonadotropin, which sustains the corpus luteum, another gland that secretes progesterone, which maintains the uterine wall and prevents menstruation's occurring.

At 6 weeks the eyes have formed. Below the eye is a large slit that could be mistaken for the beginnings of a mouth. It is, in fact, the ear. As the head further develops, the eyes will move around to a frontal position. Arms and hands, more advanced in their development than legs and feet, show up as short stumps with paddlelike ends. Parallel grooves in these "paddles" will split into the fingers and thumbs. The nervous system, which began forming about 18 days after conception, is now well enough developed to control the baby's muscles. This marvelous communication system, with its millions of nerve cells, is vital to the baby because it integrates the actions of most other systems.

The one-celled zygote formed at conception has now developed into millions of cells organized into groups—each with a particular function—the nervous, muscular, circulatory, digestive, and skeletal systems. This is perhaps the most decisive period of development, in which all systems are laid down and from which will form a well-integrated individual (Figure 2.4).

The Fetal Stage

The beginning of the fetal stage occurs in the ninth week and lasts until birth. The "baby" is now about 2 to 2½ inches long. The first bone cells appear, and the embryo becomes a **fetus.** Everything found in the fully developed baby is now present. The face is formed and the eyes have moved to the front of the head. Arms and legs are now well developed and fingers and toes almost completely formed. In the third month many specialized functions of the body are developing. Stomach and liver cells that will produce digestive juices are perfected, and the fetal kidneys begin to function. It is at this time that dramatic changes in sex organs occur. Inspection could now show whether the new baby will be a boy or girl. At about the ninth week the genes on the Y male **sex chromosomes** trigger a spurt of the male hormone androgen from the gonads (sex glands) and cause the gonads to develop into **testes.** There is no hormonal action in female babies since they do not have the Y chromosome. At about the tenth week the female gonads turn into **ovaries.**

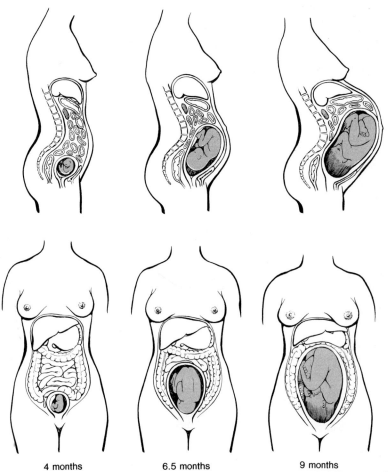

4 months   6.5 months   9 months

Figure 2.4 Development of the fetus. Views of relative size and different positions of the fetus in the mother's uterus from 4 months to term. (Source: After Louise Zabriskie, *Obstetrics for Nurses,* Lippincott, 1960 in *From Conception to Birth: The Drama of Life's Beginnings* by Roberts Rugh, and Landrum B. Shettles. Copyright © 1971 by Roberts Rugh and Landrum B. Shettles. Reprinted by permission of Harper & Row Publishers, Inc.)

The fourth to the sixth months of pregnancy are called the *second trimester.* Features such as hair, fingernails, toenails, and the teeth buds begin to form. About this time the mother begins to feel the fetus moving. The skeleton is well formed and hardening.

The *third trimester,* the last three months of prenatal development, is mainly a time of further growth and development of already well-established systems. The mother is very aware of the presence of her baby. Movements on the surface of her abdomen indicate the pushing of the baby's head and hands and the kicking of the feet.

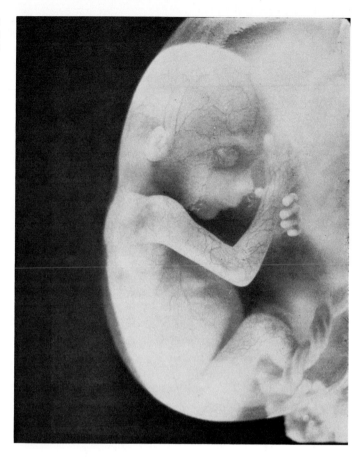

Photo of 10-week-old fetus showing hands and feet. (© Donald Yeager)

Prenatal Health

One or both of the sperm and ovum that join to produce the fertilized zygote may contain genetic defects. If these defects are serious, the zygote may be cast off early in the germinal stage or later during the embryonic stage. Certain illnesses can also lead to such spontaneous abortion.

Spontaneous Abortion

In some cases, usually between the second and third months of pregnancy, the embryo becomes detached from the wall of the uterus and is expelled through the vagina. This is called a **spontaneous abortion.** What causes a spontaneous abortion?

Hertig and Sheldon (1943) reported on a study of aborted specimens from 1000 women admitted to the Boston Lying-in Hospital. Abnormal defects were found in 61.7 percent of all cases. They suggested that the two most likely causes for these were either a defective germ cell from a parent or accidental injury to a normal embryo during a critical period of development. Many spontaneously aborted embryos and fetuses show chromosomal abnormalities. In a study of 227 aborted embryos, Carr (1966) found 22 percent had such defects.

More is known about the maternal factors that cause spontaneous abortion than about fetal or environmental factors (Cavanagh & Comas, 1977). A number of viruses are known to cause malformations or abortions of the fetus. Rubella, or German measles, has received most attention; the others are cytomegalovirus, herpes, mumps, hepatitis, and polio. With respect to German measles, the most common virus, the most important method of control is prevention.

The effect of the so-called German measles virus is to cause "clumping" of blood vessels, called *hemagglutination*. In the absence of a virus such as German measles, no clumping of blood vessels occurs. To prevent hemagglutination, the expectant mother should be vaccinated in order to prevent or block the virus that causes this condition. All women of childbearing age should be screened for the presence of rubella by the *hemagglutination-inhibition test*. If the results show absence of immunity, the woman should be vaccinated against rubella between pregnancies (Cavanagh & Comas, 1977, p. 322).

About 96 percent of all abortions are spontaneous. Having once experienced a spontaneous abortion, a woman has a 60 percent chance of having a succeeding full-term pregnancy. There must be some reason for abortions occurring in succession, and it is possible for an obstetrician to uncover and in some cases correct the malfunction.

Mother's Influence on the Fetus

Although doctors agree that the wisest advice to a pregnant mother is to live as normal a life as possible, she can take certain precautions to ensure a safe environment for the developing fetus. The mother's diet, along with drugs she may take, alcohol she may drink, tobacco she may smoke, and physical or emotional illnesses she may suffer can all have some effect on the fetus.

Diet. Swanson (1974) suggests that any detailed counseling on diets for pregnant women is suspect because in general the overall caloric intake and types of food that make up an adequate and balanced diet for nonpregnant and pregnant women differ very little (Table 2.1). The most important aspect of the pregnant woman's diet is its nutritional content. Because of an increase in blood supply, extra iron is required. In late pregnancy when the fetus is growing rapidly, extra proteins, vitamins, and minerals become important. Obstetricians might prescribe prenatal capsules containing vitamins A, B, C, and D plus calcium, phosphorus, and iron if they are considered necessary.

Table 2.1 Daily Dietary Allowances Recommended by the National Research Council

	Nonpregnant Females				Pregnancy	Lactation
	11–14 yr[a]	15–18 yr[b]	19–22 yr[c]	23–50 yr[d]		
Energy (kcal)	2400	2100	2100	2000	+300	+500
Protein (gm)	44	48	46	46	+30	+20
Vitamin A (I.U.)	4000	4000	4000	4000	5000	6000
Vitamin D (I.U.)	400	400	400	400	400	400
Vitamin E (I.U.)	12	12	12	12	15	15
Vitamin C (mg)	45	45	45	45	60	80
Folacin (mcg)	400	400	400	400	800	600
Niacin (mg)	16	14	14	13	+2	+4
Riboflavin (mg)	1.3	1.4	1.4	1.2	+0.3	+0.5
Thiamin (mg)	1.2	1.1	1.1	1.0	+0.3	+0.3
Vitamin B$_6$ (mg)	1.6	2.0	2.0	2.0	2.5	2.5
Vitamin B$_{12}$ (mcg)	3	3	3	3	4	4
Calcium (mg)	1200	1200	800	800	1200	1200
Phosphorus (mg)	1200	1200	800	800	1200	1200
Iodine (mcg)	115	115	100	100	125	150
Iron (mg)	18	18	18	18	+[d]	18
Magnesium (mg)	300	300	300	300	450	450
Zinc (mg)	15	15	15	15	20	25

[a]Weight 97 lb (44 kg), height 62 in. (155 cm).
[b]Weight 119 lb (54 kg), height 65 in. (162 cm).
[c]Weight 128 lb (58 kg), height 65 in. (162 cm).

[d]The increased requirements of pregnancy cannot usually be met by ordinary diets; therefore, the use of supplemental iron is recommended. *Source:* Committee on Nutrition. *Nutrition in Maternal Health.* American College of Obstetricians and Gynecologists, 1974.

Inadequate nutrition is almost always linked to some extent with poverty. But in the United States, and probably elsewhere in the world, malnutrition and the high frequency of mother and infant deaths are associated not only with poverty but with other factors such as poor sanitation, ignorance, and inadequate medical care (Birch & Gussow, 1970). Studies have shown that babies of severely malnourished mothers have underdeveloped nervous systems and fewer brain cells than normal babies (Dobbing, 1973, 1974; Winick, 1976).

It has been suggested that such babies will suffer from abnormal mental development in later life. However, there is no clear-cut evidence of the long-term effects of malnutrition on a child's development. The results of a study by

Stein and her co-workers (1975) suggest that at least short-term, severe starvation suffered by pregnant mothers has no ill effects on the mental development of those children who survive at birth. In 1945, toward the end of World War II, parts of the Netherlands experienced severe famine while under Nazi occupation. Food restrictions were limited to certain cities and were not prolonged. It was expected that babies born to women who were undernourished would suffer from some impairment to mental development. The IQ scores of Dutchmen at age 19 born to women in the famine-struck cities were compared to those of men of the same age from nonaffected cities. There were no real differences—in fact, the scores of men from the famine cities were slightly higher. However, birthrate in the famine cities was very low following the food restrictions, and it can be presumed that there were many spontaneous abortions resulting from malnutrition.

These results do not prove that prenatal malnutrition never affects later mental development of affected children. Environmental effects in the form of good homes and schools may overcome immediate impairment. But when early deficiencies are followed by malnutrition during infancy and when children come under the influence of adverse social and environmental conditions, it is likely that abnormal development will occur (Winick, 1976).

Weight.   At one time physicians and obstetricians commonly advised expectant mothers to restrict their weight gain during pregnancy to no more than 15 to 18 pounds. We now know that insufficient weight gain during pregnancy can result in small, premature, and high-risk infants. Today optimal weight gain during pregnancy is considered to be 24 to 27 pounds (Haynes, 1977, p. 313). Higher or lower weight gains may lead to increased risk of various pregnancy complications.

Teratogens.   The word *teratogen* comes from the Greek word monster. *Teratology* literally means the study of monsters or more generally the study of birth defects. *Teratogens* are drugs, viruses, chemicals, and radiation (*hundreds* of varieties) that can cross the placental barrier and invade the embryo or fetus and cause it harm. Damage from tetragens is most serious during the first eight weeks of embryonic life. However, teratogens can also cause severe defects to parts of the body including the brain, genitals, and eyes during the third trimester. A number of the most harmful and well-known teratogens are mentioned here.

Great care is usually taken to test the effects of drugs that might be prescribed during pregnancy, especially newly discovered drugs. Tests are conducted on pregnant animals, especially rats and mice. However, even when results from such tests appear favorable, the drugs cannot always be considered entirely safe.

Thalidomide.   One of the most shocking adverse effects of drugs taken by mothers during pregnancy was the thalidomide tragedy. **Thalidomide** is a tranquilizer used to counteract nausea (early morning sickness) and insomnia and was prescribed to expectant mothers in England, Europe, and Australia during the late 1950s and early 1960s. Tests on pregnant rats had produced no adverse side effects. This turned out *not* to be the case for pregnant women! The drug mainly affected the development of babies' limbs during that crucial embryo period about the sixth week of pregnancy. The effects were devastating; no arms or legs, stunted growth of limbs, and defects of sight and hearing. In some cases eyes and ears had not developed (Lenz, 1966; Schardein, 1976). Fortunately for expectant mothers in the United States, strict government controls on new drugs had prevented the distribution of thalidomide. Doctors have now been warned not to prescribe other tranquilizers such as Valium, Tofranil, and Librium, especially during the early months of pregnancy. Aspirin and certain antinausea drugs are also known to cause abnormalities in the fetus (Erikson, Catz, & Yaffe, 1973; Zimmerman, 1976).

Hormones. **Hormones** are chemical substances that predispose the body to be either male or female. Sex hormone treatments, including use of birth-control pills, can cause limb malformation during early pregnancy (Janerich, Piper, & Glebatis, 1974). Exposure to hormones during pregnancy was found to take one of three forms: (1) continuing to take birth-control pills after fertilization has occurred but not realizing that it has occurred; (2) using estrogen or progesterone hormones for the treatment of reproductive system disorders; or (3) taking pregnancy tests that used hormones. As is the case for other drugs, the exact effects of hormones introduced into the body of the fetus are not yet known. Further evidence linking hormones and birth defects is needed.

Other drugs such as antibiotics, barbiturates, and excessive amounts of vitamins can also be harmful. Some women believe they should increase their vitamin intake during pregnancy by taking pills. This is not necessary for most women who are eating a well-balanced diet, have no special dietary problem, have a history of good nutrition, and know the nutritional value of certain foods. A specialist's advice on diet and vitamin intake may be necessary for some expectant mothers.

On an optimistic note we should remember that most women are concerned about the well-being of their unborn babies. If the expectant mother believes a drug is necessary for some reason, the best rule is to ask her doctor's advice and to take only drugs that have been prescribed.

Alcohol and tobacco. Before ever becoming pregnant, many women have already developed drinking and smoking habits. Social drinking in the amount of a couple of glasses of wine with a meal or a before-dinner cocktail does not seem to have any adverse effects on the fetus. Drinking large amounts of alcohol, however, is quite a different matter. We do not know as yet how much alcohol can be drunk before the amount becomes dangerous. The best advice at present seems to be to drink if you must with great moderation.

We do know that *excessive* drinking by pregnant women usually results in retardation of growth in unborn babies. After birth these babies do not catch up on weight and size. Other defects that have been observed in these cases are small head size, heart defects, and problems with bone joints (Jones, Smith, Ulleland, & Streissgurth, 1973).

It has been shown that most babies born to mothers who smoke are smaller and several ounces lighter at birth than babies of nonsmoking mothers. Results of tests show that the expectant mother's smoking just one cigarette can both increase the fetus's heartbeat and slow down circulation because of the constriction of blood vessels. These cardiovascular effects are more pronounced during the eighth month of pregnancy. There is also some evidence to link spontaneous abortion with mothers who smoke (U.S. Department of Health, Education, and Welfare, 1973, 1979). The question, as with alcohol, is "How many cigarettes a day can I smoke for them to be nonharmful to the baby?" There is no straightforward answer. Although babies born of mothers who do smoke excessively tend to be smaller, they are just as healthy as babies of nonsmokers. Given the recent research results linking smoking to lung cancer and heart diseases, the more compelling argument seems to be to give up or seriously cut down on smoking for the good of the mother's health as well as that of the unborn child.

Marijuana. The effects of marijuana or "pot" on prenatal development have not yet been determined. Research on animals has indicated a relationship between intake of marijuana and a reduced growth rate of the fetus. Results from animal studies cannot accurately be applied to humans, but they do point to a potential risk from the use of this drug during pregnancy.

LSD. The effect of LSD (lysergic acid diethylamide) on prenatal development in humans is not known. Lubs and Riddle (1970) observed 22 babies with chromosomal abnormalities out of 4,500 births. None of the parents of these babies had taken LSD. There were 14 cases of babies whose parents had taken LSD, but these infants had normal chromosomes. A study by Berlin and Jacobson (1970) reported the effects of LSD on 127 babies born to 112 women. Of the 127 pregnancies, only 62 were live births. Six of these babies had congenital abnormalities, and one died within a few hours of birth. Many parents admitted taking LSD before and at the time of conception, but only three of the mothers took LSD during the crucial first trimester of pregnancy. However, the fact that 81 percent of mothers in this study smoked, 25 percent used narcotics, 36 percent had received extensive x-ray investigations because of abdominal problems, and many had histories of disease and malnutrition makes it impossible to draw any satisfactory conclusions regarding the possible effects of LSD on fetal development. In a similar study of 120 live births to mothers who were users of LSD, McGlothlin, Sparkes, and Arnold (1970) found a lower proportion of birth defects than was the case in the Berlin study. The number and type of birth defects among these babies were very like what might be expected in the case of nonusers of LSD. However, the rate of spontaneous abortion for LSD users was higher than for nonusers (15 percent for medicinal and 50 percent for black market LSD). As Dishotsky, Longhman, Morar, and Lipscomb (1971) have pointed out, the effects of LSD are conflicting since many of the mothers using this drug also used other drugs, contracted diseases during pregnancy, were undernourished, and used "street" drugs that usually contain impurities. Pure LSD appears to have little teratogenic effect on the fetus. The same cannot be said for illicit LSD.

Heroin and methadone. Expectant mothers who are addicted to drugs such as heroin and methadone are likely to have premature babies. It has been reported that babies born to addicts are themselves addicted, showing withdrawal symptoms such as breathing difficulties, convulsions, excessive crying, and fever (Henly & Fitch, 1966; Schulman, 1969). These infants can be soothed by a medication such as *paregoric.* Addicted infants have also been found to be less alert and responsive to stimuli that can be seen or heard than normal babies (Strauss, Lessen-Firestone, Starr, & Ostrea, 1975). However, the rate of abnormal births to mothers on methadone-maintenance programs has been found to be similar to that among nonaddicted mothers of the same age, color, and socioeconomic status (Brecker, 1972).

One problem with the results of studies on the effects of addictive drugs, as well as marijuana, is that mothers in these studies are often "the worst specimens of motherhood an experiment in prenatal development could imagine" (Annis, 1978, p. 114). Symptoms that are attributed to heroin or methadone may also be linked to other symptoms such as heavy smoking, malnutrition, and infections such as syphilis. It has not yet been determined how detrimental to prenatal development addictive drugs might be (Blinick, Wallach, & Jeres, 1969). Nevertheless, there is enough evidence to suggest that expectant mothers should avoid using them.

Diseases and illnesses. A number of common diseases and illnesses that can affect the developing fetus can be prevented if diagnosed in time.

Anemia. One of the common deficiencies caused by pregnancy is a loss in the mother's supply of iron. For many women heavy losses of blood in the monthly menstrual cycle can lead to an iron deficiency. Measures of hemoglobin values in early pregnancy indicate that the majority of women enter pregnancy with partial or complete depletion of iron reserves (Danforth & Holly, 1977, p. 411). The developing fetus takes part of the iron availability from the mother making it more likely that an anemic condition will result in the mother. Since anemia is a reduction in the number of red corpuscles that carry oxygen in the blood, obviously necessary for the well-being of the fetus and the mother, a doctor will usually prescribe a dose of between 30 and 60 mg of iron daily (usually to be taken in tablet form) for the anemic mother. A diet of well-balanced nourishing foods is also of prime importance. Anemia must be corrected as soon as possible; therefore, it is in the best interests of the pregnant mother to have hemoglobin values monitored regularly throughout pregnancy.

Diabetes. The correct medical term for this disease is *diabetes mellitus.* The term *diabetes* comes from the Greek word for "a passer through" and *mellitus* from the Latin meaning "sweet as honey." Diabetes is characterized by a deficiency in the supply of a hormone called *insulin,* which is secreted by the pancreas. Insulin controls the processing of sugar, and deficiency leads to high levels of sugar in the blood and urine. The term then is very apt since the excess of sugar "passes through" the kidneys into the blood and urine.

What causes diabetes? It was long believed that diabetes resulted from an inherited trait. As a result of research findings in recent years, this view has changed somewhat. Heredity is still considered to be a factor predisposing certain people to this disease, and it has been noted that the genotype for diabetes has doubled in less than ten generations (Nesbitt, 1977, p. 451). However, it has been discovered that many cases of diabetes may occur following a virus infection such as mumps, Cosackie B4, and mononucleosis (Lowenstein & Preger, 1976; Silvian, 1977). Three out of four adults who become diabetic are overweight. It used to be assumed that obesity could result in diabetes for some people. It now appears more likely that in these cases diabetes was already present and led to excessive hunger and a gain in weight, which in turn resulted in an observable diabetic condition (Lowenstein & Preger, 1976, pp. 153–154). The treatment for most diabetes is a suitable diet, exercise, and weight control. In some cases insulin injections to remove excess sugar from the blood to the liver are also necessary.

Before a method of manufacturing insulin was discovered by Banting in 1923, it was rare for a diabetic woman to have a successful pregnancy. Now the majority of diabetics can expect successful pregnancies. A classification system for evaluating pregnant diabetics has been devised by Dr. White of the Joslin Clinic in Boston, Massachusetts. This system takes into account the severity and length of the disease and how it has been controlled (Table 2.2).

A complication of diabetic pregnancies is miscarriage. The chance of a miscarriage for women in classes *A* and *B* is about 10 percent, which is the same rate as that for pregnancies in general. Women in class *C* have a 24 percent chance of miscarriage; those in class *D,* a 30 percent chance; and those in classes *E* to *T,* a 74 percent chance (reported in Silvian, 1977, p. 89).

Women in a prediabetic condition without previous symptoms often develop diabetes during pregnancy. On the other hand, if a woman is known to have diabetes, the condition should be brought under control before pregnancy occurs. In both cases the women should be treated by a specialist who will set up a program to control glucose levels in the blood, to determine the amount and rate of insulin injections, to advise on diet (usually higher in proteins and vitamins and lower in carbohydrates), and to monitor weight gain.

At delivery diabetic women in classes *A* and *B* usually have a normal delivery. Women in classes *C* through *E* usually have labor induced, and the physician decides whether delivery will be vaginally or by Caesarian section. Many babies

Table 2.2 Classification of Pregnant Diabetes[a]

Class	Onset of Diabetes	Duration	Complications	Control
A	Pregnancy	Gestation		Diet
B	Over 19 years of age	Less than 10 years		Insulin Diet
C	10 to 19 years of age	10 to 19 years	Hypertension; calcified leg vessels; benign retinopathy	Insulin Diet
D	Under 10 years of age	More than 20 years		Insulin Diet
E–T	Any age	Any	Pelvic vascular calcification; diabetic nephropathy; habitual spontaneous abortions; premature deliveries; heart disease	Insulin Diet

[a]Classification system according to Dr. White of the Joslin Clinic, Boston, Massachusetts. Adapted from Silvian, *Understanding Diabetes*. Copyright © 1977 by Lenore Silvian. Reprinted by permission of Monarch Press, a Simon & Schuster division of Gulf & Western Corporation.

of diabetic women are larger than normal at birth, probably because of the abnormally high sugar content in the mother's blood. These babies are often delivered by Caesarian section.

The survival rate of infants born to diabetic women who are in good health and who receive good prenatal care is close to the 95 percent level of those delivered to nondiabetics.

German measles. In 1942 doctors in Australia noticed that severe congenital defects of the eyes, ears, and heart occurred in many infants whose mothers had had German measles (rubella) in early pregnancy. Doctors all over the world rapidly confirmed these findings (Gorbach & Feinbloom, 1979, pp. 166–167). German measles shows up as a fleeting rash, enlargement of the lymph nodes in the back of the neck, and aching in the joints. However, many pregnant women who contract German measles show no clear symptoms.

The risk to the baby comes in the first three months of pregnancy. After the third month there is little likelihood of complications. It is usual nowadays for a woman who expects to become pregnant to have a test for antibodies to rubella well in advance of the pregnancy. If she is not immune, she is given an injection of vaccine, but only if there is some guarantee that she will not become pregnant within two months since the vaccine virus can harm a fetus.

Radiation. When we discuss gene combinations later in this chapter you will discover that many possible combinations can occur. One type of change in the embryo's or fetus's genes might be a *mutation,* which produces special physical characteristics that are not normal. A well-known mutation, Down's syndrome, is described later.

Radiation can cause gene mutations. The greater the amount of radiation, the higher the rate of genetic change. Although the amount of radiation in diagnostic x rays is relatively small, some doctors advise against a pregnant woman's having pelvic x rays. However, other specialists insist there is nothing to worry about from having even several diagnostic x rays during pregnancy. X rays and radium treatment, however, should not be given unless absolutely necessary.

The Rh factor. The **Rh factor** is an inherited protein substance in the blood. If it is present, the person is classified as Rh positive, and, if absent, as Rh negative. (The Rh factor was discovered in Rhesus monkeys in 1940 by Drs. Hunsteiner and Weiner, which is how it got its name.) Studies have shown that 85 percent of the white population in the United States are Rh positive and the remaining 15 percent are Rh negative; for blacks the ratio is 93:7 percent, with the Rh positive factor being dominant over the Rh negative factor. The Rh factor becomes important only in cases in which an Rh negative person receives an injection of Rh positive blood. This causes the system to produce antibodies against the incompatible blood. When an Rh negative woman has an Rh positive partner, it is possible that she may conceive an Rh positive fetus. In such cases it sometimes *(but not always)* happens that late in pregnancy some fetal blood is introduced into the mother's blood because of tears in the chorionic blood vessels (Swanson, 1977, p. 246). (The chorion is shown in Figure 2.13.) It is unlikely that any damage will be caused to the fetus in a first pregnancy since it takes about two weeks for antibody production to be effective. In second and subsequent pregnancies the dangers to the fetus are usually greater because of the likely occurrence of greater leakages of blood and a higher rate of antibody production as a result of previous immunization. The concentration of antibodies may become great enough to "attack" the fetus and result in a disease called **erythroblastosis fetalis.** Abnormalities from this disease include anemia, jaundice, heart defects, and mental retardation. In some cases spontaneous abortion or stillbirth may occur.

If any of the baby's Rh positive red blood cells are going to pass through the placenta and into the mother, it is likely to occur at the time of labor and delivery rather than earlier in the pregnancy (Gorbach & Feinbloom, 1979, p. 154). Stillbirth has always been the major problem for Rh negative mothers. To prevent a stillbirth, the baby is delivered prematurely by Caesarian section. If necessary, a blood transfusion can be given to the baby at this time.

The problem of **erythroblastosis** is now preventable. Tests during pregnancy can determine whether the condition has occurred or is likely to occur. If the baby is in danger, preventive injections or intrauterine blood transfusions may be given. This is an exciting breakthrough in preventative medicine. Rh negative blood can be transfused to the baby weeks before delivery and ensure survival (Apgar & Beck, 1974). However, the most common control of this condition is *Rhogam vaccine,* which immunizes the pregnant woman against the production of antibodies.

Father's Influence on the Fetus

It is well known that as a woman grows older the risk of conceiving a fetus with chromosomal defects increases (Inset 2.1). A number of studies have shown also that *genetic* abnormalities are more likely to occur with the increasing age of a father. The reasons why this happens are not clear, but is supposed that the longer a man lives the more likely it is that genetic errors will occur during *meiosis* (the process of cell division that occurs when new sperm are produced). Some of these genetic errors may be caused by radiation, infection, drugs, and chemicals. With aging, there is a likelihood of an accumulation of errors (Evans & Hall, 1976, p. 48).

Certain rare, dominantly inherited diseases have been associated with the increasing age of a father. These include *Achondroplasia* (a type of dwarfism), *Marfan syndrome* (height, vision, and heart abnormalities), *Apert syndrome* (facial and limb deformities), and *Fibrodysplasia Ossificans Progressiva* (bony growths). Unfortunately, to date there is no way of predicting which of the many possible mutations may occur as a result of increased paternal age. "The only encouragement geneticists offer parents over the age of 35 is that if a new mutation does occur in one of their children, there is no increased risk that their subsequent children will have the same defect" (Evans & Hall, 1977, p. 48).

The further development of early detection procedures will be greatly welcomed. The genetic counselor plays an important role in attempting to diagnose possible chromosomal defects in the gametes of older parents—and all parents who suspect that they may carry defects.

The Genetic Heritage

At the moment of conception the baby-to-be acquires characteristics from both parents that are determined by *genes* contained in the chromosomes found in all living cells. Genes control the growth of the body and specific physical characteristics such as body proportions, height, color of eyes and hair, and shape of nose. Contained in each parent's chromosomes are genes passed on to them from their respective parents and from grandparents and great-grandparents

"While it is well known that older mothers risk having children with chromosomal defects, less publicized is recent research relating congenital malformations and genetic diseases to advanced *paternal* age. At a recent meeting of the American Society of Human Genetics, researchers from both Europe and the United States reported studies utilizing a new chromosomal-staining technique that showed that the extra chromosome which causes Down's syndrome actually can come from the father rather than from the mother. Other studies indicated that genetic mutations seem to occur more frequently with the increasing age of a man, thus increasing the chance of a mutation's being present in a sperm cell which can cause a genetic disorder in his child.

"Geneticists aren't sure what causes mutations in the father's genes. Men are constantly producing sperm, and the continuing division of cells may allow errors in copying genes to occur. In addition, the longer a man lives the more opportunity he has to come into contact with mutation producers in the environment, such as radiation, infections, and certain drugs and chemicals. With time and aging, the errors may accumulate in the genes of the cells that divide to make sperm.

"Advanced paternal age has been associated with such rare dominantly inherited diseases as Achondroplasia (a type of dwarfism), Marfan syndrome (height, vision, and heart abnormalities), Apert syndrome (facial and limb deformities) and Fibrodysplasia Ossificans Progressiva (bony growths)."

The average age of fathers of children with achondroplasia has been observed to be 36 years; studies have found an average age of fathers of children with Marfan syndrome to be 36 years; and other research has indicated that the older father is a factor in sporadic cases of other conditions that involve severe structural abnormalities.

"Does this mean that men over 35 should forget about having children? Not necessarily. Whatever the age of the father, new mutations in his offspring are a rare occurrence—probably less than 1 percent, even among very old men. But potential parents should be aware that the likelihood of a man's fathering a child with a new mutation probably increases tenfold between the ages of 30 and 60."

Source: Evans, G., and Hall, J. G. "The Older the Sperm," *Ms* Magazine, January 1976, Vol. IV, No. 7. Reprinted by permission.

through a genetic heritage reaching into the distant past. Admiring onlookers might comment that a newborn baby looks "so much like his father," or "She's so like her mother," or perhaps, "He's got his grandfather's nose." A humorous story is told of a letter written by an attractive woman to George Bernard Shaw, the playwright, suggesting they marry and commenting that their children would be well *endowed* with his brains and her beauty. He declined with the observation that it would be unfortunate if they were born with his beauty and her brains. Shaw was quite correct; we cannot predict which traits the baby will receive from the parents' genetic heritage.

As we will see, genetic material has a basic substance of deoxyribonucleic acid—or **DNA** for short. This acid is composed of sugar and phosphate molecules

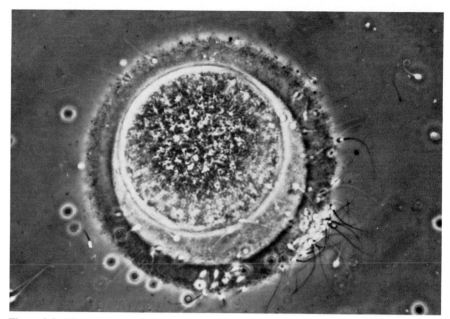

Figure 2.5 Photo of ovum being penetrated by sperm. The ovum is much larger than the sperm. Sperm are structured to move themselves so that it is possible for them to make contact with an ovum. However, only one of the hundred or so sperm that make contact will penetrate and fertilize the ovum. (American Museum of Natural History #2A 6259)

arranged in a special pattern that can be thought of as a code for the transmission of genetic information. Although the codes are determined by the parents' genetic heritage, how they will combine to form the baby's own special set of genetic instructions cannot be predetermined. First, we will consider the structure of cells in which the genes are to be found.

The Structure of Cells

The human body is made up of cells that constantly divide and produce new cells. There are two types of cells: the **somatic cells** compose parts of the body such as the skeleton, muscles, and respiratory, digestive, and nervous systems; **gametes** or *germ cells* are composed of the male *sperm* cells and the female *ova* or *egg cells*. These two types of cells have different structures and divide in different ways.

The ovum is much larger than the sperm (Figure 2.5). It is filled with food and ready for rapid cell division. Sperm are the smallest of body cells, streamlined in shape and structured to move easily. The gametes contain all the hereditary material necessary for the production of a baby. Each unit of inheritance is called a *gene* arranged along a stringlike thread called a **chromosome.**

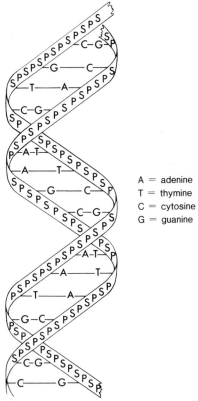

A = adenine
T = thymine
C = cytosine
G = guanine

Figure 2.6 The spiral ladder model of DNA. The sides of the ladder are made up of sugar and phosphate molecules. The rungs of the ladder are made up of two different pairs of chemical bases, *adenine* ⟷ *thyamine* and *cytosine* ⟷ *guanine*. The pattern of these pairs is the determinant for genetic transmission. Adapted from James D. Watson, *The Double Helix*. Copyright © 1968 by James D. Watson. (New York: Atheneum, 1968). Reprinted with the permission of Atheneum Publishers.

The DNA molecule. An exciting breakthrough in scientific research of the structure and composition of genes occurred in the 1950s (Watson, 1968). It was known that the chemical DNA (deoxyribonucleic acid) occurred in chromosomes and very likely was the stuff genes were composed from.

Francis Crick, an English biophysicist, and an American biologist named Watson worked together over a number of years at Cambridge University, England, to try to identify the structure of DNA. They eventually constructed a model of the DNA molecule that showed it to be an intertwined, ladderlike structure (Figure 2.6), often referred to as the "double helix." The DNA molecule consists of chemical elements and can be made up of thousands of different arrangements. These different arrangements result in differences among genes. The information carried by DNA molecules determines both the general structure of the human organism and the unique traits or distinguishing characteristics of each individual.

Cell division. The somatic or body cells each contain 46 chromosomes. When a somatic cell is about to divide, each of the 46 chromosomes splits longitudinally into two strands. When the split occurs, each part is reconstructed to make a complete chromosome identical to the original. This process of somatic cell division is called **mitosis,** which is a Greek word for "thread formation." The new cells must be exact replicas of each other (Figure 2.7) in order to ensure normal body growth.

Each gamete contains 23 chromosomes. These cells divide in a special process called **meiosis** to produce ova or sperm. In this process there are two divisions of the germ cell (Figure 2.8). Before the first division the chromosome pairs combine in a process called *crossover*. This pairing results in an exchange of various sequences of *genes*. At the next division four different combinations result from each chromosome pair. Because there are thousands of genes in each chromosome, there are thousands of possible exchanges and an almost endless number of possible combinations in the production of sperm and ova. In the second part of the process of meiosis, the two cells from the first division further divide—this time into ova or sperm. In each ovum or sperm there will be 23 chromosomes.

Gene Combinations

The end result of this pairing and crossover process is an astonishing selection of possible genetic mixings. Then we must add to this selection the multiple possible combinations that can occur when ovum and sperm unite to form the zygote. The child that results (twins are discussed later) will obviously be unique. At the same time, there will be a resemblance to the parents since it is from their mixed genes that the child develops.

The transmission of traits. As we know, the genes within the 23 pairs of chromosomes that form the zygote come from both the mother and father. In turn the mother and father received genes from each of their parents—the grandparents of the child yet to be born—and so on back through family ancestry. The complex combinations of genes become part of each individual's ancestry. Which of the genes, now combined in the zygote, will determine the unique characteristics of the child? Will the child eventually look more like Mom than Dad, what color will the eyes and hair be, how tall will the child grow up to be?

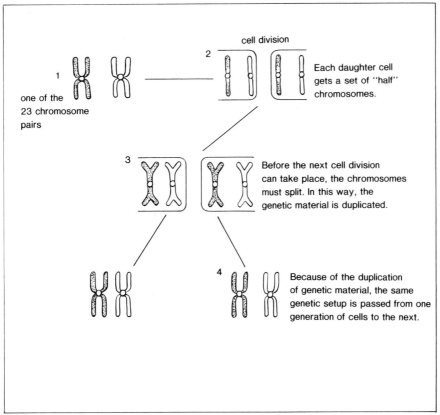

cell division

2 Each daughter cell gets a set of "half" chromosomes.

1 one of the 23 chromosome pairs

3 Before the next cell division can take place, the chromosomes must split. In this way, the genetic material is duplicated.

4 Because of the duplication of genetic material, the same genetic setup is passed from one generation of cells to the next.

Figure 2.7 Mitosis. (Source: From the book *A Child Is Born* by Lennart Nilsson. English translation copyright © 1966, 1977 by Dell Publishing Company, Inc. Originally published in Swedish under the title *Ett Barn Blir Till* by Albert Bonniers Forlag. Copyright © 1965 by Albert Bonniers Forlag, Stockholm. Revised edition copyright © 1976 by Lennart Nilsson, Mirjam Furuhjelm, Axel Ingelman-Sundberg, Cales Wirsen. Used by permission of Delacorte Press/Seymour Lawrence.)

Cross-fertilization. Probably the two most important biological discoveries have been DNA and the defining of the gene as the bearer of hereditary traits. It was in 1856 that a monk, Gregor Mendel, began experimenting with the *cross-fertilization* of plants at the monastery of Brno in Moravia, now part of Czechoslovakia. Mendel, a farmer's son, was interested in plants. He had guessed that each characteristic of a plant is controlled by two "particles," which he called genes. Each parent plant contributes one of these particles to the new plant. If

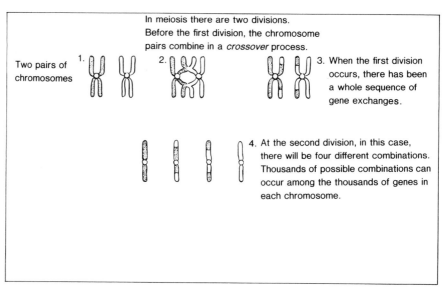

In meiosis there are two divisions.
Before the first division, the chromosome pairs combine in a *crossover* process.

Two pairs of chromosomes

1.

2.

3. When the first division occurs, there has been a whole sequence of gene exchanges.

4. At the second division, in this case, there will be four different combinations. Thousands of possible combinations can occur among the thousands of genes in each chromosome.

Figure 2.8 Meiosis. (Source: From the book *A Child Is Born* by Lennart Nilsson. English translation copyright © 1966, 1977 by Dell Publishing Co., Inc. Originally published in Swedish under the title *Ett Barn Blir Till* by Albert Bonniers Forlag. Copyright © 1965 by Albert Bonniers Forlag, Stockholm. Revised edition copyright © 1976 by Lennart Nilsson, Mirjam Furuhjelm, Axel Ingelman-Sundberg, Cales Wirsen. Used by permission of Delacorte Press/Seymour Lawrence.)

the two particles are the same, the new plant will be exactly like the parent plants. But suppose the particles are different? Mendel began his experiments to find an answer by cross-fertilizing garden peas.

He chose peas with different characteristics—shape of seed, color of seed, height of plant, and so on. For example, he crossed tall and short pea plants. He found that the first generation of *hybrids* all grew to be tall. He then knew that the character "tall" was *dominant* over the character *short*. The character short, in this case, is called *recessive*. The second generation of hybrids, fertilized from the first generation, were not uniform in height. Mendel found that about two thirds were tall and one third were short. He found this ratio of 3:1 held true when other traits were crossed. (This is always the case, both in plants and animals.) Thus a most important characteristic of genetic transmission was discovered.

Mendel's experiments helped explain how meiosis works. An important function of meiosis is the passing on of *hereditary instructions* by each specific gene for a particular trait such as blood type or eye color. Instructions are not always the same, and alternative instructions that are possible from each gene are called **alleles.**

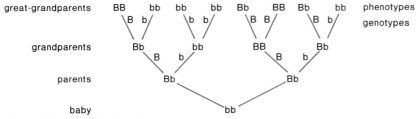

Figure 2.9 Eye-color dominance.

Combination of alleles. The position a gene occupies on a chromosome is called the *locus*. Each specific gene locus contains information for a particular trait such as eye color, height, or blood type. However, since the zygote receives genes from each parent, *instructions* regarding characteristics are not usually the same. Each characteristic or trait will have two or more instructions (alleles) at a specific locus. It is generally the case that each individual will have at least two alleles for each trait, one from each parent. For example, each child will have at least two sets of instructions for eye color, one on each chromosome containing the eye-color locus. Children with alleles for brown eyes from both parents are said to be **homozygous** for brown eyes. If the alleles differ, say one instructs for brown eyes, the other for blue eyes, this case is called **heterozygous.**

Dominance and recessiveness. How does the combination of alleles affect eye color? Alleles that provide information for the production of the pigment of the iris (always brown) are **dominant alleles.** Those that govern unpigmented irises (blue in appearance) are **recessive alleles.** If the father and mother of a baby are both homozygous with respect to genes either for brown or blue eyes, the baby will be homozygous at the eye-color locus—and will, of course, have the eye color shared by both parents. But, if the father's sperm carries a gene for brown eyes and the mother's ovum a gene for blue eyes, the baby will be heterozygous at the eye-color locus. Let us imagine how the trait of eye color might be passed through three generations (Figure 2.9). Remember that at mitosis the chromosome pairs separate. This means that both sets of genes could be carrying a dominant or recessive trait, or in some cases 50 percent of the genes could be carrying a dominant trait and 50 percent a recessive trait. In Figure 2.10 we begin the story of the baby's inheritance of eye coloring with four sets of great-grandparents whose eye coloring you can see in the first set of **phenotypes.**

We are going to suppose that these great-grandparents passed on to their children—the baby's grandparents—the *genotypes* that are indicated.

In turn the grandparents pass on to their children—the baby's parents—the genotypes *Bb* for both the mother and father. This particular baby has inherited the genotypes *bb* and so must have blue eyes.

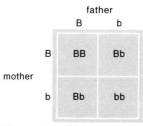

father

	B	b
B	BB	Bb
b	Bb	bb

mother

Figure 2.10 Example of combination of genotypes to produce brown or blue eyes. A baby inheriting *BB* genotypes can only have *brown* eyes. If the genotypes are *Bb* the possibilities are either *brown* or *blue* eyes. And, of course, *bb* genotypes can only result in *blue* eyes.

Beginning with the great-grandparents, there could have been different combinations of genotypes. There are four possible combinations for each set of parents. The combinations of genotypes it is possible to inherit from this baby's parents are shown in Figure 2.10. You can readily see why the baby could only have blue eyes, even though each parent has brown eyes.

When some character (phenotype) of the child is produced by a combination of several genes located on different chromosomes, an *incomplete dominance* of genotype occurs. For example, traits such as height, skin color, and hair color are often products of an intermediate dominance in combinations of genes.

Genotypes and phenotypes. If we knew the alleles that a child carried for certain traits, we would be able to describe the child with respect to those traits. But this is not always possible. Each baby has a unique combination of genes called a **genotype.** As we have seen, the child homozygous for brown eye color would have the genotype *BB,* and if both alleles were for blue eyes *(b),* the genotype would be *bb.* A child heterozygous for eye color would have the *Bb* genotype. The physical description of a child's particular traits is called the **phenotype.** So we might say that a child had the phenotype of brown eyes, or curly hair, or tallness.

As mentioned earlier we have heard people comment that a child looks just like one of his or her parents or has some physical feature such as a shape of nose or ears or a way of walking that seems to have been inherited from a grandparent. In some cases such inherited traits are more obvious than in others. What this means is that, within a limited number of possible physical traits, one or more has a clear-cut *dominance* over others. It is only possible for a child to inherit one quarter of the genes from any one grandparent, but it may so happen that a fixed portion might contain a high percentage of dominant genes that are related to certain prominent physical features (Rugh & Shettles, 1971, p. 205).

Table 2.3 Some Dominant and Recessive Traits

Dominant Traits	Recessive Traits
Hair	
Dark-brown hair	Light-brown and red hair
Curly hair	Straight hair
Normal head of hair	Baldness
Eyes and Ears	
Brown eyes	Blue eyes
Hereditary cataract	Normal
Astigmatism	Normal vision
Deafness	Normal hearing
Normal color vision	Color blindness
Nervous System	
Normal	Cerebral sclerosis
Epilepsy	Normal
Migraine	Normal
Muscular	
Normal	Progressive muscular dystrophy
Normal	Spastic
Normal	Infantile muscular atrophy
Diseases	
Diabetes insipidus	Normal
Hypertension	Normal
Normal	Diabetes mellitus
Immunity to poison ivy	Susceptibility to poison ivy
Blood Diseases	
Normal blood clotting	Hemophilia
Normal blood cells	Sickle-cell anemia
Pernicious anemia	Normal
(reduction in red blood cells)	

What is more important is the fact that each child has a genetic heritage of thousands of hereditary influences, most of which are not prominent. The complete genetic makeup (the genotype) is not revealed. The phenotype only displays the more prominent dominant genetic influences.

Over a considerable number of years geneticists have compiled a list of dominant and recessive traits (Table 2.3). Although there are exceptions to the rule, in most cases desirable genes are dominant and undesirable ones are recessive. This may be the result of natural selection. If closely related persons marry, there is a greater chance that two recessive, usually undesirable or harmful, genes will be passed on to their offspring. This is why in certain states it is unlawful for relatives closer than first cousins to marry.

Sex-Linked Characteristics

It has been mentioned that the human somatic cell is composed of 46 chromosomes. Of these, 22 pairs determine the general physical and mental characteristics of each person, and for this reason they are called **autosomes**. The remaining two chromosomes are called the *sex* chromosomes because they primarily determine the individual's sex characteristics.

How does a child come to be a boy or girl? It always depends on the sperm that penetrates the ovum. Each of the mother's germ cells contains two *XX* chromosomes. In the father's case there is one *X* and one *Y* chromosome. At meiosis each ovum gets one of the two *X* cells but each sperm will carry an *X* or a *Y* chromosome. If an *X*-carrying sperm combines with the ovum, the end result is a girl. The combination of a *Y*-bearing sperm with the ovum means there will be a boy (Figure 2.11).

More male than female babies are born. It has been established that about 106 boys are born for every 100 girls, and the difference is even higher for firstborn children. There has been much discussion about these different percentages. It has been discovered that the proportion of *X* to *Y* sperm is not always 50–50, but that often more *Y* sperm are produced than *X*. Also, the *Y* sperm are smaller and faster moving than the *X* sperm, and it may be assumed that these *Y* sperm have a better chance of reaching the ovum (Rugh & Shettles, 1971; Schuster & Schuster, 1972). Another possibility for the imbalance is that more boys than girls are aborted and, in general, the death rate for male babies is higher than that for girls (Scheinfeld, 1972). Thus nature may be compensating for this apparent advantage for male conceptions. More remains to be learned about sex determination, but it can safely be assumed that it is not a random occurrence (Furuhjelm, Ingelman-Sundberg, and Wirsen, 1977).

Sex-Chromosome Abnormalities

In addition to determing the sex of the child, the *X* and *Y* chromosomes also determine characteristics such as color-blindness and hemophilia (a failure of the blood to clot, which causes prolonged bleeding). These two abnormalities are caused by recessive genes in the *X* chromosome. A man can transmit color blindness or hemophilia to his daughters but not his sons because the *Y* chromosome does not carry these traits. However, such daughters would be *carriers*

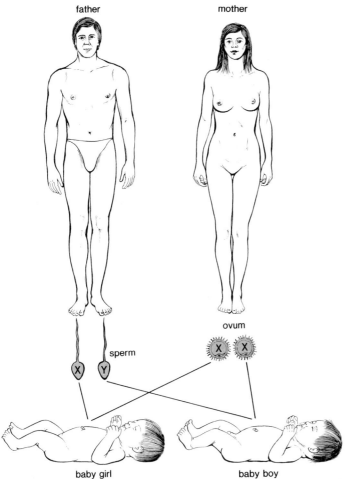

Figure 2.11 Sex determination of the baby. The twenty-third pair of the mother's and father's twenty-three chromosomes are the so-called sex chromosomes. The mother has two *x* chromosomes and the father has one *x* and one *y* chromosome in his pair, each of which goes to a separate sperm. At the moment of fertilization, if an *x* sperm penetrates the ovum (always *x*), the result is a girl (*xx*). If the sperm happens to be a *y*, the result is a boy (*xy*).

rather than color blind or hemophilic themselves (Rugh & Shettles, 1971, p. 205). These are sex-limited characteristics since they are *usually* limited to one sex (there are many more boy than girl hemophiliacs).

There is a particular chromosome abnormality known as *trisomy*, which is the presence of an extra chromosome related to one of the usual 23. Extra *X* or *Y* chromosomes result in a number of male and female abnormalities.

Male sex-chromosome trisomies. There are two well-known types of abnormal male sex-chromosome trisomies. In the first type there is an extra *Y* chromosome giving an *Xyy* pattern, sometimes referred to as *supermale*. Boys with this pattern are usually tall and have a tendency to be retarded and antisocial. When there is an extra *X* chromosome *(XXy),* the result is called an *intersex*. This pattern is better known as *Klinefelter's syndome,* which results in the boy's having undescended or sterile testes, female characteristics such as breast development, and a tendency to be of low intelligence.

Female sex-chromosome trisomies. Two types of sex-chromosome defects in girls are the *XXX* and *XO* patterns. The first trisomy is known as *superfemale*. However, rather than having an abundance of female attributes, girls with an extra *X* chromosome have underdeveloped breasts and small genitalia. The *XO* type is not actually a trisomy but a case of a missing chromosome and is known as **Turner's syndrome.** Girls with this condition are usually short in stature, with short fingers and folds of skin in the neck area. At puberty they develop small, immature breasts, abnormalities in the ovaries, and a lack of secondary characteristics such as pubic hair. These children are usually of normal intelligence, with pleasant personalities.

Autosome trisomies. The majority of inherited autosome trisomy abnormalities are associated with the chromosome pairs numbered 4, 5, 13, 14, 15, 17, 18, 21, and 22 (Rugh & Shettles, 1971, p. 210). The trisomy of chromosome 21 is known as **Down's syndrome.**

Down's syndrome. Down's syndrome occurs in about 1 out of every 600 live births (some authorities put it at 1:1000). The individual risk of having a Down's syndrome baby varies depending on the mother's age (Table 2.4).

Virtually all cases of Down's syndrome are associated with the trisomy of chromosome (autosome) 21 (Figure 2.12). About 4 percent of cases occur because of the *translocation* type in which all or part of one chromosome becomes attached to another. Although it is known that this abnormality occurs as a result of defective cell division during meiosis or during the early stages of development, why it occurs is not understood. Parents of Down's syndrome children usually have normal chromosome patterns, as do their unaffected children. Since affected children are usually sterile or are unable to procreate, the chances of inherited Down's syndrome are exceedingly slight.

Table 2.4 Mother's Age and Risk of Having a Down's Syndrome Baby[a]

Mother's Age	Risk
Under 20 years	1:2,300
20–29	1:1,500
30–34	1:800
35–39	1:250
40–44	1:100
45 and over	1:50

[a]Source: Reprinted with permission of *Patient Care Magazine*.
Copyright © 1977, Patient Care Publications, Inc., Darien, Ct.
All rights reserved.

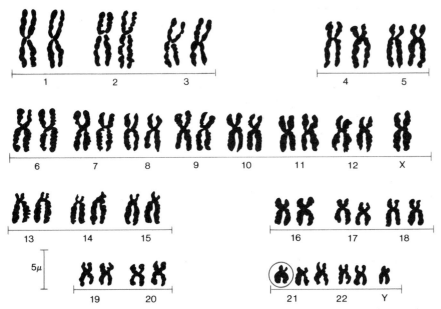

Figure 2.12 An extra chromosome at "pair 21" shown in this karotype indicates the presence of Down's syndrome in a male child. This is why the abnormality is labeled "trisomy 21." (Source: Reproduced by permission of the State Laboratory of Hygiene, Madison, Wisconsin, 1980.)

At birth the characteristic slant-eyes and oval faces are easily identified. (These facial features have led to this condition sometimes being referred to as mongolism.) Other characteristics include short stature, small misshapen ears, a short thick neck, and flattened nose. These children are always mentally retarded. However, many of them are placed in regular school classrooms (mainstreamed—see Chapter 14), where they usually develop much higher levels of competencies in self-help and mental and social skills than is the case for institutionalized Down's syndrome children. Most Down's syndrome children have a happy disposition, delight in all kinds of activities, and are easy to manage (Emery, 1968).

Down's syndrome and **spina bifida** (Inset 2.2) are the most prevalent birth defects that can be diagnosed by amniocentesis (see page 85).

The genetic heritage determines the physical characteristics of a child. We are less sure of the extent to which genes influence the development of personality and intellect. This topic is discussed in the section on the influences of nature (heredity) compared to those of nurture (the environment). An interesting topic we now turn to is that of multiple births. The conception of twins is of interest because (1) it appears that certain women have this tendency, which is inherited (Pritchard & Macdonald, 1976), and it occurs in only about 14 of 1000 births (Hamilton & Mossman, 1972), and (2), more importantly, twins have been studied in an attempt to determine the relative effects of heredity and environment.

The most common and severe type of *spina bifida cystica* is meningomyelocele. With this condition, the newborn baby has a skin or membrane-covered sac containing cerebrospinal fluid and, in most cases, imperfectly formed meninges (membranes that cover the spinal cord) and spinal cord.

Spina bifida is more common than Down's syndrome, occurring in 2 to 5 percent of live births. The underlying causes of this abnormality are not yet known, but it is believed to result from a combination of environmental and genetic causes. It is possible to detect the presence of spina bifida in the fetus by inspection of amniotic fluid. In severe cases the spinal cord appears as a ribbon of spongy, red tissue lying in a deep groove. In such cases the baby dies shortly after birth. In other instances, the rupturing of the spinal area may be slight and, whenever possible, surgical closing of the sac is done within a few days of birth to prevent meningitis (an inflammation of the membranes which envelope the spinal cord and brain) and hydrocephalus (excessive accumulation of fluid in the ventricles of the brain causing enlargement of the cranium). There is some evidence to suggest that prompt closure reduces impairment to the nervous system. The degree of impairment depends on the location of the meningomyelocele on the spine. The higher it is, the greater the impairment.

Hydrocephalus is the most common complication of spina bifida. This condition can be treated successfully, but not without some danger to the baby.

About 40 percent of babies born with spina bifida die before age 2. About half of the babies that survive have normal intelligence but severe handicaps—the most notable being urinary incontinence and impaired locomotion requiring full-time use of a wheelchair. About 20 percent are less severely impaired while the remaining 30 percent are mildly to moderately retarded with quite severe physical problems. The chances of parents having recurring babies with this abnormality are between 2 and 5 percent.

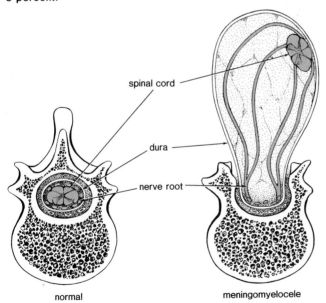

spinal cord

dura

nerve root

normal   meningomyelocele

Inset Figure 2.2 Spina bifida cystica. Spina bifida occurs in 2.4 percent of live births. The most common and severe type of spina bifida cystica is *meningomyelocele*—a skin-covered sac containing cerebrospinal fluid and, in most cases, imperfectly formed meninges and spinal cord. (Source: Reprinted with permission of *Patient Care* magazine. Copyright © 1977, Patient Care Publications, Inc., Darien, Ct. All rights reserved.)

Identical twins look alike and share the same sex. Fraternal twins may be of the same sex or of different sexes and usually have quite different physical features. (Photo, left, by Robert Eckert/EKM-Nepenthe; photo, right, by Allen Ruid.)

Twins

The frequency of twin births is about 1 in 90. Mothers who have conceived twins usually have more severe symptoms of pregnancy, such as excessive morning sickness, than is the case for a single conception. A doctor may suspect a double pregnancy if, during a regular examination of the uterus, he or she finds that the uterus has become larger than expected at that point in a pregnancy. The doctor may then attempt to confirm this initial diagnosis by means of various techniques. The most obvious and straightforward one is by using a stethoscope to listen for two heartbeats. A more complete and usually more reliable examination can be made by obtaining a fetal electrocardiogram, a sonargraph, or a radiograph.

There are two types of twins. Identical or **monozygotic** twins result when a fertilized ovum splits and becomes two zygotes. This split is believed to occur in the first week after fertilization. Fraternal or **dizygotic** twins come from two separately fertilized ova and are about four times more common than identical twins. Some women tend to ovulate more than one egg each month, and therefore they have a greater tendency to have double (or multiple) pregnancies. The fact that fraternal twins occur in some families more frequently than in others suggests this is an inherited trait. Monozygotic twins are identical because they are produced from a single fertilized ovum. They share the genetic mix of the zygote. Dizygotic twins, because they come from two separate fertilized ova, are as unique genetically as any single-birth siblings (Figure 2.13).

Many scientists interested in the relative effects of heredity and environment on the human organism's growth and development have studied twins. Not only have there been studies of the behavior of identical twins, but comparisons have

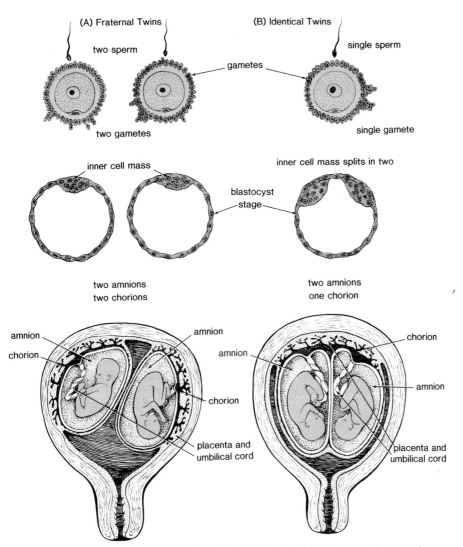

Figure 2.13 Development of fraternal and identical twins. (*A*) Two eggs (gametes) are each fertilized by two separate sperm. Two blastocysts are embedded in the wall of the uterus and fraternal twins result, each with its own placenta and chorions. Fraternal twins may be same or mixed sex. (*B*) One egg (gamete) is fertilized by a single sperm. One blastocyst, the inner cell mass of which it has split, is embedded in the wall of the uterus. Identical twins result. Each has a separate placenta, but share a single chorion. Identical twins are always the same sex. (Source: From *Human Reproduction: Biology and Social Change* by Harold D. Swanson. Copyright © 1977 by Oxford University Press, Inc. Reproduced by permission.)

been made between identical and fraternal twins. For example, if you discovered that a particular behavior trait occured in identical twins raised in families far apart but that the trait was absent in fraternal twins raised together, what might you assume about that trait? The obvious answer is that it is inherited. This would come as no surprise since we expect the same hereditary makeup for twins who both came from the same fertilized egg. If, however, we observed that certain behavior traits were not shared by these identical twins, we might assume that the difference was due to their being raised in different environments.

Interpreting the results of twin studies is not as simple as this. Identical twins may differ considerably from each other for a number of reasons. When the single egg divides, the separate zygotes become embedded in different parts of the uterus. To some extent the developing organisms compete for room, for nutrients, and for oxygen. One twin may get more than a fair share of such requirements and become more strongly developed than the other. One twin must be born first. The second twin to be born is often smaller and may suffer some lack of oxygen while waiting its turn to be born. Although identical twins share the same genetic endowment, during development in the uterus, at birth, and after birth, they have different experiences that result in their being distinct individuals (Wolff, 1979, pp. 244–245).

The trait resemblances that we are sure twins share are mainly physical; they usually look alike, seem to age in much the same way, and share many incidental behaviors. The IQ's of identical twins are also much closer than is the case for fraternal twins (Scarr-Salapatek, 1975). We can assume, therefore, that part of our makeup can be attributed to the genes we inherited. But it is difficult to separate genetic effects from environmental effects, even in studies of identical twins.

Nature and Nurture

The influence of heredity on the developing child is an age-old question. Philosophers in the sixteenth century believed that the father's sperm contained a microscopic but completely formed human being (a *humunculus*). Development in the mother's womb was supposed, therefore, to be predetermined, as was behavior after birth. Questions, some of them similar to these original questions, are still at issue: To what extent is future development determined at birth? Are such important characteristics as intelligence, personality, and appearance genetically fixed? How much influence can the environment have on molding development after birth?

These questions cannot easily be answered. As we have seen we can be quite sure about the effects of genetic heritage on some traits, and we can predict the likelihood of certain future traits occurring. For example, we can do this very easily for eye color, but less easily for hair or skin color. For most traits no simple gene is operating, but effects are produced by genes in relation to other genes. When it comes to behavior and personality traits, the picture is much more complex.

Even in the uterus the developing baby is exposed to environmental effects. It has been reported that unborn babies can be conditioned to kick when they hear a particular sound through the wall of the mother's abdomen (Wolff, 1979, p. 245). There has also been some speculation about the effect of the mother's emotional state on the unborn baby. It has been shown that emotions affect the amount of hormones produced by the mother's endocrine glands, which in turn can affect the development of the fetus.

The most controversial issue is related to intelligence (Scarr-Salapatek, 1972, 1975). Some specialists believe that intelligence is genetically determined (e.g., Herrnstein, 1973; Jensen, 1969, 1973). Jensen argues that there are two types of learning that can be associated with inherited traits. The first he calls *associative* or *Level I learning,* which includes relatively simple mental skills such as short-term memory, attention, rote-learning, and the ability to associate objects together according to simple relationships. The second type is called *cognitive* or *Level II learning* and includes mental skills such as abstract thinking, concept learning, processes of symbolization, use of language, and problem solving. Jensen has suggested that, whereas Level I learning skills are inherited by most children irrespective of social class and ethnic group, Level II learning skills are more likely to be found in middle- and upper-class Caucasians than lower-class or black American groups. On the basis of results from studies of twins he has estimated that between 70 and 80 percent of intelligence can be attributed to heredity and the remainder to environmental influences. Others argue very strongly that intelligence is influenced mainly by the environment, or that it is not possible to estimate the different effects of genes and environment (e.g., Block & Dworkin, 1976; Kamin, 1974). Another controversial issue concerns the development of language. As we will see in Chapter 4, some linguists claim that language cannot be taught, yet all normal children learn their native language, beginning at about 2 years. Other linguists insist that language is primarily learned from the culture the child is born into. The same can be said about personality differences.

Thinking back to the various theories of development and learning introduced in Chapter 1, you will realize that each theory, from its own particular point of view, made some direct or indirect reference to the relative influence of heredity and environment on child development and learning. We will return to this topic in several of the following chapters.

When specialists choose to disagree so strongly, we can assume the issue is extremely complex. At present, methods are not adequate enough to clearly separate the effects of nature (genetic influences) and nurture (environmental influences).

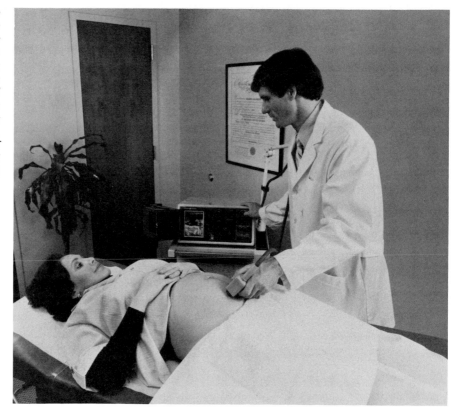

Genetic Counseling

Prospective parents who have a family history of hereditary illnesses or genetic defects can now get advice from genetic counselors regarding their chances of producing a normal or defective child. *Genetic counseling* may be done by pediatricians, family doctors, obstetricians, or geneticists.

The first step is for each partner to collect as much information as possible about the family history of particular diseases, occurrences of abortions, babies born with abnormalities, and so on. This is followed by a physical examination. We have already seen that urine and blood samples can provide information about the presence of certain abnormalities. In some cases samples of skin tissue are also taken; from these chromosome patterns can be prepared and photographed. The chromosome patterns are arranged on a chart called a *karyotype,* and possible genetic disorders can be identified. These tests are given prior to possible conception. Two tests used during pregnancy to diagnose any possible developmental abnormalities are amniocentesis and fetoscopy. Results from both types of tests can be useful in genetic counseling.

Brody (1969) describes the counseling of parents who had experienced the birth of an abnormal child. The mother, aged 20, had a firstborn with Down's syndrome. Four days after birth the baby died. The parents were reluctant to have another baby even though their doctor assured them that there was only a slight chance that a second baby would also be abnormal.

Eventually the parents were persuaded to visit a genetic counselor who pointed out that the chances of a 25-year-old woman's having a Down's syndrome child were 1 in 1,500. The woman was not completely reassured and asked for further evidence of the unlikelihood she would conceive an abnormal baby. The geneticist first drew up genetic ancestry charts for both parents going back through as many generations as possible. This indicated that there was no evidence of inherited chromosomal defects.

A chromosomal analysis was then done for samples of cells taken from both parents. The diagnosis showed that the husband had normal cells. The wife had 22 normal chromosomes including the *XX* sex chromosomes. But she also had a twenty-third *pair* of chromosomes that appeared defective. Indeed, it could be positively ascertained that she was a *carrier* of a rare form of Down's syndrome that results from an inherited genetic defect. Down's syndrome usually occurs as a result of a genetic accident at conception. The prediction from the counselor was that the couple had a one in three chance of conceiving another Down's syndrome baby.

Understandably, the prospective parents were opposed to taking such a chance. The counselor then pointed out that there was a relatively new technique called amniocentesis for determining defects in the developing fetus during early pregnancy. He described the process for draining a sample of fluid from the amniotic sac, the separation of cells (shed by the baby) from the amniotic fluid, and the biochemical and chromosomal analyses of the cells that would indicate the presence or absence of chromosomal abnormalities.

The couple decided to have another baby. Amniocentesis diagnosis in the early stages of pregnancy indicated no abnormalities. Eventually, the woman gave birth to a healthy baby girl.

Brody's description is based on a true case. It is worth considering what might have been this couple's reaction to being told after amniocentesis that the fetus of the second baby was also abnormal. How do you think you might react to such a situation?

Source: Brody, J. E., "Will Our Baby Be Normal?" Copyright by *Woman's Day*, 1969. Reprinted by permission.

Amniocentesis

Amniocentesis is usually performed between the fifteenth and eighteenth weeks of pregnancy. Ultrasonic location of the placenta's and fetus's head is usually made prior to amniocentesis or during the process itself (see Figure 2.14). A hollow needle is gently pushed into the uterus at right angles to the abdominal wall. Resistance to the needle will be felt at the skin, fascia, and peritoneum followed by a sense of "give." A syringe is then attached to the needle and 10

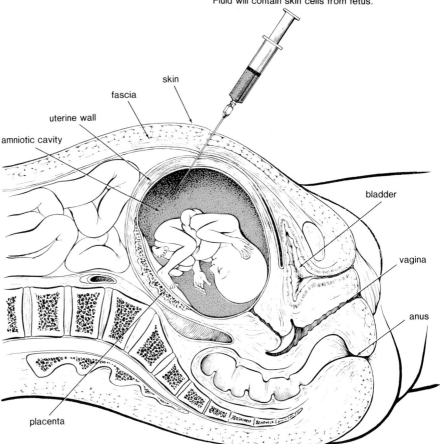

10–15 ml of amniotic fluid withdrawn using a syringe.
Fluid will contain skin cells from fetus.

skin

fascia

uterine wall

amniotic cavity

bladder

vagina

anus

placenta

Figure 2.14 Amniocentesis. The amniocentesis needle meets resistance at three points during insertion—at the skin, fascia, and uterine muscle—followed by a sense of "give" indicating that the needle has penetrated into the amniotic sac. A sample of amniotic fluid containing some of the cells shed from the skin of the fetus is withdrawn. Diagnosis of this sample permits detection of many genetic diseases, but it cannot indicate the severity of the disease in the fetus. (Source: Wickware, D. S. *Amniocentesis: For Whom, By Whom.* Reprinted with permission of *Patient Care* magazine. Copyright © 1977, Patient Care Publications, Inc., Darien, Ct. All rights reserved.)

to 15 ml of amniotic fluid withdrawn from the uterus. Floating in the amniotic fluid are skin cells from the fetus. These are prepared in a laboratory for chromosomal and biochemical studies.

Amniocentesis is offered to mothers who risk giving birth to physically or mentally handicapped children. The prospective mother will be advised to have an amniocentesis test after both parents have received expert genetic counseling. What are the most common reasons for advising pregnant women to have this test? Women between 35 and 40 have a 1:250 chance of having a baby with *Down's syndrome* (see Table 2.4). At age 45 the chance is 1:50. If there is a family history of *hemophilia*, the risk of a male baby with this disease is 50 percent. The risk of a baby's being born with *spina bifida* (see Inset 2.2) or *anencephaly* is about 4 percent if there is an affected parent or sibling. A test is advisable when the family history shows there has been a previous baby with either of these congenital malformations (Heimler & Lieber, 1978). This procedure is also used prior to planned cesarian births to detect the age of the fetus.

The importance of careful diagnosis and counseling should be emphasized. Results from large surveys show that about 5 percent of women tested had a fetus with abnormalities. This means that 95 percent of those tested were reassured. In the cases where an abnormal fetus was detected, 25 percent of the women decided to have the pregnancy terminated (Loxova, 1979, p. 251). Many parents decided to go through with the birth of the child despite their knowing it will be born abnormal. The benefit to these parents is knowing in advance that there will be something wrong with their child. They can be advised and prepared for the responsibility of raising a physically or mentally handicapped child.

Is amniocentesis always safe? The answer is yes if done expertly; otherwise it can be a hazard. It is recommended that a physician should assist in a dozen or more procedures before attempting one alone (Wickware, 1977, p. 57). There are also emotional and ethical hazards. It has been mentioned that this procedure is most useful in diagnosing Down's syndrome in the fetus. However, once the information is given to the pregnant woman and her family, they then have to "grapple agonizingly with the question of voluntary abortion" (Wickware, 1977, p. 16) or face the anxiety-provoking planning for a baby who will have a serious abnormality. Many obstetricians emphasize the need for great care in advising patients to undergo amniocentesis diagnosis, not only for prospective parents in counseling, but for those who have been diagnosed as carrying a fetus with some abnormality.

Fetoscopy

Amniocentesis has certain limitations as a diagnostic examination. For example, with this method about 40 percent of sickle-cell anemia cases are undetected.

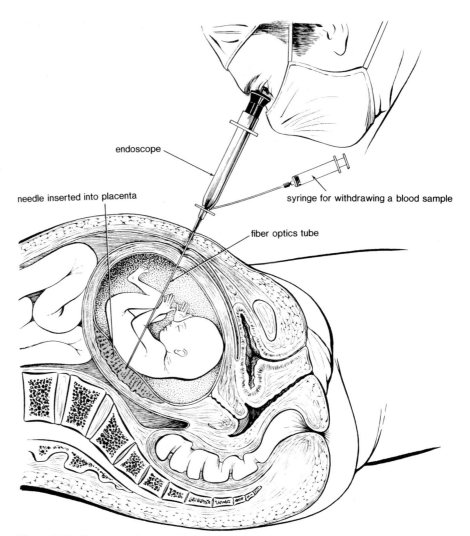

endoscope

needle inserted into placenta

syringe for withdrawing a blood sample

fiber optics tube

Figure 2.15 Fetoscopy. Fetoscopy makes it possible for the physician to actually see the fetus in the uterus and ascertain its condition. Samples of blood and tissue can be taken from the fetus or from the placenta. From these samples a diagnosis can be made of diseases such as epidermolytic hyperkeratosis—a severe skin disease—and the 40 percent of sickle-cell anemia cases missed in amniocentesis diagnosis.

A new diagnostic method called **fetoscopy** is now available. Using this method physicians can directly examine the fetus and take skin and blood samples. From the samples such diseases as *epidermolytic hyperkeratosis* (a severe skin disease), hemophilia, and sickle-cell anemia can be diagnosed.

Like amniocentesis, fetoscopy is performed between the fifteenth and eighteenth week of pregnancy. An ultrasonic-sound scan locates the fetus, umbilical cord, and placenta. A tube containing an *endoscope* and a hypodermic needle is inserted into the amniotic sac. The endoscope tube contains fiber-optic bundles that transmit light and also allow the physician to see tiny areas of the fetus and placenta (see Figure 2.15). Samples can be taken from the fetus's head where there are no major blood vessels. Using a hypodermic needle, inserted through the tube, the physician can draw a small blood sample from a fetal vein in the placenta.

The immediate benefit is to the mother. As in the case of amniocentesis, about 75 percent of cases diagnosed by this method indicate no diseases. It is hoped that future use of this method will help physicians detect abnormalities such as *muscular dystrophy* and *albinism* (a lack of pigment sometimes associated with sight and hearing problems and, in a few cases, mental retardation). It is also hoped that as the fetoscopy procedure is improved it might even be possible to perform minor surgery. Administering blood transfusions while the fetus is still in the womb is already possible.

Summary

Following conception, the germinal stage of prenatal development lasts two weeks and culminates in the implantation of the zygote into the wall of the uterus. During the embryonic stage, second to eighth week, the major systems, such as the nervous system, rapidly develop. During the fetal stage, ninth week to birth, these systems continue to develop and the fetus assumes the shape of a baby.

If spontaneous abortion occurs, this usually happens between the second and third months of pregnancy. Causes of spontaneous abortion include chromosomal abnormalities and the effect of viruses such as rubella (German measles).

A pregnant woman's diet should be similar to that of a nonpregnant woman. In late pregnancy extra protein, vitamins, and minerals may be required because of the rapid development of the fetus. Iron is prescribed for most pregnant women to offset anemic conditions. With an adequate, balanced diet, the expectant mother can expect to gain between 24 and 27 pounds during pregnancy. Babies of malnourished mothers have been observed to be somewhat retarded in development. However, the long-term effects of maternal malnutrition are not known.

Teratogens are drugs, viruses, chemicals, and radiation that can cause harm to the fetus. The pregnant woman should be advised on the use of drugs by her physician, who will also keep a close watch for possible teratogenic effects and treat these if necessary.

A number of common diseases and illnesses such as anemia, diabetes, and German measles can have an effect on the developing fetus. These diseases can be prevented (controlled in the case of anemia) or successfully treated if diagnosed early.

Excessive radiation can cause chromosomal damage and resulting defects.

The Rh factor (a protein substance) may be present in a person's blood (Rh positive) or absent (Rh negative). A problem may arise during pregnancy when an Rh negative women conceives an Rh positive baby. If fetal blood gets into the mother's blood (usually late in pregnancy, or even at birth), antibodies are produced. These are unlikely to affect the first pregnancy but can seriously affect subsequent pregnancies. If a baby is in danger from antibodies, a blood transfusion can be given (even before birth). However, it is more usual for the expectant mother to be immunized against producing antibodies by a Rhogam vaccine shot.

The aging of both parents increases the likelihood of conceiving a baby with chromosome abnormalities. One reason for this is the higher rate of genetic errors that occur during meiosis in older people.

Somatic cells each contain 46 chromosomes. These cells divide into exact replicas of each other in a process called *mitosis*. The body also produces *germ cells* or *gametes*. In the male these are called *sperm,* in the female *ova* (or egg cells). Gametes each contain 23 chromosomes that divide in a process called *meiosis*. This process involves two divisions during which there is an exchange of *genes* with multiple possible combinations. Further combinations of genes are possible when sperm and ovum unite at conception to form a *zygote*.

The zygote contains genes not only from the mother and father but also from the genetic ancestors of each parent's family. The complex combination of genes becomes the baby's unique set of traits. Each trait will have two or more sets of instructions called *alleles*. When the alleles for a particular trait (such as eye color) from both parents are the same, the child is said to be *homozygous* for that trait, and when they differ, *heterozygous*.

Certain alleles are dominant, others recessive. Dominant alleles determine particular traits. When a trait is determined by a combination of alleles, incomplete dominance results.

Each individual's unique combination of genes is called the *genotype*. The child's physical characteristics (most obviously) reflect the *genotype* in the form of the *phenotype*.

Forty-four of the 46 chromosomes (autosomes) in each somatic cell determine the child's physical and mental characteristics. The remaining two determine sex characteristics. Male sperm carry either an X or Y sex chromosome and the female ovum always an X. A YX combination at fertilization produces a male baby and an XX combination a female baby. Certain fetal abnormalities can result from either recessive genes in the sex chromosomes or from sex-chromosome trisomies. Autosome trisomy abnormalities such as trisomy 21, which is known as Down's syndrome, can also occur.

Twin conceptions may be either identical (monozygotic), resulting from the splitting of a single zygote, or fraternal (dyzygotic), resulting from the fertilization of two separate ova. Studies of twins have been conducted to gain information about the relative effects of heredity and environment on development. The respective influence of nature (heredity) and nurture (environment) remains unresolved.

Prospective parents with family histories of hereditary illnesses or defects and prospective parents older than 35 can get advice and diagnosis from a genetic counselor regarding the chances of conceiving an abnormal baby. During pregnancy amniocentesis and fetoscopy procedures can be used to diagnose the presence of some disease or abnormality in the developing fetus.

Questions for Review

1. Briefly describe the stages of prenatal development. What is particularly important about the embryonic period?

2. Describe some of the better-known effects of teratogens on the developing fetus.

3. With reference to anemia or diabetes, describe the onset and cause of the disease and the usual treatment for it.

4. Describe the two main types of cell division. What is so important about the process of *crossover* during meiosis?

5. How are traits transmitted? Describe the function of gene dominance with respect to a particular trait.

6. What are the differences between a baby's genotype and phenotype? Give examples of each.

7. How is a baby's sex determined? Describe three of the better-known sex-chromosome abnormalities and explain their occurrence.

8. If possible, arrange a visit with one or each of the following:

(a) a pregnant mother

(b) a genetic counselor

(c) an instructor for a course on prepared birth. Find out as much as possible about one or each person's knowledge and experience with pregnancy. If you have only been able to visit one of these people, try to exchange information with friends who have visited the other two. Prepare an account of pregnancy from these three viewpoints.

Suggestions for Further Reading

Annis, L. F. *The child before birth.* Ithaca: Cornell University Press, 1978. A concise account of the prenatal period. Provides clear descriptions of maternal and environmental influences on the developing fetus. Of particular interest is her summary in Chapter 6 of recently developed techniques for ensuring a normal birth in cases where abnormalities are likely to occur.

Apgar, V., & Beck, J. *Is my baby all right?* New York: Simon & Schuster, 1975. Describes possible prenatal problems and birth defects and various ways of treating them.

Bing, E. *Six practical lessons for an easier childbirth.* New York: Bantam, 1967. An excellent account of natural childbirth and how it might be achieved.

Nilsson, L., Furuhjelm, M., Ingelman-Sundberg, A., & Wirsen, C. *A child is born,* 2nd ed. New York: Delacorte Press/Seymour Lawrence, 1977. A straightforward text accompanies an excellent photographic record of prenatal development from conception to birth.

Swanson, H. D. *Human reproduction: Biology and social change.* New York: Oxford University Press, 1974. A biological view of human reproduction. An excellent text covering all aspects of the human life cycle from gamete formation to birth. Emphasis is on personal and social problems related to reproduction.

Birth

3

Soon the baby comes down through the wide-open cervix and appears in the pelvic outlet; one sees it bulging at each contraction. More and more of the baby's crown with its tufts of hair is coming into sight. Now the woman feels like pushing out her whole abdomen. "Come on, just a little more—good—push harder—now relax, the contraction is over. Breathe deeply, get plenty of oxygen—here you go, just come on, push again. . . ."

Nilsson, L., Furuhjelm, M., Ingelman-Sundberg, A., and Winsen, C., *A Child is Born.* Copyright © 1977 by Dell Publishing Co., Inc.

It has usually been the case that mothers in our Western societies have expected quite intense pain during childbirth—pain that must be relieved by tranquilizers and pain-killing drugs. Research has shown, however, that drugs administered during labor can be harmful to the baby; and many prospective parents have, in recent years, been attracted by prepared birth or natural childbirth as an alternative to traditional methods. Natural childbirth substitutes preparedness for drugs. Programs for natural childbirth provide information on the birth process, muscle-strengthening and muscle-relaxing exercises for the mother, and a method of breathing to reduce pain during labor. The father is trained to participate in helping the mother through the period of labor. This chapter opens with a description of the history of this approach to childbirth, and mention is made of the various prepared-birth programs now available to prospective parents.

Whether the expectant mother presumes to have her baby delivered by traditional methods or some modern method of childbirth, she will almost certainly be paying more and more attention to the impending birth during the last few months of pregnancy. The questions that become uppermost in her mind are, "When will the labor begin? How will I know for sure it has begun? Will I get to the hospital in time? Will the baby be normal? Will I be a good mother?" The first birth may take as long as from 10 to 12 hours although some first babies do not take nearly so long to arrive in the world. Usually the mother has plenty of time to get to the hospital. Stories of first babies being delivered in ambulances, in the backs of cars, or other more unlikely places become good copy for news reports, but these occurrences are very few.

In this chapter we will follow the stages of labor from its onset to the birth of the baby. We will note the methods used to assess the newborn baby and briefly describe the baby's physical appearance and basic internal systems such as the nervous system. Next we will discuss birth complications, individual differences among newborns, and states of the newborn. In the final section we will examine family reactions to, and relationships with, the expected and the newborn baby.

Preparing for Birth

No childbirth is completely free from pain and analgesia, anesthesia and forceps have long been used to reduce labor pains. But in 1933 Grantly Dick-Read, a British obstetrician, suggested a method of almost drugless childbirth, with the father present in the delivery room to coach the mother during labor and birth. He had asked himself: Is a woman's labor easy because she is calm or is she calm because her labor is easy? Is labor a painful and frightening experience because the woman is in pain and afraid, or is she pained and frightened because the labor is indeed painful? He concluded that fear was the main cause for the pain experienced at childbirth—a vicious circle with fear causing pain, which caused fear (1972).

Most pregnant mothers look forward to the birth of their babies with excitement and some anxiety. (Photo by Jean-Claude Lejeune)

During the 1950s Russian specialists began using a similar type of training called **psychoprophylactic conditioning.** *(Psychoprophylaxis* means psychological preparation to prevent illness. The term is used, less precisely, to mean prevention of pain.) During the training program the expectant mother is conditioned to a contrived stimulus to offset the painful stimulus of labor. The stimulus is a way of breathing in quick pants to offset the discomfort of the labor contractions along with a program of relaxing exercises.

Lamaze

During the early 1950s psychoprophylactic conditioning was further promoted by a Frenchman, Dr. Fernand Lamaze (Parfitt, 1977). Classes in the **Lamaze** method quickly spread throughout Europe and eventually to the United States (Karmel, 1959).

Lamaze courses are quite standard. Parents begin the course about two months before the expected birth. One main objective is instruction in the physiology of

labor by means of films, diagrams, and anatomical models. Emphasis is given to the sequence, nature, and rhythm of uterine contractions, which are referred to in a later section on stages of labor. The idea is to provide the mother with exact information about the birth process so she can recognize the stages of labor as they occur and so she will know what to expect and be less frightened.

The father, as a partner in the Lamaze lessons, becomes practically and emotionally very much a part of the prenatal preparations and the eventual birth of the baby. The benefits of a prepared birth can be shared by both parents. The mother is conscious and aware of what is happening during labor, and the father can help her through the stages of labor and enjoy the wonder of also being able to observe their child being born.

Some specialists believe that prepared birth is little more than a fad and that the exercises and breathing techniques have little direct effect on the birth process (Buxton, 1962; Brant & Brant, 1971). Others have reported that the benefit to mothers is not only a sense of achievement in a relatively carefree birth (Tanzer & Block, 1976) but also the need for less medical intervention, a shorter period of labor, and a reduction in the rate of birth complications (Cronenwett & Newmark, 1974; Enkin, Smith, Dermer, & Emmett, 1971). Many parents who have taken preparation for childbirth testify to its benefit. Giving the mother something "useful" to do during the labor and birth and having the husband present to provide encouragement and comfort can certainly do no harm. Lamaze, or similar preparation (see Gilgoff, 1978) for birth, does not guarantee a painless

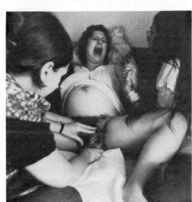
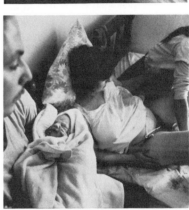

labor. However, should it prove necessary, small doses of analgesics or anesthesia may be given without denying the experience of a "prepared birth." And, of course, all modern obstetric techniques are available should there be complications. The mother can enjoy natural childbirth, confident that these benefits are on hand if needed.

Some women give birth to their babies at home, attended by midwives who are specially trained in obstetrics. Midwives in the United States stress "prepared birth" and invite fathers and children of the family into the delivery room. (Photos by Robert Eckert/ EKM-Nepenthe)

Midwives

During the pregnancy the expectant mother receives regular medical examinations to monitor her health and the development of the fetus. Most mothers, at least in the United States, expect to have their babies in a hospital while attended by a physician. In some hospitals the pregnant woman will be attended by a **midwife** during labor and childbirth, though a doctor may also be present, at least for the delivery stage. Some women elect to have their babies at home, cared for by a midwife, who is almost invariably a woman trained to provide assistance during childbirth. Midwifery is usually a special segment of a nursing program which provides training in obstetrics.

Birth **99**

A historical perspective. "Throughout history, women have always helped other women deliver their babies. In most other countries they still do—the U.S. is the only place in the world in which midwives have *ever* been outlawed. Midwives deliver about 80 percent of babies born in the world. . . .

"Though midwives have been in almost total disrepute here until recently, and our American babies have been delivered in the most scientific manner ever devised, the infant mortality rate in the United States is significantly higher than in many countries that rely heavily on midwives [such as] Sweden, Finland, the Netherlands, Japan, Iceland, Norway, and many countries of Europe, England, and New Zealand.

"In Europe for many centuries, and in the early days of America, too, lay midwives were the people who practiced obstetrics" (Brennan & Heilman, 1977, pp. 18–19).

It was not until the late nineteenth century in the United States that obstetrics became recognized as a medical specialty and were taken over by male physicians. Mortality rates for mothers and infants were high at that time and the "granny midwives" were blamed and forced out of business.

The comeback of midwives in the United States began in the 1960s, when there were only a few hundred, to a few thousand . . . with a professional organization, the American College of Nurse—Midwives.

What do midwives give? "Because we are ourselves women trained to help other women give birth as easily and happily and normally as possible, we have helped to humanize the system. . . . The new way is to deliver bright, alert babies to awake and aware mothers . . . to invite fathers to join the family, for newborn babies to feel the love of their parents right there in the delivery room. . . . Though midwives first came into the hospitals because of an impending shortage of obstetricians and

Because of a high infant and mother mortality rate in the United States during the nineteenth century, midwives were phased out of the business of delivering babies. They are now back on the scene, still in rather small numbers, principally expressing support of "natural birth" and allying themselves with physicians and the back-up services that come with hospital delivery rooms. However, some do attend pregnant women at home and arrange for them to have their babies there. (See Inset 3.1.) Laws in some states do not allow midwives into homes for a home delivery without a doctor being also in attendance.

Labor and Birth

Labor and birth occur in three stages. At the *onset* of labor the mother is alerted to the impending birth of her baby by labor pains that are caused by the first contractions of the uterus. These contractions produce the first stage of labor, the **dilation** of the cervix and vaginal canal, which is followed by the *delivery stage* and the final stage when the placenta is expelled.

a projected baby boom, we are not sought out because women like who we are and what we give. . . . We have had enough obstetric experience to know that while nature has designed a wonderful and complex process for reproducing ourselves . . . scientific research over the years has made it possible to save many mothers and babies who wouldn't make it otherwise" (pp. 52–63).

What are some of the main objectives of midwives? As Brennan and Heilman put it—"We stress prepared childbirth. . . . We are noninterventionists: our orientation is towards childbirth as a normal, natural physiological event. . . . We are a team with the doctors. . . . We are flexible: we assure (patients) that they can deliver as they want. . . . We provide low-cost service" (pp. 64–71).

Hospitals versus home. At least in the opinion of Brennan and Heilman, the risk of having a baby at home is too high. Some women see the home birth as warm and family oriented and the hospital birth as cold and impersonal. The point is made, however, that no birth is normal until it is over, and the best place for a newborn to be, if there are complications, is a hospital with a doctor available and all other necessary services.

There is a trend in America today to have babies at home, and there are physicians and nurse—midwives in some communities who are delivering babies at home. In most other Western European countries, and in England, the majority of normal births are at home, but there are extensive systems of trained midwives, and obstetric "flying squads" in cases of emergency.

Ninety-nine percent of pregnant American women still continue to check into hospitals for the birth of their baby. Those who choose home births must do so knowing the risks as well as the joys.

Source: Brennan, B., & Heilman, J. R. *The Complete Book of Midwifery.* Copyright 1977 by E. P. Dutton. Reprinted by permission.

Onset of Labor

During the last few weeks before the onset of labor the mother will, every so often, experience a contraction of the uterus. She will also very likely experience some back pains. In some cases the contractions may appear to be occurring with some frequency. The expectant mother may become convinced the labor has begun, only to have the pains disappear. This is called a "false labor" and may lead to a woman going to the hospital, only to return home again. The pains of a false labor are usually erratic. If the mother walks around and the pains go away, this is a sign the labor is false.

At the beginning of true labor the contractions, each of which lasts about one minute, occur with regularity at about half-hour intervals. After a few hours (the duration varies) the time between contractions gets shorter and shorter; when the contractions occur about every 5 or 10 minutes, the time has arrived for birth, at least for the first baby. For later babies, it is advisable for the expectant mother to go to the hospital, or to call in a midwife or doctor for a home birth, earlier than this.

Stages of Labor

The first stage of labor, called the *dilation stage,* is the longest and usually the most difficult. The cervix and vaginal canal must open, or dilate, to allow the baby to pass through. During pregnancy the cervix is closed by a *mucous plug* that is expelled as **effacement** occurs (the "show"). Effacement of the cervix is the shortening of the cervical canal from about 2 cm long to a circular opening and is the first phase of dilation. For the average full-term baby, the cervix must dilate to a diameter of about 10 cm, at which stage the cervix is said to be *fully dilated.* At the beginning of labor the child's head is usually down toward the cervix. Each contraction has the effect of pushing the upper walls of the uterus downward toward the cervix, which, in turn, forces the baby in that direction and pushes the head into the cervix and vaginal canal. For a first birth, this stage may take 8 to 10 hours, but it is usually much shorter (4 to 6 hours) and less difficult in subsequent pregnancies.

Figure 3.1 Stages of

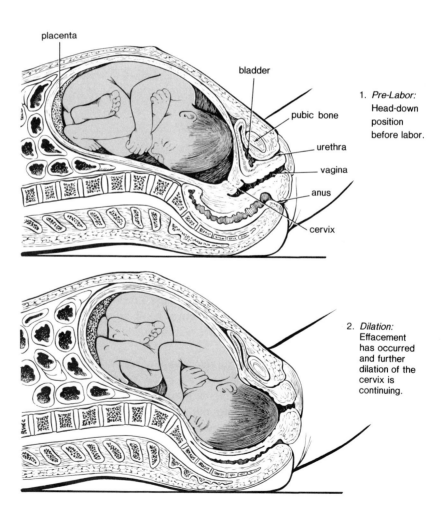

placenta

bladder

pubic bone

urethra

vagina

anus

cervix

1. *Pre-Labor:* Head-down position before labor.

2. *Dilation:* Effacement has occurred and further dilation of the cervix is continuing.

During the course of labor, pressure from the baby's head may rupture the membranes of the **amniotic sac** and there will be a gush of colorless fluid. Early in labor, this "bursting of the waters" may be taken as a sign that birth is imminent. This may not be so. A "dry birth" may take place some considerable time later. Occasionally, the sac remains intact until after delivery.

The second stage of labor is called the *delivery stage* and usually lasts from one to two hours during the first labor, although it may be as short as a few minutes in subsequent pregnancies. As the baby's head begins to distend the opening to the cervix, the mother gets the urge to push, or "bear down." In traveling down the vaginal canal the baby's face should be pointing downward, which provides the easiest birth. If this is not the case, the doctor will probably turn the baby. When the baby's head appears in the vaginal opening, just a few more pushes will slip the baby out (Figure 3.1).

When the baby's head is about to emerge from the vagina, it is usual for the doctor (or midwife) to perform an *episiotomy*. This requires the cutting of the

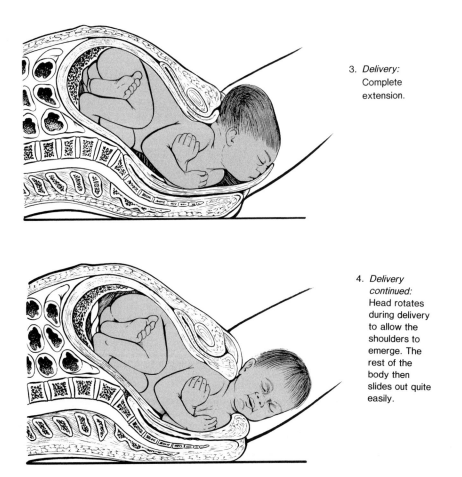

3. *Delivery:* Complete extension.

4. *Delivery continued:* Head rotates during delivery to allow the shoulders to emerge. The rest of the body then slides out quite easily.

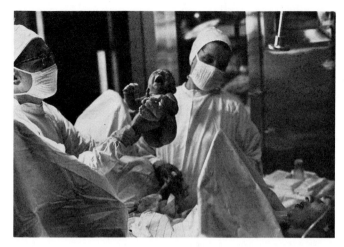

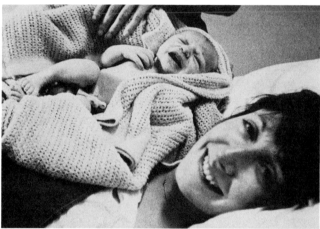

skin at the lower end of the vaginal opening, to enlarge the opening and prevent jagged tearing that may occur as the baby's head emerges. As soon as the baby is fully emerged, the incision is sewed up.

With the baby delivered, the birth is not yet quite over. During the third and final stage, which usually takes just a few minutes, further contractions of the uterus result in the expulsion of the umbilical cord and the placenta (sometimes referred to as the "afterbirth"). If this does not occur spontaneously, the usual method is for the doctor to use a pushing movement on the upper part of the uterus while gently pulling on the umbilical cord.

Immediately after delivery, mucus is cleared from the nose and throat of the baby. The usual procedure is for the doctor to hold the baby upside down by the feet to allow the mucus to drain out of the respiratory passages or to suck the mucus from the nose, mouth, and throat with a soft, rubber syringe. When the baby's lungs have begun to function, the **umbilical cord** is tied and cut. The newborn baby can now be given to the mother and enjoyed by both parents if the father is allowed into the delivery room. In some cases the baby is washed by a nurse before it is handed to the mother. (When the baby is born it is still covered in a protective "ointment" called *vernix caseosa*. While the baby is still in the womb, its hair and skin are kept soft and protected from the amniotic fluid by this oily substance. It especially sticks to the hairs on the head and around the eyes.)

This traditional method of delivering a baby has been criticized as being too insensitive to the shock of birth for both the baby and the mother. Alternative, supposedly less traumatic methods of easing a baby into the world have been suggested. One particular method that has received much publicity is that advocated by LeBoyer (1975). See Inset 3.2.

Assessing the Newborn

Most babies are born healthy, with less than 10 percent having any abnormality. Most systems are functioning normally within moments of birth. For a few babies there will be complications, and the doctor will need to recognize any danger as quickly as possible.

A simple test for measuring the degree to which the main body systems are functioning normally at birth was devised by Dr. Virginia Apgar in 1953 (Apgar, 1953). The **Apgar Scale** is now used in most hospitals (Table 3.1).

Table 3.1 The Apgar Scale

	Characteristic	Score		
		0	**1**	**2**
A	Appearance (color)	Blue, pale	Body pink with extremities blue	Pink all over body
P	Heart rate (pulse)	Absent	Slow:less than 100 beats per minute	Rapid:over 100 beats per minute
G	Reflex action or irritability (grimace)	No response	Grimace	Coughing, crying, sneezing
A	Muscle tone (activity)	Limp, flaccid	Weak and inactive, or some flexion of extremities	Strong flexion, active motion
R	Breathing (respiration)	Absent	Irregular and slow	Good breathing; baby is crying

Source: Adapted from Apgar, V., "A proposal for a New Method of Evaluation of the Newborn Infant." Copyright © 1953 by *Current Research in Anesthesia and Analgesia.*

Frederick LeBoyer (1975) has described the more usual methods of delivering the baby as the "torture of the innocents." In LeBoyer's opinion, birth is quite traumatic for the baby and should be reduced as much as possible. How is this to be achieved? He is opposed to the practices of holding the newborn upside down by the heels to aid the removal of mucus from the nose and throat, of startling a baby into breathing by a sharp slap, of putting silver nitrate into the baby's eyes to prevent infection and possible blindness, and the removal of the baby from the mother.

The delivery room should be as quiet as possible and only dimly lit. After birth, rather than cutting the umbilical cord immediately, LeBoyer maintains that the baby should be placed on the mother's stomach to be caressed by the mother until the cord stops pulsing. Once the cord is tied and cut, the baby is placed in a bath of warm water to relax. This is meant to simulate the warm fluid of the amniotic sac. Salter (1978) has reported there is some evidence to suggest that babies delivered in this fashion are more alert during the first 36 hours after birth. However, Cohn (1975) has criticized the dim lighting of delivery rooms since it may cause doctors to miss vital signs of distress at birth. He also opposes the laying of the baby on the mother's stomach or in the bath of water because this may expose the baby to sources of infection.

Without using the LeBoyer procedure, in most hospitals doctors and nurses try to ensure as gentle a birth as possible. It is not uncommon for the newborn baby to be placed on the mother's stomach, to delay the cutting of the umbilical cord, to allow both parents to share the birth experience, and to allow the mother to hold and caress the baby for some time after the birth.

At 1 to 5 minutes after delivery the doctor or attending nurse will "administer" the test. This requires observation of the baby's appearance (color), pulse (heart rate), grimace (reflex action), activity (muscle tone), and respiration (breathing). (As you can see the first letter of each measure makes up the name Apgar.) A rate of 0, 1, or 2 is given for each measure for a maximum score of 10. Over 90 percent of newborns receive a score of 7 or above. A newborn receiving a score of 4 or less needs immediate treatment and intensive care. However, the test is not predictive, and these babies may develop normally.

The Newborn Baby

The parents and the attending physician are naturally concerned about the well-being of the newborn baby during the first days and weeks following birth as a transition is made from life in the uterus to life in the outside world. Monitoring of the baby's health continues partly by the parents and also by the physician. Special attention is paid to the appearance of certain physical characteristics and also to the functioning of the basic body systems.

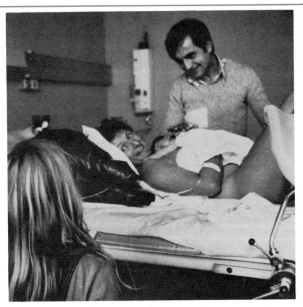

Leboyer insists that the newborn should be placed on the mother's stomach immediately after birth until the umbilical cord has stopped pulsing. The baby should then be placed in a bath of warm water to relax it. These procedures are supposed to reduce the effects of the trauma of birth for the baby. (Photos Woodfin Camp and Assoc. © Irene Barki)

Physical Characteristics

Two of the more obvious physical characteristics of the newborn that concern parents are the appearance of the baby's skin and the shape of the body.

Skin markings. The newborn baby is not all that appealing in looks—although the mother and father might choose to disagree. Even after the vernix is washed off, the baby may have some skin discoloration. Small red spots and blotches can be seen on the eyelids, the neck, over the nose, and on the forehead because of initial inefficiency in the blood circulation. These markings disappear after a few weeks as the blood circulation improves.

After a few days large red blotches often show up on the baby's skin; these are commonly called *strawberry nevus*. The blotching becomes more prominent when the baby is crying because of hunger or being uncomfortable. The condition is probably caused by an early immaturity in blood flow, and it eventually disappears.

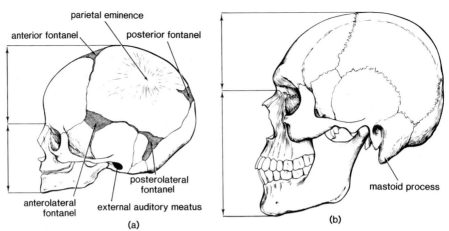

Figure 3.2 Infant skull compared to adult skull. The infant's skull bones are separated by gaps filled with fibrous connective tissue called *fontanels*. These allow the bones of the skull to mold themselves to the shape of the narrow birth passage of the mother as the baby is born. The fontanels are not filled in by growth of the skull bones until about the end of the first year of life. (Source: Sinclair, D. *Human Growth after Birth*. Copyright 1978 by Oxford University Press. Reprinted by permission.)

Bone structure.   The shape of the baby's body will largely depend on the structure of the skeleton. What is the extent of normal skeletal development at birth?

We may think of the baby's skull as being a single, molded bone, but this is not so. As you can see in Figure 3.2 a number of separate bones make up the skull. At birth these bones are not knitted closely together, although they become so later. The places where the bones come together are called the *sutures,* and the spaces between the bones are covered by connective tissue called *fontanels.* The tissue covering is tough and can be pressed without causing any damage. The advantage of this arrangement at birth is that it allows movement or molding in the baby's skull during passage through the birth canal. The fontanels close up as the baby gets older, and the process is complete at about 1 year.

The most important characteristic of the newborn's skeleton is pliability. This is very obvious in the shape of the legs. In the fetal position the legs are bowed, and they stay this way until the baby begins to walk when the legs straighten out.

Body Systems

The **body systems** that invite most attention, especially in the early days and weeks of infancy, are the nervous system, respiratory system, circulatory system, and digestive system. It is not unusual for certain abnormalities to occur in these systems as physical development continues and as the baby adjusts to the new environment.

The nervous system.   The doctor observes the baby's movements to see if they are limp and weak or strong and active. This provides an indication of muscle-tone condition and a first hint of the functioning of the nervous system. The brain and central nervous system are highly developed at birth in the normal baby (Kessen, Haith, & Salapatek, 1970). Signs of this development are reflected in certain coordinated reflex actions controlled from the lower brain centers. The doctor can check these reflexes with some appropriate stimulation. For example, shining a bright light into the baby's eyes results in reflex shutting of the lids. A newborn will focus on a red or yellow object dangled before its eyes, and follow the object when it is moved. (A detailed description of reflexes in infancy appears in Chapter 4.)

Breathing and circulation.   During pregnancy the baby was provided necessary oxygen in the blood supply brought in through the umbilical cord. When the cord is tied and cut a few minutes after birth, the lungs usually take over immediately. If this does not happen, the doctor will give the baby a slap on the buttocks. The result is a short cry and a sucking in of air—the lungs are in operation. Alternatively, the doctor might start the baby's breathing by massaging the chest or using some other artificial means such as mouth-to-mouth resuscitation.

The doctor checks the baby's breathing with a stethoscope and, at the same time, checks the heart in the same way. Sounds and rhythm of the heart are noted. Irregular heartbeats, referred to as heart *murmurs* in newborns, are quite normal. Before birth the baby's blood circulation almost completely by-passes the lungs, but after birth the blood must circulate through the lungs and pick up oxygen; at this time passage of the blood through the heart is reorganized. This reorganization takes a few days, and blood passing through partially opened or closed ventricles causes the sound called a heart murmur.

The digestive system.   The baby is born with a strong sucking reflex. In some cases the first feeding is given between 12 and 24 hours after birth, though many babies are given their first feeding on the delivery table. It has been usual for babies born in a hospital to be given the first feeding as a bottle of sugar water by a nurse. This practice is changing, however, because it is now considered important that the baby be returned to his or her mother immediately after birth. It is more likely, therefore, that the baby will get his or her first feeding from the mother.

If the mother has decided to breast-feed, she at first produces a thin, watery liquid called *colostrum,* which is rich in protein. It is not until the third or fourth day that she begins to produce milk. The newborn will probably lose a little weight in the first week or so. This is normal, and the mother need not worry.

The first feces passed by the baby are composed of a greenish-black, sticky waste called *meconium,* which is formed in the intestinal tract before birth. Once it has been passed, usually within the first 24 hours, the feces become a light golden color. Failure to pass stools within the first 24 hours may indicate an obstruction in the bowels.

By about the second or third day, over 50 percent of normal newborns develop a **physiologic jaundice** caused by the immature functioning of the liver. The symptoms are a yellowish discoloration of the skin and eyes and usually disappear in a few days. The physical cause of these symptoms is the presence in the blood of a yellow chemical called *bilirubin.* This is a normal condition, although in premature infants the condition may be more intense. Bilirubin is carried by the blood to the liver where most of it is extracted. What remains goes to the bile and from there into the intestine, from which it passes out in the feces. The livers of some newborns have not yet developed sufficiently to process bilirubin. After a few days the *enzyme,* a protein substance that helps process the bilirubin, increases in the liver and the symptoms disappear. Severe cases of high levels of bilirubin (hyperbilirubinemia) usually result in spasticity and lack of muscle coordination. These symptoms occur more frequently in premature babies. Treatment is either by blood transfusion or phototherapy. *Phototherapy* uses light from a concentrated source to penetrate the baby's skin and appears to reduce the bilirubin level (Pritchard & MacDonald, 1976, p. 813).

Complications at Birth

In most cases the pregnant mother can expect to have a normal labor and to give birth to a healthy baby. But for some mothers there will be complications at birth and their effects may continue at least for the period of infancy. Only two of the major birth complications are mentioned here; this section closes with a brief reference to a number of the more common infections of early infancy and the usual methods of treatment.

For some women labor becomes extremely prolonged, which can have harmful effects on the baby. There are also various reasons why some women cannot be allowed to experience a normal labor and birth, in which cases the baby must be removed surgically from the uterus.

Induced Labor

The amniotic sac is a membrane that protects the developing fetus during pregnancy. In almost 50 percent of the cases this membrane ruptures before labor begins. When the period of labor takes only a short time after the sac breaks, there is little chance of infection of the baby from vaginal bacteria. If labor is prolonged, however, there may be some danger of infection. When this is the case, the doctor will usually *induce* labor (begin it artificially) by injecting the mother with a drug called *pitocin*. This is a hormone that almost immediately produces labor contractions.

Cesarean Section

A **cesarean section** is the delivery of the baby through a surgical incision made in the wall of the uterus. The most common reason for this surgical operation is that the pelvic opening is too small to allow the baby to be delivered normally. [Some specialists believe it is unnecessary, that mothers with small pelvises can achieve a normal delivery although labor will be slower than usual (Gorbach, 1979).] When the baby has not attained the necessary head-down position for birth at the time of labor, or when there are complications in early labor such as *anoxia* (a deficiency in the oxygen supply), the doctor decides that a cesarean section is necessary.

At one time many babies delivered in this way died because of various complications. This is no longer the case since modern medical treatment can handle most emergencies. A criticism of the cesarean section operation now is that, because it has become so safe and easy to perform, physicians decide to use it for even minor complications in pregnancy. Furthermore, in the United States, following a first cesarean delivery, 98 percent of women who conceive again undergo a subsequent cesarean delivery, even though cesarean deliveries are now performed in a way that makes possible normal labor and delivery in subsequent pregnancies. In 90 percent of cases the surgeon makes a horizontal incision in the lower abdomen called a bikini-cut; this is the modern alternative to the previous method of making a vertical or T-shaped incision. However, some doctors still fear that no matter how the initial incision is made a subsequent normal delivery may result in the rupture of the incision. It is advised that women who prefer to attempt a normal delivery following a previous cesarean birth, or whose doctors advise them that this is possible, should certainly be in a hospital, where an emergency cesarean may be performed if necessary.

Some women wish to be aware of the birth of their child at the time of cesarean section. This is made possible by the use of a local *epidural anesthesia* (an injection in the lumbar region). Even while the surgeon is sewing up the incision, the mother can watch her baby being attended to. After the Apgar score has been determined, if all systems are found to be normal, the baby is returned to the mother. In some hospitals the father is allowed into the delivery room and the recovery room soon after the cesarean delivery to remain with the mother as she gives the baby its first feeding.

Premature Births

The due date for the birth of a baby is calculated as being 40 weeks from the first day of the mother's last menstrual period. This calculation assumes that ovulation occurs two weeks after the beginning of a period. However, the actual date of birth may be between a few days and up to three weeks on either side of the calculated due date, especially for women whose menstrual periods are irregular.

Babies born more than three weeks before the due date are considered premature. However, since errors can be made in calculating this date, a more precise measure of prematurity is the baby's birth weight. Babies weighing less than 5½ pounds (2500 grams) at birth are premature, and babies of low birth weight born close to the due date are called *small-for-date*. A premature birth is considered the most important complication of pregnancy. Of all births in the United States, between 5 and 15 percent are premature. **Prematurity** can result from various causes such as malnourished or overworked mothers. Other causes associated with premature births are mothers who smoke heavily, who are poor (associated with poor diets and untreated diseases), and who receive little or no prenatal medical care. However, the question of what the actual causes of prematurity are remains unanswered.

What are the characteristics of a premature baby? In premature babies certain functioning parts of the body such as the kidneys, lungs, and muscles may not be working as well as would be the case for a normal baby. Their skin is often thin with little underlying fat. There may also be malformations of the heart or other congenital disorders. Most premature babies have some type of respiratory problem probably caused by immature development of the brain centers that regulate breathing. Unlike a normal baby's temperature, which remains quite stable after birth, the premature baby's temperature fluctuates. Reflexes such as sucking, swallowing, and coughing are also very immature, and premature babies have difficulty breathing because of mucus blocking air passages. For these reasons premature babies are placed in *incubators* (sometimes called **isolettes**), "isolated" in an environment in which humidity and temperature are controlled and in which they are protected from infection. The special equipment and skilled care ensures a very high chance of survival during the period of further development outside the uterus when reflexes and other systems mature to the point at which the baby can exist in a normal environment.

Most premature babies are born to mothers living in impoverished conditions with all the disadvantages mentioned previously. Not only do these babies come into the world with a disadvantage, but they are taken home to grow up and develop in "at-risk" environments. Working with prematures born to such disadvantaged mothers, Scarr-Salapatek and Williams (1973) gave the babies extra stimulation and contact during their stay in the hospital. After the mothers had taken their babies home, they were visited and given counseling on how to care for their babies. It was found that the initial stimulation and contact and later care instruction helped overcome the handicap of a premature birth for these babies.

A very real problem for the premature baby is feeding. The smallest "preemies" usually just do not have the strength to suck. It is necessary to insert a tube (called a gavage) through the nose and down into the stomach through which the baby can be fed. Feeding is begun with small amounts of glucose that are given every two or three hours. The amount is gradually increased, and after a few days a weak milk solution (for which milk from the baby's mother may be used) is substituted. When the baby is strong enough, breast- or bottle-feeding can then begin.

The birth of a premature baby can be quite traumatic for the parents. The baby may be very weak and for a critical period be in danger of dying. Parents may overreact to the baby's condition and continue to treat it as frail and ailing even when the baby has matured enough to be taken home. It is very important for parents to receive good counseling about the continuing care of their baby. One of the parents' concerns should be to give the baby every chance to grow and develop in a normal fashion and for them to avoid being overprotective.

As we shall see in Chapter 5, early contact between mother and newborn baby may be important for establishing a baby's emotional attachment with the mother (Klause & Kennell, 1976). In the case of premature babies initial isolation of the baby in the intensive care incubator makes this early contact virtually impossible. To mitigate against the lack of contact with the mother and normal physical caring experiences, premature babies have received such artificial stimulation as hearing the tape-recorded heartbeats the infant would have been exposed to in the mother's uterus (Barnard, 1973), rocking, and handling and cuddling (Rice, 1977; Scarr-Salapatek & Williams, 1973). Infants exposed to such types of stimulation have been observed as being more advanced in mental and neurological development compared to premature infants who received no additional stimulation (Rice, 1977).

Long-term effects of prematurity. It has been claimed that many premature babies, once they are over the worst of the first few weeks, catch up with the development expected of the normal child. The ranks of great scientists, artists, and statesmen are studded with prematures—Charles Darwin, Isaac Newton, Renoir, Victor Hugo, Napoleon, Winston Churchill, to mention a few (Feinbloom, 1979). However, a number of investigations of the long-term effects of prematurity and early separation from the mother have provided evidence of varying degrees of retardation in development.

In one study Taub (1977) found no differences between premature and normally born children in verbal intelligence when these children were between 7½ and 9 years old. However, the premature group did not fare so well as the normal group on measures of motor development. With matched groups of premature

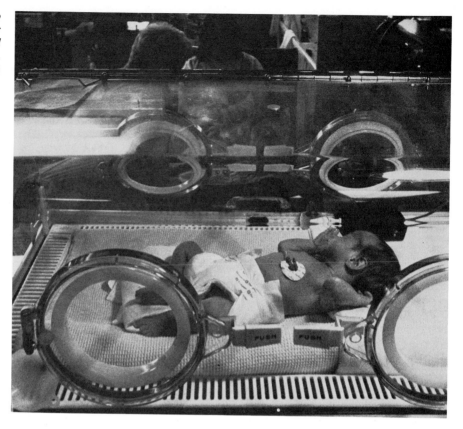

and normal-birth children aged 10 years, Wright (1960) found more prematures experiencing mental retardation, poor school performance, and visual defects. Ruben et al. (1973) found similar impairments in mental development and school achievement associated with low birth-weight children. It should be mentioned that the effects of prematurity on IQ are greater for infants born to lower-class mothers (Drillien, 1964). Social problems have also been associated with premature births (Berges et al., 1972), although children with such problems were found to outgrow some of the early appearing developmental problems over a lengthy period of time.

On the positive side, and of some encouragement to parents of premature babies, Sameroff and Chandler (1975) have commented that "self-righting influences are powerful forces toward normal human development." With proper care and attention these "self-righting influences" can be expected to favor eventual normal development. It is premature babies who go to live in unstable homes, with families living in a deprived environment and with mothers who have below normal intelligence, that are usually found, in the long run, to be deficient in health and in social and mental development (Braine, Heimer, Wortis, & Freedman, 1966; Sameroff & Chandler, 1975).

A special case of premature birth is *abortion,* which can be spontaneous or induced.

Abortions. We have already mentioned that spontaneous abortion occurs very early in pregnancy, in some cases probably even before the zygote is implanted, and that a high proportion of spontaneous abortions occur because of some serious congenital defect in the embryo. For various reasons an established pregnancy can be terminated by induced abortion.

The method used to induce an abortion depends on the stage of pregnancy. The most frequently used procedure for terminating a pregnancy during the first three months is by **vacuum aspiration** (sometimes referred to as **suction curettage**). A narrow flexible tube is inserted into the uterus by way of the vagina and the embryo and placenta are removed by suction. The woman is given either a general anesthesia or a local anesthetic to the cervix, and the procedure takes just minutes and presents little or no discomfort or danger.

An earlier method still used by some physicians is to dilate the cervix with tubes of increasing size and then to insert a spoon-shaped curette (cutting instrument) to remove the embryo and placenta. This procedure may be necessary after a vacuum aspiration if the physician believes that parts of the embryo and placenta still remain in the uterus.

Induced abortion after the third month is more difficult because of the size of the embryo and surrounding tissue. A method still commonly used in the United States to effect abortion during the second trimester is to infuse a strong saline solution into the amniotic cavity. This solution kills the fetus and causes contractions that expel the fetus in over 80 percent of all cases. However, serious complications for the mother have resulted from this method, including death (Pritchard & MacDonald, 1976, p. 505).

An alternative procedure is to use *prostaglandin,* a hormone that stimulates contractions. Amniocentesis is performed and prostaglandin is injected slowly through the syringe. After the fetus has been expelled *oxytocin* (another hormone also used to stimulate uterine contractions) is injected to aid in the expulsion of the placenta and to minimize bleeding (Duenhoelter, Grant, & Jiminez, 1976). However, this method is also not without complications (Fraser & Brash, 1974; Shapiro, 1975).

In certain cases, especially with very late abortions, the fetus can be removed by surgical incision. With late abortions it is more likely that a saline solution will be used. Whatever method is used, abortion is neither completely safe nor simple. There are also legal and moral problems related to induced abortion. The subject of abortion will continue to be debated, and it is safe to say that no easy solution is likely to be reached.

Infections

Before birth the baby receives a plentiful supply of **antibodies** from the mother via the placenta to help combat infection during the last month of pregnancy. These antibodies last until the newborn begins to manufacture its own antibodies (at about 3 months) in response to coming into contact with bacteria and viruses in the environment.

A host of various types of germ colonies soon establish "living quarters" on the baby's skin, nose, throat, mouth, and in the intestinal tract. These are normal germ *flora* that are not dangerous if the baby is healthy. Other germs, however, can be *virulent*—that is, can cause disease. The baby needs extra protection to combat such germs. Sometime in the first few months after birth, the baby should receive a DPT injection. The *diphtheria, pertussis,* and *tetanus* injection causes the baby to build up antibodies. Without this safeguard the baby might contract any of these viral infections. Diphtheria is an acute infection of the tissues of the nose, throat, and mouth; whooping cough is the common term for pertussis; and tetanus is a bacterial disease that causes severe, painful muscle spasms. Feinbloom (1979, p. 373) has commented that

By law we require widespread immunization that, in this country [United States], have all but eliminated some of mankind's worst scourges. Since the introduction of the vaccine in the 1950s, the once-dreaded poliomyelitis (infantile paralysis), which crippled or killed thousands of children every year, has become almost a concern of the past. Measles, which almost any mother could diagnose on sight only a few years ago, is so rare that today's medical students cannot recognize it.

Individual Differences

Newborns have many individual differences. Some infants are very active, some are passive, some develop certain motor activities more quickly than others, some are more responsive and alert to stimuli than others, some are very irritable and cry frequently while others are quite placid and smile frequently (Korner, 1969; Wolff, 1969). These differences are all variations among normal, healthy infants.

Many of these differences may have little relationship to later development. But the response of babies to certain stimuli may influence later development. It is also clear that the way infants behave has some effect on the way parents behave toward them. "In the short span of the first six months of life, the infant emerges as a social human being" (Stern, 1977, p. 1). The interaction between infant and parents is a two-way process. But before the infant has learned to initiate a social interaction, parents already have begun to respond to the infant's spontaneous behavior. These responses are different for the placid versus the excitable baby, the active versus the passive baby. Parents may be accepting or disapproving of their baby's temperamental traits; and the way parents react to these traits probably has an effect on the baby's personality development.

One group of investigators (Thomas, Chess, & Birch, 1970) identified nine characteristics of temperament that can be observed in infants: (1) level of motor activity; (2) quality of mood (for example, is the baby happy or irritable?); (3) acceptance or rejection of something new; (4) regularity or irregularity of behavior; (5) adaptability of behavior; (6) level of response to stimuli (for example, does the baby pay attention to a colorful toy?); (7) intensity of reaction (for example, how much attention does the baby pay to a toy, or how does the baby respond to having a toy placed within reach?); (8) distractibility; (9) attention span and persistence.

These nine characteristics were used to rate the personalities of 141 children in New York City from birth until they were 10 years old. It was discovered that two thirds of these children had temperamental traits that fell into one of three categories—*easy* (40 percent), *difficult* (10 percent), and *slow to warm up* (15 percent). About 35 percent of the children could not be readily classified into just one of these three categories.

The easy children were cheerful, regular in their habits, and adapted quickly to change. The difficult children were much the reverse—irregular in behavior, easily frustrated, and generally negative or withdrawing in new situations. The slow-to-warm-up children were quiet and had a tendency to withdraw from new situations.

For most of these children the temperamental traits obvious at birth remained as they grew older. In many cases certain traits became more prominent than others. This does not mean that early appearing traits altogether determine the later development of behavior characteristics. The development of behavior is complex and influenced by many factors. (These include social training by parents, the child's imitation of parents' behavior, peer-group pressure, and so on. Personality and social development are discussed in greater detail in Chapter 5.)

We might suppose that the easy children are easiest to bring up. However, parents sometimes set too high expectations for these children and become over demanding. This may result in the children's eventually rebelling. Whatever temperamental traits children have, it seems important to allow them some range to develop their own personalities.

What is important is the interaction between the . . . child's own characteristics and his environment. If the two are harmonized, one can expect healthy development of the child; if they are dissonant, behavioral problems are almost sure to ensue (Thomas, Chess, & Birch, 1970, p. 109).

When parents think it necessary to teach appropriate behavior, respecting children's individual temperaments while trying to effect changes in behavior is likely to achieve the best results.

States of the Newborn

If you observe an infant for a few hours, you will notice that there is a cycle of wakefulness, sleepiness, alertness, and varying types of movement. The mother of a newborn baby very quickly becomes aware of her baby's pattern of behavior, from being wide-awake—legs kicking, arms moving, head turning, eyes wide, crying, feeding, lying quite still, sucking a thumb—to sleeping. This range of activities has now come to be known as *states of the newborn.* These behaviors occur regularly and repeatedly and are apparently triggered by "internal forces" (Schaffer, 1977, pp. 30–31). Although there are individual differences in changes of state, the range of behaviors is very similar for all normal infants.

It is important to consider the state of the newborn because interactions with the environment during early infancy vary, depending on changes of state during each day. It is also necessary to consider the various states of the infant before taking a closer look at the infant's array of reflexes and range of sensory and perceptual abilities, which are discussed in Chapter 4.

Classification of States of the Newborn

To better understand the range of behaviors of the newborn, we can take a look at a classification of states by Wolff (1966).

1. During regular sleep the baby is relaxed, lying still with eyes closed and breathing regularly.

2. During irregular sleep gentle movements and slight muscle twitches can be observed. Facial grimaces and smiles are quite frequent, and breathing is irregular.

3. During drowsiness the baby is in a semi-sleep state; yet often the eyes are open and the baby is obviously aware of certain stimuli such as a radio playing or movements close by. In this state the baby's breathing is either irregular, or regular but faster than it is during regular sleep.

4. During alert inactivity the eyes are open and more focused, looking at objects in the immediate environment. However, the baby is not too active, but rather quite content to lie or to sit supported.

5. During waking activity the baby is very active and responds vigorously to external stimuli, or internal stimuli such as hunger or a pain.

Another state, not included in Wolff's list, is crying. The hungry baby, the uncomfortable baby with a soiled diaper or pain, the cold or too-warm baby cries; such crying is usually accompanied by the vigorous thrashing of arms, legs, and body.

*Infants behave in different
ways—sometimes sleeping,
sometimes relaxing, and
sometimes fretful or crying.
(Photo, top left by Rick
Smolan; top right and bottom
by Jean-Claude Lejeune)*

Development of States

Most newborn infants sleep about 70 to 80 percent of the time, although this regular sleep will be broken by short periods of irregular sleep and drowsiness. The rest of the time the baby is alert, may fuss or cry, and may need to be fed. Periods of regular sleep diminish over the first year so that, for most infants, by the end of the first year a pattern of sleeping through the night and remaining awake most of the day is established. Parents look forward to this schedule, including nap time in the afternoon since "it makes the baby much easier to live with" (Schaffer, 1977, p. 28).

As the baby matures physically, sensorimotor activity also changes. The baby becomes more perceptive of what is going on around it and establishes relationships with objects and events, which is considered crucial for later mental and social development. This interaction with the environment is a two-way affair that is sometimes initiated by the baby, sometimes by stimuli in the environment. The type of interaction and its outcome depend to a considerable extent on the baby's state. A crying, fretful baby is concentrating on an internal state of feeling uncomfortable. The crying is a signal to the parent or caretaker that the baby needs attention. But the baby's attention is really on itself. A quiet, alert baby can direct perception outward. At this time it is important to provide various stimuli for the baby to interact with. A number of studies indicate the importance of handling, cuddling, cooing and talking to the baby and providing the baby with a rich variety of stimuli (Kagan, 1972; White, 1978; Stern, 1977). It is important for both parents and others who care for infants to realize that not only will a state have some influence on how the infant interacts with the environment but also that the state can be influenced by the environment and that normal development appears dependent on relationships between both.

The Newborn and Family Relationships

Especially in infancy, it is the family that has the greatest influence on the baby's development. The baby needs caring for and initiating into the "tribe." These needs are taken care of primarily by the parents, but they may also be the responsibility of other adult caregivers and of siblings.

However, this is not a one-way process—infants have considerable influence on the quality of a marriage and of family interaction (Bell, 1974; Lamb, 1979). There is now a triadic rather than a dyadic interaction. Interaction between parents and their baby is not one way but reciprocal. The way a baby interacts with parents can have a considerable influence on their individual behavior and how they relate to each other. For example, a placid infant is easy to deal with; but if the baby is a boy, the father may expect him to be active and even welcome some irritability in the baby, perhaps assuming this to be a sign of aggression,

Infants are cared for primarily by their parents, but they may also be cared for by surrogate parents, older brothers or sisters, and sometimes grandparents. (Photos top and bottom left by Jean-Claude Lejeune; bottom right by Robert Eckert/EKM-Nepenthe)

which the father may value. The mother, on the other hand, may find it distressing to look after an irritable or very active baby. Another influence on family interaction is the beliefs parents have about child rearing. You can imagine the difference it makes to both parents and baby whether parents agree or disagree about how to rear their child.

Yogman et al. (1977) observed differences in infants' frowning and smiling at mothers and fathers compared to strangers as early as 2 months. It was also noticed that infants' smiles, vocalizations, and body movements differed depending on whether they were interacting with mother or father. Schaffer and Emerson (1964) reported that at about 9 to 10 months infants showed more anxiety at being separated from mothers than from fathers. Kotelchuck (1972, 1976) has found that infants express as much concern at being separated from either parent. Lamb (1976) has suggested that preference for either mother or father at separation is likely to be due to the extent of attachment to a particular parent and is more likely to occur when separation is particularly stressful as in a strange situation. However, further research is needed to more clearly point out differences between mother-infant and father-infant interactions that might result in a preference being shown for one parent. As Parke (1979a) indicates, the extent to which infants may prefer one parent to another is likely to vary, depending on such factors as familiarity of the setting, the social context (for example, how many people are present), and the infant's age and sex.

Research has strongly indicated that fathers play an important role in the development of their children's intellectual development. Boys appear to be more

---

**Inset 3.3
Mothering
and Fathering**

In the John Enders Research Building close by the Harvard Medical School, a 14-week-old baby named Eddie is gazing intently at his father. Two television cameras are capturing these moments on videotape. James, his father, talks to him, "Bet you're glad to see me! Were you good with Mommy?"—taps him, tickles him, smiles at him.

The investigators at the Child Development Unit of Children's Hospital Medical Center in Boston are recording the vocalizations and facial expressions of James and Eddie as part of an investigation on fathering and mothering. They know already that a father's typical interaction with a child is different from the characteristic pattern of a mother's interaction.

Investigators at the infant laboratory at the Educational Testing Service near Princeton, New Jersey, are doing similar research but in the homes of the parents and their children. They have found that fathers talk more to their sons than to their daughters and children talk less to fathers than to mothers, or to one another.

In a laboratory at the University of Wisconsin, a father sits observing a television monitor. His heart rate, skin conductance, and blood pressure are being monitored. A 6-minute videotape of a 5-month-old baby is being shown. The infant looks around, squirms, and soon begins to cry. Loudly. Insistently. Interminably. Although the baby he is watching is not his, the father tenses, his heart rate increases, and his blood pressure soars. After testing 148 fathers and mothers under these conditions, it turns out that there are no physiological differences between the reactions of a father and mother to the sight of a squalling baby. To both, it is equally distressing.

There has been an increase in research on fathering in recent years. The impact of this research is beginning to be felt in courts of law, in hospitals, and in universities, which face the task of redirecting the training of a new generation of doctors, pediatricians, psychotherapists, health-care professionals, and teachers.

---

affected than girls (Radin, 1976). According to Parke (1979a), fathers may influence their daughters' intellectual development indirectly through affecting the daughter-mother relationship—thus reminding us of the importance of viewing the family as a social system (p. 575). The father not only provides a model of maleness and paternal role behavior, he can also encourage femininity in his wife and encourage her to influence feminine behavior in a daughter. In this sense paternal masculinity is related to daughters' femininity, which is consistent with complementary role theory (Lamb, Owen, & Chase-Lansdale, 1979).

Lamb (1976, 1977a) also argues that infants have important relationships with fathers and that we should take notice of them. In reviewing the father's role in influencing the development of the child, Lamb concludes that the effects of mothers and fathers on their children are different and both are needed for normal growth and development.

Michael Lamb has found differences between mothering and fathering. Mothers apparently hold their infants primarily for activities like changing, feeding, or bathing; fathers most often hold their infants to play with them, and they tend

In a number of studies Kotelchuck and his colleagues (1972; Kotelchuck, Zelazo, Kagan, & Spelbe, 1975) found few significant differences in the ways infants attached to mothers and fathers. In fact, they demonstrated that children have extended social worlds and can attach equally well to siblings, peers, and other figures.

Ross D. Parke has also observed fathers with their infants (1979; Parke & O'Leary, 1976). He reports that fathers and mothers differ little in the ways they interact with their children. Fathers touch, look at, and kiss their children as much as do mothers; and they are as protective, giving, and stimulating as mothers are.

Thus, although there are interesting similarities in infants' relationships with both parents, there are also some important differences. T. Berry Brazelton says, "Mother has more of a tendency to teach the baby about inner control . . . she then builds her stimulation on top of that system in a very smooth, regular sort of way. Father adds a different dimension, a sort of play dimension, an excitement dimension, teaching the baby about some of the ups and downs—and also teaching the baby another very important thing: how to get *back* in control" (Collins 1979, p. 52).

All the evidence is pointing to the fact that fathers can be equally effective as parents—they just have different styles from mothers. Michael Lamb stresses the point that, "Perhaps it's really not fathering or mothering—it's parenting" (Collins, 1979, p. 65). However, he believes the number of fathers who take on a large share of what is involved in parenting is still depressingly small.

It is James Levine's hunch that the issue of fatherhood is becoming more a question for mothers than for fathers as more mothers enter the work force. The biggest push for changing the present role of many fathers is economic pressure— the necessity for both parents to work—and the associated necessity for both parents to share the responsibility of parenting their children in all the aspects of that role.

to initiate more physical and idiosyncratic games than mothers do. Boys are held longer by their fathers, and fathers begin to show a preference for boys at 1 year of age and this subsequently increases.

Prenatal Period

Susan Arbeit (1975) asked a number of women during their first pregnancy about their feelings in regard to approaching motherhood. Three themes were common in their responses. First, they reevaluated their relationships with their own parents—especially their mothers. They expected to adopt a parenting role similar to their mother's role. Second, they gave imaginary personal characteristics to the fetus. (There seems to be a need to provide an "emerging definition of the fetus as a child.") Third, they also had a need to maintain a personal identity. It was as though they were insisting that there is not just us, there is me and there is the baby.

Lamb suggests that most parents who are preparing for the birth of their *first* child tend to adopt a traditional attitude toward parenthood. This makes it relatively easy for them to agree on how to be parents since there are many sources of information to guide them. Parents who expect to adopt nontraditional roles are less likely to agree about appropriate ways of parenting, which may cause marital stress (Lamb, 1979, p. 141).

Postnatal Period

The birth of a baby has a profound impact on the parents. This is quite clear from the initial interactions between parents and their newborn (Parke & O'Leary, 1976), in the way they touch, caress, smile, and talk as they interact with their baby. Parents also have quite definite expectations about how their baby should behave, whether they enjoy an active or passive baby, look for a lot of smiling, or spend a lot of time stimulating their baby to engage in playful activities. Several investigators have shown that parents respond differently to children depending on such characteristics as sex (Condry & Condry, 1976; Lamb, 1977b) and state (Thomas, Becker, & Freese, 1978). An important finding from these observations is that infants are able to control adult behavior.

Many investigators have reported interesting mother-infant interactions. When mothers are feeding their babies an exchange of gazes and facial expressions occurs (Brazelton, Tronick, Adamson, Als, and Wise, 1975; Jaffe, Stern, & Peery, 1973). Mothers and infants gaze at each other in a *turn-taking* sequence, rather like the sequences in adult conversations. When the mother does not respond to the baby's gaze or cooing, the baby intensifies its efforts to gain the mother's attention (Brazelton et al., 1975; Carpenter, 1974).

We do not yet fully know what the baby is trying to achieve in eliciting responses from adults. Some investigators believe that babies simply use certain behaviors (such as cooing or crying) to draw attention. Others believe that babies actually check for possible relationships between their own and adult behavior in order to engage in reciprocal interaction sequences (Lamb, 1979, p. 150). For example, a baby will look for facial expressions in a parent when he or she is in a "playful" mood and seek to catch the parent's attention so as to instigate a "game." It does seem certain that by at least 3 months infants have developed expectations about how adults will behave toward them. The infant learns to expect playful gazing, smiling, "talking," playing with a toy, peekaboo games, and so forth. When these reciprocal social activities do not occur, the infant may become distressed (Lamb, 1979). By 6 months of age there will have been quite a dramatic improvement in the infant's ability to indicate social interactions.

The repertoire of social behavior shared by infants and adults, the ways in which infants and parents influence one another, and the effect of these interactions on the child's intellectual, social, and personality development are discussed in succeeding chapters.

Summary

Various methods of preparing parents for childbirth, such as Lamaze, have become popular. Both parents receive information on the birth process, and the mother is trained in exercises that are supposed to improve muscle tone and in breathing techniques that are expected to reduce labor pains. There is some disagreement among specialists about the benefit of prepared childbirth. However, giving the mother something "useful" to do during labor can be an effective distraction, and having the father present to encourage and comfort does seem to help in many cases.

Most pregnant mothers are prepared for giving birth and attended during labor by a physician in a hospital. In some hospitals the pregnant woman is attended by a midwife. There has also been a slight increase in the number of pregnant women who elect to have their babies at home and to be cared for by a midwife.

There are three stages of labor—dilation, delivery, and expulsion of the placenta. The dilation of the cervix is the longest and most difficult. During the delivery stage the baby is pushed down the vaginal canal and out into the world. At this time, as part of the birthing procedure, mucus is cleared from the baby's nose and throat. In the final stage the umbilical cord is tied and cut and the placenta is expelled.

Immediately after birth the baby's vital functions are checked. One scale used for this is the Apgar scale. Any observed malfunctions must receive immediate attention.

Parents are concerned by the appearance of their baby at birth. They may be anxious about skin markings and the shape of the baby's head. However, red blotching on the skin and elongatation of the skull caused by the passage through the vagina both quickly disappear. A number of important functions are carefully checked at birth. These include the nervous system, respiration, and blood circulation. Reflexes are checked, as are the functioning of the heart and the baby's feeding and defecation. A quite usual, mild abnormality that occurs soon after birth is physiologic jaundice caused by the as yet immature functioning of the liver. These symptoms usually clear up quickly.

At about 3 months the infant should receive injections to safeguard against diphtheria, pertussis, and tetanus. Immunization has almost eliminated most of the worst infantile infections.

Premature birth is the most important complication of pregnancy. Babies weighing less than 5½ pounds at birth are premature. Associated with prematurity is the delayed development of certain body functions. To provide a stabilizing environment, premature babies are placed in incubators (isolettes) for a few weeks after birth. Initial isolation of the premature baby can make important early contact between the parents and the child virtually impossible. In cases in which artificial stimulation has been provided, this appears to have advanced the mental and neurological development of premature babies. Long-term effects of prematurity, such as retardation of motor and mental development, are more likely to occur as a lasting effect in the case of babies growing up in deprived environments. For most premature babies there appears to be a powerful "self-righting" effect which can be enhanced by proper care and attention.

When the mother's pelvic opening is too small to allow normal birth with ease, the baby is usually delivered by cesarean section. This method of delivery is also used if prior diagnosis indicates certain abnormalities in the fetus, if labor complications develop, or if the baby has not attained the necessary "head-down" position. The modern procedure of making a horizontal incision in the lower abdomen may make possible normal delivery in subsequent pregnancies.

If a surgical abortion is performed during the first three months of pregnancy, it is usually induced by *vacuum aspiration.* An alternative method is to remove the embryo and related tissue by a *curette.* After the third month, abortion is usually induced by infusing a strong saline solution into the amniotic cavity. This kills the fetus and induces contractions that expel the fetus. In very late abortions the fetus may be removed by surgical incision. Induced abortion is neither safe nor simple, and there are associated legal and moral problems not easily resolved.

Normal babies are born with a number of sensory capabilities which they use to learn about and discriminate among various stimuli in the environment. There are, however, important individual differences in the temperamental traits of newborns. For healthy development there should be harmony in the interaction between the child's individual personality characteristics and the environment.

The newborn baby has a pattern of behaviors ranging from being wide-awake through states of relaxed inactivity, drowsiness, and irregular sleep to regular sleep. Although there are individual differences, these *states* of behavior are very similar for all newborns. During the first year changes in these states include longer periods of wakefulness during the day and regular sleep through the night. Interactions between the baby and the environment are affected by these various states, which have some implications for ongoing development.

The period of pregnancy and the arrival of a new baby have important implications for the quality of a marriage and family interactions. Mothers strive to keep separate the identity they attach to the developing fetus and their own personal identity. When preparing for their first baby, most parents adopt "traditional" parenting attitudes. Those parents who adopt nontraditional roles may experience marital stress because of disagreements about appropriate parenting behaviors.

Babies are both influenced by and also influence their "socializers." Although the mother-infant interaction is very important, so are other interactions among the baby, father, siblings, and other care givers. Father-infant relationships have assumed greater importance in recent years. The evidence from research suggests that fathers and mothers have different styles of parenting but that both can be equally effective as parents.

By 3 months the baby has formed expectations about interactions with "socializers." An even more dramatic unfolding of infant social behavior occurs between 3 and 6 months. By this time the baby is well established in infancy—a period of rapid development.

Questions for Review

1. In what way is "gentle birth," as advocated by LeBoyer, different from the more usual method of delivery?

2. Describe the main features of the normal birth process from the onset of labor to the final phases of delivery.

3. What are the characteristics of normally functioning systems of the newborn, such as the nervous, circulatory, and digestive systems?

4. What are the characteristics that distinguish a premature from a normal baby? What special care needs to be provided for a premature baby?

5. Describe how infant "states" are classified and how they develop.

6. What kinds of important relationships occur between parents and their infant?

7. Try to find mothers to talk to about the birth of their child (or children). Include as far as possible mothers who experienced a traditional birth, a premature birth, a birth by cesarean section, and a natural birth. Compare their experiences.

8. Ask the same mothers about the effects the birth of the newborn had on their families. If possible, ask the fathers this question also. For the families you interview, describe the implications the birth of a newborn seemed to have for family relationships.

Suggestions for Further Reading

Brennan, B., & Heilman, J. R. *The complete book of midwifery*. New York: E. P. Dutton, 1977. An account of midwifery by two midwives. Describes the early history of midwifery in the United States and the reasons behind its recent resurgence. The pros and cons of home birth attended by a midwife are also discussed.

LeBoyer, F. *Birth without violence*. New York: Knopf, 1975. Describes the procedures advocated by LeBoyer for reducing the shock of birth for the baby.

Macfarlane, A. *The psychology of childbirth*. Cambridge, MA: Harvard University Press, 1977. An excellent review of prenatal development, the stages of birth, and the first days of life. Includes a section on mother-infant relationships.

Swanson, H. D. *Human reproduction: Biology and social change*. New York: Oxford University Press, 1974. Read especially Chapter 7, "Pregnancy and Birth," and Chapter 9, "Revolution in Reproduction: Double-Edged Swords." Selections of chapters from the readings suggested for Chapter 2 can also be read in connection with this chapter.

Physical and Intellectual Development

4

We shall not cease from exploration
And the end of all our exploring
Will be to arrive where we started
And know the place for the first time

Development in infancy is comprised of changes in both body and behavior. It takes a month before a human infant can lift its chin. But a little more than a year later the infant can walk by itself. Within the same time the infant learns to speak the rudiments of a language and to develop certain reflex actions, such as crying and smiling, into more complex forms of communication. In the first months after birth the infant does not discriminate between caregivers, but by about 6 months of age infants develop a strong attachment to parents and a fear of strangers. These complex, coordinated changes are physical, intellectual, social, and emotional. In this chapter we will examine the physical and intellectual development during infancy, and in Chapter 5 we will explore the social and emotional changes of infancy.

Dramatic physical changes take place in body growth. The infant's height nearly doubles and its weight triples within two years. Physical changes also take place in learning *motor control*, the neurological and muscular control of movement. You know that learning to play a musical instrument or developing a good serve in tennis requires learning new moves and new motor control. The infant learns similar, but much more basic, motor control; and this causes changes in behavior such as crawling and walking. The infant also develops physically through its improving mechanisms of sensing. You may remember how it felt to look through a microscope the first time, to learn how to adjust the light mirror and to focus the lenses, and then how to figure out visually sights you had never seen before. The infant learns a great deal more in a short time about all of its senses—vision, hearing, taste, smell, and touch. Physical development in infants and throughout childhood and adolescence involves body growth, abilities in movement, use of the senses, and the like, which are expressed in related changes of behavior.

The infant's intellectual development is even greater than its physical development. Intellectual development concerns the increasing capacity to acquire and use knowledge. This process begins with the infant's growing perceptual powers, its ability to select and interpret what its senses tell it. This capacity eventually includes the processes of awareness and judgment and of remembering, imagining, and reasoning. These intellectual abilities and processes are called *cognition*. The infant's cognitive development progresses from inborn reflexes to primitive skills and from "nonsense" sounds to beginning sentences by means of memory and intention. The acquisition of language interests psychologists as cognitive development (rather than social development) because infants learn so much so quickly. In this chapter we will describe language development as part of intellectual development. In later chapters we will describe its function in social development.

As we describe physical and intellectual development, you will see that some psychologists give a particular emphasis to the influence of maturation on development and learning (maturation being the natural, unfolding pattern of growth), and that others, while not ignoring maturation altogether, place greater importance on environmental influences on learning and development. Still others point to combinational effects of maturation and environment—placing different degrees of importance on one or the other. In all cases you will be able to investigate for yourself what it is that makes the maturation vs environmental learning issue an important theme in child development.

Physical Development

Observations of infants have made it clear that there are two basic principles of physical and motor development. The first principle is called *cephalocaudal*, a Latin word meaning "head to tail." This direction of development proceeds from the head downward to the lower trunk. The head, neck, trunk, and leg muscles are gradually brought under control in that order. According to a second principle termed *proximodistal* (from the Latin, "near to far"), development also occurs from the *center outward*. The head and trunk develop ahead of the limbs. At first, the baby makes reaching and arm-waving motions. Grasping and finer control of the fingers and thumb to pick up and release objects come later.

However, a word of caution is needed here. In general, both of these principles of physical development are true some of the time, but the evidence available suggests we can be more certain about the principle of cephalocaudal development than we can be about proximodistal development (Cratty, 1979, p. 64).

Body Growth

The infant's body proportions are very different from an adult's. The length of a newborn's head accounts for about a quarter of the overall body length, whereas the head is only one eighth of the length of a full-grown adult (see Figure 4.1).

There are quite dramatic changes in the length and weight of the infant during its first 2 years. During the first year the baby's trunk grows fastest; this is followed by growth in the legs during the second year. The baby will be about 20 inches in length at birth, and this will have increased to about 34 inches by age 2—an increase of 70 percent. The average weight of a newborn is 7½ pounds and that of a 2-year-old, 27 pounds.

Some fascinating changes also occur in the development of the skeleton. At birth the baby's bones are primarily in the form of soft cartilage. The cartilage slowly begins to harden into bone (ossify) through mineral deposits. The first baby teeth appear when the infant is between 6 and 9 months old.

At birth the infant's brain weighs almost 1 pound (about 350 grams), which by age 2 will have increased by almost 200 percent. Most of this rapid gain occurs as the result of cell division and an increase in the white, fatty substance called **myelin**. Myelin sheaths all nerves in the nervous system and speeds transmission of nerve impulses. For example, the early involuntary (uncontrolled)

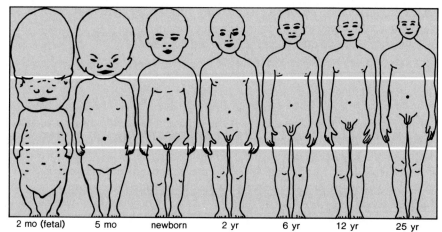

| 2 mo (fetal) | 5 mo | newborn | 2 yr | 6 yr | 12 yr | 25 yr |

Figure 4.1 Changes in body shape, form, and proportion from infancy to adulthood. (Source: Adapted from *Morris' Human Anatomy,* 12th ed., edited by B. J. Anson. Copyright © 1966 by McGraw-Hill, Inc. Used with permission of McGraw-Hill Book Company.)

movements of the hands occur because of myelination, a formation of the sheath between the nerve and muscle. The formation of new brain cells can be slowed by malnutrition during early infancy. Malnutrition will restrict the size of cells if it continues (Dobbing, 1973, 1974).

The nervous system develops *downward* from the primary centers of the brain. This accounts for the sequence in motor development from the upper part of the body to the lower limbs.

Motor Development

A momentous occasion is to see an infant stand for the first time or step falteringly in learning to walk. Of course, before this point in motor development is reached, parents will have been excited by the baby's increasing ability to use muscles in other ways such as grasping, smiling, rolling over, crawling, and flexing the legs to stand as the parent holds the baby's hands. Motor development follows a quite well-defined sequence that parallels development in the nervous system (Pickler, 1972). Remember, the overall sequence is head-downward and center-outward. The facial, neck, and shoulder muscles are first controlled, and the legs and toes are last. Similarly, voluntary control of the arms is achieved before control of the muscles in the fingers.

An interesting study conducted by Mary Shirley (1931) with a group of 25 infants illustrates the predictable sequence in motor development (see Figure 4.2).

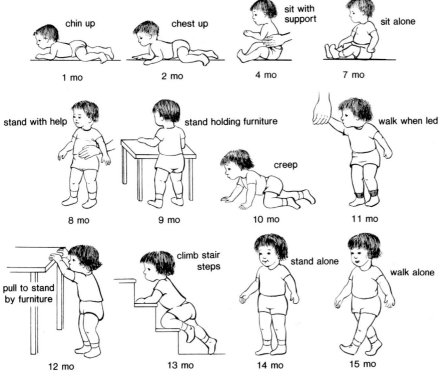

Figure 4.2 Sequence of infant locomotor development. (Source: Shirley, M. *The First Two Years.* Copyright 1933 by the University of Minnesota Press. Reprinted by permission.)

By 2 months infants can raise their heads and chests off a mattress. At 4 months they are able to sit if supported, and at 5 or 6 months they are able to sit without support. At 11 months they are walking with support, and at 15 months they are usually walking alone. This picture of the development of *locomotion* (the ability to move from place to place) fits all normal babies, suggesting a strong maturational influence on motor development. However, rate of development varies for individual babies. Some babies walk alone before 15 months, others begin later. This suggests the possibility that environment may have an influence and that there may be an *interaction* between maturation and learning.

Effects of maturation and learning.   Researchers have used different methods to determine the respective influence of *maturation* and learning on development—including studies of twins. In a study by Gesell and Thompson (1934) one twin was given a large amount of early practice on block-handling and climbing activities. The second twin was later given only a brief period of practice. Both twins performed equally well on these tasks when they were tested. Wilson (1972) studied 261 pairs of twins, of whom 100 were identical. Development of motor skills was almost identical for the monozygotic twins and the dizygotic twins.

Minerva (1935) found that a group of trained twins showed more improvement than a group of untrained twins on complex throwing tasks. However, there was little difference between these two groups on simpler jumping tasks. Minerva concluded that the more complex the task, the more likely it is that training, that is, influence from the environment, will improve performance.

Are the pattern and timing of infant motor development the same in different cultures? Dennis (1940) describes the development of walking in Hopi Indian babies. It is traditional for Hopi parents to bind their babies to cradle boards during the first months. The baby is unwrapped only once or twice a day for cleaning and a change in clothes. For quite some time, then, the babies' movements are very restricted. Some Hopi parents, affected by European ways, do not bind their babies to cradles. Dennis compared infants from both groups. You may be surprised to learn that both groups of infants walked at about 15 months. It appears from this study that walking, like other early motor skills, is mainly determined by maturation. We must remember, however, that all babies in both these studies had a chance to practice movement. Even Hopi Indian babies, when taken from the bindings, are played with and allowed to move.

Brazelton provides a most interesting contrast to the Hopi Indian study. He went to East Africa to observe babies and their families living in the bush. In the following description by Brazelton notice that the infant can support its head and shoulders shortly after birth, although according to the Shirley study this would not be "normal" until 4 months. (See Figure 4.3.) Brazelton says that at birth they

. . . were limp, poorly responsive, fragile appearing neonates. We . . . were stunned by their psychological state and their psychological unreadiness. . . . Within 24 hours after delivery a mother would pick up the limp, wobbly infant, set him on her hips to sit upright; wind a dashiki around her's and the infant's waists, leaving the infant's shoulders and head unsupported. The floppy infant would respond by adjusting his head, and straightening his back and shoulders. . . . By her expectations of his capacity to respond, she had changed him from a floppy, fragile neonate to one who was effectively supporting his shoulders and head. . . .
We saw two 5-month-old infants who took several steps without support. This . . . was in response to their grandmother's stimulating their walk reflexes and propelling them forward to a reflex walking response (1977, p. 49).

Goldberg (1972) reports that Zambian babies are carried in slings on their mothers' backs until they can sit. They are then left sitting for long periods and given opportunities to practice motor skills. These infants also show an early development of motor skills. Other studies have demonstrated that it is possible

Figure 4.3 Babies who spend much of early infancy wrapped in tight swaddling clothes or carried in slings, such as these Peruvian babies or Zinacatecos babies of Mexico, usually show a lag in motor development. However, these effects disappear by late childhood or sooner. (Photo by Derek Furlong from Black Star)

By about eleven months of age, a baby is ready to practice walking with support. (Photo by David A. Corona)

to accelerate motor development by providing certain types of experience (Sayegh & Dennis, 1965; Zelazo & Kolb, 1972).

Brazelton (1972) describes the experiences of infants in a Mexican culture—that of the Zinacantecos. The mothers carry these babies in tight swaddling clothes with their faces covered for the first 3 months. The intent is to have a quiet infant. The result is a quiet baby who shows a lag in motor development compared to infants in other cultures. Kagan and Klein (1973) paint the same picture of Guatemalan infants, also swaddled and kept in darkened rooms during the first year of their lives. Although retarded in motor and general development at 15 months, these effects had disappeared by the time these children were 11 years of age. The assumption, in this case, is that certain forms of early deprivation can be overcome without any special intervention.

In general the rate of motor development is influenced by early maturation, but it can be enhanced or slowed by particular environmental and learning experiences. We can conclude that motor development is influenced by an interaction of maturation and learning.

Reflexes. Specific, involuntary reactions to certain types of external stimuli are called *reflexes*. They are extremely important in helping the newborn survive.

Some reflexes directly sustain life: breathing, rooting, sucking, swallowing, and evacuating body wastes. Some help indirectly as protective reflexes, such as smothering-avoidance, righting, and pain-avoidance reflexes. Other reflexes help the baby as it first encounters the world socially, for instance, head turning, smiling, and crying.

Three reflexes are associated with feeding. If the baby is touched, or stroked on the cheek or around the mouth, this causes **rooting** (turning the head and mouth in the direction of the stimulus in search of the nipple). (See Figure 4.4.) Once the breast or bottle nipple is located, the baby starts to *suck* and to *swallow*, the other two reflexes. Pediatricians monitor these reflexes, along with heart rate, breathing, muscle tone, and so on, as important routine tests for normal development.

There are also several reflexes present during early infancy that have no survival value to the baby but whose absence may signal certain kinds of defects. If the baby is startled or roughly handled, the back arches, the head is thrown back, and the arms are flung rapidly outward and then hugged across the body. This is called the **moro reflex**. If it is absent or weak during early infancy, the infant may have damage to the central nervous system.

When an infant firmly grasps a finger or object placed in its hands, he or she is using the **palmar reflex**. The **plantar reflex** is a grasping by the toes of objects (such as a finger) when the objects are placed in the groove between the infant's toes and the sole of the foot. (See Figure 4.4.) The **Babinski reflex** is a spreading of the toes when the outside of the infant's sole is stroked. The swimming reflex is a paddling movement of the arms and legs, made when the infant is placed in water. These all disappear in normal infants after the first few months. However, absence during early infancy of the plantar and Babinski reflexes indicates possible defects in the lower spine, and absence of the palmar reflex has been noted in depressed infants.

In early infancy eliminating body wastes from the bladder and bowel is an involuntary reflex. When these organs are full, sphincter muscles open automatically, and sphincter-muscle *control* is not usually achieved until about 20 months. Control of elimination does depend in part on maturation, therefore, but it also depends on learning. The young child has to learn to recognize the feeling of a full bladder or bowel, and how when necessary to tighten the sphincter muscles to prevent elimination. How soon can young children be toilet trained to control elimination and to get rid of body wastes in the socially acceptable manner?

Oppel, Harper, and Rider (1968) surveyed 859 children in Baltimore to determine at what age these children achieved daytime and nighttime "dryness," indicating control of elimination. Eight percent of 1-year-olds stayed dry during the day and night. Over 50 percent of 2-year-olds were dry through the day, and 40 percent at night. It was not until after the age of 5 that all children achieved day and night dryness.

Training speeds up control of elimination somewhat, but the older the child, the sooner toilet training is achieved. It takes about seven months to achieve

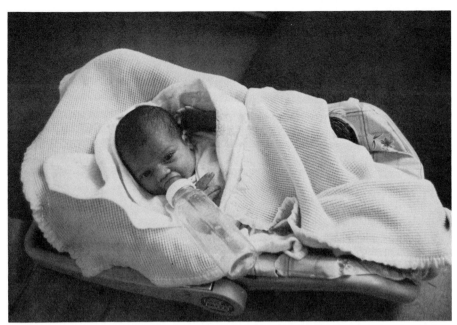

Figure 4.4 Important infant survival reflexes are *rooting* for the breast or bottle nipple and sucking on the nipple to feed. If the baby is startled the back is arched, the head thrown back, and the arms flung outward in the *Moro* reflex. The baby will also grasp an object placed in its hand (*palmar* reflex) or between foot and toes (*plantar* reflex). Absence of such reflexes may indicate damage to the central nervous system. (Photo by Robert V. Eckert/EKM-Nepenthe)

success when training commences at about age 12 months, whereas training begun with 20-month-old infants is achieved within about five months (Sears, Maccoby, & Levin, 1957). More recently it has been reported that quite rapid success can be achieved by using operant condition methods (Benjamin, Serdahley, & Geppert, 1971).

One method used takes the form of a quick sequence of events initiated close to urination or a bowel movement. The sequence is as follows: (1) Each time urination begins an auditory alert sounds from a signal device worn by the infant, and the trainer moves rapidly to the infant calling "no." The result is a mild startle effect that has the outcome of stopping elimination. (2) The trainer quickly moves the infant to a toilet facility. (3) The infant is placed before or on the potty or toilet ready for urination (or a bowel movement). (4) Urination is begun again or continued quietly, and the infant is approved. (5) After a number of such training events, the infant follows through the appropriate behavior of urination or voiding without the trainer's intervening. The auditory signal device is replaced by cotton training briefs, and the trainer teaches the infant to remove and replace the pants at the appropriate times (Van Wagenen, Meyerson, Kerr, & Mahoney, 1969).

An important point to keep in mind is that punishing or scolding a child for spontaneous bladder and bowel movements is not successful in toilet training (Sears et al., 1957; Azrin & Foxx, 1971), and many toilet-training techniques cause emotional disturbances that last into later childhood.

Mechanisms of Sensing

Perceptual and sensory development is of the utmost importance to the infant. Although the infant's perception and senses are limited by physical development, rapid changes are taking place. Even in the first few months, for example, the baby's ability to distinguish shape and pattern at varying distances rapidly improves, as do seeing, hearing, taste, and smell. But of more interest are those skills that remain constant. The fact that visual perception of size, depth, shape, and color, for instance, remains constant from birth suggests that the baby's world is not so confused as James suggested in 1980 when he called the infant's world a "blooming, buzzing confusion."

A distinction needs to be made between perception and sensing. **Perception** is the intellectual function of processing information that has been sensed. **Sensing** is the purely physical response to a physical stimulus. For example, an infant perceives a sound when he or she hears the sound, interprets it as mother's voice, and responds by turning to see if mother is near. However, a mother may call to her baby and get no response if the baby is absorbed in playing with some attractive toy. The infant hears mother's voice as a sound but does not perceptually process it as a voice or as mother's voice. Newborns can see, hear, taste, and smell from the moment of birth, and they actually react to certain stimuli such as sound and degrees of heat while still in the uterus. In this section we will describe sensory development from birth through infancy.

Vision. In the first weeks of life infants can focus their eyes, pay attention to some target object, and switch attention to new objects. When shown a blank visual field, the infant appears to *scan* it, that is, to make a sweeping search in an attempt to find some contrast, some "thing" to look at.

Haith (1976) has suggested that certain rules appear to govern the way in which infants in the first couple of months use their eyes for perceiving objects. (1) If the baby is awake and the light is not too bright, the eyes are open; (2) when the field of vision is dark or shadowed, the baby searches rather intensively for objects; (3) if there is an area of light with no clearly defined edges, the baby gazes around in an uncontrolled fashion; and (4) if the baby finds an *edge*, the baby gazes attentively at it by tracking back and forth along it (Figure 4.5). Indeed, during the first 2 to 3 months, the baby seems to be "programmed"

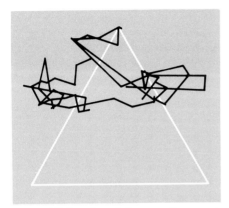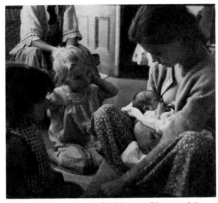

Figure 4.5 Newborn infants prefer scanning edges and corners of objects. Pictured is the way one newborn baby scanned part of the triangle. (Source: Kessen, W. "Sucking and Looking: Two Organized Congenital Patterns of Behavior in the Human Newborn." In H. Stevenson, (ed.) *Early Behavior: Comparative and Developmental Approach.* Copyright 1967 by John Wiley & Sons. Reprinted by permission.)

Figure 4.6 During the first weeks after birth the infant can only focus on objects a few inches away. During feeding, the closeness of the mother's face provides an important focal point for the infant to gaze at. (Photo by Robert V. Eckert/EKM-Nepenthe)

to focus on lines, edges, corners, and areas of contrasting color (Haith, 1976; Kessen, 1967; Kessen, Haith, & Salapatek, 1970; Salapatek & Kessen, 1966).

During the first months the baby is limited in its visual abilities by the weakness of the muscles that control the shape of the eye lenses. By 4 months distant vision is still only 20/150 (Salapatek, 1977). Infants have considerable difficulty in adjusting the focus of the eye lenses to gaze at objects at varying distances and in controlling the amount of light entering their eyes (Haynes, White, & Held, 1965). But in the first weeks of life infants can focus quite easily on objects between 7 and 15 inches away from them. When feeding, the baby's face is about 8 inches from that of the parent (Figure 4.6). Stern comments that the parent's face assumes a very real importance as an initial focal point, "the infant's early construction of his visual . . . world" (1977, p. 36).

Use of the eyes develops rapidly in the first 2 years. Time spent scanning increases from about 5 percent at birth to 35 percent at age 2. Over this period there is also a marked improvement in the ability to control head movements and eye focusing, track moving objects smoothly, and maintain attention (White, 1971).

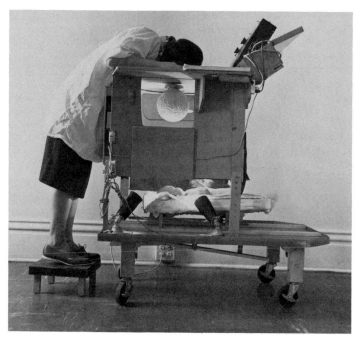

Figure 4.7 *Looking Chamber* that Fantz used to test infant's viewing interests. The infant lies in a crib looking at objects hung from the ceiling of the "looking chamber." The observer, watching through a peephole, records the attention given each object. (Source: Fantz, R. L. "The Origin of Form Perception." *Scientific American,* May, 1961, p. 71. Copyright © 1961 by Scientific American, Inc. All rights reserved. Photo © David Linton)

Fantz (1958; Fantz, Fagan & Miranda, 1975) became interested in the question of what infants preferred looking at. Infants put into a crib were then placed in a **looking chamber** so that they could view objects hung from the ceiling above them (see Figure 4.7). Their preferred way of viewing objects could be observed through a peephole. Fantz discovered that by 2 weeks infants preferred looking at a "real" face rather than a "scrambled" face (Figure 4.8), that by 8 weeks they preferred looking at a bull's-eye rather than a set of stripes (1958), that they attended more to three-dimensional than two-dimensional forms (1965), that at 3 months they looked longer at patterns of thin stripes than at a gray patch (1965), and that by 4 months they preferred looking at a facelike shape rather than other varied round shapes (see Figure 4.9).

It was mentioned earlier that infants concentrate their gaze on certain parts of patterns. When looking at pictures or drawings of real faces (see Figure 4.10), infants pay more attention to features such as eyes, nose, and mouth than to

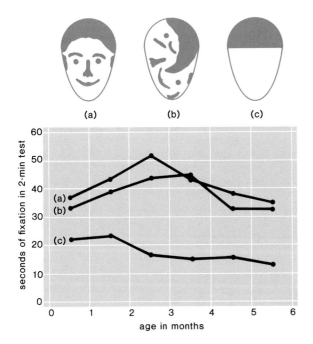

Figure 4.8 Infants' viewing preferences for faces. Adaptive significance of form perception was indicated by the preference that infants showed for a real face (*a*) over a scrambled face (*b*), and for both over a control (*c*). The results charted here show the average time scores for infants at various ages when presented with the three face-shaped objects paired in all the possible combinations. (Source: Fantz, R. L. "The Origin of Form Perception." *Scientific American,* May, 1961, p. 72. Copyright © 1961 by Scientific American, Inc. All rights reserved.)

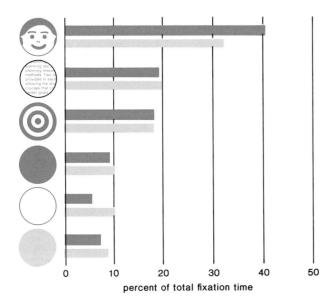

Figure 4.9 Infants' perceptions of patterns. Importance of pattern rather than color or brightness was illustrated by the response of infants to a face, a piece of printed matter, a bull's-eye, and plain red, white, and yellow disks. Even the youngest infants preferred patterns. Black bars show the results for infants from 2 to 3 months old; gray, for infants more than 3 months old. (Source: Fantz, R. L. "The Origin of Form Perception." *Scientific American,* May, 1961. Copyright © 1961 by Scientific American, Inc. All rights reserved.)

Physical and Intellectual Development   **143**

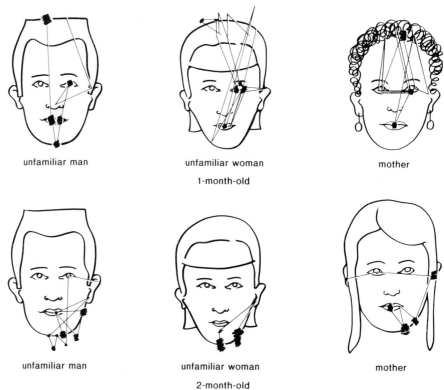

Figure 4.10 One-month-old infants tend to fixate on general features of faces of unfamiliar males and females, but show more attention to the eyes and mouth of their mothers. Two-month-old infants show an increased interest in facial features, such as eyes, nose, mouth, ears, and hair, of unfamiliar males and females, but pay more attention to the eyes and mouth of their mothers. (Source: Personal correspondence with Daphne Maurer, 1981. Reprinted with permission.)

other parts of the face. However, this is more pronounced at 2 months than at 1 month. From the results of these various studies we can be quite confident in saying that infants do show preferences in their viewing and that these preferences change over time. Changes in viewing preference can be associated with a growing awareness and understanding of the world around and with the development of social behaviors such as looking at mother's face and making eye contact with her (see Table 4.1).

Bower (1966) has shown in a series of experiments that infants have both perception of depth and shape constancy. In one study 6-week-old infants were trained to respond with a head turn when they saw a rectangle with one end further away than the other. They were then shown three other shapes as illustrated in Figure 4.11, as well as the shape on which they were trained. The

Table 4.1 Emergence of the Ability to Focus on a Figure

Age	Ability
2 months	Smiles at two eyes on a blank background
3 months	Reacts to mask with eyes and a nose
5 months	Reacts to full faces
7 months	Reacts only to familiar faces
9 months	Reacts only to faces with a pleasing expression

Source: Adapted from Ahrens, R. *Beitrage zur Entwicklung des Physiognomie und Minikerkennens. Zeitschrift für Experimentelle und Augewaudte Psychologie,* 1954.

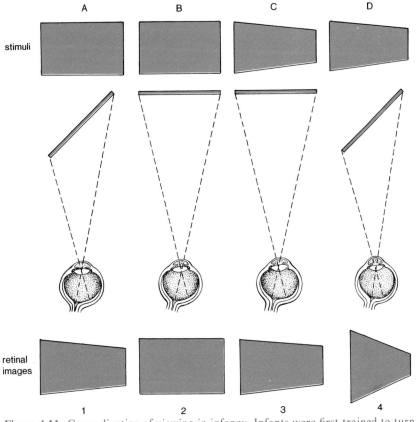

Figure 4.11 Generalization of viewing in infancy. Infants were first trained to turn their heads to view a rectangle slanted at an angle as shown in *A*. They were then tested for generalization of their viewing to this same shape *A* and three other shapes *B*, *C*, and *D* as illustrated in the figure. They looked more at shapes *A* and *B*, those with the same *real* shape as the shape they had been trained to view. They spent little time looking at shapes *C* and *D* even though the image produced by *C* was identical to that of the original training shape. This suggests that infants have a *constant* view of the world and are not easily fooled by "optical illusions." (Source: From *Human Development* by T. G. R. Bower. W. H. Freeman and Company. Copyright © 1979).

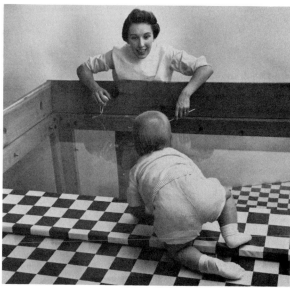

Figure 4.12 The visual "cliff." An infant crawls confidently toward his mother across the raised portion of the "cliff" but hesitates to cross the glass sheet on the "cliff side," which suggests infants are able to perceive depth. (Photos by William Vandivert.)

infants paid more attention to shapes *A* (shape trained on) and *B* (right shape, wrong position in depth) and very little attention to shapes *C* and *D*. Shape *D* had the right position in depth but the wrong shape. The infants were not fooled by shape *C*, which had the right shape but not the right position in depth.

A very interesting study by Gibson and Walk (1960) involved the use of a piece of apparatus they called the **visual cliff**. As you can see in Figure 4.12, the apparatus includes a large sheet-glass table with a barrier around the edges. In the center of the table is a slightly raised plank covered in a checkerboard pattern. On one side of the plank, immediately under the glass, the checkerboard pattern is continued. On the other side of the glass, the same pattern occurs, but about three feet below the plank. This is the "cliff." The infant (6 to 14 months old) is placed on the slightly raised center plank and is called to by the mother from both the "same level" side and from the "cliff" side of the table. She tries to induce the baby to crawl to her. Although babies in the study would crawl across the "same level" section of the table top, none of the 36 babies could be coaxed onto the cliff side, even when the surface below the glass was raised to a few inches below the center plank. The babies could obviously notice the difference. Would an infant younger than 6 months of age also be able to discriminate "same level" and "cliff" side?

In a study using the visual-cliff apparatus, Campos, Langer, and Kravitz (1970) placed infants aged 2 to 8 months (precrawlers) on both the shallow and deep sides and measured changes in heart rate. They found that, when placed on the deep side, infants' heart rates increased. We might conclude from these two studies that depth perception is innate even though its development may be influenced by learning experiences. There is a third study that needs to be mentioned, the results of which suggest that certain experiences do play a part in the development of depth perception.

Scarr and Salapatek (1970) used a series of fear-provoking situations for infants aged 2 to 23 months; one of these situations included the "visual cliff." From their observations Scarr and Salapatek concluded that infants aged 2 to 8 months could indeed distinguish between the deep and shallow sides of the cliff but that they showed no fear or avoidance of depth. Nor did simply growing older and developing locomotion (beginning with crawling at about 8 months) lead to a fear of depth. Fear of the cliff was related to length of experience with a particular mode of locomotion—creeping or walking. It was experiences of walking and crawling related to exploration of objects by tactile and visual exploration, including a growing awareness of vertical and horizontal surfaces, that produced fear. Although we can still argue that depth perception appears to be innate, reactions to heights (and depths), such as fear of a cliff drop, develop independently and appear to be strongly influenced by environmental experiences.

Hearing.   From birth babies can hear, can discriminate between sounds, and can "filter-out" sounds they get used to. Newborns turn their heads toward the source of certain sounds (Bower, 1974; Leventhal & Lipsitt, 1964; Wertheimer, 1961), but their response to sound depends on the pitch and duration of sound (Clifton, Graham, & Hatton, 1968). Continuous, low-pitched sound has a soothing effect, whereas high-pitched sudden noises produce a startled response.

By about 6 weeks of age babies can discriminate sounds such as *pa* and *ba* (Eimas et al., 1971) and *bah* and *gah* (Moffit, 1971). They also seem to listen to adult speech and, from the very first day of life, synchronize their body movements to the patterns of adult speech (Condon & Sander, 1974; Stern, 1977). Stern (1977) describes an incident in which a mother was bottle-feeding her infant. At first the mother was still and the baby concentrated on sucking. Then she began to talk to him. The baby broke the rhythm and stopped sucking, letting go of the nipple. He gave the faintest suggestion of a smile and as he watched her face and listened his eyes opened wider and he raised his eyebrows. The mother said "Hey!" opening her eyes, raising her eyebrows, and throwing back her head. Almost simultaneously the baby responded tilting his head with a broad smile on his face. Now his mother said, "Well hello! . . . helloo! . . . helloooo!" raising the pitch of her voice and laughing the "hellos." With each change the baby "experienced more pleasure, his body responding almost like a balloon being pumped up, filling a little more with each breath. . . . His head lurched forward, his hands jerked up, and a fuller smile blossomed" (Stern, 1977, p. 3). These observations demonstrate how early the infant tunes in to speech sounds, and therefore how early social and language development begin.

Taste and smell.   As in the case of other senses, taste and smell are quite acute at birth and improve with age. The preferences of newborns show the ability of their senses. It has been noticed that from birth babies prefer to suck on sweet rather than sour fluids (Desar, Maller, & Andrews, 1975), and it just so happens that the mother's milk is sweet. During the first months of life babies also get used to certain foods and show surprise by facial gestures if they are fed substitutes. Much the same can be said about smell. Week-old babies learn to notice the difference between smells (licorice, garlic, vinegar) and show preferences for sweet smells over others (Engen, Lipsitt, & Kay, 1973; Engen & Lipsitt, 1965).

The senses of taste and smell appear to be interwoven with social development. Babies can recognize the smell of the gauze pads worn by their own mothers inside their bras between feedings. They also quickly learn to tell the difference between the smell of their mother's breast pad and that of another woman (Lipsitt, 1977). In a similar study by MacFarlane (1975) the breast pad from a 1-week-old baby's mother and that from another nursing mother were placed just above the baby's head so the baby could smell the pad. Each infant in this study spent longer gazing at its mother's pad than at that of a stranger. Infants, so early in their lives, are already beginning to learn the characteristics of the major care giver. This probably forms part of the pattern of developing an attachment to the mother or major care giver. More will be said about attachment and social development in Chapter 5.

Perceptual Development

Through perception the infant processes information that its senses have given it. This processing is an intellectual activity, a bridge between sensing, the physical mechanism of receiving information, and cognition, the more complex intellectual processes concerned with memory, imagining, and reason. The process of perception can be, for the sake of description only, broken down into the function of attention and selection and the function of organization and interpretation. As we analyze perception you will see some of the elements of cognition come into play, in particular, memory and imaging.

Attention and Selection

Have you ever in the middle of some difficult parallel parking maneuver turned off the radio so that you could *see* better? If you have, you have felt how filtering out or stopping one stimulus, the radio, cleared up your perception of another stimulus, seeing how to fit into the parking space. If you were to let in all the stimuli you are capable of sensing, your world would be very much like the "blooming, buzzing confusion" James imagined for babies. It would be a world of confused perception; it would be information without understanding.

No one does let in all stimuli at once. Instead we select some to pay attention to and we filter out others. This is part of the act of perception, and even newborns have some capacity for selective perception as you will see when we examine what they select and pay attention to and how their preferences change as they develop.

As infants grow older they become interested in many different objects. (Photos by Jean-Claude Lejeune)

Novelty. Unfamiliar experiences with objects, tastes, sounds, sights, and events are novel to the infant. Fantz (1964) discovered that infants older than 2 months gaze longer at the new picture in a pair of pictures. Although infants younger than 2 months prefer looking at familiar rather than novel objects, preference for novelty increases with age (Wetherford & Cohen, 1973). After 2 months infants select and prefer to give their attention to novelty.

Habituation. Newborn babies soon get used to objects and events that are repetitive. If the infant is repeatedly presented with the same objects, interest in and attention to them wane. This is called **habituation**. This inhibition or decline in attention applies to all responses. For example, if the baby is first startled by a loud sound and the sound continues, the baby will become accustomed to it. We may be surprised at seeing a baby's sleeping peacefully well within earshot of a rather loudly playing radio or with mother's rattling pans and cutlery. If part of the baby's routine is to spend part of "sleep time" in the kitchen, sounds that initially may have been disturbing or startling become habituated to.

Discrepancy and complexity. Changes often occur in objects and events that have become well known to the infant. In addition the infant may experience alternate forms of similar objects. The ability to distinguish these discrepancies begins at about 3 months or even sooner and appears to develop as the infant grows older, as in the case of the visual cliff described in terms of depth perception.

The infant appears to be interested in the "mismatch" between objects. When the infant sees a novel object, it is as though the infant attempts to figure out whether it fits with expectations or familiar objects. By paying attention to objects and attempting to resolve match/mismatch evaluation, the infant continues to learn about objects.

Complexity is another factor affecting attention. Young infants seem to prefer looking at simple shapes, but as they grow older they change their preference to more complex shapes and patterns. This is illustrated by the example of infants' responses to pictures of faces as illustrated in Figures 4.9 and 4.10.

Organization and Interpretation

How can we account for changes in perception? It was mentioned earlier that two interacting features of development during infancy are maturation and learning. Certain restraints are placed on the infant's behavior by the sequence and timing of physical growth, but learning from the environment is also necessary. More opportunities to interact with the environment become available as the baby grows, and the environment itself can provide experiences that facilitate, tempt, and provoke changes in behavior.

Learning from the environment requires both organization and reorganization of new and previous experiences. For example, during the first two months of life the infant focuses on parts of objects (as in the Kessen study mentioned earlier), but by about the third month the infant begins to pay attention to complete figures or forms (remember Fantz discovered that 4-month-old infants preferred looking at complete shapes, especially a facelike shape). It may be that the baby now has a better memory for patterns seen before (Day & McKenzie, 1973; Salapatek, 1973) and that the baby is better able to organize and store sensual information in memory. Organizing and storing information enables the infant to compare new information with old and in turn to interpret or understand what it is perceiving.

In what manner do infants seem to remember figures and forms? Jerome Kagan (1970) has suggested that they construct and retain a mental representation of objects and events they have encountered. He terms these representations *schematic images*. Subsequent experiences are *interpreted*, that is, organized with reference to these schemas. By exposing babies to novel objects, such as mobiles or faces, and by varying the degree of change in arrangements of these objects, Kagan has obtained results that support this theory. When a baby is between the ages of 2 and 8 months it is no longer the extremely novel objects that "catch the eye," but those that are moderately novel. Kagan has called this preference the *discrepancy* theory of attention. The infant seems to prefer to pay attention to objects or events that show some discrepancy between an existing schematic image in memory and what the infant is sensing. In other words, the infant now prefers something that is similar to but different from an object already seen rather than something that is "entirely different or novel." According to Kagan (1972), when the infant is about 8 to 9 months old, there occurs a further phase in the development of perception that goes beyond the mere attention to discrepant objects. The infant begins to pay more attention to objects that have become familiar, such as human faces and toys. This is just as true for Guatemalan and Bushpeople's babies as for American babies. Infants now begin to recognize and be curious about differences in familiar objects, and Kagan suggests that infants begin to form hypotheses (ideas) about how or why the objects are different. In this way familiar objects seen in new configurations, circumstances, or situations are *fitted into* previous experiences with these objects. (See Inset 4.1.)

Up to six months of age the differences among infants in motor and cognitive development are fairly independent of the child's social class, his ethnic origin, and even some aspects of his rearing conditions. . . . Nine months seems to be a frontier that announces the child's ability to generate simple hypotheses. . . . (1972, p. 82).

Kagan supposes that this change in perception marks the beginning of intellectual activity. Piaget and Bruner have their own differing theories about cognitive development, and these are discussed in the next section.

Intellectual Development

As the infant continues to interact with the environment and to grow, intellectual abilities develop that help the infant to make sense out of the objects and events it experiences. Opinions among theorists differ about how intellectual development proceeds.

By manipulating and investigating objects, children come to discover what things feel like, look like, sound like, taste like; they learn how the parts make up the whole, how components fit together, how mechanisms work. Their focus in experiences of exploration is on the qualities of objects themselves. They are, so to speak, assimilating and accommodating to physical environments. By practicing motor skills the young child develops the skill itself and learns how to apply it appropriately to suitable objects. In the mastery of these skills the child also learns about the characteristics of objects and about certain fundamental physical laws and concepts. Here are several excerpts illustrating typical explorations of young children and their mastery of motor skills.

Exploration

Lisa is 12 months old. She is fascinated by the feeling of a damp metal surface. It feels cold and slippery. But how does it sound? She finds out by banging a metal spoon first on the metal tray, then, for contrast, on a plastic surface.

Lisa is sitting in a high chair as her mother feeds her baby food. Lisa slides her finger on the damp surface of the feeding tray which her mother has just wiped. Lisa starts to bang a spoon in her other hand on the metal tray. She eats and continues banging. Mother says, "That is a spoon." Lisa eats and bangs the spoon on the plastic bowl and listens to the different sound it produces. Lisa smiles and continues eating and banging alternately on the tray and bowl, chuckling with delight at the contrast in sounds.

Nora is 18 months old. She is studying the cat's tail and how it moves when she pulls it. She also imitates the rhythmic movement of the cat's tail with her hands.

Nora crawls under the kitchen table and sits near the family cat. She pulls up the cat's tail and brushes her stomach with the tail. The cat meows and moves away. Nora hits the cat and says "Don't." Nora again picks up the end of the cat's tail but the cat pulls away. Nora pulls again and the cat pulls away again, bristling up in annoyance. She watches intently as the cat's tail flicks back and forth. She laughs and moves her hand back and forth, almost in rhythm with the cat's tail. Nora clicks her tongue and calls "kitty, kitty," babbling to the cat. She strokes the cat and drinks from her bottle.

Piaget's view is that it progresses in *stages* that are determined by maturation and the infant's experiences interacting with the environment. For normal cognitive development to occur the infant must have many and varied experiences with the environment, with the pace and timing of development influenced by a maturational effect. The first stage of development is expected to take from birth to about age 2 years (though Piaget only intends these chronological age limits as approximate boundaries to stages).

Bruner (Bruner, Olver, & Greenfield, 1966) takes a view somewhat similar to that of Piaget but differs with him on fundamental issues. For example,

Linda, who is 2 years old, is investigating the mysteries of a flashlight by taking it apart and trying to put it back together.

Linda picks up a flashlight from the living room couch. She unscrews the head and takes it apart. She looks inside where the light bulb is, then looks at the empty compartment where batteries are normally kept. Linda looks at the head then tries to screw it back on without success. Linda puts the wrong side of the head against the battery compartment and tries to screw it on. She looks at the light bulb, takes it out, examines it, then fits it back on the head. Linda turns the head to the right side against the battery compartment and tries to screw it on again. She continues struggling with the flashlight.

Mastery

Becky, 12 months old, is trying to fit a finger puppet into a container that is much too small to hold it. Although an adult can clearly see the impossibility of the task, Becky, with her infantile understanding of size relations, cannot.

Becky tries to fit a finger puppet into a miniscule plastic toy trunk. She manages to put the bottom part of it in, then tries to push the trunk top down on it by force. The puppet is too big for the toy trunk, and as soon as Becky lets go her hand, the puppet pops up again. Becky tries to squeeze the puppet down inside the trunk several times. She looks puzzled, then toddles away to join a ball game her sister is starting.

Benjamin, 18 months old, is playing with a set of nesting cups at the kitchen table.

Benjamin takes off the lid of the largest cup, sets it down, and places the cup to one side. He then does the same with the next two cups, stacking the lids and setting the cups in a row of three from smallest to largest. Ben now takes off the lids of the remaining three cups and stacks the lids on the previous three. He adds the remaining three cups to his row of three, arranging them in ascending order from smallest to largest. Ben gets down from the kitchen table, runs to his mother and returns at full speed, his mother following him.

He now turns the largest cup of the row upside down. Mother observes and questions: "What are you making, Ben?" Ben replies: "Tower," and begins stacking the cups, the largest one at the bottom, and the others in descending order of size.

Source: Carew, J. V., Chan, I., & Halfar, C. Observing Intelligence in Young Children: Eight Case Studies, © 1976, pp. 19, 24, 26, 27, 31, 32. Adapted by permission of Prentice-Hall, Inc., Englewood Cliffs, NJ. Quotes used with permission.

whereas Piaget claims that development proceeds mainly because of an internal push due to maturation, with the help of some pull from the environment, Bruner says, "We take the view that cognitive growth . . . occurs as much from the outside in as from the inside out" (Bruner et al., 1966, pp. 1–2). The behaviorist view (for example, Bijou & Baer, 1965; Gewitz, 1969; Skinner, 1953) attempts to account for cognitive development mainly in terms of the lasting effects of the child's previous experiences. Let us first take a look at what Piaget has to say.

Physical and Intellectual Development **153**

Piaget's View

Piaget began his study of intellectual development in 1923, in Geneva, Switzerland, by carefully observing his three children, Jacqueline, Lucienne, and Laurent, playing with household objects. His aim was to develop and test certain hypotheses about how young children develop ways of knowing and acquiring knowledge.

Piaget (1963) has suggested that there are four stages of intellectual development. These are set out in Table 4.2. It is the stage of sensorimotor development that occurs in infancy (which Piaget says lasts from birth to about age 2 years). Before describing the features of this first stage, we need to clarify the concepts of stage, schema, and structure.

A stage of cognitive development is a period of time during which the child acquires a particular way of thinking and reasoning about the world. During infancy this is achieved by sensorimotor actions. No matter what objects and events the infant experiences, knowledge about them and how to organize them comes *always* from motor actions upon them that are linked to a sensorial processing of information.

According to Piaget, cognitive stages occur in a particular sequence. The order reflects the developing cognitive capabilities of the child and is always the same (invariant). Each stage must be passed through before the next can be attained. The way the child thinks during a particular stage is related to, but different from, his or her way of thinking during other stages of development.

As we have mentioned, Piaget believes that the infant first gains knowledge of the environment through direct motor actions and immediate sensory perceptions. Thus he uses the term *sensorimotor* to describe the first stage of cognitive development. The infant organizes experiences through motor actions and sensory perceptions in what Piaget calls schemas. Piaget tells us that a **schema** is an abstract image by which the infant assimilates new information (1967, 1973). Piaget distinguishes between structure and schema. He has chosen to call those actions such as grasping, reaching, and searching, which are organized during the first 2 years of life, schemas. The term **structure** is used in a particular sense to describe organized thinking and reasoning, which first makes an appearance at about 6 or 7 years.

Both schemas and structures include items (objects and events) linked by one or more relationships. For example, all the coordinated actions of extending and flexing an arm organized by the infant to reach a toy can be called a schema. The older child might relate wooden blocks according to the properties of shape, color, size, texture, or any other appropriate property by using the process of classifying, which is called a structure. These organizations, whether schema or structure, show themselves to be stable (remain essentially the same) and enduring (long-lasting in memory). Now that we have defined Piaget's terms, we can turn to the question of how schemas and structures are organized.

Table 4.2 Piaget's Stages of Intellectual Development

Sensorimotor Period	Repetition of reflex actions results in the acquisition of an assortment of action schemes.
	Increased exploration of objects in the environment is related to an improvement in the coordination of sensorimotor actions.
	Exploration of new objects and events is related to the use of schemes of sensorimotor actions already organized in memory. Imitation becomes deliberate and more systematic as this period progresses.
	Exploration becomes linked with intention. Various actions are repeated as part of exploration. Improvement in the ability to accommodate to new situations occurs.
	Toward the end of this period there emerges the ability to represent objects, events, and actions upon objects as mental images. There is a more active seeking for results from particular actions upon objects.
Preoperations	Ability to represent objects and actions upon objects improves, but the focus of attention is upon the immediate environment. The use of language appears, but the child is not yet able to form true concepts or consistently assign a word to a class of objects.
	Changes in the form of play and the use of rules and imitation are related to improvements in thinking and reasoning. But reasoning is from the particular to the particular without any logical association between objects or generalization.
	Toward the end of this period the child begins to form some concepts, but these are limited by what is perceptually obvious. Thinking is egocentric—children see their environment only from their own point of view.
Concrete Operations	In this period there is an improvement in the ability to mentally represent classes of objects, relationships between classes, and operations that can be performed upon objects—such as classification, serially ordering objects on some continuum, and conserving some property of an object even when other properties of the object have been changed (transformed) in some way.
	Play becomes focused more on the representation of objects and events and is more strongly rule-governed.
	Understanding of spatial, number and time concepts improves. There is a decline in childish egocentric thinking.
Formal Operations	A change from concrete to formal operations is marked by a growing ability to think about thinking. One form of this is hypothetico-deductive reasoning. This requires the setting up of hypotheses and the testing of them by scientific (inductive) reasoning. During this period the adolescent acquires a better understanding of relations between relations and the related ability to use propositional logic.

In his description of the psychology of the child, Piaget (1969) begins by emphasizing how change in simple motor actions, schemas, and structures occurs. According to his view, there are two processes of organization, assimilation and accommodation. *Assimilation* is a process of incorporating new experiences into a previous experience related in some way. For example, the infant sucks on a nipple to feed. In a short space of time the infant will have had many sucking experiences not only on a nipple but also on any object brought to the mouth such as a thumb or a pacifier. Each sucking experience is assimilated (made similar) to a general way of sucking.

As each action is accomplished, the infant modifies the general action by including the new, related experience—thus making it more effective for future use. The modification of the internal schema (or later structure) is called *accommodation*. For example, Piaget observed Laurent:

As early as the second day . . . seek with his lips the breast which has escaped him. From the third day he gropes more systematically to find it. . . . He searches in the same way for his thumb which brushes his mouth (1953).

In this case various experiences of "searching for" an object to suck on are assimilated into a more general and more *efficient* schema of "searching for."

Piaget describes six substages of the stage of **sensorimotor development**. Each of these substages has the characteristics we applied to the term *stage* (Table 4.3).

I and II. Reflexes and primary circular reactions. Together these two stages last from birth to 4 months of age. Soon after birth the infant has a tendency to repeat reflex actions (sucking, crying, grasping). In this first month of life the infant sucks on any object and, by practicing in this way, becomes more and more efficient at sucking. However, the infant also learns to discriminate between sucking on objects that provide food and sucking on objects that do not provide food. Other reflex actions are similarly practiced and improved.

As the infant's vision improves, exploration with the eyes begins. At this stage new activities appear that are not directly connected to reflexes. By coordinating actions of the arm and mouth, for example, the infant can suck its thumb when it likes. Vision and hearing also become coordinated. When hearing a voice, the infant only looks to the person's face if it has seen the face before. Cycles of such actions Piaget calls *primary circular reactions*. He believes they mark the dawning of memory (1952), the first component of cognition.

III. Secondary circular reactions. Primary circular reactions are used just for their own sake. When the infant is about 3 to 6 months old actions become centered on getting a result. When given a new object the infant explores it by

Table 4.3 Piaget's Stages of Intellectual Development.
Sensorimotor Period (Birth–2 years)

Substage	Description	Types of Behavior
Substage I (birth–1 month)	Reflex actions	Repetition of reflex actions such as sucking and grasping. Development of schemes of actions.
Substage II (1–4 months)	Primary circular reactions	Coordination of actions—the first *adaptations*. Leads to successful cycles of actions.
Substage III (4–8 months)	Secondary circular reactions	Schemes of actions are used to achieve some objective. The range of actions is helped by the development of hand-eye coordination.
Substage IV (8–12 months)	Coordination of secondary schemes	Uses different means to achieve some objective. Assimilates schemes in exploring new experiences. Imitates new actions and changes existing actions. Plays simple games.
Substage V (12–18 months)	Tertiary circular reactions	Seeks new results from actions by experimentation. Actions that lead to new results are *assimilated* and *accommodated* into existing schemas—which, by this process, are themselves changed (reorganized).
Substage VI (18–24 months)	Invention of new means through mental combinations	Mental combinations of *images* of actions, rather than sensorimotor actions, are used to solve problems. Remembers sequences of events, has expectations of the result of actions, can remember objects when out of sight and actively search for them.

using many different schemas. If a satisfying result is obtained from an action, the infant attempts to reproduce it. This substage occurs between 4 and 8 months of age.

For the first time Laurent sees the paper knife. He grasps it and looks at it, but only for a moment. Afterwards he immediately swings it. . . . He then rubs it by chance against the wicker of the bassinet and tries to reproduce the sound heard, as though it were a rattle (Piaget, 1955).

Eye and hand movements become better coordinated. The infant also now develops a sense of expectancy (or anticipation). The mobile hanging above the crib is not only grasped and pulled downward but pushed to see the swinging movement repeat itself. A hungry baby, seeing his or her mother appear, will cry in anticipation.

This baby is pulling on a cloth to get a toy that was placed out of reach on the cloth. However, when the toy was placed out of reach but next to the cloth, the baby still pulled on the cloth (right), fully expecting to be successful again. The use of the cloth to get an object out of reach is still magic to babies less than nine months old. They do not understand the spatial relations between the cloth and toy necessary for the pulling strategy to work. (Source: Bower, T. G. R. Human Development, 1979. With permission.)

Other new abilities emerge at this time. One of these is the recognition that objects have some permanence. Previously the infant believed "out of sight" meant "out of existence." Now if the infant loses an object after holding it, a searching action begins; but if the object is not found at once, the infant stops searching (see Inset 4.2).

By 6 months of age the infant stops making this kind of error, but other odd errors with respect to object and spatial relations persist. For example, if a toy is placed under one of two cups while the baby watches, the baby will reach out and take the toy from under the cup and will repeat this action. If the toy is then in front of the child and is placed under the second cup, the baby looks under the first cup again and shows surprise at not finding the toy there. Some infants are still making this type of error at age 12 months, as we will see in the next section.

Although between the ages of 4 and 8 months the infant develops notions of causality, these are also limited. When a toy is placed on a cloth, the baby quickly realizes that pulling on the cloth (the cause) brings the toy closer (the effect) and within reach. If the cloth is put back in the same place and the toy is placed out of reach but next to the cloth, the baby still pulls on the cloth expecting to get the toy again (Bower, 1979).

IV. Coordination of schemas. During this substage, which lasts from about the eighth to the twelfth month, the two most important changes in development are the emerging skills of *intention* and *imitation*. Piaget (1953) noted that at 8 months Jacqueline was capable of carrying out an intention.

Jacqueline tries to grasp a cigarette case I presented to her. I then slid it between the cross strings which attach her dolls to the hood of the baby buggy. Unsuccessful in trying to reach the case, she grasped the strings, pulled and shook them until the cigarette case fell down, which she then grasped. In this way the schema of pulling (strings) and grasping (the case) are combined, and a *new schema* is formed—"pulling in order to grasp." As a result of this type of exploration, schemas become more mobile, more intercoordinated to achieve different intentions. (Author's additions).

158 Birth and Infancy

The infant also begins to imitate, far more, the actions of others.

Laurent imitates sounds with approximately the right number of syllables.
Jacqueline imitates actions of putting a finger on the mouth, yawning, rubbing her eyes, sniffing. . . .

Although infants now look more successfully for objects that are hidden, they cannot deal successfully with displaced objects. For example, if an object is hidden first under one cushion and then a second cushion, the infant looks under the first cushion. Not finding the object there, the infant does not look for the object, which was "displaced" from under the first cushion to be finally hidden under the second cushion.

V. Tertiary circular reactions.   From about the twelfth to the eighteenth month, the most notable achievement is the capability to solve new problems by accommodating to new situations. The infant now actively "experiments," seeking out new activities and making discoveries. Each new activity, once discovered, is repeated. Unlike the first set of circular reactions these are not exactly similar repetitions but have new forms. The child is interested in what might be found by varying actions.

Laurent . . . grasps a succession of objects: a celluloid swan, a box, etc., stretches out his arm and lets them fall. He distinctly varies the position of the fall. . . . He lets (an object) fall two or three times . . . in the same place as though to study the spatial relation; then he modifies the situation (Piaget, 1953).

In this period infants spend much time experimenting, showing both perseverance and assurance (see Inset 4.3).

VI. Invention.   Remember that in the first 18 months the child's development has been intertwined with sensorimotor acts. Change in mental constructs comes about by external actions on objects and events. From now until about the start of the second year, the infant acquires a growing ability to solve problems by inventing new mental combinations of schemas.

This is a most fascinating change. The child can now represent the external world in terms of **images** and memories. These can be combined without, necessarily, the need for associated actions. Thus the child gains the ability to imagine, to remember better.

As adults you can remember objects and events that you have previously seen and experienced even though they are no longer present. Piaget describes this feat of memory as **object permanence** and claims that it is an important feature of development during the sensorimotor stage. The sequence of development is as follows:

1. Substages I and II (0–4 months). When an object is out of sight, it is out of mind.

2. Substage III (4–8 months). Infants do not search visually or manually for an object (e.g., rattle) hidden under a cover (e.g., blanket). They search manually if they were already moving toward the object when it was hidden—and usually if the object is only partially hidden.

3. Substage IV (8–12 months). Infants search manually for an object hidden under a cover. If the object is placed successively under *several* covers, the infants only search under the *first* cover. (See Inset Figure 4.2.)

4. Substage V (12–18 months). If an object is hidden successively under several covers, infants search under the last cover. If the infants cannot *see* the object in some of the moves (e.g., hidden completely in the hand or a container), they do not search for the object under the last cover.

5. Substage VI (18–24 months). Infants search under the last cover used for hiding, even though they were unable to see the object during some of the moves.

Failure or success can be explained in two different ways. According to Piaget, success depends upon the presence of an underlying *competency*—arriving at a stage in development where the infant now has an understanding of object permanence—which was previously absent. A different explanation suggests that infants of say 6 and 12 months *all* have an understanding of object permanence but that younger infants have not yet had a chance to practice and refine certain necessary supporting skills such as motor coordination and memory; that is, the competency is present but the performance has not yet been achieved.

Do results of research support the competence or performance explanations? In a number of studies Bower and his colleagues (Bower, 1967, 1971; Bower, Broughton, & Moore, 1971; Bower & Patterson, 1973) have looked for performance explanations of why infants sometimes fail to search for hidden objects. In one experiment they passed an object along a track and through a tunnel to the other side. They noticed that infants followed the object to the point where it disappeared into the tunnel and continued tracking to the other end of the tunnel, even when the object had been stopped in the tunnel and *did not emerge*. They later discovered that infants continued to follow the apparent course of a stopped object when the object *was in full view* and there was no tunnel. They concluded that, once infants begin to follow an object, they have difficulty stopping the movement of their eyes.

In other experiments it has been shown that (1) searching for a hidden object depends on the location of an object (e.g., under a cloth—difficult, or behind a screen—less difficult, Bower, 1974); (2) searching for an object hidden in successive

places depends on the difficulty of a task (infants in substage IV searched successfully for an object hidden successively in *two* plastic dishes, Gratch et al., 1971, 1974); (3) seeing an object hidden in several places may be too difficult a *memory task* for infants (Harris, 1973, 1974).

What can we conclude from these studies? The complicated competence versus performance question has not been fully resolved. However, it is clear that test difficulty and severe demands on memory do account for some failures to search for hidden objects. So, although further research is needed, we have learned that in some cases limitations in performance can cause failure to demonstrate an understanding of object permanence.

Inset Figure 4.2 Object permanence in infants 8–12 months.
(Source: *Human Development* by T. G. R. Bower. W. H. Freeman and Company. Copyright © 1979. Reprinted by permission.)

Inset 4.3
Experiences of Experimentation

From experiences of mastery we turn now to experiences of experimentation, in which the child's interest no longer lies in mastering a skill but rather in trying out varying ways of acting on familiar objects to test what effects his or her actions bring about. As part of this experimentation the child anticipates novel outcomes from different combinations of objects and actions. The child now deliberately *creates* new experiences. Here are some of the questions which 1- and 2-year-old scientists consider worth investigating.

At 12 months Dean is experimenting with the laws of gravity and trajectory by throwing toys out of his playpen and watching them fall.

Dean sits in the playpen. His older sister comes in with an armful of toys and puts them into the playpen. Dean picks up a spoon and a toy chicken. He throws the chicken out of the playpen onto the living room floor and leans forward to watch it fall. He mouths the spoon. He bends down to pick up a small wooden doll and the toy chicken and throws them out onto the floor. His mother sees this and says to him in a pleasant voice, "Uh!—Now, you haven't got them." Dean looks at his mother and claps his hands. Mother claps her hands back and calls, "Hey, Dean!"

Mark is 2 years old and has a similar research project. His materials are toy cars, a cushion for an incline, and his own body to test firsthand the sensations of rolling.

Mark pushes a seat cushion off the couch in the living room, so that it lands on the floor and leans on the couch at an incline. Mark slides a toy car down on the incline, then another, then another. He gets on the couch and slides himself down on the cushion incline. He gets up and picks up all the cars and repeats the game. Mark lines up two cars on the top of the incline and pushes them down at the same time and then slides the other cars down one by one. Mark picks up the cars and slides them down again and then slides down himself on his tummy.

Lucy, at 12 months, is intrigued by the phenomenon of object permanence. She is playing a game dear to generations of children—peekaboo. Her fascination with this game is in making the room and her mother vanish each time she covers her eyes and reappear each time she pulls off the cover. Lucy probably already understands that her mother is not doing a disappearing act but continues to exist even while she, Lucy, cannot see her. This realization is a short step toward understanding concepts of monumental significance to a child—such as that her mother continues to exist even when she, Lucy, has been put to bed; or that her father will come home again even though she cannot see him while he is at work; or that her toy doggie will still be there when her mother brings her back from shopping.

Lucy goes to her mother who is making the double bed. Lucy pulls the sheet and puts her head under it. Mother exclaims, "Oh!" and Lucy covers her head again. Mother asks, "Are you helping Mommy?" and makes the bed. Lucy kneels down by the bed and pulls a corner of the bedspread and covers her head with it. Mother says, "Peekaboo!" They laugh and Lucy repeats the game many more times. Mother says, "Come on," and removes the bedspread from Lucy. Lucy pulls it to cover her head again. Mother puts a diaper over Lucy's head and repeats, "Peekaboo!" Lucy continues playing the peekaboo game with the diaper.

Source: Carew, J.V., Chan, I., & Halfar, C. *Observing Intelligence in Young Children: Eight Case Studies*, © 1976, pp. 19, 24, 26, 27, 31, 32. Adapted by permission of Prentice-Hall, Inc., Englewood Cliffs, NJ. Quotes used with permission.

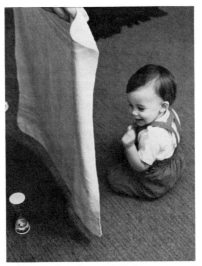

Figure 4.13 For the very young infant, an object placed out of sight means out of mind. From about age eighteen months, infants begin to search persistently for hidden objects until they are found. This means that infants are now able to represent objects and events in terms of images and memories (*object permanence*) and searching in terms of action schemas. (Photos by George Zimbal, Monkmeyer Press)

For example, Piaget noted that Lucienne was able to find a chain hidden in a match box left slightly open:

She looks at the slit with great attention; then several times in succession she opens and shuts her mouth, at first slightly, then wider and wider! By imitating this schema of opening with her mouth, Lucienne thinks out a solution. Soon after this phase of . . . reflection, Lucienne unhesitatingly puts her finger in the slit . . . [and] pulls so as to enlarge the opening. She succeeds and grasps the chain (1955).

So, for Piaget, it is at about this time that infants begin to remember with more certainty objects previously seen and search persistently for hidden objects even when displaced. However, it has been observed that some infants younger than 2 years seem to have an understanding of object permanence (Bower, 1967, 1971; Bower & Patterson, 1973; Harris, 1975; Kagan et al., 1978). (See Figure 4.13.)

Problems with stage theory. Some theorists question whether children pass through stages in this fashion. They say that intellectual development is not very "stage-like" (Flavell, 1980). Rather than proceeding in an invariant sequence, it is more likely that "unevenness is the rule in development" (Fisher, 1980, p. 510). By unevenness they mean something like the old saying, "two steps forward, one step back."

Bower (1976) has demonstrated that at age 1 year the infant has no notion of the concept of weight but has an understanding of this concept six months later. At about age 3 or 4 years this understanding has apparently disappeared again only to reappear later at about 6 or 7 years. Also, we know that training and practice in certain skills can significantly change an infant's behavior and that these changes can remain permanent over long periods. Infants may, in fact, know more, or be capable of learning more, than Piaget gives them credit for (Flavell, 1977), with his emphasis on maturation and strict stages of development.

However, it is true to say that Piaget has provided us with a major theory of intellectual development. We must keep in mind that a useful theory will inevitably continue to help in the generation of hypotheses. In testing these hypotheses we might expect some changes and modifications to be made to the theory. Even if Piaget's theory were to completely disappear, to be supplanted by an alternative theory, it would have served a most important purpose.

There does not seem to be a smooth transition from one stage to the next, nor does stage development appear to be invariant. What has been learned from certain experiences may not be applied by the child to subsequent similar experiences because of differences in the content, context, and level of difficulty of problems. Finally, it appears that we do not have to wait for the relatively slow unfolding of cognitive ability due to maturation. Substantial changes in infants' thinking and reasoning can occur quite quickly as a result of training.

Bruner's View

Bruner attributes the growth of "early skilled action partly to physical and partly to social influences" (1974). Early skills such as sucking and grasping beyond the reflex level are achieved with little experience. It seems very likely, then, that initial "learning" reflects wired-in genetic instruction. But the infant quickly begins to adapt actions to various situations. For example, the physical, internal influence on motor and mental growth is quickly tempered by experience with objects, events, and care givers.

What is the course of this change? First, according to Bruner, there is the arousal of intention by an object. Something about an object, such as a rattle, catches the infant's interest and attention. The infant might want to catch hold of the rattle and "play" with it. With this intention in mind, as it were, the infant appears to anticipate the outcome of actions necessary to grasp the rattle. A way of achieving this intention is selected; for example, leaning forward, crawling toward the rattle, stretching and grasping to pick it up. In trying to achieve this intention, the infant sustains the selected behavior toward achievement and, in fact, substitutes different ways of achieving the intention (Bruner & Koslowski, 1972; Kalnins & Bruner, 1974).

The infant's first attempts at achieving an intention are loosely or randomly ordered. Later they become serially ordered, but not in the correct order for success. For example, first attempts to coordinate the hand and arm to capture an object invariably fail. In time and with practice, actions become coordinated and the act is successful (Bruner, 1969).

After the first success there appears to be a reorganization of the various "steps" in the serial order, and a modification occurs in the pattern. The effects of the modification are threefold (Bromwich, 1977):

1. There is an increase in anticipation. For example, "the hand now begins to close gradually to the shape of the objects as it approaches, rather than after it gets there" (Bruner, 1974, p. 171).
2. The action is "smoothed-out," made more economical.
3. The successful act (a pounce-reach) is soon replaced by a new pattern of action, which may include the old pattern. The infant (now 6 or 7 months old) reaches in two steps. First the hand is extended out toward the object, then it closes in on the object with the hand held ready for picking the object up. Under stress, or if failure occurs, the original pounce-reach reappears (Bruner & May, 1972).

The infant begins from what Bruner has called a "launching-stock" of responses that date back through a long evolutionary history. From these "wired-in" responses new patterns of actions emerge, "with an adaptive, serially ordered structure that reflects some internal principle of organization that is triggered by the environment" (Bruner, 1974, p. 172).

The emphasis here seems to be on **quantitative change**. That is, the infant improves upon initial, simple actions because an impetus is provided by the environment. The early pounce grasp is predominantly reflex action. The later, smoothly coordinated reaching–grasping action is influenced by an organized pattern.

Bruner (1975) claims there is enough evidence to suggest that, starting at about 3 months of age, there is a strong tendency for infants to form and test hypotheses. This is a "generalized state of readiness to respond selectively to classes of events in the environment" (1973, p. 93). In the example of the development of the "pounce-reach" to pick up and retrieve objects just mentioned, the infant orders sensorimotor actions according to hypotheses. With practice in reaching, the infant coordinates actions and memory. This information is used to anticipate (hypothesize about) future events and to "formulate a plan for guiding action to an intended goal" (1971, p. 3).

The Behaviorist's View

Those theorists who believe all knowledge is learned from the environment focus their attention on what the infant comes to love, fear, remember, or forget; how such learning occurs; and what its long-lasting effects are. You will readily see that this view is different from that of either Piaget or Bruner. Two particular kinds of environmental learning exist, those of classical and operant conditioning.

Classical conditioning. The description of classical conditioning is attributed to Pavlov (1927). He noticed that a dog would salivate at the taste of food. He found that if a bell were rung just before or as food was given to the dog, the dog would eventually salivate at the sound of the bell only. The dog had learned to associate the food with the bell. This kind of association is called **classical conditioning**.

The objects in the world (in this case, food and a bell) are called **stimuli**. In our example the food is the *unconditioned stimulus* because it is a natural stimulus to the dog; it is already present. The salivation of the dog when eating is the *unconditioned response*, the natural response already present. The dog then becomes conditioned to salivate when the bell is rung. The bell's ringing is called a *conditioned stimulus* because it acquires a new meaning for the dog. The salivation of the dog to the ringing bell is the *conditioned response*, the response the dog learns to make. If the dog learns to salivate at similar sounds (for example, a buzzer), *generalization* of the stimulus has occurred. If the bell is constantly rung but no food provided, the dog will stop salivating to the bell's ring. In this case, the dog has now been conditioned *not* to respond to the stimulus. Therefore, the response has been *extinguished*.

How does the concept of ***conditioning*** relate to human development? A most obvious example is a fear that has become associated with such things as sounds, smells, and objects. An infant may naturally be frightened and cry at a loud and sudden voice. Crying or fear is an unconditioned response to the unconditioned stimulus, the loud, sudden sound. An infant may learn to fear and cry at the sight of a particular object, say a puppet, because the infant heard a loud, frightening noise when first seeing the puppet. Fear and crying (conditioned response) became associated with the puppet (conditioned stimulus). However, it has been suggested by Sameroff (1968) that conditioning during infancy is more likely to occur as a result of operant conditioning than classical conditioning.

Operant conditioning. We know that babies are born with certain reflexes; they suck to get food, and they respond with a startle reflex (the body "jumps") to a sharp or loud noise or to a bright light directed at their eyes (there is an immediate tight, reflex closing of the eyes and averting of the head). They already have these ways of operating. **Operant conditioning** depends on a person's already having a way of behaving or operating, an operant. If, as soon as the operant occurs, it is *reinforced* by some reward such as a smile, it becomes increasingly likely that the operant will occur again.

It is quite certain that infants' behavior can be shaped or modified through operant conditioning. For example, sounds such as cooing are a way of behaving the infants already possess. In other words, the sounds of cooing are the operant. In one case experimenters reinforced the sounds made by 3-month-old infants (Rheingold, Gewirtz, & Ross, 1959). (The researchers introduced rewarding sensations, smiling and tickling the infants' stomachs, whenever the infants made the sounds. The smiling and tickling were the reinforcements.) In just two days the number of sounds made by the infants greatly increased. At this point no further reinforcement was given. The number of sounds then decreased to about the original level.

In another study by Bower (1966) the baby's operant was turning the head to the left. By saying "peekaboo" to the baby as soon as the head turning occurred, the operant was reinforced. In this case, as the baby got used to the "game," habituation seemed to set in and the reinforcement lost its power.

Although conditioning cannot fully explain all development and learning, many psychologists believe that many infant responses can be attributed to operant conditioning. We will return to this subject in chapters 6 through 8.

Language Development

Language, according to *Webster's Seventh New Collegiate Dictionary*, is "a systematic means of communicating ideas and feelings through the use of conventionalized signs, gestures, marks, or especially articulate vocal sounds." It is clear that language is a highly structured and complex operation. In order to be capable of language a person has to be capable of memory and intention, of some form of classification or a symbolism, of recognizing and applying rules, and of physically sophisticated vocal expression. You can see that language presents to the infant a great many of the components and tasks of cognition. How the infant acquires language, therefore, can tell us a lot about how the infant functions and develops intellectually.

Characteristics of Infant's Language

One of the first reflexes is the "cry." Many babies cry at birth. Babies cry when they are hungry or uncomfortable. They learn to use crying as a signal. But at age 3 months there is a marked decrease in crying. The baby begins to make all kinds of odd sounding noises called **cooing**. Infants around the world coo in much the same way—probably because of formation of the vocal chords in the first 2 or 3 months (Sachs, 1976). At 6 months cooing changes to sounds called **babbling**: sounds like *da, di, ma, gagaga, yayaya, dadada.* These differ from culture to culture, unlike the sounds of cooing. At 9 months infants' sounds come to have a recognizable meaning. For example, an infant may consistently make a particular sound in reference to a toy or the family car. Toward the end of the first year of life, infants begin to speak their native language, each utterance consisting of a single word—*dada, mama, bye-bye.* Not until infants are about 18 months old do they begin to use two-word utterances. An infant at 18 months says, "bye-bye" (slowly). He repeats, "bye-bye (long pause) *Daddy*" (said very loudly and followed by a big smile) (Wood, 1976, p. 27). Although it is baby talk, this is a great intellectual accomplishment because it expresses the beginning of an understanding of language itself.

There is considerable difference in the rates at which language develops during infancy. Nelson (1973) describes two quite distinct types of language that emerge at this time. Some infants between 10 and 15 months learn a large number of words that are labels for objects. Other infants use more words that have a social context. Not only is it interesting to find these differences occurring so early during infancy, but they also appear to have importance for future language, social, and personality development. As the infant grows older there is an unfolding of ability, partly affected by maturation and partly by learning in a particular environment. Let us take a closer look at these phases.

The first sounds. There is no doubt that language is, to a certain extent, *genetically* determined because only humans use real language. For language to develop it appears we need not only "speakers" but "listeners." The infants' development of language is in part elicited by parents and care givers. *Vocalization* by care givers to elicit language from the infant appears to have three important characteristics. It is exaggerated in its display, it is exaggerated in time, and it is very limited (Stern, 1977, p. 14).

Usually, it is mothers who have been observed vocalizing with their infants. Around the world mothers all seem to talk a version of baby language (Ferguson, 1964). They begin with short sentences making them progressively longer over the first two years (Nelson, 1973). Even when the infant does not vocalize, the mother vocalizes as though a conversation were taking place:

Mother   "Aren't you my cutie?"
Pause   (.60 second)
Imagined response from infant: "Yes" (.40 second)
Pause   (.60 second)
Mother   "You sure are."
(Stern, 1977, p. 17)

The care giver exaggerates salient sounds but limits the repertoire as though preparing the infant with such experience for the sounds adults use (Stern, 1977, p. 15).

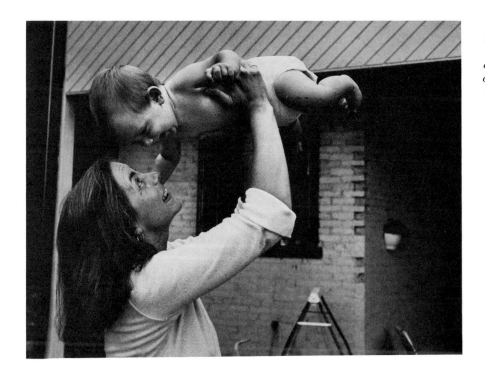

From imitation to one-word utterances.   Out of babbling emerge the first consistent sounds—used appropriately and with some purpose. Most of these are "nonsense sounds." Only a few are derived from adult language. Many of these sounds are now repeated in similar contexts and come to have a recognizable meaning—at least for parents (Bloom, 1970; Halliday, 1975). Halliday believes that this development is at least partly due to operant conditioning. Adults reinforce the sounds by imitating them and by associating the sounds to meanings adults assign to the sounds. Adults tend to translate some of these sounds into an adult form making possible systematic imitation. By the end of this phase, which lasts from 1 year to 18 months, the infant is able to produce dozens of one-word sentences, called **holophrases**. This term is used to indicate that the single words used may mean something beyond the meaning of the word itself. Saying "Dada," with arms outstretched may mean, "Come here, Dada; pick me up," or "Dada; pick me up, I'm frightened" (with a stranger close by).

Duo sentences.   Quite suddenly for most infants, at about the age of 18 months, a "grammar" emerges (Bower, 1979, p. 231). By this we mean that the infant shows an understanding that in some way there are rules that govern the expression of meaning in languages, *grammar*. The infant demonstrates this understanding by putting together two-word sentences called **duo sentences** or *duos* (paired words). Duos show that the infant is trying to communicate an idea.

Many researchers in the 1960s interpreted children's use of two-word sentences in terms of **pivot grammars**. According to this interpretation of sentence structure, duo sentences are made from two classes of words, one called the *pivot class*, the other, the *open class* (Table 4.4). Pivot words always appear in a fixed place in a sentence, either first or last (Braine, 1963; Brown, 1973), whereas open-class words have no fixed place. For example, the child might say *coat on, shoe on, hat on* or *allgone cake, allgone shoe* or *allgone coat*. For this child, in the first set of duo sentences the pivot word is *on* and in the second set, *allgone*.

Table 4.4 Duo Sentences*

Pivot Words	Open-Class Words
a	boy
allgone	boat
bye bye	coat
big	come
more	dolly
my	dolly's
night-night	hot
pretty	knee
see	mommy
this	pretty
that	sock
the	shoe
wash	tinkertoy
wet	toy
you	

Some Duo Sentences

allgone shoe
that dolly's
night-night mommy
see toy
my sock
pretty coat
you come

---

*Pivot words always appear in a fixed location, either always first in a duo sentence or second, but seldom used in both positions. Once a child begins to use duo sentences the number of utterances used increases dramatically because the child can *create* them.

Although pivot grammars have been widely used to describe the structure of children's duo sentences, they are inadequate (Dale, 1976, p. 22). There are two problems with these grammars. First, pivot grammars cannot adequately describe most children's speech (Bowerman, 1973), and, second, even in cases where pivot grammars are adequate for this purpose, they still fail to describe all aspects of children's language use (Bloom, 1970). For example, it has been observed that some children produce sentences such as *mommy byebye, kitty byebye* but also *byebye again* and *byebye birdie*, which is an instance of a pivot word *byebye* not appearing consistently in a fixed position (Dale, 1976, p. 22). A pivot grammar can be used to describe children's language, but it says very little about the relation of words in a sentence—and, therefore, very little about the meaning of sentences (Dale, 1976, pp. 22–23). Bloom (1970) provides an example of how context is important for understanding the meaning of duo sentences. One child she observed, Kathryn, said on two different occasions *mommy sock*, once when she picked up one of her mother's stockings and again when her mother put one of Kathryn's own socks on her foot. The two different meanings of this duo sentence are quite obvious. We can see how important it is to take into account not only the structure of sentences but also their meaning.

Theories of Language Development

By age 2 the infant is well on the way to mastering language. How does language come about? There is no straightforward answer, which is the case for other characteristics of child development. A number of theorists have attempted to describe the growth and change of language development.

The behaviorist's view.   Skinner (1957) explains language development in terms of operant conditioning. Certainly some of the examples already provided of cases of habituation and imitation would seem to support this view. For example, if the infant says *dada*, the parents are likely to repeat this and show approval. Skinner recognizes that, because language develops so quickly, such slow shaping could not account for all of language development. He points out (1957) that infants generalize rules taught by reinforcement. For example, an infant taught the plural of one word may generalize the rule for plural endings of other words. In this way Skinner attempts to explain the complexity of language acquisition. Other theorists find this explanation insufficient.

The nativist's view.   Chomsky (1957, 1965) maintains that the ability to develop and use language is **innate**, or native, to the infant. One argument he puts forward in support of this *nativism* theory points out that the speed with which infants acquire language strongly suggests that it is naturally endowed (Miller, 1964). So much is expressed in such a short period that the source must be already present, not acquired.

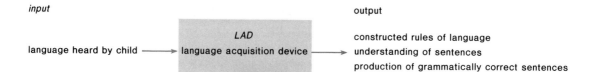

input

output

LAD
language heard by child ⟶ language acquisition device ⟶ constructed rules of language
understanding of sentences
production of grammatically correct sentences

Figure 4.14 Chomsky's model of a language acquisition device (LAD). According to Chomsky (1969), the LAD is an *innate mechanism for the production of language* that all children have no matter what language they speak.

According to Chomsky (1975, Ch. 1) infants are born with a special **language acquisition device (LAD)**. This is a hypothetical model meant to describe the mental functions involved in acquiring language. This helps the infant come to an understanding of language heard, to construct rules, and to construct an appropriate language to use (see Figure 4.14). The ideas about language the child acquires by listening to linguistic utterances and processing them using LAD are a set of principles common to *all* languages—for example, the subject-verb relationship. The fact that, in developing speech, infants and children produce as well as receive and imitate is accounted for by LAD. For example, the infant at age 2 may use the two-word sentence, "Daddy work" to mean either "Daddy is working at his desk" or "Daddy has gone to work." The infant tests this sentence out to see if another person understands its meaning. For example, the infant will say "Daddy work" to mother. She might misunderstand and say "No, Daddy has not gone to work. Daddy is at home." The infant might then reply, "Daddy work," pointing to the den or tugging mother there to show her.

Lenneberg (1967), who also argues that language development can be attributed to *innate mechanisms*, claims that the understanding, acquisition, and production of language is due to an inherited characteristic because language seems to develop in much the same sequence and at about the same rate in all cultures. Babbling for all children begins at about 6 months, first words appear at 12 months, duo sentences at between 18 and 24 months (with a rudimentary understanding of grammar), and a substantive use of grammar at between 4 and 5 years of age.

The cognitive structuralist's view. Piaget believes that language grows out of intellectual development. He says that the infant must first be capable of mental representation (images) before utterances can be considered language. As we saw in a previous section of this chapter, such representations do not occur until substage VI of the sensorimotor period between 18 and 24 months. The infant's sensorimotor "action" experiences are considered essential for the growth of representation. The way the child uses words (holophrases) and simple sentences (duos) *reflects a sensorimotor way of thinking.* In Piaget's view language does not influence cognitive development during infancy and early childhood but "springs out of" cognitive development.

Vygotsky (1962), a Russian psychologist, has an alternative view. In his opinion the way the infant thinks and the way language is used develop in a parallel fashion. From early capacities—such as sensorimotor schemas—the infant develops thought and speech separately in two parallel "streams." These two streams of development come together when the infant is about 2 years old and becomes more conscious of what words stand for. Unlike Piaget, Vygotsky believes language can then aid the child's reasoning.

Bruner's description of the development of *representation* and language is closer to Vygotsky's idea of language development than to that of Piaget (for example, Bruner et al., 1966). Bruner identifies three forms of representation: enactive, iconic, and symbolic. At first these develop one after the other although some overlapping can be expected.

The infant begins to represent the world through action (for example, the "feel" of objects may be represented by stroking actions, the hardness of objects by banging actions, and the availability of objects by reaching actions). This is called **enactive representation**. At first actions (such as grasping) occur one after the other in a serial order. Later they are organized into schemas such as the "pounce-reach" and retrieval of an object.

In Bruner's view the infant learns to remember general, external events such as grasping, shaking, and so on. In other words, enactive representation is based on memory. During the second year of life the infant develops an ever-improving ability to represent the world by *images* or *spatial schemas*. For example, in play routines the infant will stack things to make a "tower," place objects in and remove them from containers, search for hidden objects, and imitate both the actions of objects and those of people. This is called **iconic representation** because the infant is imitating an image of an object. For some time these image memories are still tied to representation through action. **Symbolic representation** (words, language) is usually associated with the use of language. Therefore, by age 2 the infant is well able to use symbols (words). But symbolic representation is just beginning to form. The infant has only an incomplete knowledge and understanding of the concepts words stand for. Although the infant may be quite precocious in the use of language as evidenced by the extent of vocabulary and the grammatical structure of sentences, the understanding of what language symbolizes is as yet naive and intuitive.

Views about the development of language reflect contrasting theories in infant cognitive development. The behaviorists tell us that language may be seen as a set of rules taught by reinforcement and then generalized to further uses of language. The nativists claim that the ability to use language is innate and "unfolds" as the infant develops. Piaget says that the infant first uses language as a means for representing sensorimotor schemas already acquired; with language development from there on, always stepping on the heels of cognitive development. The Russian psychologist Vygotsky supposes that during the first two years of life, the development of speech and thought are unrelated, after which they become fused and interdependent. Finally, Bruner believes that language as symbolic representation follows the infant's representation of the world first by action and then by image, and that as it develops from its first appearance at about age 2 can influence the course of cognitive development.

Summary

During infancy physical, motor, perceptual, and intellectual development occur very rapidly. The rate of physical growth sets both limits on and provides opportunities for other features of development.

Although some studies have shown that motor development is strongly influenced by maturation, other studies have shown that early stimulation can speed up locomotion by as much as six to eight months. Although it is certain that involuntary reflex actions are "wired-in" at birth, these also can be influenced by learning.

Mechanisms of sensing, such as vision, hearing, taste, and smell, are physical responses to physical stimuli. These mechanisms appear to be strongly influenced by environmental experiences. Changes in sensing competencies are related not only to mental but also to social development.

Perception, as distinguished from sensing, is the intellectual function of processing information that has been sensed. The baby's perception appears to be "programmed" at birth to function in set ways. At first governed by *operating principles*, perception is later organized through a process of habituation.

The novelty, discrepancy, and complexity of objects and events all play a part in perceptual development. It is claimed that infants organize perceptual experiences into schemas or schemes, at first based on the discrepancy between novel objects similar to but different from previously seen objects. Later, in paying attention to familiar objects, infants appear to form hypotheses about differences they notice in configurations or different situations in which the objects appear. In resolving the problem of "do I know this object," the infant fits objects into previous experiences with these same objects.

Piaget claims that intellectual development proceeds through an invariant sequence of stages. The infancy stage (birth to 2 years) is called the stage of sensorimotor development. According to Piaget, cognitive structure is organized into sensorimotor schemas. The *organization* of knowledge in terms of schemas is accomplished first by *assimilating* new experiences into previous experiences and then by modifying previous experiences to include the new, related experience in a process called *accommodation*. Development is influenced both by maturation (the rate of development) and the amount and diversity of *interactive* experiences with the environment.

Bruner emphasizes that infants quickly learn to adapt actions to meet their own intentions and the demands of the environment. Actions improve with practice, and change is influenced more by prompts from the environment than by a maturational factor. During the two years of infancy three forms of representation are developed—enactive, iconic, and symbolic, in that order. The infant is predisposed to represent the world by action (enactive), but the other two forms of representation, though rudimentary, have been established by the end of the second year of life.

Environmental learning theories describe development mainly in terms of cumulative learning based on previous experiences. Learning occurs as a function of either classical or operant conditioning. Skinner, a behaviorist, believes that changes in behavior are best explained as a result of operant conditioning. In a controlled learning situation behaviors considered worth developing can be reinforced and shaped by operant conditioning.

Infant vocalization begins with cooing and babbling noises. At between 12 and 18 months of age the infant begins to use holophrases, single words thought to stand for more than the meaning of the word itself. Holophrases are followed by duos; paired words. This is the beginning of "grammar."

Behaviorists explain language development in terms of operant conditioning while nativists claim that language is innate, unfolding in the process of maturation. Piaget maintains that language emerges when the child can construct *mental representations*. This is at a *later stage* than infancy, and the emergence of language is dependent on the development of sensorimotor intelligence. Vygotsky believes that language and cognition develop in a parallel rather than sequential fashion, coming together when the infant is about 2 years old. Finally, Bruner describes language development as emerging out of three ways of representing the world: through action (enactive), through images (iconic) and through symbolism (the predominant form being language). All three forms are used by the infant but only in a simple fashion.

Questions for Review

1. Briefly describe the major reflex actions of early infancy. Why are reflex actions so important at birth?

2. How have infant specialists explored the effects of both maturation and learning on development?

3. What do the results of the "visual cliff" experiment tell us about perceptual development during infancy?

4. Describe the main features of an infant's vision.

5. Why is the development of object permanence considered to be so important? Summarize the results of experiments that have explored the development of object permanence.

6. What are the main features of sensorimotor development according to Piaget?

7. According to Bruner, how does modification occur in the development of early skilled action?

8. If possible, observe infants aged 3 and 6 months attempting to get hold of an object placed some distance from them. What differences do you notice in levels of interest and attention, apparent anticipation of how the object will be reached, attempts to obtain the objects, and ability to grasp, hold, and move the object?

9. Try to observe an infant between 1 and 2 years of age who is using language. Keep a record of the utterances used: sounds, holophrases, duos, perhaps longer sentences. Also note the way infant–adult verbal interactions are structured. For example, does an adult appear to be helping the infant with its utterances?

Suggestions for Further Reading

Brazelton, T. B. *Infants and mothers: Differences in development*. New York: Delacorte, 1971. Especially written for parents. Different rates of development for an active, passive, and normal infant are described.

Carew, J. V., Chan, I., & Halfar, C. *Observing intelligence in young children: Eight case studies*. Englewood Cliffs, NJ: Prentice-Hall, 1976. Describes the everyday experiences of "ordinary" children from a wide variety of backgrounds. Contains many examples of young children's behavior and language in their normal, everyday environment.

Cratty, B. J. *Perceptual and motor development in infants and children*, 2nd ed. Englewood Cliffs, NJ: Prentice-Hall, 1979. The emphasis is on motor behavior, motor performance, and motor learning. This edition includes a chapter on theories of Piaget and Bruner.

Dale, P. S. *Language development: Structure and function*, 2nd ed. New York: Holt, Rinehart and Winston, 1976.

Ginsburg, H., & Opper, S. *Piaget's theory of intellectual development*, 2nd ed. Englewood Cliffs, NJ: Prentice-Hall, 1979. Provides a clear discussion of Piaget's description of cognitive development.

Social and Personality Development

5

Your children are not your children.
They are the sons and daughters of
life's longing for itself.
They come through you but not from
you,
And though they are with you yet
they belong not to you.

You may give them your love but not
your thoughts,
For they have their own thoughts.
You may house their bodies but not
their souls,
For their souls dwell in the house of
tomorrow, which you cannot visit, not
even in their dreams.
You may strive to be like them, but
seek not to make them like you,
For life goes not backward nor tarries
with yesterday.

You are the bows from which your
children as living arrows are sent
forth.

Let your bending in the archer's hand
be for gladness.

In Chapter 4 we described various threads of development—physical, motor, perceptual, and intellectual—as they occur during infancy, the time between birth and 3 years. Now we turn our attention to the development of social behavior. *Social behavior* is any behavior in which interacting with other people is a crucial part of both the purpose and the process of the behavior. Dancing at a club, eating pizza with friends, and running in a race are all examples of social behavior. People eat together not only to satisfy hunger more efficiently but also to interact with other people—to socialize. It is obvious that social behavior is an important part of our adult lives. Is it also an important part of an infant's life?

Infants are born with certain reflexes that attract what they need from **care givers.** Infants instinctively seek to be fed by crying out; and parents respond to this crying reflex. Infants also use their innate reflexes, such as crying or smiling, to attract caring attention for its own sake—beyond its usefulness to basic, bodily survival (Gewirtz, 1965; Schaffer, 1971; Wolff, 1969). Infants seek to be handled, talked to, looked at, and cuddled. This kind of interaction with parents is their social behavior, the beginning of their social development, and it is as vital to them as the other threads of development.

This process of socialization begins from the time of birth (Ainsworth, 1973; Bowlby, 1969; Brazelton, 1973; Lamb, 1978 a and b). Stern (1977) describes its importance during the infant's first six months. "We have learned that the purely social interactions, sometimes called 'free play,' between mother and infant are among the most crucial experiences in the infant's first phase of learning." Most infants learn to walk during their second year of life. They also begin to talk and develop reasoning. They gain a greater awareness that other people influence them and that they influence others. Social development, in other words, goes hand in hand with advances in physical and mental development. These changes enable infants to become more active as social persons.

What are the most important characteristics of social development during infancy? This chapter will explain that attachment and self-image are the most crucial aspects of infants' social development. It will also consider the roles of parents and others in supporting social development and the role of culture in shaping social development. Finally, the chapter will examine the effects of social deprivation and the effects of day-care on infants' development.

Attachment

Through free play, as well as regular physical care, the infant's interaction with the person who is giving care develops into a desire to be physically close to the care giver. At age 2 the infant expresses this desire by staying near the care giver. The degree of security the infant derives from this closeness is what we call *attachment.* The infant's experience of attachment varies according to the environment and the care giver. It may be characterized by reliable pleasure

The young infant has a strong desire to stay close to a parent, especially in strange places. This closeness provides a sense of security and it is from this base of close attachment and security that the infant will later venture forth to explore the environment. (Photo by Robert Eckert/EKM-Nepenthe)

and security or by an unreliability that causes anxiety. In either case attachment affects further social development and development in general. In order to understand what attachment is and its importance to development, we will describe the origins of attachment, the relation of attachment to general development, the consequences of separation, attachment to the father, and theories about the significance of attachment.

Origins of Attachment

Human beings have a biological heritage. By observing attachment in animals, scientists have come to a more complete understanding of attachment in humans. According to Harlow's research (1958), soothing physical contact is crucial to creating attachment in rhesus monkeys.

Contact and interaction. Harlow (1958) observed young rhesus monkeys separated from their mothers who were provided with two forms of a **surrogate parent** (a substitute mother, in this case). One surrogate was made from a wooden block, covered with rubber and overlaid with terry cloth to provide comfortable contact. The second surrogate was made from wire mesh to avoid giving "contact comfort." Each surrogate had a bottle of milk protruding from the figure's front. Both figures were essentially the same except for the "covering."

Figure 5.1 Rhesus monkey clinging to surrogate mother. (Photo by permission of the Primate Laboratory, University of Wisconsin, Madison.)

Four newborn monkeys were placed with each "mother," but all had the opportunity to visit the opposite surrogate. All the monkeys sought the cloth mother. Unexpectedly, when nourishment was provided only from the "wire mother," the infant monkeys still spent more time with the "cloth mother." Harlow (Harlow, 1958; Harlow & Zimmerman, 1959) also observed that the infant monkeys, when frightened, rushed to the cloth mother. Harlow concluded that soothing contact with the terry cloth mother was satisfying for its own sake (beyond bodily need for food) and resulted in a firm attachment (see Figure 5.1). In one experiment a "bear monster" was used to frighten the infant monkeys. Although the first reaction was to rush to the mother, the infants gradually, but warily, approached the toy bear. Infants with the "wire mother" pushed the fear-provoking figure away, but they did not cling to the "wire mother." Instead, they rocked back and forth, clutching themselves (see Figure 5.2).

Harlow and Zimmerman studied the strength or endurance of attachment in a similar experiment (1959). They separated infant monkeys from their surrogate mothers after six months. Infants raised with the "cloth mother" always returned to her when she was placed back in the cage, even after a long interval (thirty days). Infants of the "wire mother," in contrast, did not go to her when she was placed back in the cage, even when they were frightened.

As interesting as these studies are, they do not tell the whole story. Human infants differ from monkeys; therefore, we must be careful in our conclusions about attachment from these observations. It will help to look more closely at

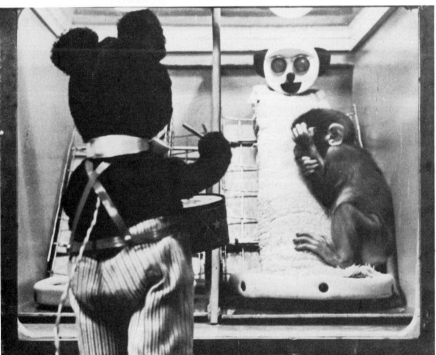

Figure 5.2 Rhesus monkey and "bear monster." (Photos by permission of the Primate Laboratory, University of Wisconsin, Madison.)

how human attachment develops. Does contact comfort also play an important part? Infants use their innate reflexes of crying, sucking, clinging, and smiling as social behavior to *elicit* care and attention and contact. In addition, infants use special smiles, varieties of *eye-brightening,* and gestures of throwing their heads back while holding their mouths open and tongues out. This last behavior seems to be more potent than a smile in attracting the mother (Stern, 1977). A mother's social behavior toward her baby consists of the way she makes "faces," uses "baby talk," moves her head and shoulders, her hands and fingers, positions her whole body, and chooses the timing and rhythm of her gestures (Stern, 1977, pp. 9–10). It is these interactions between infant and parents that lead to attachment.

To discover how important the earliest infant-parent contact and interaction might be, investigators observed the interactions of mothers and infants in the hospital right after birth. They found that for most parents and their newborns immediate contact does not appear to be crucial for an eventual, lasting attachment (Macfarlane, 1977). In the short run, however, there are noticeable benefits to contact as studies by Marshall Klaus and his colleagues show.

The usual practice in many hospitals is to take the newborn to a nursery after a brief contact with its mother following birth. The mother then sees her baby only at feeding times. Klaus used this situation for his research. In two studies (Klaus, Kennell, Plumb, & Zuehlke, 1970; Klaus & Kennell, 1976), one group of infants were left with their mothers in a quiet place for one hour following birth. Another similar group of infants were placed in the hospital nursery away from their mothers according to usual hospital practice. The researchers observed that the first group of mothers spent more time looking closely at their babies, touching them, and caressing them. In another study meant to examine the consequences of contact (Kennell et al., 1974), two groups of mothers and their babies were compared, one having extended contact after birth, the other normal hospital care. During the first year of their infants' lives mothers in the *extended-contact* group spent more time soothing their babies, looking at them, picking them up, cuddling them, and in general showing more enjoyment in caring for their babies. These babies scored higher on tests of physical and mental development after one year than did babies from the other group, and these advantages seemed to continue through the second year. Margaret Ribble (1943) also studied newborns in hospitals. At the time of the study hospitals separated infants from their mothers for long periods. Infants were kept most of the day in a hospital nursery on a flat surface with little stimulation of touch or movement. Ribble found that about a third of the 600 newborns she observed suffered from severe muscular tension. She believed that if this muscular tension persisted a condition called *marasmus* would occur. Marasmus causes protruding belly, poor muscle tone, and poor skin color. The Ribble study suggests what can occur in cases of excessively lengthy separation and lack of contact. Maccoby (1980, p. 50) maintains that immediate separation of mother and infant after birth followed by

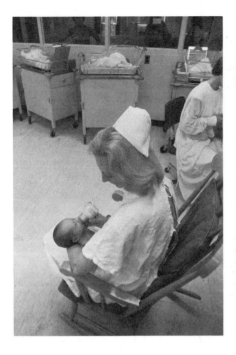

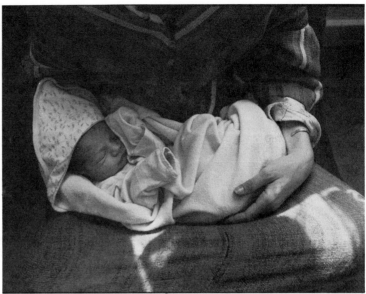

periods of contact and further separation may create handicaps for the child, but these handicaps are usually overcome in the long-term course of normal care giving.

Questions about the importance of contact between the mother and her newborn baby have not been fully answered. Apparently, however, infants seek out and benefit from social interaction expressed in physical contact, just as the monkeys who sought "contact comfort" in the Harlow experiment suggested they might.

Four stages of attachment. There is some controversy among researchers about the onset of infants' recognition of parents and other care givers. For example, Schaffer (1971) claims that during the first two months of life infants are not able to distinguish parents or other care givers from unfamiliar adults. They seek and respond to whoever holds them or is near. However, as we saw in Chapter 4, although newborns are only able to coordinate eye movements briefly, and can only focus on objects a few inches away, they do show a preference for looking at certain objects. It appears that by the age of 2 weeks an infant is able to recognize its mother's face (Carpenter, 1975). But it is not until the age of 2 months that an infant can *discriminate* parents' faces from strangers' faces and mother's from father's (Yogman, Dixon, Tronick, Als, & Brazelton, 1977). It is this change from indiscriminately responding to people in general to discriminating between care givers and strangers that appears to be crucial for the

In many hospitals, newborns are taken to a nursery soon after birth. The mother usually only sees her infant at feeding times, and sometimes the infant may be fed by a nurse. It is believed that early, frequent contact between parents and their newborn is important for the development of attachment. (Photos by Robert Eckert/EKM-Nepenthe)

development of attachment. Bowlby (1969) and Ainsworth (1967, 1973) have identified four stages in the development of attachment.

1. *During the first few months* the infant relates favorably to everyone, but especially to someone who is smiling.

2. *By the sixth month* the infant has formed a special relationship with the mother or primary care giver. The infant achieves interaction with cries, smiles, babbling, and special posturings of the body (Stern, 1977).

3. *Before the twelfth month* the infant has learned to catch mother's attention from some distance away. When mother enters the room the baby greets her with great enthusiasm. At the same time the infant *begins to fear* strangers.

4. *During the second year* attachment to mother comes to play an important role. It is from mother that the infant launches into explorations; and it is to the mother, as a safe "harbor," that the infant returns in times of fear or distress. Strangers now create a greater tension, causing the infant to cling to its mother.

A continuum of growth. Attachment evolves as the infant's social behavior becomes more purposeful, and the infant begins to show **social discrimination.** In the process of forming a secure attachment infants need to gain the attention of care givers. Two important attention-getting signals in *early* infancy are *crying* and *smiling,* the first being by far the stronger.

Crying and smiling. There seem to be three types of crying (Wolff, 1969): hunger, anger, and pain. Most mothers appear to be able to tell them apart and to respond accordingly. At first the infant is unaware of this (Schaffer 1971, p. 79).

In the early weeks, crying and smiling serve as signals only in the sense that other people will almost invariably be impelled to react to them. They are not yet signals in the sense that the infant uses them purposely in order to summon help and attention.

Another very important signal appears about the second month—the baby begins to *smile.* There are two views about why the baby smiles, or how the baby learns to smile. The first view is not likely to be attractive to parents. Some studies have shown that babies will smile at any object that has *contrasting* areas. For example, a baby will smile at a crude mask (see Figure 5.3) or at a card with six dots on it (Ahrens, 1954). Watson (1973) also discovered that playing such games as touching the baby's nose each time the baby opens its eyes wide, or poking or blowing on the baby's tummy when the baby waves its arms, results in vigorous smiling. Infants who were given mobiles they *could control,* compared to infants who were unable to control the mobiles, showed

Figure 5.3 Infant smiling at mask. (Photo by Bob Coyle)

clear smiling and cooing (Hunt & Uzgiris, 1964). These results indicate that infants will smile in response to *any high-contrast stimuli,* including human faces. However, Bower (Bower, 1979; Dunkeld & Bower, 1979) suggests we can only make sense out of a smile by looking more closely at *all those smiles* used by the baby in different situations: social smiles, smiles of amusement, smiles of satisfaction, flirtatious or coy smiles, and so on.

The second view suggests that smiling is a response to voices and faces (Wolff, 1963). It is true that smiling and babbling, which often go together, lead to extensive social interaction. No doubt parents like to believe that smiling is a sign of recognition and affection. Once infants begin to smile, the time parents spend with them increases remarkably (Newson & Newson, 1963). And there appear to be no differences between the ways mothers and fathers respond to their infants' smiling and crying (Frodi et al., 1978). By the fourth month most infants show a preference for familiar faces by smiling and cooing more when they see them or hear the persons' voices (Bower, 1974).

Between the third and seventh months crying and smiling assume the importance of real signals. Infants now begin to discriminate among adults and to prefer adults who are familiar to them. They no longer smile indiscriminately but learn to use this contact selectively as a signal. Crying becomes a signal of protest at being separated from attachment figures or as a sign of fear. Infants at 6 or 7 months are now able to discriminate among situations that guarantee

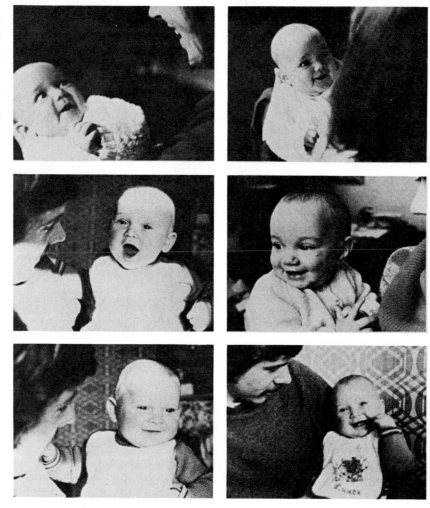

attachment and those that provoke separation and cause anxiety. It is true that at about the sixth or seventh month of infancy it becomes very noticeable that most infants cry when a stranger appears and especially when parents try to leave them with strangers. But infants' anxiety over strangers and separation has been observed in much younger infants.

Carpenter (1975), as mentioned earlier, showed that at two weeks—much earlier than the two months other scientists observed—infants could clearly distinguish between the mother's face and that of a female stranger. Using a viewing box such as the one in Figure 5.4, the researcher showed the infant six different faces: (1) the mother's silent face; (2) a female stranger's face; (3) the

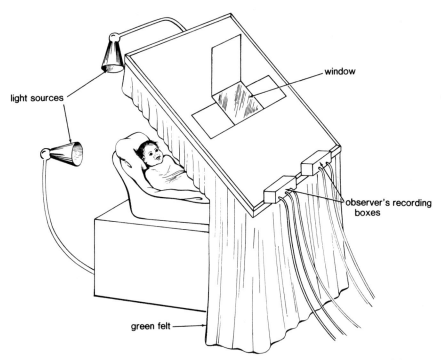

Figure 5.4 Carpenter's viewing box. Carpenter used the viewing box for studying infants' responses to faces and voices of mothers and strangers. Infants could look at faces as they appeared in the "window." (Source: "Mother's Face and the Newborn." Carpenter, G. C. In R. Lewin (Ed.) *Child Alive*. Copyright 1974 by IPC Magazines Ltd. Published by Maurice Temple Smith Ltd. Reprinted by permission of IPC Magazine Ltd.)

mother's face talking to the infant; (4) the female stranger's face talking to the infant; (5) the mother's face talking to the infant, but with the stranger's voice; and (6) the stranger's face talking to the infant with the mother's voice. The infants paid most attention to their mother's talking face, and next to the mother's silent face. The infants *tried as hard as possible* not to look at both the mother's face with the stranger's voice and the stranger's face with the mother's voice. Bower (1979) suggests that the infants' reaction to these two faces (numbers 5 and 6) appears to be fear. Therefore, although infants are usually more than 3 months of age before they begin to show fear of strangers, this social behavior begins to form at a much earlier age. Close observation of the growth of infants' social behavior suggests that the development of attachment is gradual and continuous—even if there are four recognizably different stages along the way.

Relation of Attachment to General Development

Research by Sroufe (1978) suggests that secure attachment by age 1 means the child will be more likely to spend time exploring the environment, including new places, and will develop a more mature personality by age 3. Sroufe observed that children 3 years old who had been rated "securely attached" at age 1 showed more curiosity, engaged in more exploration, were more autonomous and self-directed, were more sympathetic toward other children, and made friends more easily. He observed that children who had experienced anxious attachment at age 1 were withdrawn and hesitant at age 3. Lamb (1977a, 1978a) has described three ways in which attachment is important for social development. First, attachment creates *trust,* an important personality trait in terms of development. Once trust exists it can be generalized to other people. This in turn leads to greater social interaction and to the ability to be emotionally intimate and to love.

Second, infants who experience secure attachment explore their environment. Their heightened curiosity and autonomy make it likely they will benefit from other experiences. Infants who feel insecure because of an anxious attachment earlier may miss out on chances to extend their experience.

Finally, when infants experience secure attachment, they accept their parents as models, enabling parents to encourage and reinforce the infants' learning (Lamb, 1977a; Mussen, 1967).

Separation

Responses to *separation* change as the infant grows older and as attachment grows. Infants younger than 6 months respond positively to contact with most people. It is during the second half of the first year that anxiety over separation from the primary care giver begins to show. By age 1 most infants cry when their mothers leave and cling to them when they return. During the second year this distress changes to searching for the mother. At about age 2 they show little distress when mothers leave, although on their return infants run to greet them and hug and kiss them (Seraficca, 1978).

Ainsworth devised a particular research procedure called the *strange situation* in which to observe the effects of a mother's and a strange person's presence or absence (separation) on an infant's behavior. The procedure involved several mothers and infants, with one mother and her infant being observed at a time.

A mother and her infant are brought into a playroom equipped with toys. The observer watches the mother and infant through a one-way mirror (Ainsworth & Wittig, 1969) during seven different episodes, which always occur in the following sequence:

1. Mother puts the infant down to play and goes to sit in a chair.

2. After a short time has elapsed, a stranger (woman) enters the room and begins to talk to the mother.

3. The stranger then tries to engage the infant in play, and the mother quietly leaves the room.

4. While the mother is gone, the reactions of the stranger and infant are observed.

5. The mother returns and her reunion with her infant is observed.

6. With the stranger gone, the mother again leaves the room for a few minutes.

7. Finally, the mother returns once again.

As you can imagine, the infants played happily with their mothers present during the first episode, staying close to their mothers at first but soon leaving them to explore the room to play with toys and returning occasionally to renew contact. When the stranger entered the room, the infants usually went close to their mothers, staying close by, clinging, or hiding behind them to peer out at the stranger. Some children quickly *warmed up* to the stranger and even responded to invitations to come and play, although others continued to cling warily to their mothers. When mothers left the room, most infants cried or showed obvious signs of being disturbed. When mothers returned, infants stayed close by. When mothers left the room again, infants cried more than on the first occasion, and when mothers returned for the final time, their babies clung tightly to them, refusing to play. Ainsworth concluded that the presence of the mother, her availability, and constant contact are important for the development of a secure attachment between herself and her infant and that separation can be harmful to the infant.

Other researchers disagree with this view, believing that under certain conditions infants may actively benefit from separation.

Morgan and Ricciuti (1969) examined anxiety over strangers in infants aged 4½ to 12½ months. While some infants were sitting on their mothers' laps and some were sitting about 4 feet away from their mothers, a stranger holding Halloween masks showing a smiling face and a distorted face approached the infants. The younger infants smiled at both the stranger and masks. The older babies tended to cry. Only the older infants showed anxiety when sitting *away from* their mothers, not the younger ones (see also Bowlby, 1969). The study indicates a relationship between anxiety over strangers and anxiety over separation from the care giver. This confirms what we know about attachment, that it develops as infants' social behavior becomes discriminating and that attachment is more pronounced at age 1 than at 6 months.

Anxiety occurs in most infants when they are separated from a parent or care giver or even a familiar baby-sitter (Feldman & Ingham, 1975), and anxiety usually increases if separation is prolonged. Does this anxiety warn us of real danger to the infant?

Bowlby (1951) stated that infants permanently separated from their families are seriously damaged psychologically. He also claimed that prolonged separation leads to a predictable infant reaction of *distress followed by depression.* Lamb (1978a) argues that this is not the case. Infants placed in stable, alternate family settings make happy new attachments. Temporary separation from parents can, under certain conditions, be helpful to the infant in developing social assurance. Lamb (1978a) has described a number of "behavioral systems" within which the baby can learn beneficially about attachment *and* separation. These are summarized in Table 5.1. At age 2 and after, infants begin to experiment with separating themselves from mother. As secure attachment leads to autonomy and exploration, separation becomes a part of social development for the infants just as attachment was earlier. Margaret Mahler, a psychoanalyst, has worked

Table 5.1 Behavioral Systems that Influence Infants' Social Interactions

Behavioral System	Social Behaviors
Attachment	Staying near, asking to be held, crying. The presence of a caring adult to whom the infant is strongly attached provides a *sense of protection*
Fear-Wariness	Avoidance of objects, persons, and situations that might be harmful. Most infants older than 7 or 8 months are cautious of or distressed by strangers. Wariness declines as the infant grows older (over 2 years) and begins to interact with strangers.
Affiliative	Smiling, vocalizing, and showing toys to persons other than those to whom infants are strongly attached.
Exploratory	Presence of attachment figures lends security to infants' first "voyages" of exploration. Based on initial strong attachment to a care giver, as infants grow older they gain more confidence in "going it alone."

Source: Adapted from Lamb, M. E. "Social Interaction in Infancy and the Development of Personality." In M. E. Lamb, ed. *Social and Personality Development*, 1978. By permission of the author and Holt, Rinehart and Winston.

with severely emotionally disturbed children. She suggests that many of her patients' disturbances can be attributed to their failure to separate themselves from their mothers during infancy (Mahler, Pine, & Bergman, 1975). She described the development of a healthy mother–infant relationship as a sequence of stages (see Inset 5.1). Mahler believes that a balance must be established between the need for a strong attachment and the infant's need also to develop a degree of independence—a balance that is necessary for normal development and which, if disturbed, can result in psychotic illness.

Attachment to Father

It was mentioned in Chapter 3 that when fathers come in contact with their infants (Parke & O'Leary, 1976), they hold, cuddle, and vocalize in much the same way as mothers do. However, fathers play a special role as playmate with their infants. They spend more time playing with them than *taking care* of them (Lamb, 1977). This is reciprocated by their infants and seems to result in a very strong attachment. For example, it has been shown that infants aged 7 or 8

Inset 5.1
**Stages in the
Psychological Birth
of the Infant**

Margaret Mahler, after many years of research with infants, has described four phases stretching from birth to about age 3 years during which infants achieve a degree of autonomy and a sense of individuality that are very important for their continuing cognitive and social development.

The first phase lasts from birth to about 8 months of age. The most important feature of this phase is *symbiosis,* which can be thought of as a mutually beneficial partnership between infant and parent. Symbiosis creates a bonding, security, pleasure, and safe anchorage. This is achieved by the infant's seeing, touching, and hearing the parent, and being looked at, touched, and "spoken" to in return. At the same time, however, parents should encourage the infant to "look outward." When the infant reaches 6 months, part of this "looking outward" becomes a tentative separation from the parent and a looking at the parent *from a distance.* The parent should encourage the infant to explore, to be fascinated by a brooch or a pendant, and to play games such as "peekaboo." During the next two months, the infant makes further distinctions between the parent and what is not the parent. At about 8 months anxiety about strangers and strange situations appears. A basic trust of the parent helps the infant through this period to gain confidence in checking out strange persons and situations with the parent's being part of this exploration.

The second phase, from age 8 to 16 months, is a period of practicing separation by physically moving away from the parent by crawling, paddling, and climbing. However, the parent should still be there to hold onto and to return to as a safe anchorage if needed. At between 8 and 12 months the infant learns to stand upright and walk freely, and a period of more extensive exploration and practice in separating from parents begins. Parents are used for "emotional refueling" and as stable points of reference for looking outward. This is when a "real love of the world begins."

months and 12 or 13 months were more attached to their parents than to a stranger but showed no preference for either parent (Lamb, 1977). This suggests that though mothers and fathers may have unique child-rearing roles, when both are consistently involved in caring for their child, there may be little difference in the strength of attachment formed.

Theories about Attachment

Beliefs about the interactions and relationships infants need to achieve normal social development have been influenced by a number of theories on socialization: psychoanalytic theory, learning theory, learning by imitation, cognitive-development theory, and ethological theory. These theories, as all theories, try to make comprehensive sense out of the information available through various kinds of research. At different times and for different groups of people each of the five theories has held importance.

The third phase sees the construction of an important link between locomotion and sensorimotor intelligence, the "two powerful organizers of psychological birth" (Spitz, 1965). During this period, from 16 to 24 months, along with a greater facility in exploration, the infant experiences increasing separation anxiety and concern about the absence of parents. For normal psychological development to continue, the infant needs the parents to share new skills and experiences. Approaching 2 years of age, the infant begins to realize there are obstacles to exploration, and he or she experiences frustration and aggression. There are things to be touched and not to touch, places to go and places forbidden. In learning social rules and regulations some incompatibility and misunderstanding can occur between parents and infant. Yet the parents should encourage the infant to be independent and outgoing, while at the same time they should remain as a definite source of emotional renewal when needed.

The fourth phase of development, from 2 to 3 years, is a period during which the infant consolidates an awareness of individuality and the beginnings of an emotional understanding of object constancy, the affective side of the cognitive awareness that "out of sight does not mean being out of existence." Along with a basic trust and confidence in parents comes a recognition that parents are permanent features of life, even when they are absent. The infant appears to recognize that parents can remain a source of emotional renewal while the infant plays happily without their being present, knowing that there will be a reuniting. Through fantasy and role play the infant's observations about the world become more real, and along with this new realization comes an ability to delay gratification and to endure separation. This paves the way for the formation of a self-identity.

Source: Mahler, M. S., Pine, F., and Bergman, A. *The Psychological Birth of the Human Infant.* Copyright © 1975 by Basic Books. Used with permission.

Psychoanalytic theory.   Sigmund Freud (1935) believed that experiences during infancy and childhood critically affect later development. Freud suggested that as infants develop, strong inner needs come into conflict with outside demands. The infant may demand the parents' attention, but the parents may impose routines and other measures of control on the infant's behavior. A major task of early childhood is the resolution of conflicts between strong, inner impulses and outside demands and controls. From Freud's point of view the conflict is resolved by the infant's *identifying* with and imitating parents and incorporating the parents' standards of behavior. It is this identification (and imitation) that is expressed in what we have been calling attachment. A more detailed description of Freud's theories is provided later in this chapter where we consider infants' development of a self-image.

Learning theory.   Skinner's learning theory, described in Chapter 4, has influenced thinking and research on social development since the early 1950s. Learning theorists are interested in explaining children's behavior by examining how the behavior changes under changed conditions. For example, an infant's social responsiveness, as indicated by smiling, depends on whether parents or other care givers pay attention to the smiling infant by smiling in return, talking to the child, or picking up the child (Gewirtz, 1965). Gewirtz suggests that these types of interactions form the basis of a strong attachment bond between the infant and care giver.

Learning theory stresses two important principles about attachment. First, attachment develops over time as a result of various satisfying interactions between the infant and care givers (Gewirtz, 1969; Whiting & Whiting, 1975). Second, learning attachment is not a one-way process but a reciprocal interaction between the infant and parents. Parents undoubtedly influence the infant, and the infant influences the parents' behavior in a constantly changing relationship (Maccoby, 1980, p. 30).

Imitation.   Bandura (1969, 1971) views attachment from a behaviorist's point of view. He has refined ideas taken from learning theory by concentrating on *imitation* as a process of socialization. Bandura concluded from an extensive program of research that children are more likely to imitate adults who are nurturing. The strength of imitation depends on the amount of control the nurturing adult has over the infant's or child's behavior. Bandura was also able to point out that in order to reinforce behavior parents must reinforce while the child is actually performing the actions. Bandura says parents are models who provide examples of patterns of behavior their children can adopt, and when children do adopt the behavior parents desire, the parents can then reinforce the behavior. Parents therefore do not merely set standards and requirements that they enforce with rewards and punishments, but they also play an important role in socialization by setting examples. When there is a secure attachment between infant and parents, it is likely that the infant will be attentive to and imitate the parents' behavior.

Cognitive-development theory.   In Chapter 4 we introduced Piaget's theory about intellectual development during infancy. Piaget has said very little about emotional and social development, but psychologists interested in his theory have related it to social development (Kohlberg, 1969; Emmerich, 1968). Since these psychologists accepted Piaget's premise that a child's thinking *and behavior* undergo systematic change in a series of stages, they expected characteristics of social behavior established in early infancy to change by age 2. Maccoby, commenting on Kohlberg's findings, says that attachment has a normal developmental sequence.

While it usually appears during the last half of the first year (of infancy), increases to a peak during the second year, and then wanes gradually as children become more competent and independent, children differ in the rate with which they proceed through this sequence (1980, p. 23).

Ethological theory.   *Ethology* is the science of animal behavior. Ethologists are naturalists who study animals in their natural environment rather than in a laboratory. Lorenz (1957) and Tinbergen (1951) are ethologists who have studied how infant animals quickly learn a particular behavior that creates a strong bond between them and their parents. For example, young goslings follow their mother from their first attempts to walk. These two ethologists sought to discover what influences this important early **bonding,** or to use the ethological term, **imprinting.**

Lorenz (1952) divided a clutch of goose eggs into two groups. The first group was hatched by the mother, the second group was hatched in an incubator. The goslings hatched by their mother followed her. Those hatched in the incubator saw only Lorenz, no other animal or person, and they followed him. Then he placed all the goslings together with the mother goose and himself. The goslings hatched by the mother moved to her and those hatched by the incubator and familiar with Lorenz moved to him. The goslings ran to the one they first had contact with after hatching (see Figure 5.5).

In this way Lorenz discovered what caused the goslings to become imprinted on (or bonded to) a mother figure: the first postnatal contact. Lorenz and Hess (1958) discovered that this early imprinting, at least in the case of geese, *must occur* within the first 3 days. In other animals, such as rhesus monkeys, bonding

Figure 5.5 Early imprinting on, or bonding to, a mother or mother figure by certain types of animals happens within the first few days of life. The goslings who made contact with Lorenz immediately after hatching followed him around as if he were "their mother." (Copyright © Nina Leen, Time/Life)

occurs over the first 6 months (Harlow, 1971). These fixed times at which bonding occurs and becomes long-lasting have been called the **critical period of development.** Other specialists (for example, Scott, Stewart, & DeGhelt, 1974) prefer the term **sensitive period of development,** especially when referring to attachment in human infants. For normal attachment to occur in human infants, it appears important for infants to maintain intimate contact with caregivers from about 4 months of age. As we have already pointed out, research on attachment between infant monkeys and their mothers has some relevance for understanding the sensitive period and attachment in human infants. As you will see when we discuss deprivation, this is especially true for understanding infants who are abandoned, orphaned, or spend long periods of time in the hospital.

Social Origins of Self-Image

In the preceding discussion of the infant's social development through attachment, at least a strong hint was given that there is an important relationship between social interactions and personality development.

Although individual differences in physiology and heredity can be expected to have some influence on the development of personality, to a great extent infants learn to see themselves as their parents see them. How parents react to infants' behavior suggests to infants how they should feel about themselves. Regular and severe scolding whenever the infant follows an impulse can teach the infant to feel shame for being himself or herself. What opportunities for exploration and learning are available in the environment also shape infants' experiences and, consequently, how they see themselves. The experiences of an only child or a firstborn are quite different from those of a second child. The second child may see himself, for example, as less important because he is physically less able than an older sibling. Primary social interactions with parents and environment strongly influence the infant's *personality*—all the characteristics that make someone a unique individual.

Self-image is a chief characteristic of personality. During infancy issues of personality arise that can profoundly affect the infant's self-image. It is generally agreed among psychologists that how parents and infants interact at these "crossroads" is crucial to the infant's developing self-image. But the components of

When parents provide regular, reliable, and loving care, infants and young children develop a confidence in their own abilities and a good feeling about themselves. (Photos, left by Robert Eckert/ EKM-Nepenthe; right by Jean-Claude Lejeune)

self-image that can influence social interaction differ according to different psychologists. According to Freud, the two main components concern *self-centeredness* and *control*. According to Erikson, they concern *trust* and *autonomy*. Two other important social components of self-image are *sex identity* and *aggressiveness,* both of which are influenced by interaction with parents. In the following section we will examine all of these social origins of self-image.

Freud's Psychosexual Theory

At the beginning of the twentieth century Freud proposed a theory of personality and personality development—his ***psychosexual development theory.*** According to Freud's theory, there are three parts to any personality: the **id,** the **ego,** and the **superego.** Each part has a unique role, and the three parts interact as the personality functions and develops.

The id is composed of biological drives and instinctual urges such as hunger, sex, and aggression. Freud considered the id unconscious because these drives express themselves as impulses, as blind urges to seek pleasure and immediate satisfaction, rather than as actions thought out beforehand. Infants display the id part of personality very clearly. They wet their diapers whenever they feel the urge, and they expect to be fed whenever they are hungry—unaware, as yet, of the realities of someone's getting and preparing food.

The ego is the "I," a conscious observer and director. The ego helps regulate the id. If people acted solely on impulse, they would not survive for long because everyone would be entirely dependent, just as infants are. The ego, therefore, considers reality, not just pleasure. It considers where, when, and how to satisfy hunger as well as the actual hunger. Parents carry the ego part of personality for the infant, helping to regulate hunger, elimination of wastes, and control of temper tantrums, until the child's ego develops.

The superego helps the ego see behavior according to an ideal. It helps the ego see beyond pleasure seeking and reality and helps to set standards of behavior according to right and wrong. The superego develops from learning the standards of behavior of parents and society. By absorbing experiences of punishment and reward, the superego constructs a set of values by which the ego can judge and direct behavior.

The development of the personality, according to Freud, depends upon a sexual energy called *libido* (Freud, 1905, pp. 584–594). During infancy "sexual feelings" are very general and include such activities as *sucking* (the pleasure of sucking on mother's breast), the passing of the body's wastes (*excretion*), and even motor activities such as *rocking*. Freud believed that personality development occurs in stages when particular issues must be confronted. Those of infancy are the **oral stage** and **anal stage of psychosexual development.** Freud was convinced that the results of those confrontations during these two stages of infancy have long-term effects on the development of personality (1965).

The oral stage. In the early months of life the infant is principally self-centered. For example, during the first months the infant's interest is particularly associated with sucking, an important behavior for obtaining the gratification of food. For this reason the period of development from birth to about 1 year has been called the oral stage. During the first six months the infant cries when hungry or when feeling some other discomfort. The infant is intent on gaining relief from tension and reestablishing a pleasurable feeling. Freud called this self-orientation infant *narcissism* (love of self).

At about 6 months the infant begins to develop a sense of others. There is a growing awareness that others take care of needs. Therefore, it is not surprising to find the infant concerned with others—who they are and where they are. The infant displays anxiety when mother (or another important care giver) leaves or when a stranger is present (Freud, 1936). The oral stage occurs between birth and 1 year.

Freud believed that if the infant does not pass normally through a stage of self-centeredness toward a recognition of others the result will be a *fixation* on, a lasting concern with, the issues of infant pleasure seeking. This fixation will be displayed in adult life by excessive nail biting, smoking and drinking, a preoccupation with kissing (Freud, 1905), or an aggressive demand for a "love object" whenever it is desired (Baldwin, 1968). These activities are all aimed at obtaining pleasure in a "babyish" fashion because they are self-centered and oral.

Bruno Bettelheim in his book *Uses of Enchantment* (1976) suggests that reading folktales to children can foster normal personality development because stories such as those by Hans Christian Andersen provide insights into the development of personality (see Inset 5.2).

The anal stage. At about the age of 1 year the infant begins to focus on the anal zone, and this focus continues into early childhood to 3 years of age. During this anal stage infants find that bowel movements are pleasurable, but they also become aware of the possibility of controlling excretion. They learn to hold onto and to get rid of body wastes. However, they do not necessarily exercise control in a way that is completely socially desirable. How infants experience toilet training depends a great deal on what social standards the parents have set for eliminating body wastes. Some parents insist on rigid rules for using a potty or toilet, while others are more accepting of occasional "accidents" after an infant begins toilet training. These experiences in turn affect the infant's self-image.

An infant cannot easily and naturally control bowel movements until a certain physical developmental level has been reached, sometime between 18 months (Sears, Maccoby, & Levin, 1957) and 22 months (Heinstein, 1966). Strict and premature toilet training tends to produce anxiety in the infant (Munroe, 1955; Sears, Maccoby, & Levin, 1957). This anxiety can lead to a fixation at the anal stage called *anal compulsiveness*. This shows itself in later life as an obsession with cleanliness and neatness. Anal compulsiveness may also express itself in harboring resentment, being overly frugal or stingy, and being anxious about the quality of one's work.

Bruno Bettelheim (1976) explains that as an educator and therapist of severely disturbed children his main task was to restore meaning to their lives. He claims that one of the richest experiences in a child's life, which endows life with meaning, is the fairy story. He points out that long ago the German poet Schiller wrote, "Deeper meaning resides in the fairy tales told to me in my childhood than in the truth that is taught by life" (*The Piccolomini,* III, 4).

The original fairy tales of Hans Christian Andersen and the Brothers Grimm not only entertain the child but also provide insights about oneself and help foster personality development. They also suggest experiences that are needed to help the child's developing personality.

One fairy story Bettelheim believes is most suitable for the young child, since it stresses the need to take those first steps to transcend primitive *oral* yearnings, is "Hänsel and Gretel."

The parents are poor, having fallen on hard times. They are no longer able to provide enough food for their two children. So Mother can no longer fulfill all their *oral* demands. This causes the children anxiety and they believe Mother has become unloving, selfish, and rejecting. Hänsel and Gretel are abandoned in the forest. They find their way home since they know they still desperately need their parents. The suggestion here is that before a child develops initiative there are attempts to return to the secure source of oral gratification.

The return home solves nothing. The mother makes further plans to abandon the children.

The second time they are left in the forest they get lost. In their wanderings they come upon a gingerbread house, which they begin to devour. They give way completely to their oral regression and ignore the soft voice which asks "Who is nibbling at my house?" The gingerbread house stands in their unconscious (id) for the good mother as a source of nourishment.

Erikson's Psychosocial Theory

Erik Erikson was influenced by Freud's theory, but his *psychosocial development theory* describes in more detail important social interactions between the child and adults. Erikson points out that there is a general development of ego at each stage. There is *incorporation* (an eager taking in) at the oral stage. It is not confined to sucking but extends to other senses—for example, the eyes and hands (grasping). At each of eight stages (Erikson, 1950), the resolving of crises influences social and personality development. These stages parallel, and go beyond, the stages described by Freud (see Table 5.2).

Trust versus mistrust. Erikson (1963) has emphasized the importance of the development of a sense of trust during the first year of infancy. For example, when parents give regular, reliable attention to feeding, diapering, and playing, the baby develops a sense of basic trust that needs and desires will be met. Unreliable care produces a sense of mistrust. Erikson also believes that babies

The story warns that unrestrained oral gratification endangers one's very existence. Danger arrives in the figure of the witch. The witch, personifying the destructive aspects of oral fixation, wants to eat up the children.

The children finally realize the witch's evil designs on their life (symbolizing their personality). To survive, they must develop initiative. They must refuse the urges of the *id* and attend to the promptings of the *ego*.

Guided by a bird, the children flee from the gingerbread house (begin to reject their oral fixation). Their way home is blocked by a ''big water.'' They had not encountered any expanse of water before coming across the gingerbread house. The water represents a *transition;* a new beginning on a higher level of existence.

A duck offers to help them across. This they must do *one at a time.* This symbolizes the need to sometimes step out on one's own. We cannot always be sharing responsibility.

The children's experiences at the gingerbread house help them break away from a preoccupation with oral gratification. Having crossed the water they arrive on the further shore as more mature children. Now they are ready to use their intelligence and initiative to solve further problems they will meet in life.

Bettelheim says that the young child who ponders the story of ''Hänsel and Gretel'' can find meaning in the symbolic representations of gratification, anxiety, frustration, overcoming fear, and developing initiative. The story addresses some of the very real fears children experience (for example, the threat of rejection). But it also makes quite clear that problems can be solved at least partly by one's own effort.

Children also need loving and caring parents as a safe base from which to venture forth. Hänsel and Gretel eventually return home where they are accepted by their parents. This is psychologically correct because the young child must work out such difficulties as the oral problem while he or she is still dependent on parents.

Source: Adapted from Bruno Bettelheim, *The Uses of Enchantment.* Copyright 1976 by Alfred A. Knopf. Reprinted by permission.

learn to trust themselves. For example, when they learn to suck without biting, to grasp without pinching and hurting, they begin to have a sense that they are "trustworthy enough so that their providers will not need to be on guard lest they be nipped" (1950, p. 248). Learning trust of parents and of self during infancy enables the child later to develop self-confidence and also intimacy with others.

Developing trust is not enough. Erikson has made it clear that the "Infant must experience a goodly measure of mistrust in order to trust discerningly" (1976, p. 23). The infant needs to develop a sense of when to trust and when to mistrust. But in the long run, for normal development to occur, the infant's experience should predominantly be trust.

Infants experience separation anxiety when the care giver leaves. When infants learn that parents are dependable, they tolerate absences better. If parents are not dependable, infants usually cling harder to the care giver in strange situations or in the presence of strangers and show panic and distress when parents leave.

Table 5.2 A Comparison of Freud's and Erikson's Stages of Development*

	Freud's Psychosexual Stages	Erikson's Psychosocial Stages
Infancy	Oral sensory	Basic Trust vs Mistrust
	Muscular-anal	Autonomy vs Shame and Doubt
Preschool years	Locomotor-genital	Initiative vs Guilt
Middle-school years	Latency	Industry vs Inferiority
Adolescence	Puberty and adolescence	Identity vs Role Confusion
Young adulthood	Young adulthood	Intimacy vs Isolation
Adulthood	Adulthood	Generativity vs Stagnation
Later adulthood and old age	Maturity	Ego Integrity vs Despair

*Both Freud and Erikson describe the stages of personality and social development as systematically related to one another, emerging in a "proper" sequence.

As we will see later, children must learn to "let go," to tolerate the absence of loved and trusted ones, and to get along with peers and adults. Although the emphasis in infancy is on learning to trust, later the children must realize that many people can be considered trustworthy. It is unlikely that an overly dependent infant will easily develop a more mature extended sense of trust in later life.

Autonomy versus shame and doubt. Freud called this the anal stage—a period when infants learn to *hold onto,* or to *get rid of* body wastes as they wish. Erikson uses the terms *holding on* (retention) and *letting go* (elimination). But he uses the terms in a more general sense than Freud would. For example, babies also hold on fiercely to objects. They sometimes just as fiercely throw them away or let them go. They pile things up and knock them down. They cling to adults and push them away (Erikson, 1959). At times infants stay close to parents; but, in learning to walk, they go off more and more to explore the world. All of these actions display the infant's new sense of autonomy, a sense of general control, not just control of excretion as Freud suggested. It is this stage, which lasts from 1 to 3 years according to Erikson, that gives infants a chance to learn autonomy.

Toilet training can become a battle between infant and parent. Erikson sees this as a time when the child wants to exert its own will yet is learning to recognize that parents have rules about behavior. The 2-year-old child might try saying "no" for an answer; but it is not easy. *Doubt* creeps in as the infant realizes he cannot control all events, or the infant feels a growing sense of *shame* in making "messes." Doubt and shame can reverse the progress of autonomy.

Parents need to firmly, but gently, help the growing child. An insensitive parent may make the infant feel *shame.* This can happen if the parent repeatedly blames the infant after an accident occurs. The following dialogue between a mother and her 19-month-old daughter is an example.

Mother calls Vicky over. Mother: "Did you go pee-pee?" Vicky pulls her pants down. Mother: "Did you go pee-pee?" Vicky shakes her head. Mother: "Get up on the couch so I can change you." Mother changes Vicky's diaper on the couch. Mother: "You want me to slap you? Peeing in your pants. . . ." Mother powders Vicky and continues scolding, "Bad baby!" as she gets up to put the dirty diaper away (Carew, Chan, & Halfar, 1976, p. 131).

This dialogue was typical of Vicky's toilet training. These researchers noticed that when Vicky was almost 3 years old she was struggling to reject the idea of herself as a "bad" person.

If a mother accepts a wet diaper as a normal accident for a 19-month-old infant and changes the child affectionately, asking after powdering the infant and putting on a dry diaper, "Does that feel good now?" there is no implication of the child's being bad, and so the child does not feel that he or she has been bad.

Sex Identity

Parents are almost as much concerned about the sex of their newborn as about its well-being. The first question asked after birth is usually "Is the baby O.K.?" (That is, is it physically well?) The second question is "What is it?" (That is, is it a boy or a girl?) Traditionally, hospitals and homes advertise the sex of the newborn—pink for a girl, blue for a boy. *Sex identity,* seeing oneself as a female or a male, usually means seeing oneself as society defines the male or female role. In the past society offered narrow definitions of male and female, but contemporary society offers broader definitions that allow for an overlap of roles. Consequently, sex identity has come to have more importance for today's parents than ever before. Many parents decide more consciously about the sex roles they want their children to learn and wonder about the best way to socialize the newborn with respect to sex identity. There are varying opinions about the options open to parents. What do we know about how sex-role adoption occurs?

Sex identity is usually well established by age 3 years. How does the infant come to accept a particular sex identity? Research indicates that the infant accepts the sex assigned to it. In most cases this is the same as the infant's anatomical sex. In some cases the sex of a newborn can be ambiguous in appearance—that is, the sex organs are not clearly male or female. The infant's actual sex can be determined by chromosomal analysis. At a time when this technique was not available Money and his colleagues (Money, Hampson, & Hampson, 1957) studied 100 infants whose sex was ambiguous at birth and for whom parents arbitrarily assigned a sex identity. They concluded from their observations of these children that a child will accept whatever sex it is told it is, and that a child's sex identity can be changed before about age 2½ years without its causing the child any psychological stress. After age 3 a child's sex identity is fully established, and any attempt to change it can be psychologically damaging. The important point is that in accord with obvious physical sex characteristics in normal infants, parents "call" the infant boy or girl.

Parents behave in different ways toward their newborn baby, depending on whether it is a boy or girl. This is called **sex typing**—encouraging the child to identify with a socially defined sex role. In what ways do parents and others sex-type infants? Several studies provide answers for us.

Luria and Rubin (to be published) observed that hospital staffs perceived newborn infants according to traditional **sex stereotypes.** They saw boy infants as having strong, large features and girl infants as having delicate, fine features—even though in most cases differences in features of size and strength or delicacy did not exist. Another example of a stereotypic perception of infants has been provided by Condry and Condry (1976). College students were shown a videotape of a 9-month-old infant's reactions to various objects, including a jack-in-the-box. Those who were led to believe the infant was a boy saw the infant's strong reaction to the jack's jumping out of the box as a sign of anger. Students who believed the infant was a girl believed the strong reaction was fear.

Researchers have observed that 14- to 22-month-old infant boys playing in their own homes were likely to play with cars and trucks and the same aged girls with dolls and soft toys (Fagot, 1974). However, others have noticed that parents tend to reinforce sex stereotypes for their infants in part by providing sex-typed toys (Money & Ehrhardt, 1972; Rheingold & Cook, 1975).

Sex typing seems to occur more during the second year. Both Lamb (1977a, 1977b) and Kotelchuck (1976) found that fathers pay almost twice as much attention to sons as to daughters at this time. Mothers, on the other hand, make no distinctions. It is not surprising, then, that boys begin to show a preference for their fathers (Lamb, 1977b).

By identifying with and imitating their fathers, boys adopt a male sex role. This relationship seems to be critical for boys. If fathers are absent about the time the infant is 2, boy infants have difficulty in adopting a male sex role (e.g., Blanchard & Biller, 1971; Santrock, 1970).

Fathers who are warm and rewarding and openly express interest in the development of aggressive attitudes in their sons most strongly influence stereotyped sex-role development in boys (Biller & Borstelmann, 1967). However, most fathers also show pleasure at the "feminine characteristics" of their daughters—their "feminine looks," being "dressed neatly," wearing dresses and pretty hair ribbons—and they encourage their daughters in stereotyped activities (Mussen & Rutherford, 1963).

In summary we can say that infants' perception of their sexual identity and much of their behavior is stereotyped. Maccoby (1980) has observed that infants believe sex-inappropriate behavior (such as boys' playing with dolls) is *wrong*. Aside from the possibility of a certain biological predisposition to behave in a certain way, such as boys' greater interest in rough-and-tumble play, infants' sex identity and sex-role behavior are strongly influenced by parents. Boys are more strongly influenced by their fathers to behave in sex-appropriate ways than girls are. Also, because of limitations in their reasoning and understanding, infants more readily conform to parental pressure.

Aggressiveness

We mentioned in Chapter 3 that infants have different temperaments and it should be added that some differences in temperament are apparently linked to genetic differences while others are linked to sex characteristics. One characteristic of temperament is aggressiveness. *Aggression* is behavior intended to threaten, frighten, or hurt another person (Maccoby, 1980, p. 116). Aggressiveness is the tendency toward this behavior.

During the early months infants are not able to direct their behavior or show intention, nor are they able intellectually to consider the intent of their actions. Infants at this age, therefore, are incapable of aggression. They show outbursts of anger but not true aggression. During the first two years infants learn to coordinate their actions, to see that one event can cause another, and to experience another person as a source of frustration.

During the second year aggression is usually shown in the form of *tantrums*, loud, disruptive fits used to block control. Other kinds of aggressive behavior are throwing, smashing, pushing, and so on. If the infant associates such acts with

"getting its own way," or "stopping parents from interfering," it is likely that such behavior will be *reinforced* and happen more often.

Bronson (1975) observed infants aged 1–2 years playing in groups of three or four in a room supplied with toys. Most "aggression" consisted of brief disagreements about ownership of toys. These encounters—such as one child's trying to take a toy from another child—did not change during the year, but children's emotional reactions became more intense. For example, as children grew older they showed more frustration and anger at attempts to take a toy away from them. But, as Bronson points out, the infant's aggression is more often directed toward an object such as a toy than it is toward another child during struggles over ownership. During struggles over possession of a toy, children often declared, "Mine! Mine!" and Bronson suggests that such experiences help older infants gain self-image through an understanding of ownership and the related ideas of "I," "me," and "mine."

In a study conducted some time ago (Sears, Maccoby, & Levin, 1957), it was discovered that aggression in infants seemed to depend to some extent on how parents behaved toward their infants. Parent–infant related behaviors were as follows:

Parent's Behavior	Infant's Behavior
1. Highly permissive	Highly aggressive
2. Uses physical punishment	Aggressive
3. Shows high anxiety about child rearing	Likely to be aggressive
4. Shows low self-esteem	Likely to be aggressive
5. Mother shows low esteem for father	Likely to be aggressive
6. Shows dissatisfaction with home situation	Likely to be aggressive
7. Mother's role lowly valued	Likely to be aggressive
8. Parents disagree about child rearing	Likely to be aggressive
9. Restrictive but does not use physical punishment	Nonaggressive or controlled aggression

The highest rates of aggressive behavior occurred in children whose parents were relatively *permissive* but who also were most likely to punish unacceptable behavior physically.

From the outset parents play an important role in the development of aggressiveness in their children. It is important, especially during the second year of infancy, for parents to help their children focus expressions of anger and limit the extent and frequency of their outbursts of anger. At the same time parents must resist being pressurized by their infants' anger and not respond punitively to occasions of anger or to tantrums (Maccoby, 1980).

It was mentioned earlier that boys tend to be involved more than girls in rough-and-tumble play, which can sometimes lead to aggression. Boys also tend to receive more pressure to be aggressive and to avoid "sissy" behavior than do girls, especially from their fathers. This pressure is strongly related to parents' identification of their infant's sex identity and their expectations about related sex-role behavior. The most strongly identified sex difference between boys and girls, which cuts across most cultures, is that boys tend to be more aggressive than girls (Whiting & Whiting, 1975).

Although aggression in infancy is partly instinctive, its development is influenced primarily by parents and by the environment infants grow up in. At least in the first two years of infancy, aggression as threatening acts or attempts to physically harm does not occur. The infant who grabs another infant's toy is interested in getting the toy, not in hurting the other child. But by about age 2½ to 3 years, infants begin to use threatening gestures and attempt to hurt or dominate other children. Aggressive behavior at this age occurs mainly during struggles for possession of toys and control of space to play in (Maccoby, 1980). The infant's sense of self and understanding of a self-image is based on such information as how he or she looks and acts. In this sense aggressive behavior is likely to be one expression of the infant's self-image.

Role of Parents and Care Givers

Thus far in this chapter we have been considering the special features of attachment and the infant's growing awareness of himself or herself. Of course, parents have been very much a part of the picture. But the spotlight has still been on the infant. Let us now take a closer look at parents and their nurturing and child-rearing behavior, called *parenting;* and also at those nurturing figures who are not parents, variously called "care givers," "caretakers," and "significant others."

Infant specialists have usually portrayed the mother as the primary person who gives care to the infant. However, it appears that the infant can get along very well with more than one primary care giver, that the father plays an important role, and that two or three other care givers can be involved. The important point seems to be that the infant's early experiences be consistent and of a certain quality.

Early in this century hardly any distinction was made between "parenting" and "mothering." John Watson, in his book, *Psychological Care of Infant and Child* (1928), stated that mothering is the essence of parenting. Recently, the father's role as a parent has become more prominent (e.g., Lamb, 1977, 1978a, 1978b) in research and in parents' concern. Let us take a look first at general aspects of parenting roles that belong equally to mother and father and care giver. A general "model" of parenting behavior suggested by Becker (1964; Becker & King, 1964) has three dimensions: warm to hostile, permissive to restrictive, and calm to anxious. The warm-to-hostile dimension concerns the parent's attitude toward the child, which can range from positive to negative. The permissive-to-restrictive dimension concerns the parent's attitude toward control—that is, to what extent the parent insists on completely controlling the child's behavior (authoritarian, in Baumrind's terms) or giving the child complete freedom (permissive). The parent's attitude toward child rearing, which may be one expression of his or her attitude to life in general, can be described as ranging from calm and confident to anxious and concerned. These three dimensions are interactive and point to a wide range of possible parenting practices. Also, it is important to keep in mind that variations in child-rearing practices are likely to occur depending on a variety of changing situations and conditions. However, individual parents do tend toward one "type" of child rearing that becomes an "atmosphere" which affects the infant's behavior and attitude toward life.

Influences on Child Rearing

Two hundred years ago parents had little understanding of development during early childhood, and information from doctors, religious persons, and family members was misleading and sometimes harmful to the child's well-being. The older infant and young child were often beaten to ensure they would grow up to be obedient good Christians (Stone, 1977). However, interest in the importance of development during the early years was growing.

Locke in the seventeenth century and Rousseau in the eighteenth were both influential in changing people's beliefs about and attitudes toward child rearing. Locke was in favor of carefully structuring and guiding a child's early experiences whereas Rousseau believed that from infancy children should be provided a great deal of freedom to develop "naturally."

Today's parents have access to many kinds of professional help on child rearing from psychologists, psychiatrists, doctors, religious persons, and child specialists' "baby books" (such as Spock, 1946). Although most parents (but especially those from the middle and upper classes) seek advice on how to rear their children from doctors in particular, they also seek information from a wide variety of books and magazines (see Inset 5.3). Of course, most parents would probably readily admit that their child-rearing practices can be traced back, at least in part, to those used by their own parents and to the advice of their parents and close family friends. Such advice and help was more readily available within an "extended family" than is now the case for the modern "nuclear family," which has often moved far away from close relatives.

Other influences on parenting include such factors as the child's age and temperament, the amount of experience they have had as parents, and social and economic influences.

Parents' behavior reflects, for example, whether their infant is easy or difficult to handle. A quiet, obedient child is often seen as easier to deal with than a noisy, assertive, and willful child. Similarly, the parents' temperament also influences their own behavior. A mild-tempered, patient parent, compared to a short-tempered impatient parent, is less likely to find a fretful baby a problem to deal with. During infancy parenting not only is focused on "care taking," such as routine tasks of feeding, diapering, bathing, but also on other activities such as playing and encouraging the development of motor activities.

Parents do seem to benefit from the experience of caring for an infant. Not only do child-rearing behaviors change as the infant grows older (which may partly reflect changing parent attitudes influenced by the infant's age), but parents tend to get better at rearing subsequent infants (Lasko, 1954; Rothbart, 1971) because of their improved understanding of what can be expected of an infant.

Maccoby has said that "among the most powerful and least understood influences on child rearing are the parents' education, income, and occupation" (1980, p. 600). It is often the case that parents of low socioeconomic status (SES) lack a good understanding of how their infants can be expected to grow and develop and often find life distressful because of insufficient money to provide for their families and the usually unstable nature of semiskilled occupations. One should, however, be very careful in labeling families of different SES backgrounds. For example, it is possible to find stable and unstable families in both low and high SES groups. But, *on the average,* low SES parents tend to be more directive of their infants' behavior, to be less warm and affectionate, to talk less to their infants, and to be less successful in dealing with day-to-day child-rearing problems (Hess & Shipman, 1967). More about the effect of SES is noted in following chapters. We can conclude here by emphasizing that education, income, and occupation directly affect parents' child rearing and in turn their infants' development. Infants learn to observe and use the same modes of adapting to the environment that their parents choose to adopt (Maccoby, 1980, p. 402).

Although parent training programs and parenthood classes have boomed during the past ten years, the most widespread means of disseminating advice about child rearing is the popular literature. Newspaper columns, pamphlets, magazines, and books all offer parents an abundance of expert opinion on child development and care. The combined circulation of the three most popular women's magazines—*Ladies Home Journal, Good Housekeeping,* and *Redbook*—is 26 million.

No question is too trivial; no issue, too controversial. Experts advise mothers on the dangers for children of mistletoe and astroturf, baby bouncers and rectal thermometers, circumcision and Zen macrobiotics.

The number and variety of books on how to raise children is similarly impressive. The titles include, of course, familiar names like *Baby and Child Care* (Spock, 1946, 1968, 1976), *Between Parent and Child* (Ginott, 1965), *How to Parent* (Dodson, 1970), *Infants and Mothers* (Brazelton, 1969), and *What Every Child Would Like His Parents to Know* (Salk, 1972).

Who is reading the popular child literature? Nearly all parents read *some* child-care books or articles, but those who are especially avid readers are parents who are highly educated; who are relatively isolated from familial support, help, and advice; and who are concerned about doing the best thing for their children.

Increased geographic mobility and age stratification in our society have led to young parents' having less contact with their own parents, grandparents, and siblings. Thus, without the guidance traditionally offered by the extended family, they turn to professional experts—in person or in books.

On the other hand, the experts want to increase parents' *confidence.* They start out with deliberate efforts to reassure parents: Parents are capable; they know more than they think they do; they should relax and enjoy their kids. But such reassurance must be carefully balanced with the other aim of these books, which is to increase parents' *competence.* Presumably, the authors also want parents to change their behavior.

These primers for parents are undeniably popular and apparently succeed in informing parents about child development in an abstract way. But there is no evidence that they provide a substitute for a real person—relative, friend, or physician—when child-rearing problems arise or when young people learn parenting skills.

Parents are eager for information about children and child rearing and are actively seeking it out. The authors of popular child-care books address *all* parents, but the underlying assumption on which their advice is based is that all readers lead model middle-class lives. Information should be responsive to parents' interests and concerns rather than to the preconceived issues of the experts. This would result in information oriented not to solving specific problems but to describing children's development and how parents might foster it.

Source: Adapted from Clarke-Stewart, K. A., 1978, "Popular Primers for Parents," *American Psychologist,* 1978, pp. 359–369.

Child Abuse

When parents discipline their children to an extreme or actually attack their children so that they cause bodily harm, that parenting behavior is labeled *child abuse.* There is also a passive form of abuse, that of neglect. When parents neglect children's health, education, and emotional well-being, they are abusing them passively but effectively. It is difficult to estimate exactly how many young children are abused each year in the United States, but the number is at least in the tens of thousands. Although children of all ages under 18 years (the technical upper-age limit of child abuse) are abused, the greater number of abused children are under 3 years of age.

Which parents are likely to abuse their children? Parents with children who are temperamentally difficult may tend to abuse them. Parents who have temperamental difficulties of their own or unreasonable expectations of their children often resort to extreme punishment of what might be considered normal infant behavior (Kempe & Kempe, 1978). Although child-abusing parents can be found in all socioeconomic groups, most abusive parents are unemployed, uneducated, poor, have a low self-esteem, and for various reasons are in great need of social support (Garbarino & Crouter, 1978). It is more likely to be a mother than a father abusing children—a mother who has had a premature baby, who has a large number of children, or who is physically or emotionally ill and is finding the care of her family distressful (Martin, 1976; Parke & Collmer, 1975).

Parents who were themselves abused, rejected, or emotionally deprived as children often become abusers of their children (Kempe, 1976). Kempe also states that many cases of child abuse can be related to a parent's suddenly losing a job. The parent sees losing a job as a rejection and therefore feels a loss of self-esteem and also anger, which becomes directed at a child.

Abusive parents need help. A method found to be effective is the emergency hot line. Parents can use 24-hour phone service to contact a counselor and seek help. Early detection of abusive parents is critical if intervention is to prove effective (Kempe & Kempe, 1978). In a study of 350 parents of newborns observed in the labor and delivery room, the Kempes identified a hundred who appeared to be "high risk," that is, potentially abusive parents. High-risk parents showed lack of love between them, or lack of interest in the newborn, or disappointment at the baby's physical appearance or sex. These parents were provided special services, and fifty of them received additional help from a pediatrician. Five of the fifty infants of parents not receiving help from a pediatrician were severely physically abused and needed hospital treatment; there were no cases of serious abuse or neglect from the other group of parents. Help from organizations such as *Parents Anonymous* and help by intervention during early infancy when warning signs are observed prove to be effective measures in assisting abusive or potentially abusive parents.

Mothering

The characteristics of a "good" mother were described by Duvall (1977) on the basis of the responses of 433 mothers to the question, "What are five things a good mother does?" Resources fell into two categories, *traditional concepts* of parenting related to the training of particular behavior, and *developmental concepts* of parenting related to children's behavior traits that can only be expected to be achieved over a fairly long period of time. Certain of these parenting practices, such as providing a nurturing environment, are clearly not directed at training specific behavior but at the child's general development. These different concepts are listed in Table 5.3.

Table 5.3 Mothers' Perceptions of a "Good Mother"[a,b]

Traditional Conceptions	Developmental Conceptions
A good mother:	A good mother:
Keeps house, washes, cooks, cleans, mends, sews, manages the household, etc.	Trains for self-reliance, encourages independence, teaches how to adjust to life, etc.
Takes care of the child physically; feeds, clothes, bathes the child; guards the child physically; etc.	Sees to emotional well-being, keeps child happy and contented, helps child feel secure, etc.
Trains the child to regularity, establishes regular habits, provides a schedule, etc.	Helps child develop socially, provides toys and companions, supervises child's play, etc.
Disciplines, corrects child; demands obedience; rewards good behavior; is firm; etc.	Provides for child's mental growth, reads to child, provides stimulation, educates, etc.
Makes the child good, instructs in morals, builds character, prays for, sees to religion, etc.	Guides with understanding; gears life to child's level; interprets, answers questions; etc.
	Relates lovingly to child, enjoys and shares with child, is interested in what child says, etc.
	Is a calm, cheerful, growing person oneself; has a sense of humor; smiles; keeps rested; etc.

[a]Doing a good job of child-rearing for some mothers means performing household chores, ensuring that their child is physically healthy, and training their child in social skills—thus taking care of immediate needs. Being a "good mother" also means taking care of a child's long-term developmental needs.

[b]*Source:* Duvall, E. M. *Marriage and Family Development.* Copyright 1977 by J. B. Lippincott Co. Reprinted by permission.

The role of the mother as viewed by *children,* in a recent study by Schvaneveldt, Freyer, & Aitken (1976), was described in a way that seems to combine traditional and developmental concepts. Eighty-six middle-class children were asked what is a "good" and what is a "bad" mother. The children described a "good" mother as one who takes care of children, helps little babies, gives kisses, cooks food, does not spank—but does keep children from doing things they shouldn't. A "bad" mother doesn't kiss children, doesn't straighten the house, and spanks. In their picture of a good mother the children cared about the traditional mother's role of performing domestic duties and meeting physical needs and also about the mother's role in producing a nurturant environment, meeting emotional needs, and disciplining with understanding.

Fathering

Compared to the number of studies on mothering, there have been very few on fathering. This can be attributed to the long-standing belief that fathers interact very little with infants and young children, so fathers have little influence on their children's development until they are much older (Lamb, 1978; Mussen, 1973; Parsons, 1958). The father's influence, or lack of it, has usually been inferred from observing families without fathers (e.g., Hetherington & Deur, 1971). But it has been observed that for intact families in which both parents work and the father only assumes the role of provider with little interaction with the children, the mother is forced to assume a double role (Bem & Bem, 1972). Since it is assumed that the father can have a positive influence on his children's development, whether the mother works or not, it has been argued that the father's relationships with the children are not merely superficial (Dahlstrom & Ziljestrom, 1967).

Current research shows that the father is not only a provider but also a nurturing parent (Mischel, 1970). Although it has been noticed that women and girls show more interest in infants than do men and boys (Feldman & Nash, 1977), it has also been observed that fathers are just as likely as mothers to hold, cuddle, kiss, smile at, look closely at, and rock their newborns irrespective of whether the baby is a boy or a girl. Fathers tend to hold and rock their infants more than mothers, who spend more time feeding their infants (Lamb, 1978; Parke, O'Leary & West, 1972; Parke & O'Leary, 1976; Parke & Sawin, 1977). Frodi and Lamb (1978) have reported that by the end of the infants' first year mothers and fathers have developed distinctive styles of play with their infants. Mothers are more likely to use toys and fathers to engage their infants in rough-and-tumble play. So, although mothers and fathers appear to be equally competent in all aspects of parenting, mothers tend to adopt the caretaking role more and fathers tend to spend more time with their infants in physical play (Lamb, 1978). These differences suggest that mothers and fathers will probably have different effects on their infants' development. However, it has been found that fathers can be just as effective as mothers in making babies feel secure enough to explore their surroundings (Kotelchuck et al., 1975). Other studies have also shown that the infant's anxiety at separation in an unfamiliar setting can be greatly reduced or even completely eliminated by the presence of the father and that babies whose fathers spent time caring for them are much more inclined to explore their environment (Spelke et al., 1973).

Role of Culture

From many studies of parenting in different cultures, we know that young children's social behavior is shaped by the culture and that the strongest impact comes from parents. However, we are not sure how the child's culture in general works to instill such characteristics as generosity, helpfulness, and social responsibility (Kessen, Haith, & Salapatek, 1970; Mussen & Eisenberg-Berg, 1977; Rutherford & Mussen, 1968).

Greenbaum has suggested that when studying infant–parent interactions in various cultures careful observation should be made of (1) the amount and type of interaction during and after infancy; (2) the special efforts, if any, that each culture makes to teach children certain skills; (3) the question of whether these skills are relevant to intellectual development in any way; and (4) the question of whether various cultures have their own built-in "intervention" programs (intense socialization in some area likely to encourage mental growth), and the timing of this intervention (1979, pp. 69–70). Keeping in mind these suggestions on what to look for, we can examine child rearing in different cultures.

The IK people of Uganda were once a close-knit tribe of hunters; they were observed to be kind, generous, considerate, and honest (Turnbull, 1972); and each new generation acquired these traits. Because of problems in obtaining food, the tribe was eventually broken up into small bands concerned only with survival. They became savage, deceitful, treacherous, dishonest; and these traits were passed on to their children (Turnbull, 1972).

Margaret Mead (1935) described two tribes living on the same New Guinea island. The Arapesh were gentle, cooperative, and generous. The Mundugamors, in comparison, were ruthless and aggressive. Mead believed that the gentleness of the Arapesh was, at least in part, a result of the greater tenderness with which Arapesh parents brought up their children.

Kagan and Klein (1973) and Kagan et al. (1979) observed the effects on infant development of living in the highlands of Guatemala, in Guatemala City, and in Cambridge, Massachusetts. Children in these various settings experienced different types of upbringing in different environments.

Two villages were selected in the Guatemalan highlands since they provided an interesting contrast to each other. San Marcos is one of the poorest villages in that region while San Pedro is one of the wealthiest and most progressive with a moderately good school. Infants in San Marcos receive little stimulation and

contact with their mothers until they are about 15 months old. Infants of San Pedro, on the other hand, are carried on their mothers' hips or in their arms as they go on errands and, in general, have more contact with mothers and other family members and receive more stimulation. As they grow older, unlike infants and children in San Marcos, those of San Pedro get to watch TV, imitate TV characters in their play, and, beginning at about age 7, go to school. Thus the San Pedro children have a decided advantage over children from San Marcos with respect to additional learning experiences from watching TV and going to school.

Infants in Guatemala City from both poor and middle-class families had similar backgrounds and experiences to white American infants living in Cambridge, Massachusetts, but very different backgrounds and experiences from infants living in San Marcos and San Pedro. The question Kagan and Klein had in mind was "Would different environments and experiences have any effect on infant development?"

Children from these various settings were given tests of recall, recognition, perceptual analysis, and perceptual and conceptual inference. It was found that at about 5 to 6 years of age the middle-class children, American and Guatemalan, did better on these tests than the Guatemalan children from poor city families and rural families. But by age 11 to 12 years, there were few differences (Kagan & Klein, 1973)! This may appear surprising, especially to an *environmentalist,* considering the differences in environmental and cultural stimulation experienced by infants in these four settings. Kagan, a *cognitive structuralist,* argues that although the differences in performance at age 5 to 6 years were probably due to differences in experience in the different environments and cultures, these differences seem to have been at least partially reversed by some later, though unspecified, *interaction* (with a Piagetian meaning) with the environment.

In a second study Kagan (Kagan et al., 1979) used simple and complex memory tasks as well as Piagetian reasoning tasks. The results are rather different from those of the first study. In most tasks Cambridge children performed much better than children in either San Marcos or San Pedro. The San Pedro children performed better than those living in San Marcos. Memory and reasoning, therefore, seem to get better, depending on the level of development of the town and the related quality of education and socialization. The apparent similarities in the intellectual performance of the older children in the first study can be accounted for by the relatively simple tasks used. The results of the later study prompted Kagan to acknowledge that environment and culture can influence intellectual performance.

Children's behavior seems to be molded and influenced by their parents' culture as the study of the IK people showed. The Guatemalan highlands study showed that no matter what culture infants grow up in, parents do have an effect on their social development. The study of the Arapesh and Mundugamors showed that cultural differences in parenting make a difference in social development.

For an understanding of parenting, how important is information about how parents bring up their children in different cultures? If we find that children's behavior seems to be molded or influenced by the way their parents behave toward them—no matter what culture they grow up in—we can be more sure that parents do indeed affect the infant's social behavior. We can also assume that, where differences in development occur, these are likely to be due to cultural differences in parenting attitudes and beliefs.

Effects of Deprivation and of Later Stimulation

Harlow noticed that when young monkeys were separated from their mothers they became socially maladjusted. He found that monkeys raised by attractive surrogate cloth mothers nevertheless behaved in odd ways in certain instances. For example, some monkeys raised in this fashion were particularly abusive to other monkeys, few appeared to be normally adjusted in social situations, and most could not mate normally (e.g., Harlow & Harlow, 1969). Early and prolonged separation from a live mother proved to be a real deprivation for the young monkeys.

Infants have also experienced deprivation, a withholding of something vital to their growth. One form of deprivation, inadequate opportunity for social development through attachment and interaction, has been studied by several researchers.

Spitz (1946) compared the development of infants in a prison nursery to infants placed in a foundling home (a home that is run by charity for abandoned and illegitimate babies). The infants in the prison nursery were cared for by their mothers (some of whom were either emotionally disturbed or mentally retarded) and by members of a professional staff. In the foundling home more than eight infants were cared for by a single adult. This resulted in insufficient attention and handling.

The infants in the prison nursery enjoyed a stimulating environment—and prospered. The experience for the infants in the foundling home was devastating. The lack of mothering resulted in depression that was characterized by a lack of appetite and a lack of interest in objects and events around them. The result was retardation in weight and height and a most serious retardation in mental development. Goldfarb (1945) also observed children, ranging in age from 3 to 12 years, who had been institutionalized since birth. He found them emotionally apathetic and extremely passive.

The picture is quite clear. Even the prison setting, with mothers considered abnormal in the aspects of their social behavior other than mothering, at least came close to a "natural environment." In some respects these infants might have been considered deprived of a "good" home. But by Western standards we might be tempted to say the same about the Guatemalan infants of the Kagan and Klein study. Both sets of infants, however, had caring parents. The consistent warm, reliable nurturing the infants received seems to have been sufficient for nearly normal development—as far as we can measure it. However, it should be added that infants raised in institutions do not usually receive the same nurturing attention common to infants reared in the home. It is more often the case that the development of institutionalized infants is somewhat retarded (Provence & Lipton, 1962).

In a study lasting more than twenty years, Skeels (1966) observed a group of children in an overcrowded orphanage who were later transferred to an institution for the mentally retarded. In this institution more opportunities were provided for learning and the children were cared for by older mentally retarded girls. After about two years the group at the institution showed more improvement, as measured by an IQ test, than a control group still in the orphanage. More importantly, twenty years later the group who had transferred to the institution had achieved higher levels of social competency, self-support, education, and income than the control group. This study showed that later stimulation could relieve effects of deprivation.

There is no doubt that many thousands of infants suffer from lack of love, from normal stimulation in their environments, from abuse, and from what Bruner (1974) has called "cultures of failure" because he believes that many of these infants suffer irreversible intellectual handicaps. The remedy for infants considered culturally deprived has been **infant intervention** or *compensatory education,* either in day-care, preschool, or the home.

The intention of most intervention programs is to include infants as young as possible, since deprived children's sensitivity to treatment seems to decline with age (Caldwell & Richmond, 1964). One such program, though now closed, operated at the Children's Center in Syracuse, New York, in 1964 and is an interesting example of an early infant-intervention program (Caldwell & Richmond, 1968; Caldwell, 1972).

This ambitious program attempted to provide systematic education for infants beginning at about 5 months of age in order to develop sensory and perceptual skills. These infants received individual adult attention and were encouraged to explore their environments—to touch, handle, reach for, and feel objects. The infants themselves were handled, fed, bathed, and talked to.

Infants entering the program were compared to infants from similar social and home background who remained at home. All the infants were rated on the *Cattell Infant Intelligence Scale* or the *Stanford Binet* (see Table 5.4) at the start of the program, and six months later. At the end of six months, infants in the intervention program had increased their scores, on the average, by 17 points compared to an average gain of 6 points by infants who remained at home. The infants belonging to the intervention program also showed greater attachment to their mothers, and these more advanced babies also had the more attentive mothers. Caldwell suggests that "normal" development goes hand-in-hand with strength of attachment. The program succeeded in demonstrating the benefits of an intervention program—increased ability and increased potential.

It has been shown that differences in infants' mental development reflect differences in physical development and prior experiences and environmental conditions. Infants from low-income families do not perform as well on some tasks as those from middle-class homes (e.g., Wachs, Uzgiris, & Hunt, 1971), and this is especially the case for infants who have a low birth weight (Drillien & Ellis, 1964). Indeed, infants from low-income families have been shown to be lacking in and have been said to have a *deficit* in physical, social, and mental skills (Deutsch, 1962; Gray & Klaus, 1965; Weikert, 1967).

The *deficit theory* has been attacked by a number of specialists because it uses American middle-class behavior as "the yardstick of success" (Cole & Bruner, 1972; Hess et al., 1971). Instead of trying to change all subcultures to a middle-class norm, critics of the deficit theory propose improving the *social environment* when disadvantageous but without altering the total cultural heritage (Stein & Susser, 1970). One program to train parents in mother–infant interaction by working within the home environment illustrates this approach.

Table 5.4 Four Items from the Cattell Infant Developmental and Intelligence Scale

1. At 6 Months
   Reaches persistently

Procedure. A cube is placed on the table just out of the child's reach. If the cube should not arouse the child's interest some other object of about the same size but of greater interest to the child may be used.

Scoring. Credit is given if the child either keeps his/her hand stretched toward the object for several seconds or, as more frequently happens, if he/she reaches toward the object several times.

2. At 12 Months
   Rattles spoon in cup

Procedure. A cup is placed before the child and a spoon moved back and forth in it, hitting the edges; then the spoon is placed beside the cup with the handle toward the child. Repeat demonstration if need be, placing the spoon on the other side of the cup.

Scoring. Credit is given if the child puts the spoon in the cup and moves it back and forth, hitting the edges in imitation of the examiner.

3. At 20 Months
   Build tower of three cubes

Procedure. Ten cubes are placed in a pile before the child. The examiner builds a tower of two or three cubes, at the same time asking and motioning the child to do the same. If he/she does not do so, he/she may be handed the blocks one at a time with the words: "Put it on here," "Make one here." Pointing to another, "Here is another, put it on too. Make a big house." etc. Several demonstration towers may be built by the examiner, but care must be taken not to arouse the child's interest in knocking down rather than building up the towers.

Scoring. Credit is given if the tower stands at three blocks or if the child adds two blocks to the demonstration tower. The tower must stand unsupported after the third block has been placed and the hands removed.

4. At 30 Months
   Stanford-Binet identifying objects by use

Procedure. This item is taken from the Stanford-Binet, Form L, the procedure of which is to show a card with six small objects attached—cup, shoe, penny, knife, automobile and iron—and say: "Show me the one that . . ." or "Which one . . ." or "Show me what . . ."
   a. . . . we drink out of
   b. . . . goes on our feet
   c. . . . we can buy candy with
   d. . . . we can cut with
   e. . . . we ride in
   f. . . . we use to iron clothes

Scoring. Credit is given if four objects are pointed to.

From: Cattell, P., 1950. *The Measurement of Intelligence of Infants and Young Children* (3rd ed.), 1950. Used with permission of the Science Press.

The Ypsilanti Carnegie Infant Education Project (Lambie, Bond, & Weikart, 1974) is "culture free"; that is, it does not inject another culture into the lives of its participants. Its objectives are to

1. Fully develop the infant's intellectual and social skills.

2. Train the mother as *teacher* so she can facilitate her infant's intellectual and social development.

3. Train people to visit homes (home visitors) to train mothers as teachers.

Home visitors took along toys and other learning materials to the homes. They demonstrated their use to encourage infants' exploration and the development of sensorimotor skills. Mothers were then encouraged to use these materials in a similar fashion. Home visitors also talked to mothers about other important mother–infant interactions such as holding, playing, and talking. There was no attempt to change the mothers' ways of behaving from their own cultural point of view. The study lasted 28 months. One group received the home-based program in its entirety. A second group received a similar, but less intense program. A third group received sporadic visits.

Mothers in the first group became more positive in interacting with their infants, followed by mothers from the second group. Similarly, infants in the first group showed the most improvement in their mental and language development, followed by infants in the second group. No differences showed up between the groups of infants with respect to motor or social-emotional development. This program shows that a culture-free intervention program can be effective in encouraging infants' development. It also shows that mothers can be trained to engage in more positive interactions with their infants.

Other intervention programs (not home based) have succeeded in accelerating infant development. For example, Saltz (1973) has had success with institutionalized infants, and Scarr-Salapatek and Williams (1973) with premature infants. There is no doubt that early intervention can significantly help in the development of infants from deprived environments. A recent report indicates that low-income children who had attended infant preschool programs in the 1960s are still benefiting in terms of intellectual and social development, school achievement, and personality development (Darlington, Royce, Snipper, Murray, & Lazar, 1980).

Some psychologists such as White (1975), although willing to make a distinction between infants from "deprived" and "natural environments," believe all infants can benefit from early stimulation. One reason for this stems from the belief that infancy is a critical period for acquiring certain intellectual and social competencies. White (1975, pp. 3–4) has said that "By the time a child (has) reached three years of age, he has undergone a great deal of education." He adds that most American families do not get their children through the first 36 months of life as well educated and developed as they could be. The answer is to educate parents to be better at the job of parenting and to supplement the benefits of the home with day care or preschool. Let us take a brief look at what a number of psychologists and educators have had to say about the effects of day care.

Effects of Day Care

More and more mothers are becoming wage earners. There has been a dramatic increase in married women in employment (see Figure 5.6). As you can image, an increasing number of babies are now being cared for not only by parents but by care givers in day-care centers. Day-care centers are places that provide daytime care (but not necessarily education) for children under school age. What effects does day care have on infant development?

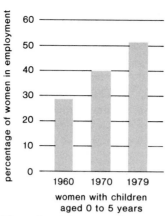

Figure 5.6 Percentage of employed women with children 0 to 5 years. Marital status includes single (never married), married with husband present, and other marital status (e.g., widowed, divorced, husband absent). (Source: United States Bureau of the Census, 1980.)

Originally, substitute care was discouraged because it was believed that day-to-day separation of infants from parents would be as disastrous to development as permanent separation (Bowlby, 1973). As we have seen, recently there has been a change in opinion regarding the influence of caretakers on infant development. What seems to be important is the quality of substitute care. There seems to be no difference in the social and mental development of infants' receiving individual, consistent, caring attention in day-care centers compared to those reared at home (Feldman, 1974; Doyle & Somers, 1975). It has even been suggested that the variety in "quality" care provided by both the home and the day-care center might, in fact, provide extra benefit to the infant's social development (Bronfenbrenner, 1975; Lamb, 1977). Even with middle-class infants, entering a full day-care program before 8 months of age has resulted in substantial social cognitive gains (Fowler, 1972; Haith, 1972). Fowler has suggested that perhaps we should question whether middle-class parents should be the sole, important care givers. The home and day-care center might be complementary environments for rearing infants and young children.

A rather different view has been projected by Kagan (Kagan, Kearsley, & Zelazo, 1978). Kagan asked the question, do infants in a well-run group day-care center, attending five days a week for more than two years, show a more advanced development than a similar group of infants reared at home? He compared infants from working and middle-class families, both Chinese and white Americans, with respect to both social and mental development. He found little difference between the two groups on any of the measures used: intellectual skills, language, attachment, separation-protest, and play. Kagan claims that

It has been suggested that time spent in a day care center might benefit the infant's social and intellectual development. (Photo by Robert Eckert/EKM-Nepenthe)

these results do "not offer much support for the view that quality group care outside of the home has an important effect on the young child's development" (Kagan et al., 1978, p. 260).

We must remember, however, that the results showed little difference in development between infants in day care and those at home. It can be argued, therefore, that at least going to a day-care center is not likely to harm the infant's development. Mothers who have to work and need to place their infants in day care should have this information. Conflicting views remain about the effects of day care on the infant's development, and the issues are still being studied.

Summary

An important feature of infant social development is attachment. Physically caring for and playing with the infant leads to a secure bond between infant and parents or other care givers. As the infant grows older attachment is marked by the infant's pleasure and feeling of security at being close to a care giver. But care givers should also encourage the infant to venture away from them and to feel secure with other nonregular care givers.

The importance of attachment to social development in particular and to general development has been demonstrated for both animal and human infants.

Harlow has demonstrated the importance of animal attachment by experimenting with infant rhesus monkeys. *Surrogate* (substitute) mothers made from wooden blocks and covered with cloth were preferred to figures made from wire mesh. "Cloth mothers" apparently provided more needed comfort. Infant monkeys forced to stay with "wire mothers" formed no attachments and developed abnormal social behaviors. Since humans have a biological heritage linked to animals, studying attachment in animals can result in a more complete understanding of attachment in humans.

Infant behaviors such as smiling, crying, clinging, and eye-brightening, and parent behaviors such as closely looking at, handling, using baby talk, and cuddling lead to attachment. Some researchers believe there is a fairly critical period immediately after birth when mother–infant contact is crucial for the development of attachment and the later development of normal social behavior. Other researchers believe that immediate separation of infant and mother at birth results in some social handicap for the infant. This setback can be overcome by later normal care giving.

Bowlby and Ainsworth described attachment as developing in a sequence of stages during infancy. The infant first learns to discriminate among care givers, then to show preferences for certain adults, which leads to protest at separation appearing at about 7 months. When infants are between 7 and 30 months old, parents (care givers) become very important to them. Originally, it was believed that strong attachment to the mother as the *primary care giver* was crucial for normal development. Now it is believed that infants fare well with substitute mothers and with a limited number of care givers. The consistency and quality of care is important.

Two important attention-getting signals used by the infant to attract parents' attention are crying and smiling. At first these have a strong survival value, but soon they become related to the development of social behavior. Smiling is interpreted by adults as an invitation by the infant to make contact. One type of infant cry is clearly associated with anxiety or fear about being separated from a care giver.

Separation causes *anxiety* in the infant. Bowlby and Ainsworth suggested that separation from the mother can be harmful to the infant. But Lamb has suggested that the infant can learn to deal with separation. Being willing to explore strange places or to tolerate strangers from a secure attachment base probably helps the development of the infant's personality and social behavior.

Fathers play a special role with their infants, usually spending more time (than mothers) playing rather than taking care. However, although fathers and mothers have unique child-rearing roles, fathers do make contact in much the same way as mothers, by holding, cuddling, and vocalizing with their infants.

There are a number of theories about attachment and its importance for infant social and personality development:

1. Freud believed that socialization occurs as the infant resolves conflicts between inner impulsive needs and external demands by *identifying* with parents and accepting their standards of behavior.

2. Learning theory emphasizes the importance of attending to and reinforcing acceptable social behavior. Attachment, an important element of social behavior, is said to develop out of long-term, satisfying reciprocal infant–care giver interactions.

3. Bandura, in focusing on *imitation* as a process of socialization, provides a particular learning theory view. Parents are seen as *models* who provide examples of acceptable social behavior. When these are imitated by their children, the desired behavior can then be reinforced.

4. The cognitive-development view of infant social development, as expressed by Kohlberg, is that behavior changes systematically in a sequence of stages as the child adapts to social requirements.

5. Ethology, the theory of how different types of animals behave in their natural habitats, has also influenced studies of attachment in humans. Ethologists have observed that there are "fixed times" for *bonding,* or *imprinting* between parents and infants. These *times* became known as *critical periods.* Imprinting in animals is long-lasting and not easily *extinguished.* In the case of human infants, it appears important that they maintain *intimate contact* with care givers from about 4 months of age. Some specialists prefer to call this a *sensitive period.* Deprivation from lack of attachment at this time may not be so "critical" for the infant. Adjustments may be possible later, as long as the loss of attachment has not been too severe and too extended.

Parenting behavior has a profound effect, for good or ill, on the development of infants' self-image, one of the chief characteristics of personality. There are a number of theories about the origins and development of personality during infancy. According to Freud's *psychosexual theory,* the infant's personality and social behavior develop during a two-stage sequence. The *oral* stage lasts from *birth to 18 months* with the emphasis in infant behavior on obtaining gratification through *oral stimulation.* The *anal* stage lasts from *18 months to 3 years* and gratification comes primarily through bowel movements. The infant is mainly "pleasure seeking," motivated by the *id. Ego* develops later through delaying gratification and by seeking to obtain gratification in various socially acceptable ways. It is believed that *fixation* during a stage can lead to a maladjusted personality in adulthood.

Erikson, in his *psychosocial theory,* focuses on *ego* development influenced by social experiences. Gratification can be achieved by more general behavior—for example, not only by sucking the nipple but also other objects, and by smiling and babbling. The infant passes through two of eight states, each marked by a crisis. From *birth to 18 months* the conflict is between *trust and mistrust*, influenced by the quality of infant–care giver interactions. From *18 months to 3 years* the conflict is between *autonomy* and a sense of *shame* and *doubt*. The infant not only learns to control bodily functions but also relationships with adults. The infant explores by itself and learns to accommodate personal desires to rules set by care givers.

Two important aspects of personality are sex identity and aggressive behavior. *Sex identity* (sex-role adoption) appears to be strongly influenced by care givers. It is during the second year that sex typing occurs. The father strongly influences the male role adopted by sons and also tends to reinforce daughters' female sex typing.

Aggression in infants is also thought to depend on how care givers behave toward infants. Permissiveness coupled with physical punishment produces the most aggression. Firm, calm care givers who set reasonable rules seem to have the best effect. In this climate normal, controlled aggression emerges.

Parenting roles are a product of personality and previous social experiences. Although "mothers" and "fathers" can be equally competent care givers, in *intact families* mothers tend to do most of the care giving and fathers tend to engage in more physical play interactions. When both mother and father are working parents, it is important for both to share the care giver role.

When parents willfully cause their children bodily harm or serious neglect, this is termed child abuse. Children of all ages, across all socioeconomic boundaries, are abused, but most abused children are under 3 years of age and temperamentally difficult. Most abusive parents are unemployed, poor, and uneducated, and they are more likely to be mothers experiencing some kind of stress. Parents who were themselves abused or neglected as children are often abusive of their children. Help can be provided by around-the-clock emergency telephone services or early intervention.

Infant social behavior is also shaped by the *culture*. Some specialists believe that culture has little effect on mental development *in natural environments* but that it certainly has effect on social skills (e.g., reading in Western society, or tool making in primitive tribes). Both mental and social development can be seriously retarded in some cultures (or subcultures). Infants reared in "cultures of failure" usually require special help if they are to attain normal (or nearly normal) development later. Help to overcome *deprivation* can be provided by group care or by training the mother in the home. For intervention to succeed infants must receive constant, quality care in a stimulating environment.

Opinion is divided about the effects of group day-care on infants' development. The weight of evidence suggests that infants from both normal and deprived home backgrounds can benefit from such care. Results from a study by Kagan suggest that day-care for both middle and working-class infants has little effect on the child's development. However, Kagan found *no adverse effects*—some consolation for working mothers who must place their infants in day-care centers.

Questions for Review

1. Briefly describe the viewpoints of psychoanalytic, cognitive-structuralist, and learning theories with respect to the development of attachment during infancy.

2. What aspects of ethological theory and research, and other research on attachment in animals such as that of Harlow, have relevance for understanding attachment in humans?

3. Describe briefly the main characteristics of the stages of development of attachment during infancy described by Bowlby and Ainsworth.

4. How does the infant's personality develop from birth to 3 years, according to Freud and according to Erikson? How do these two theories differ in the description of personality development?

5. In what respects are mothering and fathering roles similar and different?

6. What effects might a father's absence have on an infant boy's development?

7. Summarize the main points of the arguments that state (1) separation always causes retardation of social development, and (2) separation can be beneficial for social development.

8. What effects do different cultures appear to have on infant development?

9. Summarize the main causes of *deprivation* during infancy. What might be done to overcome the effects of deprivation?

10. What are considered to be the effects of day care on infant development?

11. If you find it possible to spend time observing infants with people, attempt the following:

    (a) Find an infant—either by contacting a "family," infant day-care center, home day-care facility, hospital, or some other suitable location.

    (b) Arrange to observe an infant (girl, or boy, or both) interacting with an adult or older child (female, male, or both).

    (c) Try to find a convenient time for observation when one particular activity is likely to occur; for example, bath time, feeding time, a general period of playful activity, etc.

    (d) Keep a "diary" of *all* observed interactions.

    (e) Interpret your observations in the light of information you now have from chapters 3 and 4 about the infants' physical, mental, and social development.

Since it is likely that you will only be able to select one infant/other person dyad (pair), it might be a good idea to arrange to share the assignment with a friend, or friends, so that you can compare observations from different sources.

Suggestions for Further Reading

Bigner, J. J. *Parent-child relations.* New York: Macmillan, 1979.
For this chapter, the whole of Part I and the first chapter of Part II would be suitable. Besides taking the typical view of the adult's effect on the child, this text also examines the child's influence on the *adult's development and growth.*

Carew, J. W., Chan I., & Halfar, C. *Observing intelligence in young children: Eight case studies.* Englewood Cliffs, NJ: Prentice-Hall, 1976.
In this text, the authors provide glimpses of the growing-up experiences of eight children. In Chapters 5–7, you will find descriptions of differences in parenting style, contrasting values for child development in different social classes, and examples of the effects of deprived environments on the young child's development.

Herbert-Jackson, E., O'Brien, M., Porterfield, J., & Risley, J. R. *The infant center.* Baltimore: University Park Press, 1977.
A detailed guide to organizing and managing an infant day-care center.

Maccoby, E. E. *Social development: Psychological growth and the parent–child relationship.* New York: Harcourt Brace Jovanovich, 1980.
Focuses on social development in the context of the family during early and middle childhood. It is suitable as further reading not only for this chapter, but also for Chapters 8 and 11.

White, B. L. *The first three years of life.* Englewood Cliffs, NJ: Prentice-Hall, 1975.
Provides a description of physical, social, and mental developments during a sequence of seven phases from birth to 3 years. Ideas in this text are derived mainly from Burton White's work as director of the Brookline Early Education Project.

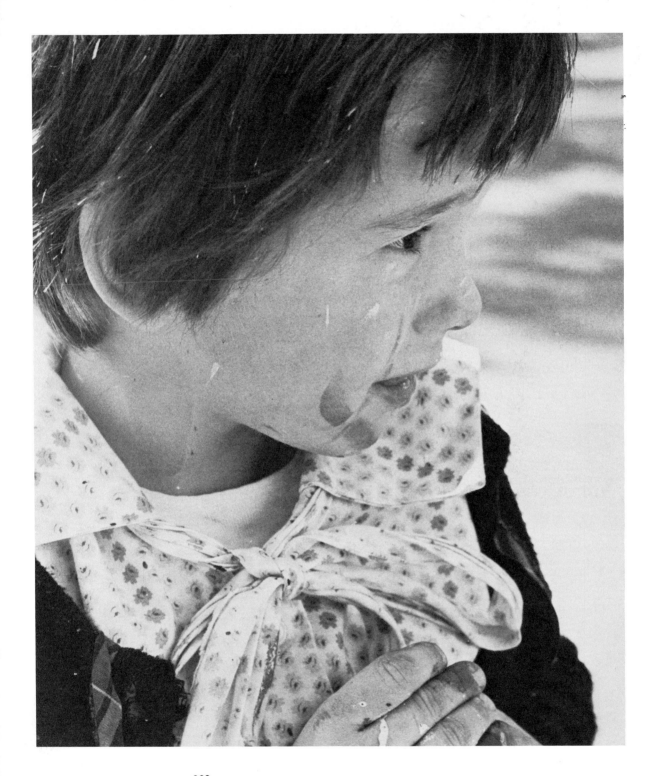

232

The Preschool Years

Physical and Intellectual Development

6 6, 7, 9, 11, 12

Motor Development

Reinforcement

Punishment

Shaping

Preoperational Development

Representation

Linguistics

Intelligence

Cognitive Style

I am a part of all that I have met;
Yet all experience is an arch
where through
Gleams that untraveled world whose
margin fades
Forever and forever when I move.

From Alfred Lord Tennyson, *Ulysses*

The years from about age 3 to 6 or 7 are usually called the "preschool years." This is really a misnomer. For one thing, not all young children at these ages go to preschool, and if they do attend a preschool or day-care center, they transfer to kindergarten at about age 5. The ages 3 to 6 or 7, which demark this period of development, should not be considered fixed for every child.

Nevertheless, psychologists have marked this period of time as a developmental period. Skinner gives it no name, refers to it as a "phase" of development containing two subphases, and suggests that at this time certain types of behavior can be expected and should be encouraged. Gesell refers to the years between 2 and 6 as the first cycle of development of alternating "better" and "worse" years. Piaget has called the years between age 3 and 6 the stage of preoperational development, and Bruner marks this time a period when children are consolidating their ability to represent the world, especially symbolically in the form of language. By their observation of children, these psychologists have detected important changes in behavior between the time infancy comes to a close, at about 3 years, and age 6 or 7.

Changes can be noted in children's physical growth during these years. From about 18 months to 3 years, the rapid growth of infancy slows down. Until the sudden acceleration of growth at puberty, physical development now continues at a steady, slower growth rate. This chapter focuses on physical, intellectual, and language development during the preschool years. It also discusses the measurement of intelligence and the variations in characteristic ways of thinking (cognitive styles).

Physical Development

The average 2-year-old is about 30 inches tall and weighs approximately 28 pounds. Over the next four years there will be a steady increase of 2 to 3 inches in height and 5 to 6 pounds in weight each year. Weight gain can be attributed mainly to increases in bone and muscle as the child loses body fat. During these years there is little difference in the height, weight, and rate of growth of boys and girls (Watson & Lawrey, 1967). However, there are cultural differences in rates of growth for children this age. American and European children are, on the average, taller and heavier than children in Eastern countries and parts of Africa (Meredith, 1978). The differences can be attributed mainly to the quality of nutrition. Undernourished children in some of the latter countries, for example, can hardly be expected to achieve their full potential of physical growth.

One aspect of growth during childhood is the changes that occur in body proportions. If we were to observe a group of children first entering preschool, we would notice that they still retain the top-heavy, stubby-legged, potbellied look of infancy. As they grow older, we would notice that their chests get bigger, shoulders broaden, legs grow longer, and stomachs flatten out. Whereas at age

2 we would think of them still as "babies," at age 6 they would become "children." Physical growth during the preschool years means getting taller, stronger, and achieving more coordinated body movements.

The preschool child's skeleton is also developing. Existing bones grow larger and the remaining cartilage from the period of infancy hardens into bone. There is a striking development in the shape of the face. The jaw becomes larger and the face lengthens, which accounts for the disappearance of the "baby face." By age 3 most children have a full set of baby teeth (sometimes called **deciduous** or **milk teeth**). Beneath the milk teeth are the 32 permanent teeth in various stages of development, which do not begin to appear until the fifth or sixth year.

As the muscles and skeleton develop, so too does the nervous system. During the preschool years, the sheathing of nerve fibers (**myelinization**) is completed.

In addition to physical growth there is the development of coordination. Muscles, bones, and the nervous system are developing in harmony to give the child the strength and mobility to explore and develop motor skills needed for engineering tasks such as building complex block structures or artistic skills that require the controlled wielding of a crayon or paintbrush. For the child to become more aware of these developing physical competencies, he or she needs space to explore, materials to practice with, and encouragement from others acknowledging his or her progress.

Motor skills develop quite slowly in the years from 2 to 6. At age 2 the child is still quite clumsy and has a tendency to fall over quite easily and has difficulty in navigating around objects. Movements typical of preschool children range from running, jumping, climbing, and throwing to building towers with wooden blocks, stringing beads, completing jigsaw puzzles, and manipulating crayons. We can distinguish among these movements and the skills they require in children's *motor development.*

Gross motor skills involve movement of the entire body and include riding bikes, climbing, throwing, catching and kicking balls, and balancing (Frankenberg & Dodds, 1967). Children of preschool age are intensely active and get lots of practice in these skills. By age 6 they can become amazingly competent at such activities. *Fine motor skills* usually involve hand-eye coordination and quite precise muscle control. At first, preschoolers have problems holding crayons, using paintbrushes, manipulating small objects, pouring liquid from one container into another, cutting with scissors, using construction tools, and getting into and out of clothes that need tying, buttoning, or buckling. The 2-year-old is better able to finger paint than to use a paintbrush, better able to assemble ready-made objects by gluing them than to construct and design them. But by age 6, given practice with various materials and help from caring adults, the child has gained control over many tools that require a fine manipulation. At the same time the child is also developing intellectual skills, for example, in representation. At age 2 the child may be more interested in just exploring a medium such as paint, crayons, or sets of objects, using them in a rather random fashion.

Preschool children enjoy running; jumping; climbing; throwing, catching, and kicking balls; swinging; and balancing—all activities that influence the development of gross motor skills. (Photos by Jean-Claude Lejeune)

At age 6 many artistic activities are intended to be representational. The child now tries to draw a detailed picture of a person, an animal, an object, or a building (Kellog, 1967).

What is the importance of motor development to the child's overall development? At one level the success of mastering various physical skills, the joy in playing physical games, the growing realization that difficult tasks requiring a fine hand–eye coordination can now be accomplished seem to have an important influence on the development of a healthy self-concept (Caplan & Caplan, 1974). At another level, as we have already seen, sensorimotor development is considered to be a necessary precursor to later intellectual development. In the next section you will find many examples of children's behavior and changes in behavior that link physical and intellectual development.

Intellectual Development

The changes that occur in thinking and reasoning between 2 and 6 to 7 years of age are even more startling than those that occur during infancy. How have psychologists viewed these changes? What have they discovered about intellectual development? In this section we will discuss four views of intellectual development. Behaviorists (environmentalists) such as Skinner believe that development can be principally attributed to operant conditioning—a most important aspect of which is positive *reinforcement* or the rewarding of appropriate behaviors. Gesell states that development is governed by maturation and that it occurs in stages. Piaget also places an emphasis on maturation as exerting some control over the rate of development; but he also emphasizes the important influence that children's interactions with the environment have on the quality of development. Bruner feels that the techniques of representing the world through action, image, and symbolism such as language, and the effects of culture are crucial for development.

The Behaviorists' View

In Chapter 4 we mentioned that Skinner believes that changes in behavior result from operant conditioning. If the child's behavior is rewarded, that behavior is likely to occur again. The reverse is also true—*punishment* discourages a particular behavior. Skinner uses two general concepts to describe these two conditions, reinforcement and extinction.

Reinforcement.   The most important feature of Skinner's theory, and the most relevant to the idea of development, is the concept of reinforcement. There are two types of reinforcement, positive and negative. When something is "added to" a response (a behavior) that is likely to make it happen again, such as a reward for good behavior, it is called a *positive reinforcer*. For example, if the preschool teacher says to the child who has been helping at tidy-up time, "That has been a great help. You've done a good job of cleaning up," the child is likely to willingly help at the next tidy-up time. Behaviors can also be strengthened by removing something from a situation; this is called a *negative reinforcer*. For example, children may come to realize that in certain situations changing from quiet to noisy play results in parents' or teachers' shouting at them. If they find being shouted at unpleasant, they can remove the shouting by playing quietly again. In this case shouting, which is a negative reinforcer, strengthens the desirable quiet behavior. The process of negative reinforcement is sometimes confused with punishment, which actually does not increase a behavior but suppresses it.

Extinction.   When behavior ceases because of conditioning, the process is called *extinction*. Punishment is one type of extinction. Punishment usually takes one of two forms, removing a positive reinforcer or using a negative reinforcer as a consequence of some behavior. It may be that the love and affection from adults, which children find so enjoyable, is not given as a consequence of certain behaviors. A child may, in a fit of temper, refuse to help clean up a playroom. The parent or teacher simply refuses to recognize the child—no smiles, no compliments, no signs of affection. If a group of children is involved, the child may see other children receiving positive reinforcement for helping to clean up the room. Over a period of time this type of punishment may suppress the temper tantrums as the child seeks to regain the positive reinforcements of being loved and accepted.

As mentioned previously, when the children's quiet play changed to noisy play, the noisy play was negatively reinforced by the adults' shouting. Suppose that a parent or teacher comes across a group of children playing noisily, perhaps fighting or breaking toys. The result may be being shouted at, being given a time-out (taken out of classroom activities; usually being told to sit quietly on a chair in a corner of the classroom), or even physical punishment. The negative reinforcer is used only as a consequence of the undesirable behavior. In your own adult world examples of punishment by negative reinforcement might include being ticketed for illegal parking, receiving a poor grade for a poorly presented assignment, or losing a part-time job for continuously arriving late for work. The important distinction between punishment and negative reinforcement is that the latter strengthens an already acceptable behavior to which it is associated while the former suppresses an undesirable behavior to which it is directly related. It has usually been supposed that punishment does not truly extinguish undesirable

behavior—that it only has a temporary effect. However, Hilgard and Bower (1975) have found that certain kinds of punishment can have effective long-term effects.

Primary and conditioned reinforcers.   Many positive reinforcers such as food, warmth, comfort, and sexual contact comprise most of our basic needs and have an important significance for development. Similarly, negative reinforcers such as pain, shock, lack of food, and extreme cold and heat also have an important impact on development. These positive and negative reinforcers are called *primary* because they are related to our basic biological functioning.

Children's behavior is complex and cannot be related merely to primary reinforcers. Skinner suggests that the wide variety of human behaviors can be accounted for by conditioned reinforcers. A *conditioned reinforcer* strengthens behavior by its being associated with a primary reinforcer. The affection, approval, and attention a child receives from his or her parents are examples of conditioned reinforcers when they are associated with existing primary reinforcers such as comfort, security, and attachment. Negative conditioned reinforcers might be a frown or a statement such as "I don't love you."

Shaping.   Inducing complex behavior through operant conditioning (*shaping*) is usually a fairly long process. The complete form of the desired behavior is not learned immediately. Each skill is usually reinforced bit-by-bit until the complete behavior is said to be shaped. A child's learning to eat with utensils develops in a series of steps. The parents may begin by praising the child for holding a spoon and dipping it into the food, next for picking up food in the spoon, and later for conveying the food in the spoon into his or her mouth. **Reinforcement must be provided for each step in a related sequence.** In some cases the sequence is a set of related but distinct activities. For example, a child may successfully pile building blocks into a cart. "That's very clever," says the teacher, who may then add, "You've got to be strong to pull all those blocks." This prompts the child to pull the blocks along in the cart, which gains praise. The child then builds a tower with the blocks—to much applause.

The child is likely to seek approval for other related sequences of actions, which results in achievement of various tasks with many parts. When sequenced actions are planned, for example, to achieve some objective such as solving a problem or to produce a design of shapes by cutting and pasting colored paper, each response in the chain of events generates consequences that affect the next response. The child's cutting is reinforced when he or she cuts out a correct shape, an accumulation of correct shapes reinforces the pasting, success with the steps in pasting reinforces completion of the design, and finally there is the reinforcement of approval from a parent, teacher, or peer (see Inset 6.1) for the finished article. These sequences of reinforced actions have been called *behavior chains* and are important to integrated sequences of performance. These are complex patterns of behaviors that, in Skinner's view, are made up of separate responses joined together in a chain. Each response in the chain affects the response that follows. For example, a child first learns to hold a pair of scissors correctly with two fingers and thumb, then to open and close the scissors, next to hold them correctly for cutting, and so on until a perfect hand-eye coordination and manipulation of the scissors results in correct, skillful cutting (Bijou, 1976; Keller & Schoenfeld, 1950; Munn et al., 1974).

Maintaining reinforcement. The best kind of reinforcement is continuous, especially to start desired behavior. But it is unusual to find children's behavior being constantly reinforced. Parents and teachers commend and applaud children's behavior intermittently. Skinner found that behavior which is only intermittently reinforced is more difficult to extinguish than continuously reinforced behavior. If parents want to set up a schedule for a child's getting ready for bed, it is probably better to continuously reinforce (reward) the desired behavior (washing, brushing teeth, putting on pajamas) at first. After the child has gotten into the habit, intermittent reward will serve to maintain it. On a negative note, if parents only respond once in awhile to a child's nagging, or some other unpleasant behavior, the child will persist in the behavior (Bijou & Baer, 1961).

R. Murray Thomas has summarized Skinner's view of child development as a process of learning increasingly complex behaviors as a result of consequences that follow the behaviors. The role of parents and teachers is twofold, "(1) to get children to try desirable acts and (2) to arrange consequences of children's acts so that desirable behavior is reinforced and undesirable behavior is extinguished" (1979, p. 390).

As reported by Lamb (Lamb, Easterbrook, & Holden, 1980), it has been known for a long time that young children can shape one another's behavior by using rewards and punishment. From research by social learning theorists in controlled settings, we know that young children instructed on how to use both rewards and punishments in connection with predetermined behaviors of other children effectively shape those behaviors (Hartup, 1970). More recently, research has focused on young children's reinforcement and punishment of one another's behaviors in naturalistic settings. Fagot (Fagot, 1977; Fagot & Patterson, 1969) has observed preschooler's reinforcement of sex-appropriate behavior and punishment of sex-inappropriate behavior. Lamb and Roopnarine (1979) have shown that reinforcing and punishing responses of preschool peers are very effective in shaping behavior. It does seem that besides parents and teachers, peers also influence one another's early socialization by these methods.

Lamb and others have further examined the types and effectiveness of reinforcement and punishment used by preschoolers (1980). Preschool children were observed in a preschool setting during free play. Observations were made of their sex-typed activities (Connor & Serbin, 1977; Fagot, 1977; Fagot & Patterson, 1969; Lamb & Roopnarine, 1979) and the ways in which peers responded to these behaviors. Male sex-typed activities included playing with cars and trucks, climbing, chasing, playing ball games, using tools, and engaging in loud, disruptive behavior. Female sex-typed activities included painting and drawing, playing with kitchen utensils, playing with dolls, playing "house," and sewing. Children's reinforcing responses to such activities were *praise* (expressing verbal approval), *joining in play,. imitating another child's play, watching another child play* (when the other child was aware of being watched), *agreeing with an activity*, and *expressing a desire to use another child's toy.* Children punished each other by *criticizing, ceasing to play with another child or threatening to do so, disapproving of another child's activity* (by comments addressed to a nearby child or adult), and *diverting* (offering a child another toy).

It was observed that preschoolers reinforced and punished one another's behavior in accord with conventional sex stereotypes in ways that proved very effective in shaping behavior. More important, both reinforcement and punishment worked best with sex-appropriate behavior. For example, when one boy refused to play with another boy in a ball game, the second boy did not stop playing. But when one boy showed disapproval of another boy's playing with "girls' toys," or refused to join in the game, the likely result was for the second boy to stop playing with those toys. Girls had similar effects on one another. Preschoolers already know the rules that affect sex-appropriate behavior and sex-inappropriate behavior and are willing to abide by these rules (Lamb & Roopnarine, 1979). Reinforcement and punishment appear to act as reminders.

Although the development of children's social behavior can be attributed to many factors, these studies show how effective reinforcement and punishment can be in shaping sex-stereotypic behavior and other types of social behavior, when used by preschool peers.

Inset 6.1
**Preschoolers Shape
One Another's
Behavior
by Reinforcement
and Punishment**

Phases of reinforcement. Skinner does not see development occurring in a sequence of stages, but as a continuous accumulation of conditioned behavior. However, with respect to the childhood years he has referred to "phases of environmental treatment" that should take the child's age into account (1948). He has suggested that from about age 2 to 4 years children's needs should be met as soon and completely as possible to ensure no frustration, anxiety, or fear. Toys should be designed to encourage perseverance in learning how to play with them. Adults must be both men and women so that the child's interactions are likely to "eliminate all Freudian problems" (1948, p. 120). From age 4 to 6 years children should assume increased responsibility for themselves and their environment and be conditioned to "good" behavior. The emphasis through these phases of development is on a continuous schedule of conditioning to produce expected ways of mental and social behavior.

Skinner has not specified particular behaviors to be conditioned during these preschool years. The assumption is that the culture, the good home, the good school know what behaviors are best—these are the ones to develop. This same assumption is made by others who have followed the Skinner tradition (e.g., Bijou & Baer, 1961, 1965).

Gesell's Stages of Development

In contrast to Skinner's behaviorist or environmentalist view of development, it is interesting to consider Gesell's diametrically opposed maturational view. From extensive and detailed studies of thousands of children at the Yale Clinic of Child Development, Gesell and his colleagues established behavior "norms" about children's behavior at various ages (Gesell, 1940; Gesell & Ilg, 1946). These gradients of growth were organized into ten categories ranging from motor development to philosophical outlook (see Table 6.1). Pediatricians and child psychologists still use these norms, which are called *aspects of development*.

Gesell believed that development is influenced primarily by *genetic* characteristics. The environment supports the child's growth, but does not directly influence development (Gesell & Ilg, 1946). All aspects of growth are governed by maturation. For example, he said that the child: "Sits before he stands; he babbles before he talks . . . he draws a circle before he draws a square . . . he is dependent on others before he achieves dependence on self. All his capacities . . . are subjects to the laws of growth" (Gesell & Ilg, 1943, p. 11). Charting this growth, year by year, Gesell noted that it appeared to proceed in *cycles of behavior*. When development was proceeding smoothly in the right direction, the child was said to be in a state of **equilibrium** (balanced behavior). When development was not proceeding smoothly, the child was said to be in a state of *disequilibrium* (behaviors being out of balance). For each of these cycles a number of stages were observed (see Table 6.2).

Table 6.1 Gesell's Aspects of Development

Category	Developmental Aspects
Motor characteristics	Physical activities Use of eyes and hands Eye-hand coordination
Personal hygiene	Sleeping Eating Evacuation of body wastes Bathing Dressing Maintaining good health
Emotional expression	Smiling, crying, and other expressions of temperament Aggression and assertiveness
Fears and dreams	Phobias Emotional disturbances Other abnormal behavior Identity Sex-role identity Self-concept Self-esteem and achievement
Interpersonal relationships	Mother-child relationships Child-child relationships Play interactions Peer group influences
Play and pastimes	Play and humor Games Pursuit of interests and hobbies Other forms of entertainment
School life	Acceptance of a school environment Behavior Achievement in school subjects
Ethical sense	Responsiveness to praise and blame Moral reasoning
Philosophical outlook	Understanding of time and space Use of language, thought, and communication Understanding of concepts such as *war*, *death*, and *god*

Source: Adapted from Gesell, A., & Ilg, F. L., *Child Development*. Copyright 1946 by Harper & Row. Reprinted by permission.

Table 6.2 Alternation of Stages of Equilibrium and Disequilibrium

Stages of Child Behavior

First Cycle Age	Second Cycle Age	Third Cycle Age	General Personality Trends	Quality of the Age
2	5	10	Smooth, consolidated	Better
2½	5½–6	11	Breaking up	Worse
3	6½	12	Rounded, balanced	Better
3½	7	13	Inwardized	Worse
4	8	14	Vigorous, expansive	Better
4½	9	15	Inwardized-outwardized, troubled, "neurotic"	Worse
5	10	16	Smooth, consolidated	Better

Source: Thomas, R. M. *Comparing Theories of Child Development.* (Adapted from Ilg, F. L., & Ames, L. B., 1955.) Copyright 1979 by Wadsworth Publishing Co. Reprinted by permission.

You will notice that within each cycle the stages alternate—better/worse. The terms *better* and *worse* sound judgmental, but they are terms that Gesell used (Ilg & Ames, 1955). The term *better stage* refers to a year in which the child seems to be well adjusted with respect to himself or herself and with other people. A *worse stage* is a year in which the child is confused, fearful, unhappy, or at odds with the world. Ilg and Ames (1955) describe the fifth and sixth years of life as follows:

1. Age 5. *Not a fearful age.* Less fear of animals and bogeymen. Concrete, down to earth fears such as bodily harm, falling down, and fear of certain animals.

2. Age 6. *Very fearful.* Fearful of all kinds of noises such as loud bangs, the ringing of a doorbell, shouting, and thunder. Fearful of ghosts and witches and of creatures hiding under the bed or in cupboards. Fearful of sleeping alone in the room, of not having a night-light when going to sleep (pp. 172–173).

Age 5 would be considered a stage of equilibrium (better) and age 6, a stage of disequilibrium (worse). In the better stages the child can be expected to move forward happily, while in the worse stages an imbalance in development occurs.

A principle of development that is strongly related to these cycles of behavior is *self-regulation,* coming to terms with the environment according to the pace of growth. Since maturation is believed to be working in its own quiet way—regulation by its own time clock—parents and teachers are advised to be patient, to take note of the child's attempts to come to terms with the environments, and to pay attention to the "norms" of growth as indicators of what behaviors to expect at various stages. Trying to teach a child too much too soon will endanger the child (Gesell, 1952).

Gesell's theory hinges on the principle of a maturation schedule. In the "bad" years there is little for a parent or teacher to do but remain patient until the next "good" phase. It is for this reason, however, that his theory has received most criticism. Evidence that suggests environmental influences are important is ignored and too much emphasis is placed on "norms," or average behavior. As Thomas (1979, p. 124) has pointed out, "No child is average or typical in every way. Each child has a pattern of characteristics that makes up his individuality. Group averages are of limited use in explaining a child's past, predicting his future status, and suggesting what should be done to guide his development."

Piaget's Preoperational Stage

Piaget proposed a ***preoperational development*** theory that emphasizes the importance of maturation to the process of development but that also recognizes the important role the environment plays in this process.

Before we discuss Piaget's stage of preoperational thinking, certain features of his theory of development must be described by way of introduction. We need to have some understanding of the concepts of **equilibrium,** *representation* (the **semiotic function**), **symbolism,** and **operation** in order to better understand the stage of preoperations and the stages that follow.

According to Piaget, development occurs because of *equilibration*. He uses this term in describing how a child adapts to his or her world and expresses it this way: "But always and everywhere adaptation is only accomplished when it results in a stable system, that is to say, when there is equilibrium between accommodation and assimilation" (1952, p. 7).

This means that the child is at that stage of development when he or she can accommodate (fit in) new knowledge to knowledge already in memory and, in doing so, make an adjustment to what is known so that it includes the new knowledge (assimilation). For example, the preschooler may already be quite competent at classifying objects according to some single property—these are all the red circles and these are all the yellow circles (in one sense there are two properties here, "circle" and "color," but, in classifying, the child has only to pay attention to color). The child may then notice a group of objects including circles that are both big and small, red and blue. In classifying these objects into big and small red and blue circles, the child is paying attention to both size and color at the same time. When the child "catches on" to this complex type of classifying, he or she assimilates the new knowledge as a kind of classifying and accommodates it to what he or she already knows about classifying because the procedure is similar to classifying objects by a single property. But in accommodating this new way of classifying to what is already known about classifying, the child extends (changes by accommodation) his or her knowledge about classifying to also include classifying objects according to two properties. This is a development change that shows a greater degree of balance (equilibrium) in the child's knowledge about classifying. Let us take a close look at what is involved in the process of equilibration as Piaget has described it and some of the problems with this aspect of development.

Equilibrium. Flavell (1977, p. 242) has suggested three major steps in this process. (1) Equilibration of thought (or action) is achieved at some level of development. You remember the example Bruner gave us of the development of flexing and grasping movements until the infant could smoothly reach and pick up an object. The final, coordinated movement is said to be a state of equilibrium—being in balance. (2) Cognitive *disequilibrium* then occurs. The child becomes aware of contradictory information that cannot be assimilated. For example, an object the child is about to reach for may be suddenly hidden. (3) When the child has developed the ability to retain an "image" of the object in memory, he or she uses reaching and grasping to *search* for the object. A new state of equilibrium has been reached. In moving toward equilibration new and more adequate ways of acting upon or thinking about objects and events are constructed (Piaget, 1970, pp. 237–249).

Flavell warns that there are problems with this concept of equilibration. For a child to achieve equilibrium it requires (1) attention to some contradictory information (the object is there to be grasped, then it is not there); (2) understanding the information to be contradictory, and therefore a problem to be solved—a reaction we cannot readily assume of the child; (3) responding positively to the contradiction as a problem and trying to solve it rather than ignoring the problem, refusing to have anything to do with it, or clinging to an initial belief (there is now no object); and (4) solving the problem (1979, p. 242). This is a complicated sequence of interactions, and it is difficult to believe that a young child will readily and always run through this sequence.

However, we must keep in mind that Piaget has chosen to describe development as occurring in this fashion. We saw that at the end of the sensorimotor period—dominated by actions upon objects and representation of objects by actions—the infant begins to represent objects and events in images and symbols. From Piaget's point of view this is an important transition stage, a period of disequilibrium that projects the infant into the stage of preoperations. One of the most important features of development during the preoperational stage, the catalyst as it were, to bring about eventual equilibration of preoperations is an improvement in the child's ability to represent and to symbolize objects and events. Let us take a brief look at Piaget's description of the representational process (the semiotic function) and symbolism as a form of representation.

The semiotic function.   *Semiotic* refers to the process of representation. The child learns to make one thing stand for or signify another. "Jacqueline inquired, 'Is that man a daddy?'—'What is a daddy?'—It's a man. He has lots of Luciennes and lots of Jacquelines" (Piaget, 1951).

Jacqueline can imagine the man as a daddy—with lots of children. She has a representation in her mind of "a daddy," which is evoked when she sees a man. We can see that Jacqueline is not yet sure exactly what a daddy is—it is a man, but are all men daddies? Piaget has called the representation of an object a *signifier*. The child either uses a word to label the object remembered ("I have a daddy"), or uses both words and pictures, or uses real objects. The objects or events themselves are called *significates*. One of the problems facing the child during this stage is to tie together, more and more accurately, the signifier with the significate.

Symbolism.   Tying together signifier and significate can occur during *symbolic play,* play that involves using something to represent something else. Piaget sees the role of play as the child's attempt to assimilate reality so that it can be imagined. For example, he observed Laurent's pretending to be a church, imitating the rigidity of the steeple and the sound of the bells (1951).

Symbolic representation develops in a particular kind of way. At first the child projects symbols onto objects. For example, the child may cuddle a doll and say, "hungry, hungry; cry, cry," and imitate the sound of crying. Later one object is made to stand for another; blocks of wood become cars, colored pebbles become candy, the child dressed in a mask becomes a monster. A more advanced form of representation occurs when the child imagines distant objects as, for example, in telling a story. "When we go to Grandma's, we can see a big lake from the porch. It has sailing boats—Oh!! and swans, sometimes." Sigel has referred to this process as "distancing" (e.g., 1970). It indicates a growing memory for objects no longer present and a means of symbolizing them in the mind.

Operations.   If we are to understand preoperations, we should understand first what an operation is. Brainerd (1978, pp. 96–99) has identified a number of characteristics of an *operation,* three of which are mentioned here. First, an operation is a *symbolic representation* of objects or events. One type of symbolic representation is a *class*. When we put objects together in a class because they share some common property, we need to symbolize that property in some way. Consider some of the objects we call fruit—apple, orange, pear, banana. When we choose to call these objects *fruit,* we must ignore their separate properties.

This process of putting objects together into a class or category is an operation—we call it *classifying*. If the child processes all kinds of objects into classes, he or she must have a symbolic representation of how to classify. Second, operations are governed by logical rules of organization, principally, inversion and compensation. We can add 2 to 3 to obtain 5 and inverse this operation by subtracting 2 from 5 to obtain 3 again. While *inversion* requires the same mental process to reverse an operation, *compensation* requires a different mental process to reverse an operation. For example, if we multiply 2 by 3 to yield 6, we can reverse this operation by dividing 6 by 3 to yield 2. Third, single operations always combine with other operations to form integrated systems called **structures of the whole.** By "structures of the whole," Piaget means that the various operations which characterize a given stage are interrelated. For example, it is supposed that as infancy draws to a close, those "schemas" (the precursors of operations) described in Chapter 4, reflexes, primary, secondary and tertiary reactions, and the beginnings of a symbol system, become interrelated to form an equilibrated structure of the whole called *sensorimotor intelligence.*

With the concepts of equilibrium, representation, symbolism operation, and structures of the whole in mind, let us now consider the stage of preoperations as it occurs when children are between 3 and 6 years of age (see Table 6.3). Piaget describes this stage as a time when children tend to think that everyone views the world in the way in which they do. At this point their language often lacks communication, and their ideas about causality and about the properties of objects are limited. The preoperational stage can be described from the points of view of limitations and of progress or traits as the next sections do.

The negative face of preoperations. Preoperational thinking is said to have several limitations. These constitute the negative face of preoperations. Piaget and his colleagues devised a task concerned with identity, in which a straight piece of wire is bent into an arc and then straightened again. The child is asked if, through the transformations from straight to bent to straight again, the wire remains the "same wire" (Piaget, Sinclair, & Vinh-Bang, 1968, pp. 5–20). Three-year-olds constantly maintained it was the same, but they did not appear to pay much attention to the change in the wire's shape. Four-year-olds frequently insisted it was not the same, referring to the changes. The majority of 5- and 6-year-olds insisted it was the same wire, but they assumed its length did not stay the same as it was bent; as the wire bent, many of these children thought it got shorter. Rigidity of thought is a typical limitation of the spontaneous thought of children at this age. It is rigid since they do not seem readily able to consider a number of properties and their changing relationships (e.g., to know that although the property of shape is changing, nevertheless, the property of length remains constant).

You can leave on a journey from home to college, spend a semester there, and later return home; a group of boys and a group of girls interacting together become one group of children but can become two groups again; five cents can

Table 6.3 The Stage of Preoperations

Cognitive Contents	Examples of Related Behavior
Egocentrism	Children think that everyone views and experiences the world in the same way that they do.
Causality	Children's thinking is *transductive:* 1. They use different arguments to explain similar cause-and-effect relationships. For example, a large boat floats because it is large; a needle floats because it is small. 2. They link unrelated objects and events: the bike moves . . . "because I sit on it; because it's a nice day; because it likes to." 3. They have difficulty with "why" type questions referring to cause and effect as though they were one and the same thing: "Why can we see the sunshine?" " 'Cos it's hot." "Can we see the sunshine when there are clouds?" "No! 'Cos there's clouds." 4. They believe all objects and events are created for a purpose: God plants stones to make mountains grow. 5. They believe that many "lifeless" objects are, in fact, *alive,* especially when they move. So clouds, running water, flying kites, moving cars, and buses all have "life."
Language and Communication	Children's language is lacking in communication. 1. They often talk to themselves for long periods of time (monologue). 2. They often rehearse aloud the same statement (repetition). 3. They hold conversations with others but without taking into account what the other person is saying.
Identity	Children have difficulty understanding that certain properties of objects remain *constant* especially when they notice other properties of those objects changing.

Preschoolers sometimes have difficulties understanding changing relationships between objects. They will agree, for example, that two pipe-cleaners are the same length, but insist that when one pipe-cleaner is bent into a circle it is shorter than the straight pipe-cleaner. (Photos courtesy of the author)

become seven cents by adding two cents, and then can become five cents again by subtracting two cents. These are all examples of **reversibility.** The preoperational child cannot deal with these thoughts. However, it will be apparent that the preschool child does know, for example, that having left home and arriving at the preschool, later there will be a journey back home again; that having spilled juice on the table at snack time, getting a cloth and wiping it up makes the tabletop clean again; that blocks can be built into a tower and knocked down again. Is not this reversibility? Of course it is. Why then do certain aspects of reversibility confuse the preschool child? In part this may be a memory problem—keeping in mind concepts of time and space in long drawn-out sequences can provide too big a memory load, so the young child may "lose sight" of the reversibility of certain action sequences. The child also seems to have problems keeping in mind a complete class and its parts at one and the same time. It may be easy to recognize a set of 3 objects and a set of 2 objects arranged close to each other. But when they are combined to make a set of 5 objects, the first two sets "disappear." The preschooler may find it difficult to think of 5 children and of 3 boys and 2 girls at the same time.

Here is another example involving amount that has to do with the **conservation** of quantity. You can see that in Figure 6.1, the two beakers marked *A* and *B* are of equal shape and cubic capacity and contain equal quantities (amounts) of liquid. The child is asked three questions: Does this beaker *(A)* have the same amount of liquid, does it have more liquid, or does it have less liquid in it than this beaker *(B)* does? The child is very likely to agree that there is the same amount of liquid in beakers *A* and *B*. The liquid from either beaker *A* or *B* is then poured into beaker *C* (a taller and narrower beaker than *A* and *B*). The same question is asked. Usually, the child responds that there is more liquid in beaker *C.* Do you realize why the child makes this error? *More* is associated with *higher.* The child is having problems paying attention to the property of amount, which is what is needed to solve the problem. As the shape of the liquid changes, the child incorrectly assumes the amount changes also.

A final example involves what Piaget has called *function*—a simple association between one thing and another. The young child may associate the weather's getting colder when leaves begin to drop from the trees during fall; or that the butter gets soft and melts if it is placed in hot sunlight; or that the light comes on when the light switch is operated. Changes in one thing are associated with changes in another. But the changes that are observed and understood are usually qualitative. Quantitative **functional relationships** are much more difficult.

Figure 6.2 is a diagram of an experiment that Piaget and his colleagues constructed to study the child's understanding of a *quantitative* functional relationship (Piaget, Grize, Szeminska, & Vinh-Bang, 1968, p. 62).

A string $(A + A')$ is attached to a spring. The string is led over a pulley and attached to a weight holder *(W)*. Different weights can be attached to the weight holder. Any weight attached at *W* causes the spring to stretch and the string to move over the pulley. This has the effect of reducing the length of the string at

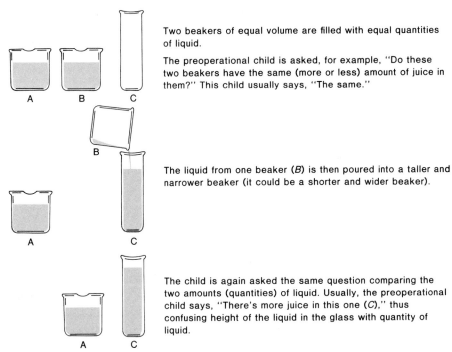

Two beakers of equal volume are filled with equal quantities of liquid.

The preoperational child is asked, for example, "Do these two beakers have the same (more or less) amount of juice in them?" This child usually says, "The same."

The liquid from one beaker (*B*) is then poured into a taller and narrower beaker (it could be a shorter and wider beaker).

The child is again asked the same question comparing the two amounts (quantities) of liquid. Usually, the preoperational child says, "There's more juice in this one (*C*)," thus confusing height of the liquid in the glass with quantity of liquid.

Figure 6.1 Conservation of quantity.

A and increasing the length at *A'* by equivalent amounts. These amounts will be recorded on the scales 1 and 2. The background at *A* is green and at *A'* red. This allows easier reference to be made to the length of string in these two segments.

Children of different ages were asked to predict what would happen to the various parts of this apparatus if weights were attached at *W*. They were also asked to describe and explain the changes they observed. Children aged 4 to 6 years could describe some functional relationships—putting a weight on the end of the string makes the string longer, as *A'* gets longer, *A* gets shorter. But the idea that an increase of length at *A* or that a movement of the pointer at 1 will be exactly equal to a movement of the pointer at 2, or vice versa (as measured by the scales), is not readily understood. The young children were not able to work out the reversibility of the action, and such *non-reversibility of thought* is a typical limitation of preoperational thinking.

Centering refers to the young child's tendency to concentrate on single objects or limited details of objects to the exclusion of other important information in a situation. You can imagine how such behavior limits a child's thinking. In the liquid task, by concentrating on first one property, the tall beaker, or on another, the wide beaker, the child may simply translate either tall or wide into the idea

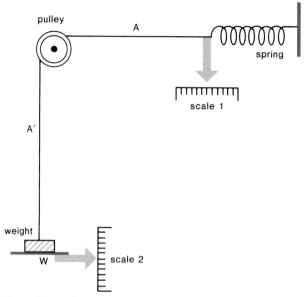

Figure 6.2 A functional relationship problem. Adding weight at *W* causes the spring to stretch. This results in a shortening of the string at *A*, which can be measured on *scale 1,* and an equivalent lengthening of the string at *A*¹, which can be measured on *scale 2.* (Source: Piaget, J., Grize, J. B., Szeminska, A., and Vinh-Bang. *Epistemologie et Psychologie de la Fonction.* Copyright 1968 by Presses Universitaires de France. Reprinted by permission.)

of *more* liquid. So the compensation of taller, but thinner—wider, but shorter— is not considered. Such thinking requires *decentering,* concentrating on more than one.

The preoperational child is not expected to be able to consider relationships among several objects and generalize a category (thinking inductively) or the reverse (thinking deductively). Rather, the child proceeds to think from particular to particular without establishing logical relationships. This is called **transductive reasoning.** For example, the child might argue that *A* is like *B* so *B* is like *A*. The black dog (*A*) barks and frightens me. Here is a black dog (*B*). It will bark and frighten me. Another example is to reason that *A* causes *B*, so *B* causes *A*. If Mary tidies her room (*A*), Mother will take her to the shop for some candy (*B*). If Mother takes Mary to the shop for some candy (*B*), Mary will tidy her room (*A*). Adults sometimes make similar mistakes. They come under such names as prejudice, bigotry, and shopping errors (such as "large items are packaged in large boxes, so large boxes must contain large items.")

Another example of the result of transductive reasoning is the construction of **graphic collections,** groupings by visual appearance. Let us suppose the young

Figure 6.3 A grouping of geometric shapes.

(a)

The child might say, "The *white* triangle goes with another *triangle*, and this is another *stripey one*, and next is another *circle*, and then a *white one* . . . ," and so on, constantly changing the criteria for placing the geometric shapes together.

(b)

Another form of graphic collection is the use of objects to represent a shape—such as a truck.

Asked to put the geometric shapes (fig. 6.6) into groups so that they go together in some special way, the preoperational child is likely to construct some form of *graphic collection* rather than *logical classes*.

Figure 6.4 Graphic collections.

preshool child is playing with a variety of geometric shapes (see Figure 6.3). The child is invited to put them together in some way, or more explicitly, to put them into groups so they go together in some special way. The result is likely to be some form of collection as shown in Figure 6.4 (*a*) and (*b*) rather than as logical classes.

You can see in Figure 6.4(*a*) that the child's reasoning might be—the triangle (striped) goes with the triangle (gray); and the stripes (circle) with the stripes (triangle); and the circle (big) with the circle (small and striped); and so on. The child keeps *changing the criterion* for grouping and so never forms a class. Figure 6.4(*b*) shows the child has constructed a shape, representing a truck. This is another type of graphic collection. Piaget says that such pre-classification activities are characteristic of this stage and show the limitations of transductive reasoning.

Sometimes the young child tells stories when making these graphic collections, adding to the array of objects fantasy figures in imaginative play (See Inset 6.2.) The child of preschool age is certainly much more involved in the here and now and spends much time in sharpening and practicing the skills acquired since infancy. Playfulness figures largely in many activities. Thus, in a spontaneous fashion, the child is more likely to construct a truck from shapes or, like an artist with nose close up to the canvas, to create arrays from objects that merge from shape into color into size.

The positive face of preoperations.   Transductive reasoning along with centering, irreversibility, and rigidity constitutes the negative face of preoperations. These preoperations are only negative in the sense that they lack the qualities of logical operations. What are the positive aspects of preoperational thought? They include egocentrism, causality, and identity. It is in these three areas that important development changes are expected to occur. In one sense these areas are negative—they restrain logical thought. But in moving away from inaccurate and illogical expressions of cause-and-effect relationships, for example, the child is making attempts to describe and explain actual cause-and-effect relationships.

Egocentrism means concentrating on "me." The young child tends to see the world "just as it looks to me." There is an inability to take another person's point of view. You may have noticed that adults sometimes act in much the same way, although the reasons are likely to be different! (We will consider adolescent egocentrism later.) Seeing the world from just one point of view obviously limits an understanding of it. Suppose two 3-year-olds, Jim and Mary, are sitting on opposite sides of a table in the center of which is a hollow pumpkin. The pumpkin has eyes, nose, and mouth cut in the side facing Jim. There is also a lighted candle inside the pumpkin (see Figure 6.5). Jim is asked to describe what view he thinks Mary has of the pumpkin. It is very likely that he will claim she can see a "funny face" and the light from the candle. A 6-year-old faced with this problem is more likely to realize that there will be a different view of the pumpkin from the opposite side of the table.

The social world of a preschool in which children learn to share, to control their aggressions by taking into account another person's feelings, and to help one another solve problems seems to help young children develop other points of view, both with respect to the affective social world and the intellectual physical world.

There are three types of cause-and-effect relationships that preoperational children at first have great difficulty dealing with and only gradually come to a better understanding of—finalism, artificialism, and animism (Piaget, 1929).

I sat one day with a 4-year-old. He had shown no predisposition to engage in classifying objects. Various geometric shapes, like those in Figure 6.3, were scattered over the tabletop. He was constructing typical graphic collections and carrying on a monologue, occasionally speaking to me. My intention was to find out if he could classify the shapes. I began by asking if he could make groups from the objects. He ignored me. I asked if I could use some of the shapes. "Sure," he said. I placed two similar shapes together and asked, "What have I got here?" He looked, but made no comment. A triangle was selected and placed at one side of the table away from the other shapes. "What is that shape called?" I asked. "A triangle," he replied. "Can you see another one like that?" I asked. He pushed another triangle in my direction. I placed it with the other. "What do we have here?" Straightaway he replied, "Two triangles." The game continued briefly with a square and a circle—to which he added a square and a couple of circles, disinterestedly. He also continued constructing collections of diverse shapes, a train, and a clown. I suppose he thought he should get more involved with me, because he said, "I'll make you a *group*." He selected a large square, then another of a different color and placed it on top of the first. Ah! I thought—he's really going to show me he can classify shapes. But the next was a circle, topped by a triangle, another circle, and finally two squares. "That's for you," he said. "And what is it?" I asked. "A deli sandwich of course," he replied; and he told me about going to a restaurant with his family the previous evening.

I was sure he could quite easily do some classifying; but how much more interesting for him to make pictures and sandwiches. This raises the question of competence versus performance. For example, does a child's performance always accurately reflect the child's competence? This is a difficult question to answer. There is evidence to show that preschool children can achieve levels of performance not usually expected at this age (Lawton, Hooper, Saunders, & Roth, 1978; Lawton & Ershler, in preparation; Lawton & Fowell, 1978). Preschool children can be helped to understand logical relationships among objects and to construct logical concepts. For example, 3-year-olds can quite easily acquire the concept of all the round objects or all the square objects, and can understand that an object can be at one and the same time both round and red, both a bird and an animal. This does not deny children the choice of also constructing "graphic collections"—we could call them patterns or collages or artistic expression. The child may use geometric shapes to represent such logical concepts as "roundness" or random patterns or the pictorial shape of a clown.

Piaget describes the child's inclination to insist on a definite cause (often unrelated) for every occurrence as finalistic thinking or **finalism.** The preoperational child answers why, what, where, and how questions with finalism but has a special difficulty with why questions. Why questions can refer to either cause or effect, but preoperational children fail to distinguish between the two. Two questions were asked of a 3-year-old who was building a tower from wooden blocks: "Why did you build the tower so high?" and "Why did the tower fall over?" The first question refers to the purpose or effect, the second to the cause. To both

Figure 6.5 An egocentric view. When the young 3-year-old boy is asked to describe what he believes is the young girl's view of the pumpkin, he describes the view from *his* side of the table.

questions the child replied, "Cos it will fall over." Further questioning made it clear that the child meant "Tall towers of wooden blocks fall over." The child knows that from experience and is relating a fact, not indicating clearly either an effect or cause and certainly not distinguishing between the two types of questions.

The child's answer is also closely related to Piaget's concept of artificialism. **Artificialism** assumes nothing happens by chance or "naturally"; flowers grow only because somebody planted them, birds fly because God made them. The preoperational child believes that events occur according to some rule, so the tower of wooden blocks falls over because that is what is supposed to happen.

Last, preoperational children often believe that certain inanimate objects actually live, which Piaget refers to as animistic thinking or **animism.** For example, preschool children say the sun gives light because it is alive, a car moves because it is alive, and clouds, too. Toward the end of this stage the child begins to discriminate between animate and inanimate objects but still makes errors with respect to certain objects; a bird is alive because it flies, a bike is not alive because we make it move, but a stream is alive because it flows *all* the time (Piaget, 1929).

You are familiar with such optical illusions as those illustrated in Figure 6.6. Optical illusions are cases of mistaken identity. Conjuring tricks, disguises, and camouflage are attempts to confuse us about the identity of objects—but we are not always fooled. As a person walks away from us into the distance, we do not

A horse of another color?

When does an ellipse become a circle?

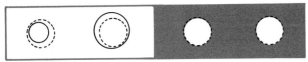

Which dotted circle is larger?

Which line is longer? Actually, both are the same length.

Do you see a vase or two faces?

Do you see a square?

Figure 6.6 Optical illusions.

believe he is growing smaller. When we view a round dinner plate from the side, it appears to be elliptical, but we know it remains round. When we see a ball of clay flattened into the shape of a pancake, we would insist there is still the same amount of clay. Preoperational children have difficulty understanding that in many cases an object's *identity* remains the same in the face of certain changes or transformations. They seem to lose contact with some crucial property that defines the identity of the object, which does not change, and focus instead on some property irrelevant to the object's identity, which is changing. Preoperational children are distracted by and center on the change, forgetting or refusing to still take into account the unchanging and identity-fixing property.

According to Piaget (1968), egocentrism, causality, and concepts of identity develop slowly during the preoperational period. We will see in Chapter 7 that when preoperational children are provided with certain types of experiences and instruction, they appear to come to a logical understanding of such concepts much sooner than might be expected according to Piaget's theory.

Since representation plays such a crucial role in intellectual development during the preschool years, we should consider Bruner's belief that representation is the key to intellectual development.

Bruner's View of Representation

It was mentioned in Chapter 4 that Bruner believes early motor action in infancy is governed by "wired-in" arrangements in the nervous system, that is, genetic traits. Very quickly, however, the development of movement, perception, and thinking then becomes dependent on *techniques* (Bruner, 1964) that are acquired and that aid intellectual (and social) development during early childhood.

Techniques of representation. The fact that a child can move is due, in large measure, to maturation. But the infant playing with a suspended mobile, the child playing peekaboo and later hide-and-seek, the preschool child selecting blocks and arranging them into a tower are all examples of actions with a goal in mind. This is going beyond maturation. Action becomes "skilled and patterned acts." For example, the young child gets to know that things happen in sequence. To build a tower from wooden blocks requires an understanding of spatial arrangements of objects so that they will balance. Such acts also require selective perceptual organization. The child learns to represent the physical environment, cause-and-effect relationships, questions and statements, and so on, through the symbols of language. Therefore, representation of the environment is not just simply a business of selecting a mode of **representation—enactive, iconic,** or **symbolic**—it also requires techniques of using representation such as the correct use of language.

Building a tower from wooden blocks requires an understanding of the spatial arrangements of objects. (Photo by Robert Eckert/ EKM-Nepenthe)

Integration of actions and thoughts.　Bruner, like Piaget, considers that the organization of thinking and reasoning is a crucial matter in development. Whereas Piaget conceived of two processes of organization, assimilation and accommodation, Bruner describes organization as a single process termed *integration*. Integration is the means whereby actions and thoughts are organized into higher-order categories. This is another way of describing "classifying." Single objects are the *lowest order*. A group of objects that form a class—such as children—is a higher order of objects. The child learns that those creatures with wings, that can fly, pick food with their beaks, and have funny three-toed feet, are called *birds;* and that those objects of various sizes, colors, and shapes that travel around the street on four wheels are called *cars;* and that helping Mom back a cake, helping set out snacks at the preschool, helping another child in an activity are all called *helping.* Birds, cars, and helping, in these instances, are higher-order categories. These acts of integration make possible the use of larger and larger units of information. These can be used more and more efficiently for solving problems (Bruner, 1964).

Effects of culture on representaton. Bruner considers that the techniques of representation the child is acquiring and the ability to integrate bits of information are very strongly influenced by *conventions* (social rules) already established by the culture the child is born into and transmitted through symbol systems that are also governed by rules. Why is this so important? There is a very practical reason. To live in a community and to be a part of it, we must abide by certain conventions (social rules). When we wish to communicate, to share our thinking, to share in the solving of problems, we use symbols such as language, which is also governed by rules (for example, grammar and syntax). Social rules, language, thinking rules, problem-solving rules are all shared.

Representation has evolved in a similar fashion in all cultures. It is transmitted to the child and acquired by the child sequentially in its three forms—enactive, iconic, and symbolic. "Their appearance in the life of a child is in that order, each depending upon the previous one for its development, yet all remaining more or less intact throughout life" (Bruner, 1964, p. 2). The ways in which representation is used are also similar. However, there are cultural differences in the levels to which representation is developed. For example, some cultures, such as Bushpeople of South Africa, have a less-advanced use of language (symbolic representation) than we have in the United States. There are also differences in the knowledge acquired by and transmitted through representation. For example, different cultures have different social rules and conventions and different artifacts with different uses and functions, all of which can be represented by enactive, iconic, and symbolic representation.

Development of representation. How does the development of representation occur? In early childhood Bruner expects that more use will be made of enactive and iconic representation. Although by age 2 the infant has a rudimentary understanding and use of language, extensive use of symbolic representation is not expected to occur until much later. Bruner has conducted a number of experiments to shed some light on the development of representation. In one experiment Bruner and Kenney (1966) examined the way in which children aged 5 to 7 years attempted to solve a problem of double classification. They used a set of glasses that could be arranged in a matrix as shown in Figure 6.7. The glasses were described to the children, and they were shown how the glasses had been placed to form the matrix. The glasses were scrambled, and each child was invited to put the glasses back in their original places (*reconstruction*). The glasses were then scrambled again. This time the glass that had been in the southwest corner of the matrix was placed in the northeast corner. Each child was asked to construct the matrix "something like it was before," but to leave the one glass where it had been placed (*transposition*). All the children found it easy to reconstruct the matrix. On the second problem almost all the 7-year-olds succeeded in constructing the transposed matrix, but most 5-year-olds failed to do so. What are the reasons for these similarities and differences?

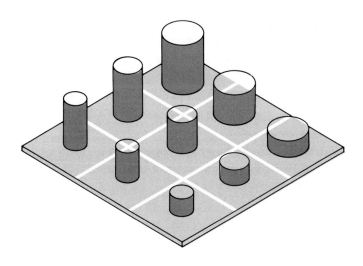

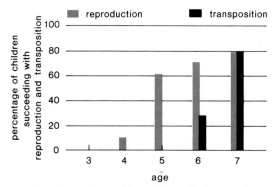

Figure 6.7 The matrix problem. The cylinders can be *ordered* by both *width* and *height* (seriation), and can be *classified* by both *width* and *height*. In this matrix there is a relationship between seriation and classification. (Source: Bruner, J. S., Oliver, R. R., and Greenfield, P. M. *Studies in Cognitive Growth.* Copyright 1966 by John Wiley & Sons, Inc. Reprinted by permission of Jerome S. Bruner.)

For the first problem all children seemed to rebuild the matrix as though remembering a copy of the original—an iconic image. For the second problem that is what the 5-year-olds still tried to do. Of course, they did not end up with a transposed matrix. The 7-year-olds paused, talked to themselves about the problem, and checked the position of each beaker with the others around according to shape and size. The second problem required the use of rules of reckoning, not simply copying. Iconic representation was no longer sufficient—the older children used symbolic representation. Bruner has suggested that it is around ages 4 to 5 years that language (symbolic representation) becomes increasingly important to thinking. Not all theorists hold this view of the importance of language for intellectual development.

Development of Language

The study of language itself is called *linguistics.* In recent years linguists have become interested in the relationship between knowing the rules of language and processes of thinking. At the same time psychologists have shown a growing interest in how language is acquired and used in communication. Specialists combining both interests have become known as **psycholinguists.** Roger Brown (1970, 1973), a well-known developmental psycholinguist, has focused his attention on how children select words and make up sentences with them.

Sentence Construction

At age 2 the child has a vocabulary of about 50 words. At age 6 this has grown to between 8,000 and 14,000 words (Carey, 1977). There is also a steady increase in the number of words used in sentences. The duos at the beginning of this period (allgone—ball, me—milk) will have been extended to three-word sentences by age 2, four-to-five word sentences by age 4, and six-to-eight word sentences by ages 5 to 6 (Miller & Chapman, 1981).

This rapid development in vocabulary and language use is remarkable. Just consider the conversation of two children, Christine (18 months) and Brian (5 years), playing in the bathtub (Williams, Hooper, & Natalicio, 1977).

Christine: "Oooh. It's still wet, 'cause still fall down. Oooh wee, I got one dry Brian. Eee I got, it's his nose go dop!"

Brian: "Dolphin, dolphin, dolphin. . . . Look at the dolphins right at the spot in the air. Dolphin, don't! Don't! No, no dolphin! . . . Oooh, I'm on the 'freet' board. What am I doing on the 'freet' board? . . . Now it's the time for the dolphin contest. She's been talking. She's gotta get down. She has to get the toughies. She got a teamwork. She got really does me too. Got two gangs . . . is what he's got."

How can the development of sentence production be charted? Brown (1973) recorded the speech of three children, Adam, Eve, and Sarah from 18 months to 6 years and discovered regularities in the development of word use and language construction during this period. The earliest sentences are termed **telegraphic sentences** because the child tends only to use essential words (just as an adult does when composing a telegram): *I see ball, I go upstairs, it raining.* Brown points out that although some words are omitted, the essential words are always in the correct order, which suggests these children were already aware of a rule for constructing sentences (Brown, 1973). The children then began to use prepositions such as *in* and *on*. By age 6 conjunctions and words for comparison, such as *more, less, big, little,* were being used. However, although children of this age understand each word, they do not yet seem to be able to use them for the purposes of comparison. Donaldson and Balfour (1968) have found that a child will use "more" and "less" to mean the same thing. Another feature of development is the achievement of using a **complex sentence.** For example, "That my ice cream, *and* that yours." "He thinks he doesn't have what I have."

As children improve in using rules of grammar, they get better at dealing with questions and using negation. Whereas at age 2 the child asks in a simplistic way, "Read dat?" "No Mommy?" at age 4 the child uses *what, where, who,* and *why* questions such as "What is that bag for?" and "Why put dust in my hair?" (Brown & Bellugi, 1964). We should keep in mind, however, that in terms of preoperations the child's thinking, reasoning, and intention when using such questions can be expected to be quite limited.

Language and Thought

We do not yet know exactly why language develops the way it does or what the relationship between language and thought is. In Chapter 4 we discussed and compared the views of a number of theorists. Let us take a further brief look at a cognitive-structuralist and learning theory view of the relationship between language and thought.

The cognitive structuralist Piaget believes that preoperational language serves two purposes. The child uses it for the purpose of self-stimulation (*egocentric* purpose) and also to communicate with others (*social* purpose) (Piaget, 1955). There are three forms of egocentric speech. When the child talks aloud to himself or herself, this is called a *monologue.* There may be other children or adults present, but the child does not direct speech toward them. The young child sometimes repeats (rehearses) a sentence over and over again. This form is called *repetition.* A third form of egocentric speech is called **collective monologue.** This occurs when the child talks to another person but does not listen to what the other person has to say. It is quite funny to listen to two preschool children jabbering away, without any apparent relationship between what each is saying!

Piaget found that whereas the 3-year-old child's speech is almost totally egocentric, virtually all the speech of the 7-year-old is social. He assumed, therefore, that there occurred a gradual shift from egocentric to socialized speech during the period of preoperations, due in part to mental development and in part to social interactions among the preschool child, adults, and peers.

Bandura, a social-learning theorist (1965, 1969), believes children can learn verbal codes and rules by listening to and imitating others (1971). The idea that children imitate others seems to be common sense. Accepting this situation, parents and teachers often correct children's utterances. But imitation cannot explain all language acquisition. For example, if a child about 3 years old is asked to repeat a sentence such as, "I can see the ball," the child is likely to respond, "I see ball" (a telegraphic sentence) (Brown, 1973).

In another investigation, Brown and Hanlon (1970) asked parents if they approved or disapproved when their children made errors such as saying "mices" or "swammed." They discovered that the parents made no attempt to correct such errors. These children eventually acquired correct grammar. Although Brown does not say so, it may well be that as children grow older, parents do more correcting or children become more attentive to adult expressions and make more effort to correctly imitate what they hear. More research is needed to understand the effects of imitation on language development.

Language and Culture

Do children acquire language in the same way the world over? No matter what the culture, the first word all children utter is a noun, a proper name, or a personal/social word such as "Hi." The purpose is usually to identify some object. Similarly, the emergence of the duo sentence occurs about the same time for all children. Slobin (1977) has identified a number of other features about language development and structure that are about the same for all children. These include

1. Children of preschool age learn their native language (or more than one language!) in much the same way.

2. A child soon realizes that speech is made up of discrete words and that these can be combined. Children make the combinations themselves.

3. All languages have a grammar. All children learn grammatical rules. "The first grammatical devices are the most basic tools . . . intonation, word order, and inflection."

4. When a child begins to use more complex sentences than the duo, the extra words fill in the gaps that were implicit in the shorter sentences. At the three-word stage, there are limits. The child can say, "Mama drink coffee" or "Drink hot coffee," but *not* "Mama drink hot coffee."

5. The basic rules of grammars emerge regularly and uniformly across different languages.

6. Young children often learn correct word endings (e.g., *come, fell, break*) at first by rote. Later, as they acquire an understanding of general rules (e.g., learning to use **ed** to indicate the past tense), they lapse into errors *(comed, felled, breaked)*. The child seeks regularities, is oblivious to exceptions, and only slowly sorts out all the rules (e.g., Bellugi, 1970).

7. Cross-cultural studies have shown that the immense amount of child-mother verbal interaction in middle-class American homes is a "relatively rare social situation in the world." In many other cultures mothers speak very little to their young children—it is children who speak to children. Does this matter? Apparently not. The rate and course of language development is remarkably similar for all cultures.

8. For some considerable time it was thought that poor black children had "verbal deficits." In most urban ghettos black children get most of their speech experiences with other children rather than parents. However, it has been found that these children learn rules of language as quickly as white middle-class children (Baratz & Baratz, 1970). Black English has a highly structured grammar system. Black children "have the same basic vocabulary . . . and use the same logic as anyone else who learns to speak and understand English" (Labov, 1970).

Measures of Intelligence

So far in this chapter we have discussed intellectual organization and its development. Some psychologists, Piaget, for example, refer to the results of organizing intellectual abilities as "intelligence". Psychologists also discuss *intelligence* as a separate term, and there have been various definitions of it. Burt (1955, p. 162) referred to intelligence as "innate, general cognitive ability," and Wechsler thought of intelligence as "the capacity of the individual to understand the world about him and . . . to cope with its challenges" (1975, p. 139). Guilford (1967) described intelligence as a structure of 120 factors categorized in three dimensions called *operations* (e.g., cognition, memory), *products* (e.g., classes, relations), and *contents* (e.g., figural, symbolic).

A child's intelligence is often inferred from his or her performance on an intelligence test as indicated by a score called the **intelligence quotient** (IQ). Items in intelligence tests are supposed to represent "intellectual" behavior of children and adults—at least in Western society. The most prized intellectual abilities in Western society are language and math skills—and these tests do measure quite accurately such skills, along with memory and problem-solving skills. They are also good predictors of academic achievement. This is not really surprising. Academic achievement is related to skills in language, math, memory, and problem solving!

There are a number of versions of intelligence tests developed by different psychologists. These tests are widely used to measure, for example, a person's "level of intelligence," to diagnose the possibility of learning difficulties, and to predict an expected level of school achievement. Two of the most widely used intelligence tests are the Stanford-Binet and the Wechsler Preschool and Primary Scale of Intelligence (WPPSI).

Two Standard Tests

Binet and Simon developed a test for the French government in the early 1900s as a measure to identify mentally retarded children (Terman & Merrill, 1937). This test has been revised a number of times and is now known as the Stanford-Binet test. The revised version, which measures both verbal and non-verbal ability, can be given to individuals from age 2 through adulthood. For example, in one item, the preschool child is shown a number of objects (toy car, dog, etc.). The adult who is giving the test asks the child to name each item. A screen is then placed between the child and the objects and the adult removes one of the objects. When the screen is taken away, the adult asks the child which object is missing (which object is hidden). The child has to give the correct answer to get credit. The complete test measures attention, comprehension, memory, and so forth, but the child is usually given an overall score.

Binet chose and arranged items in his test according to the concept of *mental age*. For example, items passed by about 50 percent of all 6-year-olds are placed in one set, those by 50 percent of all 7-year-olds in another set, and so forth. If a 6-, 7-, and 10-year-old child each gets the same number of correct items up to and including the set for the average 6-year-old, then all three are said to have a mental age of 6. The IQ score is computed by dividing the mental age score (MA) by the child's chronological age (CA) and multiplying by 100.

$$IQ = \frac{MA}{CA} \times 100$$

In the above example the 6-year-old has an IQ of 100, which is an average performance, the 7-year-old an IQ of about 84, and the 10-year-old an IQ of 60—which is diagnosed as *retarded* intelligence.

David Wechsler designed a test of adult intelligence in 1939. This was followed by a version for school-age children (WISC) in 1949, and one for preschool and primary-age children (4 to 6½ years old) in 1967 (WPPSI). The WPPSI has two sections, verbal and performance. Thus three IQ scores can be obtained: verbal IQ, performance IQ, and a general IQ.

Two other tests are often used with preschool (and elementary school) children. The Ravens Progressive Matrices and Peabody Picture Vocabulary Tests. The RPMT is supposed to measure underlying cognitive competence (an example is given in Figure 6.8).

As you might imagine, the PPVT measures the child's vocabulary. Children's responses, as for the vocabulary items of the Stanford-Binet, are considered predictors of general intelligence. A sample item is shown in Figure 6.9. The child is asked to look at the four pictures. The adult who is giving the test says a word, and the child merely has to point to whichever illustration the word seems to fit.

IQ and Culture

Children from lower-class and economically disadvantaged minority groups obtain lower IQ scores than middle-class children. Also, black children in the United States have IQ's about 15 points lower than do white children. Jensen (1969, 1977) has argued that genetic factors account for about 80 percent of intelligence and that environmental influences on IQ are small. Jensen's argument that the differences in IQ between ethnic groups can be attributed to heredity has caused considerable controversy. An alternative point of view is that low levels of performance on IQ tests may reflect the expectations and traditions of a particular culture or subculture.

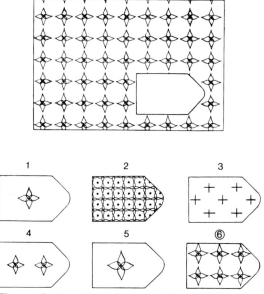

Figure 6.8 Items from the Raven Progressive Matrices Test. The child is asked to point to one of the six numbered choices of pattern that best fits the space in the larger pattern above. (The correct choice number is circled.) (Source: Raven, J. C. *Raven Progessive Matrices Test.* Copyright 1962 by A. P. Watt, Ltd. Reprinted by permission.)

Douglas (1967), for example, found that if there was a higher proportion of middle-class children than lower-class in a school group, the lower-class children's level of achievement was about the same as that of children from the middle-class—much higher than the average level of achievement in a completely lower-class group! The reverse was also found to be true. Golden and Birns (1976) have demonstrated that differences in performance on IQ tests are more likely to be related to social class than to race. In the United States many black children come from disadvantaged environments. The IQ test items are phrased in white middle-class language and are related to middle-class experiences and values thus favoring white middle-class children. It has been noted that black children learn a different set of rules for "black English" and a different style of thought (Scarr-Salapatek, 1971). Therefore, differences in IQ between black and white children seem to be related to differences in cultural and environmental

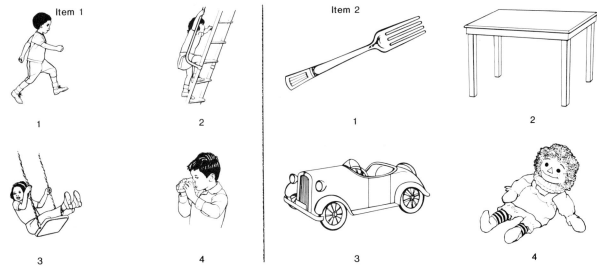

Figure 6.9 Examples of items from the Peabody Picture Vocabulary Test. For each item, the child is asked to look at all four pictures. The examiner says a word and the child is asked to point to (or say the number of) the picture that best illustrates the meaning of the word. The word for item 1 might be *climbing,* and the word for item 2, *fork.* (Source: Dunn, L. M. and Dunn, L. M. Copyright 1981 by American Guidance Service. Reprinted by permission.)

experiences (Anastasi, 1976). In an interesting study by Scarr and Weinberg (1976) it was found that black children adopted by middle-class white families as infants had average IQ's of 106 by the time they reached school, compared to an average of 90 for black children raised by their own parents. Scarr and Weinberg also found that black and white infants adopted by white middle-class families have similar IQ's.

A child's IQ is also expected to predict future achievement. As we have seen, both IQ scores and levels of achievement can vary as a result of cultural and environmental experiences. However, intelligence tests are still widely used. Used carefully, they can give some indication of mental capacity and future achievement, though certain myths have grown up around their use (see Inset 6.3). Results of IQ tests should be used tentatively and not as the sole indicator of a child's potential mental development or future achievement.

Standard IQ tests purport to measure "intelligence," which is widely viewed as the key to adult success. As a result children with low IQ scores are the subjects of anxious solicitude from their parents, while groups that test badly, notably blacks, are constantly on the defensive. This is doubly true when, as usually happens, those who do poorly on IQ tests also do poorly on school achievement tests that measure things like reading comprehension and arithmetic skills.

Parents' and teachers' anxieties have been further intensified as a result of claims that IQ scores are largely determined by heredity. If an individual's genes determine his or her IQ, and if IQ then determines the individual's chances of adult success, it is a short step to the conclusion that there is nothing he or she can do to improve future prospects. Moreover, if life chances are determined at birth, many recent efforts at social reform have obviously been doomed from the start.

The controversy over IQ and achievement tests has become so bitter that it is almost impossible to discuss the subject rationally. Neither social scientists nor laypeople seem to have much interest in the actual facts, which are extremely complex. The best currently available evidence contradicts a number of commonly accepted myths about IQ.

Myth 1: IQ tests are the best measure of human intelligence.

IQ tests measure only one rather limited variety of intelligence, namely the kind that schools (and psychologists) value. Scores on the tests show remarkably little relationship to performance in most adult roles. People with high scores do a little better in most jobs than people with low scores, and they earn somewhat more money, but the differences are surprisingly small.

Cognitive Style

Before concluding this chapter we should consider the concept of *cognitive style.* Earlier in the book we mentioned that we can expect individual differences in children's development. In discussing intellectual development and intelligence the emphasis has been on normal development; that is, on how intellectual development occurs on the average. However, it has been noticed that children adopt different styles of processing information and solving problems irrespective of their level of development or intelligence.

Differences in cognitive styles among children can be related to level of maturation, memory, attentiveness, personality, social class, and age.

The best-known description of cognitive style has been provided by Kagan (1966, 1971). He distinguishes between *impulsive* children who tend to respond quickly and with many inaccuracies (**impulsive cognitive style**) and *reflective* children whose thinking is more deliberate and accurate (**reflective cognitive style**). Reflective children take more time in trying to solve a problem and appear concerned about getting the answer or solution correct. Impulsive children, on the other hand, show little anxiety about making mistakes (Messer, 1970). It

Myth 2: The poor are poor because they have low IQs. Those with high IQ's end up in well-paid jobs.
The poor are seldom poor because they have low IQ scores, low reading scores, low arithmetic scores, or bad genes. They are poor because they either cannot find adequately paying jobs, cannot work, or cannot keep such jobs. This has very little to do with their test scores.

Myth 3: One's IQ is overwhelmingly determined by genetic endowment.
Claims that "IQ scores are 80 percent hereditary" appear to be greatly exaggerated. Test results depend almost as much on variation in children's environments as on variations in their genes.

Myth 4: The main reason black children and poor white children have low IQ scores is that they have "bad" genes.
While differences in the environments that children grow up in explain much of the variation in their test scores, differences in their school experiences appear to play a relatively minor role. But even socioeconomic background has a quite modest impact on test scores. Many factors that influence the scores seem to be unrelated to either school quality or parental status. At present nobody has a clear idea what these factors are, how they work, or what people can do about them.

Myth 5: Improving the quality of the schools will go a long way toward wiping out differences in IQ and school achievement and therefore in children's life chances.
If school quality has a modest effect on adult test scores, and if test scores then have a modest effect on economic success, school reforms aimed at teaching basic cognitive skills are likely to have miniscule effects on students' future earning power.

Source: Adapted, with permission, from Bane & Jencks, 1973, pp. 32–34 and 38–40. Copyright © 1973 by Harper's Magazine. Reprinted from the February 1973 issue by special permission.

has also been suggested that reflective children generate more hypotheses in attempting to solve problems, pay careful attention to important properties and details, and persevere more in trying to find a solution (Ault, 1973). For these reasons they do better than impulsive children on Piagetian tasks of discrimination learning, reasoning, and conservation (Pascual-Leone, 1973).

A typical test of impulsivity-reflectivity is Kagan's Matching Familiar Figures Test (Kagan et al., 1964. See Figure 6.10). This test measures both anxiety over errors and the speed of information processing. Given items to look at, such as those in Figure 6.10, reflective children carefully compare each picture in the six-item array with the standard item before responding. Impulsive children make random, quick comparisons often not checking all of the six items.

Children do not tend to become more reflective as they grow older, but differences in cognitive style can be found among children at every age. There are certain tasks that demand a measure of reflective thinking, but there are other problems that can be solved adequately by an impulsive style of thinking. It has

Figure 6.10 Items from the Matching Familiar Figures Test. The child is asked to find the object in the six-object array that is identical to the object above them. (Source: Kagan, J., Rosman, B. L., Day, D., Albert, J., and Phillips, W. "Information Processing in the Child: Significance of Analytic and Reflective Attitudes," *Psychological Monographs*, 1964, *78*, 1–37. Copyright 1964 by the American Psychological Association. Reprinted by permission.)

been shown, for example, that on the Matching Familiar Figures Test, if a change in one of the six items is inside the figure (such as the shape of the nose on the teddy bear), a reflective child is more likely to notice it. But, if the change is to the contour of the figure (such as a change to the height of the back of the chair), an impulsive child is more likely to notice it (Zelniker & Jeffery, 1976).

Since many learning tasks require careful attention to detail and perseverance in the step-by-step solving of problems, impulsivity is likely to be a drawback to the child. However, the results of some studies have shown that children who tend to be impulsive in their thinking and problem solving can be trained to be more reflective (Messer, 1976; Nelson, 1968; Zelniker & Oppenheimer, 1976).

There are other dimensions of cognitive style. Children differ in the way they organize information to be learned in terms of such trends as simplification versus complexity, consistency versus inconsistency, and in the way learned information seems to be organized in memory. Another dimension of cognitive style that appears to have important implications for learning is the tendency for children to be generalizers or particularizers or somewhere between these two extremes (Ausubel & Schwartz, 1972). This means that some children show a preference for paying particular attention to the general aspects of some idea while others focus on particular details. In tasks such as the comparison of amounts of liquid problem in Figure 6.1, children need to attend to the general aspect of quantity and to realize that the particular details of various forms of transformation are of no consequence.

It remains to be established whether a child's particular cognitive style generalizes to *all* learning situations and the extent to which cognitive style may constrain or help learning.

Summary

The rapid growth rate of infancy slows down after age 2, and there is a slower but steady physical development during the preschool years. Body proportions change so that children look less top-heavy, and the lengthening of the face and jaw development result in the loss of the "baby face." Motor skills are also developing. The clumsiness of movement at age 2 gives way to increasing competence in a wide range of body movements. Changes in hand-eye coordination are also lending more control to fine motor skills. These changes in physical development seem to influence in important ways the child's self-concept and growth in social and intellectual competencies. Some psychologists, such as Piaget and Bruner, believe that sensorimotor development is a necessary precursor to later intellectual development.

From a behaviorist point of view intellectual development between 2 and 6 years is being fashioned by operant conditioning. Desired behavior should be developed first by continuous reinforcement and later by intermittent reinforcement. Integrated sequences of reinforcement are usually called behavior chains. Skinner describes development as a continuous accumulation of conditioned behavior, although he believes that there are phases of environmental treatment during childhood for each of which the child's age and previous experience should be taken into account when planning reinforcement schedules.

A counterpoint to Skinner's view is Gesell's belief that development is influenced almost completely by genetic factors. The child's behavior "unfolds," controlled by a "maturational clock." Parents and teachers should not interfere with development. Using "norms" of expected behavior, they should wait for particular behaviors to emerge—and then support them. A criticism of this theory is that Gesell places too much emphasis on norms and ignores evidence that suggests environmental influences are important.

Preoperations, as described by Piaget, have both a negative and positive side. The negative side shows the child's thinking as rigid, irreversible, centering, and transductive. The positive side emphasizes the fact that the preschool child is now able to represent objects and events symbolically, even though the child tends to view the world only from his or her own point of view. However, during these years there is a decline in egocentric thinking and the child shows a growing ability to handle cause-and-effect relationships and a better understanding of the identity of objects.

According to Bruner, the preschool years is a period of development of representation. Although able to use three forms of representation, the preschool child tends to make more use of enactive and iconic representation than symbolic representation. The child is also learning to use techniques of representation such as patterned acts and the rules of grammar and syntax and to integrate thinking and reasoning into higher-order categories. Techniques the child uses have evolved within cultures and are transmitted to the child by the culture he or she grows up in.

The study of language development and language use is called psycholinguistics. During the preschool years there is a steady increase in the child's vocabulary, the number of words used in sentences, the construction of sentences, the uses of questions, and an understanding of both the meaning of words and the finer points of communication.

Piaget found that children's speech changes from egocentric to social during these years. This shift in the type of speech and other aspects of language development such as the use of grammatical rules and the understanding of word meanings is said to be due primarily to mental development and partly to social interaction. Thus, language development follows mental development. Learning theorists, such as Bandura, hold an opposite view that language development is influenced by children's imitating adults' speech.

There appear to be many factors affecting language development. However, langauge seems to develop the same the world over, although there are obviously cultural effects as in the case, for example, of black English.

There are various definitions of intelligence, and a number of tests have been developed to measure intelligence. Two frequently used tests are the Stanford-Binet and Weschler intelligence tests composed of items that measure verbal and nonverbal skills. The score a child obtains on such tests is called an intelligence quotient or IQ. Social and cultural backgrounds can affect a child's IQ. Low IQ scores for children from poor and disadvantaged environments may "cloak" actual intellectual competencies.

Children bring to their thinking, reasoning, and problem solving different cognitive styles which appear to be related to factors such as motivation, memory, personality, age, and social class. Kagan has described two cognitive styles, impulsive and reflective. Impulsive children tend to respond quickly, are careless in their thinking and problem solving, and tend to make many errors. Reflective children take more time, more care, generate more hypotheses when solving problems, and show anxiety about getting correct answers and solutions. Children do tend to become more reflective with age although both impulsive and reflective children can be found at all ages. It has been shown that impulsive children can be trained to become more reflective. Other dimensions of cognitive style are simplification/complexity, consistency/inconsistency, and generalization/particularization. The extent to which a child's cognitive style generalizes to learning situations or affects various types of learning tasks is not yet clearly known.

Questions for Review

1. Describe the main features of development from ages 2 to 6 years.

2. Why is the process of development of behavior by operant conditioning often a lengthy process? What procedures can parents use to ensure the continuous accumulation of conditioned behavior?

3. What implications does Gesell's theory have for parents' and teachers' treatment of young children's intellectual behavior?

4. Briefly describe the main features of the stage of preoperations as described by Piaget. Why are preoperations sometimes referred to as "negative"?

5. In this chapter two examples were given of problems the preoperational child has with the concept of quantity. Suppose you wanted to find out if a young child would have similar problems with *number*. What would you do to find out? Describe some of the errors (and their probable causes) the child might make.

6. Try out a matrix problem with two children aged about 4 and 6. Draw up a matrix board with nine boxes (see Figure 6.7 in this chapter). Cut out *nine* rabbits (or any suitable shape) so that you have three sets of three colored rabbits. For each set have the rabbits sized from largest to smallest. Make sure all the large rabbits are of equal size—and the same for the middle-size rabbits and small rabbits (see Figure 6.11).

Figure 6.11 A second matrix problem. The rabbits are shown *ordered* in size from biggest to smallest and by color from black through dark gray to light gray. They are also *classified* by size and by color.

Record the children's actions in attempting to place the rabbits in the matrix—for reconstruction and transposition. Ask them about their constructions and record their responses. Compare your results to those obtained by Bruner and Kenney.

7. If possible, ask two children aged about 3 and 6 years to tell you a short story or to describe some incident they have recently experienced, which you will record on a tape recorder. Transcribe the recordings and compare the two samples with respect to words used, meanings given to words, and types of sentences used.

8. What does Kagan mean by impulsive and reflective cognitive styles? Give a number of preschool aged children a problem or set of problems such as those referred to in questions 5 and 6 above. Observe their "style" of trying to solve the problem(s) and see if you can determine when a child (a) tends to be either impulsive or reflective, and (b) is attentive to general or particular aspects of the task.

Suggestions for Further Reading

Anastasi, A. *Psychological testing,* 4th ed. New York: Macmillan, 1976. Provides a comprehensive description of psychological tests and discusses problems with psychological testing, such as intelligence tests.

Brown, R. *A first language: The early stages.* Cambridge, MA: Harvard University Press, 1973. Describes the development of a child's first language with particular emphasis on the development of grammar and syntax.

Bruner, J. S. *Beyond the information given,* selected and edited by J. M. Anglin. New York: Norton, 1973. Particularly chapters 18 and 19 which deal with the development of representation and the course of cognitive growth.

Nye, R. D. *What is B. F. Skinner really saying?* Englewood Cliffs, NJ: Prentice-Hall, 1979. Discusses the basic concepts and underlying assumptions behind Skinner's view of behaviorism. Considers some of the controversies and misunderstandings that have surrounded Skinner's work.

Piaget, J. *Play, dreams and imitation in childhood.* New York: Norton, 1951. An account of the relationship between play and development from Piaget's perspective.

Piaget, J., & Inhelder, B. *The psychology of the child.* New York: Basic Books, 1969. Piaget's own account of the developmental process from infancy through adolescence. This book will also be of use in succeeding chapters.

Sinclair, C. B. *Movement of the young child: Ages 2 to 6.* Columbus, OH: Charles Merrill. Provides a clear description of physical and motor development during the "preschool" years, and also provides suggestions for assessing these types of behavior.

Learning and Instruction

7

We take a handfull of sand from the endless landscape of awareness around us and call that handfull of sand the world.

Once we have the handfull of sand, the world of which we are conscious, a process of discrimination goes to work on it. This is the knife. We divide the sand into parts. This and that. Here and there. Black and white. Now and then. The discrimination is the division of the conscious universe into parts.

Shades of color in different piles—sizes in different piles—grain shapes in different piles—subtypes of grain shapes in different piles—and so on, and on, and on. You'd think the process of subdivision and classification would come to an end somewhere, but it doesn't. It just goes on and on.

From R. Persig, *Zen and the Art of Motorcycle Maintenance* (New York: Bantam, 1975), pp. 75–76.

There are two schools of thought about learning. According to the environmentalists best represented by the *behaviorists* (e.g., Skinner), the young child learns about concepts and rules that the culture creates. For example, the child learns that in the world around him or her there are concepts like color, shape, dog, cat, bug, pet, dad, mom, and so forth. He or she also learns that there are rules governing the structure and use of language and rules for problem solving. The culture (in the form of parents, teachers, care givers) has the responsibility for transmitting knowledge to the child.

The cognitive structuralists, on the other hand, are concerned with ways in which the child interacts with the environment and from this interaction constructs intellectual skills to help him or her in logically representing the world. In infancy these skills are action schemes, during the preschool years they are preoperations, and later they become more sophisticated in the form of concrete and formal operations. Parents and teachers can help the child construct this type of knowledge by providing a stimulating environment, by encouraging curiosity and exploration, and, by asking certain kinds of questions, pointing the child in the right direction for generating important interactions with the environment. Piaget says that for intellectual skills to be meaningful rather than stereotyped or rotely learned, they should not be directly taught—the child must construct them, not the adult. The concept of self-construction of knowledge epitomizes development, and Piaget claims that development controls learning. "Learning is no more than a sector of cognitive development which is facilitated by experience" (1970, p. 714).

Other theorists such as Gagné, Bruner, Ausubel, and Montessori view learning as falling somewhere between these two perspectives. What this middle group shares is the belief that learning does imply changes in behavior, which result from certain kinds of experiences, and that what has been learned is called knowledge. The group differs in their beliefs about the relationship between development and learning and their descriptions of knowledge.

Descriptions of organized systems of learning invariably include descriptions of methods of instruction and the teacher's role in these two related processes of language and instruction. As we will see, teachers may be trained professionals working in school settings or they may be parents.

This chapter presents descriptions of both environmentalist and cognitive-structuralist theories of learning, as well as those theories that fall between. Where appropriate, we have indicated distinctions and relationships between development and learning. We have provided examples of various attempts that have been made to apply theory to practice in the form of preschool or day-care programs. A section is devoted to a discussion of "parents as teachers." This is followed by a look at play as a particular form of learning. This chapter concludes with a description of special education programs for those children who are both intellectually and physically handicapped.

The Conditioned Response

You are now familiar with the main features of *operant conditioning.* Skinner believes that children's learning at any age can be shaped by a series of reinforced experiences (1968). Keep in mind that from Skinner's viewpoint development is a process of learning increasingly complex ways of thinking and behaving as a result of consequences that follow attempted behaviors. "The role of parents and teachers is therefore twofold: (1) to get children to try desirable acts and (2) to arrange consequences of children's acts so that the desirable behavior is reinforced and undesirable behavior is extinguished through nonreinforcement or punishment" (Thomas, 1979, p. 390). This, in a nutshell, is both the essence of organized learning and the method of instruction.

One method of achieving this type of learning is through the use of **programmed learning materials,** which are lessons prepared to teach specific skills in a specific order and do not depend on the child's discovery. These can be presented to the child on work sheets, in books, or by the use of teaching machines (Keller, 1968; Skinner, 1968). The important feature of these programs is that they provide immediate reinforcement for correct answers by providing the correct answer as a check (Figure 7.1).

We're going to talk about vehicles.

a. Point to the airplane. This is a vehicle.
Point to the house. This is not a vehicle.
Point to the tree. This is not a vehicle.
Point to the car. This is a vehicle.
Point to the truck. This is a vehicle.
Point to the train. This is a vehicle.

Get ready to tell me which objects are vehicles.

b. Point to each object and ask:
Is this a vehicle?
The children are to answer yes or no.

Error

Children give the name of an object.

Correction

1. You're right. It is a (name of object).
But it is also a vehicle or
But it is not a vehicle.

2. Repeat *a* and *b*.

Now let's look at some more vehicles. Turn the page quickly.

Figure 7.1 Item from the Distar Language Instructional System. Showing the teaching method for instructing children in *classification.* (Source: From *Distar ® Language 1: An Instructional System* by Siegfried Engelmann and Jean Osborn. Copyright © 1976, 1972, 1969, Science Research Associates, Inc. Reprinted by permission of the publisher.)

Point to each vehicle and say:
This is a vehicle.

c. Point to the car.
Is this a vehicle? Touch. *Yes.*
Say the whole thing. Touch.
This is a vehicle.

d. What kind of vehicle is this? Touch.
A car. Yes, this vehicle is a car.
Say the whole thing about **this vehicle.**
Touch. *This vehicle is a car.*

e. Repeat *c* and *d* until all children's responses are firm.

f. Point to the bicycle.
Is this a vehicle? Touch. *Yes.*
Say the whole thing. Touch.
This is a vehicle.

g. What kind of vehicle is this? Touch.
A bicycle. Yes, this vehicle is a bicycle.
Say the whole thing about **this vehicle.**
Touch. *This vehicle is a bicycle.*

h. Repeat *f* and *g* until all children's responses are firm.

i. Point to the motorcycle.
Is this a vehicle? Touch. *Yes.*
Say the whole thing. Touch.
This is a vehicle.

j. What kind of vehicle is this? Touch.
A motorcycle. Yes, this vehicle is a motorcycle. Say the whole thing about **this vehicle.** Touch.
This vehicle is a motorcycle.

k. Repeat *i* and *j* until all children's responses are firm.

Another method is by programming both learning activities and the teacher's presentation and control of learning materials along the same lines. For example, the teacher provides information, states requirements or asks questions, and gives immediate feedback. An example of this didactic approach is given in the next section.

An approach to learning that is at once both strongly behavioristic and yet bridges a gap between carefully controlled conditional learning and discovery learning is that taken by Gagné (1974). This section begins with examples of programs based on a behavioristic approach and follows them with a description of Gagné's variation.

The Bereiter-Engelmann Approach

Preschool programs based on a behaviorist theory have a set of behavioral objectives, descriptive statements of specific changes in children's behavior following learning. In some cases each objective is associated with a carefully planned *direct-instruction technique,* which is a step-by-step set of the teacher's actions or statements and the student's responses (Bereiter & Engelmann, 1966). For example,

Behavioral objective: To move from one-word responses to complete affirmation and negative statements in reply to questions.

Teacher Says		*Child Responds*
What is this?		Ball.
Say it all.		This is a ball.
Is this a ball?		No.
Say it all.		This is not a ball.

Many of the behaviorally oriented preschool programs were organized for disadvantaged children (e.g., Bereiter & Engelmann, 1966; Bushell, 1973; Garber & Heber, 1977; Sapon, 1968). A variety of such programs, however, has also been used with normal children and has achieved impressive successes (see Table 7.1).

Table 7.1 Examples of Behavior Modification Early Childhood Education Programs

Researchers	Children	Type of Modification	Effects of Program
Bushell, Wrobel, & Michaelis, 1968	Preschoolers	Token rewards for correct behavior	Increased rate of study behaviors; independent task involvement; attending to instructions
Chadwick & Day, 1971	Elementary school underachievers	Rewards and social reinforcement	Substantial increase in work time; improved accuracy in performance
Edlund, 1972	Primary-grade children	Immediate reinforcement for correct responses on Stanford-Binet Scale	Significant improvement in IQ
Kazdin, 1973	First, third, and fourth graders	Reward system of reinforcement	Improvement in study behaviors; attention to and involvement in tasks
Knight, Hasazi, & McNeil, 1971	Preschoolers	Systematic presentation strategies and immediate feedback by mothers to children concerning correct and incorrect letter and word recognition	Improvement in reading skills

Source: Adapted from Evans, E. D., *Contemporary Influences in Early Childhood Education.* 1975. Copyright, 1975, Holt, Rinehart & Winston. Reprinted with permission.

Whereas the Bereiter-Engelmann program (now called the Engelmann-Becker Model at the University of Oregon) relied primarily on teacher-directed learning to achieve objectives, other behavioral programs, which we describe next, have arrangements of different learning situations.

The Primary Education Project

One of the best-known behaviorist programs is the *Primary Education Project* (PEP) (Resnick, Wang, & Rosner, 1977). This program was designed for preschool through the early elementary grades. Although intended for use with disadvantaged children, it can be adapted to the needs of normal children. What are its special features?

The PEP has its own theoretical base. Instructional sequences for the PEP program were derived from an analysis of learning tasks explicitly designed to "teach children the skills and concepts that underlie intelligent school performance." Learning is expected to be cumulative (Gagné, 1968) in the sense that early-appearing abilities and knowledge are the prerequisites for later learning (Resnick, 1973). The authors of this program also claim that its sequence is based on Piaget's theory of development, since certain information-processing skills derived from Piaget's theory, such as classification and quantification, are taught. Furthermore, these skills are introduced in the order Piaget claims to be the natural course of development.

Curriculum objectives for the program are stated in connection with three general classes of skills: perceptual motor skills, conceptual linguistic skills, and orienting and attending skills.

Perceptual motor skills include a wide range of sensori-discriminations and constructions and a variety of gross and fine motor skills. *Conceptual linguistic skills* include classification, reasoning, and memory skills along with the language skills that allow the child to express these competencies and that, we might suppose, influence the development of conceptual competencies. *Orienting and attending skills* are those abilities that allow a child to pay attention to a learning task, to follow directions, to be persistent, and to accept delay in achieving rewards. They also include self-motivation traits—ability to work autonomously, to have confidence in one's own ability to succeed, and to complete tasks.

The content of the PEP program consists of a combination of formal, structured curriculum and informal, child-selected activities. The structured curriculum includes an introductory math curriculum (quantification), concept learning (classification), and motor activities (**perceptual-motor skills**). Table 7.2 shows examples of content and related behavioral objectives. Informal *exploratory* activities are intended to promote generalized skills in communication, social development, and problem solving.

PEP defines roles for both teacher and child. To guide children in self-directed activities, *prescription tickets* are given out at the beginning of each session. The child "follows" a code on the ticket to complete an activity at his or her own pace. These self-scheduling systems operate rather like a programmed learning system in that children are learning to perform assigned tasks according to a particular sequence. However, this type of scheduling is intermixed with child-selected activities. Some children may require more direction than others, but the overall goal is to encourage children to plan their own time and accomplish certain tasks within a reasonable time limit, working at their own pace. The teacher's role is to manage activities. This can be accomplished by direct programmed instruction, help with the self-scheduling system or in organized traditional group activities such as ball games. The emphasis is on demonstration,

Table 7.2 Examples of Objectives for a Classification and Quantification Curriculum

Unit	Given	Objective The Child Can
Classification *Unit 2* *Shape and Size* *Discrimination*	A. Basic shapes and matching outlines B. Irregular shapes and matching outlines C. Two sizes of rods and instructions to superimpose D. Two sizes of a shape and instructions to superimpose	A. Place the shapes on the appropriate outlines. B. Place the shapes on the appropriate outlines. C. State whether they are the same or different size and give the reason. D. State whether they are the same or different size and give the reason.
Units 6–9 *Big and Little* *Long and Short* *Tall and Short* *Wide and Narrow*	A. Two objects different in size B. Two objects different in size C. Two objects different in size D. Several sizes of an object	A. Point to the "big" ("long," "tall," "wide") object. B. Identify the "little" ("short," "narrow") object. C. Describe them according to size using the term "big" or "little," etc. D. Seriate them in order from biggest to smallest.
Quantification *Units 1 and 2* *Counting and* *One-to-One* *Correspondence*	A. Set of moveable objects B. A numeral stated and a set of objects. C. Two unequal sets of objects D. Two unequal sets of objects	A. Count the objects, moving them out of the set as they are counted. B. Count out a subset of stated size. C. Pair objects and state which set has more. D. Pair objects and state which set has less.
Unit 6 *Seriation and* *Ordinal* *Position*	A. Three objects of different sizes B. Objects of graduated sizes C. Several sets of objects D. Ordered sets of objects	A. Select the largest (smallest) objects. B. Seriate the objects according to size. C. Seriate the sets according to size of objects. D. Name the ordinal position of the objects.

Source: Adapted from Resnick, L. B., Wang, M. C., & Rosner, J., in *The Preschool in Action: Exploring Early Childhood Programs,* Second Edition, edited by M. C. Day and R. K. Parker. Copyright 1977 by Allyn and Bacon, Inc. Reprinted by permission.

Table 7.3 Levels of Complexity in Learning Intellectual Skills

Level	Examples of Intellectual Skills
Problem Solving	Using rules to solve problems. For example, rebounding balls from a wall to see in which direction they will roll.
Using Rules	Relating concepts in learning a principle or rule. For example, relating *ball* and *round* when learning the rule that round things roll.
Concept Learning	Learning the logical relationships between objects and being able to construct classes of objects. For example, learning that an insect is an animal with six legs and three body parts—and applying this criterion to identifying groups of insects.
Making Discriminations	Learning to perceive similarities and differences between and among objects and events. For example, realizing there are different types of dogs that are nevertheless all called "dogs"; and also realizing that dogs and cats are different and called by different names.
Making Verbal Associations	Associating words with the objects they refer to. For example, calling a dog "dog."
Chaining	Putting together a sequence of stimulus-response associations. For example, reaching for an object, forming the hand for grasping, grasping the object, bringing it back to the mouth.
Making Stimulus-Response Connections	Learning various stimulus-response connections. For example, seeing a rattle and reaching for it; learning to recognize mother's face and smiling.
Signal Learning	Involuntary reflex actions of early infancy. For example, a rooting reflex prior to sucking on mother's nipple or bottles.

Source: Adapted from Gagné, R. M., *The Conditions of Learning.* Copyright 1970 by Holt, Rinehart and Winston. Reprinted by permission.

explanation, and praise (reinforcement). Although this program is based in part on a behavioristic theory of learning, it is more flexible than highly structured program-learning approaches such as those Bereiter and Engelmann used. Having enjoyed a certain degree of success, the program has now been revised and adapted in the light of previous experiences.

Using an abacus requires an understanding of number sets, relationships between numbers, and rules of computation. (Photo by James L. Ballard)

Cumulative Learning: Gagné's Hierarchies

Gagné has suggested that a useful trend in learning can be ensured by building on learning skills learned at a subordinate level. Learning proceeds from the simple to the complex (1974, 1977). This is called **cumulative learning** as in the PEP. Gagné also feels that both programmed and discovery methods should be used in planning hierarchical sequences of learning (1977).

Gagné divides learning into eight levels arranged in a hierarchy (see Table 7.3). You can see from this hierarchy of types of learning that there is an emphasis on operant conditioning. But the more complex types of learning do not seem so dependent on conditioning. This partly depends, however, on the method of instruction. Even problem-solving techniques can be learned from programmed instruction.

Gagné (1977) distinguishes among the subject matter of objects, events, and skills (or rules) for processing information. For example, the preschool child might correctly apply the verbal labels "one," "two," "three," "four," and so on, to sets containing those numbers of objects. Thus, it will be apparent that the child possesses some concept of numbers. However, a more comprehensive understanding would include a knowledge of the relationships between numbers and rules for establishing these relationships. Three, for example, is a combination of $1 + 1 + 1$, or $1 + 2$, or $2 + 1$. Thus number concepts and number computation are interrelated, but the first is subject matter and the second involves information-processing skills.

Gagné's theory sets up special conditions considered essential for meaningful learning. The most important is that hierarchies of concepts and skills point out sequences of instruction and learning. Sequence of instruction can be built up by analyzing the requirements of a learning task. The steps from simple to complex learning and the links between them must be identified. It has been mentioned that the PEP was based, in part, on Gagné's concept of cumulative learning. Figure 7.2 illustrates how two units in the PEP, one on quantification and one on classification, were organized according to this concept.

Bruner's Theory of Learning: First Levels

In considering the learning process, Bruner first comments on *readiness for learning.* Just consider your own learning at this time. Do you ever think, "Yes, I'm ready to learn this subject," or "I don't think I'm quite ready to tackle that subject"? What does being ready to learn mean?

Bruner relates readiness to both development and learning. It is a given fact that the preschool child has a characteristic way of viewing and explaining the world. But this changes between the time the child first enters preschool at about age 2 and the transition to kindergarten at age 5. Learning proceeds, *in part,* according to the child's way of viewing things, that is, on development. Remember, that according to Bruner, the child at age 2 has just mastered, at a simplistic level, three ways of representing the world. But the child still shows a dependence on enactive and iconic representation rather than symbolic. New learning experiences, and the materials that go with them, should reflect this dependency. "The task of teaching a subject to a child at any particular age is one of representing the structure of that child's way of viewing things" (Bruner, 1960, p. 33).

However, Bruner also points out the idea of readiness:

[It] is a mischievous half-truth. It is a half-truth largely because it turns out that one *teaches* readiness or provides opportunities for its nurture, one does not simply wait for it. Readiness in these terms consists of mastery of those simpler skills that permit one to reach higher skills (1966, p. 29).

This concept of readiness and the way it is related to both development and learning sets Bruner's theory apart from Piaget's. The most important difference is the greater emphasis Bruner places on the influence of the environment on development. An important environmental influence is instruction. According to Bruner, instruction plays an important role in aiding development.

1. Hierarchy of Classification Units

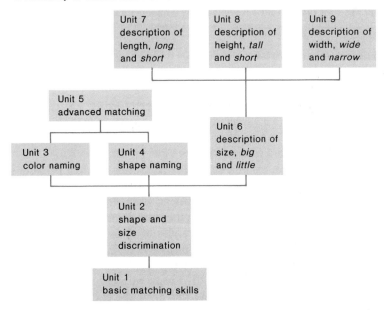

2. Hierarchy of Quantification Units

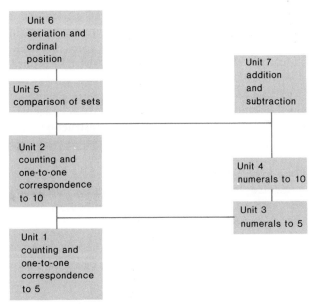

Figure 7.2 Hierarchial relationships of classification and quantification units. For both classification and quantification, units must be taught in a sequence beginning with unit 1. Where two units are shown at the same level—as is the case for units 2 and 3 in the quantification hierarchy—either can be taught first since the skills in each unit are at the same level of difficulty. Both units must, however, be taught before unit 4. (Source: Resnick, L. B., Wang, M. C., and Rosner, J. In *The Preschool in Action,* M. C. Day, and R. K. Parker, eds. Copyright 1977 by Allyn & Bacon, Inc. Reprinted by permission.)

Instruction . . . need not follow slavishly the natural course of cognitive development in the child. It can also lead intellectual development by providing challenging but useable opportunities for the child to forge ahead in his development (1960, p. 39).

If instruction is so important, how should one proceed to organize learning experiences for the child? Four principles of learning stand out:

1. *Identify basic concepts.*

Concepts can be in terms of subject matter or in terms of skills. For example, take the problem of centrism we associate with the preoperational child. The child, in focusing only on one aspect of an object or event at one time, makes errors. How will learning a basic concept help?

Consider these two examples: (a) If a child only paid attention to a penguin's swimming, he might call it a *fish*. Helping a child to also pay attention to other relevant properties of a penguin, that it has feathers, wings (that do not help it to fly, but to swim) and that it lays eggs will help the child come to the realization that some birds, at least, can swim. Other examples of birds such as ostriches will help the child realize that, in fact, not all birds fly. Flying is not a critical property of a bird. (b) Suppose the teacher asks the child, "How far is it from school to your house?" and the child replies, "If I walk with my mom, its a long way. But if we run it's not so far." In making this error the child is mixing up *speed* with *distance* (a lack of conservation). Inhelder, a colleague of Piaget, has suggested that providing the child with simple learning experiences such as showing the child that a penguin is a bird that can swim, or an ostrich and a penguin are both birds that cannot fly, or that walking or running a certain distance does not make the distance shorter or longer, "can speed the child towards attending to several features of a situation at once" (reported in Bruner, 1960, p. 43).

2. *Take into account the child's readiness to learn.*

Ensure that the organization of learning, and of learning materials, is in keeping with the child's present level of development to begin with. Instructional sequences for the preschool child should progress from the enactive to the iconic to the symbolic.

3. *Organize the curriculum in a spiraling sequence.*

Basic concepts should be presented and re-presented in a **spiraling curriculum** sequence from simple to ever-increasing abstract levels (see Figure 7.3).

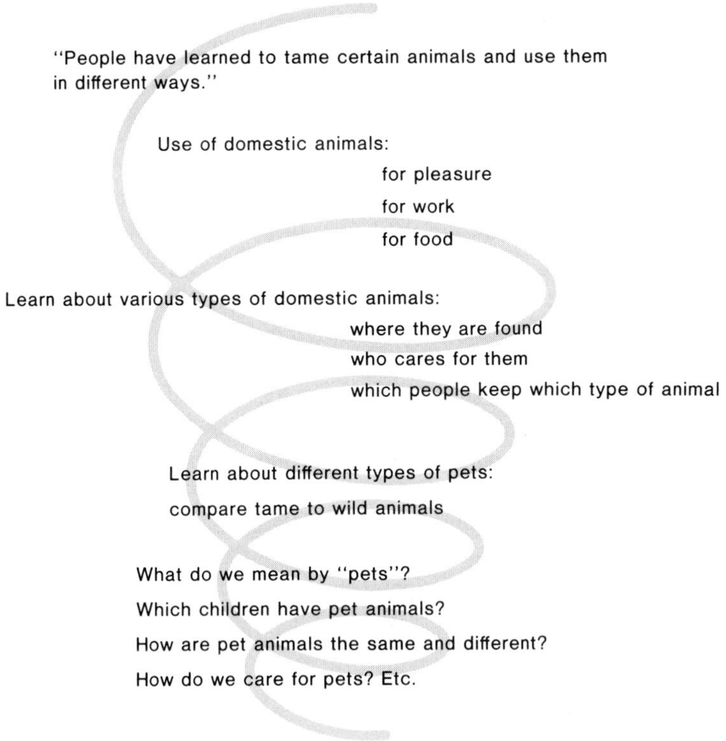

"People have learned to tame certain animals and use them in different ways."

Use of domestic animals:

for pleasure

for work

for food

Learn about various types of domestic animals:

where they are found

who cares for them

which people keep which type of animal

Learn about different types of pets:

compare tame to wild animals

What do we mean by "pets"?

Which children have pet animals?

How are pet animals the same and different?

How do we care for pets? Etc.

Figure 7.3 The spiraling curriculum. Beginning in early childhood, curricula should be built around important ideas that are developed over periods of time. Ideas and related concepts, first introduced at a relatively simple level, should be reintroduced again and again at increasingly complex levels.

An idea that might form part of a preschool curriculum can be put this way: "*People* have learned to *tame* certain *animals* and *use* them in different ways." There are a number of possible ways of developing this idea. One suggested sequence of development is shown in the illustration.

4. *Encourage informed guessing.*

The child should be encouraged to make informed guesses and try to find answers to them. This principle combines two of Bruner's important ideas about learning. One is the notion of going beyond the information given, and the other is that *discovery learning* is an important form of learning. For example, the preschool child may know how to check whether the contents of two sets of objects are the same, and the two sets can be arranged in a linear fashion next to each other with same objects side by side (see Figure 7.4).

Each example in Figure 7.4 shows a "one-to-one correspondence" between two sets of objects. The child can demonstrate by one-to-one correspondence arrangements that, for those examples, the sets in each pair are the same as each other. In this way, the child may also come to an intuitive understanding of "equal sets." With respect to a new series of paired sets, the child may use the one-to-one correspondence procedure to find out which sets are equal and which are unequal. This may be considered a simple step beyond the information given, and for the preschool child it can be an important discovery. Part of **discovery learning,** then, is inferring relationships among and between objects—for example, deriving the consequences of cause-and-effect relationships from testing possibilities or arriving at logical conclusions (see Inset 7.1). The joy of self-discovery can be a form of positive reinforcement to a child's learning.

Learning by Subsumption

In Chapter 1 we mentioned that Ausubel is a theorist who sees an interrelationship between development and learning. He describes a sequence of three stages of development: preoperational, concrete operational, and a final abstract logical stage. As you might imagine, the use of these terms is based on the meaning that Piaget gave them. However, there is little correspondence between Ausubel's and Piaget's description of development. A brief description of Ausubel's theory of development is included here because it is important to realize that, like Bruner, he assumes that there are certain developmental constraints on a child's ability to learn.

Figure 7.4 One-to-one correspondence. (Source: Adapted from Lavatelli, C. Copyright © 1973 by the Center for Media Development. Reprinted by permission of Delta Education, Inc.)

1. Line up five dolls in a row. From a group of seven chairs, take out enough chairs so that each doll has one to sit on.

2. Line up two rows of six pennies in 1-to-1 correspondence. We can say that each row of pennies has an equal "amount" or "number" of pennies. Of course, all cases of 1-to-1 correspondence illustrate *equal sets*.

3. *Double seriation and 1-to-1 correspondence.* Place the six children in raincoats and boots in order from biggest to smallest (or tallest to shortest). From the six umbrellas (or some larger number), give each child an umbrella that is the right size for him or her.

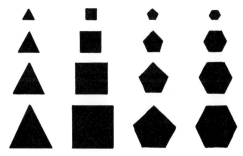

4. *One-to-one correspondence in a matrix puzzle.* First, place the objects into groups according to the number of sides each object has. Then put the objects from each group in rows next to each other from *biggest to smallest* and from *least to most number of sides*.

Learning and Instruction   **297**

Bruner (Bruner, Olver & Greenfield, 1966) has described an experiment by Olver (1966) that illustrates how children make inferences in going beyond the information given. The experiment "was carried out with the aid of a simple piece of apparatus: a rectangular board of five columns and five rows of small lightbulbs. Each bulb, upon being pressed by the child, either lights up in brilliant scarlet red or remains unlit, depending upon whether the bulb is part of a pattern or not. The child's task is to discover, by pressing as few bulbs as possible, which one of several patterns presented to him are hidden in the bulb board. Only one bulb can be pressed at a time. Figure 7.5 shows the board with two (of a number of) alternative patterns." The child must press the bulbs to determine which of these two patterns is on the board.

This task was given to 3-, 5-, and 8-year-old children. Inferential reasoning differed according to the children's age, characterizing major turning points in their development.

The 3-year-old searches the board for bulbs that will light up, looking for a pattern to "spring out" like one of the alternative patterns. The young child seems to be simply inferring that any of these alternative patterns might appear as the bulbs are pressed. The 5-year-old proceeds differently. Now the child tests each one of the alternative patterns one at a time eliminating or accepting the results, but too often accepting some result on insufficient evidence. For example, if a row of bulbs lights up across the top, the child may infer that this proves it is the horizontal-bar model and not test the vertical column of bulbs in the middle to check if it is the *T* model. But the 5-year-old does set up a series of hypotheses based on the information supplied and tests each in turn, but bases expectations only on some *particular* image. What is striking about the 8-year-old children is that they seem able to take into consideration *all* the available information rather than just single images. They deal simultaneously with all the possible patterns, considering exclusion and overlap in order to isolate distinctive features.

Going beyond the information given to the making of inferences appears to be tied to the child's preferred way of representing information. The 5-year-old is particularly dependent on sensorimotor, and iconic representation and expectations are bases on the immediate and obvious. By age 8 the use of symbolic representation allows the child to fuse together the set of alternative images and base inferences on them.

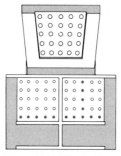

Figure 7.5 The bulb pattern board. (Source: Olson, D. R., In Bruner, J. S., and Oliver, R. (eds.), Studies in Cognitive Growth. Copyright 1966 by John Wiley & Sons. Used with permission.)

Source: Bruner, J. S., Olver, R. R., Greenfield, P. M., et al.
Studies in Cognitive Growth, 1966.

This preschool boy is applying primary concepts of color to separate the blocks into groups according to their color. (Photo by Robert Ekert, EKM/Nepenthe)

Stages of Development

The three stages of development, preoperational, concrete operational, and abstract logical, are supposed to coincide with the preschool, elementary, and high school years (Ausubel, 1963; Ausubel, Novak, & Hanesian, 1978). The principal characteristic of change is a move away from relying upon concrete examples to understand concepts and the relationships among them, and using them to solve problems. Change moves toward performing those "operations" without needing the concrete examples. Concepts the preschool child is capable of acquiring and using are called **primary concepts.** Before describing these concepts and the way in which they are learned, we should briefly consider Ausubel's concept of readiness.

According to Ausubel, there are two types of readiness which are interdependent. The first is *developmental readiness,* which is expected to change with age and experience. The preschool child's level of developmental readiness is the ability to learn primary concepts. As we will see in chapters 9 and 12, during the middle and adolescent years, developmental readiness is related to the child's improving ability to deal with **secondary concepts** and later abstract concepts. *Subject-matter readiness* refers to the child's knowledge of specific subject-matter ideas in some particular subject-matter area.

During the preschool years children are only able to form primary concepts. These are concepts the child learns in the presence of concrete examples. For example, suppose the child is playing with wooden blocks of different colors and learns to separate them into classes by color. If some of the objects are colored red, then the property red is used to form the class of red objects. Red is the primary concept. What must the preschool child be provided with to learn the primary concepts *big* and *small?* Whatever the concept being introduced, the child must learn the critical properties of that concept, which must be clearly and concretely exemplified.

Subsumption Learning

Ausubel's learning theory emphasizes the learning of subject matter. He believes that the concepts contained in any subject matter should be learned by a process of **subsumption learning.** The obvious question you may ask is, "What is meant by subsumption?" Consider the following example of learning the concept *fish*. The teacher knows that a fish is

An animal that
is usually found in water,
has gills for breathing,
usually has scales covering its body,
has fins that help it swim.

These are *general properties* because they apply to most fish; when you use them to describe fish, you provide a general idea of fish. The preschool child needs to have each and every property concretely exemplified one at a time. The teacher must therefore provide examples of animals (including fish) and non-animals and examples of all the properties of fish by using illustrations, films, and real objects. The child is then shown many examples of fish (names are not important) not previously seen, along with other animal and non-animal objects. If the child recognizes the examples of fish objects as fish because they have the fish properties the child has learned initially, each new fish example is *subsumed* into the general idea of fish or fishness. This requires the child to **discriminate** fish from other examples of animals and non-animals. The child may forget the names of particular fish or specific properties such as color, size, and shape. Such forgetting is not important. The important thing in subsumption learning is to remember the general idea. General ideas are remembered longest, even when particular concepts and facts are forgotten.

You may already have recognized that this subsumption learning is hierarchical. Ausubel believes that we quite naturally organize information in our minds into hierarchies. This means that we construct general ideas, or **superordinate concepts** such as fish, animals, transportation, plants, and insects (bugs), and organize under each superordinate concept related **subordinate concepts** and facts. Two examples of such hierarchies are illustrated in Figure 7.6.

1. Living and Nonliving Things

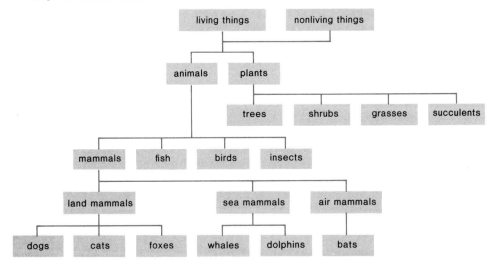

2. Hierarchical Classification

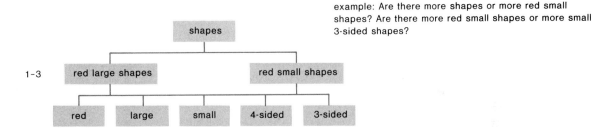

1. Compare subordinate and superordinate concepts. For example: Are there more shapes or more red small shapes? Are there more red small shapes or more small 3-sided shapes?

2. Construct superordinate concepts from subordinate concepts.

3. Construct subordinate concepts from set of shapes.

4. Identify properties of objects to use as criteria for constructing subordinate concepts.

5. Identify different properties of all the objects in a set of shapes.

Figure 7.6 Two hierarchies of concepts.

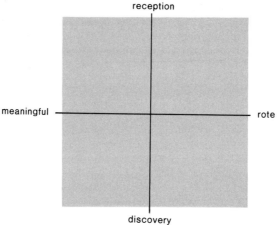

reception

meaningful ————————————————————— rote

discovery

Figure 7.7 Four dimensions of learning. **Reception learning** can range from such activities as the direct teaching of relationships between sub- and super-cordinate concepts to the direct teaching of multiplication tables. According to Ausubel, the first activity would be meaningful and the second would be rote.

Discovery learning can range from such activities as the guided discovery of how to apply rules or strategies to the solving of problems (meaningful) to using trial-and-error in attempting to solve problems (rote).

We should keep in mind that learning is usually *more-or-less* meaningful or *more-or-less* rote.

If the child has arrived at an understanding of the *logical* relationships among and between concepts and facts in a *hierarchy,* learning is said to be *meaningful.* This is not the only form of learning that can occur. Ausubel describes a dimension of learning from *meaningful* to *rote* and a dimension of a method learning from *reception* to *discovery* (see Figure 7.7).

Dimensions of Learning

Imagine that the preschool child has learned a new "bit" of knowledge—for example, some objects are called *dog.* The child kept pointing to dogs, asking, "What's that?" Mom and Dad replied each time, "That's a dog." If the child does not relate that new "bit" of knowledge to any other knowledge previously learned, we say that the new knowledge is *rote,* and the learning has been **rote learning.** For example, were you to memorize a telephone number or directions for how to get some place, which were not related to previous knowledge, that would be rote learning. Sometimes we attempt to learn even more important types of knowledge in this way. How would you respond to the question, "With respect to Piaget's theory of development, what is an operation?" If you merely respond with a ready-made definition without fully understanding the critical properties of an operation, or could not recognize an operation even when a child was truly demonstrating such a behavior, then your knowledge of this concept would be to some extent rote. A **meaningful learning** of the concept "operation" requires an understanding of the concept's critical properties and an ability to recognize those operations that are an important feature of Piaget's theory.

According to Ausubel, how does learning occur? The child may learn by reception or discovery of knowledge. When the child is directly instructed, learning is predominantly by *reception*. The child may also spontaneously, or by encouragement, seek knowledge and discover it by self-direction. Both types of learning may occur in a relatively rote or meaningful fashion. We can see then that there are, according to Ausubel, four dimensions of learning: meaningful reception, meaningful discovery, rote reception, and rote discovery (see Figure 7.7). It would be unusual for the child to be learning entirely in one of these forms. It is more likely that the child's learning includes various combinations of these forms.

Since Ausubel does not believe that the young child, because of developmental constraints and lack of experience, is capable of organizing self-directed learning very efficiently, he emphasizes the importance of meaningful reception learning.

Meaningful Reception Learning

Like Bruner, Ausubel believes that important knowledge that is worth learning exists in the culture and should be transmitted to the child. Instruction therefore is important. However, unlike Bruner and Piaget, he does not believe the child is very capable of discovering knowledge in a meaningful fashion, but rather by reception learning.

Meaningful reception learning has some special features. When preparing a learning experience for young children, the teacher has to select content, in terms of both subject matter and skills. Each learning experience must be organized and presented according to certain principles:

1. Analyze content and identify superordinate concepts, that is, the most general concepts.

2. For each concept, identify the properties to be learned (as in the case of the concept "fish" mentioned earlier).

3. For each concept, select a number of concrete objects that exemplify the concept. The important properties of the concept should be easy to identify in each object.

4. Organize this content into a lesson, that is, into a presentation.

5. Select content that is related to these basic concepts, which contains many *particular* examples of each basic concept.

6. Organize this content into various related learning activities. (Lawton, Lewis, & Deibert, 1976; Lawton & Wanska, 1979; Lawton, Hooper, Saunders, & Roth, 1978; Lawton & Ershler, in preparation; Fowell & Lawton, in preparation.)

Suppose the content (step 1) is animals and the superordinate concepts identified are mammals, fish, birds, and insects (a limited selection). The teacher might decide to first teach the superordinate concept, "mammal." At step 2 the teacher must identify the properties of a mammal. A mammal is an animal that

a. has hair on its body;

b. gives birth to young of its own kind;

c. in the case of the female, suckles the young.

Mammals live on land, fly in the air, and also live in the water. No matter where they live, they all share the properties of "mammal." The teacher must select examples of all kinds of mammals to show to the children when he or she is teaching the properties of mammal (step 3). This material can then be organized into a lesson called the **advance organizer lesson** (step 4). The advance organizer lesson presents the superordinate concept *in advance of* related subordinate concepts and facts. An example of part of such a lesson is provided in Table 7.4.

Examples of related subordinate concepts (land, air, and water mammals) and facts (a land animal is a fox, a rabbit, a bear, etc.; an air mammal is a bat; a water mammal is a porpoise, a whale) are selected and organized into related activities (steps 5 and 6). For example, suppose a related activity involves a board game. It is a traditional "follow-the-route" board game. The winner is the first child to arrive at the "finish" line. This board game has spaces with a name and a single example of some species of mammal, land mammal, air mammal, and water mammal. When a child lands on one of these spaces after the throw of a die, he or she must select an example of that "animal" from picture cards showing species of animals to be found on the board, plus some that are not included in the game. After selecting a picture card, the child must explain *why* it can be chosen as, say, a land mammal by referring to its special properties. These properties are, of course, general properties, learned during the advance organizer lessons. Having various related activities serves two purposes. First, it allows the child the opportunity to meaningfully subsume new knowledge under the initially learned general idea or superordinate concept. This helps clarify the general concept and more firmly "anchor it" in memory. Second, it provides a chance to find out if the child has learned and understood the superordinate concept. If this has been the case, the child will recognize subordinate concepts and facts in terms of the properties of the superordinate concept that they share. It is these shared properties that allow the child to meaningfully relate them into a superordinate concept. It almost goes without saying that a responsibility of the teacher is to organize both advance organizer and related activities into presentations that are suitable for and attractive to preschool children.

How does such learning aid development? It appears to do so in two ways. First, it leads the child to a meaningful understanding of logical relationships between objects and events. To understand the content (subject matter) of a task has an important impact on the child's attempt to solve whatever problem the task poses (Wason & Johnson-Laird, 1972). Second, in constructing superordinate and subordinate classes the child must understand the rules of hierarchical classification (see Figure 7.6 bottom). Practicing general rules of hierarchical classification on a variety of subject matter, which can be classified into hierarchies of related super and subordinate classes, can facilitate the child's performance of this operation (Ausubel, Novak, & Hanesian, 1978, pp. 249–250; Lawton, Hooper, Saunders, & Roth, 1979; Lawton & Ershler, in preparation). According to Piaget's theory, such operations are not yet available to the preschool child. But it appears likely that certain types of instruction and related learning experiences can play a significant role in bringing about a transition from one stage of intellectual development to another. Vygotsky (1962) pointed out that there is a reciprocal relationship between development and education.

Piaget's View of Knowledge

Piaget holds a different view about the relationship between development and learning. He differentiates between development, which he sees as a general process, and learning, which he sees as a specific process: "Development is a process which concerns the totality of the structures of knowledge . . . learning is provoked by situations . . . it is a limited process—limited to a single problem, or to a single structure" (1964, p. 7). What does Piaget mean here by "structures of knowledge"? He is referring to arrangements of knowledge that he has described as taking three forms, social, physical, and logico-mathematical (structures of operations).

Three Forms of Knowledge

Piaget does not consider himself a psychologist but rather a *genetic epistemologist,* someone concerned with the biological foundations of knowledge. He asks the question, "What is knowledge and how does it develop in humans?" *Social knowledge* results from the creation of conventions (social rules). It is a convention to have a calendar with months, weeks, days, and dates; it is a convention to call this book a book. This portion of social knowledge is arbitrary. If we all decided to call this book a "mook," that would be its name. We also usually agree about socially acceptable rules and norms, and established sets of moral values. We cannot change such social knowledge at the drop of a hat, and so it can be considered nonarbitrary. *Physical knowledge* is knowledge of objects and events. It is a "physical" fact that if I release this book from my hand it will drop to the floor. This is an external reality.

Table 7.4 An Advance Organizer (AO) Lesson and Related Learning Activities for Preschoolers

AO Lesson: Teacher's Guide	Examples of Lesson Materials	Example of an AO Lesson Taught to Children	Related Learning Activities
1. Sometimes we may wish to place objects into groups. This helps us remember how objects go together in some way. There is a special way we can use to put objects together into groups. 2. First look at *all* the objects we have. 3. Look to see what properties they have (children have learned the concept, *property*). 4. Look to see if any of the objects have a property they share. 5. Collect together all the objects that share that property. 6. Make sure to choose *all* the objects that share that property. 7. When choosing the objects, keep thinking about that *one* property. Do not change from that property to another property. 8. Make as many groups as you can in this way.	1. Geometric shapes— *properties* are color, size, and shape 2. A set of animals (e.g., different types of fish)— properties are size, shape, and coloring 3. Plants (picture cards showing different types of flowers)—properties are color, shape, size, and type (flowers children are familiar with such as daisy, African violet, tulip, rose, daffodil, lily, etc.)	The teacher might choose to teach the general rules for identifying and using properties of objects for the construction of classes in the form of a story: "This is the story of Mr. Jacobs, who owned a flower shop, and Sally, who liked to help Mr. Jacobs arrange the flowers on the shelves. (Cutout figures are stuck onto a display board to illustrate the story and provide concrete examples of objects and their properties.) Sally arrived at Mr. Jacob's shop one day just as a van was delivering some flowers. Mr. Jacobs was glad to see Sally because he needed help in arranging all the flowers on the shelves. He explained to Sally how she was to put the flowers into *groups* and place them on the shelves. She was to begin by collecting together all the African violets. How would Sally know which were the African violets? (Teacher and children discuss the *properties* of African violets	Following the AO Lesson, children move on to *related learning activities*. A number of activity centers are set up with various *game-like materials* all of which require classifying. Children are required to complete each game before moving on to the next. In a *self-directed* fashion they are encouraged to attempt to apply the general rules learned in the AO Lesson to the solving of the various problems presented in the games. For example: *Find the Animals:* This is a board game showing a roadway running through woods and fields. The roadway is divided into sections. There is a starting and ending point to the roadway. A box contains picture cards showing different types of animals, and there is a large die. Children roll the die in turn and move a figure along the roadway the correct number of spaces according to the number on the die. Sometimes

and how Sally needs to carefully look for *all* these particular flowers.)

Sally next collected all the daffodils together and placed them in the shop window. . . . (So the story continues with the teacher's demonstrating and discussing with the children how Sally would look for the different types of flowers by identifying each type by its properties, and would carefully collect *all* the flowers of each type and place them into a group. The teacher emphasizes the general rules for constructing classes as indicated in the *teacher's lesson guide*.)

A number of short stories are told in this fashion with the teacher's showing that the same set of rules is used in each case even though the *content* of the stories is different. Children are also *actively* involved in the AO Lesson, helping the teacher construct the illustration for each story, role playing the characters in the story, and getting a chance to retell the story to one another.

they land on a space that shows the picture of an animal. From the picture cards the child chooses the same or a similar animal. At the end of the game each child has to arrange the animals he or she won into groups according to species. One child might have a couple of mammals, three insects, two birds, and three reptiles. The teacher may discuss the various classes of animals the children have constructed, ask the children to describe to one another the classes of animals each has won, or ask the children to show the subclasses of some general class such as mammals. Not only are children actively involved in constructing classes in this way, they also get the chance to verbalize about both the content of the classes and how they are constructed. The teacher can also use each activity as a means for evaluating childrens' understanding of the general rules for constructing classes.

Note: The lesson described here takes about 15 or 20 minutes to teach. It is one in a series of lessons used to teach *general rules* for classifying and dealing with hierarchical classification to preschool children. This particular lesson is used to help young children *organize* in memory general rules for constructing classes of objects by identifying properties and using them consistently. This organization of strategy for constructing classes is taught *in advance of* a series of activities, all requiring the construction of classes of objects, which is why the lesson is called an *advance organizer lesson.* Its most important feature is that it presents *general rules* that have the potential for helping the child transfer the skill of constructing classes to various sets of objects.

Logico-mathematical knowledge is the most important of the three forms, and the meaningful learning of social and physical knowledge is dependent on this form of knowledge. To understand logico-mathematical knowledge, we should begin with the idea of operation. An operation is a logical process governed by logical rules that Piaget derived from the science of mathematics—therefore, the term logico-mathematical. An operation, you will remember, involves an interaction between the child and objects in the environment. Is the result of an operation, therefore, knowledge about the objects that were partners in the interaction? Not exactly. Piaget describes it like this:

[Logico-mathematical] knowledge is not a copy of reality. To know an object, to know an event, is not simply to look at it and make a mental copy, or image, of it. To know an object is to act on it. To know is to modify, to transform the object, and to understand the process of this transformation, and as a consequence to understand the way the object is constructed. An operation is thus the essence of knowledge; it is an interiorized action which modifies the object of knowledge. For instance, an operation would consist of joining objects in a class, to construct a classification. Or an operation would consist of ordering, or putting things in a series. Or an operation would consist of counting, or of measuring. In other words, it is a set of actions modifying the object, and enabling the knower to get at the structures of the transformation. . . .
Above all, an operation is never isolated. It is always linked to other operations, and as a result it is always a part of a total structure (1964, pp. 7–8).

Schemas and preoperations also fit into this category of knowledge except that they are pre-logical.

How do preschool children learn these three forms of knowledge? A great deal of social and physical knowledge is learned by "simple abstraction." The child points to objects and for each one asks, "What is it?" For example, names of objects and events, as well as rules for crossing the road safely, are learned directly from the environment. For the meaningful learning of logico-mathematical knowledge, the child itself must create relationships. Piaget (1970) argues that if such knowledge is presented to the child by demonstration or direct teaching, the child will not learn about relationships meaningfully; the learning will be more rotelike.

Finally, it should be made very clear that although Piaget distinguishes among the three forms of knowledge and how they are learned, he says that the three are also inseparable. For example, when the child throws a ball and watches it roll across the floor, the fact that the round object—ball—rolls is a physical knowledge fact. In playing a target game with balls the child might make the

following predictions: the faster I throw, the farther the ball will roll; if I roll it against the wall from here, it will bounce (rebound) over to there. When testing these predictions, the child will be dealing with relationships. These relationships include both physical and logico-mathematical knowledge and need to be *worked out* in the mind.

Although Piaget has written about the educational implications of his theory (e.g., 1970, 1973), it has been left to others to devise educational programs based on his ideas (e.g., Ershler, McAllister, & Saunders, 1977; Furth & Wachs, 1974; Kamii & DeVries, 1977, 1978; Lavatelli, 1973; Copple, Sigel, & Saunders, 1979). There are many Piagetian preschool and elementary school programs. A careful study of them shows that there are also many variations on this theme. Converting Piaget's theory of development into educational practice is not easy (Kuhn, 1979; Murray, 1979, see Inset 7.2).

There appear to be a number of difficulties in attempting to apply a theory of cognitive development, such as Piaget's, to the practice of education. These difficulties have been attributed to ambiguities and imprecision in the description of the sequence of stages of development and the intellectual skills that characterize each stage (Kuhn, 1979; Murray, 1979).

Piaget, after more than fifty years spent developing his theory, made the modest claim that he had, "Laid bare a more or less evident general skeleton (of development) which remains full of gaps" (Sinclair-deZwart, 1977, p. 1). The theory, therefore, remains open-ended and tentative. However, a number of educational programs, mainly for preschool and elementary-grade children, have been based on this theory, which, if not directly proscribed by the theory, are at least compatible with it. (Copple, Sigel & Saunders, 1979; Ershler, McAllister, & Saunders, 1977; Forman & Kushner, 1977; Furth & Wachs, 1974; Kamii & DeVries, 1977, 1978; Lavatelli, 1970).

What is the task facing educators who attempt to apply Piaget's theory of cognitive development to educational practice? Diane Kuhn (1979) has described it under two headings: (1) specify the objectives of the educational process, and (2) specify the methods for attaining the educational objectives.

Educational Objectives Based on Piaget's Theory

Educational objectives for preschool programs derived from Piaget's theory are all aimed, primarily, at promoting children's acquisition of pre- and concrete operations. Kuhn argues that these objectives are inappropriate since all children eventually achieve pre- and concrete operations without a Piagetian or any other type of preschool education. It can also be argued that acquiring concrete operations does not in itself guarantee success in dealing with all *real-life* problems, or, indeed, with all types of Piagetian tasks [see, for example, the "beans in the bottle" (Figure 9.6) and the "area and perimeter" (Figure 9.7) problems]. Murray (1979) points out that an important consideration for the teacher in developing a curriculum is the selection and organization of content. It has been shown that the content of learning activities affects the way children learn and solve problems (Wason & Johnson-Laird, 1972). So emphasizing the development of *operations* through learning does not, in itself, appear to be sufficient.

Case (1975) has also observed that young children often use reasonable but inadequate strategies when attempting to solve Piagetian problems. Training children to use more efficient, teacher-manufactured strategies—based on children's original inadequate strategies—leads to quite remarkable improvements in performance.

Educational Methods Based on Piaget's Theory

What processes of learning can be derived from Piaget's theory? The preschool programs mentioned earlier provide opportunities for children to *actively* construct relationships between and among objects and events from which activities it is expected concrete operations will eventually emerge. In some Piagetian preschool programs (e.g., Kamii & DeVries, 1977; Furth & Wachs, 1974) children are "left alone" to direct their own learning activities in an *enriched environment*. The teacher is expected to encourage the child to *interact* with the environment in various ways by asking interesting questions and making suitable suggestions, *but never directly teaching*. Furth and Wachs state that it is the teacher's responsibility to provide activities that "are developmentally appropriate so as to challenge the child's thinking" (Furth & Wachs, 1974, p. 47), and Kamii and DeVries express a similar view when they say, "We derive from Piaget's theory the moral that it is fruitless to try specifically to organize content for children . . . children organize things for themselves because they constantly try to make sense out of their world" (Kamii & DeVries, 1977, p. 406). Kuhn also criticizes this approach to the process of learning and the method of teaching because (1) it is clear that there are many children who acquire concrete operations who cannot be called active, curious, independent, self-directed learners, and (2) it is not at all clear what is meant by such statements as "self-directed learning."

If children are to be encouraged to direct their own learning in a "free environment," we need to know what children do intellectually when they are left alone, what learning activities they spontaneously engage in, and whether these self-selected and directed learning activities result in desirable cognitive development. Kuhn points out that "Since, by and large, we do not know very much, recommending that children be left alone to direct their own learning activities runs the risk of being found a meaningless educational prescription" (Kuhn, 1979, p. 351).

Murray (1979) has suggested that the only certain recommendation that one can make, based on Piaget's theory, is that educational practice should be based on a "natural process of development" such as the one Piaget has tried to describe. In spite of the difficulties of trying to relate Piaget's theory to educational practice, the effort must be made. Teachers cannot afford to wait for all the issues to be resolved. But in venturing to tackle this difficult task, teachers should be aware of the ambiguities that will inevitably follow in the wake of their practices.

Piagetian Preschool Programs

Constance Kamii and Rhita DeVries (1977) direct a program at the University of Illinois at Chicago Circle. Recently they published a description of their "science" curriculum (1978). Kamii is opposed to "science" as it is usually taught to preschool children (e.g., making crystals, using electric batteries to make bells ring and to light bulbs). She substitutes physical knowledge for science. Types of physical knowledge activities are movement of objects (mechanics), changes in objects, and activities between these two categories.

Target ball is an aiming game that involves the throwing of balls at targets. Building a target by stacking is itself a physical-knowledge activity. Jack set his target about 1½ feet from the wall. Figure 7.8 shows a boy attempting to knock over a target. His second attempt produced a ricochet. According to Piaget, angles of incidence (as in the rebound from a ricochet) are not understood by the preoperational child (Inhelder & Piaget, 1958). After many unsuccessful attempts at ricochet shots, Jack concentrated on straight shots.

What was learned from this activity?

1. Targets were made. Building simple and elaborate targets involved achieving balance and other relationships between objects.

2. Various experiments were pursued. Jack varied his distance of throw, angle of aim, overhand-underhand throws, rolls, and bounces. All involved working out relationships.

3. Other children invented their own problems. Predictions were made and children tried hard to get solutions. Bobby, unable to hit a target throwing the ball, hit the target with the ball in his hand!

Which of the three types of physical knowledge can be associated with this activity?

Celia Lavatelli believed that the task of the preschool is to provide a foundation for the emergence of logical operations. She hinted that these do not emerge simply by virtue of the child's growing older; "There are children of 8 and 9 years who still think preoperationally. They are considered handicapped in school learning" (1970, p. 35). She expected that preschool children can learn logicomathematical knowledge *when they are directly taught,* as long as the child acts upon the explanation and makes it his or her own.

Lavatelli devised an early childhood curriculum divided into five areas: number, space, classification, seriation, and measurement. Teachers using this curriculum are encouraged to provide learning through active interactions with concrete objects. The responsibility for organizing learning, however, rests with the teacher, not the child. The teacher demonstrates the correctness of interactions, minimizes the making of errors, and avoids selecting learning experiences that encourage children spontaneously to make errors. As we have already seen,

Figure 7.8 Children experiment with overhand throws, underhand throws, and underhand rolls to find out how easy or difficult it is to knock down various targets. (Source: Kammi, C., and DeVries, R. *Physical Knowledge in Preschool Education.* Copyright, 1978, by Prentice-Hall, Inc. Reprinted by permission.)

left to their own devices, preoperational children tend to be easily distracted from a task by irrelevant properties of objects. Exercises in the Lavatelli curriculum help the child concentrate on relevant properties of objects when he or she is trying to solve a problem. For example, a child shown a row of toys and an equal number of pennies placed in a pile near the row of toys may claim, "There are more toys than pennies." The teacher might ask "If each toy costs a penny, do we have enough pennies to buy these toys?" Being instructed to move the pennies one-to-one beside each toy may cause the child to reconsider; now there is one penny for each toy. After piling up the pennies again he can now realize that for each toy there is still a penny despite the perceptual difference. His thinking has been challenged by operating on real materials in an enjoyable activity (1970, p. 4).

The main aim of Lavatelli's program is to help the preschool child move from preoperations to concrete operations, a practice criticized by other Piagetian educators, such as Kamii and DeVries (1974), who consider their approach a more orthodox application of principles derived from Piaget's theory.

Sigel's preschool program is based on a *constructivist learning* perspective. **Constructivism** is the belief that knowledge is the result of an active process of construction of relationships among objects (Sigel & Cocking, 1977). During the process of construction, discrepancies occur between what the child expects to happen and what actually happens (remember Jack and his ricochet shots). Resolving discrepancies results in development. We must remember that from a Piagetian point of view the child's chances of finding a resolution depend somewhat on current expectations and knowledge, in which the limits are set by the child's present stage of development. However, trying to resolve a discrepancy usually leads to new experiences and a move forward in understanding.

Children have a knowledge of the world and understand their world through representation of it. Representation develops in an orderly sequence and as a result of the child's interaction with physical and social environments. Competence in representation grows as the child becomes better able to remember objects and to construct relationships between and among objects in their absence. Sigel has called learning situations that require the child to deal with objects and events separated in time and space from the present *distancing events* (Sigel, 1970; Sigel & Cocking, 1977; Copple, Sigel, & Saunders, 1979).

A series of "science" activities is shown in Table 7.5. The basic principles that guide the selection of such activities are reflected in the principles governing problem solving:

Principles

Active Construction	1. Choose activities that allow the child to be the cause of the action and employ a "hands-on" approach.
Resolve Discrepancies	2. Choose activities and materials that allow the teacher to ask the child questions that focus attention on discrepancies and on the actions in the situation.
Distancing Events	3. Choose activities that help the child focus on the transformations, on changes from one state to another rather than on the beginning and end states.

Table 7.5 Science Problem-Solving Tasks

Science Problem-Solving Procedures	Cognitive Processes Engaged	Science Problem Tasks
Identify Problems	Notice discrepancies, inconsistencies, and incongruities.	Notice that magnets do not pick up some metal-looking objects.
Explore through Observation	Analyze objects visually. Compare and note similarities and differences.	Inspect objects that float. Inspect objects that float and those that do not.
Manipulation	Integrate visual and motor activities.	Pour fixed amount of liquid specified in recipe.
Generate Hypotheses	Anticipate outcomes. Relate previous experience to current (re-presentation); infer relationships.	Anticipate what will happen when ice is left in a warm place. Recall what happened when a structure was built with too heavy a top.
Test Hypotheses; Experiment	Notice effect of different combinations. Plan and decide what to do next. Seriate. Compare alternatives, attend to changes, and generate transformations.	Vary amount of salt in play dough. Collect different objects before testing magnets. Arrange weights from increasing to decreasing heaviness. Use a magnifying glass with a variety of objects.
Collect Data	Attend to outcomes of manipulations.	Watch to see effect of changing heat and cold on mercury in a thermometer.
Interpret Data and Make Conclusions	Infer causality. Generalize. Classify.	Infer that things sink *because* they are heavy. Conclude that *all* heavy things sink. Create two classes: sinking things and nonsinking things.

Source: Copple, C., Sigel, I. E., & Saunders, R. A., *Educating the Young Thinker.* Copyright 1979 by D. Van Nostrand Co. Reprinted by permission.

Developmental Interaction: A View from Bank Street

Bank Street College is located in New York City. For many years a demonstration laboratory school for children aged 3 to 13 years has been operated there. **Developmental interaction** has come to be identified with Bank Street, although many educators share this approach, which stems from the **progressive movement.**

John Dewey (1938) advocated educational practice that demands "changing positions in changing times"—therefore, the name, progressive. He was opposed to the drill methods used in schools during the early part of this century. He stood for cultivation of expression, learning of general techniques, making the most of life's opportunities, and becoming acquainted with a changing world. Harriet Johnson, influenced by this philosophy, expressed the purposes of the first nursery program at Bank Street as follows:

[The child's] introduction to the world should be so made that he will hold his thread of a familiar experience as he goes out to find a new one . . . the significance of one experience . . . lies in its relationship to others (1934).

How has the modern counterpart of that first program evolved? What is the significance of the title, a "developmental-interaction program"? *Developmental* refers to both the growth of knowledge about the world and the qualitatively different and increasingly complex ways of organizing experiences (i.e., concepts and skills). *Interaction* refers to the child's interaction with the social and physical world and the interaction between emotional and cognitive development (Cuffaro, 1977).

Learning materials and activities would appear, at face value, to be like those found in many preschool programs: blocks, clay, paints, crayons; cooking, dramatic play, trip taking. Some of these materials, such as blocks, paints, and clay are provided for the children to *explore freely*. There are also structured materials, such as puzzles, pegboards, and lotto games, that encourage differentiation, comparison, ordering, and evaluation.

The curriculum reflects themes of "how," "what," and "why" explorations of the physical and social world. There is an emphasis on the development of cognitive functions—ordering, judging, reasoning, problem solving, and using systems of symbols (Shapiro & Biber, 1972). The major elements of the curriculum and instructional principles are summarized in Table 7.6.

Table 7.6 Examples of Goals and Related Learning Experiences for a
Developmental-Interaction Preschool Program

Learning Goals	Examples of Learning Experiences
1. To provide the child with opportunities to interact physically with the environment: (a) Explore the physical world (b) Engage in constructive and manipulative activities with objects	Children climb, ride and steer tricycles, slide, swing, balance, heave. Children play with rough sand, smooth soft cloth, hard wooden blocks, soft play dough; contrast colors when painting; construct and manipulate objects of changing/unchanging form, consistency, and pattern.
2. To promote the child's potential for ordering experiences through cognitive strategies: (a) In a variety of sensorimotor–perceptual experiences, focus on observation and discrimination	Children look for similarities and differences when standing beside a fish tank and watching the fish, or when listening to running water (rain on windowpanes, water swirling down a drain).
(b) Represent by gesture, two-dimensional drawing and three-dimensional clay molding	Children move to different musical rhythms imitating a kangaroo, a lame person, the rushing wind; use paints or crayons to represent two-dimensional objects; use wooden blocks to represent three-dimensional objects.
(c) Link words to the concepts they stand for so as to organize experience and information	Children order the *content* of experience (e.g., classify, seriate, deal with change) and verbalize about it; use "if-then" thinking when solving problems, in social situations and in play activities; verbalize about the ordering of events in a sequence.
3. To provide opportunities for learning through play: (a) Set the stage for and encourage children to participate in dramatic play. (b) Use the fantasy of play to rehearse and represent reality.	Children engage in self-initiated dramatic play reliving meaningful aspects of their experiences—play moms and dads, doctors and nurses; pretend to be babies, tigers, engineers, getting sick, getting well. Through dramatic play express and deal with emotion; dramatize in a symbolic way both positive and negative experiences.

Source: Adapted from Biber, B., in M. C. Day & R. K. Parker, eds. *The Preschool in Action.* Copyright 1977 by Allyn & Bacon, Inc. Reprinted by permission.

The teacher can help the preschool child understand how to use structured materials so as to encourage differentiation, comparison, ordering, and evaluation. (Photos courtesy of the author)

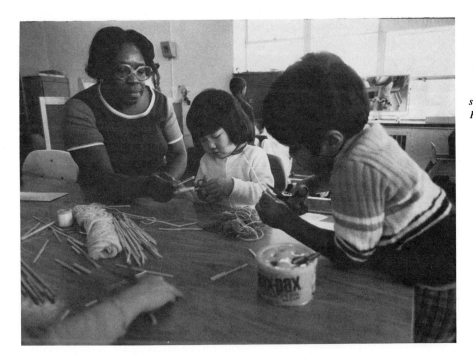

The developmental interaction *approach to learning provides children with opportunities to freely explore certain types of materials and also to classify, order, and evaluate other structured materials. (Photo by Robert Eckert/EKM-Nepenthe)*

Here is an example of how the program's developmental goals are implemented during instruction.

A cooking episode: In part one of the episode children and teacher are planning the episode. It begins at lunchtime.

The fresh *pears* at lunch evoke the comment from Fernando, "Apples!" "Well this is a fruit," said Miss Gordon, "but it has another name. Do you remember the apples we had last week?" Rosina added; "And we made applesauce."

"This fruit is called a pear, Fernando." The teacher responds to what is correct in the child's response, valuing his category association. The children relate to previous experience. Miss Gordon explains that tomorrow they are going to buy lots of apples and make applesauce. She asks the children how they will take it home. Rosina suggests food jars.

"A good idea," said Miss Gordon. "Let's write a note to tell mom we need jars tomorrow."

Rosina dictates a note: "I got to bring bunches of jars to school. We are going to make applesauce. I love you, Mommy."

The teacher helps the children to think ahead to steps in a process. The children also learn that writing is a recording of meaning and a way of communicating. The children estimate how many jars they will need, in terms of people they want to give applesauce to. You can see how much representation will be required—in the absence of applesauce and people and jars.

The next day they go to buy apples at the store. They buy Golden Delicious and Red MacIntosh—all apples (but with similarities *and* differences). They follow a chart for the cooking process (using symbols); they measure out quantities of water and sugar (relationships between amount and effect); they eventually taste the applesauce. "Mine's sour," declared Fernando. "What does it need?" asks Miss Gordon. "More sugar" (The process involves making judgments, making comparisons, dealing with cause and effect.) (Biber, 1977, pp. 446–451).

Montessori's Theory of Learning

While studying for a medical degree at the University of Rome, Maria Montessori (1870–1952) came in contact with mentally retarded and disturbed children. Her interest in their learning problems led her to develop sets of learning materials based on those of Seguin, a French psychiatrist, but materials intended to fit her theory of learning and related method of instruction.

In 1896 Montessori became the first woman in Italy to earn a medical degree, and in 1898 she became director of the Orthophrenic School in Rome, an institution for subnormal or retarded children. She subsequently became well known because of her phenomenal success in fostering the development of these retarded children, a success that was attributed to her learning materials. People argued that if these materials were so successful with retarded children, how much more successful they might be with normal children.

Montessori's philosophy of education followed that of Rousseau, Pestalozzi, and Froebel, which emphasized the innate potential of the child. She believed the child's learning is influenced by an internal pattern of unfolding. However, although she held that this pattern sets the limits for development, she insisted that it only provides a potential not a guarantee for development (1964). The child is not expected to achieve the full potential for development by self-directed, spontaneous, and incidental experiences. Development and *guided* learning must go hand in hand.

According to Montessori, development and learning pass through a series of what she called **sensitive periods** when the child is particularly "tuned-in" to order, taste, touch, exploration, walking, and the interest in and observation of small and detailed objects. Although development is expected to be sequential, phases of development are said to overlap. Though she believed that children are predisposed to develop and learn, Montessori emphasized the need for assistance from adults (1963). If for any reason a child's development is inhibited during a sensitive period, Montessori expected that the child's later development will be handicapped. She did not want learning experiences left to chance.

To promote learning in the child, Montessori developed a *prepared environment* with specially constructed learning materials and furniture scaled to the child's physical level of development. In this environment the teacher has two functions. One is to demonstrate the proper use of the learning materials and the environment. The second is to serve as a resource person. The child is expected to respond to the teacher's demonstrations and then to take advantage of the learning materials.

The Montessori instructional materials are called **didactic learning materials** because they are constructed in such a fashion that they guide the child's use of them. There is usually only one right way for each set of materials to be used. For example, each of a set of wooden cylinders fits into a drilled hole of the same diameter in a wooden block; graded color cards are to be arranged from darkest to lightest color (and vice versa).

The teacher introduces each set of materials to the child and carefully demonstrates the correct use of them. At first the teacher does not correct errors but re-teaches the use of materials if the child shows a lack of understanding. When the child has learned to use the materials, the teacher immediately corrects any error. Montessori saw no virtue in making errors. "After a period of repetitive

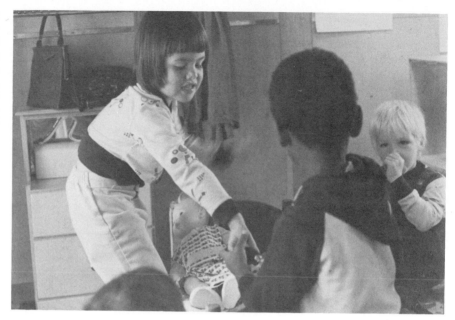

use . . . the child will begin to create new ways in which to use materials" (Lillard, 1972, p. 68). The teacher may, of course, have to encourage by suggestion, clues, and the like, what Lillard called a "burst of creative activity." This is the main characterization of the **fundamental lesson,** with an accent on demonstration.

Further learning experiences that are associated with the fundamental lesson then follow. There is a special sequence to related activities; this is called the *three-period lesson.* First, the teacher points out to the child the relationship between new materials and the general idea introduced during the fundamental lesson: for example, the idea of *rough, smooth,* or the idea of *seriated order* as demonstrated by the wooden cylinder blocks. Second, the teacher may say, for example, "Find me a rough object" or "Find me a smooth object." This is to find out if the child can find examples of objects having the properties described in the general idea. The teacher does not correct errors at this point. If errors are consistently made, the fundamental lesson is re-taught. Why do you think this is necessary?

Third, the teacher ensures that the child can use the idea for many different types of objects which share that general property. Do you think the fundamental and three-part lesson sequence is in any way similar to the advance organizer-related learning activity sequence described earlier?

Playing *with objects can be linked to such types of learning as creativity, problem solving, and language learning. (Top photo by Robert Eckert/ EKM-Nepenthe; bottom photos courtesy of the author)*

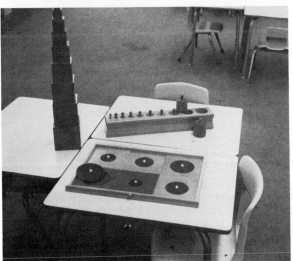 

Preschool Children's Play

Most if not all preschool programs include playful activities. Some educators believe that all preschool children's activities can be described as play in one form or another. This section describes characteristics and types of *play* and considers relationships between play and learning.

Young children seem to have a very compelling wish to *reproduce* their experiences in play. In fact, they spend so much time playing that it becomes a completely absorbing business that includes all aspects of feeling, thought, and action (Maier, 1969).

But what is play? Catherine Garvey (1977, p. 2) has provided this humorous dialogue between a mother and her 6-year-old son:

"Tom, I want to clean this room. Go out and play."
"What do you mean, go out and play?"
"Just go out and do whatever you do when you're having too much fun to come in to dinner."
"You mean toss the tennis ball against the garage? Finish painting my bike? . . . Check out the robin eggs? . . ." Tom left quickly, sensing a certain mood in the way his mother looked at him!

Play certainly includes those activities. It also includes such activities as the target ball game, dramatic play, spontaneous imitative behavior, and so on. But it is really not enough to simply list play activities. What do these activities have in common? Do they have any unique features?

Characteristics of Play

Observations of children's playful behavior has produced a variety of descriptions of the characteristics of play. Fein (1979) distinguishes between the stylistic attributes of play and the structural characteristics of play. Over a given period of time the *stylistic attributes* can be measured by (1) the number of different actions a child uses, (2) the number of different objects a child uses, and (3) the action/object changes that occur. *Structural characteristics* are defined in terms of the features of Piaget's stages of development: thus children may be involved in sensorimotor exploration, pretend-type activities associated with preoperations, or later emerging symbolic types of play (1979, p. 71).

Gardner has described preschool children as being patterners or dramatists (Shotwell, Wolf, & Gardner, 1979). *Patterners* show a strong curiosity in the design and mechanical features of objects. For example, when such children are given a set of variously shaped blocks, they tend to explore features of patterns and balance—such as creating a design by matching a number of smaller blocks to a larger block. *Dramatists* are more interested in the dramatization or narration of interpersonal events. For instance, given the same set of blocks, dramatists might call a large one "mommy" and a small one "baby," and have them reenact a shopping trip (Shotwell et al., 1979, p. 130).

Garvey (1977) and Sutton-Smith (1979a) have both summarized in some detail the characteristics of play as they see them. Garvey describes them as follows:

1. *Play is pleasurable and enjoyable.* Young children's play is free from rules. Play has no consequences. The child can enjoy playing various roles, even such roles as the "loser" in a mock battle. These performances are *free* from consequences (Bruner, 1972).

2. *Play has no extrinsic goals.* The child enjoys play for its own sake. Piaget has identified three forms of play—sensorimotor, symbolic or representational (the preschool years), and rule-governed play.

   Describing one of his infants "playing," Piaget says, "He brought his head back to the upright position and then threw it back again time after time, laughing loudly" (1951, p. 91). Symbolic play *"reproduces* what has struck the child or *evokes* what has pleased him or enabled him to be more fully a part of his environment" (Beard, 1969, p. 44). At first play is more or less unconscious, since in the early part of preoperations behavior is egocentric. Later in this period children begin to use rules in games. They learn rules from older children. Pretend play declines, and children begin more and more to imitate reality.

3. *Play is spontaneous and voluntary.* Young children do not engage in formal play. They move spontaneously from one activity to another, all of which can be called some form of play—building with blocks, painting, playing with puzzles, sociodramatic play.

4. *Play involves active interaction with an environment.* This is a most important characteristic because it links play to such types of learning as creativity, problem solving, language learning, and learning social conventions (Garvey, 1977, pp. 4–7).

As we will discuss, other psychologists interested in play describe certain types of play as being rule-governed. Using Garvey's description of play characteristics, the closest type of learning to which we can bring such play is children's spontaneous and incidental learning. As we have seen, many psychologists and educators believe it is important for preschoolers also to engage in structured, goal-directed learning, which may also be considered playful.

Sutton-Smith (1979b) has based his description of play characteristics on the major types of play theory:

1. *Reframing.* Events are reframed, that is, given different connotations. A child may grimace and roll around on the floor pretending to be hurt. This is socially acceptable as play rather than proper behavior.

2. *Reversals.* There are many examples of reversal behavior in children's play—reversal of roles (pretending to be a fire chief, a monster, or an animal), reversal of rules (trying out different ways of sharing), and reversal of tactics (learning a more flexible approach to routine behavior by playfully changing the routine).

3. *Abstraction of Prototypes.* When a child plays a different role, such as being a doctor or a monster, actions that are used in play are abstracted from the object being represented—the child acts like a doctor or like a monster.

4. *Theme and Variation.* We can often see a child in play focusing on some central action or object—for example, making a "horrible" face and growling or pushing an object along and making "car-engine noises." The child may then produce variations on these themes—the monster waves its long arms, stomps its feet, or becomes another form of monster; the object is a car, a firetruck, an airplane, and the engine noises vary accordingly.

5. *Boundaried Space-Time.* Objects set limits on play and children set limits on their play by some frame of reference. A toy fire truck cannot really function like the real thing, nor can the child actually do the job of a real doctor; and the monster must not be too frightening and is not capable of injuring or biting playmates. Similarly, there are times for playful behavior and times for proper behavior.

6. *Modulation of Excitement.* When children play they are aroused by the activity and excited by the pleasure they get from play. During the preschool years children learn to control the tempo of excitement. In playing games excitement must be modulated, and if the game is also a task there is likely to be a cumulative or growing sense of excitement until a climax when the task is completed (adapted from Sutton-Smith, 1979, pp. 15–22).

Types of Play

Children's playful activities can be placed into two broad categories: exploratory and rule-governed play. Remember Jack's experimenting with ricochet shots in the target ball game. He was exploring cause-and-effect relationships. A child spontaneously cutting patterns out of paper, mixing liquids together to see what happens, dressing up and trying to play a role, is engaging in **exploratory play.**

Children of all ages engage in playful activities that have no apparent objective. Although indulged in by young children more than older preschool age children, "let's pretend" role play involves all children in representations of the physical environment. The same holds true for playing with materials. For example, in carefully constructing towers with building blocks only to knock them over, the child may also be rehearsing representation. The building blocks represent skyscrapers, knocking them over represents an earthquake, and the falling blocks are accompanied with flailing arms and earsplitting yells, representing the collapse of the skyscrapers. Children pretend to be ambulances and fire trucks. Having driven to the scene of an "accident," they suddenly turn into ambulance attendants and fire fighters. Exploration of materials and exploration of behavior during pretend play has significance for mental and social development.

Rule-governed play is particularly the domain of the older preschool child. It has been mentioned that rules governing play are learned from the culture the child lives in. Some rule-governed activities are more like problem solving than play (Gardner, 1971). For example, the child might be engaged in shaking a set of tin cans, each containing a different number of beans, and attempting to arrange them from loudest to softest (quietest) noise; or he or she might be sorting picture cards illustrating animals into classes of animals; or the child might be learning how to operate a pogo stick; or he or she might be "zooming" around the play equipment in the outside area following a "map." Do you feel inclined to call some of these activities "play" but others not? They all involve problem solving and are governed by rules. Well, it is often difficult to distinguish between whether the child is playing (not goal-directed) or problem solving (goal-directed). The two obviously overlap to some extent.

The important point is that "playful" activities of various kinds help the child in seeking information, learning concepts, learning about rules and how they work, resolving conflicts, and relieving frustration. Whether the child is engaged in exploratory or rule-governed play, some form of learning is also occurring. A question often asked is, does play (or playful learning) follow development or can certain types of instruction influence the child's type of play? There have been many research reports which suggest that it is the child's emerging ability to use symbolic representation that ties together play and such forms of cognition as social cognition (Saltz & Johnson, 1974), divergent thinking (Dansky, 1980), classification ability (Rubin & Maioni, 1975), and intelligence (Johnson, 1976). This research has been principally in the Piagetian tradition of looking mainly at children's free play, when they are free to select their own activities. A consideration that had not been addressed seriously until recently is the effect of different types of instructional program on children's play and the relationships between play that is influenced by particular types of instruction and play that is influenced by development. Johnson and his colleagues (Johnson, Ershler, & Bell, 1980; Johnson, Ershler, & Lawton, 1981) recently observed children's play in a formal-education program, which included meaningful reception learning (as described earlier in this chapter) and a discovery-based program, based on principles derived from Piaget's theory of development. For this research play was described in terms of Smilanski's cognitive play categories—*constructive, functional,* and *symbolic* (1968). **Constructive play** is goal-directed. Children have some interaction in mind such as role-playing doctors, nurses, and patients, and, as you might expect, much of this type of play is governed by rules. It has features of both exploratory and rule-governed play described previously. In **functional play** children are engaged in learning about the physical and social environment through observation and by "acting-upon" objects—playing with objects to find out about them. These types of experiences are considered to be prerequisites for the development of later cognitive abilities, as demonstrated in constructive play (Forman & Kushner, 1977). **Symbolic play** can be imitative (based on real-life experiences) or fantastic (based on impossible or improbable events). This type of play involves changes or transformations to objects and events. For example, the child might pretend to be a monster—or suppose that another child is a monster—or pretend that a wooden-crate is a car, or pretend to be driving a car without any props. In their research Johnson and his colleagues found that more children in the formal education program engaged in constructive play and used more transformations in their symbolic play (see Inset 7.3 and Table 7.7), suggesting an important influence of certain types of structured learning on development.

We have been looking at how "normal" children learn. However, many children are handicapped in some way and need help in developing intellectual and social competencies. Chapter 14 is devoted to a description of abnormalities in childhood and how these affect general development. The final section of this chapter looks at the other side of the coin—how attempts are being made through special education programs to treat *certain* types of handicapped children. Only part of the story can be told here.

It is understood that children's play behavior aids development (Jackson & Angelino, 1974). The amount and type of play to be encouraged in preschool settings is less well understood. In examining this issue Johnson and his colleagues (Johnson, Ershler, & Bell, 1980) observed preschoolers in both a discovery-based and formal-education preschool program during free-play activities. The objective was to discover if any relationship existed between the preschool curriculum and type and amount of play. It was expected that children's preferred play behavior in these two preschool programs would differ because of differences in curriculum, organization, and teaching methods.

The curriculum of the formal-education program included long-term sequences of learning activities related to advance organizer lessons (Lawton, 1978). An important objective of the program was to instruct children in certain content areas and the use of logical reasoning. In contrast, the discovery-based program provided the opportunity for spontaneous interaction of children with materials, teachers, and peers in planned, child-directed activities.

Based on the educational objectives of the two programs, children in the formal program were expected to engage in more goal-directed play while those in the discovery-based program were expected to show more functional play. The results of the observations are shown in Table 7.7. It is clear that children in the formal-education program engaged in more constructive play than did children in the discovery-based program who were more likely to engage in functional play. Children in both programs were equally involved in symbolic play, although children in the formal program used a greater amount and variety of symbolic representation.

These results suggest that the type of educational program provided by the preschool can influence children's play behavior in important ways, which may be significant for both intellectual and social development.

Source: Olver, D. R., in Bruner et al. Studies in Cognitive Growth. Copyright 1966 by John Wiley & Sons. Reprinted with permission.

Table 7.7 Percentage of Time Spent in Different Types of Play

Type of Play	Discovery-based Program	Formal-Education Program
	Percentage of time	Percentage of time
Constructive Play	30.7	57.9
Functional Play	36.3	12.3
Symbolic Play	11.5	14.9

Source: Adapted from Johnson, J. E., Ershler, J. A., & Bell, C., 1980. With permission.

Special Education

Children considered in need of *special education* include both the handicapped and the specially gifted. Reference will be made here only to handicapped children. Children who come from poverty backgrounds and others who are disadvantaged by certain types of early experience are considered handicapped children. So also are children diagnosed as having physical and mental disorders.

Project Head Start and Follow Through

Project Head Start began in 1965. It was intended as an intervention program to provide compensatory education; that is, education to compensate for a range of disadvantages in the environments of many children. These children were almost exclusively from poor families. Head-Start programs shared a common major goal, to improve the child's intellectual development and performance on learning tasks. These programs were organized for preschool-aged children based on the belief that the earlier intervention begins the better. (It is well known that performance differences, instead of diminishing with school experience, actually increase.) It was hoped that by the end of the preschool years, the disadvantaged child would no longer be disadvantaged. **Project Follow Through** was initiated in 1968 as part of the compensatory program. The reason for *Follow Through* was to provide a long-term, diversified program to sustain gains made by preschoolers in the Head-Start programs. An important feature of the twenty-two Follow-Through programs was the idea of "planned variation and educational alternatives" (Evans, 1975; Maccoby & Zellner, 1970).

In the early 1970s Head-Start programs began to receive much criticism; it was claimed that immediate gains from learning in these programs are either short-lived or not big enough to make up for differences between disadvantaged and advantaged children (Bronfenbrenner, 1974). Recent reports (Lazar & Darlington, 1979; Darlington et al., 1980) indicate that such conclusions were premature. Reexamination of the effectiveness of the preschool programs for low-income children has been conducted by means of direct measures of children's actual school performance. What do the results show for low-income children who participated in preschool intervention programs almost two decades ago? The major findings were that early education programs

1. significantly reduced the number of children assigned to special education classes (see Figure 7.9);

2. significantly reduced the number of children retained in grade (see Figure 7.9);

3. significantly increased children's scores on fourth-grade math achievement tests and some improvement on reading tests;

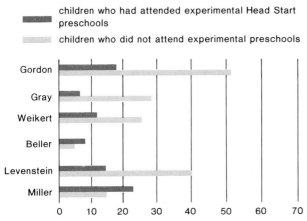

children who had attended experimental Head Start preschools

children who did not attend experimental preschools

1. Percentage of children assigned to special education classes

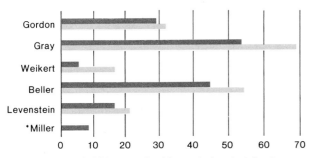

2. Percentage of children retained in grade (grade failure) at least once

Figure 7.9 Effect of preschool intervention on later school performance. In general, fewer children who had attended these six Head-Start preschool programs were (1) later placed in special education classes than children who had not attended; or (2) held back a grade (due to grade failure) at least once during their later school career. (Source: Adapted from Lazar, I., and Darlington, R. *Lasting Effects after Preschool*. Final Report, HEW Grant 90C–1311. USDH, Education and Welfare, DHEW Publication No. [OHDS] 79–30179, 1979.)

4. improved children's IQ scores compared to children not attending Head-Start intervention programs—and this difference is maintained from between three and fifteen years after the preschool program ended; and

5. resulted in low-income children's being more likely than control children to give achievement-oriented reasons for being proud of themselves.

6. The high-quality Head-Start programs surveyed were about equally effective in helping low-income children (Levenstein et al., 1979, pp. 19–20).

These existing results indicate very strongly that children who participated in special education preschool programs were better able to meet the minimal requirements of later schooling than were children who did not attend such programs. At a time when public opinion seems to be reflecting a feeling of disillusionment about Head-Start programs, policy makers' commitment to preschool children, especially low-income children, seems worth a continued investment (Levenstein et al., 1979, p. 20).

The involvement of parents in Head-Start programs appears to improve the chances that children will benefit from this special education. As a result of comparing Head-Start programs with and without parental involvement, Bronfenbrenner (1977) recommends that long-term intervention programs should (1) establish a child/parent relationship during the first three years centered around challenging activities with the parent mainly responsible for teaching, and (2) provide a cognitively oriented preschool program with a continuation of the parent's role as teacher. Results from other studies such as Gordon's (1977) and Radin's (1972) support the conclusion that parent training and involvement in intervention programs results in more lasting benefits to the child. Radin reported that

In general the findings of this study suggest that a parent education component is important if the child is to continue to benefit academically from a compensatory preschool program. . . . A parent program does appear . . . to enhance the mothers' perception of themselves as educators of their children. . . . Thus, perhaps, new maternal behaviors are fostered which are conducive to the child's intellectual functioning (1972, p. 1363).

Educational Programs for Physically and Mentally Handicapped Children

There are many ways in which a child's learning can be adversely affected by **physical** and **mental handicaps** such as cystic fibrosis, muscular dystrophy, heart disorders, amputations, visual and auditory impairments, genetic defects (like thalidomide effects), Down's syndrome, cerebral palsy, autism, and schizophrenia.

Physical handicaps.   Working with physically handicapped children presents special problems for the parent, teacher, and special aide. Many of these children suffer pain and frustration and may be prone to temper tantrums. Parents may become hostile to such children and in some cases abuse them. When this occurs, the children are usually particularly hard to care for, overly active, and difficult to supervise. They threaten the parents' self-image because "they fail to respond to care, to thrive, and to show normal growth and development" (Johnson & Morse, 1968).

Children with visual and hearing handicaps are usually less difficult to deal with. These children are very like children with normal sight and hearing. With careful training, even the severest cases can become self-sufficient and achieve normal or near normal mental and social development. It is important for parents and teachers to be on the lookout for visual impairment. It is easy to recognize the completely blind child, but careful observation is needed to detect symptoms of the partially sighted child. Symptoms listed by Jones (1969) include the following. The child

1. develops mentally at a rate below that expected for children of the same age;

2. covers or shields one eye habitually when looking at objects;

3. appears clumsy or awkward moving around;

4. has poor eye-hand coordination;

5. thrusts head forward and squints when looking at objects;

6. stumbles or trips often.

Children with auditory handicaps appear to be at a greater disadvantage than those with sight impairments. Ninety percent of these children fail to achieve a reading age above fourth grade, and 30 percent remain illiterate (Berg & Fletcher, 1970).

It is important to identify children with sight and auditory handicaps as early as possible. If special training is not initiated before the child is 5 or 6 years old, for most children it is too late. When such problems are attended to in the preschool years, improvements in learning can occur.

Retardation.   There are various degrees of retardation, a subject discussed more fully in Chapter 14. Only the particular cases of retardation due to Down's syndrome, cerebral palsy, **spina bifida** (not always resulting in retardation), autism, and schizophrenia are discussed here.

For many parents the birth of a Down's syndrome child comes as a bitter blow (Drotar, Baskiewicz, Irvin, Kennel, & Klaus, 1975; Solnit & Stark, 1961), which is also the case when children are born with other types of mental handicaps. Ann Gath (1972), in an exploratory study of families with Down's syndrome children, found that for most of the mothers "The memory of how they heard the news of the retardation was still very painful." Without exception all parents in a further group Gath studied (1974, 1978) regarded having a child with Down's syndrome a bitter blow, and experienced long-lasting grief. In some cases grief was followed by denial and aggression toward the child (1979).

Down's syndrome is the most common condition among children in schools for the retarded. But many of these children are now to be found in preschool programs for normal children, which is termed "mainstreaming."

Much has been done in recent times to provide better "intervention" programs for preschool handicapped children. Two particular model demonstration projects for handicapped children from birth to 5 years are illustrative of this trend (Foster & Berger, 1979). The Family Intervention Project at Georgia State University and the Family and Infant Program at North Metro Children's Center, Atlanta, both use parent-mediated intervention strategies in the home setting. Children in these programs have conditions such as Down's syndrome, cerebral palsy, spina bifida, autism, and schizophrenia. Rather than focusing on a special *dyad* interaction of, say, mother and child, Foster and Berger involve the whole family. This approach is based on the family as a system (Minuchin, 1974). They believe this is important for a number of reasons:

1. Many reported failures of child behavioral (modification) programs have been attributed to problems within the family as a whole.

2. Staff in early intervention programs are being asked more and more to deal with families, not just the handicapped child.

3. Preschool programs are in a unique position to offer preventative as well as remedial programs. It seems possible to prevent rigid family arrangements, which may not best influence the child's *and the family's* development, by involving the whole family.

Here is a case example of a rigid family system and the method used to effect changes in the family:

Case Example: In a family where a young retarded child was progressing at a very slow developmental rate, the educational program being implemented by the mother was continually undermined by the grandmother who babied the child and reinforced tantruming and dependent behavior. Though the mother demonstrated skill in behavior modification and teaching techniques, she did not use these techniques systematically with the child in the home where the grandmother also lived. The father was generally uninvolved in the child's program and not available to support the mother when her behavior with the child was opposed by the grandmother. Structurally, the grandmother and child were in a cross-generational alliance against the mother with the father distant from the whole family.

The goal was to strengthen the marital and parental subsystems, allowing the parents to be more in charge of the child, and to support the grandmother in moving out of parental role. In structural terms, this meant changing the family configuration from one where the grandmother was close to the child and the parents distant, to one where the parents were closer and the grandmother more removed. The kinds of strategies used to effect changes in this family included:

Encouraging the parents to spend one evening each week together without the children in an activity that was enjoyable to both of them.

Commending the parents in each other's presence for instances when they competently handled parenting tasks (e.g., managing illness in the child) and expressing puzzlement when they would give over responsibility at other times to grandmother who was so much older and less capable of dealing with young children.

Setting up a behavioral program for the parents, particularly the father, to implement with the child: the task was framed to the parents as our (the staff) needing help because we had been unsuccessful in teaching the skill to the child. But the chosen target behavior was one that would guarantee rapid parental success: an already emerging behavior.

Focusing the family's attention on a minor behavioral problem in another child in the family and requesting the grandmother to serve as a "consultant" on how to help this child.

The first three tasks served to bring the father into the family and to strengthen the marital dyad and the parents' sense of their own competency in the parenting role. The task for the grandmother gave her another focus away from the target child, but consistent with her previous behavior. These moves altered the family structure sufficiently for the parents to begin to take charge of the child's behavior and educational program themselves with subsequent positive changes in the child's developmental status. (Foster & Berger, 1979, pp. 54–55)

Whatever kind of handicap is afflicting the child, many people are involved in helping the child achieve the highest levels of development possible, independence, and happiness—parents, teachers, therapists, pediatricians. The sooner the child is diagnosed as being in need of special care the better. Very often it is not just the child who needs special help, but the parents and siblings also. Care of the handicapped child is a "family" concern. There can be great joy and satisfaction in being a part of even the slightest gains in development and learning made by a young child who is struggling to overcome a handicap.

Summary

Two schools of thought dominate ideas about how children learn, the environmentalist and the cognitive structuralist. The behaviorist theories, based on an environmentalist view of learning, are those developed by Skinner and Gagné. Skinner has emphasized the sequencing of learning through reinforced experiences. Gagné has proposed a learning theory built around a hierarchy of concepts and skills. The sequence of learning proceeds from the simplest level to the more complex levels of knowledge.

Bruner suggests new learning should be *matched* with the child's present view of the world but instructional sequences should proceed from the enactive to the iconic to the symbolic. The child should first be taught basic concepts, rules, and learning strategies. Informed guessing and seeking for solutions should also be encouraged. An important function of instruction, according to Bruner, is to help improve the child's development and learning.

Ausubel describes three stages of development: preoperational, concrete operational, and abstract logical, loosely based on that by Piaget. At the preoperational (preschool) level, the child's learning is confined to acquiring primary concepts. Readiness for learning is described as a composite of developmental and subject-matter readiness. Of the four dimensions of learning, meaningful reception, rote reception, meaningful discovery, and rote discovery, Ausubel claims the most profitable is meaningful reception learning. By using this method general concepts are taught *in advance of* related concepts at a particular level.

According to Piaget, there are three forms of knowledge: social, physical, and logico-mathematical. He has emphasized that the three forms of knowledge are inseparable.

Several specialists have arrived at different interpretations of how to apply Piaget's theory of intellectual development to learning and instruction. Lavatelli supports direct teaching of all three forms of knowledge. Kamii would like the teacher to encourage the child to learn through active interaction with objects and events. According to Sigel, the child learns best by active construction of relationships among objects, and the resolution of discrepancies, transformation, and changes.

The developmental-interaction approach is based on the philosophy of the progressive movement, championed by John Dewey, and is best extolled by the Bank Street approach to learning and instruction. Development is influenced by the different ways in which the child comes to organize experience. Learning occurs when the child actively interacts with the social and physical world. Learning materials are of two types: materials to explore freely, such as paint, and structured materials such as puzzles.

Montessori has held that the sequence of development is by way of sensitive (overlapping) periods. Learning is fostered in a prepared environment that includes didactic learning materials. Instruction is organized according to a method called the fundamental and three-period lessons.

Play is considered to be a dominant form of young children's behavior. Therefore much of learning can be considered playful activities. Play is said to be pleasurable, spontaneous, and voluntary and to have no extrinsic goals. Children also use the medium of play to reframe experiences, reverse the roles of proper behavior, indulge in role play, invent various themes and variations on themes. Children accept limitations on play and learn to control the tempo of play. Play can also be related to such activities as creativity and problem solving. There are two basic forms of play, exploratory and rule-governed.

There are special forms of preschool education for disadvantaged and physically handicapped children. The main objective of Head-Start and Follow-Through programs has been to help disadvantaged preschool children get a head start before kindergarten and the early elementary grades. Recent analyses of the results of intervention programs begun in the early 1960s have proved them to be successful in reducing the number of low-income children assigned to special education classes or held back a grade. Children from these intervention programs perform well in later school subjects and are proud of their achievements. Involvement of parents in Head-Start programs appears to improve the chances of their children's success.

Children with visual and learning impairments are usually less difficult to deal with than those with hearing impairment and serious physical disabilities. Early screening is important to identify handicapped children. If special training is not initiated before the child is 5 or 6 years old, then it is almost too late.

The birth of a baby with Down's syndrome or a baby whose development is retarded from such handicaps as spina bifida, cerebral palsy, autism, and schizophrenia is a most painful experience for many parents. Parents find it difficult to relate to these children. Much has been done recently to help these families and provide special intervention programs for their handicapped children.

Questions for Review

1. Briefly describe methods of applying Skinner's operant conditioning view of development and learning to the organization of preschool programs. In your view what is the single most crucial principle of instruction derived from this theory?

2. A very important factor affecting learning is the child's *readiness* to learn. How is *readiness* described by Bruner, Ausubel, and Piaget? Do you notice any similarities or differences among these three psychologists' views?

3. What does Bruner mean by "going beyond the information given"?

4. From Ausubel's point of view, what is the relationship between the preschooler's level of development and the learning of primary concepts?

5. Using an example of a learning activity, describe the steps in the process of *meaningful reception learning.*

6. What is the relationship between *development* and *interaction* according to the "Bank Street view"? How is the concept of developmental interaction applied to the organization of Bank Street programs for preschoolers?

7. How would a preschool teacher trained in the Montessori method relate the notion of *sensitive period* to the preparation of a fundamental and three-period lesson? Give examples of activities.

8. What is presently being done to provide educational opportunities for low-income-family children and preschoolers who are physically and mentally handicapped?

9. If possible, make arrangements to visit two or three preschools or day-care centers in your area (a mixture of preschool, day care, Montessori preschool, and traditional preschool would provide interesting contrasts). Spend at least thirty minutes in each center and write down what you see teachers doing, children doing, and how you see teachers and children interacting. Try to use short, descriptive sentences related to *what actually occurred.*

Using this information, try to answer the following questions:
(a) What did the children appear to be learning from the activities they engaged in?
(b) Does there appear to be any possible relationship between the learning activities you observed and children's development?
(c) What were teachers' behaviors apparently aimed at achieving (for example, did teachers ask questions, and what were the questions asking)?
(d) How did teachers and children interact, and what seemed to be the purpose of the interactions?
(e) What similarities and differences did you notice among the centers you visited?

Suggestions for Further Reading

Boegehold, B. D., Cuffaro, H. K., Hooks, W. H., & Klopf, G. J., eds. *Education before five*. New York: Bank Street College of Education, 1977. Contains brief chapters on the behavioral, Piagetian, developmental-interaction, and Montessori method approaches to preschool education. Also includes interesting chapters on day-care, infant-toddler programs, and home-based programs.

Bruner, J. S. *The process of education*. Cambridge, MA: Harvard University Press, 1966. In this book, considered one of the most influential works on education, Bruner answers the question, "What shall we teach and to what end?" Especially important for this chapter is Bruner's Chapter 3, "Readiness for Learning."

Bruner, J. S. *Towards a theory of instruction*. Cambridge, MA: Harvard University Press, 1966. A companion book to *The Process of Education*. Read particularly Chapter 3, "Notes on a Theory of Instruction."

Day, C. M., & Parker, R. K. eds. *The preschool in action: Exploring early childhood programs,* 2nd ed. Boston: Allyn and Bacon, 1977. The second part of this book includes chapters describing programs based on behavioral, Piagetian, and developmental-interaction views of learning and instruction.

Garvey, C. *Play*. Cambridge, MA: Harvard University Press, 1977. Shows how the changing forms of play help the child cope with a physical and social environment. Many anecdotal illustrations and examples taken from videotapes of children's play.

Social and Personality Development

8

who are you, little i

(five or six years old)
peering from some high

window; at the gold

of november sunset

(and feeling: that if day
has to become night

This is a beautiful way)

The well-cared-for infant is initiated gently into a social world. The infant forms attachments with primary care givers and, usually, the infant's experience with others is contained within a fairly narrow scope. When he or she feels secure from these first social experiences, the infant ventures forth and explores other social contacts. It was pointed out in earlier chapters that social behavior is related to physical and mental development. As infancy draws to a close the child has become physically more mobile and more able to think and reason about the world around—including social relationships. The child about to leave infancy behind has already acquired a whole range of skills for engaging others into playful, social activities. A most important skill is language, and adults become fascinated by the young child's attempts at conversation—filled with questions, often interrupted with "ums" and "ahs," and all at once coy, earnest, and humorous. Although much of speech is egocentric, the child attempts to communicate with others.

We have mentioned that during the preschool years the child's play changes from fantasizing with objects to sociodramatic pretend play. This involves the ability to act out previous experiences and also to experiment with role playing and various kinds of social encounter—some of which in the real world, with *proper* behavior, might be threatening.

Development of social skills follows an awakening notion of others' social behavior, and the need to respond. The child's own social behavior becomes steadily enmeshed in that of others (Hinde, 1974). The family's role in bringing about changes in the child's social behavior is considerable. Parents teach the child acceptable ways of behaving, set limits on social behavior, establish themselves as models the child can identify with, and provide the first opportunities for broadening social behavior by interacting with other persons (Lamb, 1978, p. 44).

Opportunities for socializing and developing new social behaviors are provided within the family, within peer groups, in school settings, and in the neighborhood. We have already seen that the child's emerging social behavior and personality go hand in hand. Various theories, which you are now familiar with, have been mentioned to describe and explain how this dual development occurs. In this chapter we will pursue these theories a little further and will introduce new ideas about the family, peer group, and the school. We will also examine the development of specific social behavior by considering sex roles, aggressiveness, and altruism.

Theories of Personality Development

The psychoanalytical views of Freud and Erikson are primarily theories of personality development, although they give great importance to the consequences of social interaction on personality development.

The Psychosexual View

According to Freud (1923, 1924), between the ages of about 3 and 6 years, the child passes from the anal stage to the *phallic* or *oedipal stage* of psychosexual development. The child now becomes interested in and gains pleasure from the genital area. Preschool children become very interested in differences between boys' and girls' genital parts, and the bathroom can often become a consulting room. There are many examples of play connected with the experience of urination and interest in that area. Here is an illustration from Lowenfeld (1967, p. 114).

Aged 5: the boy found that while he was playing with water the rubber dog got water inside it. As he squirted it out, he said excitedly, "Oh, he's tiddling." . . . He turned it [the dog] upside down, dragged its legs apart, pointed to the part where the penis should be, and laughed.

Freud distinguished between the features of this stage for boys and for girls. From about the fourth to the sixth year, Freud claimed, a boy starts to take a great interest in his penis, "so easily excitable and changeable, so rich in sensations" (1923, p. 246). He may get pleasure from "showing-off" his penis, comparing it to those of other boys, and attempts to see the sexual organs of girls and women. Freud also supposed that the young boy becomes fearful of the size of his father's penis and dreads the possibility of having his own cut off (castration). He directs his attention toward the main source of gratification, his mother. He "falls in love" with her and fantasizes about marrying her and being in bed with her (1909). Freud named this phenomenon the *Oedipal complex* after the Greek myth about Oedipus, a king's son who, during infancy, was given to foster parents. In later manhood while on a journey he met the king, his father. Oedipus did not recognize him because he was in disguise. They quarreled, and Oedipus killed the man. Later he married the widowed queen, not realizing she was his mother. When he discovered their true relationship, in horror he put out both his eyes and went into exile. Freud associated the story with his belief that all young boys fall in love with their mothers and wish to get rid of their fathers.

Although he was less sure about the way this complex affected a young girl, Freud (1924) believed that a girl, by about the age of 5, begins to fear her mother and turns her affections to her father. Her fear stems from the fact that her mother no longer appears to provide a constant love, and she also suddenly realizes she does not have a penis—which she blames on her mother. The young girl, according to Freud, fantasizes about marrying her father and getting rid of her mother. Freud referred to the imagined relationship as the *Electra complex*. Freud also took this title from Greek mythology. Electra persuaded her brother to kill their mother and stepfather to avenge the murder of their father. Ruth Monroe (1955) doubted this aspect of Freud's theory. However, one day she was bathing her 4-year-old daughter in the same bathtub with her brother. The girl, comparing herself with her brother, suddenly stated, "My weewee (penis) is all gone." She would not be reassured by her mother and for a number of weeks strongly objected to being called a girl. Freud called this state, *penis envy* (1933).

How do children resolve these complexes? Freud (1924) believed a boy learns to repress his unrequited sexual love for his mother. He realizes she loves him, and he loves her in return, but in a socially acceptable way. The boy also begins to identify more with his father and at this time begins to acquire a strong male, sex-role identity. In the case of a girl, incestuous desires are suppressed out of a fear of losing parental love (1933). For both boys and girls these acts of suppression lead to the development of the **superego** (conscience). Children, under the influence of the superego, learn to accept moral values, usually those provided by the parents' teaching.

The newfound superego is rigid at this stage of development. This rigidity shows itself in children's compulsiveness about neatness, about "wrong things," and in their concern with guilt. Children also continue to experience conflicts between the standards set by their superego and the still lurking Oedipal and Electra complexes. As we will see, according to Freud, these conflicts break out at puberty, resulting in the problems of adolescence.

The Psychosocial View

As we have already seen, Erikson (1963) was influenced by Freud's psycho-sexual theory, but, unlike Freud, Erikson emphasized the positive social development of children that emerged from relationships with parents. According to Erikson, during the preschool years there is a single major psychosocial conflict that the child needs to resolve for normal social and personality development to occur—the conflict between *initiative* and *guilt,* between the impetus of self-expression and exploration and the feelings of blame and failure.

During this period parents and care givers can play an important role in helping the child deal with complicated feelings that include hate and guilt. What the child is striving for is a feeling of self-confidence. Mental development is moving on at a pace, thinking and reasoning becoming more logical, and there is a growing facility in using language. The child's imagination is rich with ideas (Erikson, 1959), his or her activities are filled with purpose, and the child shows much initiative in generating all kinds of activities.

However, the child also has feelings of doubt still, and fears of punishment for wrongdoing. Erikson believes that some of the child's ambitions are influenced by the Oedipal complex. The child finds that certain behaviors violate social regulations. It is in acknowledging social rules and conventions that the child develops a superego. The crises of this stage are generated by experiencing failure. Erikson's warning to parents is to use their authority carefully, explain rules and regulations to their children as rationally as possible, and offset restrictions with

opportunities for the child to develop initiative. It is a good idea for parents and children to share activities and to generate shared endeavors.

In becoming more aware of social roles and learning rules of social behavior, a main theme in children's lives is what Erikson has called "making and making like" (1959). As the child continues to explore the world around, aided by further physical and mental development and a growing sense of initiative, success breeds confidence. As children strive for self-confidence, they become very aware of themselves as having an *identity,* a sameness or oneness of being, an understanding of who and what they are as a person. Bigner (1979, pp. 137–145) has suggested that the child's development of a sense of initiative and identity can be helped by learning several important tasks. These include the following:

1. *Discovering personal capabilities.*
The child has a consuming interest in testing the boundaries of initiative. Erikson has called this energy, *intrusiveness.* Preschool children are very active in seeking to explore their environment. They *intrude into* every space physically—charging in where angels fear to tread! They *intrude* intellectually by asking many questions, often repeating the same question ten times over. When they paint, they paint everything including themselves; when they paste, they get stuck to the paper; when they socialize, they impress themselves verbally onto people. Yet, although young children may often appear to have boundless confidence, suddenly they can appear shy and withdrawn. They judge their own behavior harshly in terms of its rightness or wrongness. Parents may alleviate a child's feeling of failure or of doing wrong, when he or she discovers limitations, by their giving greater concern for the child's effort and exploration and less concern to results that the child feels are failures.

2. *Learning to establish routines and taking responsibility for personal actions.*

In helping children learn the boundaries of their limitations and some of the reasons for their existence, parents and teachers would do well to establish routines. They can nurture feelings of success by helping their children experience personal responsibility for their accomplishments.

Children may respond immediately to certain requests, especially if they consider them fun to do, or they may strongly object to tasks. Established routines allow for this fluctuation in feeling and for eventual pride in accomplishment. Preschool children take great delight, for example, in dressing and undressing themselves. During wet or snowy weather, this may take the whole of "outside playtime." Putting on and taking off snowsuits, two pairs of socks, and a pair of heavy boots takes some doing! But even 3-year-olds, all thumbs, sometimes succeed. Adults should try not to nag or scold too severely, which can create unnecessary feelings of guilt or failure. Establishing habits and routines can be very helpful in controlling behavior and in encouraging initiative.

3. *Learning to discriminate between various social roles and how to interact properly with others.*

When people interact they assume different roles depending on the situation. Children can learn about the changing face of role taking within the family, the school, and other social settings. It is mainly within the family setting that the young child learns about social interaction.

Theories of Social Development

Social learning theory is the environmentalist's view of *socialization,* the process of being trained to form and to become aware of cooperative and interdependent relationships with others and with society. We will examine this view of the preschool child's social development and then we will examine the child's moral development.

Moral thinking is considered by various cognitive structuralists to be an area of overlap between cognitive development and social development. Piaget believes that moral rules are learned from the culture maintaining that the types and diversity of experiences involving moral judgments will significantly affect the child's moral development. Piaget has said that the level of children's moral reasoning goes hand in hand with the level of intellectual development, but he places a sharp emphasis on the influence of adult-imposed rules on children's social behavior. Kohlberg, whose view of the development of children's moral reasoning and related social behavior stems from Piaget's theory, stresses the relationship between the ability to reason and moral development, linking the two together in parallel stages. As you will see, moral development gives a clear view in stages of the process of socialization, of the child's training in and learning of the values of parents and society.

Socialization According to Learning Theory

Some psychologists believe that the best indicator of children's social knowledge and social behavior is the extent to which children behave like their parents. This is, of course, a behaviorist's view of learning and development. Miller and Dollard (1941) made an important early study to determine whether children would imitate certain types of behavior when their imitative behavior was reinforced. They found that children learn sex roles and moral behavior when they are rewarded for appropriate behavior and punished for inappropriate behavior. More recently, Bandura (1969, 1971, 1977) has focused his research on children's imitative behavior. He discovered that preschool children imitate unfamiliar adults who are affectionate and caring. Imitation is more strongly reinforced by adults who exert firm control over things the child desires. By the preschool years children have begun to learn to associate satisfaction (feeling good) with behavior adults approve of. Children shun other behaviors because they result in dissatisfied feelings. During the preschool years children develop an internalized control over their behavior rather than depending on external praise, criticism, or punishment. We can see that social learning theory is strongly influenced by psychoanalytic theory and its focus on love, satisfaction, and power.

It is not simply a case of parents' and other adults' influencing children's behavior by their setting up behaviors to be imitated and enforcing these demands by rewards and punishments. Social learning theorists acknowledge that preschoolers are able to, and likely to, pick models to imitate, and they do this quite spontaneously, especially if they see people being rewarded for what they do (Bandura, 1969; Mischel, 1920).

Moral Development

As was the case in all his studies on children's behavior, Piaget investigated children's moral thinking by observing their behavior in various situations. He considered various aspects of children's moral judgments in relation to rules, lying, cheating, punishment, and so forth (1932).

Piaget began his study of the development of moral judgment and related social behavior by studying how children (boys) played the game of marbles. (For many years both in Europe and England marbles was a game played exclusively by boys.)

Children take games such as marbles quite seriously—especially as they grow older. Piaget discovered that moral behavior was closely associated with an understanding of rules and a willingness to play by the rules. From his observations of children's game playing, he concluded that moral development, like mental development, develops in a series of stages.

Piaget's stages of moral development.   During the preschool years there are two stages of moral development, the egocentric stage and the incipient (cooperation) stage (see Table 8.1).

Table 8.1 Piaget's Stages of the Development of Moral Reasoning

Stage	Moral Concepts
Moral Realism (a) 3-5 years (Egocentric stage)	Children lack any real understanding of rules and how they operate or of the relative seriousness of various kinds of transgression. Acts are believed to be right or wrong based on the say so of some external authority but without any consistency of judgment. Children simply conform, more or less, to rules and standards set by adults without any consideration for why these are required.
(b) 5-9 years (Incipient cooperation stage)	Children now show more respect for and understanding of rules. They still believe rules are set by some external authority, usually parents, but they now see rules as consistent and unchangeable. Children now begin to take into consideration the consequences of acts before judging their relative rightness or wrongness. Acceptable social behavior is judged solely from an egocentric view without taking other people's feelings and views into consideration.
Morality of Cooperation or Autonomy 9-11 years	It is now understood that social rules are arbitrary and can be questioned and even changed if necessary. Children believe it is possible to make personal decisions about obeying rules and that obedience to some external authority is not always necessary or desirable. However, children do show respect for authority, realizing its necessity for social order. They also now take other people's feelings and views into consideration. Punishment for wrongdoing is related to the intention of the wrongdoer and the consequences of acts. By early teenage-hood children become very concerned about equal justice for all.

Source: Adapted from Piaget, J., *The Moral Judgment of the Child.* Copyright © 1932 by Kegan Paul. With permission.

As children grow older they learn to play according to mutually accepted rules. (Photo by Paul Buddle)

Piaget was interested in discovering whether the young child understood the rules of a game, if the child was willing to play a game according to rules, and if the child was willing to change them. He observed pairs of boys playing the game of marbles. At the *egocentric stage* children do not apparently fully understand rules, even though they state that they do. Nor do they necessarily play together, but rather play their own individual version of a game according to different sets of rules. They see nothing improper in this disparity, since the aim of the game is not so much winning as enjoying oneself. That is why Piaget called their moral judgment egocentric, similar in pattern to the speech of children of the same age.

At the second stage of moral development, **incipient cooperation,** the child is more likely to play according to a set of socially accepted rules. There is a willingness to define acceptable rules and to play cooperatively with a partner according to a common set of rules. At this stage a child believes that rules are absolute and unchangeable. However, a child may accept that the marbles can be placed in a circle rather than a square. This is not breaking the rules, but another version of the same rule. The child does not yet understand that this is a real change which may require altering the rules.

To find out how children think or reason about moral behavior, Piaget invented stories with a moral, each story having two versions; he told the stories to the children and then asked them their opinion about an incident. Here is an example.

A little boy named Augustus noticed his father's inkpot was empty. One day he decided to help by filling the inkpot. In opening the ink bottle he spilled some ink on the tablecloth, making a large blot.

A little boy named Julian thought it would be fun to play with his father's inkpot. At first he played with the pen. He dipped it into the ink and made a blot on the tablecloth (Adapted from Piaget, 1932, p. 122).

After hearing both stories, the child was asked, "Which boy was the naughtier"? Children in the first two stages of development gave two types of answers. The first type merely takes into account the *results* of the act.

"Which is the most naughty?—*The one who made the big blot.*—Why? *Because it was big"* (Piaget, 1932, p. 126).

Older children are more willing to take into account the motive for the action, as well as the outcome. In this case, Augustus would be less guilty because he had good intentions.

Young children's moral judgments are influenced by rules as adults apply them to children. These rules work in two ways. The adult is apt to punish a child merely for the magnitude of a wrongdoing—ignoring intention. For example, the child may mischievously crumble a cookie over the floor and gain a mild rebuke. On another occasion, helping to tidy the garage, the child might inadvertently smash a set of clay flowerpots and suffer quite a severe rebuke. So it is the result rather than the intention that is punished. It is this association between result and punishment that influences the child's moral thinking and judgment. But this is not the complete picture. Suppose that the child lied to cover up a misdemeanor. Parents tend to punish children for telling lies. Exaggeration, however, is never punished. Indeed, the child may be "rewarded" for telling some fantastic story, as though this were "cute" or clever. The child, however, may think that exaggerations are naughtier than lies. In a sense they are *bigger* lies. The young child, unable to discriminate between the value of the result of behavior and the value of the intention, not the various positive and negative relationships that exist between them, is likely to be confused by adults' different reactions to various behaviors that the child sees as being similar. Cognitive structuralists would argue that the child is, in fact, faced with a cognitive conflict in the situations described above. As children grow older (between the ages of 9 and 11), they begin to take into account both intention and result of behavior.

Kohlberg's stages of moral development.　Influenced by Piaget's work, Laurence Kohlberg (1969, 1971) has also studied moral development. Like Piaget, Kohlberg considers that children's social (moral) behavior does not simply reflect rules imposed by their culture, but that children also form their own moral judgments through the development of reasoning. From this point of view social development is strongly influenced by intellectual development.

Over a period of twelve years Kohlberg studied the moral reasoning of a group of boys aged between 10 and 16 years when the study began. He used a method of ascertaining the development of moral reasoning similar to that Piaget used—he posed a moral dilemma by way of a story. One of the best known of Kohlberg's stories is called "Heinz Steals the Drug." It goes as follows:

In Europe a woman was near death from cancer. One drug might save her, a form of radium that a druggist in the same town had recently discovered. The druggist was charging $2000, ten times what the drug cost him to make. The sick woman's husband, Heinz, went to everyone he knew to borrow the money, but he could only get together about half of what it cost. He told the druggist that his wife was dying and asked him to sell it cheaper or let him pay later. But the druggist said no. The husband got desperate and broke into the man's store to steal the drug for his wife. Should the husband have done that? Why? (1969, p. 376).

Children of different ages were asked to tell how the main character of the story should act and to give a justification for the actions. This required the children to take the part of the character in the story—to see the dilemma from the character's point of view. Not so easy for the egocentric preschool child! Kohlberg analyzed responses to these moral dilemmas. He was not interested so much in the children's judgment of "good" or "bad" acts, but in how they reason about moral dilemmas. We must keep in mind that these children were on the

Table 8.2 Kohlberg's Six Stages of Moral Reasoning

Stage	Moral Concepts
Level 1. ***Preconventional Morality.*** (Ages 4 to 10 Years) Stage 1: Concern with obedience and punishment	Children determine the badness of actions by the degree of punishment that results. Good behavior is associated with avoiding punishment.
Stage 2: Concern with satisfying needs	Good behavior is associated with satisfying one's own desires and needs without considering the needs of others. Although children show some awareness of fairness, it is usually in the sense of what they get out of the exchange: "You can play with my action-man if I can play with your new soccer ball."
Level 2. Conventional Morality (Ages 10 to 13 Years) Stage 3: Concern with the "good-boy, nice-girl" image	Children behave in accordance with rules and standards in order to gain the adults' approval rather than to avoid the physical consequences of bad behavior. There is a growing awareness of the need for rules, and the goodness or badness of behavior is judged in relation to the intention of acts.
Stage 4: Concern with law and order	At this stage children have an unquestioning attitude toward authority and to social rules. All laws are made to be obeyed and that is the duty of each person without any exceptions being possible.
Level 3. Postconventional Morality (Ages 13 to Young Adulthood or Never) Stage 5: Concern for the rights of the individual	Good behavior is now defined in terms of the rights of the individual according to rules and standards agreed upon by society in general. It is now considered acceptable to change rules or laws if this is necessary for the greater good, or even to break the rules in certain circumstances—though intention then becomes very important.
Stage 6: Concern for ethical principles	Decisions about one's actions are now based on *personal* ethical principles derived from universal laws, which are consistent with the general good and with concern for others. Personal moral beliefs and values are steadfastly adhered to even when they are sometimes contradictory to laws established to preserve social order. For example, a man may steal a drug to save the life of his wife because preserving human life is a higher moral obligation than not stealing.

Source: Adapted from Kohlberg, L., in D. A. Goslin, ed. *Handbook of Socialization Theory and Research.* Copyright 1969 by Rand McNally. With permission.

verge of or into early adolescence. However, from the results of his studies, and in keeping with Piaget's theory of moral development, Kohlberg identified three levels (each with two stages) of moral reasoning spanning the years from age 4 to young adulthood (see Table 8.2).

According to Kohlberg, at the pre-moral level, within stage 1 (the preschool years) the child confuses moral judgments with other judgments. Rules are changed as the facts in the story change. This is an interesting example of centration. Rather than take all facts into consideration, the child takes each fact separately, judging each one on its own merit, and so confusing the overall picture.

Like other social psychologists, Kohlberg believes that children become so-cialized by learning rules of social behavior from their culture and by imitating other people's behavior. The environment is expected to have an important in-fluence on children's social behavior. In exploring cultural effects on the devel-opment of moral reasoning Kohlberg discovered that

In four different cultures, middle-class children were more advanced in moral judgment than matched lower-class children. . . . Middle-class and working-class children seemed to move through the same sequences, but the middle-class children seemed to move faster and farther (1971, p. 190).

However, as we have already mentioned, like Piaget, Kohlberg also believes that the level of moral reasoning is closely aligned to the level of intellectual devel-opment. Even the most advantageous environment is not expected to "speed up" development by all that much. It would be unlikely that we would find preschool children using a stage 2 type of moral reasoning.

Family's Role in Socialization

The family, whatever its strengths and weaknesses, whatever its structure, whatever its membership, provides the first referent for the child's social devel-opment. By the time the child is 3 years old the family relinquishes part of its primary control over the child's social behavior. Peers and teachers begin to play a significant role in the child's socialization. Although it has been suggested that as the young child is introduced more and more into the large community, the community replaces the family as the most important influence on the child's social development (Cohen, 1976), the more generally held belief is that the family retains the primary socializing role. Clausen has observed that the family continues to provide a continuity of care and adjustment (1966) and that a wide range of children's tasks and achievements which contribute to socialization are closely linked to various aims of parenting activities (1968). For example, the development of trust is linked to the parents' nurturing; intellectual development is linked to parents' teaching; the development of the child's awareness of how to adapt behavior to the demands of the social environment is a result of the parents' orienting the child to the world of kin, neighborhood, and community; and the achievement of a measure of self-control results from parents' providing the guidance and help in formulating goals and planning activities (1968, p. 141). However, although the family apparently dominates the child's social develop-ment at this time, the child is also faced with accommodating the social influences of the community with those of the family. The extent to which the child achieves success in learning to adapt to both social milieus can be attributed in no small measure to the supportive strength of the family.

Family: Structure and System

Although at one time mother–child relationships were considered all important, it is now believed that each family member's influence on and contribution to the family social setting should be considered. *Family structure* is quite complex. It includes *membership* (both parents or one, step-parents, number of family members, spacing and sex of children, and extended members such as grandparents), *role relations* (for example, responsibilities accepted by both mother and father, and older siblings), and *strength of relationships* (between husband and wife, between parents and children, and between siblings).

Socialization within the family is not a one-way system—it is not simply a case of parents' socializing their children. Social relationships between parents and children are reciprocal. But the process of socialization is even more complex than this two-way system. The whole family can be considered an interacting system (Minuchin, 1974).

Relationships among individual members affect all family members. A parent's interaction with a child will change or be reinforced depending on how the child reacts (Bossard & Boll, 1966). The parent's personality also enters into the relationship. A parent who feels the need to be authoritarian may have that attitude reinforced by the child who always obeys. Another parent may initially start out with strict rules for behavior but relax them and become more permissive as the child learns the rules and accepts them. Husbands and wives who share beliefs about parenting have a different effect on a child's social development from parents who differ about child rearing and constantly openly bicker about their differences.

Zilbach (1968) has charted a sequence of phases through which a family system might pass. Immediately after marriage the husband and wife need only consider each other in establishing a partnership, the birth of the first child marks the beginning of the second phase, and the preschool years mark the third phase. If further children are born, they also mark phases. For example, children with brothers and sisters learn how social power is used to discriminate age and sex roles within the family (Bigner, 1974; Sutton-Smith & Rosenberg, 1965, 1968), and firstborn children learn to use certain social tactics to achieve their own social goals when they are interacting with younger siblings (Bigner, 1979). Each phase creates new family patterns of relationships. The *family-system* approach attempts to trace the effects on family life and on the social behavior of family members and to trace the effects of events that occur in these various phases.

Effects of Parenting Styles

In Chapter 5 we discussed the effects of certain kinds of parenting on the child's sex identity and the development of aggression. Although we still have much to discover about how parents acquire parenting behavior, certain basic styles of parenting have been observed. Parenting styles are usually described in terms of a series of dimensions: consistent–inconsistent, warm–hostile, anxious–relaxed, overprotective–neglectful, effective–ineffective (Baumrind, 1967, 1971; Sears, Maccoby, & Levin, 1957).

During the early part of the twentieth century parents, on the whole, were quite restrictive. Their attitudes toward young children have been illustrated by such well-worn phrases as "A child should be seen but not heard." Rules of behavior were firm but also very narrow, with the autonomous child being strongly discouraged. By the middle of the century the influence of psychoanalytic theory and the writings of child experts such as Spock (1946) resulted in a shift to more permissive parenting attitudes. Children were encouraged to experiment, explore, follow their own initiatives, and fulfill their own wishes, even if the results were not always acceptable to parents. A strong interest developed among researchers about the effects of different *parenting styles* on children's social behavior.

The picture of child-rearing practices is complex. Parents are never simply loving or abusing, strict or permissive, attentive to a child's needs or detached. Parenting styles not only run the gamut of each dimension but are like a fabric interwoven with various strands of parenting behaviors. However, for various reasons, in their efforts to better understand parenting styles and their effects on children, investigators have individually come up with general dimensions of child-rearing practices. There have been a number of important studies on child rearing that paint somewhat different pictures of the dimensions of parental behavior and arrive at different conclusions about how parenting styles affect children's social development.

General dimensions of parenting behavior on which studies have usually focused are democratic–controlling, restrictive–permissive, and warm–hostile. What has been discovered about the effects of these general styles of parenting on children's social behavior?

Democratic or controlling parents. Baldwin (1948; et al., 1945) conducted a longitudinal study of children's social development from birth until later childhood. Parents were interviewed and observed at home interacting with their children several times during the study. A particular dimension of parenting identified was that of *democracy–control*, across which there were many variations. For example, many families who adopted a democratic style of child rearing also exerted a strong measure of control over their children's behavior. In these cases there was a certain interrelationship between these two facets of behavior.

Some parents are quite restrictive in controlling their children's behavior, while other parents are more relaxed. (Photos by EKM-Nepenthe)

Democratic parents used a great deal of verbal communication with their children, frequently consulted their children about social rules and regulations, offered explanations for the setting of rules, were always willing to answer children's questions about family rules, included their children in decision making, and encouraged their children to be self-reliant and to control excessive emotional behavior. *Controlling parents* (whether in a democratic or authoritarian manner) emphasized and clearly explained restrictions on their children's behavior.

Children of highly democratic parents were well organized, aggressive, fearless, successful, and highly social. In some cases children were too forceful and coercive, showing insensitivity toward other children. Children of highly controlling parents were obedient, suggestible, fearful, nonaggressive, and lacked tenacity.

A problem with this study is that Baldwin did not clearly represent cases in which parents may have been democratic but lacking control (permissive) and highly controlling without any democracy (authoritarian), or other cases that clearly represent various degrees of relationship between both these parenting styles. He made it clear that he did not favor authoritarianism; in extolling the virtues of giving children scope for self-determination of activities and a voice in deciding family rules, he provided support for permissiveness in parenting.

Restrictive or permissive parents. The study by Sears, Maccoby, and Levin (1957) and subsequent studies by other investigators such as Bronson (1972) and Kagan and Moss (1962) have pointed out that *restrictive* parents tend to have obedient, polite, and conforming children while *permissive* parents tend to have aggressive, very expressive, and uninhibited children. As you might imagine, many parents were observed who struck some balance between the two extremes.

Baumrind (1966) used an interesting approach to her study of child-rearing practices. She began by observing preschool children aged 3 to 4 years. Their behavior was rated according to certain characteristics of personality such as impetuosity, self-reliance, aggressiveness, withdrawal, and self-control. Three types of children were identified:

1. competent children who were usually happy, self-reliant, and self-controlled;

2. withdrawn children who were usually sad, infrequently approached other children, and engaged in solitary activities;

3. immature children who were usually lacking in self-reliance and self-control.

The next step was to observe interactions between these children and their parents. Initial ratings of parents' child-rearing behavior such as controlling, demanding mature behavior, and nurturing were later modified to represent three distinctive **parenting styles—authoritarian, authoritative,** and **permissive** (Baumrind, 1971, 1973). See Table 8.3. It is important to realize that no parent fit neatly into one of these categories but, depending on situation and circumstances, might at one time or another adopt all three styles of parenting—or some combination (see Inset 8.1).

According to the characteristics of parenting style described in Table 8.3, extremes of authoritarian (restrictive) or permissive child rearing appear to be equally destructive of normal social development (Baumrind, 1971). Both strict and permissive parents have unrealistic beliefs about young children. They do not seem to understand the importance of a parent model for the preschool child, or the child's inability to understand certain kinds of demands. Authoritarian parents are concerned with strict control and are quite detached from their children, who tend to be discontent and withdrawn. Permissive parents are quite the opposite—undemanding, providing little control, but warm and affectionate. Their preschool children are immature, uncontrolled, and lacking in self-reliance. The parents who come out best are those with authoritative attitudes. These parents attempt to provide realistic guidance to their children. When they lay down firm rules, they explain why. They do not combine firmness with threats of punishment for wrongdoing, and they encourage the child to discuss policy about behavior.

However, the picture is not quite so straightforward. Baumrind also discovered that black girls raised by authoritarian parents were self-assertive and independent. Not only is the family system complex but so too is the interrelationship between the family and the sociocultural environment. In order to get a clearer picture of the interrelationships between parents and their children it is also necessary to consider the effects of subcultures on both children and family (Lamb & Baumrind, 1978, p. 59).

Table 8.3 Parenting Styles

Authoritarian Style		Authoritative Style		Permissive Style	
Characteristics	Features	Characteristics	Features	Characteristics	Features
Desire to control the child.	Make the child conform to absolute standards of conduct. Enforce rules. Insist child pays attention.	Desire to become "expert" about the child's development.	Learn about children by listening to and observing the child. Permit the child to be a socializing agent. Modify parenting role in response to child's coaching. Respond to child's suggestions and complaints. Transmit flexible norms to child.	Make few demands on children and are lax in controlling behavior.	Adopt a laissez-faire attitude to child's behavior. Do not enforce rules when child is disobedient. Tend to spoil child by allowing too much freedom of choice.
Insist on unquestioning obedience.	Forcefully punish bad behavior. Show annoyance to child. Express impatience. Restrict the child's autonomy. Assign household chores to teach child respect for work.	Are willing and able to behave rationally, and explain to the child rationale for values and norms.	Know basis for demands made of the child. Ensure child knows, within reason, why demands are made. Are willing to discuss decisions with child.	Are willing to help the child but do not consider themselves as models for the child's behavior.	Usually accept bad behavior, taking a detached attitude toward it. Explain reasons for rules. Do not show annoyance at disobedience. Discuss decisions with the child without setting up definite principles.
Remain detached from child and ignore child's demands. Tend to provide an unenriched environment.	Do not explain rationale for rules to the child and keep rules inflexible. Do not take child's opinion into account. Child must be self-entertained. Cultural activities are not planned with child.	Value self-assertion and willfulness in the child.	Help child toward independence. Discipline firmly, but respect child's abilities and capacities. As child develops, increase expectations for competence, achievement, and independence.	Are quite warm in their attitude toward the child. Have no definite standards for the child to attain.	Are mostly nondemanding of the child.
Children are hostile, uncooperative, discontent, but reasonably achievement oriented.		Children are very friendly, cooperative, purposeful, self-reliant, self-assertive, and highly achievement oriented.		Children are hostile, uncooperative, lacking in self-control, aimless, and not very achievement oriented.	

Source: Based on Baumrind, D. "Effects of Authoritative Parental Control on Child Behavior," *Child Development,* 1966; "Authoritarian vs. Authoritative Control," *Adolescence,* 1968; and "Current Patterns of Parental Authority," *Developmental Psychology Monographs,* 1971.

Inset 8.1
Is There a Best Way
to Raise Children?

Baumrind's results from her research on parenting styles were reported by the mass media with a certain amount of exaggeration. As Baumrind pointed out when speaking at the Children's Community Center, Berkeley, California, headlines such as ''The Best Parents are Authoritative,'' or ''Kids Thrive in Strict Homes'' are meaningless. They also suggest that the researcher knows the *best* way for parents to raise children.

In responding to the media reports and commenting on the differences between the three basic parenting styles she has identified—the authoritarian, authoritative, and permissive parent—Baumrind offered the following clarifications on her research findings:

1. First, there is no such thing as a *best* way to raise children. Each individual family's total life situation is unique. . . . It is each parent's responsibility to become an expert on his own children, using information in books, or parent-effectiveness encounter groups, or best of all, by careful observation and intimate communication with the child. . . .

2. Second, the generalizations which I make have a reasonable probability of being true for a particular sample, but the extent to which that sample is representative . . . remains in question. . . .

3. Third, to have any research meaning at all, research findings must be *interpreted*. . . . Yet the interpretations I make of my findings may well be disputed. . . . Each of you must evaluate the relevance (of these findings) to your own family. . . .

    I should tell you that my *subjective* assurance about what I say rests as much upon my personal experience as a parent as on my research findings. I have three daughters . . . (and) my theories and my practice coincide rather well (I think), and I am subjectively satisfied with the effectiveness of what I call ''authoritative parental control'' in achieving my *personal* aim.

She went on to say that what gets in the way of most parents who do wish to control the behavior of their children more effectively is lack of expertness as parents,

Baumrind (1977) further observed a group of the preschool children from her original study (1967) when they reached the age of 8 to 9. Instead of describing the children's behavior in terms of social competency as she had before, Baumrind turned her attention to what she calls agency, of which there are two forms:

1. **Social agency** is the tendency for the child to take initiative and show leadership in group activities and to be socially interacting.

2. **Cognitive agency** is the tendency for the child to have a sense of identity, to respond positively to intellectual challenges, to set high standards in intellectual activities, and to show originality and creativity in thinking and reasoning.

indecisiveness about the application of power, anxiety about possible harm resulting from demands and restrictions, and fear that if they act in a certain way, they will lose their children's love. "Nowadays I think more parents are concerned about maintaining the approval of their children than vice versa. . . ."

In comparing the "authoritative" to a "permissive" style of parenting, Baumrind took as her model of a permissive adult A. S. Neill, famous as the founder of *Summerhill* in England, a school run along very laissez-faire lines.

Neill has expressed his views on rearing children as follows:

I believe that to impose anything by authority is wrong. The child should not do anything until he comes to the opinion—his own opinion—that it should be done (1964, p. 114).

Clearly, Baumrind suspects that such absence of control of children's behavior will not, in the long run, be effective in influencing the development of social competencies.

Baumrind also mentioned that, originally, Spock (1946) advocated the psychoanalytic view that full gratification of infantile sucking, excretory, and sexual impulses was essential for secure and healthy adult personalities. By 1957 he had changed his mind and stated that, "A great change in attitude has occurred, and nowadays there seems to be more chance of a conscientious parent's getting into trouble with permissiveness than with strictness."

In opposing parental permissiveness toward children and arguing for an authoritative style of parenting, Baumrind pointed out that there is no evidence from research to support the assumption that strict social training during childhood causes later neuroses, that punishment is harmful to the child, and that only unconditional love is beneficial to the child. Unconditional commitment is a more constructive objective. By this she means that there must be a give-and-take between the parents' concern for the child and the child's respect for the love and concern shown by parents (adapted from Baumrind, 1977, pp. 248–255).

Baumrind found that children could be ranked from high to low according to these characteristics. Children's interactions with parents during the preschool years and at ages 8 or 9 were then analyzed to discover why types of parenting styles were associated with various levels of agency behavior. At both preschool age and at ages 8 or 9, high-, medium-, and low-level cognitive and social agency corresponded with authoritative, authoritarian, and permissive parenting practices, respectively (1977).

Warm or hostile parents.   There is no doubt that *warm* and *affectionate* parents most often have children who are socially competent and well adjusted. How can we best define the *warmth* of parenting? Maccoby (1980, p. 392) has suggested a number of characteristics. A warm parent is

Children seem to benefit from being instructed by their parents in social and intellectual skills. Affectionate parents have children who are usually socially well adjusted. (Photos, left by Paul Conklin; right by Robert Eckert/EKM-Nepenthe)

1. deeply committed to the child's welfare;

2. willing to spend time (within limits) in joint enterprises of the child's choosing;

3. responsive to the child's needs;

4. ready to show enthusiasm over the child's accomplishments and acts of altruism;

5. sensitive to the child's emotional states.

Hostility is both the lack of such commitments to the child's well-being and openly expressed feelings of rejection or hostility. Some of the effects of warm nurturance have already been mentioned. One of the first signs is a secure attachment of the child to parents (Ainsworth, Bell, & Stayton, 1971; Clarke-Stewart, 1973). Children of affectionate parents also learn social rules with acceptance and apply these rules appropriately to their behavior in various situations. In order to take into account the child's feelings a parent or teacher might *explain,* "You must not grab the toy away. Mary is using it right now and she hasn't finished playing with it. You can have a turn later. Why not ask Mary to give it to you when she is finished with it," rather than telling, "No, don't grab the toy, that's naughty. If you keep doing that you'll get a time-out." The explanation identifies a rule of sharing, which requires taking into account another person's feelings, learning to delay gratification, and becoming aware of self-control. The "no" linked with a threat of punishment provides no explanation and no sensitivity to the child's feelings so the child does not know what "naughty" means. Parents who are accepting and affectionate tend to have children with a high degree of self-esteem, who are considerate of other children and who refer to moral standards for their behavior rather than fear of punishment (Hoffman & Saltzstein, 1967).

Influences on Parenting

The emphasis so far has been on the effects of parenting styles on children's social behavior. But there are a number of factors that influence parents' child-rearing practices. Maccoby (1980, pp. 395–405) has described a number of factors that appear to affect parents' behavior such as characteristics of the child, previous experience as parents, socioeconomic status, and family stress.

Characteristics of the child.   As the child grows older changes in parents' behavior reflect changes in the child's needs and competencies. Parental control during infancy, for example, consists primarily of physical intervention such as carrying the infant away from "mischievous" activities, putting fragile objects out of reach, and occasionally spanking the child. During the preschool years parents increasingly use reasoning, an appeal to moral values, and the withholding of privileges.

Although many changes in parenting are linked to the child's physical and cognitive development, parents are also influenced by their perceptions of their children's temperament and responsiveness. For example, a group of mothers of preschoolers stated that they had found stubbornness in their 2-year-olds cute, but now that their children were 3 or 4, they did not find their stubbornness amusing. One mother remarked, "Now it seems intentional"; another said, "I feel I'm being manipulated." These inferences about their children's behavior go beyond mere observations of children's responsiveness; they are also attributing meaning to behavior and this significantly affects their parenting practices (Maccoby, 1980, p. 396).

In the early preschool years children have little understanding of authority. They come to believe that they must obey parents because adults are bigger and more powerful. Only toward the end of this period do children begin to understand that there are good reasons for being obedient (Damon, 1977). These changes can be attributed to the parents' training, and parents are likewise influenced by changes in their children's behavior.

Previous experience.   Lasko (1954) contrasted parents' treatment of firstborns with that of siblings observed at the same age. She discovered that firstborns were treated differently from their siblings. Firstborns received more attention, affection, and verbal stimulation. They were also expected to be more mature and their behavior was more controlled and coerced by their parents. Other investigators have observed similar differences in mothers' behavior toward newborns (Rothbart, 1971).

Table 8.4 Effects of Socioeconomic Status on Parenting Styles

Socioeconomic Status	Child-Rearing Practices
High Compared to Low SES Parents	Parents are more democratic and tend to be either permissive or authoritative (in Baumrind's terms). They are more likely to point out the effects of a child's actions on others and appeal to the child's desire for the well-being of others.
	Parents talk to their children more, reason with them more, and use more complex language. Parents tend to show more warmth and affection toward their children.
	Parents are more likely to stress happiness, creativity, ambition, independence, and self-control.
Low Compared to High SES Parents	Parents are more controlling, power-assertive, authoritarian, and arbitrary in their discipline, and they are more likely to use physical punishment.
	Parents talk less to their children, insist on the child's behaving in a certain way with no reasons given. They use simple language. Parents tend to be more distant and cold, and they infrequently show affection toward their children.
	Parents tend to stress obedience, respect, neatness, cleanliness, and staying out of trouble.

Source: Adapted from *Social Development: Psychological Growth and the Parent-Child Relationship* by Eleanor E. Maccoby. Copyright © 1980 by Harcourt Brace Jovanovich, Inc. Reprinted by permission of the publisher.

It appears that with experience in dealing with their children, mothers learn to take into account the developmental level of their young children. However, parents' behavior can also change as a result of the timing of subsequent children. For example, a second child following close on the birth of an earlier child causes greater displacement of attention and related child-rearing practices than when children are not so close together in age. When there is quite a gap in time between births, lastborns seem to receive more favored treatment simply because they are not competing for attention (Lasko, 1954).

Socioeconomic status. Among the most powerful and least understood influences on parenting practices are parents' education, income, and occupation, which are frequently related and altogether are referred to as socioeconomic status (SES). Comparisons between parents of high and low socioeconomic status have revealed consistent differences in parenting as illustrated in Table 8.4. These differences hold true, on the average, irrespective of race or culture (Hess & Shipman, 1965; Kamii & Radin, 1967). However, families of both low and high SES differ among themselves in important aspects of parenting. For example, some low SES families live stable, organized lives while others are unstable and have many problems such as illness, unemployment, and drug and alcohol abuse.

Parents in high-status jobs from high SES families are usually self-directed. They are more likely to reason and negotiate with their children—skills they use in connection with their jobs—and to emphasize self-reliance. But there are also high SES families who are disorganized and erratic in child rearing. Children with social problems come from all walks of life, but usually there are more problem children with more severe types of problems in low SES families.

Family stress. Tired, worried, or ill parents, parents who feel they have lost control of their lives are likely to be impatient, lacking in understanding, and even hostile toward their children. Zussman (1978) observed parents with their preschool aged and infant children in an artificially produced stressful situation. Parents became less responsive to their preschool children and interacted less with them. They interacted with the toddlers just as much as usual, but they were more critical and interfering.

A more severe family stress is divorce. This stress usually persists for a lengthy period, including both the lead-up to divorce and its aftermath. Hetherington, Cox, and Cox (1976, 1979) compared 48 recently divorced families with 48 intact families; both groups had children in the same preschools. The parents of both groups were similar according to age, education, and length of marriage. It was discovered that divorced parents were more anxious, depressed, angry, and self-doubting, and were less affectionate toward their children, made fewer demands on them, and communicated less. During the first year following divorce there were frequent parent–children conflicts, and mothers imposed more punishments (negative control). Fathers, trying to maintain some affectionate relationship with their children, became highly permissive and indulgent. Toward the end of the second year following divorce, the parent–child relationship had almost returned to the positive relationship that existed before the divorce—but more so for girls than for boys.

Just as Baumrind cautioned against taking her results and their interpretation too literally, Maccoby cautions that there is no best way to bring up children. She also believes the case for parental influence on children's social development tends to be overstated.

Parents as Teachers

There are two views on the role of *parents as teachers.* Some psychologists and educators believe that, at least during the preschool years, parents should be deeply involved in the education of their children. Gordon (1969) has suggested that parents can be involved in early education at several levels: as an audience, receiving information from teachers; as a reference, supplying teachers with information; as a teacher of their children; as volunteers in the classroom; and as decision makers in helping to devise a curriculum. Bronfenbrenner (1976) provides a rather different view of parents as educators. He asks a telling question, "Who cares for America's children, who cares?" His answer is not only parents,

but also "the general public." We will discuss why this is so and how people in general can help care for young children. First, let us return to the more particular idea of the parent as a teacher. Why is there a strong belief in the need for parents to help educate their children, and how are they expected to go about this task?

Along with changes in the structure and position of the family in society have come changes in children's levels of development and achievement. Children from certain minority and low-income families are especially at a high risk of physical, intellectual, emotional, and social damage. But, as Bronfenbrenner puts it, "the signs of progressive disarray are not limited to the poor and nonwhite . . . [there is a] decline in academic achievement . . . among pupils in all segments of our society" (1976, pp. 6–7). White (1975) also makes the same case when he says that *all* children can benefit from education during the early years. He claims that as many as nine out of ten children have early experiences that are not considered suitable for their needs. Therefore, *all* parents should be helped in some way to become involved in the education of their children. To do so, they also need training in certain parenting skills that they do not have simply by right of parenthood.

Honig (1979) has listed five child-rearing "tools" parents need: knowledge of child development, observation skills, skills for controlling children's behavior, knowing how to use the home for learning experiences, and knowing how to use language to help children's thinking and reasoning (which includes teaching children how to use language).

364 The Preschool Years

1. Knowing fundamental information about a child's physical, intellectual, emotional, and social growth should help parents set realistic expectations for their children and help them achieve certain competencies.

2. Observing a child's present behavior is a first step toward ascertaining probable future behavior and setting realistic goals for children's achievement. If a parent has knowledge of child development, observational skills should be sharpened and make possible more appropriate decisions by parents as to when and how to help a child toward some development goal.

3. Most parents are very concerned about discipline, about setting rules and reputations that govern their children's behavior, and about the day-to-day management of children's behavior.

4. Parents can benefit from knowing how to take advantage of usual settings, routines, and activities in the home to create learning and problem-solving opportunities for children.

5. The single most important tool for helping children's development is language. Parents can communicate with children in various ways to encourage thinking and reasoning—by explaining, by asking questions, by discussing. Parents can also teach their children how to use language competently.

However, we must keep in mind the fact that it is becoming increasingly difficult for parents to find time to educate their children (see Inset 8.2). About one in every three mothers of a child aged 3 or less is working. For children between 3 and 6 years the figure is a little over one in every two mothers (Bronfenbrenner, 1977). We can add the fact that one in every six children in the United States lives in a single-parent family (Schlesinger, 1975). Less and less time is spent in nurturing, guiding, socializing, and teaching children. It has been reported that many mothers of preschool children spend no more than about fifteen minutes a day communicating with their children (Woodward & Malamud, 1975). It is for these reasons that Bronfenbrenner makes the plea to emphasize not merely the education of parents to be better at parenting but to reeducate the community to better support the family.

How can we begin to try to achieve such an objective, so startling in its widespread implications for social change? Bronfenbrenner proposes that much more use can be made of television to present to the general public, as realistically as possible, family living conditions and information on how the community can help families—families helping families. Another approach is to get people and organizations in the community to think about and become more aware of their present role and potential role in helping families and children. But to begin at the beginning, what is also needed in our schools is a "curriculum for caring." A young person should, as part of becoming educated, learn about the need all humans have for comfort and care, how this can be achieved, and acquire the motivation, sensitivities, and skills to engage in caring.

Anne Morris and Joseph Glick have described the setting up of a pediatric clinic program in the Department of Pediatrics at the Mount Sinai School of Medicine in New York.

The scene is familiar to almost everyone who has ever had a child or visited a pediatric outpatient setting: the waiting room overflowing with restless children, wailing infants, and mothers alternatively bored and nervous. In a pediatric clinic, the mother may park some or all of her children in the playroom while she absentmindedly thumbs a long outdated magazine, always waiting.

The waiting seems unavoidable; but couldn't this time be spent more constructively? Under the directorship of Anne Morris, the playroom in the pediatric clinic at Mount Sinai Hospital was transformed from a parking lot for children into a learning laboratory for parents, children, and staff. But, first and foremost, it is a place where a "captive" audience of low-income parents can pick up essential pointers on ways to help their youngsters develop intellectually and emotionally. Parents have responded enthusiastically to this innovation.

This demonstration project provides learning experiences for 2- and 3-year-old children aimed at improving their IQ's and helping them later to perform well in school. And it does so with the help of parents. Parents are invited to participate in the "playroom program" where they learn play skills they can use at home with their children. They visit the playroom on a regular basis every two to three weeks for six months, with visits coordinated as far as possible with pediatric appointments.

Parents first are observers while their child undergoes a "developmental evaluation" which serves to identify cognitively handicapped children requiring special medical and psychiatric services of the clinic. At subsequent appointments, the playroom trainers work individually with parents, who then use their new skills with their own children. A parent will work with the same playroom trainer throughout the training cycle. Parent and trainer go through a set curriculum which exposes the parent to a progression of play approaches, each of which focuses on a particular toy which the parent may borrow, use at home with the child, and return at the next session. (Some expendable books and toys are given outright.)

Creating and operating such a program requires several critical components:

Low-income parents of 2- and 3-year-olds willing to participate in the training program

A pediatric setting where they can be recruited and trained

A playroom where training takes place

A playroom staff of trainers who recruit and work with the parents

A training curriculum consisting of a special sequence of exercises for parents to learn in conjunction with a carefully chosen group of toys

A program coordinator responsible for establishing and operating the program, for training and supervising the playroom staff, and for assuring that the program is functioning well and integrated into its host setting

The Basic Program

The program emphasizes the importance of the parent-teacher providing the child with rational explanations and optional solutions as part of his learning experiences during play activities. Parents are advised to attach words to actions because the children require direction and instruction to learn. The mother becomes aware that the concepts her child learns, such as matching colors, are the result of a particular interaction she began by directing the child's attention to certain features of a toy. Although the activities are play for the child, they are not random behavior for the parent, who becomes aware of the cognitive needs of her child at a particular stage of development.

Twelve sequentially graded exercises for each age group concentrate on perceptual-motor and language skills and problem solving. Each toy selected has a primary feature so that parents with limited education experiences can immediately perceive the relationships of the different elements. For example, the openings in "the shape box" indicate clearly where each differently shaped block is to be placed . . . The activities for each exercise are broken down into small steps that lead to a goal such as matching colors or shapes.

The Program's Impact

The demonstration program at Mount Sinai Hospital showed that

1. Parents are willing and able to participate in such a training program, even when it requires extra trips to the clinic with their children.
2. Parents react enthusiastically to the training provided.
3. Children react positively to the new toys and skills their parents bring home.
4. The program apparently also brings behavioral benefits to the children.
5. The program helps parents to accept greater responsibility for their role as their children's teachers.

Parents consistently reported behavioral changes in their children. They said the program had helped them as well as their children to learn.

The importance of programs such as this is that they can influence the parents' view of themselves as the primary educators of their child.

Source: Adapted from Rosenfeld, A. H., *Parent Education in a Pediatric Clinic.* United States Department of Health, Education and Welfare, 1979.

Whatever view we take of parents as educators, it has become abundantly clear that children need skillful parents if they are to develop to their fullest potential, that parents do not have parenting skills by virtue of being parents, and that support systems of various kinds must be set up in our communities to provide education for the community about the conditions and needs of its families.

School's Role in Socialization

There appear to be certain similarities between the family and preschool. Cohen (1976) maintains that, like the family, the school is a self-contained unit. The structure of the school imposes certain roles, expectations, and rules on the child.

School: Structure and System

Because for over ten years the school is to the child a continuous institutional, social environment, it has been ranked second to the family in influencing social and personality development (Swift, 1964; Glidewell, Kantor, Smith, & Stringer, 1966). The teacher, like the parent, plays an important role in helping the child learn and practice social skills as well as cognitive ones. So, to a certain extent, learning how to adapt to various social situations and interpersonal relationships in a school setting will determine the child's progress in developing social competencies (Swift, 1964, pp. 250–281). However, just as in the family system, the influence is not a one-way process since preschoolers also influence teachers' behavior. Beyond this relationship there are the more complex teacher, child, peer group, environment interactions and their multiple influences on social behavior.

Effects of Teaching Styles

It can only be expected that teachers will differ in their methods and *teaching styles.* But, in general, teaching styles turn out to be very much like the categories of parenting styles described earlier in the chapter. Lewin, Lippitt, and White, as long ago as 1939, identified three teaching styles they termed authoritarian, democratic, and laissez-faire. The characteristics of these styles sound very much like those of Baumrind's three general parenting styles (authoritarian, authoritative, and permissive), and they were found to result in similar behavior responses from children (see Table 8.5).

Table 8.5 Teaching Styles

Teaching Style	Teaching Behavior
Authoritarian	Teacher determines rules and standards of classroom behavior and deals with classroom organization. Decisions are taken one at a time so that future decisions are always uncertain to a large degree. Teacher decides the roles students will take in the classroom; praises and criticizes the behavior and activities of students while remaining aloof from taking part in group activities. This type of teacher tends to be friendly but impersonal.
Democratic	Teacher encourages all students to participate in discussion of classroom matters and to make joint decisions about classroom procedures. Once classroom decisions are agreed on, all students become involved in achieving their set goals. Teacher takes initiative in suggesting alternatives to resolve problems as they arise. Students are left free to decide the best ways to fulfill responsibilities—such as working on an activity—and they may do this alone or with other students. Teacher tends to be fair and objective in praising and encouraging students without, necessarily, becoming involved in their activities.
Laissez-faire	Teacher tends not to take a leadership role. Students are given complete freedom to do more or less as they wish. Although providing some material support and advice when asked, teacher tends not to take part in discussion about objectives nor in helping students achieve their goals. Teacher tends not to comment on activities undertaken by students nor to interfere with the course of events.

Source: Adapted from Lewin, K., Lippitt, R., & White, R. K., "Patterns of Aggressive Behavior in Experimentally Controlled 'Social Climate.' " *Journal of Social Psychology,* 1939, *10,* 271-299. With permission.

More recently, Hendrick (1980, pp. 99–139) has used similar descriptions of teaching styles. She describes four preschool teaching styles: authoritarian, overpermissive, inconsistent, and competent.

Authoritarian teachers tightly control children's classroom behavior. Such teachers have many unexplained rules such as "Don't run," "Don't make a noise," "Be quiet," "Sit down," "Take turns," "Tell him you're sorry!" They tend to use severe punishments and often claim that parents expect them to use such control. Children respond with restlessness, tension, and aggression. They become very dependent on the teacher for direction and, if left to their own devices with some activity, tend to be disruptive, disorganized, lack persistence, and frequently fail to complete tasks.

Overpermissive teachers are often confused about the difference between freedom and license. Such teachers fail to make it clear that freedom means working constructively and not interfering with the other children's rights and freedom. What children learn from this style is lack of control, lack of self-esteem, anxiety,

Young children can be helped in developing a sense of empathy toward each other. One expression of empathy is the understanding by the child that the other child needs help. (Photo by Vivienne della Grotta)

or that they need to be aggressive to get their own way. Permissive teachers tend to produce anxious or very aggressive children (Bandura & Walters, 1963; Patterson, Littman, & Bricker, 1967).

Inconsistent teachers are erratic in classroom organization and management. Children are allowed to use materials and move from one activity to another about as much as they please. Misbehavior may be punished one day, ignored the next. Rules governing both cognitive and social activities are also inconsistent. Inconsistent teachers are also likely to foster aggression among children (Parke & Duer, 1972).

Although Hendrick does not identify competent teachers by a descriptive term such as authoritative, she makes a number of suggestions about the characteristics of preschool teachers who competently teach appropriate skills. Competent teachers help children learn to be generous and to share equipment and experiences. Teachers can provide good models for generosity (Midlarsky & Bryan, 1967), which appear to increase this behavior in children (Rosenhan, 1972). Competent teachers also help children develop empathy, to understand what another child is thinking or feeling or why the child is acting in a certain way. This is a most important skill for preschoolers to learn, beset as they are with a tendency toward egocentric thinking (Flavell, Botkin, Fry, Wright, & Jarvis, 1968; Hetherington & McIntyre, 1975). Children learn that it feels good to help others. Teachers can teach this by such simple activities as "passing juice (or cookies)" at snacktime or by encouraging one child to help another with some task or to comfort another child. Along the same lines, competent teachers teach children that all the children in the preschool have rights, which must be respected. Children can be taught that rules apply to everyone through activities such as learning the rule that each child may go only into his or her own cubby.

Using competition to manipulate children's behavior can develop rivalry as a favored response among children. So it is best to avoid comments like "I bet you can't pick up as many blocks as I can." or "It's time for a snack. Whoever washes his or her hands first can sit by me." Again, the teacher can provide an excellent model of cooperation by emphasizing the value of cooperation and compromise rather than competition and rivalry. Children become more interested in having friends as they grow older, and the demonstration of friendship seems to pass through a number of stages (Youniss, 1975). It can help when the teacher points out ways of encouraging friendship when children are in pairs or small groups.

During the preschool years children are developing many concepts related to sexual identity. Questions facing the competent teacher are: How do I respond to shifts in values and role descriptions occurring within society? Do I let my own personal convictions regarding sexual identity and role affect what I teach in the classroom? Helping children develop an understanding of sexuality and value their own particular sexuality is not always easy. As far as possible, the teacher has to take into account each individual child's home background, family structure, and parents' wishes (Hendrick, 1980, pp. 124–137).

Competent teachers also teach children how to think, how to organize their actions, how to interpret events, how to make judgments—all necessary skills not only in acquiring social knowledge but in getting to know how to use it.

School and Home as Social Settings

The social setting of the school compared to that of the home provides the child with a contrast. These two social systems have distinct norms of social behavior (Hess, Block, Costello, Knowles, & Largay, 1971). Parental pressures and expectations of their infants in the first two or three years of life result in children's strongly identifying with them (Money & Ehrhardt, 1972). Long before they arrive at a preschool or day-care center, children have learned to behave in certain ways according to rules and regulations parents have set. They have also developed a self-image and expectations about their intellectual and social competencies. They take to school a personality fostered in the home. Teachers, like parents, have specific expectations about children's behavior (Powell, 1978). These tend to be more systematized, however, to control groups of children at one time and to ensure an orderly running of the school program. Children have to get used to the particular social demands on them in a school environment that the teacher imposes but without the intimate relationships that exist with a family (Lightfoot, 1975). A collaborative relationship is needed, therefore, between parents and teachers to help the child adapt to the social transitions (Almy, 1975; Keniston, 1977). If the child perceives incompatible models of appropriate behavior and experiences inconsistent styles of care giving, this creates problems for the child (Lippitt, 1968).

To find out more about interpersonal relations between parents and teachers, Powell (1978) examined the communicative behavior of 212 parents and 89 day-care teachers (care givers). The findings are quite startling. He found few attempts to coordinate children's socialization experiences. Teachers and parents just did not communicate very well on these matters. Day-to-day communication at the "transition point" where parents drop off and pick up their children was superficial. It appeared sufficient for parents to merely greet the teacher with "Hello" or "How's it going?" Messages between parent and teacher at that level had little impact.

The image that emerges, according to Powell, is a set of social experiences that are *fragmented* and discontinuous for the child because the individual child's family, families of other children, and the day-care center are all independent social systems. However, this need not be interpreted necessarily as a negative picture. In learning to adapt to several social settings that are similar in certain ways yet different in others, the child may arrive at a more general understanding of social knowledge and in the process acquire a flexibility of social behavior.

The Peer Group

Parents and teachers certainly have an important influence on children's social development. But during the preschool years children begin to form close friendships and acquaintances in pairs and groups. For the first time the **peer group** also begins to have an effect on children's social behavior.

Parents asked why they send their children to preschool or day-care usually give as one of the first reasons, "The school provides a chance for social contact with other children." Piaget has expressed the opinion that peer interaction is important during the preschool years because it helps the egocentric 3-year-old to take into account other children's points of view. (School also provides an environment in which the young child can contrast social demands and regulations.) Whereas the school strives to preserve normative patterns of behavior, the peer group allows for individual behavior patterns.

Young children form peer groups quite spontaneously (Hartup, 1970). This is more noticeable in the neighborhood since the school is an environment in which children are "thrown together." What purposes do peer groups serve? Ausubel and Sullivan (1970) have suggested that early peer-group associations serve five functions. They provide

1. status and identity;

2. **self-esteem;**

3. a source of values and standards;

4. training opportunities;

5. experiences in trying out personal social bonding.

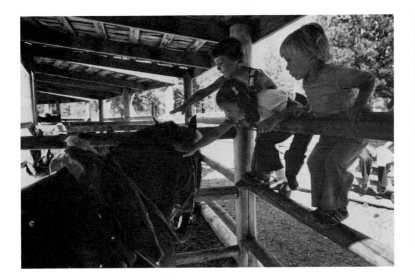

We know that the family can also serve these functions. However, the peer group forms a complementary function to the family (Cohen, 1976). In the company of peers the child can test previously formed attitudes and social behaviors (Cambell, 1964). The child must also take into account the differing behaviors of other children.

Young children gain a sense of identity, self-esteem, and the importance of social values from early peer-group associations. (Photo by Bob Ekert/EKM-Nepenthe and Jean-Claude Lejeune)

Peer interactions increase in frequency between 2 and 5 years and, of course, the types of social behaviors change. This is never so obvious as when one observes a social function such as a 3-year-old's birthday party in comparison to a 5-year-old's. A group of 3-year-olds is really a set of individuals making few brief social contacts. A group of 5-year-olds is much more a set of socially relating children. Three-year-olds revolve around one another, briefly "touching." They talk *at* each other, quickly love and hate, and make no firm friends. The 3-year-old's firmest friend may still be a "comforter," such as a piece of cloth or a blanket or a soft toy, which the child carries around with him wherever he goes. By age 5 the child has acquired quite a few social graces, a number of firm friends, and probably a temporary best friend. Early peer relations appear to serve as prototypes for later, more formal group associations. They provide the child the opportunity to exercise social choice and an acceptance or disapproval of interpersonal bonds (Cohen, 1976).

Sex-Role Development

In Chapter 5 we considered how a child becomes aware of a particular sexual identity and has a particular **sex-role adoption** during infancy. Learning that "I am a boy" or "I am a girl" is no problem for most children. However, learning how to behave as a male or female can provide some difficulties. How do children come to adopt certain types of sex-role behavior?

Social and Personality Development   **373**

Preschoolers' Sex-Role Adoption

Sex roles are both adopted and prescribed. Children have expectations about how they should behave as boys or girls, and adults have expectations about how boys and girls should behave. To what extent do children conform to adults' expectations?

Most preschool-age children's understanding of sexuality is stereotypic. They associate a person's gender with the person's clothes, hairstyle, or occupation. For example, in spite of many parents' attempts to eliminate sexist ideas about occupation from their children's thinking, 3- to 5-year-olds still cling to beliefs in traditional sex roles (Kohlberg, 1966; Kuhn, Langer, Kohlberg & Haan, 1978). Both boys and girls believe that

Girls wear frilly dresses, play with dolls, help mother clean the house, cook dinner, take care of babies, and become nurses.
Boys wear trousers, help father mow the grass, play with toy cars and airplanes, fight, are naughty, grow up to be doctors.

Damon (1977) wondered if young children's stereotypes about sex roles were as "set in stone" as they appear to be. To children aged 4 through 9 he told a story about a boy called George who liked to play with dolls. George's parents told him that boys should not play with dolls, and they bought him toys that boys play with. George, however, continued playing with the dolls. The children were asked whether they thought it was all right for George to play with dolls—"Is there a rule that boys shouldn't play with dolls? Where does it come from?" "Is it fair for George's parents to punish him for playing with dolls?" (1977, p. 242).

Children's responses to such questions changed with age. Four-year-olds thought George should be allowed to play with dolls. Most 6-year-olds stated that it was *wrong* for George to play with dolls or dress like a girl: "He [George] should stop playing with the girls' dolls and start playing with the G.I. Joe" (Damon, 1977, p. 255). They also believed the parents had the right to tell George to stop playing with dolls. But by age 9 children take a more reasonable attitude. They argue that George can play with dolls if he likes, or even wear a girl's dress to school. However, they are very aware of social pressure to conform to certain sex roles. They also point out that "guys" will think George odd for preferring dolls to cars and trucks, and that one day at school in a dress should suffice to make George realize he shouldn't wear it again because the other "kids" would laugh at him and make him embarrassed.

During the preschool years children have highly stereotypic views of sex roles which become less rigid over time. The development of attitudes toward sex roles and children's sex-role behavior appears to be linked to other changes in thinking and reasoning.

Influences on Sex-Role Adoption

We have seen that preschoolers come to believe that parents can set rules about sex-role behavior such as the kinds of toys boys and girls should play with. Parents set the conditions for sex-role identification by providing distinctive toys and clothes for boys and girls (Rheingold & Cook, 1975) and by being models for their children to imitate (Bandura & Walters, 1963; Mischell, 1970). Preschoolers have been observed performing exaggerated sex roles of mothers and fathers in their play (Garvey, 1977).

However, at least within the preschool years, it seems that children do not necessarily imitate or identify with the same-sex parent. According to Freud we would expect the reverse but this is only partly true. A study of preschoolers by Sears, Rau, and Alpert (1965) found that if parents strongly repressed their children's sexual and aggressive impulses, both sons and daughters developed extreme feminine behavior. A later study by Hetherington (1967) found this to be true for girls but not for boys. She also found that children imitated the most dominant parent irrespective of any same-sex relationship.

Parents do strongly determine and reinforce what they consider to be appropriate sex-role behavior; in the preschool years this is particularly so with respect to play. It was pointed out earlier that beginning in late infancy fathers rather than mothers engage in rough-and-tumble play with their children, especially boys (Lamb, 1978b). Most fathers emphasize masculinity in their reactions to older sons' toys and games (Fagot, 1978). At the same time, fathers expect their daughters to be feminine, wear feminine clothes, play with "girls'" toys, and play games that girls play (Hetherington, 1967; Maccoby & Jacklin, 1974; Mussen & Rutherford, 1963). Mothers do not show as much concern about clearly defined sex-role play.

If there are siblings in the family, relationships among them are important in "shaping" social behavior. It appears that during the period from about 2 to 10 years siblings exert most influence on one another. Siblings can serve as role models (Sutton-Smith & Rosenberg, 1970; Rosenberg & Sutton-Smith, 1972). Their appropriateness as role models may be because they demonstrate the "little-boy" or "little-girl" roles young children are expected to adopt (Lamb & Urberg, 1978).

The number of siblings in a family and birth order can also affect children's social development. Brothers and sisters learn from one another how social power and a person's functions are used to discriminate age and sex roles in the family (Bigner, 1974; Koch, 1960). Firstborn children learn to use high-powered social tactics in achieving their own wishes over younger siblings. These tactics include bossing, verbal threats, and using physical force (Bigner, 1979).

Younger siblings learn from older siblings that males have higher social power than females and that females are more socially interactive while males are usually more disruptive (Bigner, 1974). Older siblings often act as teachers to younger brothers and sisters (Circirelli, 1972).

In Chapter 5 it was mentioned that infants are not truly aggressive in their behavior but that some aspects of their behavior, such as grabbing for a toy, are suggestive of aggression. During the preschool years the expression of true aggressive behavior becomes more noticeable. But so, too, does children's unselfish concern for the welfare of others—which we call *altruism*. In the next section we will trace these two interesting features of social behavior through the preschool years.

Aggression and Altruism in Early Childhood

Children's aggressive behavior takes different forms. It may be physical, showing itself as hostile attacks aimed at hurting, harming, or injuring another child, or destroying objects. It may be nonphysical, as in the case of verbal abuse such as taunts, teasing, or humiliation.

Theories about the origins of *aggression* are controversial. Freud believed that life is influenced by two instincts, *Eros* (life) and *Thanatos* (death). The will to survive or the need to relieve feelings of tension result in aggressive acts (Freud, 1927). Lorenz (1966) also believed aggression to be an inherent drive that cannot be prevented, suggesting that aggression should be controlled but not eliminated. Skinner (1953), however, insists that aggression is not an inevitable type of behavior. It is a socially learned way of acting and can be readily eliminated if it is not rewarded. Other theorists such as Bandura (Bandura & Huston, 1961) believe that aggression is learned by imitation. Parents are important role models for their children. Also, parents' behavior toward their children appears to crucially affect the degree of aggressive behavior and whether the child learns to control aggression.

Children can also learn to share, help, and be sympathetic to other people's feelings. This is not an alternative to aggressive behavior but another feature of social interaction which is usually referred to as *prosocial behavior* (e.g., Mussen & Eisenberg-Berg, 1977) or **altruism** (e.g., Zahn-Waxler, Radke-Yarrow, & King, 1979). How do aggression and altruism develop? What seems to motivate such behavior? Is aggressive and altruistic behavior learned?

Development of Aggression

During the preschool years social difficulties with peers trigger most angry outbursts. Many quarrels among children generally have to do with possession of objects, but this is more likely to be the cause of aggressive-like behavior in younger children. Aggression among older preschoolers is more likely also to involve physical violence.

A study by Hartup (1974) found further evidence supporting these basic developmental changes. Young preschool children are more likely to get involved in **instrumental aggression** usually aimed at retrieving an object, territory, or a privilege. Older children are more likely to engage in **hostile aggression** (directed toward a person). This seems to be caused mainly by frustration or the assumption that another child has intended to be aggressive (therefore, there is retaliation). Other investigators have noticed the same, general course in development of aggression from tantrums, to hitting, pushing, kicking, to seizing toys and other possessions, to more violent physical and verbal aggression (e.g., Feshbach, 1970).

Parental Influences on Aggression

You may realize from previous descriptions of aggression during infancy (Chapter 5) that parents can seriously influence children's aggressive behavior. The large-scale study by Sears, Maccoby, and Levin (1957) found that parents differed in their views about the desirability of aggression in their children, or how to control it. One mother said:

I just told them in no uncertain terms that it was something that was never done (p. 235).

Another mother's attitude was

I think there's a certain amount that should be allowed. I think that it's something they have to get out of their system (p. 236).

Many parents were observed using aggression to control their children's behavior—hitting a child, taunting, humiliating, and verbally abusing a child, provide examples of aggression "at the very moment they are trying to teach the child not to be aggressive" (Sears, Maccoby & Levin, 1957, p. 266). There is no doubt that children learn to imitate parents' aggressive behavior.

Effects of Models of Aggression

In an interesting series of studies, Bandura and his colleagues (Bandura & Huston, 1961; Bandura, Ross, & Ross, 1961, 1963) have examined the effects of models on children's aggressive behavior. Two studies are mentioned here.

Study 1:

Two groups of children, each with an equal number of boys and girls, experienced playing with toys with an adult model. With the first group the adult model played quietly. With the second group, the adult model first played quietly but then acted very aggressively toward an inflated rubber toy called a bobo doll. The doll was punched, kicked, and hit over the head with a mallet. A third group of children played with toys with no adult model present.

Later, the children in the second group were much more aggressive in their play behavior than the other children, and this was more noticeable when the adult model had been male rather than female. Boys and girls expected men to be aggressive but showed surprise at the "lady's" behavior! Also, boys were more aggressive than girls.

Study 2:

Children were shown films of "live" models and "cartoon-character" models behaving aggressively toward a bobo doll. In both cases children imitated the model's aggressive behavior but were more prone to imitate real models rather than cartoon models.

The filmed sequences Bandura used raise the question about the effects that violence on television might have on children's behavior. Feshbach (1970) found that there are hardly any long-term effects from such modeling behaviors as those children observed in the Bandura studies. But what about the usual diet of films and cartoons that children watch on TV?

Friedrich and Stein (1977) showed groups of preschool children one of three types of television programs daily over a period of four weeks. One group saw aggressive-type cartoon films such as "Batman" and "Superman." The second group saw "Mister Rogers" with its emphasis on prosocial behavior. A third

group saw "neutral" films (neither prosocial nor aggressive). Children's aggressive behavior was measured before viewing began. As you might expect, the "neutral" films had no apparent effects on behavior. The "Mister Rogers" programs influenced prosocial behavior. Children who viewed this show worked harder and longer on tasks, became more obedient, and more willing to delay satisfaction. Children who watched the aggressive cartoon films were less likely than the "Mister Rogers" group to obey rules, and were less tolerant of delays in achieving satisfaction. Other studies have also indicated that watching TV can have an effect on both children's aggressive and prosocial behavior (Drabman & Thomas, 1976; Liebert, Neale, & Davidson, 1973; Stein & Friedrich, 1975). The effects seem to be heightened when children already have dominant parents who are either aggressive, prosocial, or both, and these effects are more apparent for older than younger children.

Development of Altruism

In spite of their propensity for egocentric behavior, preschoolers can also be seen helping, sharing with, and comforting each other. In one study of children's altruistic behavior (Zahn-Waxler, Radke-Yarrow, & King, 1979), mothers of children between the ages of 15 and 20 months were asked to describe incidents in which their children experienced other people expressing feelings of anger, fear, sorrow, or discomfort (mothers tape-recorded descriptions at the time they occurred). Mothers of children as young as 2 years observed their children reacting to other people's distress with concern. This was more likely to be the case for children whose mothers explained the situation rather than using reprimands, and who frequently saw their mothers offering help to others, comforting them, or sharing possessions with others. Both direct teaching and modeling of altruistic behavior can be very effective in engendering altruism in young children.

Trends in the development of altruistic behavior, or for that matter moral behavior in general, are hard to establish. It does appear that there is consistency in altruistic behavior as children get older. However, while it has been possible to measure changes in children's altruistic thinking (Mussen & Eisenberg-Berg, 1977), there is not always a clearly discernible pattern of development of altruistic behavior.

Summary

The preschool years are associated with the Oedipal stage of psychosexual development. According to Freud, boys "fall in love" with their mothers, and girls with their fathers. Children resolve these relationships by learning to repress the sexual aspects of the desired love. This results in the emergence of the superego. The child's superego is very rigid, and the child may be tormented with guilt feelings after wrongdoing.

Erikson's psychosocial view emphasizes children's personalities and social development through their relationships with parents. The child becomes purposeful and interested in initiating various activities. Feelings of doubt still linger, but the child, full of energy, tends to intrude into all kinds of situations. But the child needs to realize there are limits to the use of initiative. These limits are acknowledged by learning to respond to social rules. In this way the superego emerges.

Learning theorists believe that children's social development results from their imitating parents, other adults, and peers. Imitation is more strongly reinforced by adults who are affectionate and caring and who exert firm control over what children desire. During the preschool years children learn to develop an internalized control over their behavior. At this age children spontaneously begin to pick models to imitate.

Piaget has said that the development of moral behavior is related to the understanding of rules. At first the preschool child does not understand social rules. Later the child learns to play according to rules. At first only the results of actions are taken into account in judging moral behavior. Later the child considers both result and motive.

Kohlberg has identified a sequence of six stages in the development of moral reasoning. During the preschool years, the pre-moral stage of development, children tend to confuse moral judgments with other judgments. During these years children develop social behavior by learning the rules of their culture and by imitating others.

During the preschool years the family remains the most important and strongest influence on the child's social development. The family structure is complex, and relationships among members of the family are interdependent and interactive. According to some theorists the family system develops in a sequence of phases. First, there is the husband and wife couple. The next phase begins with the arrival of the firstborn child. The third phase is the preschool years. A subsequent phase would begin with the arrival of another child. (Many factors such as divorce, childlessness, the death of a child, and adoption of children may influence the development of the family system.)

Baumrind has described three parenting styles—authoritarian, authoritative, and permissive—that affect children's social development in different ways. Children's social behavior resulting from various parent–child relationships can be described in terms of social competency or social and cognitive agency. Self-reliant, controlled, affectionate, high-achieving children are usually the product of authoritative parents. However, parent–child relationships are complex. There is no single correct way to raise children. Parenting behavior can be affected by various factors including characteristics of the child-parenting experience, the socioeconomic status of parents, and family stress.

Parents can also function as teachers. This role has been found appropriate and supportive of children's intellectual and social development in both socially deprived and socially enriched environments. However, it appears that many parents need some training for this role. Also, it is the case that, since in many families both parents work full-time, there is little time available for parents to fulfill this role. Some psychologists and educators believe that the community and its social agencies should be better trained, or at least made more aware of the support that families need.

The school system is similar to the family system. For example, rules are imposed, there are codes of behavior, there is training in social behavior, and the system is continuous. Teaching styles can be described in terms similar to those used to describe parenting behavior. Democratic (authoritative) teachers competently teach social skills and set consistent standards for social behavior. Competent teachers also teach children how to use appropriate social behavior in various social settings. However, it has been shown that the home and school can be incompatible models, making the socialization of the child somewhat fragmented and discontinuous.

Peer interaction also has an important effect on the child's social development. Peer interaction increases in frequency during the preschool years with early relationships serving as prototypes for later more formal group associations. The peer-group structure can be viewed as being complementary to the family system.

In the peer group the child can test out social behavior learned elsewhere. Associations formed among peers and the overall influence of the peer group can affect the development of identity, self-esteem, values and standards of behavior, and an understanding of social relationships.

Sex roles are both adopted and prescribed. Preschoolers learn sexual identity and sex roles from the culture they live in, but at this age their understanding of sexuality is highly stereotypic. However, children also have their own expectations about sex-role behavior even though they are influenced by parental, sibling, and social pressures.

Aggression may develop from the tantrums of infancy to social differences with peers in later childhood, though this idea is controversial and further research is needed on the development of aggression. Usually, aggression is described as consisting of two types—instrumental and hostile. Instrumental aggression is related to retrieving objects, territory, and privileges. Hostile aggression is directed toward a person. Children can also learn to share belongings and be sympathetic toward others' feelings. This type of behavior is referred to as prosocial behavior or altruism and can be observed in children as early as two years.

It is generally believed that aggression is learned. If parents provide models of aggression, it is likely the young child will imitate them—and more strongly if rewarded. Parents have different views about aggression. Some are totally opposed to any form of aggression, some consider it is necessary, most believe it should be controlled. Gentle but firm control, coupled with explanations about desired behavior, seems the best way for parents to control children's aggressive behavior. Children's viewing of aggression in TV shows does seem to result in aggressive behavior. However, it is more likely to heighten the aggressive behavior of children who already have aggressive parents, and of older children rather than younger.

Children's altruistic behavior is learned from parents and other people. Trends in the development of altruism are difficult to establish.

Questions for Review

1. Compare Freud's psychosexual view of social and personality development during the preschool years to Erikson's psychosocial view.

2. According to learning theory, what are the most important factors that influence children's social development?

3. What emphasis does Piaget place on learning rules as an influence on young children's social development?

4. According to Piaget and Kohlberg, in what ways is the development of pre-moral reasoning related to changes in children's social behavior during the preschool years?

5. How has Baumrind chosen to describe parenting style, and what effect, according to Baumrind, does parenting style have on children's social competency?

6. What are the factors Maccoby believes influence parents' child-rearing practices?

7. What might cause "fragmentation" of children's social experiences in the home and nursery school? If fragmentation occurs, is this likely to be a negative influence on children's social development?

8. In what ways can parents become involved in the education of their children?

9. To what extent does the peer group appear to influence the child's social development during the preschool years?

10. Compare the factors that appear to influence the development of aggressive and prosocial or altruistic behavior during early childhood.

Suggestions for Further Reading

Bettelheim, B. *The uses of enchantment: The meaning and importance of fairy tales.* New York: Knopf, 1976. This book invites us, indeed entices us, to re-read the fairy stories of our childhood with a different eye to meaning. The stories of Hans Christian Andersen are interpreted from a Freudian perspective.

Erikson, E. *Childhood and society,* 2nd ed. New York: W. W. Norton, 1963. Traces psychosocial development through "eight ages of man" from the first demonstrations of trust during infancy to the ultimate ego integrity that can occur in later life.

Fisbach, S., & Singer, R. *Television and aggression.* San Francisco: Jossey-Bass, 1971. An interesting appraisal of a controversial subject.

Hendrick, J. *The whole child: New trends in early education,* 2nd ed. St. Louis: The C. V. Mosby Company, 1980. Includes chapters that discuss the important influence of preschool education on the child's moral and social development.

Maccoby, E. E. *Social development: Psychological growth and the parent-child relationship.* New York: Harcourt Brace Jovanovich, 1980. Focuses on the child's social development in the context of the family during early and middle childhood.

Rutherford, Jr., R. B., & Edgar, E. *Teachers and parents: A guide to interaction and cooperation.* Boston: Allyn and Bacon, 1979. Includes detailed descriptions of procedures that teachers can use to foster cooperative efforts with parents to help children's development.

384

The Middle Years

Physical and Intellectual Development

9

The children who explored the brook and found
A desert island with a sandy cove
(A hiding place, but very dangerous ground,

For here the water buffalo may rove,
The kinkajou, the mangabey, abound
In the dark jungle of a mango grove,

And shadowy lemurs glide from tree to tree—
The guardians of some long-lost treasure trove)
Recount their exploits at the nursery tea

And when the lamps are lit and curtains drawn
Demand some poetry please. Whose shall it be,
At not quite time for bed? . . .

From T. S. Eliot, *To Walter de la Mare.*
(London: Faber & Faber), p. 232.

In this chapter we will continue to trace the child's physical, intellectual, and language development through the years of middle childhood to the threshold of adolescence. The gradual, uneventful physical growth of the child that marked the preschool years continues through this period. Many books on human growth give the middle years scant attention; but a number of interesting changes in physique and in motor development do occur and are worth mentioning. We must also keep in mind that as the child's body grows and changes, as motor skills such as throwing, catching, running, and jumping become better coordinated, intellectual abilities are also developing, and the child's social world is also changing. Children become more aware of their bodies and compare themselves with other children. There is much more involvement in rule-governed games that are quite competitive and require fairly sophisticated levels of physical and motor competencies. Consideration of "physical" success or failure, although not as intense as the emotional conflicts that some adolescents experience, can affect other aspects of the child's development before the middle school years come to a close.

Between the ages of about 6 and 12 years children are very actively involved in intellectual activities. They are better able to remember and to represent objects and events. The narrower boundaries of previous thinking are pushed out. It is with more certainty of understanding that children now form concepts. They can sustain a criterion for forming a class and, when necessary, switch criteria for forming classes more easily, remember more than one property of objects at a time, and classify objects on the basis of more than one property. They also need other intellectual skills. Consider how important understanding the concept of *change* is. It takes a considerable amount of time for the child to understand the intricacies of *reversible change,* such as realizing that daffodils and tulips can be "flowers" and also two separate classes at the same time, and to understand *irreversible change,* such as realizing that when two colors are mixed together we cannot separate them again. However, this understanding, according to Piaget, is complete by the end of the middle years. At this time children also become more aware of and fascinated by their improving ability to solve problems. We will look at intellectual development from four different viewpoints, first the behaviorist's view, then three cognitive structuralists' views (Bruner, Ausubel, and Piaget).

An important function of language from its very first appearance has been to regulate behavior. At first the child uses language to regulate others' behavior and others use language to regulate the child's behavior (Bower, 1979, p. 246). But during these middle years the child comes to use language in a self-regulatory way: "I do what I say." And, of course, language comes to be used more for communication.

There are many changes occurring during the middle years in children's physical development and in their thinking and reasoning. Although for the sake of description we need to consider each form of change separately, we should keep in mind that these diverse changes are often interrelated.

Physical Development

In describing *physical growth* there are inevitably going to be quite a few references to "averages." You have heard people refer to young children as being tall for their age, or small for their age, or just about average, but reference to averages is overstated. There is really a range of possible levels of normal growth and development (Tanner, 1970, 1973). Elementary school children come in all shapes and sizes. Variations in growth are even more noticeable when watching, say, a mixed-sex soccer team of 9- or 10-year-olds where a tall girl in defense might be seen very effectively placing passes up field to rather diminutive, scurrying boys who are trying their best to score goals.

There are three aspects of growth: children grow in size; they grow up, which means that various parts of their bodies change with respect to proportion; and they grow older, which means that their bodies go through different stages of maturation when body tissues register the passage of time (Krogman, 1972, pp. 3–4). During the middle years children grow and physically mature steadily but slowly, with very little change in body proportions. The most obvious aspects of physical growth are changes in size—in height and weight. Size can be affected by a number of factors, which include age, sex, socioeconomic group, and genetic ancestry. So, too, can the rate of growth in size.

Growth in Height and Weight

Parents are often concerned about the eventual height to which their children will grow. Certain professions such as ballet set restrictions on height, at least for ballerinas (Sinclair, 1978, p. 31), and above-average tallness is certainly an advantage in basketball. Leaving such considerations aside, excessive tallness in girls or shortness in boys may result in emotional problems. If a child's predicted height is shorter than or in excess of "acceptable" limits, hormonal treatments can be used to modify growth (Sinclair, 1978, p. 148). Tanner and his colleagues (1975) constructed a scale for use in predicting height based on a child's height at a particular chronological age, which also took into account the parents' height since there is a strong genetic influence on growth. A boy's height at age 6 will be about 65 percent of his eventual maximum height, while for girls it will be about 70 percent. At age 12 the percentage of height reached will be 84 percent and 93 percent, respectively. The *average* 6-year-old boy and girl are about the same height—3½ feet. By age 12 the girl will be a little taller at 4 feet 10 inches compared to the boy's 4 feet 8 inches. During this period a boy's weight will increase from 40 to 80 pounds (20 to 36 kg) by age 12.

The child's ethnic heritage and socioeconomic background will affect growth in height and weight. Immigrants from the Scandinavian countries of Europe are usually taller than those who trace their origins to countries around the Mediterranean; variations in stature of native African tribes are reflected in

Children of the same age grow at different rates—as can be seen by the appearance of these two eight-year-olds. (Photo by Robert Eckert/ EKM-Nepenthe)

American black people who can trace their roots to Africa; and people from countries such as China, Japan, Mexico, and Puerto Rico are, on the average, below average height and weight. We can expect children to follow the patterns of growth set by their ethnic heritage.

What about socioeconomic background? Circumstances of nutrition, health, health care, and parent–child relationships can all affect the child's growth. Insufficient food, an inadequate supply of calories, protein, amino acids, and vitamins can seriously retard normal growth and development. If we add to that poor sanitation, inadequate health care, even emotional factors such as a broken home, rejection by parents, or a lack of recreational facilities, we can see that children's normal growth can be affected by very complex situations. We know that if severe and long nutritional deficiency occurs early in a child's life, this can have profound, permanent detrimental consequences (Scrimshaw & Gordon, 1968). However, outside of those pockets of great social and economic need, American children are showing a trend to grow taller and heavier, which can be attributed to better nutrition, health, and living conditions.

Maturational Growth

Not all children run the "growth race" at the same rate. Three children whose chronological age is 10 years may have biological "ages" of say 8, 10, and 12 years. Individuals register passage of time through changes in their body tissues, and **maturation** or biological age varies. But there are ways to measure age by considering skeletal and dental growth.

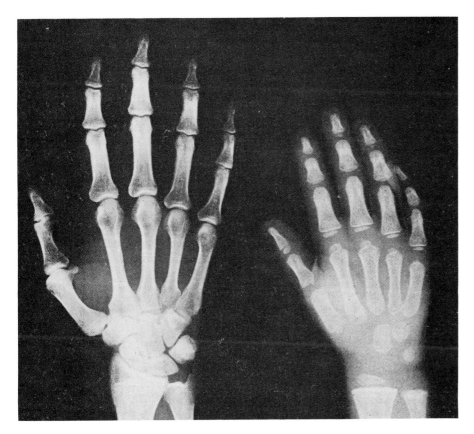

Skeletal age. A child's biological age is unique to that child and is part of an individual identity. It is also a better predictor of physical behavior than chronological age. The body system that provides the best measure of growth timing and rate is the **skeletal** or **bone age,** which can be obtained by taking X rays.

The bones of the skeleton of a newborn baby continue to form (**ossification**) until full growth is reached at about 18 years of age. A child's skeletal age can be determined by examining the amount of bone growth or ossification that has occurred and how closely the ends of bones have become united. An X ray of the hand and wrist is usually used for this purpose and for several reasons. The hand is the easiest part of the skeleton to X ray and the appearance of bone growth and the union of bones are clearly defined. Also, the total process of assessing bone age for the hand and wrist has been standardized, and atlases of hand–wrist maturation are readily available (Krogman, 1972, p. 51).

The hand–wrist X rays of normal, healthy children can be used not only to establish their maturational age but also to predict future growth. Let us suppose that the three 10-year-old children in our example are all boys who are presently 4 feet 8 inches tall. We would predict that their ultimate height would be the reverse of their present bone age; that is to say, the child of 4 feet 8 inches with a bone age of 8 years is very likely to grow to be the tallest of the three children.

Dental age.   Another *index* of maturity that can be used to estimate the child's growth is the appearance of primary and secondary teeth—the **dental age.** It is often said that the 6-year-old child's mouth is "full of teeth" since at this time there are more teeth in the jaw than at any later time. At this age primary teeth are about to begin falling out and the secondary teeth, more or less fully formed in the jaw, are growing. You must have seen many "gap-toothed grins" of 6-year-olds.

The first secondary tooth to erupt is the first permanent molar in the lower jaw; this occurs at about age 6. The rest of the teeth appear in sequence from front to back during the years from 7 to 12. This sequence is not invariable, however, but differs somewhat among individuals. Although a radiograph of the developing jaw can be used to give an estimate of a child's maturational age, most estimates are based on the appearance of certain teeth. Even though there is some variability in sequence of tooth appearance, certain teeth do appear at closely predictable times. For example, the second permanent molar erupts when a child is about 12 years old and used to be called "the factory tooth." In England, under the terms of the Factory Act in the early nineteenth century, when the second molar appeared, children were then considered old enough to go to work!

Obesity

A particular growth problem for about 5 percent of American children is **obesity.** The amount of fat deposition just below the skin in obese children is usually between two to three times that of normal children. There seem to be a number of reasons why obesity occurs. For some children it can be attributed to over feeding during infancy (Jelliffe & Jelliffe, 1974; Penick & Stunkard, 1973); in other cases it can be a combination of types and quantity of food eaten and attitude toward food (Weil, 1975). For example, when some children (and adults) get upset, they eat more. It has also been shown that obesity can have a genetic origin (Seltzer & Mayer, 1964).

Whatever the causes of obesity, most excessively fat children, beginning in middle childhood, resent their size. It is common for these children to be teased, and they are more likely to be rejected than befriended. Obesity is difficult to treat and for many cases requires medical, nutritional, and psychological counseling.

Motor Development

The slow, regular physical growth during the middle years allows for a marked improvement in motor skills and coordination. This is a time for individual and team sports that demand motor skill. During this period of *motor development,* boys' muscular strength doubles. Girls' muscular strength also increases but not quite to the same extent. One cannot help noticing the zest with which children this age engage in ball games, move from one place to another invariably at a run, speed around on bikes, climb all kinds of obstacles, and continuously add finesse to such exacting activities as gymnastics and ballet. Their energy seems limitless. No less remarkable is the continuous improvement of finer motor skills necessary for writing (the joys and tears of learning cursive handwriting!), drawing, painting (see Inset 9.1), sewing, cutting, hammering, and using a whole variety of tools. To some extent improvements in motor skills can be associated with improvements in intellectual competencies that are also occurring at this time.

Investigators have used various tests to examine the development of motor abilities, most frequently measurements of balance, jumping, and hopping; running speed and agility; and throwing, catching, kicking, and batting balls (Cratty, 1979, pp. 201–219). In general, it has been found that improvement in motor skills keeps pace with maturation, though practice in many skills can produce quite startling changes in ability levels. For example, somewhat uncoordinated attempts to kick a ball improve very quickly with practice. However, this does not hold true for all skills. Most children this age, for example, find it easier to throw than catch or to simply kick a ball rather than to kick it accurately at a target. Part of the problem has to do with **reaction time** or the speed at which a child reacts to some movement. To a large extent maturation determines reaction time, decreasing as age of maturation increases (Astrand, 1976; Surwillo, 1974).

Motor activity is closely associated with play. During middle childhood rules of play become more formal and play becomes more competitive. With increasing age children also tend to form more complex and larger groups when playing. Motor coordination continues to improve during childhood with no sex differences until about age 11 years, when boys tend to improve their coordination more than girls (Espenschade & Eckert, 1967). The relationship between motor skills and ability at games is not straightforward. At one time very few girls played soccer, and their attempts to kick a ball, compared to boys, suggested real differences in level of coordination and gross motor skills. Today many girls play soccer skillfully. During the middle years there are no differences in skill level in playing soccer when both boys and girls have had adequate practice. In the teenage years most boys are physically stronger and faster at running than girls,

An interesting feature of children's motor activities is the development of scribbling and drawing. By about 18 months infants are exploring and using many objects with their hands. At this time they are likely to grasp an object, such as a crayon, that when touched to a surface makes a mark. They then proceed with vigor to mark every surface in sight, often to the consternation of parents! The stages through which children pass in acquiring scribbling, drawing, and writing abilities are as follows:

Inset Table 9.1 Emergence of Scribbling, Printing, and Drawing

Year	Examples of Activities	Printing and Writing
Infancy 1-2 years	Scribbling emerges as repetitive radial or circular patterns. Multiple and single-line crossings are made. A variety of scribbling patterns are used.	
Preschool Years 3-5 years	Simple crosses may be drawn using two lines. A variety of patterns of enclosed spaces emerge. Figures are placed in simple combinations of two figures. "Suns" are drawn, sometimes forming faces. Crudely drawn human figures emerge. Crudely drawn buildings and houses appear. Circles and squares may be drawn. Animals and trees also appear in drawings. Drawings of objects become more refined.	Can print various large-sized numbers and letters arranged irregularly (end of fourth year). Able to print names of objects in irregular manner (age 5).
Middle Years 6-12 years	Better drawings of objects are made. Triangles are drawn reasonably well. Diamonds are drawn. Three-dimensional geometric figures are drawn. Linear perspective is seen in drawings.	Many 6-year-olds can print numbers from 1 to 20 and letters of the alphabet, and many can copy words in large irregular letters. By age 9 children can copy numbers and letters in correct alignment. At age 12 children are printing numbers and letters fluently; beginning to learn cursive writing.

Kellog (Kellog & O'Dell, 1969) has listed three basic steps in the acquisition of hand-eye control seen in drawings and writing—stages of scribbling, of combining or forming aggregates, and of making pictures.

The Scribbling Stage

At this stage children scribble horizontal and vertical lines, attempt to obliterate a pre-drawn shape or balance it with a scribble, or try to scribble within its boundaries.

As more control of hand-eye coordination is gained, children attempt to *enclose* space first by *squiggles,* then by *circular repetitive loops,* and by age 4 by using imperfect circles and squares.

Stage of Combines and Aggregates

Once children have mastered the drawing of simple geometric figures they attempt

to combine more than one shape into a pattern and include (aggregate) three or more shapes into a design.

The Pictorial Stage

As children improve in their drawings of designs, it is not unusual to find the shapes taking the form of objects in their world. Circles become "suns" and "faces," big loops become bodies, straight lines become arms and legs, fingers and toes, and squares and triangles are put together to make houses.

Paralleling efforts at drawing are the attempts of children to print letters and numbers. When printing letters, the 4-year-old is likely to scatter them around the page slanting at varying degrees or resting on their sides. Many 5-year-olds can print their first and last names, numbers from 1 to 20 and all the letters of the alphabet—although they often have problems in distinguishing between b and d and p and q. They also find it easier, generally, to print capital rather than lowercase letters.

Printing and writing can be improved more easily with younger children than with children of 9 years or older (Cratty, 1979, p. 181). One of the most helpful models for improving printing is that suggested by Birch and Lefford (1963) and Cratty and Martin (1975), in which partly formed letters of dark broken lines are used to guide printing efforts and are then gradually removed.

Source: Cratty, Bryant J. *Perceptual and Motor Development in Infants and Children,* 2nd ed. Copyright © 1979, pp. 168–186. Adapted by permission of Prentice-Hall, Inc., Englewood Cliffs, NJ.

During the middle years, boys and girls become equally competent in physical skills they practice. In sports such as soccer it is not unusual to find boys and girls playing together in mixed teams. Boys tend to play more aggressively and run faster, especially as they grow older, but girls can be equally skillful at playing the game. (Photo by James L. Shaffer.)

but girls can remain equally skillful at soccer. We can assume that maturation influences the development of motor skills, but there also seems to be some influence by the culture in which the child grows up.

Intellectual Development

Most of what needs to be said about behaviorist theory and Bruner's and Ausubel's theories has already been mentioned in chapters 4, 6, and 7. A number of ideas from these three theories, particularly relevant for the middle childhood years, are briefly described. The greater part of this section concerns a description of the stage of intellectual development that Piaget called *concrete operations.* There are at least three reasons for doing so. First, Piaget's description of this stage is very detailed and rather complicated, so any discussion of his theory cannot be passed over lightly. Second, a fairly detailed description of fundamental Piagetian concepts should help the reader grasp what is meant by concrete operations. Third, there is no doubt that Piaget has provided us with one of the most thorough descriptions of intellectual development. Gaining an understanding of this theory provides the chance to put it to practice by observing and working with young children.

However, to begin this section on intellectual development during the middle years, we are going to turn again to behaviorist theory and consider a most important concept to which we have not yet referred in any detail—***transfer of learning.***

A Behaviorist's View of Transfer

Suppose that you are a behaviorist psychologist and have been observing the learning behavior of a child from infancy to 6 years of age. You have noticed that much of the child's early learning occurred in many new and particular situations. You refer to the accumulation of learning from these situations over this time period as development. You also have noticed that as the child grew older the child dealt with many new experiences with objects and events in terms of previously learned behaviors. You realize that when this occurred the objects and events were similar in some way to those the child had previously experienced. For example, having learned to eat with a spoon and drink from a cup, the child also quickly learned to use other eating and drinking utensils. In fact, you noticed that as the preschool years went by the child became more and more adept at responding correctly, in ways previously reinforced, to similar stimuli when they appeared in a whole variety of new situations. You note in your observations that the child *transferred* previously learned skills and knowledge of the world to new situations as they arose.

Our hypothetical child has to learn to adapt general responses to similar situations that are also different in important ways. For example, the child may have learned to ride a bike that is stopped by using a handbrake. The child asks to ride a friend's bike that can only be stopped by peddling backwards. Too late the child realizes that there is apparently no brake to stop the bike . . . an inevitable crash! Hopefully there are no major injuries but just a case of having clothes dusted, and bruises and pride attended to. The "unusual" braking system is pointed out, the bike is mounted again, and the reverse peddling tried out. It works, confidence is regained, and soon the child is speeding around once more, braking correctly when necessary. Before long the child has learned to ride bikes with various braking mechanisms, and you are able to make a note that there has been a marked improvement in the child's ability to *discriminate,* being able to recognize both similarities and differences between objects and events. Discrimination is important for transfer of learning.

Changes in learning behavior can, in fact, come about from three forms of transfer: generalization, horizontal transfer, and vertical transfer. Rohwer, Amman, and Cramer (1974) have described these mechanisms of change as follows. If a child has learned to associate a word with a particular object (stimulus)—circle, square, red flower, and so forth—and then uses the word to define or describe new, but similar objects, that would be a generalization of response. For example, here's another circle, this square is bigger than the other, this flower is different from the other but it is also red.

Suppose a child has learned the rule for identifying the animals called "fish," as described in Chapter 7. This rule is applied to discriminating, say, guppies and goldfish from newts and water snails. On a visit to the aquarium the child sees, for the first time, new examples of fish. In identifying them as fish the child does not have to relearn the rule about the properties of "fishness." Similarly, if the child has learned to convert feet to inches, there is no need to relearn that rule when converting yards to inches. This kind of transfer is called *horizontal transfer* because what has been learned in one situation is transferred to a new, similar situation in which the complexity of content and skills are at the same level as previous related learning experiences.

Children who are studying one unit on Eskimo people and a second unit on Bushpeople who live in the Kalahari desert are asked to state similarities and differences between these peoples and also to compare them to the community in which the children live. The children arrive at the concepts of *tribal* and *industrialized* cultures. They combine the rules for identifying the Eskimo and Bushpeople communities into a rule for identifying tribal people. This is a *higher-level* concept. The previously learned skills of forming individual concepts (simple classifying) have been combined with other skills into a higher-level rule of hierarchical classification that involves combining subordinate concepts into superordinate concepts because of shared, common properties. This combining is called *vertical transfer* because low-level *subordinate* concepts are combined "upwards," as it were, into *superordinate* concepts.

Generalization is a form of transfer, but both horizontal and vertical transfer have a very special feature. Taken together they allow us to understand how, from a behaviorist's point of view, development occurs because both vertical and horizontal transfer are particular examples of cumulative learning (which was mentioned in Chapter 7). The result of these forms of transfer would be new, higher-level concepts and skills. In their turn these new forms of knowledge allow the child to perform at a more advanced level.

Bruner has also commented on the importance of transfer of learning. He has pointed out that beginning at about 6 years of age children show remarkable improvements in their ability to use symbolic representation.

The Development of Symbolic Representation

According to Bruner, by about 2 years of age the child is able to use three forms of representation: enactive (by action), iconic (by imagining), and symbolic (by using symbols, particularly words). He is quick to point out that the young child uses language almost as an extension of pointing. It is only by about the age of 5 or 6 years that the child uses words to represent a more complete understanding of concepts as classes of objects (1966). Even then, the child's *symbolic representation* is influenced by his or her egocentric view of the world, which seems to persist until the child is 9 years of age or older (1964). Bruner seems to be saying two things. First, the child passes through a stage of egocentric thinking, which gradually diminishes between 6 and 12 (a qualitative change). Second, the child gets better at using symbolic representation (a quantitative change). For example, the 6-year-old tends to group objects—say apple, potato, milk—by perceptual features (color, size, pattern) and only by age 12 years groups objects according to how things function. For example, apple, potato, and milk are not just "food," but "You can eat them. They are good for you. They help you grow" (Bruner, 1964, p. 9; Olver, 1961; Rigney, 1962). See Figure 9.1. Between the ages of 4 and 12, language, as a form of representation, plays an increasingly important role in the development of knowing and as a tool to express and apply what is known to the learning of new knowledge.

Ausubel's Stage of Concrete Operations

The *concrete-operational development* stage, as described by Ausubel, covers the elementary school years. The main feature of development during this stage is the child's growing capability in using secondary concepts such as "equality of sets," or "tribal" and relationships between them. How does the child learn a secondary concept?

The preoperational child learns primary concepts by seeing many actual examples of a concept and by abstracting the properties of a concept. There are three reasons why the concrete-operational child's learning of a concept is qualitatively different from the younger child's learning. New concepts are learned when

1. The actual properties of a concept are learned, *not* the particular instances of the concept.

2. Only a single example of each property is provided to illustrate a concept as opposed to multiple examples of the concept itself. For example, third graders are likely to understand the concept of *nomad* after learning that people who are called *nomads* wander from place to place usually caring for flocks of animals such as sheep, goats, and cattle, or hunting for food; they live off the products of their animals or the animals they kill in the hunt and sometimes trade with other people. When you present 8-year-old children with information about such people as the Bedouin, Central Eskimos, or Bushpeople of the Kalahari, they will then quickly recognize that these people are nomads.

3. The properties of a concept are remembered—and can be used to identify actual examples of the concept whenever this is required (Ausubel, Novak, & Hanesian, 1978, pp. 222–234). The child can now also learn propositions more easily. A proposition is a statement of a relationship between two or more concepts.

In the following examples of propositions the main concepts are italicized. For the concrete-operational child, one or two concrete examples of the properties of each concept should be sufficient for understanding the concepts and their relationships.

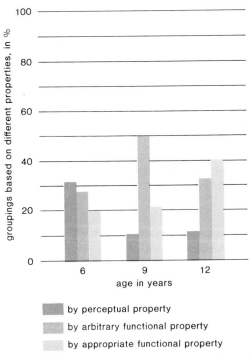

y-axis: groupings based on different properties, in %

x-axis: age in years

■ by perceptual property

▨ by arbitrary functional property

▧ by appropriate functional property

Figure 9.1 Features of objects used by children of different ages as a basis for placing objects into groups. The youngest children rely more heavily on perceptual properties than do others. As children grow older their grouping of objects come first to depend on *arbitrary* functional properties—what you or I can do to objects that make them alike. With increasing maturity children shift to a more *appropriate* conventional function or use of objects and less egocentric function. (Source: Adapted from Bruner, J. S. *The Course of Cognitive Growth,* 1964.

"*Fish,* like other *animals,* go through a *life cycle* from *birth to death.* Many *bigger fish* eat *smaller fish* as part of a *food chain.* So *some fish* die when they are eaten as part of a *food chain.*" Other concepts in these propositions, such as "go through" and "part of" may also have to be learned as secondary concepts. Prerequisite learning is important for the meaningful learning of secondary concepts. The child's understanding of relationships between secondary concepts, as they are expressed in propositions, will depend upon very recent or concurrent direct experience with related primary concepts. At first the young concrete-operational child may need such concrete examples handy so that he or she can refer to them during learning. As the child's experience and knowledge increase, there will be less need for what Ausubel has called *concrete props.*

There are similarities between Bruner's and Ausubel's views. For one thing, we might suppose the 6-year-old could learn functional as well as physical properties of objects—fish as fish and fish as part of a food chain. Learning primary concepts depends a great deal on enactive and iconic representation—the child needs many concrete examples to illustrate the properties of concepts being learned. In learning secondary concepts the child begins to rely more heavily on words—labels that stand for concepts, and relationships between concepts. However, Ausubel emphasizes that there is still, nevertheless, a dependency on concrete examples to illustrate concepts—though fewer are needed and dependency on them is lessening. This view differs somewhat from that of Bruner.

Both Bruner and Ausubel describe changes in thinking that are qualitative—for example, using functional rather than perceptual properties of objects (Bruner) or using secondary rather than primary concepts (Ausubel)—but they also stress quantitative change. Bruner talks about using new ways of representing recurring regularities; for example, getting to know and understand concepts in a symbolic form that were first represented enactively. Ausubel points out that the concrete-operational child's understanding of concepts such as *fish* or *food chain* will be quantitatively different from that of the preoperational child; it is a matter of understanding at a more abstract level the same concepts first learned at a concrete level.

Piaget's Stage of Concrete Operations

We must keep in mind that the concepts Piaget is most concerned with are those he calls operations, what we refer to "loosely" as intellectual skills. Piaget believed that between the ages of 6 and 12 years the child becomes capable of performing certain actions (operations) on objects (and events) as long as they are actually concretely present. That is why he called this phase of development the *stage of concrete operations* (see Table 4.2).

Piaget wrote extensively about this stage of development and described its features in great detail. Also, the amount of research related to concrete-operational thinking is truly phenomenal. Given the mass of available information about the concrete-operations stage, our discussion has to be selective. The following types of concrete operations will be described: classification, relations, transitive inference, conservation, number concepts, spatial concepts, and movement–time–speed concepts.

According to Piaget, the stage of concrete operations spans the years from about 6 to 12 years. As we will see in Chapter 10, a considerable amount of research has pointed to the fact that under certain kinds of conditions preschool children appear to be able to meaningfully acquire concrete operations. However, we should also keep in mind a point that Flavell made about the expectations we should have in regard to development at this time. The child now has a better understanding of what a problem is; to solve a problem requires reasoning and the use of some strategy; and choices can be made, often need to be made, about how to attempt to solve a problem (Flavell, 1977, p. 86).

Classification.   **Classification** involves a number of basic processes that include constructing a class of objects, constructing hierarchical classes of objects and cross-classifying (or multiple classification). We will consider each of these in turn.

Any class of objects has two properties. The first is the criterion (property) that defines the class—for example, geometric shapes. Piaget refers to this criterion as the **intension of a class.** The second criterion is the number of objects (almost always relative) that make up the class—for example, a 6-year-old's concept of the class of geometric shapes may include just eight objects. Piaget refers to this criterion as the **extension of a class** (the extent of the number of objects in a class). When a person is classifying any particular group of objects, it is important to pay attention to both the intensional and extensional properties of each class as it is constructed. Let us look at an example.

In Figure 9.2*(a)* fourteen geometric shapes are displayed. This group of objects can be formed into classes that include the following:

	Property
Intension	*Extension*
Geometric Shapes	14
Squares	6
Large squares	2
Small squares	4
Small black squares	2
Small white squares	2
Triangles	3
Circles	5
Large black circles	3
Small black circles	2

As each class of objects is constructed, both the intensional property of the class (e.g., squares) and the extensional property (e.g., the number of squares) must be attended to. The importance of being clear about the intensional and extensional properties of classes will become apparent as you read through the description of hierarchical classification.

The first example of class in Figure 9.2 is "geometric shapes." This class includes (extension) all the shapes in the array. How can the child best construct and organize these classes? A child who truly understands how to construct hierarchies of classes would explain as follows:

"Well, first you have *all the shapes* (this is a superordinate class since it contains all other classes in that group of geometric shapes). You can put these into groups so you have *large shapes* and *small shapes* (this is the first breakdown of the superordinate class "shapes" into two subordinate classes). Or you can have two groups of *white shapes* and *black shapes.* You can also have groups of *squares, triangles,* and *circles* (a less inclusive set of classes; that is, each of these three classes contains fewer of the shapes than the previous classes). These can be made into smaller groups of the *big squares,* the *small squares,* the *one big triangle,* the *small triangles,* the *big circles,* and the *small circles.*"

That would be quite remarkable for a 6-year-old, but most 12-year-olds would find it quite easy. (The author knows quite a few 6-year-olds who find such a task easy; they will be mentioned in Chapter 10.)

No doubt you have noticed that our hypothetical child began with the largest class (the superordinate class), all the shapes, then described the biggest subordinate classes (such as large shapes) followed by the smaller subordinate classes (such as triangles) to the smallest subordinate classes (such as the small squares). This is called **hierarchical classification.** Hierarchies of concepts represent a two-way process of class composition—you can add objects together to form subordinate classes, and subordinate classes together to form superordinate classes. You can also reverse the composition to form subordinate classes from superordinate classes and objects (facts) from the subordinate classes. This two-way process of class composition is called **reversibility,** and a full understanding of hierarchical classification means that the child must also understand reversibility.

Let us take a closer look at reversibility as part of the process of classification since Piaget has said that reversibility and conservation are the best indicators of concrete operations. Suppose the young child who did so well with the geometric shapes is now shown an array of picture cards illustrating rabbits, some brown and some black. The child readily sorts the group into two classes and also explains that the black rabbits and brown rabbits together are the group of rabbits. However, according to Piaget, true composition with reversibility requires that the child knows, at one and the same time, that you can have *rabbits* and *brown rabbits* and *black rabbits* as separate, yet related, classes. To find out whether a child had such understanding, Piaget would ask the question, in this form, for example, "Are there more rabbits or more brown (or black) rabbits?" Of course, the whole class, rabbits (superordinate concept), and the two subclasses, brown and black rabbits (subordinate concepts), cannot exist in reality

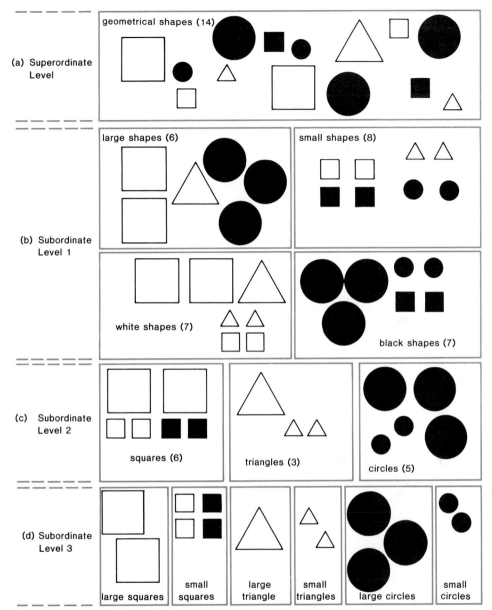

Figure 9.2 A hierarchy of geometric shapes. The geometric shapes pictured include *all* the shapes (14), the class of large shapes (6), the class of small shapes (8), the class of white shapes (7), the class of black shapes (7), the class of squares (6), the class of triangles (3), the class of circles (5), and finally, the least inclusive classes of large squares (2), small squares (4), large triangle (1), small triangles (2), large circles (3), and small circles (2).

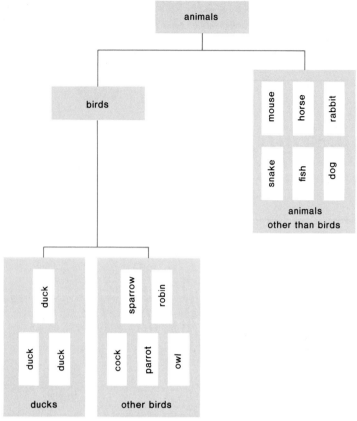

Figure 9.3 A hierarchy of animals. (Source: Adapted from Piaget, J., and Inhelder, B., *The Child's Conception of Space*, 1956, pp. 110–118.)

at one and the same time. If the child has composed the class rabbits and is asked to compare it with say, the class black rabbits, this subclass must be "imagined" for the child to compare the whole with one of its parts. To imagine a class that does not concretely exist in reality is, according to Piaget, beyond the capabilities of a 6-year-old. It is only toward the end of this stage that children are expected to have developed the competency of dealing with abstractions.

Piaget (Inhelder & Piaget, 1964) refers to this relationship of subordinate and superordinate concepts in a hierarchy as **class inclusion.** It always involves superordinate and subordinate classes, which are related. In one of Piaget's original well-known experiments (Inhelder & Piaget, 1964, pp. 110–118), the classes were three or four ducks, other birds (cock, sparrow, parrot, etc.), and animals besides birds (snake, mouse, fish, horse, etc.). Consider how many classes there are altogether here. As the series of classes are identified, there are *five* classes altogether. Their hierarchical relationship is shown in Figure 9.3.

It turned out that children in the study knew the names of each class. But Piaget found that only the older children (about 10 years of age) properly understood the hierarchical system and class inclusion. In order to find out if a child understood class inclusion, Piaget asked the following questions:

Are there more birds or more animals?
More animals or more ducks?
More birds or more ducks? and so on.

Children have difficulties with this form of question (Markman, 1973; Siegel, 1978; Siegel, McCabe, Brand, & Mathews, 1978).

The error young children most often make in responding to the class-inclusion question is to compare subordinate classes that are part of the superordinate class mentioned. They then call one of the subordinate classes by the name of the superordinate class. For example, the superordinate class *birds* includes *ducks* and *other birds*. The child is asked, "Are there more birds or more ducks?" (Remember, there were 3 ducks and about 5 other birds.) The child may respond, "More birds." If the child is asked, "Which are the birds and which are the ducks?" he or she is likely to point to the ducks (3) as the ducks and to the *other birds* (5) as the birds. If the ratio were ducks (5) and other birds (3), the answer would likely be more ducks than birds. It appears that the young child cannot keep in mind, at one and the same time, the superordinate class, *birds,* and one subordinate class, *ducks*—and compare them. Now in Piaget's experiment the children who could not deal with the hierarchy of animals had no problems with a hierarchy of flowers. He says, "Their difficulty in comparing the part with the whole in this domain must be due to the fact that zoological classes are not very clearly defined for them"; and, "the level of reasoning varies with the character of the content to which it applies" (Inhelder & Piaget, 1964, p. 114). It might be supposed that if Piaget had taken time to familiarize these children with the zoological classes referred to, they would have fared just as well with this problem as the flower problem.

Young children also have difficulty understanding relational terms such as *more than* or *less than* (Donaldson & Wales, 1970; Palermo, 1973, 1974; Siegel, 1977). It has been shown, for example, that preoperational children can solve problems of class inclusion if the traditional and seemingly confusing question "Are there more____ or more____?" is changed. In one study (Siegel, McCabe, Brand, & Mathews, 1978) 3- and 4-year-old children were shown an array of candy that included *M & M's* and jelly beans. Rather than ask the question, for instance, "Is there more candy or are there more *M & M's*?" the researchers asked the children, "Would you rather eat the candy or the *M & M's* (or jelly beans)?" The children almost always chose the candy and explained correctly, in class-inclusion terms, why. However, their responses to the traditional form of the question were incorrect.

Figure 9.4 A matrix of rabbits showing cross-classification. To compare a cross-classification matrix such as this with a **double-seriation** matrix, take another look at figure 6.11.

Another important feature of classification is multiple classification or cross-classification as it is sometimes called. When a child constructs a hierarchy such as the "rabbits" example, more than one property of the objects being classified must be taken into account. Apart from the property *rabbit,* there are also the properties *brown* and *black*. But there is only one major class—rabbits—and when dealing with color this property can be taken for granted. Sometimes, however, more than one property of a subclass can be (needs to be) attended to. Suppose that among both brown and black rabbits some were shown *sitting* and some *standing*. The child can now classify these rabbits on *two dimensions* at the same time using the properties of color (brown–black) and position (standing–sitting). This type of classification is called **cross-classification** or **multiple classification** and is illustrated in Figure 9.4 (see also Figure 9.5).

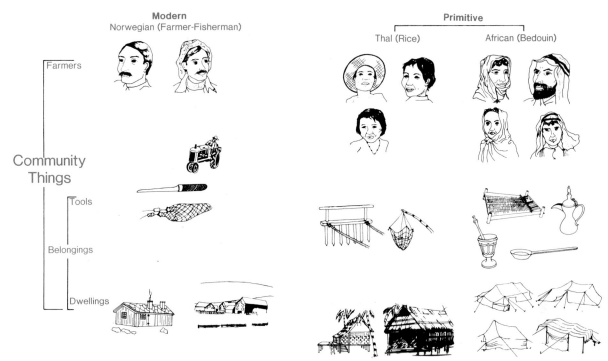

Figure 9.5 A cross-classification of three farming communities and their belongings. (Source: Lawton, J. T., and Wanska, S. K. Facilitating the Learning of Meaningful Verbal Materials and Logical Operations by the Use of Advance Organizers: A Replication and Expansion Study. Wisconsin Research and Development Center for Individualized Instruction, Madison, Wisconsin. 1979.)

Multiple classification expressed in matrices can be used effectively in various elementary school projects. For example, third grade children may be doing a project on how various communities satisfy certain basic needs. Comparisons are going to be made of the types of people in three communities, Bedouin nomads, Thai rice farmers, and Norwegian farmers—fishing people; also the tools and shelters (dwellings or homes) that these people use. The children use a "retrieval chart" (in effect a matrix) to organize information (Figure 9.5). The children can paste small pictures or words and sentences onto the chart to represent findings. Each picture, word, or sentence must be doubly classified—by need and by community. To answer a question such as, "Why do these three communities of people need shelter?" children have to generalize about similarities in three different communities' needs for shelter. To compare, say, the clothing of Bedouin nomads to that of the children's families, the children first have to identify (isolate) that information at the intersections of clothing with Bedouin nomads and then compare it to information about clothing worn by the children's families. Being able to cross-classify obviously has important implications for children's thinking, reasoning, and problem solving.

Relations.　There are certain operations that children can perform on objects which involve ordering the objects on some dimension such as biggest to smallest, widest to narrowest, one to ten, and the reverse of these orders. Such relationships are concerned both with differentiating (for example, this ball is bigger than that ball) and with ordering (for example, this is the biggest ball, next comes the middle-size ball, then the smallest ball). Once the direction of the dimension has been decided (for example big $\rightarrow$ small, or small $\rightarrow$ big), it is unidirectional. If, for instance, a child notices that "The black dog is bigger than the brown dog," the reverse cannot be true. Suppose the child also noticed a gray dog and said, "It is smaller than the brown dog." If there is a true understanding of the unidirectional relationship of the order of size of the three dogs, the child is able to argue that

If the black dog is bigger than the brown dog,
And the brown dog is bigger than the gray dog,
Then the black dog is bigger than the gray dog.

There are a number of types of **relations: seriation,** additive seriation, one-to-one correspondence, multiple-relations, and **transitive inference** (Inhelder & Piaget, 1964; Piaget, Inhelder, & Szeminska, 1960). Examples of each type are illustrated in Table 9.1.

Conservation.　Researchers have said that the best indicator of whether a child has developed concrete operations is the child's ability to deal with **conservation** (Inhelder & Sinclair, 1969). Here is an example of two 6-year-olds faced with a problem of conservation. Bill and Margaret have been chasing around the yard playing a game of tag on a very hot summer's day. They come rushing into the house, asking for a drink. Their mother happens to have just finished a course on child development and remembers a problem she saw demonstrated to illustrate what Piaget meant by conservation. She decides to play a trick on the children by surreptitiously presenting them with a conservation problem. Getting two glasses of the same shape and size, she fills each to the same level with orange juice. She then places nearby a tall, narrow beaker (see Figure 9.6). She first asks her two thirsty children which of the two same-size glasses they prefer. With a quick glance at the levels of juice, Bill says he doesn't mind which one he gets. Margaret says she doesn't mind which one she gets either. Mother then asks the children to watch carefully as she pours one glass of juice into the tall, narrow beaker. Both children now decide that for sure they prefer the tall, narrow beaker, "cos that's got most juice in it." In this situation neither child could conserve amount or quantity of liquid. What caused the children to believe the tall, narrow beaker contained more orange juice than the shorter beaker? They were confusing quantity with height of the beakers—shorter mean less juice and taller meant more juice. For example, just as the rabbits could be transformed

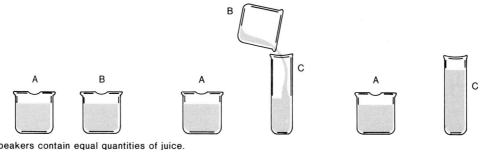

Two beakers contain equal quantities of juice.
The juice from beaker *B* is poured into a tall, narrow beaker.

Does beaker A have the same amount (quantity) of juice as
beaker C?

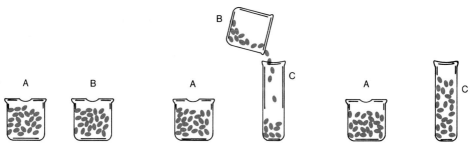

The two beakers contain equal quantities of jelly beans. The
jelly beans from beaker *B* are poured into a tall, narrow
beaker. Does beaker A have the same amount (quantity) of
jelly beans as beaker C?

Figure 9.6 Conservation of quantity. Children who insist, for the first example, that
beaker *C* contains more juice than beaker *A* may claim, in the second example, that
beakers *A* and *C* contain the same amount (quantity) of jelly beans. Can you think of
reasons why this might be so?

Remember that you have already seen an example of conservation in figure 6.1.

into the two subgroups of brown and black rabbits—and back again into the
total group of all rabbits—without losing a rabbit (!), so the juice can be transformed from its short, wide shape in one beaker to its tall, thin shape in a second
beaker—and back again into its original shape—without losing a single drop of
juice (thus the quantity is conserved). See Inset 9.2.

Table 9.1 Types of Relations

Relations	Objects	Problem	Solution
Seriation: requires ordering objects along some dimension.		Order the squares from largest to smallest.	
Additive Seriation: requires one or more objects to be added to a series.		Add these two pencils to the already seriated pencils.	
One-to-One Correspondence: requires that a second set of objects be placed in a one-to-one correspondence with an already seriated set of objects.	(1)	Place the four balls below the four boxes so that each ball goes with the right size box.	
	(2)	Counters and numbers must be arranged in a one-to-one correspondence with the dotted squares from 4 to 1.	
Double-Seriation: requires that a set of objects be placed in a matrix to show a seriated order in *two* dimensions.		Picture cards of trees are to be arranged in the 3 × 3 matrix to indicate (1) classes by size of tree and number of apples, and (2) seriation by size of tree and number of apples as a *double-seriation*.	
Transitive Inference: requires that an inference be made about a relationship between two objects in a set of three objects after each of the two objects has been compared to the third object but not to each other.	A B C 50 grams 100 grams 150 grams	The child is asked to compare A to B to determine which is heavier. The child does this by holding one ball in each hand. The child is then asked to compare C to B to determine which is heavier. The question then asked is "Which is heavier, A or C?" The child is not allowed to compare A to C directly by holding those two clay balls, one in each hand, but must make an inference.	Children who reason that, "A must be lighter than C because B is lighter than C but heavier than A" are capable of transitive inference.

Since about the mid-1960s a series of experiments, mainly by North American researchers, have been aimed at training children to acquire Piagetian concepts such as class inclusion, transitivity, and conservation (e.g., Brainerd, 1972a,b, 1974; Bucher & Schneider, 1973; Inhelder, Sinclair, & Bovet, 1974—colleagues of Piaget; Lawton, 1977; Lawton & Wanska, 1979; Siegler & Liebert, 1972; Youniss, 1971). What is the source of such interest in children's *learning* of Piagetian concepts through training of some type as opposed to acquiring these concepts without instruction of any type in the normal course of development?

Learning experiments associated with Piaget's theory have been mainly in response to Piaget's claim that development always imposes constraints on children's learning. One such constraint is that a child at one stage of development cannot meaningfully learn concepts that emerge during a subsequent stage. However, Piaget and his co-workers in Geneva have acknowledged that children in a transitional stage can be trained by a self-discovery procedure to acquire concepts they already have some understanding of (Piaget, 1970; Inhelder, 1972; Sinclair, 1973; Inhelder, Sinclair, & Bovet, 1974).

To questions about concrete operations concepts such as, "Are there more flowers or more tulips?" (class inclusion) or "Do we now have the same (more or less) liquid?" (liquid quantity conservation), children in a transitional stage give certain types of responses. They

1. frequently change their minds—"There's more to drink in this glass . . . no, more in the other one . . . no there's the same in both . . ." (and so forth);
2. sometimes answer correctly in one case (more flowers) but incorrectly in another case (with 6 horses and 2 cows—"Are there more animals or more horses?"— "More horses");
3. can be influenced too easily by the "teacher" to change their minds whether they have responded correctly or not (Inhelder et al., 1974, pp. 281-282).

The "self-discovery" training approach usually asks children to predict a solution to a problem, test their prediction by physically manipulating objects in whatever way they imagine is helpful, and state their conclusions as evaluations of their initial predictions. At no time does the "teacher" directly teach or demonstrate a correct solution to aid the understanding of a concept. Piagetians are opposed to what they call *tutorial methods,* which means any teaching (training) procedure that uses direct instruction, demonstration, or both. You can imagine that this position will tempt researchers to investigate which teaching procedure does work better.

Inhelder et al. (1974) investigated the self-discovery approach in eight experiments but did not compare this teaching method with a tutorial approach. Brainerd (1978, pp. 91-93) has compared two of the experiments by the Genevan group with similar experiments by Sheppard (1973, 1974), who used a tutorial training procedure.

The results were as follows:

1. Training conservation of liquid quantity

Instructional Approach	Complete Progress	Partial Progress	No Progress
Self-Discovery Inhelder et al., 1974	21%	33%	46%
Tutorial Sheppard, 1974	30–40%	Almost all remaining children	—

2. Training class inclusion

Instructional Approach	Complete Progress	Partial Progress	No Progress
Self-Discovery Inhelder et al., 1974	37%	37%	26%
Tutorial Sheppard, 1973	40%	20%	40%

All of the children in the first two groups of the Inhelder et al. experiments had previously solved correctly *some* quantity, conservation, and class-inclusion problems, thus showing they were transitional. The children in Sheppard's experiment failed all previous problems of these two types. So Sheppard was able to produce better learning results with children who knew far less about conservation and class inclusion to begin with (Brainerd, 1978, p. 93). The fact that concrete operations concepts have been learned by both elementary and preschool children who showed no prior understanding of them before training suggests that learning can influence development.

If a particular property of an object remains unchanged when other properties are changing (being transformed), then the particular property is said to be conserved. If the same can be said for the particular property shared by two similar objects when irrelevant properties of one of the objects are changed, that is also a case of conservation (compare the two quantity conservation examples in Figure 9.6). The simple, straightforward rule for *conservation* is that at the time an object is transformed (certain properties being changed), if nothing is added to or taken away from some particular property, that property is conserved. At this point in your reading you are probably begging for some examples. The example of the children's choosing which beaker of juice they preferred is an example of a problem involving quantity. Conservation concepts that occur most frequently are quantity, number, substance, weight, length, area, and volume. Each of these concepts is illustrated in Table 9.2.

At the beginning of the stage of concrete operations, children have problems with the concept of conservation. They are too easily distracted by irrelevant perceptual changes, as in the case of Bill and Margaret. Later children begin to understand this concept, but sometimes they conserve and sometimes they do not. It is also true that they begin to "catch onto" some types of conservation such as quantity before others such as weight and volume (Brainerd & Brainerd, 1972; Gruen & Vore, 1972; Chittendon, 1964; Uzgiris, 1964). Toward the end of this stage, at least in theory, children have no problem with conservation. As with the case of class inclusion, they supposedly develop the competency of remembering some particular property of an object in an abstract form and understanding it has not changed when other properties of the object are transformed. That children achieve such a level of understanding is questionable. In Chapter 10 you will find a number of problems children have with conservation concepts that we can associate as much with learning as development. But here is a conservation problem you can try to solve. If you have any difficulties with it, note them down, ask yourself why such problems might have occurred, and ask your friends if they had any difficulties.

Look at rectangles *A* and *B* in Figure 9.7. They have sides of equal length; therefore, they are equal in area, and both perimeters (perimeter of each rectangle is the total length of the four sides) are of equal length. If a section of rectangle *B* is cut off and placed along an edge of the rectangle in the three positions shown in *C*1, *C*2, and *C*3, will—

1. The area of rectangle *A* be the same as (more or less than) that of the transformed rectangle *B*—as shown in *C*1, *C*2, and *C*3?

2. The perimeter of rectangle *A* be the same as (more or less than) the perimeter of the transformed rectangle *B*—as shown in *C*1, *C*2, and *C*3?

The answers to the problem can be found at the end of the Summary section.

Inset Table 9.2 Types of Conservation

Type of Conservation	Examples of Equivalence	Transformations and Questions of Conservation
Conservation of Quantity	See Figure 9.6.	See Figure 9.6.
Conservation of Number	Six pennies arranged in one-to-one correspondence	One row of pennies is spread out over a longer distance Are there the same number of pennies in each row?
Conservation of Substance	Two balls of clay of the same amount and shape	One clay ball is changed into a "sausage" shape. Is there the same amount of clay in the "sausage" as in the ball?
Conservation of Weight	Two clay balls weigh the same	One clay ball is changed into a "sausage" shape. Does the "sausage" shape weigh the same as the clay ball?
Conservation of Length	A B A B Two pieces of string, or two rods of the same length	A B One straight-shaped string is changed Is the string at *B* the same length as the string at *A*? A B One rod is broken into three pieces. Is *B* rod the same length as *A* rod?

Conservation of Area

A   B

Two grass yards of the same area.

One yard (B) is rearranged to look like this.

Is there the same amount of grass to cut at B as at A?

Conservation of Volume

Two clay balls of equal amount are placed in two beakers of water. Water level in each beaker rises to the same level

A   B

One clay ball is changed to a "sausage" shape. If it is placed in the beaker (B) will the water level be the same as in beaker (A)?

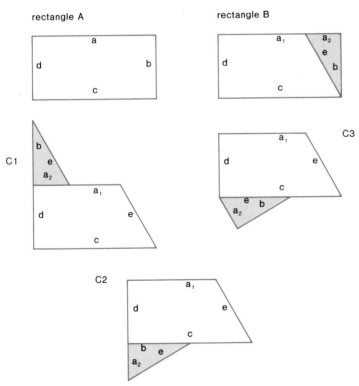

rectangle A

rectangle B

C1

C3

C2

Figure 9.7 Conservation of area and perimeter problem.

Ordination is a special case of seriation. Preschool children may find seriating different sized wooden cylinders easy, but seriating coins according to their value rather than size (ordination) is difficult. (Photos courtesy of the author.)

Number concepts. From a Piagetian point of view the concept of numbers or the act of numbering is a special relationship between classification and seriation (Piaget, 1952; Piaget & Inhelder, 1956; see also Brainerd 1978, pp. 155–168). You may remember that in describing classes and classification we used the term extension in reference to the question of "how many." When numbers are used to define a class of objects (or refer to themselves), they are called *cardinal* numbers. A child might say, for example, "I have five cents. See, I can count them, one, two, three, four, five." Another name for counting is **cardination.**

Suppose a child has been given four coins—a quarter, dime, nickel, and penny. The child may say, "I have some coins (class of *coins*); I have four coins (class of *coins* and *four*); I can place them in order of value—first the quarter, then the dime . . . and so forth (seriation)." Another way of saying seriation (a type of relations) is **ordination.** However, it should be mentioned that preschoolers who can easily seriate objects according to, say, size and length may have great difficulty seriating coins according to their value. If they do not understand the value of a coin, they are more likely to pay attention to the relative sizes of the coins. So an important aspect of acquiring concrete operations is the synthesis of classification (cardination) and relations (ordination).

Spatial concepts. A 6-year-old realizes when a cookie jar is *open* and when it is *closed* and has an intuitive notion that grannie lives *far away,* that walking to the elementary school does not take too long because the school is *close to* home, and that the hose dad uses for watering the lawn needs to be *connected to* the water outlet. By first grade the child can also measure distance—and knows that a person walking away into the distance is *not* getting smaller. Spatial operations include topological, Euclidean, and projective concepts which we now consider.

The preoperational child can only deal with **topological concepts** such as nearbyness, separation, succession, enclosure, and continuation (Piaget & Inhelder, 1956). Readers familiar with preschool learning materials will no doubt know what a "feely-box" is. Various objects are placed in a box with an aperture through which the child can get his or her hand without being able to see the objects. The child, by feeling the objects, attempts to ascertain what each one is. This type of activity is concerned with the topological properties of objects. Older children might be discussing an area of countryside comparing hilly sections to flat sections, wondering about the problems of driving on curving roads with many steep gradients, or considering why cities like Chicago grew to be so large.

An introduction to geometry would focus on topological concepts. But as children develop a greater ability to deal with number and measurement, **Euclidean concepts** such as measuring the distance between two objects can also be introduced. Elementary school children are quite capable of handling problems like the following. The child is shown two model houses (*A*) and (*B*), or a picture of two houses, some distance apart. A toy doll is shown going from one house to the other. A third house (*C*) is placed between the first two. The child is asked, "Will the doll now have as far to go (not as far or farther) from this house (*A*) to this one (*B*)? However, 6-year-olds may have difficulty with this type of problem and other Euclidean concepts such as conservation of area (see Table 9.2). Another Euclidean spatial concept 6-year-olds have problems with is the relationship between horizontal and vertical. No doubt you have seen kindergarten children's drawings of trees or people or other objects arranged on a slope at an angle to the horizontal—for example, mountaineers putting their best foot forward but defying gravity! (See Figure 9.8.) Often children turn the drawing paper so that the slope of the hill is made to appear flat or horizontal in order to draw objects upon it. By age 12 children find such drawings humorous. They are able to handle many types of problems with Euclidean concepts and to use measuring instruments such as rulers, compasses, and protractors.

The first grade child knows very well how to get home from school but has great difficulty describing the journey to another child. Perhaps you have noticed some adults have similar problems when you have asked directions to some place. Describing the pathway of a journey, with all its twists and turns, requires an understanding of **projective spatial concepts.** Perspective is another example of a projective spatial concept. When drawing, perspective is beyond the capabilities of many children in the early elementary grades, and not all 12-year-olds can

(a)

This drawing is a typical one of those produced by young elementary school children that shows a lack of awareness of the relationship between horizontal and vertical in this kind of situation.

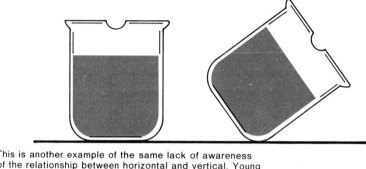

This is another example of the same lack of awareness of the relationship between horizontal and vertical. Young elementary school children draw the water level in the tipped beaker as shown above rather than in this correct relationship.

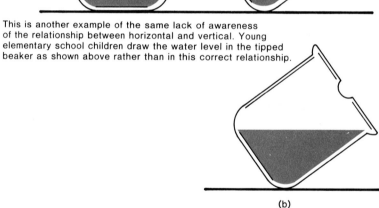

(b)

Figure 9.8 Children's concepts of horizontal and vertical.

handle this concept successfully. A well-known example of a projective relationship problem used to test children's understanding of this concept is "the three mountains problem" (see Figure 9.9).

Three "mountains" are set out on a table with a chair at each of the four sides of the table. The child (*A*) sits on one of the chairs and another child (*B*) sits in turn on each of the other three chairs. When the other child (*B*) is in each

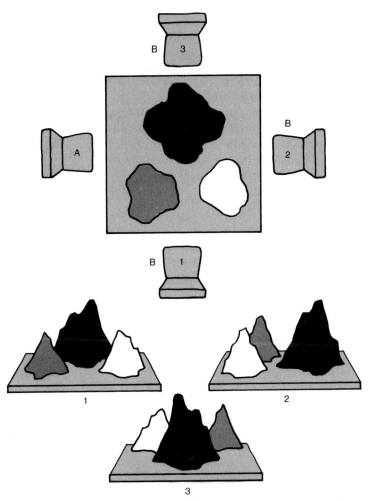

Figure 9.9 The three mountains problem. One child sits in the chair at *A*. Another child sits first at *B-1*, then at *B-2*, and finally at *B-3*. On each occasion the child sitting in the chair at *A* is asked, "How does child *B* see the mountains from where he or she is sitting?"

Child *A* is shown drawings or three-dimensional models as in this illustration to choose from, or is asked to draw what is considered to be the view from child *B*'s position.

position in turn, child (*A*) is asked, "How does (*B*) see the mountains from where he or she is sitting?" The child can respond by drawing the other child's eye view, by selecting from drawings depicting possible views (including the correct one, of course), or by constructing what is considered the other child's view from three similar "mountains." Usually only children aged about 10 to 11 years can spontaneously identify with ease the correct eye views of the other person. You will, no doubt, recognize the relevance of the concept of "egocentrism" with this problem.

Movement, time, and speed. Finally, it should be mentioned that at the beginning of their middle years children experience difficulties understanding concepts of movement, time, and speed—and especially relationships among them. Perhaps you have heard the story of the child who was asked by the teacher, "Is it far from school to your home?" The child replied, "Well, if I walk it's quite a long way, but if I run it's not all that far!" Toward the end of this period children can make close estimates of the length of time of journeys and know who is the fastest runner in the class and how this can be ascertained; at least some of them take pleasure in solving problems such as — "Two cars leave towns A and B at the same time and are traveling toward each other along the same highway. The towns are 200 miles apart. Car X is traveling at 35 miles per hour and car Y at 55 miles per hour. How far will car X have traveled by the time it meets car Y?"

So much for concrete operations. In looking back over this section, you may decide that you have been taken on a tour of problems. There is a reason for all the examples. First, I believe that when most adults are first introduced to Piaget's theory they become very concrete-operational. They need lots of concrete examples to begin to understand concepts such as class inclusion, transitive inference, and conservation. I certainly found this to be the case for myself, and perhaps you did also. (By the way, Ed Labinowicz's book, *The Piaget Primer: Thinking, Learning, Teaching* (1980), is full of interesting examples of concrete-operation type problems.) Second, children come to an understanding of concrete operations by solving problems—if you are willing to accept "interactions with the environment" as problems. Every question a child asks is the acknowledgment of a problem to be solved. A child's world is full of questions. And, finally, as a follow-up to that last point, development occurs because of the interacting processes of assimilation and accommodation as the child wrestles to better understand the environment and to act upon it.

You may have noticed that in all the problems introduced here questions were asked, responses were made, and discussions of objects and events were pursued, all through language. Language is an important tool we use to communicate. How is *communication* progressing at this time in the child's development?

Language Development

Language development involves both the learning of a native language and skills in using language to communicate. By age 5 or 6 children have a good understanding of the rules of grammar and syntax. But children also need to realize language is a tool that can be used to communicate.

As Bower has emphasized, "The whole point of language is communication" (1979, p. 241). Children appear to become more eloquent when they are actively trying to communicate. Consider the following conversation.

Brian (age 6): Hey, let's play zoo.

Brad (age 8): I'm the zookeeper, you two are the monkeys.

Brett (age 6): I'm the monkey, we're different animals in here, and we fight! I'm a tiger, you're a lion.

Brian: Uh-h I'm a gorilla.

Brad: Hey! Hey, I have an idea.

Brett: I'm a monkey.

Brad: Hey, I have an idea; see, a monkey is a gorilla's son.

Brett: (To Brian who is hitting him) Gorillas don't hurt monkeys. Listen, gorillas don't hurt monkeys.

Brian: Gorillas are monkeys and they both fight (screeches).

Brad: Don't Brian, you're gonna hurt him. The zookeeper's gonna get ya!

Brian: You gotta be an animal. You can't get in here, or you're trapped (Williams, Hopper, & Natalicio, 1977, p. 23).

By age 5 or 6 the child has mastered most syntactic rules and his or her grammar is almost complete. What does this tell us about the substance of communications? It tells us very little in itself. We need to know the answer to questions such as these: What is the child trying to communicate? Is the child attempting to describe some object or event? Is the child trying to explain some phenomena—perhaps a "cause-and-effect" relationship? Does the child seem to understand the concepts that the words he or she is using stand for? How competent is the child at constructing verbal propositions (relationships between concepts)? In order to find some answers to these questions, let us take a look first at two important but contrasting ideas about communication development.

Referential Communication

An important aspect of communication between people is **referential communication,** which requires that one person describes a referent (such as dog, the red circles, the mammals that live in water) so that another person can select it (an object or a class) from a set of referents. Various methods have been used to find out how children use referential communication such as telling them to draw a picture, construct a model, assemble objects according to specific instructions, and follow a "map." Children's referential communication skills include both sending and receiving information. The following example of a referential communication game (Hess, Dickson, Price, & Leong, 1979) illustrates one method for testing children's ability to send and receive information. Two notebooks with sets of four pictures are placed on a table so that two people sitting across from each other can see the set of four pictures facing each of them but not the set facing the other person (Figure 9.10). The pictures in each set are the same but placed in a different sequence to prevent identification of a picture by its location rather than by the properties of the object in the picture. Under each picture on the receiver's side is a push button connected by a wire to a light under the corresponding picture on the sender's side. The object of the game is for the sender to select one of the four pictures and verbally describe it so that the receiver will push the button under the correct picture at the first attempt. Let us suppose two children are playing the game. The child who is playing the role of the sender is instructed to describe a selected picture by referring to the properties of the object in the picture. For example, in the set of four pictures in Figure 9.10 let us suppose the selected picture is the one marked with a black dot. The child might say:

There's a monkey.

It's hanging in the cage.

It's holding on by its paws.

The monkey's looking at you.

Do you think that these referents would be sufficient for the child who is receiving the communication to select the correct picture? This is unlikely. What referents would you use? What referents would you use for the pictures in the two sets of Figure 9.10? It should be clear from considering how the game is played or playing it yourself with a friend that accuracy in referential communication is important for understanding (see Inset 9.3).

A number of researchers have investigated children's referential-communication abilities (e.g., Dickson et al., 1979; Flavell et al., 1968; Glucksberg et al., 1975; Kraus & Glucksberg, 1969). A frequently stated possibility for children's errors on such tasks is that because of childish egocentrism, the sender does not fully take into account the listener's informational needs. Another possibility is

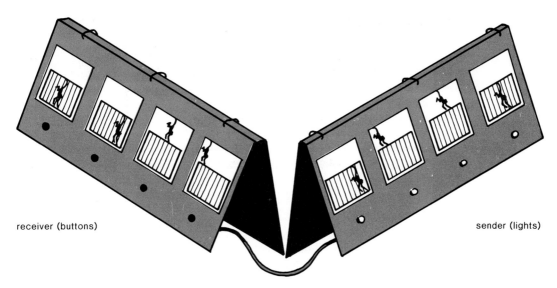

receiver (buttons)   sender (lights)

(a) Communication game set up with sample referent set of
pictures

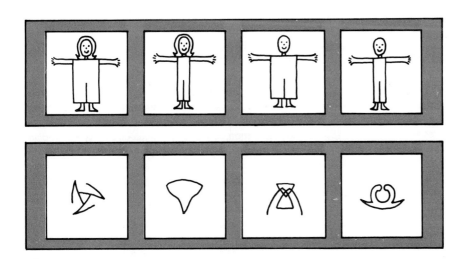

(b) Two further sample sets of referent pictures

Figure 9.10 Referential communication game. (Sources: (*a*) Material for the game,
monkeys, and people referent sets of pictures: Dickson, W. P., 1974; Hess, R. D.,
Dickson, W. P., Price, G. G., and Leong, D. J., 1979. (*b*) Referent set of abstract
pictures: Krauss, R. M., and Glucksberg, S. *The Development of Communication:
Competence as a Function of Age.* Copyright © 1969 by the Society for Research in
Child Development, Inc. Reprinted by permission.)

Communication involves two or more people. A major function of communication is the exchange of information about objects or events. This is achieved by a *speaker* describing discriminating properties of objects and events to a *listener.* In many communication situations there is an exchange of this type of information. A little girl may ask her mother, "Where is my doll?" Mother seeks clarification by asking, "Which doll?" and the little girl replies, "The one with golden curls and a blue dress." Mother says, "Oh, yes! I think you will find that doll in the toy chest in the closet in your bedroom." If the little girl goes to her bedroom and locates the doll she has been searching for, we can say that her mother's "referential communication" was *accurate.* Accuracy of communication is measured in terms of the correctness of the listener's responses.

Although there have been many studies of communication accuracy (e.g., Glucksberg, Krauss, & Higgins, 1975; Dickson, 1979a), most of these studies were on children communicating with other children. Few have focused on communication between parents and children. One study did examine how accurately mothers and their 4-year-old children communicated about a target picture in sets of four pictures in a communication "game" (Dickson et al., 1979). Measures of both the mother's accuracy of sending messages and the children's accuracy in this regard were obtained. In two cultures (Japanese and American) with quite different communication styles a strong relationship was found between communication accuracy and cognitive development one and two years later. The conclusion was this: "How accurately parents and children communicate may be important in all cultures; however the cultures may differ in their styles of communication" (Dickson et al., 1979, p. 58).

Accuracy of communication between parent and child may influence the child's intellectual development by the meaningful transmission of information, clarification of word meanings, and the provision of good "models" of communicators (Dickson et al., 1979, p. 54). Children who develop good communication skills are better able to abstractly represent their environment and engage in sustained and meaningful conversation with others (White & Watts, 1973).

In contrast to accuracy of communication, *style* of communication is defined in terms of how something is communicated—the form of a communication (Dickson, 1981, p. 120). One form of children's communication, for example, is the asking of questions. Results from other studies of communication (e.g., Flavell et al., 1968; Maratsos, 1973) suggest that the style of a communication can influence its effectiveness. For example, the relative ineffectiveness of preschool children to communicate in certain situations has been attributed, at least in part, to their egocentric view of the world. Communication improves quite remarkably as egocentric styles of communication decline during the middle years. As Dickson (1981) notes, our understanding of the development of children's communication abilities and the importance of parent–child communication would benefit from the study of relationships between communication style and accuracy.

that there is an important difference between *speaking* (sending the referents) and *listening* (receiving the referents), which may give rise to errors in communication (Dickson, 1978; Glucksberg & Krauss, 1967; Glucksberg et al., 1975). Both speaker and listener skills seem to be relatively poorly developed in preschool children but show considerable improvement during the elementary school years (Patterson & Kister, 1981). It has been shown that listener skills can be improved by means of brief instructional procedures or modeling techniques (Cosgrove & Patterson, 1977, 1978) and that training can improve accuracy of referential communication in both adult–child and child–child pairs (Patterson & Massad, 1980).

In "real-life" situations same-age children communicate at the same level using a variety of communication skills. In communicating with younger children, taking into account that younger children's ability to communicate might be quite limited, older children often modify their speech patterns. (Photos by Jean-Claude Lejeune)

Sociolinguistic Communication

Other researchers have been interested in how children communicate in a variety of social settings. In other words, they have set out to examine broad aspects of social communication. This view takes communication development to mean more than just referential communication. **Sociolinguistic communication,** as it is called (Flavell, 1977; Halliday, 1973; Shatz & Gelman, 1973), includes many of the aspects of referential communication such as using various types of questions, identifying and describing properties of objects, and using such features of language as analogy (its like a . . .). Other skills of communication used in a wide variety of social situations are making promises (Haliday, 1973), understanding indirect requests (Ervin-Tripp, 1974), older children's modifying speech patterns when communicating with younger children (Shatz & Gelman, 1973), changing word meaning (Brown & Berko, 1960), using spatio-temporal words and phrases, such as, *first it goes here, then you put it there,* (Clarke, 1972; Donaldson & Wales, 1970; Wood, 1976), and propositional reasoning (Corrigan, 1975). These investigators have tended to use communication tasks that "closely mimic the natural real-life communication situations the child encounters at home or at school" (Flavell, 1977, p. 174). An important contrast between the results of studies in these two traditions of referential and socio-linguistic communication is that children often communicate less egocentrically in the sociolinguistic situations. The following two examples of communication problems clearly illustrate this difference.

Experiments in Communication

In one study (Flavell et al., 1968, pp. 82–102) the experimenter taught 7- and 14-year-olds how to play a board game by playing it silently with them. No verbal explanation of how to play or descriptions of rules were given. The children then had to explain the game verbally to adults who did not know the game. Some adults were allowed to see the board game, others were blindfolded. The older children were much better at explaining the game than the 7-year-olds. They also produced longer, more detailed descriptions for the blindfolded adult players. The young children tended to use much the same descriptions whether the adults were blindfolded or not. This was taken as a sign of egocentric communication.

In a second study by Maratsos (1973) the experimenter put a wooden hill with a toy car on the table. The experimenter told the child, "We're going to play a game with this hill and this car and some toys. This is how the game works. I want you to sit there and catch the car coming down the hill, O.K.? I am going to put some people and animals on top of the hill. . . ." The experimenter then either continued with his eyes open or closed. The children could see whether the experimenter's eyes were open or closed. For the eyes-closed case the instructions continued— "Then I'll close my eyes, and you tell me which one I should put in the car" (Maratsos, 1973, p. 697). Two or three toys were then put on top of the hill. The experimenter said, "O.K., now who gets first turn?" When the experimenter's eyes were open the children indicated their choice of who got a ride by merely pointing. When the experimenter's eyes were closed the children carefully described which toy was to get a ride. In almost all cases their verbal communication was adequate.

These children adapted their instructions to the listener's situation, just as Flavell's first graders did. However, Maratsos's children were aged just *3 years!* Can this be so? Non-egocentric 3-year-olds? Flavell offers three explanations of what influences children's performance in communication and perhaps also in the Maratsos's experiment. The first concerns *information-processing load,* that is, the sheer amount or complexity of the information. Flavell's board game was more complex than Maratsos's game with the hill. As the information-processing load increases, even adults regress to egocentric forms of communication. Can you think of recent instances when this has happened to you? Second, other factors may affect the level of quality of communication. The naturalness of the communication situation, the child's familiarity with the content of what is communicated, and the meaning of the messages to the listener influence performance and may have reduced egocentricism in Maratsos's experiment.

Finally, egocentric communication may decrease as a result of a growing ability to use, what Flavell calls, meta-communication. Rather than just communicating—saying what comes naturally—*meta-communication* involves knowing about communication; for example, having skills in analyzing a message, knowing that first tries at communication may need changing, or adapting in response to that look on the listener's face which conveys a "what are you trying to say" message. The listener needs to have this skill as much as the communicator. When a listener does not understand a message, it is important to fashion a useful question (or set of questions) to get at the meaning of a message.

Summary

During the middle years children grow and mature slowly but steadily with little change in body proportions. Physical growth is marked by changes in height and weight. Children on the average increase their height by 26 percent and double their weight, with girls being a little taller and heavier by age 12 years. Individual differences in size and rate of growth are affected by various factors, which include age, sex, socioeconomic background, and genes.

The maturational or biological age of a child is a better predictor of physical behavior than chronological age and is indicated by skeletal or bone age, usually measured by assessing an X ray of the child's hand and wrist. Another index of maturation is the sequence of appearance of the secondary teeth.

There are also marked improvements in motor skills and coordination during this period. Children engage in both individual and team sports that demand quite sophisticated levels of motor skill. Evidence of the development of fine motor skills can be seen in children's drawings and the way they use tools. In general, motor skills keep pace with maturation.

According to behavioristic theory, not all learning produces development. Important for development is the ability to generalize or transfer previous learning to new learning situations. In behavioral theory we find reference to three types of transfer: generalization, horizontal transfer, and vertical transfer.

Bruner emphasizes that improvements in children's ability to represent their world mark the course of development. At about age 5 or 6 children begin to acquire a better understanding of the relationship between the word as a symbol and what it refers to. By age 12 there will have been significant improvements in children's use of symbolic representation and in the use of language as a tool.

According to Ausubel, the concrete-operational stage of development is marked by the elementary school child's growing ability to use secondary concepts, which require less reliance on concrete examples, and in the learning and use of propositions. Both Bruner and Ausubel distinguish between qualitative changes, such as an improvement in children's abstract thinking, and quantitative changes, such as a better understanding of certain concepts that the child continues to learn and use.

Piaget describes the stage of development that spans the middle school years in terms of concrete operations. During this phase children acquire competencies in classifying, dealing with relations, conservation, number concepts, and spatial and time concepts, and they become less egocentric in their thinking.

The point of acquiring language is to communicate. By age 5 or 6 children have mastered the fundamentals of grammar and syntax. However, they still have a long way to go in developing communication skills.

Two important traditions of research related to referential and sociolinguistic communication have provided some notable insights into communication development. Referential communication research focuses on the child's ability to correctly send and receive referents such as the names of objects, the properties of objects, and the characteristics of classes of objects. Sociolinguistic communication research is broader in scope and includes such features of general social communication as asking questions, making demands, adapting levels of speech, propositional reasoning, and so forth.

From the results of research in both traditions, Flavell has identified three factors that appear to influence children's communication performance: (1) information-processing load; (2) the naturalness, familiarity, or meaningfulness of the communication situation; and (3) the extent to which communication requires awareness of communication itself (meta-communication).

The Conservation of Area and Perimeter Problem

The answer to this problem is as follows. Let us suppose that a rectangle has the measurements shown in Figure 9.11. The triangle to be cut from one end of the rectangle has the measurements also shown in Figure 9.11. Figures 9.11 (a)–(c) show the triangle placed on edges of the rectangle in two different positions and three different sides of the triangle.

Since the area of the triangle remains the same whether it is part of the rectangle or in any of the three positions shown in Figure 9.11, the area of the remainder of the rectangle plus the area of the triangle will always be the same as the area of the original rectangle. Although there have been three transformations in the shape of the figure, the area remains the same in each case.

This is not so for the perimeter. In Figure 9.11 (a), the length of perimeter is 28 cm, which makes it longer than (or *more than*) the length of the perimeter of the rectangle. In Figure 9.11 (b), the perimeter is 26 cm—also longer (more than). But in Figure 9.11 (c), the perimeter is 24 cm—the *same* length. So the property of the original figure (rectangle) that we call perimeter sometimes changes and sometimes stays the same as transformations occur.

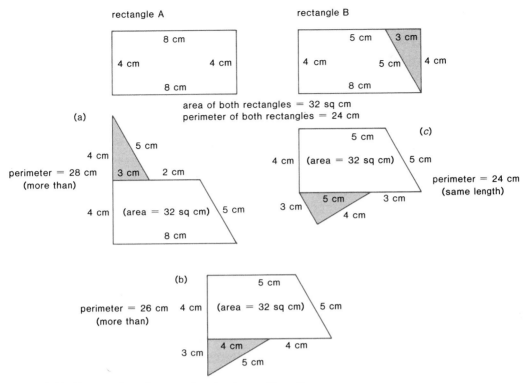

Figure 9.11 Conservation of area and perimeter problem: the answer.

Perhaps you found it easy to conclude that the area would not change as the triangle was moved. But to be sure about the length of the perimeter, you just have to measure it each time the triangle is moved. Because the lengths of all sections of the sides (perimeters) of Figures 9.11 (a)–(c) are given, all you have to do is a simple addition sum each time. Even this is likely to be difficult for a 6-year-old. Otherwise you either would have had to *deduce* the measurements or use a ruler. These are even more difficult tasks for a child.

The important point here is that, although this is indeed a conservation problem, it has an additional dimension to those examples of Piagetian conservation problems provided in this chapter. With this problem you also needed to have an understanding of certain geometrical and mathematical concepts; in the case of the question of perimeter, you had to be able to add, subtract, and make measurements. Without these skills, which have nothing to do, *per se,* with conservation, the child who is able to solve other types of conservation problems would surely fail this one. And we must keep in mind that, being exposed to it for the first time, some adults fail it also!

Questions for Review

1. Describe the differences among growing in size, growing up, and maturation.

2. What are the main characteristics of physical and motor development during the years from 6 to 12?

3. What is meant by skeletal age and how is it measured?

4. Briefly describe the three forms of transfer of learning from a behaviorist viewpoint. How are these forms of transfer interrelated?

5. What particular aspect of development does Bruner emphasize as occurring during the middle years?

6. According to Ausubel's theory of learning, what are the differences between learning *primary* and *secondary* concepts? In what sense is the growing capability to learn and use secondary concepts both a qualitative and quantitative change?

7. What is meant by *reversibility* as part of the process of classifying and conserving?

8. What are the main features of spatial concepts? Describe some of the problems the young child seems to have in dealing with such concepts.

9. Choose a couple of Piagetian problems—for example, hierarchical classification and cross-classification. Ask a friend your own age and a child between 4 and 7 years of age to attempt to solve the problems. Note very carefully how the older and younger person set about solving the problem. Compare the two sets of information, and suggest reasons for any similarities and differences you find.

10. What is meant by (a) referential communication and (b) sociolinguistic communication? Give examples of both types of communication.

11. Children as young as 3 years have been observed taking another person's point of view into consideration when involved in "sociolinguistic communication." What explanations have been offered to account for this unusual non-egocentric communication?

Suggestions for Further Reading

Brainerd, C. J. *Piaget's theory of intelligence.* Englewood Cliffs, NJ: Prentice-Hall, 1978. A comprehensive introduction to Piaget's theory. An explanation and evaluation of the theory is also provided.

Copeland, R. W. *Diagnostic and learning activities in mathematics for children.* New York: Macmillan, 1974. Contains activities grouped in the four areas of space, number, logical classification, and measurement. The activities are based on Piaget's theory of development.

Flavell, J. H. *Cognitive development.* Englewood Cliffs, NJ: Prentice-Hall, 1977. A very readable overview of Piaget's theory. Provides interesting accounts of language development, communication, and memory not found in other textbooks dealing with this theory.

Labinowicz, E. *The Piaget primer: Thinking, learning, and teaching.* Menlo Park, CA: Addison-Wesley, 1980. Intended particularly for teachers, but the illustrated sequences depicting children's thinking and learning should be of interest to the general reader.

Learning and Instruction

10

"Grasping the structure of a subject is understanding it in a way that permits many other things to be related to it meaningfully. To learn structure, in short, is to learn how things are related." How can the role of structure be made central in teaching? "The answer to this question lies in giving students an understanding of the fundamental structure of whatever subjects we choose to teach. This is a minimum requirement for using knowledge, for bringing it to bear on problems and events one encounters outside a classroom—or in a classroom. The teaching and learning of structure, rather than the mastery of facts and techniques, is at the center of the classic problem of transfer."

From Jerome S. Bruner, *The Process of Education*, 1960

435

At the start of the middle years, when children make the transition from nursery to kindergarten, the learning environment usually changes. The kindergarten program is likely to be more structured and more teacher directed. This is even more so the case when children move into the elementary school grades. Learning becomes associated with subject matter that is organized into separate disciplines, such as science, math, language arts, and social studies. Both the home and school systems now suggest to the child, with varying degrees of emphasis, that learning is competitive. Clearly defined achievement levels spur the child's learning. The questions parents ask about their children change from, "How is he doing? Does she get along O.K. with the other kids? What was that interesting sounding project you were doing last week?" to "How is he doing in math? Is he at grade level?" Teachers tend to emphasize ideas about learning and teaching methods and seldom, if at all, talk about development, as the term has been described in this book. Teachers do make comments such as, "Oh, Mary's behavior has really improved recently. She now pays more attention in class and has stopped interfering with other children when they are working"; or "I have seen a real improvement in Jamie's understanding of math concepts"; or "I was amazed to see how tall Sarah had grown during the summer vacation." All of these comments suggest that teachers notice something developing in children; Mary's behavior became more socially acceptable; Jamie developed a better understanding of math concepts; and Sarah developed physically. But the descriptions of development are in "lay" terms, and do not have the more precise meaning given to the term "development" by theorists.

As we saw in Chapter 9, changes in intellectual development during the middle years are quite remarkable. As the years go by between the ages of 6 and 12, children become able to handle large amounts of information. These intellectual changes are related to factors that include increased attention span, increased memory span, an awareness of the need to remember, developed ways of organizing information, and an improved ability to solve problems.

When we consider the process of learning, it is also important to consider the processes of development and instruction. These three processes are influenced by such factors as heredity, maturation, family structure, school structure and organization, peers, and the environment. These three basic systems, along with the other factors mentioned, combine in various ways to influence the child's physical, intellectual, and social behavior (see Figure 10.1). How do these three basic processes fit together? How easy or difficult is it to apply theories about these processes to the practice of "education"? Part of the answer to these questions was touched upon in Chapter 9, especially when we briefly considered Piaget's views on learning.

In this chapter we are going to take a closer look at the relationships among development, learning, and instruction in order to answer these questions and a number of related questions: Does developmental change influence learning? Can learning influence change in development? Can development and learning be accelerated by instruction, and, if so, is this of any lasting benefit to the child?

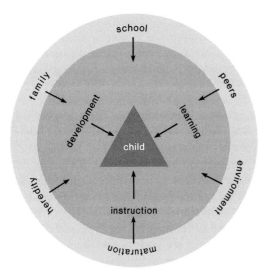

Figure 10.1 Three basic interacting systems of development, learning, and instruction. Developmental, learning, and instructional systems interact and combine to influence changes in children's behavior. Other factors such as heredity, maturation, family systems, school systems, peers, and environment are also interwoven into these three basic systems.

We will examine these themes in the theories of Gagné, Bruner, Ausubel, and Piaget and then in the work of researchers who study the development of memory.

Gagné's Theory of Learning and Instruction

Environmentalists like Gagné state that learning is cumulative. Gagné distinguishes eight types of learning and arranges them in a **learning hierarchy** from complex to simple. (For examples of each level, see Table 7.3.)

8. Problem Solving

7. Using Rules

6. Concept Learning

5. Making Discriminations

4. Making Verbal Associations

3. Chaining

2. Making Stimulus–Response Connections

1. Signal Learning

An important principle associated with *cumulative learning* (Gagné, 1977) is that learning is not related to age but to experience. Gagné and others, who write about cumulative learning, expect that children's many learning experiences during infancy and early childhood frequently include their acquiring simple intellectual skills such as making stimulus–response connections and associating words with the objects they refer to (levels 2, 3, and 4). They also believe that preschool children can deal with tasks of learning rules and solving problems (levels 7 and 8). *Any* learning task is a reasonable one for a child, if the child has learned the prerequisite skills for that task. However, older children have more finely tuned capabilities than younger children. A child in the early elementary grades is likely to be more frequently involved in discrimination learning (level 5) than a child in, say, the eighth or ninth grade. Older children tend to spend more time learning concepts and rules (levels 6 and 7). However, "The general principle is that the kind of learning that may be required can be predicted, not from age, but only from the nature of the performance being taught" (Gagné & Briggs, 1974, p. 50). This view of learning is very similar to Bruner's, and, as you may recognize by now, is very different from Piaget's. According to Gagné and Bruner, changes in learning will be quantitative and development should be measured in terms of increasingly complex intellectual skills acquired through learning.

Four Levels of Learning

The types of intellectual skills and subject-matter concepts associated with levels 1 through 4 of Gagné's eight-level hierarchy of learning are "not normally expected to play a substantial role in school learning" (Gagné & Briggs, 1974, p. 37). According to Gagné, during the school years learning experiences should provide children with opportunities to acquire intellectual skills and subject-matter concepts at the four higher levels of complexity—discrimination, learning concepts, using rules, and solving problems. Learning at each level is dependent on learning that occurred at prior levels.

As you read through the following descriptions of learning at each of these four levels, you will notice similarities to descriptions of learning by other theorists such as Piaget, Bruner, and Ausubel. We will begin with the level of discrimination learning.

Making discriminations.   When a child notices a difference between two objects, that is one form of discrimination. For example, the child may say, "That is a bird and that is a butterfly." Another form of discrimination occurs when a child matches an object with another object because they are similar in some way.

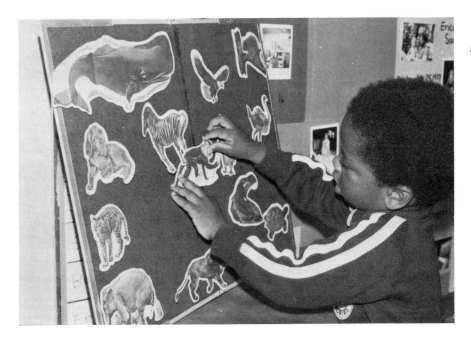

The child may be playing with a red ball. The teacher asks the child to pick out another red object from various objects in a group that is like the ball in some way. The child may choose a red hat.

Learning concepts. Gagné calls the general properties of objects *concrete concepts*. These are properties such as round, smooth, rough, color, and so on. If a concrete concept has been learned, the child should be able to point to many objects that all have at least one property in common. Another type of concrete concept is object position. Sometimes an object has a special property associated with its "spatial" relationship to other objects. The child may be able to point to an object as being inside of, at the front of, behind, to the side of, or below another object.

Suppose the child arrived at school and announced to the teacher, "I had to walk in the roadway coming to school this morning, 'cause they're repairing the sidewalk." We can be pretty sure the child knows the meaning of the concepts, *roadway* and *sidewalk*. However, Gagné makes the point that when a child is learning concepts for the first time, it is necessary to have the child demonstrate the concept. What does this require the child to do? We earlier referred to the concept of *mammal*. The child may have been learning this concept. The teacher wishes to know if the child can define it. It is not sufficient to simply ask the question, "What is a mammal?" The child may reply, seemingly correctly, but only knowing a word chain (rote learning). For example, the child might say, "A mammal has hair on its body. The mother mammal provides milk for her babies." The child may know that animal-mammals are covered in hair, but may not include humans as examples of mammals. Also, the child may not fully understand how the mother-mammal provides milk. Being able to give a verbal definition (a chain of words) of a concept does not guarantee that the child fully understands the concept. A *defined concept* is a concept in which the meaning has been demonstrated. For example, to be sure the child really can define the concept meaningfully, the teacher should have the child

1. Identify a mammal, using illustrations (or live mammals) among nonmammals. This can be done by pointing and using word labels.

2. Identify properties of mammal by pointing out these characteristics in illustrations (or live mammals).

3. Distinguish among different kinds of mammals, again using concrete objects (Gagné and Briggs, 1974, p. 42).

Using rules.   A rule is the underlying principle of logic or consistency within a concept or a skill. For example, if the child consistently identifies mammals, or any other concept, correctly, we can be sure that the child has learned the rule that governs the structure of these concepts. The child not only knows the intensional properties that define a single instance of the concept, but can generalize it for many instances (extensional properties).

Another form of rule might be the one governing the construction of a hierarchy of concepts. Indeed, there are many kinds of rules, which include rules of language, algorithms in math, such as the rule for subtraction (see Figure 10.2), and rules of social behavior. Obviously, a defined concept is an example of a rule. You have heard and probably used the expression, "As a rule." Almost invariably, whatever statement you make includes a defined concept. Try it!

Solving problems.   One of the most important aims of education should be to teach the child how to solve problems; or it should be to invite the child to discover how to solve problems. (Unfortunately, although many teachers recognize the importance of this objective, children are often taught simply to follow rules.)

If a child has learned the rule that governs the construction of the concept *mammal* and is then faced with the task of identifying mammals among many other types of animals, would you call this a problem? Of course it is. But you would no doubt agree that it is a simple problem. The child cannot solve many problems facing him or her by applying a single rule (also called a low-level rule). Take, for example, the cross-classification problem with brown and black rabbits, some sitting and some standing, referred to in Chapter 9. The child may know the rule for classifying and the rule for seriating. To cross-classify, the child must acquire the rule that when two classes intersect, the object at the intersection must have two properties, with each one being shared by only one of the two classes involved. The rule is similar for double-seriation. To construct a matrix that requires both double classification and seriation means combining the rules for double-classification and double-seriation into a more complex or high-order rule.

Instructional Sequences

In order to organize for learning at each of the four levels, Gagné has suggested that the teacher should design sequences on instruction according to a number of procedures.

1. *Identify performance objectives.*
Whether teaching skills or subject-matter concepts, each unit of instruction should have a **performance objective** consisting of five elements: situation, learned capability, object, action, and tools.

For example, the child, given a battery, light bulb, socket, and pieces of wire (situation), demonstrates (capability) the making of an electric circuit (object) by connecting wires to battery and socket and testing the lighting of the bulb (action)—the child may use a pair of pliers (tool) (Gagné & Briggs, 1974, p. 90).

2. *Construct learning hierarchies.*
Gagné suggests that making intellectual skills (rather than subject-matter concepts) the organizing focus is perhaps the best way for planning a lesson. In keeping with the principle that all learning proceeds from subordinate to higher-level skills, a sequence of learning can be set out as a learning hierarchy (Gagné, 1968). One such hierarchy, intended for use with kindergarten children, is illustrated in Figure 10.2. Gagné states that, for the child, "The process of learning becomes highly reinforcing . . . because he is frequently realizing that with apparent and satisfying suddenness he knows how to do some things that he didn't know before" (Gagné & Briggs, 1974, p. 108).

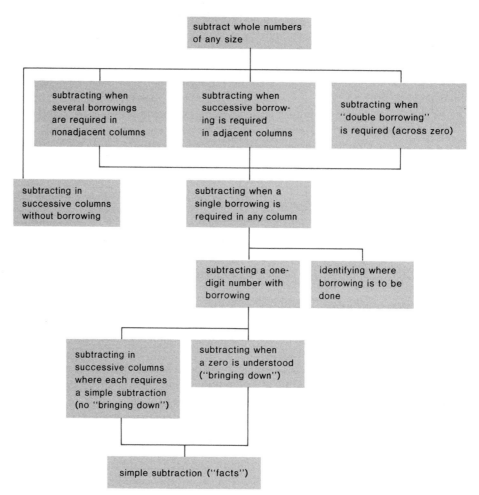

Figure 10.2 A learning hierarchy for subtracting whole numbers. It is evident that learning the skill of subtraction requires the learner to combine a number of simpler skills. (Source: Gagné, R. M., and Briggs, L. J. *Principles of Instructional Design.* Copyright 1974 by Holt, Rinehart and Winston. Reprinted by permission.)

Table 10.1 A Sequence of Instructional Events

Instructional Events	How the Learner Proceeds
1. Gaining attention	Various ways of gaining a child's attention can be used such as changing the stimulus or appealing to a child's interests by asking various types of questions.
2. Informing the learner of the objective	Make sure the child knows what is to be learned and how it is to be learned.
3. Stimulating recall of prerequisite learning	The child should be reminded of previously learned skills that are related to the new skill to be learned or the child should be encouraged to remember by being asked a question.
4. Presenting the stimulus material	The material to be learned should be presented as clearly as possible.
5. Providing learning guidance	The child should be helped to learn in a manner most appropriate for the demands of each particular learning task.
6. Eliciting the performance	When the child has achieved the learning task, the teacher says "show me" or "do it" or "tell me," so that the child might demonstrate that correct learning has occurred.
7. Providing feedback about performance correctness	It is important to provide information to the child about the correctness or incorrectness of performance—and, if the latter, suggestions about how to correct performance.
8. Assessing the performance	As carefully as possible, the teacher should assess whether the child's performance is appropriate or not as it relates to a particular learning objective.
9. Enhancing retention and transfer	Provide the child with opportunities to practice, review previous learning, and apply what has been learned to a variety of new, related learning tasks.

Source: Gagné, R. M., & Briggs, L. J., 1974, pp. 123-132.
Principles of Instructional Design. Copyright 1974 by Holt,
Rinehart and Winston. Adapted by permission.

3. *Identify a sequence of instructional events.*
The instructional events that make up an instructional sequence follow very straightforwardly from the structure of the learning hierarchy. The intention of the sequence of events is to move the child from "where he or she is" at the beginning of a lesson to the attainment of the lesson's objective. The usual order for instructional events is shown in Table 10.1, and an example of the application of this order to the teaching of a lesson is provided in Inset 10.1. These events apply to all types of learning situations. It goes almost without saying that the teacher would be expected to arrange these sequences.

According to Gagné, the first thing a teacher should do in planning instruction is to decide on performance objectives. For each performance objective, the teacher needs to set out the sequence of instructional events as they will occur within a lesson. Gagné (Gagné & Briggs, 1974, p. 123) has described ten instructional events and how they function to influence learning. He has related them to an example of a first grade science lesson taken from the 1967 AAAS Commission on Science Education Curriculum for elementary schools—*Science, a Process Approach.*
Title of Lesson: Linear Measurement

Instructional Event	*Lesson Activity*
1. *Gaining attention* by introducing a novel situation, appealing to children's motive for mastery of their environment.	A large cardboard box is placed on one side of the room, a table on the other. Children are asked how they could tell, without moving box or table, whether the box would fit under the table. Suggestions are asked for, discussed, and verified.
2. *Stating the objective.*	Children in groups are given "measuring sticks" varying in length from 5 to 100 cm. They are asked to think about how they could use the sticks to measure the height of the box.
3. This activity stimulates *recall* of a previously learned capability, in which lengths of unit sticks are ordered from shortest to longest. In addition, the children are being asked to *recall* the counting of numbers, in reporting how many units are contained in the length they measure. They are learning to select shorter or longer units and to place them end-to-end, both subordinate skills that will be readily *recalled* in the next activity.	Measurements obtained by different groups of children are found to be different. The suggestion is made that different "units" be given different names. A table is made of measurements obtained by children, reporting the number of units they obtained in measuring a designated length.
4. The *stimuli* for the learning are presented: the sticks and lengths to be measured.	Children are asked to measure strips of tape placed on the floor (a little over 1.5 m long); and also to measure the length of new pencils.

5. The "tries" made by the children, which are more or less successful, depending on the units they work with, provide for discussion in which some amount of *guidance* is given.

6. The *performance* sought is elicited by the question "Which is more suitable for measuring these tapes?" The selection of appropriate units is the objective in this case.

Different groups of children have different-sized measuring units (5 cm to 100 cm). The children discuss the appropriateness of different lengths being measured.

Finally, they are asked to compare the suitability of 15-cm sticks and the 100-cm sticks in measuring the tapes on the floor. The 15-cm sticks and the 100-cm sticks are laid end-to-end on each side of the tapes, and the children are asked which units are more suitable.

7. *Feedback* is given for selection of units that result in more successful and less successful measurement attempts.

8. *Assessment* of the learning has been carried out in an immediate sense, in this lesson, by asking for the measurement of (1) pencils, and (2) tapes on the floor. The assessment is continued, in order to increase confidence in its reliability, by the additional "appraisal" portion of the exercise.

Following the learning, additional appraisal is carried out by marking different chalk-lengths on the floor, and asking the children to select appropriate unit sticks to report their measurements in number of stick-lengths.

9. *Transfer of learning* is the functional aim of this and other measurements which might be employed. Note the intention of using varied situations for these additional activities.

A "generalizing experience" is suggested, consisting of measurements of the span of the child's outstretched arms, and also his height. The children must choose the "stick units" and make the measurements.

10. *Retention* is enhanced by scheduling review in a subsequent lesson. For example, Measurement 4 is entitled "Linear Measurement Using Metric Units."

Source: From Gagné, R. M., and Briggs, L. J. *Principles of Instructional Design*, 1974, pp. 133–134. Copyright ©, 1974, Holt, Rinehart & Winston. Adapted with permission.

Bruner's Theory of Learning and Instruction

In Chapter 6 we made a brief mention of basic concepts that Bruner has suggested for organizing learning experiences. We can now go a step further and consider how Bruner's ideas of development, learning, and instruction fit together. We can also consider how they might be applied to developing curriculum units at the elementary school level. First we must begin with the relationship between development and learning.

Benchmarks of Intellectual Growth

Bruner ties intellectual development very closely to learning procedures that the culture has developed. To describe what is involved in intellectual growth, Bruner (1966, pp. 5–6) has selected six benchmarks.

1. *Growth is characterized by an increased ability to represent the world.*
The high point is, of course, symbolic representation. Apart from representation there is the related ability to deal with transformations (such as conservation). This means that the child not only uses language as a tool to represent objects and events and to communicate but also uses skills such as classification and conservation.

2. *Growth depends upon remembering objects and events in a "storage system" that corresponds with the environment.*
There you have an environmentalist view, quite different from Piaget's cognitive-structuralist view. A simple example would be remembering a hierarchy of related concepts arranged under the superordinate concept, plant. Teaching should move the child closer and closer to an understanding of what the term *plant* refers to—what it represents.

3. *Growth involves an increasing ability to communicate, by means of words or other symbols, what one has done or intends to do.*
This means that, in attempting to communicate, the child comes to realize the importance of logical necessity—of making sense. For example, an 8-year-old who has seen the transformation of a quantity of liquid from one container to a container of a different shape might say, "Well, there's still the same amount of water. The shape has changed but no water has been added or taken away."

4. *Growth depends upon an interaction between the child as learner and a teacher as instructor.*
Development and learning join hands. The teacher organizes learning, helps the child learn, and thus influences development. According to Bruner, a great deal of responsibility for development rests with the teacher.

5. *Teaching is vastly facilitated by the medium of language.*
The child uses language, not only for communication, but to bring order into the environment. Bruner insists that language is a powerful "tool" that serves cognitive development. A number of examples of how language can be used as a

"tool" have already been given. But one further example can be added here since, according to Bruner, it is in the middle school years that propositional reasoning, which requires the use of language in a special way, can flourish. Consider the use of *if . . . then . . . because*. This is a language tool for stating a prediction (*if*), setting conditions for what is predicted (*then*), and using information to reason that the prediction is probably correct (*because*). Suppose that first grade children have been learning about tribes of people such as the Bushpeople of the Kalahari Desert. They have an understanding of dry desert conditions supporting little vegetation and widely distributed plant and animal life. They know that Bushpeople are nomadic because of their environment, that they are good hunters, but that they use simple weapons for hunting. The teacher asks, "Why do Bushpeople of the Kalahari Desert spend so much time in hunting for food?" In some cases even 6- and 7-year-olds can argue, "*If* Bushpeople live in a desert with not much water, and animals are wild and hard to catch, and there's not much water, *then* they have to go searching for food, *'cause* it takes a long time to hunt wild animals that run away or find grubs and berries to eat—oh, and water's hard to find." Such a long statement may sound surprising for a 6-year-old, but with training even children this young can learn to use the tools of language, and in using tools such as "if . . . then . . . because" they can construct such completely reasoned statements (Lawton, 1977b).

6. *Growth is marked by increasing capacities to deal with several alternatives simultaneously, to deal with several sequences at once, and to give enough time and attention to these multiple demands.*

This benchmark refers to the qualitative differences between the "one-track" thinking of the young child and the 10-year-old's ability to deal with a complex world. In Lawton's study (1977b) the **propositional reasoning** of 10-year-olds was compared to that of 6-year-olds and found to be much more advanced.

Organizing Instruction

With these benchmarks of development and learning in mind, we can consider the main features of Bruner's theory of instruction. Bruner asks why we need a theory of instruction if we have been provided with theories of development and learning. He explains that theories of development and learning are descriptive, but not prescriptive. For example, a theory of development might describe most 6-year-olds as lacking an understanding of reversibility. A learning theory might describe what the child needs to learn (say, concepts and rules) in order to understand reversibility. There would also need to be a related theory of instruction. A theory of instruction should attempt to set out the best means for completing necessary learning, such as reinforcement schedules, advance organizer lessons followed by related activities, some type of discovery method, and so forth. "A theory of instruction, in short, is concerned with how what one wishes to teach can best be learned, with improving rather than describing learning" (1966, p. 40). Bruner's theory of instruction has four major features:

1. *Instruction should specify learning experiences most likely to predispose the child to learn.*
One example would be to facilitate and regulate exploration of alternatives such as discrimination or different types of problem-solving strategy. Guiding the young child to attend to particular properties of concepts when classifying or attempting to solve conservation problems should help the child learn.

2. *Instruction should specify the structure of knowledge to be learned.*
"Optimal structure" is the set of basic ideas in a subject area from which a larger body of knowledge can be generated. Many ideas and problems can be presented in a simple enough form (enactive, iconic, symbolic) so that any child can understand them. For example, with 6- or 7-year-olds there is probably more need to give many concrete examples of new concepts they are learning than might be required with 12-year-olds who, because of previous learning and experience, are better able to deal with new abstractions. Ausubel also makes this point when he distinguishes between learning primary and secondary concepts.

3. *Instruction should specify learning sequences that are considered to be effective in producing desired learning outcomes.*
One important sequence of learning is from the enactive, to the iconic, to the symbolic modes of representation. But Bruner makes it clear that a sequence of learning can have many forms, depending on the desired objective for learning. However, it is certainly a good rule of thumb to follow carefully this sequence with children who are just moving into the middle years.

4. *Instruction should specify rewards and punishments related to the process of learning.*
Whether the child makes use of the results of learning depends upon when and where corrective information is received. The form and pacing of reinforcement is important. A great deal of responsibility rests with the teacher to correct, or help the child correct errors, to clearly teach and demonstrate correct information, to provide some rewards for success, and also to help children to be independently satisfied with their successes through intrinsic rewards (Bruner, 1966, pp. 40–53).

Applying Theory to Practice

How can Bruner's theories of learning and instruction be applied to the ***curriculum development*** of elementary schools? It just so happens that Bruner had a strong hand in the development of a social studies curriculum (K–12) called "Man: A Course of Study" (1966, Chapter 4; 1971). The structure of the course is built around three basic questions:

Children learn to represent objects and events actively, as in pretending to be monsters; and iconically and symbolically, as in drawing monsters and writing the name monster. (Photos by Jean-Claude Lejeune)

What is human about human beings?

How did they get that way?

How can they be made more so?

Five subjects associated with the evolution of human beings are explored: tool making, language, social organization, the management of prolonged human childhood, and the human urge to explore the world. These five "great humanizing forces" all include, in Bruner's opinion, examples of **cultural amplifiers** so important to development and learning. For example, language is considered to be a cultural amplifier for two reasons. First, the culture has constructed or invented it, and, second, language serves to emphasize knowledge that the culture needs to live, survive, and enrich itself.

Children study such topics as the "Netsilik Eskimos and Bushpeople" and the "Life Cycle of the Salmon." The life of the Eskimo, for example, provides a sharp contrast to life in a technological society. It is advised that the teaching method should emphasize the following:

Concept learning so that children meaningfully understand concepts such as *life cycle, life-styles, nomads,* and so forth.

Making contrasts such as comparing the life-styles of Eskimos, Bushpeople, and the children's own communities to come to a better understanding of differences and similarities in life-styles.

Making informed guesses (inferences) in cases where, knowing something about, say, the Bushpeople's life-style, children hazard guesses as to why the Bushpeople spend so much time searching for food—the *if* part of reasoning.

Seeking evidence to support or reject guesses, which requires children to consider the *because* part of reasoning.

Establishing causal explanations, which requires children to organize information they have collected in such a way that they can argue, "Well, if . . . then . . . because . . ." According to Bruner, involvement in this type of learning, with careful instruction and guidance from teachers, underpins development. This is because the explanation of cause-and-effect relationships requires the statement of a hypothesis (if), the organization of supporting information (then), and some kind of justification (because). Another term for this process is *problem solving*; and, as we have seen, psychologists are in agreement that this represents the highest form of reasoning.

Ausubel's Meaningful Learning

We described the main features of Ausubel's learning theory in Chapter 7. According to this theory, the main advantage of the subsumption process of learning is that the child should recognize new instances of learning as being related to previously learned general concepts, or high-level rules. This is what makes learning meaningful. Since Ausubel does not believe that discovery learning is easy for most young children, he suggests that reception learning should pay better dividends. Three further ideas from Ausubel's theory will be mentioned: how different types of concepts are acquired, the interrelated processes of remembering and forgetting, and planning for instruction.

Learning Concepts

There are two ways in which *concept learning* occurs—by **concept formation** and by **concept assimilation**. Concept formation is the act of recognizing that certain objects share a property or a number of properties and of forming classes of objects on the basis of shared properties. For example, "These are all the red shapes; some of them are circles." According to Ausubel, concept formation is characteristic of preschool children's thinking (Ausubel, Novak, & Hanesian, 1978, pp. 92–94) as they form concepts inductively from experiences. A young child asks, "What is that?" and is told it is a dog. The child asks the same question in relation to other animals, some of which are dogs. The child deduces from these experiences that some animals are the same *and* are called dogs. Concept assimilation occurs when a child who knows the properties of a class of objects then sees (experiences) examples of the concept and recognizes them as members of the concept. For example, a child may know that a fish is an animal that swims in water, has scales on its body, and has gills for breathing. This child then sees "fish" that he or she had not previously seen but recognizes them as fish because they all possess the properties of fish—can swim in water, have scales, have gills for breathing. These new instances (examples) of fish are assimilated into the child's already existing concept of fish.

The preschool age child learns many concepts spontaneously by asking "what" type questions. From the responses to such questions, the child forms intuitive ideas about classes of objects (concepts). For example, Johnny aged 3, may have a pretty good idea what a dog is.

The process of learning concepts by assimilation can occur in a spontaneous fashion as well as in an instructional situation. Children in the elementary grades can be expected to learn new concepts by being presented with the properties of the concepts. Only a limited number of illustrations of each property need be used, and in some instances even these may not be necessary. You might find it useful at this point to consider for a moment the similarities and differences between concept assimilation and Gagné's description of the learning of "rules."

Remembering and Forgetting

An important aspect of subsumption, or assimilation learning, not previously mentioned, is that some information tends to be remembered and some forgotten. Ausubel, like many other theorists, makes the assumption that the child (and, likewise, the adult) tends to reduce information to the form of basic concepts. This makes it easier to remember information, since the initial mass of detail has been reduced.

When a child learns a general concept in an advance organizer lesson, the next step is to provide a series of related learning activities during which the child is presented with many instances of a general concept. The child may have learned the general properties of a concept such as *insect*, or *equal to*. At some point during subsequent learning the child may have solved problems involving ladybugs, ants, flies, and other insects, or that $2 + 2 = 4$, $3 + 1 = 4$, $6 - 2 = 4$, $2 + \square = 4$ (the child has to deduce the missing number to place into the box, which in this case is "2"). For a while the child will remember each particular example of insect, its name, and each instance of equality. But it is likely that the child will forget some instances. Indeed, the child need not remember all instances—if he or she remembers the general idea of "what an insect is" or the rule for "dealing with equality." Ausubel claims that general concepts are easier to remember; if the child is given practice in applying the general concept, or high-level rule, to many related instances, this helps remembering. Knowing the general concept should help the learner recall, recognize, or find again particular examples whenever this becomes necessary.

Many teachers overemphasize the remembering of detail and of low-order concepts and facts. Ausubel offers a "gardening hint" to these teachers. Emphasize the learning of general ideas such as, "Eskimos formerly met many needs through hunting. Today, these people, like people of our community, meet many of their needs through the exchange of goods and services" (Durkin, 1969—for grade 3). For children to learn such important ideas, they need to consider many low-order concepts and facts. They might see a film on "Eskimo Life" showing Eskimos hunting *seals* with *harpoons*, building *igloos*, making clothing from *seal skin*, traveling by *sled*, meeting other people who are not Eskimos, *bartering* for *goods*, and so forth. They need not remember in specific detail how Eskimos hunt, the tools they use, or exactly how they cut ice blocks for igloos. However, only by considering the detail, do they come to a meaningful understanding of the general idea. This general idea can be related to many different communities of people—the specific facts about Eskimos are only relevant for that group of people! To put this principle in a nutshell—organize learning so that children can afford to forget (specific facts and low-order concepts), but, in their forgetting, they will remember what is worth remembering (general ideas and high-level concepts). How does this actually translate into sequences of *instruction*?

Planning for Instruction

Ausubel and educators interested in his theory have suggested a plan for organizing concepts that is different from Gagné's learning hierarchies. You may have noticed that the concepts in a learning hierarchy are always unidirectional, from a simple to a complex level, or the reverse. An alternative way is to illustrate an organization of linked fundamental ideas as shown in Figure 10.3. These are not in a single, unchangeable hierarchy. Their relationships can be changed depending on the teacher's plans, and what is considered useful to teach to a certain group of children. No sequence is indicated, and planning the instructional sequence is left to each individual teacher. The advantage to this type of curriculum plan is that various related ideas can be built into whatever sequence is decided on. Thus, naturally arising related "themes" can be taken into consideration. Children are interested in questions such as "Why are some mammals wild and some tame? Why can baby mammals look after themselves much sooner than human babies? Does the father always help look after the baby mammals, or is it just the mother?"

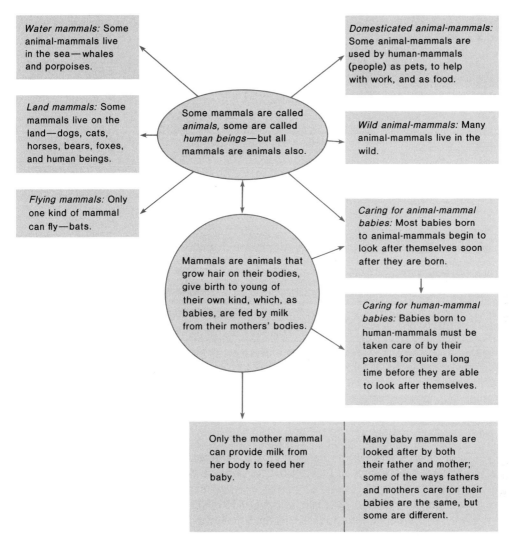

Figure 10.3 Relationships between fundamental ideas about mammals. (Based on an idea for organizing related ideas in Ausubel, D. P., Novak, J. D., and Hanesian, H. *Educational Psychology: A Cognitive View,* 1978, pp. 362–63. Holt, Rinehart and Winston. Used with permission of the authors.)

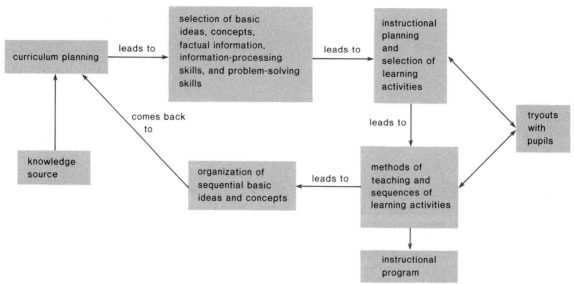

Figure 10.4 Cycles of decision making in curriculum and instructional design. (Source: Adapted from Ausubel, D. P., Novak, J. D., and Hanesian, H. *Educational Psychology: A Cognitive View,* Holt, Rinehart and Winston, 1978, p. 367. Used with permission of the authors.)

How can the teacher take into account the dual problems of selecting content for curriculum units and organizing related instructional procedures? One method, as shown in Figure 10.4, is to use a "cycle" of decision making that takes into account curriculum and instructional planning at one and the same time. Care should be taken, in selecting significant concepts, not to include so many concepts that the relationships among fundamental ideas are too complex for the child to understand. Once the concepts and sequence of introduction have been decided upon, then hierarchies of related concepts can be constructed. Teaching then follows a meaningful–reception–subsumption procedure as described in Chapter 7.

Piaget on Education

As we have already mentioned, Piaget, in writing about education (e.g., 1951b, 1970a, 1973b), clearly distinguishes between development and learning. A major constraint that development imposes on learning is that a child cannot learn a Piagetian concept that is within a stage in advance of the stage the child is

presently in—thus, a preoperational child cannot meaningfully learn concrete operations. We must keep in mind that this is a theoretical position and that we need proof of theories to establish their validity. Experiments such as those by Inhelder, Sinclair, and Bovet (1974), Sheppard (1973, 1974), and others, mentioned in Chapter 9, were attempts to validate Piaget's theoretical position. As we saw, the results of experiments suggest that children can meaningfully learn, in advance of their supposed stage, Piagetian concepts from direct teaching.

Nevertheless, Piaget remained opposed to teaching methods that emphasize showing, demonstrating, or telling. He put it this way: "An education that is an active discovery of reality is superior to one that consists merely in providing the young with ready-made wills . . . and ready-made truths" (1970b, p. 26). He calls the first approach to education the new school or active school; the second, the traditional school or receptive school.

Children in the new school should be actively and spontaneously involved in pursuing activities that arise from their own personal needs and interests. The teacher must present subject matter that is easily assimilable by children of different ages. The teacher must take into account each child's readiness by encouraging his or her participation in activities at the child's individual level of development. The teacher should encourage the child by asking interesting questions aimed at promoting active exploration and by setting up learning materials that lend themselves to the discovery of logical relationships. But the teacher should never attempt to teach directly such relationships.

Unfortunately, in setting up an alternative (unacceptable) form of education, Piaget uses as his model the traditional type of school that existed throughout Europe and Britain in the early part of the twentieth century. As he quite rightly

Learning and Instruction **455**

says, such schools imposed work on the child. Too much emphasis was placed on rote learning. Children chanted verbal slogans they could not begin to understand, and sang their way interminably through "times tables." It is also true that these schools could be criticized for overemphasizing "verbalism, that dismal scholastic fact—a proliferation of pseudo-ideas hooked onto a string of words lacking all real meaning [which] explains one of the fundamental reasons for the active school's reaction against the receptive school" (1970b, p. 164). Some schools today could receive the same sort of criticism, but teaching methods and curriculum in many present-day "traditional" schools have improved in comparison to the European schools of the early part of the twentieth century. In considering Piaget's criticism you will also have to compare it with such "receptive" teaching methods as those advocated by Ausubel (meaningful reception learning), Bruner (careful instruction in skills and subject-matter concepts so that children might better attempt to discover knowledge), and Montessori (the fundamental lesson approach to learning).

Training Methods, Genevan Style

It has been left to Piaget's colleagues to experiment with new school *training* methods. The essence of these training methods is that the child makes discoveries about objects and relationships among objects (as in classifying, seriating, dealing with multiple classification, and conservation) by using prepared materials and by being guided by the teacher. The most important rule for the teacher is to guide, not to tell. This is how they began: "We started with the idea that under certain conditions an acceleration of cognitive development would be possible, but that this could only occur if the training procedures in some way resemble the kind of situation in which progress takes place outside an experimental setup" (Inhelder, Sinclair, & Bovet, 1974, p. 24). What kind of situation did they have in mind?

First, the child must interact actively with learning materials. *Active interaction* means the child establishes relations in both a physical and mental (thinking about) way. Second, the child should not be coerced into accepting "correct" responses that the teacher provides. The teacher observes errors and uses them as a foundation for further instructions. Third, training procedures should steer the child in the right direction, even if this initially leads to errors. Fourth, the teacher should ascertain the child's present stage of development through diagnosis before training begins. There is no point in teaching the child concepts that he or she already understands. After training, the child receives a number of tests.

1. A test should be given to see if the child has learned the concept taught by the new school method. For example, class inclusion. This test should include materials the child has not seen during training. For example, the child might have been trained in generalizing by using flowers and might be tested by using animals.

2. A second test should be given soon after (about three weeks) the first test to find out if the child continues to remember the concept taught (stability of memory).

3. A test should be given of a concept related but not identical to the concept taught. For example, if the child is taught the concept of class inclusion, a test might also be given of the child's ability to deal with cross-classification. In this case both tests are in the same category of classification.

4. A test should be given of a concept different from that taught but in the category of concepts associated with the stage that the original concept is associated with. For example, having taught the child the concept of class inclusion, a test might be given to measure the child's competency on a conservation task (adapted from Inhelder, Sinclair, & Bovet, 1974, p. 28).

In Chapter 9 it was mentioned that Inhelder and her colleagues believe it is only possible to train children who are on the verge of understanding a concept—who are in a transitional point between stages. An example of their training procedure is provided in Inset 10.2.

Alternative Training Methods

It was also mentioned in Chapter 9 that Piaget and his co-workers compare the self-discovery training method they use to what they call "tutorial methods" of training. This second term is a little misleading. To provide a better picture of some alternative methods of teaching Piagetian concepts, a number of examples are referred to here.

Beilin introduced the method of rule instruction to the teaching of Piagetian logical concepts (1965) and achieved success with this method (1965; 1971). This requires teaching the child an "operation" such as conservation as a rule or set of rules. For example, four rules that might be taught to the child in connection with the number conservation problem are

1. "When we shorten *this* line of pennies, if we don't add any pennies or take any away, then there will still be the same amount."

2. "If we put the pennies like this [shortened row] and then back like this [original positions], we see the number of pennies has not changed."

A correct understanding of class inclusion implies that the child understands that each object in a group of objects belongs to both a subclass (subordinate concept) and a more general class (superordinate concept). To train children to this understanding, Inhelder et al. (1974, pp. 172–176) had children aged 6 to 8 years perform certain types of actions (on objects) that could be progressively corrected. The following materials were used in the training sessions: ten apples (A); eight peaches (P); seven other fruits (O—two lemons, two tangerines, two plums, one apricot and non-apples and non-peaches); two dolls (a boy and girl); and two baskets. Training was in three parts.

First Part: The teacher began by putting into the basket of one of the dolls a collection of fruit consisting of two subclasses (several examples of a collection were used as indicated below) say, two apples and four peaches. The number of fruit in each subclass of fruit was varied. The teacher then asked, for example,

Collection	Request
AAPPPP	Give me more apples from the doll's basket, but the same number of fruit.
or	
AAOOOO	As above.
or	
AAAAPP	Give me fewer apples but just the same number of fruit.
or	
AAAAOO	As above.

Children were also instructed to, "Show me the apples. Now show me the fruit." In this first part children were actively involved in making up collections of fruit and comparing subclasses of fruit.

Second Part: Once children this age have constructed two subclasses from a general class (physically or mentally), they can no longer compare one of the subclasses to the general class since the general class has, as it were, "disappeared." To help with this problem two dolls with two baskets each having similar collections of fruit were used. With the girl and boy doll each having four apples and two peaches, the teacher asked:

3. "When we shorten *this* row of pennies we have just shoved the pennies closer together. So the shorter the row the closer the *same* number of pennies."

4. After shortening one row of pennies, and before the child is allowed to respond, the teacher might say, "Now before you make up your mind whether there are now fewer pennies in this row [shortened], or the same number of pennies in this row [unchanged row], count the pennies in both rows."

Does someone have more apples?

Does someone have more fruit?

Does someone have more peaches?

The boy eats all his apples and the girl eats all her fruit; who eats more?

Inhelder and her colleagues hoped, of course, that the child, in comparing a subclass (say apples) to a general class (fruit) would realize that the two collections of fruit could be used to represent subclasses and general class at the same time, and use them to help in making this type of comparison. Can you imagine how this teaching method might actually confuse the child?

Third Part: With only one collection of fruit present (e.g., AAAAPP), the teacher asked:

If the doll wants to eat the most, what must she say:

I'm going to eat all my apples or I'm going to eat all my fruit?

In the doll's basket are there more apples or more fruit?

If the child made a mistake, the teacher said,

Show me the apples. Show me the peaches. Show me the fruit.

If incorrect answers were made, the teacher drew the child's attention to the error. For example, "But look, if the girl eats all her fruit there is no more left, but if the boy eats all his apples he still has two peaches. So you are not correct." When children were unsuccessful the number of fruit in collections was reduced, but when children were correct in their responses the number was increased.

Most improvement following training was shown by children aged 7 to 8 years. However, only two of the five children this age were completely successful in arriving at an understanding of class inclusion, and they were in a transition stage before training began.

Rochel Gelman (1969) attempted to train 5-year-old children in the conservation of length and number. By testing a large group of children aged 5 on problems of conservation, she found a group who could not conserve. Remember that Inhelder does not believe it likely that such children can be meaningfully trained to learn a logical concept such as conservation. Gelman believed that children often make errors in conservation problems because they pay attention to irrevelant properties of objects. She therefore attempted to train these children to focus on relevant properties that had to be attended to during a transformation.

The children were divided into three groups, with each group being trained by a different procedure.

The first group practiced "oddity" learning. When they were shown various sets of three objects, in which two were always the same (two red blocks and one yellow block), they were asked to point to two objects that were the same. Correct responses were rewarded (reinforcement).

The second group was also shown sets of three objects, two identical and one different. The same type of question was asked as for group one, but half the problems required the children to attend to number (e.g., two rows of five objects and one row of three), and half the problems required attention to length (e.g., two 3-inch sticks and one 1-inch stick). There was no verbal information from the teacher about the rule, but the children were, in fact, getting extensive training in rules for conserving number and length. They had to pay attention to the properties *number* and *length*; to make sure this was the case, Gelman introduced irrelevant properties into the objects—color, shape, size, and arrangement. These children were also rewarded for correct responses.

The third group received similar training to the second group, but no reinforcement. They were told they had played the game well, but they were given no information about correct responses. These children, therefore, had no way of knowing (or learning) which properties required their attention.

Gelman tested the children on length conservation twice, one day after and about three weeks after the training. She also tested them on conservation of liquid one day after training. The results are shown in Figure 10.5. It is quite obvious that the second group learned a rule for conservation of length. More importantly, they seem to have learned a general rule for conservation because they performed well on the liquid conservation problem.

Benefits from Training

You might have noticed that Gelman's method of training was based on environmentalist learning theory. It was partly behavioristic, and she was, indirectly, teaching a rule for conservation. Other studies have reported success from training using other types of environmentalist learning methods. For example, in a study by Lawton and Wanska (1979), children were taught general social studies concepts and high-level rules for constructing hierarchies and comparing superordinate and subordinate concepts (for class inclusion). The teaching method was based on Ausubel's theory of learning, and advance organizer lessons were used. The most successful type of training was to teach both general subject-matter concepts and high-order rules *together*. In other words, being familiar with the content of the problem and knowing the rule for constructing superordinate and subordinate concepts was better than just knowing one or the other. This method was very successful with kindergarten, third, and fifth grade children.

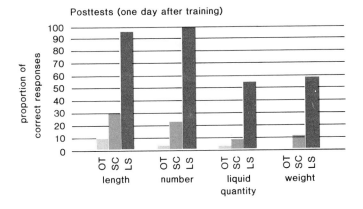

Posttests (one day after training)

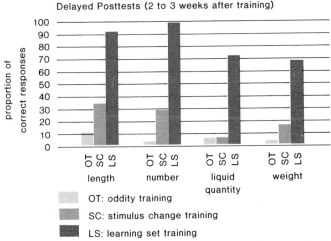

Delayed Posttests (2 to 3 weeks after training)

OT: oddity training

SC: stimulus change training

LS: learning set training

Figure 10.5 Results of Gelman's conservation training method. (Source: Gelman, R. "Conservation Acquisition: A Problem of Learning to Attend to Relevant Attributes." *Journal of Experimental Psychology*, 1969, 7, pp. 167–168. Adapted with permission.)

Piaget raises a number of questions regarding the real benefits to children resulting from training. He insists that training effects should (1) persist after training, (2) remain in the child's memory over long periods of time, and (3) generalize to problems and materials not met during training. In the two training experiments mentioned, children's performance met these three requirements. In the Lawton and Wanska study the trained children were performing as well on class-inclusion tasks with different content six months after training as they had been just after training was completed.

One further question remains. Will children acquire certain competencies in the natural course of events without special training? There is no straightforward answer. Consider the following case first. Lawton and Wanska found many

11-year-old children who failed class-inclusion problems! But we know preschool children can succeed with such problems (Inhelder, Sinclair, & Bovet, 1974).

The older children in the Lawton and Wanska study were presented with picture cards that included illustrations of Bushpeople, Eskimos, and people from an advanced technological community; the simple and complex tools these people used; and the dwellings these people lived in. With these picture cards, class-inclusion problems involved comparing such concepts as "Are there more *people* or more Bushpeople? More *simple tools* or more *Bushpeople's tools*? More *simple dwellings*" or more *dwellings*?" The complexity of these materials and the 11-year-olds' unfamiliarity with the content probably contributed to their initial failures. The 6-year-olds in Geneva compared concepts from materials such as flowers, fruits, and animals. These materials can be considered less complex and reasonably familiar to young children. Many researchers have found that as the content and complexity of problems change, so does children's performance. Just by increasing the number of objects children have to attend to can change performance.

Now a second case. Sometimes a problem may require more than one skill, more than one rule, to solve it. College students are well past the stage of concrete operations. Here is a concrete operational problem for you to solve. Consider the two bottles in Figure 10.6. Bottle *A* contains 20 red beans and bottle *B*, 20 blue beans. Here is the problem.

1. Five red beans are taken from bottle *A* and placed in bottle *B*. Bottle *B* is then shaken to distribute the red beans among the blue beans.

2. Suppose *5 beans* were taken from bottle *B*. If those 5 beans were placed in bottle *A* would there then be
   (a) More red beans in bottle *A* than blue beans in bottle *B*?
   (b) Fewer red beans in bottle *A* than blue beans in bottle *B*?
   (c) The same number of red beans in bottle *A* as blue beans in bottle *B*?
      (e.g., see Murray & Armstrong, 1978; Odom, Astor, & Cunningham, 1975).

You will notice this is a conservation problem. The solution can be found at the end of the Summary. Try the problem on your friends as well. If you fail to solve the problem, ask yourself why. It does not mean that you cannot conserve. But adults make errors on some conservation tasks and also on many other types of tasks. There is no simple straightforward reason for this. To solve the beans-in-the-bottle problem you have to use math knowledge. The math rule that helps is *in addition* to the rule for conservation. You have to use more than one rule. When a child, or an adult, makes errors in trying to solve problems, this may happen because of not knowing any of the relevant rules, knowing some but not all the rules, knowing all the rules but not realizing that a particular known rule would be useful in helping solve a problem, and so on.

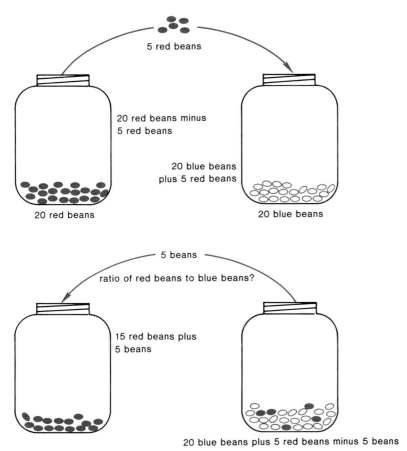

5 red beans

20 red beans minus
5 red beans

20 blue beans
plus 5 red beans

20 red beans

20 blue beans

5 beans

ratio of red beans to blue beans?

15 red beans plus
5 beans

20 blue beans plus 5 red beans minus 5 beans

Figure 10.6 The beans in the bottles problem.

Since children seem to fail to solve problems for a whole variety of reasons, what can we do about this? Robbie Case (1975, 1978) has come up with an interesting suggestion.

Instruction That Works Around Developmental Limits

Many theorists have pointed out that young children use reasonable strategies on intellectual tasks but that these are usually oversimplified. Also, young children are only capable of handling a few items of information at one time (Case, 1978, p. 439).

Visual Array	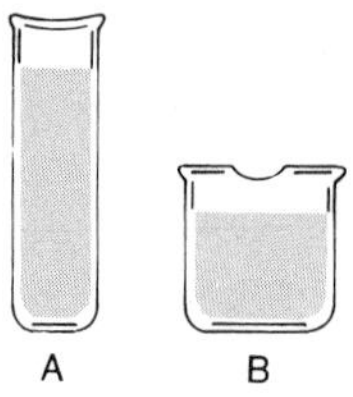	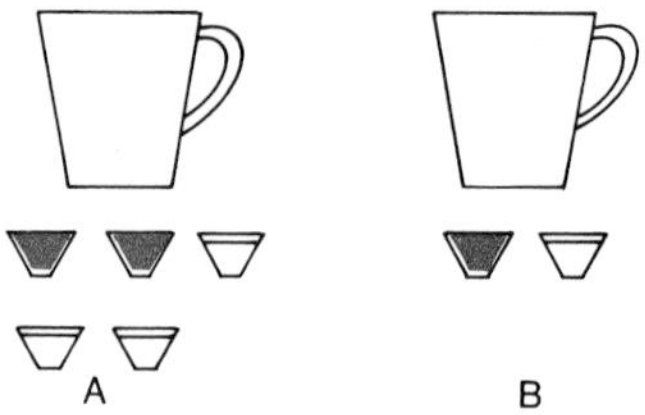	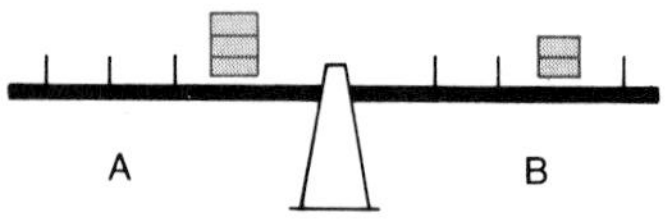
	A B	A B	A B
Task Question	Which beaker has more water to drink?	Which mixture will taste more strongly of orange juice (indicated by shading)?	Which side will go down?
Response 5–6 years	A has more because it's taller.	A will taste more. It's got two juice. B's only got one.	A will go down. It's got more weights.
7–8 years	B has more. A is a bit taller, but B is much fatter.	B will taste more. A's got more water than juice. B doesn't.	B will go down. It's only got two weights, but they're so far out. A has three, but they're right in close.

Figure 10.7 Children's strategies for solving Piagetian problems. Young children spontaneously choose strategies to solve Piagetian problems such as these, which are not so much incorrect as they are incomplete. (Source: Case, R., *A Developmentally Based Theory and Technology of Instruction.* Review of Educational Research, Summer, 1978, pp. 439–463. Copyright 1978, American Educational Research Association, Washington, D.C. Reprinted with permission.)

Examples of young children's strategies used on three Piagetian-type tasks are presented in Figure 10.7. For the first problem (Piaget, 1957), most 5-year-olds compare simply the height of the liquid in each beaker and choose the one in which the liquid is higher. This strategy works well when beakers are the same size. Usually, at home or at school, this will be the case. For the second problem (Noelting, 1975), most 5-year-olds compare only the number of cups containing orange juice and ignore the total number of cups. This is also a reasonable strategy—when the number of cups is equal in the two sets. Finally, for the balance beam problem (Inhelder & Piaget, 1964; Siegler, 1976), children age 5 invariably count the number of weights on each side and simply choose the side with the greater number of weights. Case points out that these are all reasonable strategies. "They are not so much incorrect as they are incomplete" (1978, p. 440).

Young children's memory also sets constraints on their ability to deal with problems. Many studies have shown that limitations in children's working memory are very severe (Case, 1975, 1978; Chi, 1978; Pascual-Leone, 1978; Scardamalia, 1977; Trabasso & Foellinger, 1978). The term **working memory** means needing to remember some information, and then continuing to remember it over a short period of time (Case, 1972a,b; Case & Serlin, 1978; Pascual-Leone, 1970). Many of the Piagetian tasks introduced in previous chapters require this kind of memory. How can young children be helped in overcoming their memory limitations?

Case's model.   If we were to observe young children, say 7- to 8-year-olds, trying to solve a Piagetian-type problem, our best guess about their present stage of development would be to reflect on the strategies they used to try to solve the problem and the conclusion they reached. Case raises the question, are the child's spontaneous problem-solving strategies the best indication of level of development? He does not believe so, for two reasons. First, the young child's thinking and reasoning are frequently interfered with by limitations of memory; second, the naive, inexperienced child spontaneously selects strategies that are along the right lines but inadequate for solving Piagetian problems. To help the child there is a need to reduce the memory load and instruct the child in more useful problem-solving strategies. The procedure for this instruction is based on three principles:

1. Before designing instruction, the teacher describes, step-by-step, the strategy he or she will teach *and* the strategies that children use spontaneously.

2. The teacher designs the instruction to clarify the limitations of children's spontaneous strategies and the necessity for teaching the strategy.

3. In selecting the strategy to be taught and the instructional sequence for teaching it, the teacher reduces memory requirements for learning to a bare minimum (adapted from Case, 1978, p. 442).

The idea that planning for instruction should begin with a detailed description of a strategy (e.g., a hierarchy of related concepts) is not new (Gagné & Briggs, 1973; Lawton & Wanska, 1979; Lawton & Fowell, 1978). What is new about Case's suggestion is the idea that the teacher should clearly describe the child's spontaneous and usually inadequate strategies (and information). The teacher should keep in mind both the child's spontaneous strategy and the teaching strategy when he or she plans the instruction. A simple rule of thumb in selecting learning materials is that the lower the number of objects, or bits of information, the child needs to attend to at any one time, the smaller the load on working memory. If the teacher reduces the amount of information for each unit of learning, it is possible actually to *increase* the total amount of information to be learned. Familiarity with the learning materials also helps working memory.

Pointing out important properties of objects that the child needs to attend to is also important. You may no doubt realize that Gelman used such techniques in her study described in this chapter and in the design of advance organizer lessons described in Chapter 7.

We must suppose that by helping children learn how to use their memories more efficiently they will get better at it over a period of time. We must also suppose that the children's learning to use efficient strategies is, in fact, intellectual development since the strategies they are learning are concrete operations. Memory improvement and strategy learning are, in essence, markers of intellectual development. Yet, according to Case, there is a maturational brake on the extent to which instruction can promote learning. For example, no matter how efficient the instruction, it is unlikely that a 6-year-old will learn to think and reason as efficiently and persistently correctly as a 12-year-old.

Case's instructional sequence. There are six steps in Case's instructional sequence.

1. *Set the task in a situation the child is familiar with in everyday life.* The goal of the task should be made clear, and the child should be able to determine on his or her own whether it has been achieved. For example, a third grade child is shown picture cards illustrating dwellings, tools, and food used by Bedouin, Thai farmers, and Canadian wheat farmers. The child is told that the picture cards are to be arranged in a matrix to show who the dwellings, tools, and food belong to. Each "cell" of the matrix must contain a card or set of cards. (See Figure 9.5.)

2. *Provide a series of problems so that, in applying the everyday strategy, the child realizes that it does not always work* (for example, a series of matrix problems).

3. *Help the child understand why the everyday strategy does not work.* One way is to ask "probing" questions such as "Do you think you could count the number of cows in each field?" (conservation of area). Another way is to provide a brief verbal rule, "Let's count the cows in both fields and see if we get the same number." Another way is for the teacher to use the child's unsuccessful strategy, wondering out loud why it does not work (a method used on Sesame Street).

4. *Demonstrate a correct procedure, or possibly a number of correct procedures* (but keep in mind limitations on working memory). These can be similar to a method such as using "advance organizers" mentioned in Chapter 7 or Beilin's method of "rule instruction" mentioned earlier in this chapter. Case makes the point that various teaching methods can be used; these include guided discovery, modeling, or didactic exposition.

5. *Explain to the child why the planned strategy works better than the child's original everyday strategy.*

6. *Provide a period of practice in using the new strategy and experience in transferring it to new and more complex learning situations.*

Although this instructional procedure has been tried out in only a few studies, so far the results have proved it to be very effective (Case, 1974, 1977).

An important concept highlighted in this theory of instruction is working memory. Memory obviously plays an important part in the process of learning. The final section of this chapter provides a brief review of memory development.

Development of Memory

A simple measurement of **memory** is the number of items that can be remembered. This is sometimes called **digit span** or **memory span**. Read over the following list of sixteen words a few times, then try to recall them; try this with a friend.

chair	Oriental	church	wedding
bells	lake	boat	car
pottery	table	spoon	fireworks
steeple	aft	Chinese	cloth

Keep track of the number of words you remember. You may attempt this by reading down or across each of the four lists, or you may decide to reorganize the words to make the task easier. For example you could put table, chair, cloth, spoon together. The strategy would be something like "four objects in the dining room." Putting table first might help because the other three objects "go with" the table. Try organizing the rest of the words like this. You will probably notice that this organization helps you remember. However, if the number of words were steadily increased, you would reach a point at which you found remembering *all* the words increasingly difficult, no matter what strategy you used to organize them. There is a limit, sooner or later, to memory span. As children grow older their use of labels for objects and classes and their ability to remember these labels improves (Flavell & Wellman, 1977).

There have been many studies of children's memory development in using words, pictures, objects, and so forth. These studies have examined not only memory span but strategies that children use to help them remember information (Brown, 1975; Flavell, 1970; Hagen, Jongeward, & Kail, 1975; Kail & Hagen, 1976). In general, results show that as children get older memory span increases and strategies for remembering get better, as does the ability to use strategies.

Children enjoy playing memory games, such as the one illustrated here, that requires them to recall pictures of objects they have seen and that are then placed face-down in some special order. (Photo courtesy of the author)

Preschool children have useful but often inadequate strategies for remembering. Older children not only realize the need to organize information to help them remember, but they can use various strategies at the same time or even make substitutions (Kreutzer, Leonard, & Flavell, 1975).

When a group of people are introduced by name, most of us find the task of remembering the names difficult. It is much easier to remember a person by his or her face, voice, or mannerisms. We can distinguish between **recall memory** (such as remembering a name) and **recognition memory** (such as remembering a face). Recall requires a process of retrieving some representation of previously learned information. Recognition is often easier because there is something out there in the environment that helps us to remember. What we can see may be providing clues to our memory.

Piaget and Inhelder (1973) have described another type of memory that falls somewhere between these two. Suppose a child has been learning a concept such as seriation by using wooden rods of different lengths. The child may be asked to recall the pattern, perhaps by drawing it. The teacher may also ask the child to pick out the pattern, previously constructed, from among a group of various patterns. This is recognition. Or suppose the child is given the wooden rods again and asked to reconstruct the pattern. This requires *reconstruction memory*, which falls between recall and recognition.

Brown (1975) distinguishes among three types of memory—memory as knowing, memory as knowing how to know, and memory as knowing about knowing. Flavell (Flavell & Wellman, 1976) uses a very similar distinction, mentioning four features of memory—basic processes (memory span, recall, recognition), knowledge (memory as knowing), strategies (memory as knowing how to know), and metamemory (memory as knowing about knowing).

Basic Processes of Memory

All of the basic capacities and processes of memory—recognition, recall, memory span—have been developed by the end of infancy. For example, it is possible during this phase to observe the emergence of memory span (object permanency), of recognition (distinguishing between a parent and a stranger), and of recall (Daddy gone work? Went in car.). Little is known about development of recall, but is seems likely that it emerges at between 18 months and 2 years. Once the capacity to recall has been acquired, the infant can store "schemas" in memory and begin to use symbolic representation. Remembering schemas requires more organization of bits and pieces of information.

Remembered Knowledge as an Aid to Knowing

An important way in which the young child acquires new knowledge is by adding to knowledge already in memory, which is using memory as knowing. For example, the young child soon learns many "categories" of objects such as bird, dog, toys, food. When the child sees a new bird, dog, or toy for the first time, he or she automatically puts it into the correct category. How excited young children are to see an unusual, or eye-catching bird such as a hummingbird or cardinal for the first time. If the children already know something about birds, learning about hummingbirds and cardinals is made easier. So what children already know has an enormous effect on what new knowledge they learn and remember. This principle is clearly applied in learning theories you have been reading about in previous chapters.

In an interesting study by Paris (1975) children were read a short story and then asked eight memory questions.

Linda was playing with her new doll in front of her big red house. Suddenly she heard a strange sound coming from under the porch. It was the flapping of wings. Linda wanted to help so much. . . . She ran inside the house and grabbed a shoe box from the closet. . . . She cut up paper into little pieces and put them in the bottom of the box . . . gently picked up the helpless creature and took it with her. Her teacher knew what to do.

The questions were as follows:

1. Was Linda's doll new?

2. Did Linda grab a match box?

3. Was the strange sound coming from under the porch?

4. Was Linda playing behind her house?

5. Did Linda like to take care of animals?

6. Did Linda take what she found to the police station?

7. Did Linda find a frog?

8. Did Linda use a pair of scissors?

You will notice that some of these questions require one type of knowledge to provide an answer—simple recall of facts in the story. For example, the story says Linda was playing with her new doll, so the answer to question 1 is right there in the story. But what about questions 4 or 5? The story does not provide a ready-made answer for either question. The children have to *infer* the answer. Hagen, Jongeward, and Kail (1975) have pointed out that children constantly make inferences, elaborations, and reorganizations in their everyday conversation. Without doing so, it would be difficult indeed to communicate.

It is also clear that such skills improve with age. In a study by Paris and Upton (1976) 5-, 8-, and 10-year-olds were read a story about a child who is raiding the cookie jar. The story begins, "Chris waited until he was alone in the house. The only sound he heard was his father chopping wood in the barn." One question about this incident asked, "Was Chris's father in the barn?" Another question asked, "Did Chris want his parents to know what he was doing?" Almost twice as many 10-year-olds as 5-year-olds made a correct inferential response to the second question. The first question referred the children explicitly to a part of the story that actually says that father was (chopping wood) in the barn. A correct answer to the second question can only be based on implication. If Chris was about to do something, and "waited until he was alone in the house," then it is quite likely he did not want his parents to know what he was doing. It has been shown that 7- and 8-year-old children sometimes find it difficult to make inferences but that they find *explication* easier than *implication*. (see Inset 10.3).

Memory as Strategy

John is in fifth grade. He has finished dinner and is settling down to some math and social studies homework. He explains to his mother that the math is easy. It is some multiplication problems. He admits he may find the social studies

During the middle years, as children grow older, they become better able to construct and infer additional information from sentences (Paris & Lindauer, 1976; Paris & Upton, 1976). This is an important information-processing strategy. Bruner (1957) has referred to **inferential reasoning** as a strategy children (or adults, for that matter) can use to ''go beyond the information given,'' which is so very important in trying to solve a great variety of problems. How does the ability to make inferences appear to develop during the middle years? A study by Paris, Lindauer, and Cox (1977) sheds some light on this question.

In their experiment a comparison was made of elementary school children's recall of sentences previously read to them when given both implicit and explicit cues. The following sentences were used to allow children to suggest plausible consequences of some action that could be stated implicitly and explicitly.

1. My brother fell down on the *playground* (and skinned his knee).

2. The teacher turned out the *lights* for the movie (and the room got dark).

3. Her *pants* were too tight when she bent over (so they ripped).

4. He accidentally played in *poison* ivy (and itched).

5. Mary dropped the *vase* of flowers (and broke it).

6. She slammed the *door* shut on her hand (and hurt her finger).

7. John sat on the *balloon* (and it made a loud noise).

8. The kitten tipped over the *dish* (and spilled the milk).

Children were either read each complete sentence so that the consequences of an action (e.g., skinning his knee from falling down on the playground) was explicitly stated, or they were read only the first part of the sentence (with the clause in parentheses omitted) so that an outcome was only implied. Children were from the second and sixth grades and college students were also included.

Two types of tests for inference making were used. In the first procedure, called *cued recall*, the children and college students were given both the main cue (the word in italics) in each sentence, and the consequence clause (in parentheses). They then had to attempt to restate the sentence as they had first heard or read it. In the second procedure, called *free recall*, no cues were given, but the children and college students were simply asked to tell as many sentences as they could. The results are shown in Table 10.2.

When the explicit cue is given for cued-recall, the performance of children and college students is quite similar. However, the young children, especially the second graders, did not use the implicit cues so easily. With respect to type of cue, noun cues were much more effective than consequence cues with the children. Recall and inference making does improve with age, at least in this experiment, and this is just as true for cued as for free recall.

Paris et al. concluded that young children were not able to use implied cues to recall sentences, perhaps because they did not understand the inferences when the sentences were first read to them. Although older children made good use of both explicit and implied information, young children's understanding was limited mainly to explicit information.

Inset 10.3
Developing an Ability to Make Inferences

Table 10.2 Percentages of Correctly Recalled Sentences

| | A. Cued Recall | | | |
| | Explicit List | | Implicit List | |
Grade	Nouns	Consequences	Nouns	Consequences
2	70.3	65.5	62.5	24.2
6	69.5	70.3	66.4	48.4
College	76.6	79.7	68.8	62.7

| | B. Free Recall | |
Grade	Explicit List	Implicit List
1	30.5	33.6
5	35.2	39.8
College	46.1	47.9

Source: Paris, S. A., & Upton, L. R., 1976. Copyright © 1976 *The Society for Research in Child Development, Inc.* Adapted with permission.

homework a bit difficult. "We have to use an index, and I wish you would help—I'm not sure how to use it properly." His mother promises to do so. "Oh, and we are starting a science project tomorrow," John says. "I need to take some things to school." He looks through his backpack to find the list of things he needs.

This is a typical array of evening activities for the elementary school child. Each activity involves the use of memory as knowing—how to do multiplication, how to use an index, and things to be collected together and taken to school for a new science project. Each activity requires different types of memory strategy. The essence of a *memory strategy* is that it is planned goal-oriented behavior (Flavell, 1970) to aid recall. Two important memory strategies are rehearsal and problem solving.

There are many types of **rehearsal strategy for memorizing.** However, a common characteristic is the naming (or labeling) of objects either aloud or in the mind. The simplest form of rehearsal is repetitive naming. The most complex is generating associations. For example, the child, shown the picture of a white dog with a black patch, might associate the word dog with the name "Spot" and rehearse both names together.

One of the most instructive studies concerning the development of children's rehearsal strategies is that by Flavell, Beach, and Chinsky (1966). Children aged 5, 7, and 10 years were first shown seven pictures. Each child was then shown two to five of these pictures to be remembered. The children were asked to recall these pictures immediately after rehearsal or following a delay of 15 seconds.

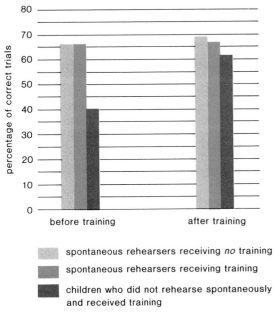

Figure 10.8 Results of training children to rehearse when they are attempting to memorize. (Source: Keeney, T. J., Cannizzo, S. R., and Flavell, J. M. "Spontaneous and Induced Verbal Rehearsal in a Recall Task." Society for Research in Child Development, Inc., 1967. Used with permission.)

The children's lips were watched for movement, which would show they were "quietly" rehearsing overtly. Only 10 percent of the 5-year-olds rehearsed as compared to 60 percent of the 7-year-olds and 85 percent of the 10-year-olds. The results from other studies have shown similar developmental trends (Cuvo, 1975; Keeney, Cannizzo, & Flavell, 1967; Ornstein, Naus, & Liberty, 1975; Ornstein, Naus, & Stone, 1977).

As children grow older they become more adept at modifying their rehearsal strategies to meet the demands of various memory requirements. Even so, given a problem such as the sixteen-word memory test presented earlier, only children aged about 12 have been observed reorganizing words into categories for rehearsal.

Instruction for rehearsal has resulted in quite remarkable improvements in memory. One study (Keeney, Cannizzo, & Flavell, 1967) identified 7-year-olds who spontaneously rehearsed, consistently rehearsed, or failed to rehearse—as indicated by lip movements. Half the rehearsers and all the nonrehearsers were trained to rehearse. Children were shown pictures and told to whisper the names of the pictures over and over until they were given the memory test. Figure 10.8 shows the results. Rehearsal training was highly effective for the original nonrehearsing children.

We have seen how children perform in laboratory studies of memory. But what about solving real-world problems that require remembering? Children from kindergarten, first, third, and fifth grades were asked the following questions:

Suppose you were invited to a birthday party for a friend. How could you make sure you remembered the party? Can you think of anything else you could do? How many different ways can you think of? (Kreutzer, Leonard, & Flavell, 1975, p. 29). Suppose your friend has a dog and you ask him how old his dog is. He tells you he got his dog as a puppy one Christmas but can't remember which Christmas. What things could he do to help him remember which Christmas he got his dog? (Kreutzer, Leonard, & Flavell, 1975, p. 36).

Developmental changes in the way these children responded to questions about the future were similar to those described in the laboratory studies. The older children were very resourceful, suggesting not only a note to help them remember, but placing it in a conspicuous place. Although half the kindergarten children suggested a note, few remarked that it should be placed in view—to help remember the note!

The last question proved to be much more difficult for the younger children. Nearly half the kindergartners were unable to suggest any ways to help the friend remember the age of the dog. However, all of the fifth grade children provided useful suggestions.

It is clear that all children use memory strategies that develop and become more sophisticated over time. It is also quite clear that children can be easily trained to use memory strategies. Kail (1979, p. 33) asks, "Why is there such a gap between what young children do spontaneously and what we can train them to do?" Part of the answer lies in what we know about metamemory.

Metamemory

Metamemory is an intuitive understanding that both children and adults have of memory and how it works—knowing about knowing (Brown, 1975). John knew that multiplication problems were going to be easy, but he was not too sure about remembering how to use an index. He also believed his mother's memory would prove useful. He might also have believed that, after further instruction and practice, his memory about using an index would improve.

According to Kail (1979, p. 35), there are three important characteristics of metamemory. The first is knowing that some situations require a planned attempt to memorize while others do not (Flavell & Wellman, 1977, p. 5). The second is knowing what makes memorizing easy or difficult. For example, the child might believe, "I have a very good memory," or "I find some things easier to remember than others." Believing, or knowing, certain types of information are easy or difficult to remember influences memorization. The third characteristic is knowing how one is progressing on a memory task. For instance, does the child know when information has been sufficiently memorized?

Even preschool children realize that some tasks require them to *do something* about remembering. However, their efforts are usually limited to such simple actions as looking and pointing (Kail, 1979, p. 40). Older children use numerous memory strategies (Appel et al., 1972).

What do children know about the ease or difficulty of memorizing? Consider this story:

Jim and Bill are in grade ___ (child's own grade). The teacher wanted them to learn the names of all the kinds of birds they might find in their city. Jim had learned them last year and then forgot them. Bill had never learned them before. Do you think one of these boys would find it easier to learn the names of all the birds? Which one? Why? (Kreutzer, Leonard, & Flavell, 1975, p. 8).

Even kindergarten and first grade children realized that relearning would be easier; "Because as soon as he heard the names they would probably all come back to him." The older children seemed more aware of different possibilities; "The kid who learned them (before) might think he knew them, and then . . . get them wrong, but the kid who didn't learn them last year might study more than the kid who *thought* he knew them" (Kreutzer et al., 1975, p. 9).

Finally, does the child pay any attention to how memory is functioning when he or she is attempting to memorize? When the child chooses a certain memory strategy, we can readily see that it might help to keep a check on whether the strategy is working. This is called **memory monitoring**.

It has been discovered that young children are not good judges of whether they have succeeded in memorizing (Wellman, 1977). Masur, McIntyre, and Flavell (1973) asked, "What do young children and adults do when they realize they have not memorized all that was expected of them?" To help find an answer they gave a memory task to children from grades 1 and 3 and to college students. The memory task was a set of pictures 1.5 times greater than the memory span for each group. There was a series of 45-second study periods, and after each period there was a recall task. In subsequent study periods following a recall task, the college students and third graders almost always concentrated on pictures that had not been recalled in the previous recall task. The first graders picked about equal numbers of recalled and unrecalled pictures.

Knowing about memory and how it works does seem to help children with memory tasks. Like other aspects of memory, metamemory develops over time. Although metamemory influences children's memory, it does not appear to be necessary for all memory behaviors. It is clear that metamemory, like other types of memory such as memory strategy, can be trained. However, the influence of training on memory needs more careful study before we can say more about its long-range benefits. "As we learn more about the development of memory, we move closer to our goal of understanding the nature of . . . intellectual change.

Furthermore, as we better understand the factors that govern the development of mnemonic and cognitive skills, we move closer to our goal of ensuring that all children develop these skills fully and use them capably" (Kail, 1979, p. 144).

Summary

Gagné believes that children of all ages have the various types of capabilities he describes. Older children, however, tend to be more capable as a result of previous learning and previous experience. Applying Gagné's learning theory to instruction means first identifying performance objectives. Instructional sequences can then be designed; these should be hierarchical, proceeding from simple to complex levels of skills and concept learning.

Bruner has identified six "benchmarks" for learning; these include increasing abilities to represent, to remember, to communicate, and to deal with many alternatives simultaneously. Instructional planning should take into account the child's readiness to learn, structure of content in terms of basic objectives, and potentially effective learning sequences.

According to Ausubel, meaningful reception learning should pay better dividends than discovery learning for children in the middle years. Whatever the approach, children first acquire concepts by a process of concept formation. Later, they are also able to acquire concepts through assimilation. An expected benefit from subsumption learning is to aid the learning of general ideas and basic concepts, which tend to remain longer in memory than low-level concepts and factual information.

Piaget has distinguished between the new school of active, exploratory, mainly self-directed learning and the traditional school, which hands out ready-made information. In the new school the child should construct, for himself or herself, an understanding of logical relationships between and among objects.

Results from various training studies have shown that it is possible to improve a child's understanding of Piagetian concepts. However, we are still not sure what long-range benefits such learning may have for the child. Actual problem-solving performance and expected level of competence often do not ride side-by-side. Even adults fail some concrete-operational problems. The reasons for such discrepancies are various. Performance can be affected by factors such as problem solving requiring multiple rules, the relative complexity of problems, familiarity with the content of a problem, and memory.

Case has suggested a method for linking instruction for problem solving to the child's level of development. This includes identifying the child's spontaneous but limited strategies, teaching a more efficient, planned strategy in a step-by-step fashion, and reducing the load on working memory.

Basic types of memory (recall and recognition) are available to the 2-year-old. Both types of memory and features of memory (basic processes such as memory span, knowledge, memory strategies, and metamemory) develop over time. As in the case of cognition, memory can be improved by training, but the benefits of such training are still an open question.

A Conservation of Number Problem: The Answer

Two bottles A and B contain 20 red and 20 blue beans, respectively.

1. *Five* red beans are taken from bottle A and placed in bottle B. Bottle B is shaken to distribute the five red beans in among the blue beans. We can represent this mathematically as

$$20R - 5R = 15R \text{ and } 20B + 5R = 20B + 5R$$

2. *Five* beans are taken from bottle B. Let us suppose that the ratio happens to be 3RED:2BLUE. Then

$$15R + 3R + 2B \quad \text{and} \quad 20B + 5R - 3R - 2B$$
$$\text{results in } 18R + 2B \quad \text{results in } 18B + 2R$$

As you can see, the result gives us the *same* number of red beans in the red-bean bottle as blue beans in the blue-bean bottle. No matter what the ratio of red beans to blue beans in the five beans taken from the bottle B at step 2, when these five beans are placed in bottle A, there will always be the same number of red beans in bottle A as there are blue beans in bottle B.

Questions for Review

1. Give examples of learning at each of the four levels described by Gagné that are supposed to play a role in school learning.

2. Describe the three parts of Gagné's instructional sequence.

3. Bruner mentions six benchmarks of intellectual growth. Give examples of children's learning associated with each of these benchmarks and describe how such learning ties in with development.

4. Using examples of the four major features of Bruner's theory of instruction, explain what he means by "instruction is concerned with improving rather than describing learning."

5. Explain the difference between concept formation and concept assimilation.

6. Describe the similarities and differences between concept assimilation and the learning of rules as these two processes of learning are described by Ausubel and Gagné, respectively.

7. Choose one example of "receptive" learning (such as advance organizer learning, reinforcement learning, or Montessori's fundamental lesson approach) and compare it to the "self-discovery" approach to learning used by Inhelder and her colleagues.

8. Describe the main features of Case's model for instruction. How has Case related learning and instruction to Piaget's description of development?

9. Give examples of memory being used to store knowledge, memory strategies, and metamemory. Why is metamemory considered so important a feature of memory?

10. How does memory appear to develop from about age 4 through 10? To help you answer this question, read again the descriptions of research by Paris and Upton (1976); Flavell, Beach and Chinsky (1966); and Kreutzer, Leonard and Flavell (1975) mentioned in the section Development of Memory.

Suggestions for Further Reading

Some of the suggested readings are taken from books mentioned in connection with previous chapters.

Ausubel, D. R., Novak, J. D., & Hanesian, H. *Educational psychology: A cognitive view*, 2nd ed. New York: Holt, Rinehart and Winston, 1978. Particularly chapters 3 (pp. 92–101) and 10.

Brown, A. L. The development of memory: Knowing, knowing about knowing, knowing how to know. In H. W. Reese, ed., *Advances in child development and behavior*, Vol. 10. New York: Academic Press, 1975. An excellent chapter describing three important types of memory.

Bruner, J. S. *The process of education*. Cambridge, Mass.: Harvard University Press, 1960. Particularly chapters 2 and 3.

Bruner, J. S. *Towards a theory of instruction*. Cambridge, Mass.: Harvard University Press, 1966. Particularly chapters 1, 3, and 4.

Flavell, J. H. *Cognitive development*. Englewood Cliffs, NJ: Prentice-Hall. Chapter 6.

Gagné, R. M., & Briggs, L. J. *Principles of instructional design*. New York: Holt, Rinehart and Winston, 1974. Describes a basis for organizing instruction derived from Gagné's theory of development and learning.

Piaget, J. *Science of education and the psychology of the child*. London: Longman, 1970. Includes two "essays," the first one tracing the development of education (mainly in Europe) since 1935, the second setting out a new method of education developed over the last fifty years or so as an alternative to the traditional methods. In connection with our Chapter 10, part II of Piaget's book is of particular interest.

Social and Personality Development

11

His earliest memory, the mood
Fingered and frail as maidenhair,
Was this—a china cup somewhere
In a green, deep wood.
He lives to find again somewhere
That wood, that homely cup; to taste all
Its chill, imagined dews; to dare
The dangerous crystal.

From "Passage from Childhood" in *Selected Poems* (1967) by C. Day Lewis. Copyright 1938 by C. Day Lewis. By permission of Harper & Row, Publishers, Inc.

The middle years of childhood are often called a period of tranquility that the child can enjoy between the effervescence of the preschool years and the turbulence of adolescence. Perhaps all three of these labels overdramatize the course of development. If you ask your friends about their memories of the middle childhood years, their responses will be very different from one another's. The usual reason for these differences is that individuals' personalities differ. So too do their social experiences. When you consider the various theories of social and personality development described in this chapter, you should keep in mind that each presents a general picture. Although each picture is of the same "season," the views are different.

What are the important features of social and personality development at this time? Many are recurring themes already discussed in earlier chapters. A most important feature of personality development is the child's growing self-awareness, as an individual and as a member of various groups. (Freud labeled this period as the *psychosexual/social latency period.*) Sex-role identity continues to develop. Social relationships outside the family are keenly sought after, and the peer group comes to assume a very important role in influencing social development. There is also a vigorous striving for achievement. Prevailing and insistent questions are not only "Who am I?" but also "What can I do?" It is a period of initiation into a wider world beyond the home, but the child continues to need support from the family. In searching for greater independency and identity, the child also needs a sense of interdependency.

This chapter picks up on social development where Chapter 8 ended. The first part of the chapter further considers the psychosexual and psychosocial views of social and personality development and then Kohlberg's view of changes in moral reasoning during the middle years. This is followed by a discussion of the influence on older children's social development of the three interacting systems you have already been introduced to: the family, the school, and the peer group. Mention is also made of further sex-role development, the relationship between self-concept and achievement, and the interplay between the effects of discipline and a growing sense of social rules, attitudes, and values.

Personality and Social Development

It is quite apparent that, as children's social behavior develops, it affects and is affected by the developing personality. How does this apply during the years from 6 to 12? In Freud's psychosexual view, as we have already seen, social behavior is influenced to a large extent by motives of self-gratification. Moral behavior is dominated by instinctual drives. Present-day psychosocial theorists, called **ego psychologists,** emphasize the emergence of the ego as influencing the development of social behavior, rather than leaving it solely to the instincts. New understandings of "self" occur when the child adopts new roles. But what influences the development of the ego? Breger, a psychosocial psychologist, puts it this way:

From what he [the child] is—more or less angry, demanding, aspiring, loving, anxious; from what the parents do—display certain principles in their own actions [or not], punish, espouse, love or reject; from all these, the child, over a period of years, transforms himself in new directions (1973, pp. 256–257).

According to Freud's theory, the interplay of anger, anxiety, and love in the child are motivated by sexual instincts or, expressed another way, a basic and primitive pursuit of self-pleasure and self-gratification. Freud chose to describe this sensual quality of early personality development in terms of the Oedipal or Electra complex, which the child has very likely resolved before age 6. The ego is very important at this time in personality development. "It allows personal adaptation (of personality) through meaningful cognitive and behavioral interchange with the demands of reality" (Cohen, 1976, pp. 25–26). The superego is fashioned from the reality of social demands, from the child's contact with social values. The child achieves standards of socially acceptable behavior by adopting the social behavior characteristics of parents and other adults. Let us take a closer look now at Freud's interpretation of children's social behavior following the genital stage.

The Psychosexual View

We must keep in mind that Freud's account of development during this period was based on interviews with neurotic adults in Europe almost a hundred years ago. He inferred from what adult patients told him of their problems that during childhood, between the ages of 6 and 12, although gratification is still associated with the genital area, the child represses sexual behavior. This total repression of sexual and aggressive fantasies (Freud, 1905) results in a period of calm. In Freud's opinion sexual and aggressive behavior is merely latent at this time, "only a lull before the storm of puberty" (Erikson, 1959). For this reason he calls ages 6 to 12 the latency period. The child's energies are directed toward working and playing with other same-sex peers. This does not appear to be the case for all children or for all cultures. Mead (1961), for example, found no "latency period" occurring for Samoan youth—at least in the terms Freud proposed. It is also quite apparent that in our present Western societies, especially in the United States, children are maturing sexually earlier than in times past. There appears to be a greater awareness of and interest in sexual behavior during these years than Freud would have us believe.

With respect to moral behavior, Freud supposed that during this phase, the superego remains quite rigid in controlling behavior—moral reasoning being very much in terms of "very right or very wrong." Playing by the rules in games assumes a great importance, with rules being made to be strictly kept.

In the normal course of events Freud believed that the Oedipal conflict should be resolved by the time the child was 12 years old. If this conflict is not resolved, the expectation, according to this theory, is that fixation can lead to certain kinds of problems in later life. For example, in the teenage and adult years the individual may avoid sexual relations with the opposite sex or feel uncomfortable with opposite-sex partners.

The Psychosocial View

Although, as you may now realize, Erikson's view of personality development is an outgrowth of the Freudian tradition, he has provided a much different description of development during these years. He believes, for example, that this is a very important period for the growth of the ego which is related to the extent of the child's confidence in striving to achieve. He calls this period between 6 and 12 the stage of industry versus inferiority.

During these middle years most children eagerly engage in all kinds of activities that seem to have some purpose. It is with an inquisitive willingness that the child steps out into the wider world intent on learning useful skills and social behavior. The child experiences

A sense of finality regarding the fact that there is no workable future in the womb of his family. . . . He develops a sense of industry. . . . He can become an eager and absorbed unit of a productive situation (Erikson, 1950, p. 258).

Erikson believes that understanding adults, who pose tasks the child can accomplish and enjoy and who provide adequate guidance, are of crucial importance. Whether the child is learning the hunting skills of the Bushpeople tribe or the tools of literacy in a technological society, much is learned from adults.

If the child is not prepared for life outside the family, if the child is too easily hurt by the inevitable failures that occur in work and play, if the child lacks adults' necessary support and help, then there occurs a sense of inadequacy and inferiority. In Erikson's opinion, if the child's potential abilities are "not evoked and nurtured during the latency period, they may develop late or never" (1959, p. 87). On the other hand, he has said that it often takes just one gifted and inspired teacher "to kindle the flame of a hidden talent" (1959, p. 87).

Moral Development

Children's social behavior is guided by the norms, standards, and values of the society they live in. Children learn, and make decisions about, what is appropriate or inappropriate behavior or, expressed another way, what is right and wrong. Moral development has to do with learning the appropriate rules and values that guide social behavior and the extent to which moral thought is reflected in behavior.

In Chapter 8 we discussed Piaget's description of stages of development of moral reasoning (see Table 8.1). Piaget was particularly interested in how children arrive at an understanding of rules (particularly in the games they play) and how appropriate they are, what is meant by telling a lie or telling the truth, and how children come to recognize authority. His observations of children led him to believe that they first imagine that all rules are imposed by some adult authority. Piaget calls the first stage (covering ages 3 to 5) the egocentric stage of moral realism because children simply conform, without understanding, to rules and standards that adults set. In the second stage, called incipient cooperation (covering ages 5 to 9), children understand something about the operation of rules but are still egocentric in their blind acceptance of authority and in ignoring other people's feelings.

It is only toward the end of the middle years that children begin to understand the nature of socially appropriate behavior which is acceptable to everyone and which they themselves can use in deciding how to behave. This important change in *conventional moral reasoning* is said, by Piaget, to parallel the course of intellectual development. When a child acts in accord with a generally accepted peer-group rule, this involves taking into account other children's points of view— which can hardly be called egocentric behavior. For a child to realize that, in spite of changes in the way another child is behaving in a game, nevertheless, no rules are being broken is one form of conservation. In other words, moral reasoning has become truly concrete operational. Piaget calls this stage the morality of cooperation. During this stage children (between 9 and 11) come to understand that social rules are arbitrary and that it is possible to make personal decisions about obeying rules. They retain respect for authority but base it on an understanding of the purpose of rules rather than on blind acceptance. It is at this time that children begin to judge acts by intention and not just their consequences (as they did in the stage of incipient cooperation). They also now consider other people's feelings when thinking morally.

With respect to the way children decide upon the gravity of lies, Piaget (1932) supposed that it is only at about age 10 that children recognize the difference between "lying" out of ignorance and "lying" with intent. However, Lickona (1976) found that first grade children included the recognition of intent in their evaluation of lies. Even so, younger children in Lickona's study had difficulty in comparing unintentional lies that accidentally resulted in no harm. When they were faced with a choice between, for example, a situation where "Bill fooled his sister into going to bed an hour ahead of time by changing the position of the hands on the clock" and "because Mary accidentally told Bill the lasagna needed another 15 minutes in the oven rather than 5 minutes, his snack got burned," younger children believed that both incidents were equally wrong. They saw the results of both the deliberate and accidental inaccuracy about time as a consequence of an intention to deceive. Older children toward the end of the stage were more aware of intention in comparing and judging such incidents.

Results such as this support Piaget's view that the development of moral reasoning goes hand in hand with intellectual development. Judging intent, taking various factors into account, focusing on the important features of behavior, and not being distracted by irrelevant information are signs of quite advanced reasoning.

Preconventional morality: stage 1, concern with obedience and punishment. We saw in Chapter 8 that preschool (preoperational) children at stage 1 of moral development are strongly influenced in their moral reasoning and social behavior by adult-imposed rules, being concerned with the obeying of rules or getting punished for breaking them. Like Piaget, Kohlberg believes that moral development coincides with intellectual development (1969–1976). In Chapter 8 we mentioned that the preschool aged child was at the stage of pre-moral reasoning or, as Kohlberg also describes it, the stage of "preconventional morality" (see Table 8.2). According to Kohlberg, during the years from 6 to 12 there is a gradual shift from preconventional to conventional levels of moral reasoning that parallels changes in intellectual reasoning from the early sub-stages of concrete operations to fully-fledged concrete operations. At the time the child is entering the stage of concrete operations (about 6 to 7 years), there is a parallel change in pre-moral reasoning to stage 2 of preconventional morality. There is still a certain amount of self-centeredness (egocentrism) in young children's moral reasoning.

Preconventional morality: stage 2, concern with satisfying personal needs. At this stage, although children are still very concerned about rules, they treat rules much more flexibly than previously. Between the ages of about 7 and 10, children judge issues in more relative terms. If asked, "Can the rules of the game be changed," they will say, "Yes, that's O.K., so long as everybody agrees." If asked whether some action is right or wrong, children now say, "Well, it all depends."

What does the rightness or wrongness of acts depend on? In part, it depends on the idea of fairness expressed in the slogan, "You scratch my back, and I'll scratch yours" (Kohlberg, 1971, p. 166). In part, it depends on the child's needs and sources of pleasure. A child at this stage might offer the judgment that Heinz (see p. 350 for the story about Heinz that Kohlberg used when formulating his theory) can steal the drug if he loves or needs his wife. But, if he wants to marry another woman, who is younger and more beautiful, then he doesn't need to (1963, p. 24). Kohlberg has referred to such reasoning as moral cynicism.

Conventional morality: stage 3, concern with "good boy, good girl" image. At about 10 years of age children, turning from egocentric thinking, begin to consider others' welfare. Children want to appear "good," and they judge their actions in terms of what a "good" person should do. In pleasing and helping others they look for approval as a measure of their "good acts." Intentions now become important, and the 10-year-old is likely to argue that poor Heinz was not really doing wrong in stealing because he was trying to save his wife's life. It is the greedy druggist who is bad, out to make a profit at the expense of others (Kohlberg, 1958).

Conventional morality: stage 4, concern with law and order. Many children, as they cross that borderline between childhood and adolescence, became righteous. They are very concerned about being fair. "You keep getting onto me about tidying my bedroom, but you *never* get onto Jane." In seeking fair play young adolescents often exaggerate the principle of the matter and not infrequently complain that "I" am not being fairly treated—shades of egocentricism! According to Kohlberg, moral reasoning changes from merely seeking approval for "good" behavior to concern for a more general social order. It is now a question of doing one's duty, respecting authority, and desiring social order for its own sake. Sometimes there are conflicts in reasoning. For example, a 13-year-old may find sympathy for Heinz without condoning his theft; and many say Heinz should steal the drug but should also go to jail for the theft (Crain, 1980, pp. 107–108). By this stage the child can assume another's role. According to Kohlberg's theory, the development of role taking is the major mechanism influencing growth in moral judgment (Kohlberg, 1969). As mentioned earlier, Kohlberg, like Piaget, believes that the development of moral reasoning parallels cognitive development. Kohlberg has also suggested that perspective-taking development also occurs in conjunction with or prior to moral development (1973–1976). Walker (1980) has described the parallel relationships among

Table 11.1 Parallel Stages in Cognitive, Perspective Taking, and Moral Development

Cognitive Stage[a]	Perspective-taking Stage[b]	Moral Stage[c]
Preoperations The "symbolic function" appears but thinking is marked by centration and irreversibility.	*Stage 1 (subjectivity)* There is an understanding of the subjectivity of persons but no realization that persons can consider each other as subjects.	*Stage 1 (heteronomy)* The physical consequences of an action and the dictates of authorities define right and wrong.
Concrete operations The objective characteristics of an object are separated from action relating to it; and classification, seriation, and conservation skills develop.	*Stage 2 (self-reflection)* There is a sequential understanding that the other can view the self as a subject just as the self can view the other as subject.	*Stage 2 (exchange)* Right is defined as serving one's own interests and desires, and cooperative interaction is based on terms of simple exchange.
Beginning formal operations There is development of the coordination of reciprocity with inversion; and propositional logic can be handled.	*Stage 3 (mutual perspectives)* It is realized that the self and the other can view each other as perspective-taking subjects (a generalized perspective).	*Stage 3 (expectations)* Emphasis is on good-person stereotypes and a concern for approval.
Early basic formal operations The hypothetico-deductive approach emerges, involving abilities to develop possible relations among variables and to organize experimental analyses.	*Stage 4 (social and conventional system)* There is a realization that each self can consider the shared point of view of the generalized other (the social system).	*Stage 4 (social system and conscience)* Focus is on the maintenance of the social order by obeying the law and doing one's duty.
Consolidated basic formal operations Operations are now completely exhaustive and systematic.	*Stage 5 (symbolic interactions)* A social system perspective can be understood from a beyond-society point of view.	*Stage 5 (social contract)* Right is defined by mutual standards that have been agreed upon by the whole society.

Source: Walker, L. J., 1980. Copyright © 1980 by the Society for Research in Child Development, Inc. Reprinted by permission.

[a]Adapted from Colby & Kohlberg (Note 1).
[b]Adapted from Selman & Byrne (1974) and Selman (1976).
[c]Adapted from Kohlberg (1976).

cognition, **perspective taking,** and moral reasoning (see Table 11.1). To examine the plausibility of these hypothesized relationships, Walker attempted to stimulate the moral development of children aged 10 to 11 years to the level of stage 3 (as in Table 11.1). He first tested these children's levels of intellectual, perspective-taking, and moral-reasoning development. All the children used in his study were at moral stage 2 but differed in levels of intellectual and perspective-taking development (see Table 11.2). Walker expected that only those children at moral stage 2 who had attained beginning formal operations and were at stage 3 of perspective taking would benefit from "training" intended to move them to stage 3 of moral development.

Table 11.2 Percentage of Children Benefiting from Moral Reasoning Training

Group	Pretest	Post-test (at 8 days)	Follow-up (at 6 weeks)
Experimental			
Beginning formal and perspective taking stage 3	25	62	63
Beginning formal and perspective taking stage 2	17	16	15
Concrete operational and perspective taking stage 2	13	15	13
Control			
Beginning formal and perspective taking stage 3	24	19	27
Beginning formal and perspective taking stage 2	19	17	11
Concrete operational and perspective taking stage 2	13	9	9

Source: Adapted from Walker, L. J., 1980. Copyright © 1980 by the Society for Research in Child Development, Inc. Adapted by permission.

Only children with beginning formal operations and stage 3 perspective taking improved to stage 3 of moral reasoning following experiences role playing the central character in moral dilemma situations.

Training consisted of presenting the children with role-playing dilemmas set at stage 3 of moral reasoning. Children had to imagine that they were the central character in six dilemma situations which they had to resolve with the help of adult advice. These dilemmas were based on the type of stories used by Kohlberg (Kohlberg et al., 1977), such as the story of Heinz mentioned in Chapter 8. As Walker expected, only children who had attained beginning formal operations and who were at stage 3 of perspective taking benefited from the training. The results are shown in Table 11.2. Walker concludes from these results that moral education programs using Kohlberg's approach can be expected to be successful only with children who have attained the same level of intellectual and perspective-taking development as the level of moral reasoning the program aims to teach. Lockwood (1978), after a careful analysis of existing programs, arrives at the same conclusion. One solution might be to construct moral education programs that incorporate logical reasoning and perspective taking.

There has been some criticism of Kohlberg's theory. Kurtines and Greif (1974), for example, are concerned at the lack of research evidence which suggests that moral judgment is related to actual moral behavior. But Kohlberg has already observed that

The fact that children do not always do what they say when the chips are down does not mean that development of judgment and development of conduct go along two different tracks. Verbal judgments may not be "trustworthy" reports of conduct, but they may still reflect the same basic developmental process (see Maccoby, 1968, p. 240).

Other critics have responded to this argument by pointing out that the moral dilemmas Kohlberg presented to children by way of stories do not reflect the type of moral conflicts children usually face in "real-life" situations. Perhaps children are better able to reason about the moral implications of actual moral dilemmas they have experienced in their lives. Damon (1977) has tested this supposition. He asked children aged 4 to 8 years how they thought amounts of candy, money, or toys might be fairly divided among a number of children. In one story the sharing of candy followed the completion of a task at which one child had worked somewhat harder than the others. One child was bigger and stronger than the others, and another child was younger and smaller. In responding to the story the 4-year-olds had little understanding of fairness with respect to sharing. The 6-year-olds usually suggested equal sharing, not taking other factors into account. However, the 8-year-olds recognized that some children in the stories were more deserving than others and, with respect to other situations, reasoned that good deeds should be rewarded but that bad deeds should not. It is apparent that, given more realistic situations to judge, children much younger than 10 to 12 were able to display a "conventional" wisdom in their moral reasoning (see Inset 11.1).

| Inset 11.1 Can the Environment Influence Moral Reasoning? | Denny and Duffy (1974) questioned Kohlberg's claim that the development of moral reasoning results from changes in the level of children's intellectual competencies. Kohlberg contends that levels (and stages) of moral reasoning do not result from environmental influences alone since, if intellectual competencies develop similarly in all children, then it is difficult to believe that these competencies develop as a result of direct learning of the moral values of a particular culture (Kohlberg, 1969, p. 354). |

It seems unlikely that parents teach the same social rules, obligations, and moral values to their 4-year-olds as they teach to their older children. Parents of young children frequently say such things as "If you hit your sister one more time, you'll come into the house," thus orienting the children toward punishment and authority. In other words, parents tend to teach young children a preconventional type of moral reasoning. It seems likely that parents adjust the implied level of moral reasoning to suit the child's age. If this is the case, then the stages that seem to occur in moral reasoning may simply reflect the level of teaching of moral reasoning selected by parents with regard to the expected level of reasoning of their children.

The purpose of the Denny and Duffy study was to determine whether parents actually do attribute different moral principles to children of different ages, and whether there is any relationship between parents' selected level of teaching and the child's level of moral reasoning.

Children aged 6, 10, and 14 years were first asked a series of questions demanding a moral judgment such as, "Kathy's parents told her that if she didn't do well in school, she would be punished. On the next big test Kathy didn't know many of the answers. When the teacher wasn't looking, Kathy copied someone else's answers.

Table 11.3 Levels of Moral Reasoning Implied by Mothers and Used by Children

Children's Age	Preconventional	Conventional	Postconventional
Number of Children at Each Level Implied by Mothers			
6	12	1	4
10	5	4	8
14	5	7	8
Number of Children Actually at Each Level			
6	15	2	0
10	7	9	1
14	5	8	4

Mothers treat children of different ages in ways that imply an expected level of moral reasoning. It has been suggested that the way parents treat their children with respect to moral reasoning may influence moral development. An alternative explanation is that the level of children's moral reasoning influences parents' expectations.

Kathy got a good grade on the test. Kathy's mother was so happy that Kathy got a good grade on the test that she took her out for an ice cream sundae. Was Kathy right to copy the answers? Why?" The mothers of these children were then interviewed to establish the level of moral principles they conveyed to their children. They were asked questions such as, "If you found out that (their child's name) had stolen something from a department store but did not get caught, what would you say or do to (child's name)?" Childrens' and mothers' responses were scored according to which level of Kohlberg's stages of moral reasoning they implied. Mother's responses were then compared to their children's responses. The results are shown in Table 11.3.

It is clear from these results that a strong relationship exists between the child's age and the level of moral reasoning that the mother implies in her interactions with her child—the older the child, the higher the level of moral principles the mother used. (It can be assumed that the mothers' responses to the hypothetical situations reflect the way they usually teach moral reasoning to their children.) This could account for, at least in part, the stages of moral reasoning children seem to pass through. Of course, an assumption in this interpretation is that children imitate their parents' moral reasoning. Another equally likely interpretation is that mothers tailor the level of teaching and explanation to suit the level of reasoning they observe in their children. (This was a correlational study and so no causality can be established.) Further research is necessary to help determine the direction of causality. Until such time, it seems reasonable to conclude that environmental factors should not be discounted as possible causes of stages in the development of moral reasoning.

This type of constructive criticism and testing of theory is all to the good. There are great difficulties in exploring the determinants of prosocial behavior and the developmental changes that occur in moral reasoning. The work of theorists such as Kohlberg contributes to an understanding of children's social behavior and moral thinking, and it continues to make progress (Mussen & Eisenberg-Berg, 1977).

Self-Image

The *self-image* is a composite of a self-concept and self-esteem, which children learn to differentiate. Let us take a look at self-concept first. A broader view of "self" is not only "What am I?" but "Who am I, what kind of person am I, how am I different from you?" Preschool children are particularly concerned with self as, "How do I look?"—the "mirror-image" of self. As they grow older, they come to recognize that they also have a "private self" that cannot be seen. Older children know that self has multiple characteristics such as "I'm a girl, I have blue eyes, I'm tall and slim." "Sometimes I'm happy, sometimes sad, I like playing checkers but not chess, and my favorite singing group is the Beatles." They accept the different components of their individuality as their **self-concept.**

Another view of self is **self-esteem,** a personal value of worth that children give themselves based on their self-concept. How do children develop self-esteem? Children with high levels of self-esteem have parents who also have high self-esteem. As in the case for other types of personality and social behavior, parents play a crucial role in influencing the child's developing self-concept. Parents who establish reasonable rules, which are fairly and consistently enforced, most often produce children with a great deal of self-confidence. Such children think well of themselves (Baumrind & Black, 1967).

Self-concept and achievement. The ability or inability to trust in oneself is a part of a developing self-concept. Children may believe that what they are, what they become, and what they can achieve is entirely in their hands, although they may hope for support from caring parents and others. Alternatively, children may assume that much of what happens to them or what kind of person they will become growing up is in the hands of "fate," or they may become overly dependent on other people's determining who they are, what they are likely to become, and whether they will achieve much or little. This sense of knowing that one is in control of one's own life and confident in oneself or that one is at the mercy of fate is referred to as **locus of control,** a most important aspect of the self-concept. By age 8 children are usually quite sure about where the locus of control rests (Nowicki & Strickland, 1973). You probably have realized that parents have an important influence on the determination of locus of control. Parents who support their children's behavior rather than determine it and who suggest possible ways of solving problems rather than offering detailed directions

Parents can help children develop self-esteem and self-confidence by involving them in jobs and activities around the home. (Photo left by John Maher/EKM-Nepenthe, right by Jean-Claude Lejeune)

or solutions foster an internal locus of control (Coopersmith, 1967; Loeb, 1975; Seligman, 1975).

Parents also influence children's levels of achievement (Baumrind, 1971). It comes as no surprise to find that children with high self-esteem are also high achievers (Taylor, 1964). Such children are obedient, have good relations with their peers, and have high expectations for their performance in various activities (Coopersmith, 1967). Parents' expressions of warmth and acceptance seem necessary for the development of self-confidence. Children lacking in self-confidence usually have parents who are harsh, who are inconsistent in establishing discipline, and who appear unconcerned (Coopersmith, 1967). These children are usually very anxious and low achievers in school (Coopersmith, 1967; Sears, 1970).

Socializing Effects of Different Family Systems

During the preschool years, as we have already seen, one important effect parents can have on children is to help in their development of self-esteem, self-confidence, and achievement. This influence is maintained with little change during the middle years (Kagan, 1978). Of course, for most children between the ages of 6 and 12 years many changes occur in the type and variety of social experiences. Children tend to spend more and more time away from home; however, although they are becoming more independent of family at this age,

children fluctuate between dependency and independency. As Bigner (1979) has pointed out, despite the fact that school-age children are looking increasingly for independence from parents, recognizing that parents can make mistakes, becoming resentful of parental demands, and showing more hostility toward their parents, they nevertheless express general approval of their relationships with parents and continue to look to them for support.

Parental Support

Children are involved in all kinds of activities that take them outside of the home for longer periods than at any previous time. One way in which parents can respond to this is by learning "to let go" (Duvall, 1977). As we have seen, children also spend more time associating with peers. Parents need to show that they accept and encourage this new social role. Yet there are many instances in which parents need to offer advice, and perhaps a restraining hand, on a child's behavior when it is indiscriminate. As Erikson has pointed out, at this stage of psychosocial development the child needs encouragement and support from understanding parents. Advice or restraint should be offered with some explanation and possible suggestions for alternate kinds of behavior.

Divorce

The number of divorces in the United States has increased sharply in recent years. It has been estimated that close to one out of every two current marriages will end in divorce. On the average, children spend about six years in *single-parent* families that result from divorce. Of these children, the majority live with their mother; only 10 percent live with their father (Hetherington, 1979, p. 851).

There is great concern about the effects of divorce on children. It has been reported that children aged 6 to 8 years are usually the most vulnerable (Kelly & Wallerstein, 1976). The distress felt at parents' separating affects boys and girls differently. Boys, more than girls, tend to become rebellious at home and pose problems for teachers in school (Hetherington, 1976; Rutler, 1970). Girls show similar reactions to their parents' divorce but are usually easier to control. In the middle years and in adolescence, girls with divorced mothers tend to be more assertive in the company of boys compared to girls from intact families. They are also likely to marry at a younger age and to develop negative views of their husbands (Hetherington, 1972).

It is widely believed, at least among certain groups of people (e.g., people with strong religious beliefs that divorce is morally wrong), that divorce is inevitably harmful to children and therefore to be avoided at all costs. It is true that children become fearful of not being wanted or loved at the time of a pending divorce, feel guilty because they believe they have caused the divorce, or feel anger toward either the remaining or departing parent. But these same deep feelings may be experienced in families in which the marriage has failed but parents are staying together "for the sake of the children." An embittered marital relationship may result in parents' showing hostility toward or rejection of their children. The likely harmful effects on children's development in such a situation can hardly be ignored (Lamb, 1977c, p. 164). Divorce is never a neat, cleanly disposed-of event. Its effects are usually felt long before divorce and for years afterward (Hetherington, Cox, & Cox, 1976, 1979). Lamb (1977c) has summarized the effects on children of a father's or mother's absence following divorce.

Effects of father's and mother's absence.   Following divorce, the courts usually place children in the mother's care. What are the implications of the father's absence for the remaining family members?

1. There is no longer a male figure whom sons can learn to imitate and daughters can learn to complement.

2. The family now lacks a major adult socializing or disciplinary figure.

3. There is almost inevitably a loss of income since most fathers are the major breadwinners. This means making do on less money and usually requires a substantial family reorganization, both being sources of stress.

4. The mother loses emotional support; another source of stress for the family.

5. Social isolation may result. In some subcultures divorce is not approved. In general, single-parent families do not usually receive as much social support as intact families (adapted from Lamb, 1977c, p. 165).

It appears that the development of masculinity in sons may be impaired by a father's absence (Biller, 1974, 1976; Lamb, 1976). However, when fathers, for some reason, refuse to interact with their sons, this has the same effect as fathers being actually absent (Blanchard & Biller, 1971). Many fathers become obsessed with their occupation and may lose interest in or alienate their families. This is one of the most frequent reasons for divorce. Such fathers, for some considerable time, are not likely to have played a significant role in influencing the social development of their children.

Children can adapt to the crisis of a divorce. Adjustment will depend on the quality of life in the single-parent family. There may be alternate support systems available in the form of relatives in an extended family, good friends who have become accepted within the family, or a prospective or actual step-parent. Alternate fathers (e.g., uncles) or stepfathers can adequately function in the same way as "real" fathers in influencing the sex-role development of sons (Oshman & Manosevitz, 1976).

Daughters are also affected by a father's absence. Girls learn feminine behavior not only by imitating their mothers but also by learning behavior that complements the maleness of fathers and brothers (Hetherington, 1967). However, although girls are affected by a father's absence, it is boys who are considerably more vulnerable.

There is very little evidence about how children adjust after divorce when it is the mother who leaves the family. On the basis of a number of case studies, Levine (1976) suggests that children left with the father can adjust readily and without being unduly disturbed. Because there are fewer cases in which children are left in the care of the father, most of these fathers will have fought for the custody of their children. Therefore, they are likely to be very devoted and committed to the upbringing of their children (Lamb, 1977c, p. 170). This is not to suggest that mothers are less committed to caring for their children in the best possible way. Single parents, whether mothers or fathers, can adjust to their new parenting role and also help their children adjust to the new family structure. Let us now take a close look at single-parent families and, since most single parents are mothers, the particular effects of divorce on the mother.

Single-Parent Families

According to Schlesinger (1975), about one in every six children in the United States lives in a single-parent family with 90 percent of single parents being mothers. In many cases the single-parent family system is transitional between

The single parent often faces the responsibilities of managing a family alone, experiences financial hardships, and feels a lack of emotional and social support. (Photo by Robert Eckert/ EKM-Nepenthe)

divorce and remarrying (Ross & Sawhill, 1975). We know very little about the effects on children of growing up in single-parent families, whether under long-term conditions with one parent or as a pattern of incidents following repeated divorce.

To date, very little research has been done on single parenting. One such study by Hetherington, Cox, and Cox (1978) pointed to the fact that single parents (usually mothers):

1. suffer from the responsibilities of managing a family usually shared by two parents;

2. often experience financial hardship;

3. are often socially isolated, with many experiencing stress from lack of emotional and social support.

It is an unfortunate fact that many of the mothers granted custody of their children by the courts have serious problems adjusting to their single-parent role (as do single-parent fathers). For many women, divorce results in ill-health and emotional upset. The psychological well-being and continuing development of children can be seriously affected by a mother's facing the stresses of health and emotional problems (Bloom, Asher, & White, 1978). In the first year following

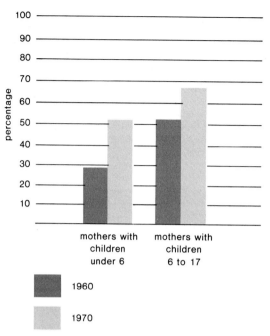

Figure 11.1 Mothers having a job. Graph includes married mothers with husband present, those with husbands absent, and those widowed or those divorced. (Source: United States Bureau of the Census, 1980.)

a divorce, mothers become depressed, less supportive, and lacking in control when dealing with their children. However, the mother's "sense of competence, self-esteem, and happiness is modified by the behavior of her children, particularly her sons" (Hetherington, 1979, p. 856). At a time when she is confronting many stresses the mother needs her children's cooperation, affection, and acknowledgment of her competence as a mother. Especially in the first year following divorce, it has been noticed that many divorced mothers and their sons are likely to get involved in an escalating cycle of aggressive confrontation, each trying to coerce the other (Hetherington, 1979, p. 856).

As previously mentioned, an inevitable result of divorce and father absence is a loss of family income. This loss is usually substantial, and because of financial hardships, many single-parent mothers need to work (Nordheimer, 1977. See Figure 11.1). The effects of mothers' working (including single parents) on children's development has recently been assessed by Hoffman (1979. See Inset 11.2). She indicates that quality of family life is not adversely affected. With mother working, single-parent families also can function very well, especially when they are helped by some support system. More research is needed to identify the sources of and types of changes and stress associated with divorce and the

More and more mothers are joining the work force. For almost a decade, over half the mothers of school-aged children, living with their husbands, have been employed. More recently, the number of mothers of preschool-aged children joining the work force has risen to about 42 percent. It is only to be expected that the greater proportion of all working mothers are from single-parent families. Single-parent families are on the increase, and there is every indication that the trend toward more mothers, including single parents, going out to work will continue (U.S. Department of Commerce, 1979). Lois Hoffman (1979) has provided an updated look at maternal employment and its effects on child development. She has this to say.

Maternal Attention

The way families organize themselves has become more efficient, and family size has diminished. It is no longer certain that today's child with a working mother lacks sufficient attention. It is interesting to note that some studies (Moore, 1975; Birnbaum, 1975) have indicated that full-time mothering can actually work against the child. Some mothers overinvest in their children, so that mothering becomes a form of smothering.

Value of Employment to the Mother

Many women feel a great need to have a job. For the single parent there are obvious economic reasons. But even in the case of women who have no great need to earn a wage, employment can provide social stimulation and a feeling of competency (Dubnoff, Veroff, & Kulka, 1978). Recent surveys have indicated that the working mother is more satisfied with her life than the nonworking mother—and so is her husband.

Effects on Child Rearing

What is happening to the preschool-aged child when the mother is at work? What is the quality of the mother-child interaction when the working mother is home with the child?

(continued)

best types of support systems for helping single-parent families achieve a satisfying and fulfilling life-style (Colletta, 1978; Hetherington, 1979).

What is being done to help single parents? There are a number of organizations whose sole purpose is to offer support to single-parent families; Parents Without Partners (PWP) and Family Life Council organizations can be found in many urban areas. There are also many church organizations set up for this purpose. Weiss (1973) has described how PWP provides support:

1. It is *sustaining* because it accepts the single parent and helps with problems.

2. It provides opportunities for mutual support. Single parents can meet and share with each other similar problems they are having.

Inset 11.2 Although numbers of children attending preschools and day-care centers have increased in recent years, most preschool-aged children of working mothers are still cared for in their own homes (U.S. Department of Labor, 1977). We do know that children who attend quality day-care centers do not appear to suffer any adverse effects (Belsky & Sternberg, 1978; Rubenstein & Hawes, 1979). It also seems to be the case that working mothers spend as much time with their children as nonworking mothers (Goldberg, 1977), and the quality of care does not differ (Cohen, 1978, Hock, 1980).

When children go to elementary school, problems of child care are considerably reduced for working mothers. Although school-aged children still need love, guidance, and a secure home base, they also need independence and a chance to cope on their own, to develop a sense of responsibility, and a feeling of competence.

Research findings have shown that, with the mother working, there is a less traditional division of family chores between husband and wife. Also, children in middle childhood are more likely to have household responsibilities (Hoffman, 1974).

Much in the situation of the working mother benefits her children. Daughters seem to do very well at school and seek occupational competence. Their mothers provide models more consistent with the roles they are likely to play as adults. Sons of working mothers are less stereotyped in their view of sex roles. They see their mothers as more competent than do sons of nonworking mothers; and they see men as warmer. It has been discovered that sons of working mothers are usually better adjusted socially and do well academically (Gold & Andres, 1978; Hoffman, 1974).

Working mothers are certainly part of modern family life. In most cases, the quality of family life is not adversely affected when mother goes out to work. What is known suggests that mother's employment is not an inevitable loss to the family. There can be benefits to all members of a family with a working mother. But it is important to realize that the fact mother works is not irrelevant to the quality of family life and children's development. More research is needed to understand more fully what children's needs are and how they can be met when the mother is employed.

Source: Adapted from Hoffman, L. W. "Maternal Employment." *American Psychologist,* 1979, *34,* 859–865.

3. It provides the single parent with opportunities to get involved in the activities offered by the organization. This may promote a sense of personal growth.

4. It provides a means of establishing new emotional attachments to others. This is most important in combating feelings of isolation, loneliness, and fear.

Socializing Effects of the Elementary School

Children with loving, caring, supportive parents tend to perform well in school. Stress caused by disruptions within the family often retards children's achievements. But although parents and the family system in general have an important influence on children's social development, the socializing effects of the school environment must also be recognized. Throughout the middle years, children spend about six hours of each school day in school. As they grow older, the effects of school on social development become more pronounced.

The *teacher role* plays a significant part in socialization. During middle years the teacher can be viewed as an alternate parent to the child at school. As with parents' care, teachers influence a child's social behavior by modeling and by reinforcing behavior.

Most teachers in the primary grades are women. They tend to reinforce in both boys and girls such traditional "feminine" behavior as being quiet, obedient, compliant, and passive (Mussen, Conger, & Kagan, 1979, p. 401). This often leads to boys' viewing school activities as feminine. For this reason, boys may have problems adjusting to school during the elementary grades.

Children's experiences of learning academic and social skills lead to a concept of ability. Children develop strong beliefs about their abilities to perform various tasks. They become very conscious, not only about their own expectations of success or failure, but also about the teacher's. The child's concept of ability is closely tied to feelings of self-esteem. Because of this the teacher should try to organize tasks in such a way that all children can achieve some success and reward. (It is important to remember that intermittent reinforcement works best.) Putting the emphasis on rewarding children for acceptable behavior is not to say that certain types of behavior may not sometimes require punishment.

Elementary school teachers see their primary responsibility as teaching children academic skills—not social skills. Bruner (1960) has pointed out that training elementary school children to use concretely and intuitively logical operations requires special skills. So too does the arrangement and teaching of various subject-matter areas so that children learn important ideas, not merely a mass of factual information. But to communicate knowledge wisely and to provide a model of competence, the teacher must be free to be creative and free to continue to learn how to teach. Children should be able to identify with the teacher as a model of someone who learns. The teacher can be a figure of a learner with whom children can compare themselves.

Who is not able to recall the impact of some particular teacher—an enthusiast . . . a disciplinarian whose order came from love of a subject, a playful but serious mind? There are many images, and they are precious. Alas, there are also destructive images: the teachers who sapped confidence, the dream killers (Bruner, 1960, pp. 90–91).

Teachers should help children develop skills in considering possibilities rather than just conclusions to develop an ability to monitor their thinking both in the classroom and in other social situations. (Photo by James L. Ballard)

Are there negative effects of the educational system? Many critics believe that the public school system leaves much to be desired. One bone of contention is "the hidden curriculum." This mostly takes the form of the teacher's expectations of certain types of behavior, such as conformity to a system the child does not necessarily understand. These systems include excessive attention to neatness for its own sake, competition for signs of achievement such as "stars," and stereotypic values attached to sex role. Illich (1971) goes so far as to argue for "deschooling." He believes that schools do not help children develop a wholesome concept of self or acquire useful knowledge.

The fact that children acquire social behavior, at least in part by identifying with and imitating adults, makes the implication for teachers fairly obvious. Ways in which appropriate social skills can be taught were described in Chapter 8, where the performance of a competent teacher was outlined (Hendrick, 1980). The belief that, in inculcating social behavior, teachers have a responsibility to help children develop both social knowledge and skills that they can take with them into the world beyond the school, has been echoed by others. Biber (1977) has suggested teaching ways of thinking concerned with possibilities as much as

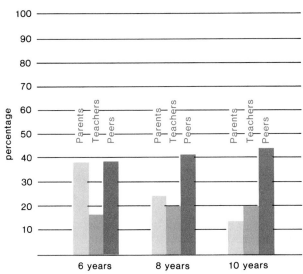

Figure 11.2 Percentage of time children spend with parents, teachers, and peers. During the middle years children spend more time with peers than with parents or teachers. As older children become less dependent on adults they seek attention and approval from peers. (Source: Adapted from Wright, H. F. *Recording and Analyzing Children's Behavior.* Harper & Row, 1967. Used with permission.)

conclusions, so that the child's thinking is flexible enough to deal with a whole variety of social situations. Flavell (1977) makes this appeal very strongly in talking about metacognition, thinking about thinking. He believes teachers should attempt to teach children to monitor their thinking not only in school but also in other social settings. For example, young children who are inclined to be egocentric can be trained to become more sensitive to other people's feelings by assuming roles. This requires them to make "good inferences about what is going on inside (other people)," in other words thinking about thinking (Flavell et al., 1975).

The Peer Group

Although parents and teachers are able to represent suitable role models for children to imitate, it has been suggested that most social learning takes place between child and child in play situations (Greif, 1977). Beginning at about age 4 and continuing through the preschool and middle years, children increasingly spend more time with their peers and less time with parents and teachers (see Figure 11.2). They become less dependent on adults and look more to other children for support and attention (Heathers, 1955). During the middle years children become more inclined to form groups. Indeed, the elementary school years are often referred to as the "gang years." Peer interaction in a social setting has been observed as early as 6 months by some researchers (Vandell, Wilson, & Buchanan, 1979) and two years by others (Eckerman, Whatley, & Kutz, 1975). But it is in the middle childhood years that the *peer group* begins to become more prominent. At first there is a lot of shifting in and out of groups, but in the later years of this period peer groups become more cohesive (Hartup, 1979).

The peer group can take many forms, from children gathering together to play games to strongly bonded pairs or groups of friends to special groups organized for team sports to delinquent gangs. The peer group provides an alternative social subculture to that of the family. Membership in a peer group means accepting certain codes, moral values, and behavior standards that can be very different from those set by parents. Children have to learn to accommodate to both systems to live satisfactorily in each, and most children do so. Having to slip from one subculture to another can develop adaptability. As children grow older and differences between family and peer group become more obvious, more important, and perhaps more strongly at variance, children must learn to work changes without becoming too compromising and risking a loss of self-esteem.

The peer group plays an important role in influencing the development of appropriate cultural behavior, which will be played out in later life. Two interesting features of peer groups is that they occur spontaneously, even when not encouraged by the culture (Hartup, 1970), and they group together by age and sex. In our Western societies groups of boys at this age make very clear their dislike of girls—and vice versa.

Five Social Functions

A better appreciation of the influence of peer interaction on children's social development has emerged in recent years (Asher, 1978; Hartup, 1978, 1979; Suomi & Harlow, 1975; Whiting & Whiting, 1975). An important function of peers is to provide playmates. In playing together children learn social rules, learn to modify aggression, and develop appropriate sex-role behavior. During play it sometimes turns out that children do not share rules and ideas about how to behave. If they remain together, somehow they have to resolve such conflicts. Peer conflicts can be particularly significant in influencing the development of role-taking behavior (Shantz, 1975).

The importance of the peer group during middle childhood in preparing children for adolescence and adulthood has been summarized in terms of five functions by Williams and Stith (1974): companionship, independence from adults, source of information, acceptance of rules, and sex identity.

Companionship. During middle childhood children begin to form very close friendships. The neighborhood gang involves children in a great deal of social give and take. A whole variety of activities from playing "night games" to collecting beer cans, from going fishing to building forts, are played together in a spirit of friendship and sharing.

Independence from adults. A most important objective of the peer group is to be self-controlling. Groups of children set up different rules from those devised by adults with respect to acceptable behavior. This is a time for testing behavior that children know is forbidden by adults. Such behavior includes swearing, pestering adults in the neighborhood with all kinds of "tricks" (the residue of smashed eggs trickled down the side of a house is very difficult to remove!), and varying degrees of vandalism. The peer group can exert a great deal of pressure on its members to "take part," be loyal, not tell tales, dress in a certain way, and, in general, behave according to the unwritten code of the group.

Source of information. Children in peer groups transmit an extraordinary amount of information to one another on a whole variety of subjects. Very often, information supplied by the peer group is more strongly believed than that offered by parents or teachers. Utech and Having (1969) attempted to assess the influence of parents and peers on decision making at different ages. Children aged between 8 and 16 years were presented with a number of dilemmas. One was presented in the following fashion:

Susan likes music and is trying to decide whether to join the band or the choir. Her parents think the band would be more fun because it plays at the basketball and football games. Susan's friends think she would enjoy the choir better since it goes to different towns for performances. What do you think Susan will decide to do? Will she join the band as her parents suggest? Will she do as her friends suggest and join the choir?

Another version had the friends suggesting the band, and parents the choir. The two versions of the dilemma were presented at different times. Children's responses to the questions indicate that compliance to parental demands or suggestions declines with age. The peer group provides this opportunity to become independent of adults' rules, values, and information.

Acceptance of rules. During the middle years children become more aware of rules and how they govern behavior. This is obvious, as Piaget discovered, in the way they play games such as marbles. It is interesting that peer-group codes are mainly a listing of "thou shalt not . . ." rather than "thou shall. . . ." Breaking the group's rules results in some form of punishment, which often includes being ostracized. Such actions serve several purposes. Children learn the value of conformity to group values. This is important for cohesiveness and can only be achieved through cooperation. Immediate punishment clearly demonstrates the results of inappropriate behavior.

When the mother is dominant in the family, boys tend to be aggressive and unfriendly. (Photo by Robert Eckert/ EKM-Nepenthe)

Sex identity. By about the second or third grade children begin to strongly discriminate group membership on the basis of sex. At least this is the case for spontaneously formed peer groups. Adult-organized groups, which include teams for various games, are sometimes of mixed sex. In the United States this seems to be more the case for soccer than, say, Little League baseball, tag football, or ice hockey. But children who are quite happy at playing on mixed-sex teams may still tend to seek membership in same-sex neighborhood peer groups. There are various explanations for such double standards. Adults may reinforce different kinds of behavior for boys and girls. Supporting mixed-sex team games is really a special case. The reasons for this type of "grouping" are particularly related to formal team sports and such groupings are not long lasting. At this age, at least from the Freudian point of view, children are establishing a clear identity, including gender. Thus, children of the same sex may share this objective and demonstrate it in terms of a strong pressure to conform to certain patterns of behavior.

Competition, Conformity, and Cooperation

Where should we look for peer groups? The most obvious place is the neighborhood. There is more time for "getting together" outside of school. Informally, schedules for times and places for meetings are arranged. The line from the old song "when we were kids on the corner of the street" describes one favorite meeting place. But any suitable place for playing together will do. These spontaneous gatherings bring together friendly and unfriendly children.

The ways in which children behave in the peer group can be affected by parental behavior. Boys from families in which the mother is dominant tend to be aggressive and unfriendly. In families in which the father is dominant, boys are usually much friendlier, but they are also dominant in exerting power (Hoffman, 1961). Such imbalances of personalities within a peer group lead to competition. It has been suggested that such competitiveness can positively influence social behavior (Blitsen, 1971; Hartup, 1964). When differences of opinion arise, children are forced to take others' behavior into account. This leads to adaptations in personal reactions, attitudes, and goals (Gardner, 1978, p. 308). A certain degree of conformity to peer-group norms is necessary. Conformity increases during the middle years, with girls tending to be more conforming than boys (Costanzo & Shaw, 1966; Hartup, 1970; Hoving, Hamm, & Galvin, 1969). However, the extent of conformity among peers depends on a number of factors, including size of the peer group, types of relationships that exist among children in the group, the issue of conformity, and the amount of pressure to conform exerted by the peer group (Hartup, 1970).

Children learn not only the rules that govern competition but cooperation as well. Children spontaneously form "teams" and are organized into groups for team games by adults. As long as competition does not become overemphasized, children can learn how to succeed by both competing and cooperating. Success, in turn, helps children enhance their self-esteem (Goldberg & Deutsch, 1977, p. 340).

The strength and value of the peer group is highlighted in societies in which the peer group has been especially organized as part of the socializing process. In the Israeli Kibbutz and day-care centers of Communist China, many social activities are organized around peer groups rather than individual children or family groups. Studies of such groups strongly suggest they have a beneficial effect in promoting social development (Hartup, 1976).

Games and Humor

Part of children's social world is playing games and sharing jokes and funny stories. It is clear that a relationship exists between intellectual development and children's exploratory play, the nature and function of the games they get involved in, and their expression of humor. This section takes a brief look at the interrelativity of social and intellectual development as it is expressed by games and *children's humor* during the middle years.

Weisler and McCall (1976) have pointed out that the novelty, discrepancy, and complexity factors, which are important influences on infants' attention and exploration, actually continue to affect the playful exploration and game playing of middle childhood. Children's reactions to new objects and events seem to be based on how moderately new, discrepant, or complex these are compared to past experiences. As children grow older their play changes to include increasingly complex materials and situations that require more abstract representation (1976). Fantasy and imagination also have a more important role in play as children mature, and they appear to influence intellectual development (Singer, 1973), or they are an outcome of changes in thinking and reasoning.

Children enjoy ritual-type games that may include chants, for example, "Ring-around-a-rosy, a pocket full of posies, a-tishoo, a-tishoo, we all fall down"—with the ending accompanied by shrieks and laughter. That particular little ritual has been handed down from the days of the Black Death. The posy of roses was to perfume the smell in the air from decomposing bodies. So many people were dying that it became impossible to move them all quickly away for burial. Sneezing was a first sign that a person might have the plague. After the sneezing came the terrible illness and, at last, the "falling down of the dead." Children of the Middle Ages realized the significance of the chant. In the process of its being passed down by tradition, the game has lost its original meaning. But children often do play games that refer to cruelty, torture, and death. In fantasy play one can dare to think of such horrors and alleviate the horror with humor.

There are many other chants and rhymes that children constantly repeat and find clever or funny. The humor of some of these ditties is often not shared by adults!

Mrs. White had a fright.
In the middle of the night.
She saw a ghost eating toast.
Halfway up a lamp post.

Children love nonsense verse.

One fine day in the middle of the night.
Two dead men got up to fight,
Back to back they faced each other,
Drew their swords and shot each other.

They also tell interminable jokes to roars of laughter. You have to be a special kind of adult to react accordingly.

When is a door not a door?
When it's a-jar.

What did the earwig say when it fell off the roof?
Earwego!

What is yellow and dangerous?
Shark-infested custard.

Why did the chicken cross the road?
(Well, your answer is as good as mine!)

It has been suggested by Shultz (1974) that *incongruity* between the supposed or imagined and the real world often plays a part in humorous expression. In the nonsense riddle, "When is a door not a door? When it's a(jar)," the obvious incongruity is in the final word and the implied difference between a door's being *a jar* and being *ajar*. The same type of incongruity is obvious in the riddle, "Why did the cookie cry? Because its mother had been a wafer so long." Shultz found that children aged between 6 and 12 years differed in their responses to such riddles. The older children were better able to detect the incongruity in the riddles and appreciate the humor in them, which suggests that the development of humor is related to intellectual development. Other researchers have arrived at the same conclusion (McGhee, 1974, 1976; Schultz & Horibe, 1974; Schultz, 1976; Sutton-Smith, 1976; Whitt & Prentice, 1977). Both games and humor involve fantasy, representation, rules, values, and social communication. They are also rich sources for social learning during this period of development.

Development of Sex Roles

As children acquire the subtleties of social behavior with family members, teachers, and friends, an important aspect of the development of social behavior is the growing awareness of *sex-role identity.* It is apparent that during infancy children are becoming aware of gender differences through early identification with parents. During the preschool years further learning of sex roles occurs through observing differences in the way adults and other children dress, in their hairstyles and in physical attributes. Adults also continue to provide models of particular sex-role behavior.

Parents assign a sex role to their infants and reinforce sex-role behavior by providing different types of clothes and toys to boys and girls (Rheingold & Cook, 1975). Apart from parent social pressure, children's understanding of sex identity and sex-role behavior is developed according to the degree a child can discriminate between parents as male and female models (Biller & Borstelmann, 1967). Boys develop sex-role preferences much earlier and with more consistency than girls. **Sex-role orientation,** the extent to which children view themselves as either male or female, is acquired, at least in part, by modeling the parent's behavior (Maccoby & Jacklin, 1974; Margolin & Patterson, 1975) and, for some children, other significant adults' behavior. But, whereas both boys and girls imitate the behavior of the dominant parent (Hetherington, 1967), this need not necessarily be the same-sex parent. This does not mean that a boy, strongly influenced by his mother, will assume female sex-role behavior, only that certain characteristics of the mother's personality will be imitated and incorporated into a more general sexual behavior, which will reflect the child's sex-role preference. **Sex-role preference** is the child's desire to behave in ways sexually appropriate to one sex or the other. Boys emulate the behavior of men, while girls emulate

To a certain extent, children acquire a view of themselves as either boy or girl by modeling the behavior of parents. (Photos by Jean-Claude Lejeune)

the behavior of women. Sex-role preference is derived from such cultural influences as peers, media models, and teachers (Cohen, 1976; Sutton-Smith & Rosenberg, 1970; Steinglanz & Serkin, 1974). During the middle years, and in later life, such distinctions help explain variation in sex-role orientation and preference (Cohen, 1976). For example, a boy may notice that his father often looks after the baby—bathing, diapering, and feeding. Such behaviors are likely to be adopted. The same boy may also be involved in peer-group activities that stress highly competitive, rough-and-tumble boyish behavior. Such contrasting sex-role behavior can obviously occur just as easily for girls. For example, many girls now play soccer, once considered a male-only sport. Depending on the strength of modeling and reinforcement, different behaviors may be adopted in different situations.

Sex Stereotyping

Sometimes sources of information used by children provide examples of sex stereotypes, although much has been done to eliminate the "male truckdriver" and "female nurse" images. However, as Maccoby (1974) has remarked, even when care is taken to exclude such information from children's learning, enough cues are available to make early **sex stereotyping** possible. In a study by Williams, Bennet, and Best (1975), children from kindergarten through second grade were asked to identify the sexual characteristics of characters in picture stories. As the age of both boys and girls increased, they tended to respond more in terms of adult sex stereotypes. Children described male characters increasingly in such terms as aggressive, strong, brave. They also described female characteristics as gentle, kind, or emotional. Avoidance of sex stereotypes and sex stereotyping is virtually impossible. However, as mentioned above, when young children are able to observe male and female adult models demonstrating, to some extent, what has been traditionally opposite-sex behavior, we can expect a more flexible attitude toward sex-role behaviors as children grow older.

Constancy of Sexual Identity

Do children believe that their individual sexual identity is unchangeable? Apparently so. Kohlberg has suggested that children continue to believe that a person retains the same sex identity in spite of changes in hairstyle or clothing (1966). According to Kohlberg, when children begin to understand the constancy of sex, there is a strong likelihood they will pay more attention to same-sex persons' attitudes and values, and more likely imitate them.

Discipline and Social Norms

Discipline has to do with setting and maintaining rules and regulations to guide children's social behavior. Since the culture sets rules and regulations, children learn them from the culture; children also learn how the rules and regulations are related to social and moral behavior. *Social norms* are the culture's conventional attitudes, values, and standards of behavior. Parents and teachers primarily transmit them. During the middle years this transmission takes place in one significant way—through discipline.

Parental Discipline

As we mentioned earlier, parents who use forceful methods to obtain obedience (authoritarian) or who are manipulative (permissive) usually have children lacking in social competence. Inculcating autonomy (self-control) in children appears to be best achieved by authoritative-oriented controls, which are reasonable limits on behavior. Parents who adopt this approach use reasoning, overt power, and reinforcement to achieve control over their children's behavior (Baumrind, 1966, p. 891).

Other researchers have reached a similar conclusion, and they have referred to two major styles of achieving parental discipline, love-oriented and power-assertive techniques (Becker, 1964). Martin (1975) describes a *love-oriented approach* as having both a cognitive and an emotional component. Parents who use this approach not only set reasonable rules for behavior but also teach these rules to their children. In doing so they invariably indicate the reasons for the rules and explain what might happen if the rules are broken. Children also learn that, if they break a rule, the parents' love will be withdrawn or parents will feel hurt at the undesirable behavior. It has been shown that a love-oriented approach leads to children's acquiring self-control.

In this author's family there are four boys who all like to play soccer. We have a number of soccer balls, which we store in the basement when they are not in use. During the winter months there is a great temptation to get a ball out and indulge in a little soccer training. We have explained to the boys that we do not like soccer balls being kicked in the house. Soccer balls should be used outside in the yard (statement of rule). If they are kicked around in the house, they can easily cause damage (reason for rule). We have also indicated that, if such behavior occurs again, they will lose certain privileges (last portion of cognitive component). Once or twice the younger boys have broken the rule. Almost inevitably there has been some damage. We have indicated, very emotionally, that we are not at all pleased and that repairs have cost money that we wanted to put to different use (affective component). The boys have helped with the repairs, and this author cannot remember the last time they gave into the temptation to organize indoor soccer.

The parent who uses a *power-assertive approach* yells and shouts, uses verbal threats, and physical punishment. It is unusual to find such a parent backing up a rule with an explanation other than "Because I said so." Children who have become used to power-assertive methods for controlling their behavior remain dependent upon an external locus of control. They respond to punishment sanctions, and they may be aggressive, which can be attributed to modeling and reinforcement of such behavior provided by their parents (Bandura & McDonald, 1963; Bandura, Ross & Ross, 1963; Becker, 1964). On the other hand, inconsistent and harsh discipline may result in a child's becoming fearful and withdrawn.

School Discipline

Teachers are just as concerned about discipline as are parents. Maintaining discipline in the classroom has been a prevalent problem over the years. An age-old method for enforcing discipline is corporal punishment. The slogan "spare the rod and spoil the child" stems from colonial days. A schoolhouse in Sunderland, Massachusetts, built in 1793, had a "whipping post" and many classrooms of the 1800s had "paddling devices" (Manning, 1959).

How much is corporal punishment used today? There are few published reports about corporal punishment. But it may come as some surprise to read the following statistics from three areas in the United States as reported by Maurer (1978).

1. There were 46,022 reported cases of corporal punishment in California schools for the 1972–73 school year. Only 5 percent of these were in high schools (Riles, 1974).

2. The Dallas school system reported 24,305 "paddlings" during 1971–72. At that time, there were 330,000 children in schools. On average, there were 2000 incidents of "paddling" every month.

3. During the first 45 days of the 1975–76 school year in Miami, Florida, 2,892 school "paddlings" were reported.

Maurer (1978) comments that, at least in the case of children from lower-class homes, there is a great deal of corporal punishment throughout the elementary school grades. Welsh (1974, 1976) has concluded from the results of a number of studies that severe corporal punishment can seriously influence the development of delinquency. In his "belt theory of juvenile delinquency" he asserts that children can become habituated to destructive and aggressive behavior by the continuing use of physical punishment. Other studies have indicated that corporal punishment in schools is associated with vandalism.

What is the relevance of discipline for the classroom? "It should be as impersonal and task oriented as possible" (Ausubel, Novak, & Hanesian, 1978, p. 508). Children should be punished when their behavior interferes with learning in the classroom. When children are punished because the teacher takes some misdemeanor personally, they usually misinterpret the reasons for the punishment and judge the teacher to be unfair (Kounin, Gump, & Ryan, 1961).

The teacher with the most effective classroom control is very like the "authoritative" parent (Kounin, 1970). However, we must remember that teachers receive groups of children into their classrooms, with varieties of already partially developed social behaviors and moral standards. Maladjusted and behaviorally disturbed children present special disciplinary problems. It is not always easy for the teacher to find a solution, or effect a "cure," and the teacher's norms for desirable behavior may be in conflict with those in some of the children's homes.

Inset 11.3
Popularly Accepted
Beliefs and
Some Alternatives
for Corporal
Punishment

Clarizio (1975) explores four of the most common myths about corporal punishment in the schools.

Myth 1: "Physical punishment is a 'tried and true' method.
It is good for students. It helps them develop a sense of personal responsibility, learn self-discipline, and develop moral character." Bongiovanni (1977) reviewed the literature on corporal punishment and concluded that it cannot be claimed to be a tried and true method in the school setting. Indeed, it most often has the opposite effect on children's behavior than what is desired. Instead of orderliness, cooperation, and commitment to learning, it breeds aggression, coerciveness, and delinquency.

Clarizio also points out that there is a great deal of evidence to support the suggestion by Feshbach and Feshbach (1973) that there is a significant relationship between the amount and severity of physical punishment that parents use and various forms of childhood psychopathology, particularly delinquency and acting out behavior. Some studies (Buttons, 1973; Welsh, 1974) have indicated a nearly perfect correlation between the amount and severity of physical punishment suffered by children between the ages of 2 and 12 and the amount and severity of adolescent antisocial aggressiveness.

Myth 2: "Occasional paddling contributes substantially to the child's socialization."
Clarizio stresses that, to be effective, punishment (unless traumatic) must be applied immediately and consistently. Yet in the school setting behavior that one wishes to eliminate can hardly be monitored closely enough to be punished each time it occurs. Therefore, the so-called "judicious" and infrequent use of corporal punishment results in a situation in which the undesired behavior is intermittently reinforced. Such schedules of reinforcement result in the continuation of the behavior. Thus, Clarizio concludes that instead of weakening the undesirable response, occasional paddling may actually strengthen the behavior that is intermittently reinforced.

Myth 3: "Corporal punishment is the only recourse in maintaining order."
Some parents and teachers apparently believe that corporal punishment is necessary in controlling children's behavior. Clarizio (1975), however, points out that in school systems that prohibit the use of corporal punishment both teacher and student survive nicely without it. Consider New Jersey and Massachusetts, which have banned corporal punishment for many years. Effective alternatives do exist and are already in use in those two states and also in many school districts throughout the nation. Some alternatives to corporal punishment are

1. Provide clear orientation to pupils and parents about school programs, school codes of conduct and the reason for having them, grading systems, special services, and extracurricular activities.

2. Ensure and reward regular school attendance.

3. Provide in-service training for teachers in appropriate classroom management techniques such as setting reasonable standards of classroom behavior and academic achievement and learning how to handle hostility in a nonaggressive fashion.

4. Try to make the curricula as relevant as possible to pupils. Academic success and disciplinary problems seldom go together.

5. School rules should be reasonable, clear, and concise. School rules should be designed to assure an atmosphere of learning. They should not reflect personal or arbitrary preferences of school authorities.

Myth 4: "Those involved with schools favor the use of corporal punishment."
Citing a study by Patterson (1974), Clarizio documents that no more than 55 to 65 percent of school officials see corporal punishment as an effective technique and favor its use. Only one third of the parents reported that they view physical punishment as an effective way to make students behave in school. Students, especially at the high school level, tended to agree with that opinion. According to Clarizio:

The small segment of students who do accept or favor corporal punishment as a means of correcting behavior may do so for a number of reasons, none of which is healthy. Some may simply accept it as a desirable way to handle conflict situations. Others may see it as an easy way out of trouble in that it does not take much of their time nor does it require them to change their behavior. Those parents who endorse the use of physical punishment in schools often use this type of discipline in the home; but it is unsuccessful, as it only produces children who misbehave in school (1975).

According to David Gil (1971), abolishing corporal punishment in schools would begin lessening the incidence of child-beating elsewhere. Research on the democratic classroom (Hyman, 1964) has demonstrated that teachers using clearly defined techniques help children to internalize controls in the classroom setting. By sharing in goal setting and accepting freedom with responsibility, the need for corporal punishment is eliminated.

There are many alternatives to corporal punishment. It is true that techniques must be matched with teachers, students, and situations. However, the variety of alternatives available is probably never exhausted by most users of corporal punishment either because of their lack of knowledge or because of beliefs based on the mythology described by Clarizio.

Source: Adapted from Hyman, I. A., McDowell, E., & Raines, B. "Corporal Punishment and Alternatives in the Schools: An Overview of Theoretical and Practical Issues." In *Inequality in Education: Center for Law and Education*, 1978, *23*, 14-19.

Excessively punishing children can only lead to grave disturbances in their development. There is strong evidence to show that the amount and severity of aggressiveness that adolescents display is closely related to the amount and severity of physical punishment they experienced between 2 and 12 years of age (Welsh, 1974). Parents and teachers should strive to foster in children positive social behavior. When we find children in homes and schools who show little aggression—though perhaps much determination—and who have the ability to emphathize with others and show concern for people's well-being, they are likely to have parents and teachers who enforce rules and regulations with a minimum amount of punishment.

Summary

In Freud's view the middle years are a period of repression of sexual and aggressive behavior and a period of calm in psychosexual development. The child's energies are now directed toward work, play, and establishing relationships with peers.

Erikson views this period as a time of active and inquisitive exploration beyond the home. The child is becoming independent of the family, yet still needs parental support to foster a sense of industry. A lack of confidence in stepping out into the world results in a sense of inferiority.

According to Kohlberg, between the ages of 6 and 12 the child's moral reasoning develops from an egocentric concern with personal needs through a phase when it is important to appear to be a "good person" to an understanding of the need for social order for the good of people in general. Changes in moral reasoning parallel changes in intellectual development.

The child develops a self-image composed of a self-concept and self-esteem. The self-concept is an understanding and appreciation of "how I look, how I feel, and how I act." The other aspect of self-image is self-esteem, an evaluation of one's worth based on one's self-concept. The development of children's self-concept and self-esteem is influenced by the way their parents treat them. When parents establish reasonable rules regarding social behavior and encourage and reward their children's achievement, the result is usually a good self-image. Children with a good self-image also have a high level of confidence in their own abilities. Although they acknowledge some dependency on parents, they also develop a strong sense of independency, a belief that they are in control of their own lives. This aspect of the self-concept is referred to as locus of control.

The influence of the family on the development of the child's self-image is maintained with little change throughout the middle years. Although children at this time are striving for independence, they also continue to rely on the family for support. Besides offering help and advice, parents should also indicate their support for children's venturing toward autonomy.

Divorce can have serious negative effects on children's mental and social development, and children between the ages of 6 and 8 are thought to be the most vulnerable. In most cases following divorce, children remain in the mother's care. The father's absence may result in problems for the children, both boys and girls, in establishing sex-role identities, in problems for the family in the loss of an important source of discipline, and in an inevitable loss of income. The mother is likely to feel stress from the loss of emotional support and the increased responsibility in caring for the children. Immediately following divorce, many mothers become depressed and often have problems relating to their children. However, single-parent families can adjust to the demands placed on them by divorce, especially when they receive support in resolving problems and avoid becoming isolated.

The socializing influence of the school becomes more marked during these years. The teacher can become the next most important adult in a child's life after the parents, providing a model for both social and learning behavior. Teachers should ensure that children not only acquire useful information and thinking skills but also an ability to monitor thinking—to think about thinking, which is useful both in school and real-life situations in a broader environment.

Peer-group relations during the middle years also have a strong influence on social development. In playing together in peer groups (almost invariably same-sex) children learn social rules, learn to compete and cooperate, adapt their behavior, and test out their independence from the family. Social behaviors learned in this way are carried into adult life.

Children enjoy playing ritual-type games and sharing jokes and humorous stories. An important aspect of children's humor is the development of an understanding of *incongruity* between the real and the imagined. It also appears that the development of humor is related to cognitive development.

Sex-role orientation is the extent to which children view themselves as either male or female and is derived by imitating parents and other significant adults. The outcome of modeling sex-role behavior on adults is a sex-role preference by boys to behave like men and girls to behave like women. As they grow older, children's sex-role preference can become adapted to various social situations and the influence of peers, media models, and teachers. Sex-stereotyped behavior can hardly be avoided since a child's culture provides so many cues. However, when children are provided the opportunity to observe male and female adults adopting traditionally opposite sex-role behavior, this can have the effect of making their sex-role behavior more flexible.

Discipline, the setting and maintaining of rules and regulations for social behavior, is important for children's social development. Parents who adopt an authoritative style of parenting, setting reasonable limits on children's behavior and avoiding corporal punishment, appear to achieve the most positive control over their children's behavior and, at the same time, inculcate self-control in their children.

Teachers also need to establish discipline in the classroom. The best type of classroom discipline seems to be impersonal and task oriented. The teacher with the most effective classroom control is very like the authoritative parent.

Questions for Review

1. Compare the main characteristics of the latency period of psychosexual development to the stage of industry versus inferiority during psychosocial development.

2. According to Piaget, how do children between the ages of 6 and 12 years develop an understanding of the rules that govern social behavior?

3. Describe the main features of Kohlberg's levels of preconventional and conventional moral development.

4. What are the effects on children's development of father's and mother's absence following divorce?

5. What problems face single parents, and what is being done to help them?

6. What effects does the elementary school have on children's social development?

7. To what extent does the peer group affect social learning in children during the middle years? How does the influence of the peer group differ from that of the family?

8. In what ways are children's games and humor expected to affect development during the middle years?

9. How does the development of sex-role orientation differ from that of sex-role preference?

10. What are the relationships between the development of a self-concept and achievement?

11. Certain kinds of discipline appear to be important for normal development. In what ways can parents and teachers use discipline most effectively to influence children's social behavior and encourage children to become self-disciplined?

12. Try to locate two single parents—preferably a mother and a father. If they are willing, inquire of them what they found to be the most difficult problems they faced on becoming single parents. Find out if they felt in need of help as a single parent; whether they sought help; if they did seek assistance, whether they received help, of what kind and from where; and how they have adapted to the role of being a single parent.

Suggestions for Further Reading

Asher, S., & Mordechai, J., eds. *The development of children's friendships.* New York: Cambridge University Press, 1981. Provides wide-ranging reports of research on children's peer relationships and the impact of these relationships on their development.

Bernstein, A. C. *The flight of the stork.* New York: Dell, 1980. Based on interviews with over 100 children aged between 3 and 12 years, the author describes what children want to know about sex and indicates stages of development in their interest of this subject.

Bossert, S. T. *Tasks and social relationships in the classroom.* New York: Cambridge University Press, 1979. Discusses the relationship between what the teacher does in the classroom and children's social development.

Erikson, E. H. *Childhood and society,* 2nd ed. New York: W.W. Norton, 1963. This book not only provides us with an interesting account of Erikson's view on psychosocial development but also delightful vignettes on such topics as anxiety in young children, apathy in American Indians, and the detection of conflict during social development through psychoanalytic methods.

Light, P. *The development of social sensitivity.* New York: Cambridge University Press, 1979. Describes the results from a series of experiments to examine individual differences in children's social behavior and factors that might explain these such as family relationships.

Maccoby, E. E., & Jacklin, C. N. *The psychology of sex differences,* Vol. 1. Stanford, CA: Stanford University Press, 1978. Provides a comprehensive review of research on the factors affecting the development of sex differences in children's behavior.

Mussen, P., & Eisenberg-Berg, N. *Roots of caring, sharing, and helping.* San Francisco: W.H. Freeman, 1977. An interesting and easy to read description and discussion of research on prosocial behavior.

Piaget, J. *The moral judgment of the child.* New York: The Free Press, 1965. Piaget's description of moral development from childhood to adulthood.

Richards, M. P. M., ed. *The integration of a child into a social world.* New York: Cambridge University Press, 1974. Provides a useful overview of the social development of the child.

Adolescence

Physical and Intellectual Development

12

It is one of those cases where the art of the reasoner should be used rather for the sifting of details than for the acquiring of fresh evidence. The tragedy has been so uncommon, so complete, and of such personal importance to so many people that we are suffering from a plethora of surmise, conjecture, and hypothesis. The difficulty is to detach the framework of fact—of absolute undeniable fact—from the embellishments of theorists and reporters. Then having established ourselves upon this sound basis, it is our duty to see what inferences may be drawn and what are the special points upon which the whole mystery turns.

"Is there any point to which you would wish to draw my attention?"

"To the curious incident of the dog in the night-time."

"The dog did nothing in the night-time."

"That was the curious incident," remarked Sherlock Holmes.

From "The Silver Blaze" by Sir Arthur Conan Doyle. Published with the permission of the copyright owner of the Sir Arthur Conan Doyle literary estate.

Adolescence spans the years of transition from childhood to adulthood. How is the child initiated into adolescence? How does the child know that childhood is over? There are a number of markers, but the most obvious one is physical change. After the preschool and middle years of slow steady growth, early adolescence is a period of rapid physical growth and sexual development. In technological societies the onset of adolescence is also associated with graduation from the elementary school. To the child, entering high school is synonymous with becoming an adolescent. Because of cultural expectations, parents' and teachers' attitudes toward the child change at this time. The child is expected to be an adolescent. Most children welcome the initiation. As novices they may feel some concern about their change in status, but they readily cast off the old skin of childhood.

In industrial societies adolescence is a prolonged period of time taken up primarily by preparation for an occupation. During the latter part of the nineteenth century and the early years of the twentieth century, working-class children left school in their early teens. They were expected to get jobs and help support the family. Working in the world of adults, they tended to model their adult counterparts. Their youthful vigor and boisterous ways distinguished them. But they were, nevertheless, looked upon as young adults.

In nonindustrial and primitive societies, adolescence is like a swift spring. Initiation into the tribe, marriage, and acceptance of adult responsibilities occur early in the teenage years. Mountain Wolf Woman, a Winnebago Indian, describes her marriage:

They had let me go to school and now they made me quit. It was then that they told me I was going to be married. I cried but it did not do any good. . . . They had already arranged it (Lurie, 1966).

In these societies marriage and other initiation rites confirm adulthood.

In this chapter we describe physical and intellectual development during the adolescent years. Physical changes are the most similar ones across all cultures for adolescents. Cultural differences, however, do appear to affect intellectual development to some degree and, in quite significant ways, social development at this time.

Physical Development

Before the onset of adolescence the pituitary gland at the base of the brain begins to secrete hormones that affect adrenal glands beside the kidneys and the male testes and female ovaries. In their turn, these glands produce hormones. Distributed by the bloodstream, these hormones stimulate the growth of axillary hair (under the arms), pubic hair, and the development of the reproductive

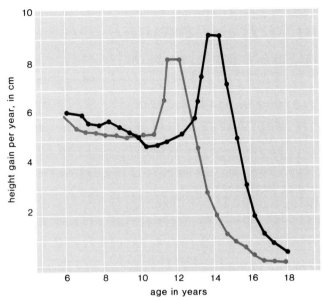

Figure 12.1 Average increase in height for boys and girls showing the adolescent growth spurt. The growth spurt occurs earlier for girls than for boys, but after it is over, boys are taller than girls by an average of about 8 percent. (Source: Tanner, J. M. *Growth at Adolescence*. Blackwell Scientific Publications, 1962.)

organs. It takes from two to four years for the adolescent to reach sexual maturity—a period referred to as *puberty* (from the Latin, *puber,* grownup; adult). During this period other physical changes occur and the body takes on a more adult form.

Physical Changes

Following the middle years of childhood, when physical growth is almost at a standstill, in the period before puberty the child experiences a sudden **growth spurt.** On the average, boys grow 8 inches between the ages of 12 and 15 years. Girls grow an average of about 4 inches between the ages of 11 and 14 years. Rates and timing of growth spurts are different for girls than for boys. The sudden increase in growth begins at about 10 years for girls, almost two years before its onset for boys. Girls of 11 years may be taller than many boys of the same age (see Figure 12.1). Can you remember the age at which you appeared to be all hands and feet, when you seemed to lack coordination, when in spite of getting taller and stronger looking you actually felt less strong and tired more quickly at physical activities? These experiences are more acute for some adolescents than for others. The rapid physical changes may, in fact, be the source of embarrassment for a while. The growth spurt in early adolescence affects the skeletal and muscular dimensions of the body also.

During the period of fast growth in height boys increase their weight by an average of 12 pounds, and girls by about 10 pounds. Part of this weight gain can be attributed to an increase in fat thickness, especially on the hips and thighs. As height increases, the shoulders and hips widen. Boys' shoulders widen faster than their hips, and the fat on their hips and legs decreases. Girls broaden more in the hips and shoulders, and the fat layer on their hips remains about the same.

The growth spurt does not affect all growing parts of the body in the same way. The peaks of growth in height and hand size, for instance, occur at about age 13 and precede those for weight and size of the head, which occur about a year later (Tanner, 1964; 1971). These differences in growth rates tend to follow a particular sequence.

As a mother knows, first the boy's trouser legs get too short. However, if she can persuade her son to put up with this *odd* look, she knows the trousers will last at least another few months before hip growth makes them too tight. Her son can then complain that bursting seams do warrant a new pair of trousers or jeans. A jacket gets too short with the peak in trunk growth, about a year after the peak in leg growth. And the jacket gets too tight soon after it gets too short since muscle growth and widening of the shoulders follows the peak in growth of the trunk. A similar sequence of growth occurs for girls, though it is less substantial (Smart & Smart, 1973, pp. 11–13).

The speed and duration of the growth spurt are influenced by heredity and nutrition, which account for individual differences in growth. Early maturing individuals of both sexes tend to be shorter than late maturers, and rate of maturation is the main factor accounting for differences in height (Tanner, 1971). Because this rapid growth makes considerable demands on the body for extra protein, calcium, iron, and other nutrients (Lambert et al., 1972), young adolescents are usually voracious eaters.

Sexual Change

Pubescence is a period of about two years during which physical changes occur that lead to puberty. There is a normal sequence of development (see Figure 12.2). The period of rapid growth comes just before **menarche,** the first occurrence of menstruation, for girls and prior to a voice change and the appearance of axillary and facial hair for boys. These changes are brought about by the secretion of hormones by the gonads. Male testes produce a hormone called **androgen,** and female ovaries produce **estrogen.**

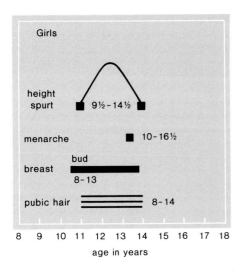

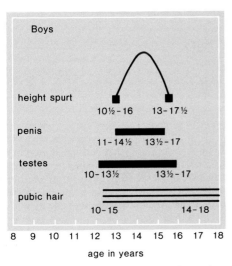

Figure 12.2 Sequence of growth of certain primary and secondary sexual characteristics in girls and boys during adolescence. The adolescent spurt in the growth of the skeleton and muscles is closely related to the rapid development of the reproductive system. (Source: Tanner, J. M. *Growth at Adolescence*. Blackwell Scientific Publications, 1962.)

The advent of puberty, the capacity to reproduce, is usually marked by the first menarche in girls, and it is also linked to the size of the breast bud (Tanner, 1970). However, there is usually a period of a year or longer following menarche during which many girls remain sterile. Puberty in boys is marked by a growth in the testes and size of the penis and in the production of semen (Tanner, 1970).

As is the case of the growth spurt, there are wide differences in the age at which puberty is reached. In Western countries about 50 percent of girls reach puberty by age 13 and the same percent of boys by age 15. In both sexes an equal proportion are either early or late maturers. In certain African tribes, such as the Bantu of South Africa and tribes in Rwanda, the average age at menarche ranges from 15 to 17 years (Hiernaux, 1968).

For girls, the onset of puberty can lead to feelings of fear or elation associated with menstruation.

When I was in the third grade I heard some other girls talking about menstruation and had no idea what they were talking about. . . . I asked my mother. She gave me a brief description, but I felt it was very incomplete; in turn, I felt some fear because I really didn't understand what was going to happen to me and why. . . . Would I really change inside? Would my feelings and actions be strange to me? Would it mean I was an adult? Did it really mean I could have a baby?

The big question was "When will I start?" Most of my classmates had already reached puberty by the eighth grade, but so far I had not. . . . I really wondered whether I wanted to grow up. . . . Childhood seemed like a good place to stay. . . . But growing up was appealing, too (Kaluger & Kaluger, 1976, p. 112).

And, from the diary of Anne Frank:

I think what is happening to me is so wonderful, and not only what can be seen on my body, but all that is taking place inside. . . . Each time I have a period—and that has only been three times—I have the feeling that in spite of all the pain, unpleasantness, and nastiness, I have a sweet secret. . . . Sis Heyster also writes that girls of this age don't feel quite certain of themselves, and discover that they themselves are individuals with ideas, thoughts, and habits (Frank, 1952, pp. 115–116).

It should be kept in mind that sexual development is not merely a physical expression. Sexuality is more completely a part of one's personality, for not only physical but also social, emotional, and cultural forces influence sexuality in important ways (Kirkendall & Rubin, 1979).

The male and female reproductive organs grow rapidly during the first two years of puberty. However, they do not fully mature until young adulthood at about age 20. Secondary sex characteristics are breasts, body hair, and a change in voice. Enlargement of the breasts occurs for both boys and girls in a sequence of stages. In the first stage there is an enlargement of the *breast bud* and surrounding *aureola*. Then the small mound of papilla and breast develop, and finally the breasts enlarge to the mature stage. Growth of the breast bud and pubic hair occur within about a year of each other.

During early adolescence, especially at the onset of puberty, teenagers develop physically at different rates. Some teenage boys, for example, are beginning to look like young adults while others of the same age retain the looks of young boys. (Photo by Paul Conklin)

The word *pubescence* comes from the Latin word that means to grow hairy. In males, soon after the testes and penis begin to enlarge, the first pubic hair appears. At first it is sparse, straight, and downy. Within a year or so it becomes darker in color, coarser in texture, and curly. Axillary hair begins to appear when pubic hair has almost grown in. Finally, facial hair appears. Some boys are very proud of being able to grow a beard and a mustache (though usually in their late teens). Girls also grow facial hair. It is more noticeable for some (especially those with dark hair) than for others, and it can be embarrassing. Facial hair is quite normal, however.

A change in voice begins during pubescence and continues through puberty. It is caused by a growth spurt of the larynx. The change is more noticeable for boys. The voice drops in tone as the vocal cords lengthen. Changes in the voice continue into late adolescence.

Another physical change that occurs during puberty is an enlargement of the *apocrine sweat glands* in the axillary and genital regions, which now secrete sweat with a strong odor. An increase in the activity of the sebaceous glands in the skin makes the skin oilier. The skin pores enlarge, and the skin becomes thicker and coarser, especially in boys. These changes frequently result in acne, which can be bothersome to both sexes.

Differing Rates of Maturation

Following the adolescent growth spurt, individual differences in physical development become more noticeable. In the fourth grade children differ in height by only a few inches. But by eighth grade teenagers can differ in height by more than a foot. There will be teenage males of the same age, some looking like young men and others like young boys. Fourteen-year-old girls can have the figures of young women or can retain the appearance of early puberty.

Personality seems to be influenced by rate of maturation. In one study of 17-year-old males (Weatherley, 1964), early maturers were more self-confident, independent, and socially adept than late maturers. The latter often had negative feelings about themselves. The same boys were studied in adulthood (Jones, 1965). The early maturers were found to be poised, responsible, and high achievers. The late maturers were exploratory, insightful, independent, and impulsive; many of the negative aspects of their earlier personality had apparently disappeared. However, it does seem that some relationships between maturity patterns of growth and personality development continue into adulthood.

For more than a century records have shown that there is an increasing tendency for children to begin the adolescent growth spurt earlier and to achieve a more advanced physical development than previous generations. These trends are stronger in the more prosperous parts of the world (Tanner, 1968).

Records of the onset of menarche from different countries show that puberty is occurring earlier (see Figure 12.3). In the United States the average age for the onset of menstruation is about 12½ years. For the mothers of these children it occurred at about 14½ years (Damon et al., 1969), and a century ago the average age was 17 (Maddock, 1973).

Boys, also, are now reaching sexual and physical maturity far sooner than used to be the case (Sullivan, 1971). Boys in the United States, for example, can now be expected on the average to grow 1 inch taller and be 10 pounds heavier than their father. For girls compared to their mothers, the differences will be 1 inch and about 2 to 3 pounds (Muuss, 1970). At the turn of the twentieth century European and American men reached full height at about age 26. In these countries adolescents are now full grown by the time they are 18 or 19 (Tanner, 1968). Similar trends toward ealier maturity have been noted in other countries such as Japan, China, New Zealand, Italy, Poland, and Britain (Muuss, 1970).

What are the likely causes for these trends? A comparison between the increasingly earlier onset of physical growth and age of maturity, and improving standards of living, shows that they keep pace with each other. Children today, at least in our Western societies, are better fed and healthier than in the past. George Orwell described conditions in England just over 40 years ago.

The basis of their diet [families in the industrial north of England] is white bread and margarine, corned beef, sugared tea, and potatoes—an appalling diet. Would it not be better if they spent more money on wholesome things like oranges and wholemeal bread? . . . The peculiar evil is this, that the less money you have, the less inclined you feel to spend it on wholesome food. . . . The results of all this [poor diet] are visible in a physical degeneracy. The physical average in the industrial towns is terribly low . . . you have a feeling of walking among a population of troglodytes. The miners are splendid men, but they are usually small, and the mere fact that their muscles are toughened by constant work does not mean that their children start life with a better physique (1976, pp. 85–87).

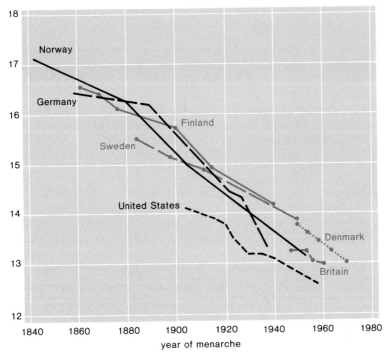

Figure 12.3 Secular trend in the average age of menarche. There has been a trend for the age at menarche (first menstrual period) to occur earlier in the United States, Britain, and Europe. On the average, girls now begin menstruation between 2.5 and 3.3 years earlier than girls did a century ago. (Source: Tanner, J. M. *Growth at Adolescence.* Blackwell Scientific Publications, 1962.)

Socioeconomic conditions can affect the **secular trend.** But other factors are also likely to play a part. It has been suggested that increasing ease of travel has had some influence on these changes. Limitations on travel resulted in much intermarriage among local families. Transmission of genetic traits thus became limited. In the nineteenth century the invention of the bicycle and steam locomotive promoted travel. Young men and women moved out of their home villages and towns, met and married mates from distant regions, and so broadened the range of genetic heritage. Tallness is a dominant trait, and travel made it more likely that this trait would reach more people. The results of this wider sharing of genetic traits is said to be a **hybrid vigor** (Tanner, 1971). It is generally accepted that these two factors, standard of living and gentic heritage, explain best the trends in physical development. Orwell commented on this possibility also:

What a set they looked! Puny limbs, sickly faces, under the weeping London sky! Hardly a well built man or a decent looking woman. . . . If the English physique has declined, this is no doubt due to the fact that the Great War carefully selected the million best men in England and slaughtered them before they had time to breed. But the process must have begun earlier than that, and it must be due ultimately to unhealthy ways of living (1976, p. 88).

We might wonder to what extent the secular trend might continue. Records suggest that there has been a leveling off in recent years, especially with respect to the change in onset of menarche.

Sexual Behavior

The child reaches puberty in adolescence, but full sexual maturity comes later. Although adolescents are capable of reproduction and sexual activity, many cultures ask them to delay these activities, while in other cultures *sexual behavior* is more freely allowed. However, Sorensen (1973), reporting on the results of a national sampling of American youth aged between 13 and 19, states that 37 percent of youth aged 13 to 15 and 64 percent of those aged 16 to 19 had experienced sexual intercourse. Many families uphold traditional social and religious attitudes toward sexual activity, linking it with marriage. There are other reasons why parents may forbid premarital sex. Many families forbid adolescent sexual intercourse for fear of an early, unwanted pregnancy. Ignorance about and aversion to the use of birth control methods are related reasons. The possible physical hardships of an unwanted pregnancy for a young girl, the fears that "shotgun marriages" are not likely to work out, and the economic, educational, and social problems of a forced early marriage are all reasons given for avoiding adolescent sexual relationships.

Standards for teenage sexual behavior differ according to culture. For example, in countries such as Ireland and Spain, where strong Catholic traditions opposed premarital sexual activities of any kind, courting couples were accompanied wherever they went by a "guardian." A frequently quoted example of non-Western cultural attitudes toward adolescent sexual behavior is Margaret Mead's description of Samoan life. In documenting her description, she observed that adolescent Samoans were permitted to engage in sex play.

Adolescence represented no period of crisis or stress but was instead an orderly development of a set of slowly maturing interests and activities. . . . To live as a girl with many lovers as long as possible, and then to marry in one's own village, near one's own relatives, and to have many children, these were uniform and satisfying ambitions (1961, p. 15).

Studies investigating adolescent attitudes toward sex indicate that young people view sexual relations as a private concern, which society should not try to control (Dreyer, 1975). However, it is quite clear that culture influences sexuality. For example, it was long believed that males had less control over their sexual desires than females, which led to the assumption that boys should have greater sexual freedom than girls; this *double standard* is still prevalent in certain subcultures. There was a decline in the double standard among teenagers in the 1970s. In Sorensen's study (1973) almost as many girls as boys (66 percent versus 76 percent) approved of living together without getting married, and Hopkins (1977) found that the number of teenage girls experiencing premarital intercourse is almost the same as for boys.

Twenty or thirty years ago cultural attitudes toward masturbation, which were influenced by medical folklore and religious beliefs, were opposed to this practice as causing mental and physical illnesses or as being immoral. Today few adolescents are affected by such beliefs (Hass, 1979; Miller & Lief, 1976).

Intellectual Development

Developments in thinking and reasoning also occur during adolescence. The most important change seen by the cognitive-structuralist theorists is the child's increasing ability to deal with abstractions. Whereas the child during the middle years focuses thought on reality, the adolescent can deal with transformations that are merely possible (Inhelder & Piaget, 1958). Ask a sixth grader the question, "What causes a pendulum sometimes to swing fast and sometimes slowly—what affects the rate of swing of the pendulum?" The answer is likely to be a simple response such as, "Oh, the way it swings," or "How you push it," and so on. These are singular reasons stated as facts. The adolescent is more likely to suggest a number of possible reasons in order to construct a logically consistent principle. This change in reasoning does not just pertain to intellectual development. Kohlberg, referring to moral development, says that the adolescent tries to construct universal and logically consistent principles that apply to all people in particular moral situations (Kohlberg & Elfenbein, 1975).

Bruner (1964), although he chooses not to describe development in terms of stages, says that as children mature they become more able to use "indirect information." They make references to possibilities of the state of things or relationships between objects that are not apparent in the immediate situation. Ausubel also assumes that the adolescent becomes less dependent on concrete examples in dealing with abstract relationships. "The intellectually mature individual becomes capable of understanding and manipulating relationships between abstractions" (Ausubel, Novak, & Hanesian, pp. 236–237). However, both Bruner and Ausubel make it quite clear that younger children in preadolescence, even as early as the preschool years, can solve hypothetical problems under certain conditions.

Skinner does not believe that distinct ways of thinking occur but that all behavior, including the cognitive, is shaped in a gradual and continuous manner by the environment (1953, p. 91). He does say that, in educating the child, age must be taken into account. More importantly, the child's current way of behaving should be noted, to which age contributes (1969, p. 89). This is about as much as can be said of the behaviorists' view of later intellectual development. Assuming that the environment continues to act on the child, learning is cumulative. By virtue of experience and practice, the adolescent becomes able to deal with an abstract environment. Thinking becomes more abstract (not exclusively, or under all conditions) and is shaped by abstractions.

The remainder of this chapter provides descriptions of adolescent development by Piaget, Bruner, and Ausubel. In contrasting these three different viewpoints, you will notice that the descriptions of cognitive functioning are not confined by the boundaries of adolescence. The reasons for this are related to the question of qualitative versus quantitative change. This will become clear as you consider each viewpoint in turn. Let us begin with Piaget's description of formal operations.

Formal Operations

A 14-year-old adolescent has been shown a pendulum set up in a special way for an experiment (see Figure 12.4). The experimenter describes the pendulum as a length of string (variable 1) that can be shortened or lengthened with a weight (variable 2) on the end, which can be decreased or increased. The experimenter also explains that the pendulum can be swung from various heights (variable 3) and, finally, that the pendulum can simply be released to swing, or given a push (velocity—variable 4).

The adolescent is told that the pendulum can swing fast or slowly. The problem is to find out which of the variables (independent) affect the rate of swing. How would you set about solving the problem?

According to Piaget (Inhelder & Piaget, 1955), the normal adolescent realizes that there are four hypotheses to be tested; these include all four independent variables. For example, "The rate of swing of the pendulum will be affected by the amount of weight." While the amount of weight is varied, all other factors must be held constant. In turn, each independent variable is tested. This is important since it is not known at the beginning whether one or more of the independent variables affect rate of swing. In this way it is discovered that only the length of the pendulum affects the rate of swing. For example, a young girl aged 16 attempting this problem for Piaget responded as follows:

[At first believes that each of the four factors is influential. She studies different weights with the same string length (medium long) and does not notice any change.] *That doesn't change the rhythm.*—[Then she varies the length of string with the same 200-gram weight and finds that] *When the string is small, the swing is fast.*—[Finally she varies the dropping point and the impetus successively, with the same medium length string and the same 200-gram weight, concluding for each of these two factors] *Nothing has changed* (Inhelder & Piaget, 1955).

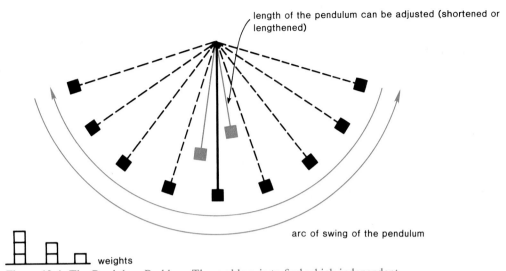

length of the pendulum can be adjusted (shortened or lengthened)

arc of swing of the pendulum

weights

Figure 12.4 The Pendulum Problem. The problem is to find which independent variable influences the *rate of swing* of the pendulum. The independent variables are (1) the length of the pendulum (shorter or longer); (2) the weight (more or less); (3) the height at which the pendulum is released (higher or lower); and (4) the force given to the swing of the pendulum (from giving it a hard push to just releasing it). This is one of the problems Inhelder and Piaget (1958) used to test for the emergence of formal operations.

In this experiment our 16-year-old identified (or accepted as given) four variables, realized the possibility that one, some, or all might affect the rate of swing of the pendulum, constructed hypotheses, and correctly tested them. Piaget calls this process of thinking **hypothetico-deductive reasoning.** This type of reasoning, according to Piaget, is exemplary of the stage of formal operations, which extends from age 11 years onward. *Formal operational development* consists of thinking about thinking, about relations among relations, and about transformations that are merely possible instead of concrete, and it involves the ability to use propositional logic. (See Table 4.2.) Propositional logic requires the use of *inferences,* that is, of passing from one proposition considered to be true to another proposition whose truth follows from the first.

What are the *problem-solving* expectations for younger children? From a Piagetian perspective, preoperational children younger than 7 will approach this task haphazardly. They may randomly push the pendulum and immediately suppose that "It swings fast, because I push it like so." In changing the weight, they may come to the same conclusion. At the concrete-operational stage the child begins to investigate a number of possibilities, measures the results, and accurately reports similarities and differences observed. But, overall, the child

is not systematic. For example, having changed the length of the pendulum, the child says, "It goes slower when it's longer." The weight is then changed, but also the length of the pendulum *at the same time*. The conclusion this time is "It goes slower when the weight's heavier—and when the string's longer" (Ginsburg & Opper, 1979, p. 180).

However, it seems that, as the child matures into the young adolescent, there is not a change to formal reasoning at first, but rather a return to simpler forms of reasoning (Brainerd, 1973; Dasen & Christie, 1972). Bower (1979, p. 207) suggests that this *regression* probably happens because of the adolescent's attempt to make concepts more precise and to free them from the real world. When concepts are always tied to the real world, there is often a chance of making errors. For example, to young children, "bigger" usually means "heavier" (some adults assume this is the case when shopping for certain products—as the packaging experts know all too well!). However, this is not always the correct relationship.

Try the following experiments with young children (say, between 6 and 8 years) and older children (10 to 12):

1. Show the child some popcorn kernels before and after popping. Ask these questions: "Do we now have more popcorn?" or "Do you think the popcorn will now weigh more?"

2. Show the child a glass of water and a cube of sugar. Ask the child to notice the level of the water (you could put a bright colored elastic band around a beaker at the water level). Put the sugar cube into the beaker and point out the change in water level. Ask the child to account for the increase in height of water in the beaker. Now wait for the sugar cube to dissolve. Ask, "Why is the water *still* higher than before we put the sugar cube into the beaker?"

3. Other examples you might use include cakes and bread *before* and *after* baking.

Piaget warns us that with these types of problems the young child tends to reason only from what he or she can see. For example, with respect to the popcorn problem, an 8-year-old responded as follows:

Will the seed keep its size?—*No, it's going to swell*—How do you explain that?—*There are grains inside, the heat makes them come out.*—Is it still the same weight?—*It's gotten heavier.*—Why? *Because it's bigger.*

The older child, however, might hypothesize about what cannot be seen. An 11-year-old put it this way:

The heat has opened it up and then it burst.—Why?—*I don't know, I've never been told.*—Are there more things in the seed than before?—*No, it's the same.*—Does it weigh more?—*It weighs the same, because this one (popped) is exactly the same as that one.*— How do you know?—*Because this one (unpopped) is in a piece, but this one (popped) has burst with the heat* (Piaget & Inhelder, 1941).

The adolescent more readily sees beyond the immediately obvious, which in the case of the popcorn is illusory. However, adolescents do not easily solve all problems that require formal reasoning. And although young children make more errors when spontaneously trying their hand at such problems, they can be trained to do better.

Some questions about formal operations.   Piaget and Inhelder (1958) used a number of formal operational tasks to investigate adolescent thinking. Martorano (1975) gave ten of these tasks to white, middle-class girls (IQ range, 100 to 120), twenty each from grades 6, 8, 10, and 12. He found that performance on tasks did improve across the age range from 11 to 18 years, especially between the eighth and tenth grades. However, these girls did not do equally well on each task. The proportion of twelfth graders using formal operational reasoning ranged from 15 percent on the task that proved most difficult to 95 percent on the easiest task. Martorano concluded that, although formal operational thinking appears to emerge during adolescence, "It cannot be said to represent the characteristic mode of thought for that development period" (1974, p. 43).

Lunzer has expressed another critical point of view (1973; 1975). Based on the evidence from a number of experiments, he concluded that, although problems of logical inference are solved more efficiently as adolescents get older, adults can appear strikingly inept when trying to solve formal problems. One type of problem in which this occurs requires the making of inferences from some information. There are two basic forms of problems, simple and complex. When information provided in a problem is unambiguous and straightforward, one can make an inference about the state of some variable. This is *simple inference*. For example, the answer to a problem such as $3 + 4 = ?$ and $3 + ? = 7$ requires a simple, straightforward inference (1973, pp. 5–6). If initial information does not allow one to make an immediate, unambiguous inference, a number of alternatives must be identified. Each one must be considered in turn before a final inference can be drawn. This is *complex inference*. For example, $? - 7 = 7 - 3$, or $576 + 495 = (576 + 382) + (495 - ?)$. The second of these two examples of complex inference math problems is more difficult than the first (1973, pp. 5–6). It was found that the first example of complex inference math problems could be solved by most 10-year-olds. The second was only solved by 16- to 18-year-old adolescents. Here is another type of complex inference problem to try your hand at.

Two soldiers are marching through the jungle. They come to a crocodile-infested river which they must cross. There is only one small boat which belongs to two small boys. The boat is big enough to carry the two boys alone, one boy and one soldier, or one soldier by himself. How do the two soldiers get across the river if the two boys are willing to help but want their boat back again? (Lunzer, 1973, pp. 26–27)

Try to solve the problem before looking at the solution at the end of the *Summary*.

We can draw a number of conclusions from the research on formal operational reasoning. Whether the adolescent solves a hypothetical problem depends in part on the content of the problem, how familiar it is, or how complex it is (Falmagne, 1976; Wason & Johnson-Laird, 1972). Adolescents and adults "Usually do better when thinking abstractly about real, concrete problems . . . than when thinking abstractly about abstract problems" (Flavell, 1977, p. 116). The problem itself may be quite simple or very difficult—so the particular problem and not just the nature of the problem can have an effect. Adolescents and adults revert to concrete operations when the content of a problem is unfamiliar or the problem too complex. Many problems, including some of those Inhelder and Piaget used, can be solved without using hypothetico-deductive reasoning. When this is the case, it is unlikely the problem solver will use a rigorous deductive approach (see Inset 12.1). With respect to problems that can hardly be solved without using hypothetico-deductive reasoning, it has been noted that not all adolescents appear to achieve the stage of formal reasoning (Niemark, 1975).

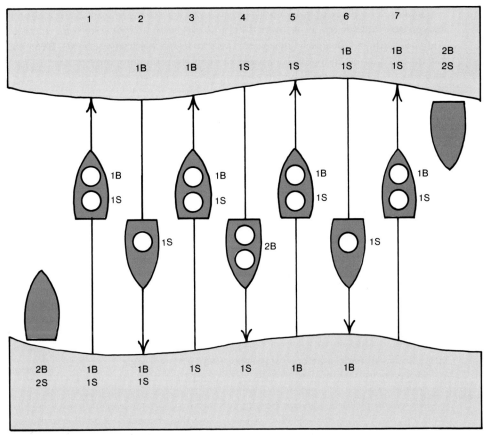

Figure 12.5 Crossing the river problem: the answer.

For the boat to cross the river it must contain two boys, one boy and one soldier, or one soldier. As you can see, it takes seven trips to get both the soldiers across the river and ensure that the two boys still have the use of their boat.

It took me three attempts to solve this problem. It is a question of manipulating the variables—2 boys, 1 boy + 1 soldier, or 1 soldier in the boat at any one time. If the chosen sequence of combinations goes wrong, it is necessary to backtrack and try another combination. Of course, it is also necessary to remember which combinations have been eliminated. This is a fairly simple example of hypothetico-deductive reasoning. Each combination of trips across the river is a hypothesis. By trying each combination, we deduce whether the hypothesis is correct and in this way eventually arrive at a correct solution.

Piaget (1972) has acknowledged that it is unlikely that hypothetico-deductive reasoning is *universal*. It is more likely to be used in industrialized than in nonindustrialized societies (Berry & Dasen, 1974; Neimark, 1975). Even in advanced societies, individuals capable of such thinking may only reason in this way when working on problems in areas in which their expertise, experience, and interest are greatest. An automobile mechanic, when troubleshooting a car, may be controlling variables and testing hypotheses, but he or she may not use this procedure on other types of problems (Flavell, 1977, p. 117).

Inset 12.1 **Using Natural Logic to Solve Real-World Problems**	As Tschirgi (1980) mentions, children and adults are involved in many daily activities that are varied and complex and that are filled with potential problem-solving tasks. Yet much of the research on children's and adults' problem-solving abilities uses specially prepared abstract deduction tasks or reasoning games that require particular strategies. Tschirgi suggests that, in natural situations, a major consideration will always be the value of the outcome of some event and that children and adults use strategies which are sensible in relation to the task at hand. However, these strategies conform to a natural logic rather than a formal logic.

Piaget has suggested that formal reasoning, based on propositional logic, does not develop until the adolescent years but then characterizes adolescent and adult reasoning and problem solving. Recent research has questioned this view in two important ways. First, many studies (Case, 1974; Scardamalia, 1977; Siegler & Liebert, 1975) have shown that children as young as 7 or 8 years can be trained to use efficient problem-solving strategies. Second, other studies have shown that adults may not, necessarily, use formal logical reasoning to solve problems (Lunzer, 1975; Mynatt, Doherty, & Tweney, 1977; Wason & Johnson-Laird, 1972).

Tschirgi asks what aspects of natural situations lead people spontaneously to choose confirming rather than disconfirming tests of hypotheses and why people sometimes choose disconfirming evidence. If one aspect of a situation is the plausible cause of a negative result, people should easily choose the logical disconfirming test. For example, "Suppose John bakes a cake using margarine, honey, and whole-wheat flour, and the cake is runny. John hypothesizes that it is the honey alone that caused the problem. To prove his hypothesis he sensibly (and logically) tests by baking another cake, continuing to use margarine and whole-wheat flour but switching to sugar" (Tschirgi, 1980, p. 2). If John's first cake had turned out to be a success, he would have confirmed this by baking another cake using the same ingredients.

It is likely that through experiences in solving such real-world problems children and adults acquire two particular strategies for solving problems—they vary one

Table 12.1 Percentages of Different Answer Types to the Story Problems.

Age	VOTAT	HOTAT	CA
7 years	36	41	23
9 years	35	37	27
11 years	50	34	16
Students	55	·38	7

Source: Tschirgi, J. E., 1980. *Sensible Reasoning: A Hypothesis about Hypotheses.* Copyright, 1980, the Society for Research in Child Development, Inc. Adapted with permission.

thing at a time (VOTAT) and hold one thing at a time (HOTAT). Rarely do they presume to change all (CA) things at the same time. To test this assumption, Tschirgi had 7- 9- and 11-year-old children and college freshmen and sophomores consider a number of story problems referring to baking a cake, making a paper airplane, making clay pots, sewing a dress, feeding a cat, planting tomato seeds, washing clothes, and going fishing. Each story could have a *good* and a *bad* outcome. For example, the bake-a-cake story could end with John's baking a "great cake" or "the cake turned out to be just terrible." Each story had three possible answers to a question such as, "John thought the reason the cake was great/terrible was the honey. What should he do to prove his point?" The first type of answer was VOTAT (he can bake the cake again but use sugar instead of honey and still use margarine and whole-wheat flour); the second type was HOTAT (bake the cake again still using honey but this time use butter and regular white flour); the third type of answer was CA (bake the cake again using sugar, butter, and plain white flour). The types of responses selected by children and students are shown in Table 12.1.

These results tell us that children and adults are sensitive to the nature of the outcome of real-life problems. Faced with a *good* result people look for the *one* thing that will make it happen again. Faced with a *bad* result people systematically search for the *one* thing they can change in order to obtain a *good* result. However, we can also see that these abilities get better as people grow older. The younger children were less able to discriminate between the appropriate VOTAT and the inappropriate CA. This suggests that young children need further experience and practice to realize the necessity of using a VOTAT strategy. We know that children as young as 7 to 8 years can be taught to use such strategies effectively.

Tschirgi concludes that hypotheses testers may not usually use formal logic in dealing with real-world problems but by following a more natural logic they have a good chance of solving many everyday problems.

Egocentrism in adolescence. Flavell has suggested "we are *at risk* (almost in the medical sense) for egocentric thinking all our lives" (1977, p. 124). One important reason is that, whereas we are directly conscious of our own points of view, we can only understand or take notice of the other person's view indirectly. Even when we try to take the other person's point of view into consideration, our own views continue to "ring in our ears" (1977, p. 125).

Young children often have difficulty distinguishing between their own point of view and another child's view. Adolescents are less prone to this blinkered way of thinking, but they are often preoccupied with themselves. This makes them either oblivious to other people or very concerned that the eyes of the world are on them. An adolescent can feel very self-conscious. Elkind suggests that

The adolescent fails to differentiate between . . . the thoughts of others . . . and those which are the focus of his own concern. He assumes that other people are as obsessed with his behavior and appearance as he is himself. It is this belief that others are preoccupied with his appearance and behavior that constitutes the egocentrism of the adolescent (1967, pp. 1029–1030).

As we have seen, egocentric thinking is not just a part of social behavior but all other forms of thinking and communication. It has been shown, for example, that adolescents and adults often attribute other people's behavior not their own to *stable, internal traits* (Kelley, 1973; Mischel, 1973). "You tripped because you are clumsy (stable, internal trait) whereas I tripped because it was dark (variable, external trait)" (Flavell, 1977, p. 124). It would be a *double standard* to label adolescents singularly egocentric. Adults can be just as obviously self-absorbed in thinking and communicating.

Other Theories of Problem Solving

There are views besides Piaget's on how adolescents solve problems that are linked to a theory of learning more so than a theory of development. We reintroduce two theorists here with whom you are now familiar, Bruner and Ausubel. Let us take a look at what they have to say about problem solving.

Bruner's view. According to Bruner (Bruner, Wallach, & Galanter, 1959), problem solving begins in early childhood with a desire to organize experiences and search for regularities. In doing this the child should be encouraged to actively discover regularities by seeking to solve problems (see Inset 12.2). This is achieved to a large extent by tools provided by the child's culture. What are these tools? One is representation, and a second is comprised of problem-solving techniques the child can learn. From this point of view we can expect reasoning to be strongly influenced by culture. "Mental growth is in very considerable measure . . . a mastering of techniques that are embodied in a culture" (Bruner, 1966).

Does this mean that young children and adolescents might use advanced, abstract forms of problem solving if they learn the techniques? For young children, the answer is no. They almost invariably use crude trial-and-error problem solving and rely on enactive and iconic (concrete) forms of representation. For adolescents, however, the answer is not a simple yes; rather, it is possible but not always so. We must remember that Bruner views development as a spiraling staircase to higher levels of reasoning, not a linear progression. At each step of the staircase the growing child can re-experience important concepts, and can meet again skills that have become good friends. This knowledge can be extended, practiced anew, and used to solve more difficult problems at increasingly abstract levels. But there is no guarantee this will be the case. The child should not be judged merely on what he knows but also on what can be generated from what he knows (Bruner, 1957).

Differences between adolescent and childlike reasoning exist because of experience and a growing tendency to have available abstract forms of representation. One of the effects of this growing ability to organize information for problem solving is the greater number of inferences an adolescent can employ. This is illustrated in the following two experiments.

Huttenlocher (1966) gave a simple problem to 6- and 12-year-old children. A board had two light switches. Each one could be in the "on" or "off" position. There was also a light bulb that could be switched on. The child was asked to tell, by turning off only one switch, what turned the light on. There are four ways of presenting the problem:

1. The light is off, a switch is turned, the light comes on.

2. The light is on, a switch is turned, the light goes off.

3. The light is on, a switch is turned, the light stays on.

4. The light is off, a switch is turned, the light stays off.

A different number of inductive steps is required to make a correct inference for each presentation of the problem:

Presentation　　　　　　　*Inferences*

1. *If* I turn this switch, the light comes on.

2. (a) *If* this switch is turned, the light goes off.
   (b) *If* this switch is turned back to its original position, the light comes on.

3. (a) *If* this switch (No. 1) is turned, the light just stays on (so it cannot be this switch that makes it come on).
   (b) *If* this switch (No. 1) is turned back to its original position, the light stays on.
   (c) So it must be the position of the other switch (No. 2) that makes the light come on.

In *The Act of Discovery* (1961) Bruner says that the most personal knowledge of all that we might comprehend is what we discover for ourselves. What does the act of discovery entail? "Discovery, like surprise, favors the well-prepared mind." What is so important to discovery is the prior arranging, rearranging, and transformation of information as it is learned in such a way as to enable a person to go beyond the information at hand, to make good guesses and hypotheses, to make inferences, and to achieve intuitive leaps.

When children are left to themselves, they discover things within limits. However, there are certain forms of child rearing in homes, schools, and the broader environment that help some children to be better at making discoveries than other children (Bruner, 1961, p. 22). Bruner emphasizes that it should be an important aim of teaching to give the child as firm a grasp of a subject as possible and to encourage the child to be as autonomous and self-propelled a thinker as possible. Only by solving problems and using the necessary effort in making discoveries do children (and adults) learn how to employ strategies of discovery. The more practice a person has the more likely it is that he or she will learn to generalize problem-solving skills to a whole variety of problems as they occur in formal settings and in daily life.

What types of discovery methods do children use? Over a period of time Bruner observed children of different ages using methods ranging from simple trial-and-error approaches to well-organized methods for testing hypotheses. These approaches can be illustrated by an example from one of Bruner's experiments in which he used a game of twenty questions. Children aged between 10 and 12 years were told that a car had gone off the road and hit a tree. The children were allowed to ask questions to which they received either a "yes" or "no" answer in an attempt to discover what caused the accident. (Most children enjoy playing this game but differ quite remarkably in the approach they take and strategies they use to find a solution.) The children in this experiment used two basic types of questions. One type of question was

4. (a) *If* this switch (No. 1) is turned, the light does not come on.
   (b) *If* this switch (No. 1) is turned to its original position, the light stays off.
   (c) *If* this switch (No. 2) is left as it is, the light stays off.
   (d) So only if this switch (No. 2) is turned does the light come on.

The more inferences the 6-year-olds had to make the poorer was their performance. On the other hand, children aged 12 did almost as well on all four presentations.

To investigate hypothesis testing, Potter (1966) used a series of color slides, with each slide depicting a familiar object (e.g., a woman looking at a cow) but

intended to locate the constraints in the problem that might lead to an eventual hypothesis and possible solution. For example, "Was there anything wrong with the car door?" The other type of question was put in the form of a hypothesis. (This form often follows the first type.) For example, "Was the (or, perhaps the) driver was rushing to the doctor's for an appointment and the car went out of control?" The approach for these questions differed. Some children organized questions carefully in a sequence with an objective in mind. Others took "potshots," asking questions randomly in a disorganized fashion. Needless to say, the children who used a well-organized approach were more successful, and usually more persistent in seeking a solution to the problem. The children who flooded themselves with disorganized information from potshot questions became confused and disorganized.

Bruner urges that careful instruction is necessary to guide the learner to be a "constructionist" in useful ways to make discoveries and to solve problems. Here is a concrete instance. A fifth grade class was working on the organization of a baboon trip (an assignment in the curriculum, "Man: A Course of Study." Bruner, 1966, pp. 158–159). Specifically, the question was "How might the baboons protect themselves from predators?" The children saw a brief film in which six or seven adult male baboons went forward to try to intimidate and hold off three cheetahs. After the film the teacher asked the children what the baboons had done to keep the cheetahs off. A boy raised his hand tentatively and asked whether cheetahs always attacked together. "Yes," the teacher replied, "although a single cheetah might follow a troop to pick off a straggler." Another child asked, "Well, what if there were four cheetahs and two of them attacked from behind and two from the front. What would the baboons do then?" The teacher might have answered the question straightforwardly, but did not do so. This was fortunate, for such questions open the deeper issues of what might be and why it sometimes is not. It is such conjecture, in this case quite unanswerable, that produces rational, self-conscious, problem-solving behavior so crucial to intellectual growth.

showing the object gradually coming into focus one slide at a time. These slides were shown in sequence to individuals ranging in age from 4 to 19 years. The subjects were asked to guess, on the basis of what they could see in the projected picture, what they thought the out-of-focus slide might be showing. They also knew they would see some more slides showing the objects gradually coming into focus in the projected picture. The responses are very interesting:

4-year-old: It's a picture. It could be a little, a little, a big round orange ball. I think it's a skunky.
5-year-old: A—some ice cream. Somebody sleeping in bed. I don't know what the white thing is. It might be sheets.
9-year-old: Oh, that looks like the shadow of a person—like in New York. Those look like people, and those look like decorations. Oh, this looks like the face of a bull, or something like that.

In this set of photos a camera is shown coming progressively into focus. As each photo is shown in this sequence young children make "potshot" guesses as to what the object is (not might be!) changing their guesses in a haphazard fashion as each photo is shown. Most older children and adults set up hypotheses about what the object might be *and test them out with the available information. (Photos courtesy of the author.)*

16-year-old: Could be a person bowling, and the pins are in the right-hand corner and the person in the left. Looks like a bull. Looks like a man with red hair looking at a bull—kind of brownish white.

18-year-old: It looks like two people in fencing outfits, with the white jacket—like things they wear. Well this looks kind of ridiculous, but it looks like a fellow in a white shirt, with red hair, is kissing a cow wearing a white nightcap.

The young children produced a multitude of uncorrected hypotheses. They got so carried away by their attempts to link the out-of-focus object with their own experiences that some of them even failed to recognize it, when at last it came into focus! The older children and adolescents indicated a growing development of related major and supporting hypotheses. They continually checked these hypotheses against the clues provided by each successive picture. "From the 4-year-old's lack of differentiation to the college student's structured integration, there is a familiar theme of development. . . . The growth of integration makes possible the maximal use of information. . . . An inferential structure can be. . . related . . . to an integrated set of hypotheses" (Potter, 1966, p. 133).

This change in problem-solving ability over time is expected to be influenced in large measure by education. The young child, says Bruner (1966), needs to be armed with a readiness to explore alternatives and search out contrasts with an expectancy that there will be something to find. The teacher must respect the growing child's trends of thought. The teacher should set forth problems that are within the limits of developing intellectual skills but that make a demand on the child. These problems should introduce new realms of experience and invite the discovery of new mysteries.

Where is development taking the child? What can we expect of the adolescent and adult? The answer is a mix of the practical, the philosophical, and the ideological. Development improves in a practical way the art and technique of inquiry and allows the child to benefit from an educational system that can profoundly aid the course of cognitive growth. The adult may apply higher levels of reasoning in later life to philosophical problems on "great issues, principles, and values that a society deems worthy of the continual concern of its members" (Bruner, 1960, p. 52). The adult may ideologically "optimize learning . . . optimize transfer or retrievability of information . . . in order to contribute to man's further evolution" (Bruner, 1966, p. 37–38). The great discoveries of science, medicine, the arts, and technology seem to be the results of adults' creative insights. These insights blossom from many years of thought, of conjecture, of half-truth, of a million prior hypotheses. Piaget might argue that adults' discoveries are the realization of the development of formal reasoning that occurred during adolescence. Other theorists, such as Bruner and Ausubel (and behaviorists such as Skinner), seem to be saying that intellectual development is a life-long endeavor.

Ausubel's view. As we saw in Chapters 9 and 10, according to Ausubel, even preschool children can understand some abstract concepts. It is also expected that they will be able to apply them to solving simple problems. In using abstract logical thinking, young children need to know secondary concepts. When they apply such concepts to problem solving, Ausubel calls this meaningful problem solving. According to this view of problem solving, can we expect differences in performance between preschool children and adolescents? A number of factors affect problem solving, one important one being that improvement in this ability takes time. Novak, who has applied Ausubel's learning theory to the development of science curriculum programs, suggests that "most children cannot engage in broadly ranging abstract logical thinking much before the age of 11 or 12, and indeed adults cannot perform in this way in subject-matter areas in which they lack secondary concepts" (1977, p. 122). Novak suggests that the learning of secondary concepts accounts for much of "formal" reasoning (see Inset 12.3).

As we have previously mentioned, instruction appears not only to help children become better problem solvers but, in many instances, to be necessary for successful problem solving. It was mentioned in Inset 12.2 that Bruner (1961, 1966) emphasizes preparing the child to "go beyond the information at hand" to make discoveries. Other theorists do not believe that this is always necessary in order for the child to acquire important and useful knowledge (Ausubel, Novak, & Hanesian, 1978; Novak, 1977).

Novak (1977), for example, believes that much of children's and adults' formal reasoning (problem solving) can be explained in terms of relating new knowledge to previously learned general ideas. Rather than going beyond the information given, people can learn efficiently and solve problems efficiently when they relate new knowledge or a problem's content and demands to a general framework of knowledge that encompasses the new experiences. In other words, to paraphrase Bruner, they stay *within* the information given rather than, as Bruner actually has it, go beyond the information given. This does not preclude making guesses, forming hypotheses, or making inferences. For example, if children are asked what might happen when various liquids are mixed together, they need to have a general notion about what is involved in combining liquids and what is involved in the process of change following mixing. They also need to know about the structure of liquids—that, for example, liquids can be "light" or "heavy" or, more precisely, have different densities. Knowing general rules or a general strategy for testing hypotheses about this type of problem should also help. Children come to this problem, then, with a general framework of relevant knowledge *within* which they can attempt to solve the problem.

To assume that children will, in general, usually discover ways to solve problems, or that, in the normal course of events, abilities to solve problems using formal logic will develop during adolescence (as Piaget tells us) seems to be asking too much. Other examples have already been given to show that adolescents and adults actually fail many Piagetian problems we would expect them to solve. Novak provides us with a further example that illustrates the likely relationship between success in problem solving and the previous learning of relevant general concepts. Lawson (Lawson, Nordlund, & DeVito, 1974) gave college students (age 18) a number of Piagetian problems, two of which we might expect them to have solved using concrete operations or formal operations (two types of conservation of volume problems) and three using formal operations (deciding what affects the rate of swing of a pendulum, what affects the extent to which various types of metals will bend, and how to keep a "teeter-totter" in balance by placing weights at different positions on the two arms of the balance). In each problem a score of 2 meant the student was fully able to use concrete operations and a score of 4, fully able to use formal operations.

The results in Table 12.2 show that most students were fully concrete operational on all five problems. But, of course, we would expect that they would have been fully formal operational. The difficulties many students had with these problems could possibly have been due to the fact that they lacked an understanding of the content of the problems, or about strategies useful for solving these problems, or both. Theorists, such as Ausubel and Novak, suggest that we can improve children's and adults' abilities to learn new knowledge and to solve new problems by making sure they have learned a general framework of concepts and problem-solving strategies into which new knowledge and problem-solving skills fit.

Table 12.2 College Students' Scores on Five Piagetian Tasks

Problem	Score[a]
Conservation of Volume 1	1.9
Conservation of Volume 2	2.8
Pendulum Problem	3.0
Bending Rods Problem	2.9
"Teeter-totter" Problem	3.0

[a]Total possible score on each task = 4.
Source: Lawson, A. E., Nordlund, F. H., & DeVito, A.,
"Piagetian Formal Operational Tasks: A Crossover Study of
Learning Effect and Reliability," *Science Education.* Copyright
1974, John Wiley & Sons, Inc. Adapted with permission.

What factors, according to this theory, appear to influence problem solving in general, and what distinguishes the adolescent from the preschooler in particular? Ausubel (Ausubel et al., 1978, pp. 565–566) has mentioned a number of factors, some of which are briefly described below.

1. In attempting to solve a problem the individual must already know and understand concepts and principles that are relevant to that particular problem.

2. As noted by other theorists and investigators, a number of intellectual and personality traits appear to influence problem solving. These would include cognitive style; the ability to organize the various parts and sequences of the problem; the ability to select a strategy, or a number of strategies that seem useful in attempting to solve the problem (flexibility); improvisation; curiosity; and an ability to tolerate frustration (sticking at it, determination).

3. Verbal ability helps problem solving. It is interesting to watch people, children, adolescents, and adults, talking their way through a problem. Verbal ability, put another way, can be called symbolic representation. We have already seen what importance both Piaget and Bruner have placed on this ability. However, we should remember that an abstract concept can sometimes be represented concretely. When young children are trying to solve problems, verbalizing about the problem is helped by having concrete examples of concepts (variables) at hand.

4. We can expect differences in problem-solving ability due to age-level trends and individual differences.

Table 12.3 Elementary Strategy for Determining Cause-and-Effect Relationships

Step	Verbal Rule
Step 1	Name the dependent variable (the "thing" you are trying to change).
Step 2	List the independent variables (the things that might influence the "thing" you are trying to change).
Step 3	Concentrate on the first independent variable. Make it take different values while changing nothing else. Each time it is changed record its value and the value of the dependent variable.
Step 4	Summarize the results of step 3 in the form of a verbal statement such as (a) "Changing A (the first independent variable) does (does not) change B (the dependent variable)." (b) "Making A (for example, the weight in the pendulum problem) greater does not change B (the rate of swing of the pendulum)."
Step 5	Take the next independent variable and repeat steps 3 and 4. Proceed through all the independent variables.
Step 6	Summarize the overall results in a statement such as "To increase the rate of swing of the pendulum it is necessary to shorten the length of the pendulum."

Source: From Ausubel, D. P., & Robinson, F. G., *School Learning: An Introduction to School Psychology.* Copyright, 1969, David P. Ausubel and Floyd G. Robinson. Adapted with permission.

5. Training young children and adolescents to use a general problem-solving strategy that can be applied to a range of related problems appears to be helpful. Ausubel believes that the effects of this type of training are likely to be limited. This will be due mainly to changes in content of problems and strategies needed to solve a wide range of problems.

Ausubel has described a general strategy for solving causal relationships such as those found in the pendulum problem (Ausubel & Robinson, 1969, pp. 160–165). As we have seen, according to Piaget, children aged about 6 to 10 years are not expected to be able to use hypothetico-deductive reasoning to solve problems. In fact, they are not expected to adequately solve problems such as the pendulum problem by any method. The most usual error young children typically make is to vary two independent variables at once—for example, the length of the pendulum and the weight on the end of the pendulum. What the problem solver needs to know (whether a child, adolescent, or adult) is that independent variables must be manipulated one at a time. An elementary strategy that can be used for this type of problem is outlined in Table 12.3.

Exceptional ability and the expression of original ideas in various pursuits is considered to be a mark of creativity. (Photo by EKM-Nepenthe/ John Maher)

General strategies can also be worked out for many different types of problems. Since it is rare to find a one-of-a-kind problem, the general strategy should prove useful in attempting to solve a number of different, but related, problems, but we should not expect to be able to apply some general strategy to all problems.

To conclude this chapter we will take a brief look at what is considered to be the "highest expression of problem solving" (Ausubel et al., 1978)—creativity.

Creativity

According to some theorists, *creativity* is a higher level of problem solving that only a few people are capable of. Other theorists believe creativity is possible for most people. To be marked as a *creative* person, the adolescent must be able to come up with original ideas that are not only unique but also considered to have some importance. Itzak Perlman, who is now a well-known violinist, was showing exceptional ability in his violin playing at the age of 5. By the age of 10 he was playing for the state broadcasting company in Tel Aviv. The music he creates on the violin is exceptional because of a unique playing ability. The music Perlman plays was composed by artists such as Mozart, Bach, Paganini— also truly creative individuals.

The characteristics of problem solving at the level of creativity are said to be originality, flexibility, spontaneity, verbal fluency, a fluency in expression, and an ability to integrate information (Guilford & Merrifield, 1960; Getzels & Jackson, 1962; Wallach & Kogan, 1965). Unlike some theorists, Bruner does not place creativity out of reach of all but a few specially endowed individuals. He would like creativity to be encouraged in *every* child, through adolescence and into adulthood. It would be a part of continuing development.

A small part, but crucial part of discovery of the highest order is to invent and develop models or "puzzle forms" that can be imposed on difficulties with good effect. It is in this area that the truly powerful mind shines. But it is interesting to what degree perfectly ordinary people can, given the benefit of instruction, construct quite interesting and, what a century ago, would have been considered greatly original models (1961, p. 30).

Others have also suggested the importance of encouraging creativity (Torrance, 1965; Torrance & Myers, 1972). Torrance (1965) describes five ways in which creative thinking can be fostered:

(1) respect unusual questions;
(2) respect unusual ideas;
(3) show individuals that their ideas have value;
(4) provide opportunities for creativity that are not, necessarily, evaluated;
(5) relate evaluation to causes and consequences (interactions and relationships between variables), not to the individual.

Torrance and Torrance (1973) have used this approach to good effect. They report that the most successful approach involves the child (adolescent or adult) in problems that require both reasoning out the problem and being emotionally involved. Usually problems need some structuring because the individual is *learning* how to be a problem solver. Very often the problem solver, lacking enough **intrinsic motivation,** also needs encouragement. When involvement in problem solving allows for practice and interaction with others (peers and adult specialists such as teachers), this appears to produce the most desirable effects.

In this chapter cognitive development during adolescence has been linked, almost exclusively, to hypothetico-deductive reasoning and other types of problem solving. This is only part of the picture.

Invention, creativity, and the less exciting day-to-day problem solving we engage in seem to be influenced, in some measure, by structured learning (not all of which needs to be experienced in classrooms). Creative problem solving also seems to be, in part, the happy coincidence of luck, of being presented with, or finding, uninvited information, and of stumbling across accidental relationships among variables.

Summary

At puberty children experience a growth spurt that affects skeletal and muscular development in a particular sequence. Sexual changes occur at this time. For girls puberty is marked by the first menstruation. For boys growth in the size of the penis and testes and the production of semen mark the onset of puberty. Secondary sex characteristics such as the growth of axillary and pubic hair and voice change also occur at this time.

Following the growth spurt, marked individual differences in maturation occur. At this time many young adolescents become concerned about their physical appearance. Some studies have shown that personality can be affected by rate of maturation.

There are cultural differences in attitudes toward sex. Adolescents in many nonindustrial cultures are quite active sexually. In Western societies, social and religious mores often place severe restrictions on adolescent sexual behavior prior to marriage.

Secular trends in maturation show an increasing tendency for the growth spurt to occur earlier in adolescence. This change seems to be related to improving standards of living and diet, especially in industrial societies. It is also claimed that a widening transmission of genetic traits has resulted in a hybrid vigor, which has affected maturation.

According to Piaget, adolescents continue to show signs of egocentrism in their behavior. Elkind has remarked that adolescent egocentrism is mainly the result of self-consciousness and an assumption that other people are preoccupied with the teenager's appearance and behavior. But both adolescents and adults have been observed attributing other people's behavior to stable, internal traits and their own to variable, external traits. Strong signs of egocentrism appear in certain adult behavior, although its source and the form it takes may differ from adolescents' egocentricism.

There are different views about the course of intellectual development during adolescence. Behaviorists emphasize a gradual and continuous shaping of cognitive behavior. Because of experience and practice it becomes possible for adolescents to reason about an *abstract* environment.

Piaget links adolescence to the stage of formal operations. Hypothetico-deductive reasoning is abstract, dealing as it does with transformations that are merely possible. It has been discovered, however, that the content and level of difficulty of problems can affect level of reasoning. Not all adolescents appear to reach the stage of formal operations.

Bruner has said that problem solving begins in early childhood. The young child can deal with *if–then* reasoning. Problem solving is dependent on forms of representation (organization and reorganization of information) and techniques learned from the culture. Representation and techniques become more abstract and information more integrated during adolescence. Instruction, which provides opportunities to go beyond the information given, is likely to strongly influence development.

According to Ausubel, young children can engage in abstract, logical reasoning if they understand secondary concepts. Adolescents are able to do so by using abstract concepts. The main differences between the problem solving of young children and adolescents is the level of abstraction of concepts used and an increasing flexibility and thoroughness in reasoning. Like Bruner, Ausubel emphasizes the importance of education in influencing the development of reasoning. Both these theorists believe it is possible to train young children, adolescents, and adults to become more efficient problem solvers.

Some theorists describe creativity as a higher level of problem solving that only a few people are capable of. Other theorists believe creativity can be and should be encouraged in every child.

According to Piaget's theory, formal operations is the final stage of intellectual development. Ausubel and Bruner believe that development continues beyond adolescence.

Questions for Review

1. What help and advice might parents give to their teenage children experiencing the age-growth changes of early and middle adolescence?

2. Describe the differences between the egocentrism of early childhood and adolescence. Do you believe that egocentrism eventually fades out during late adolescence? Support your views with examples.

3. What are the main characteristics of formal operational thinking?

4. Summarize the arguments opposing the stage of formal operations as a complete model of adolescent thinking and reasoning.

5. Compare the views of Piaget, Bruner, and Ausubel on adolescent reasoning.

6. See if you can persuade two groups of people to try to solve two problems—the pendulum problem and the crossing the river puzzle. For example,
(a) ages 8 to 10 versus 12 to 18
(b) teenagers versus old people (aged about 60 plus)
(c) teenage boys versus teenage girls
(d) professional adults with a university degree versus blue-collar or working-class adults.
Compare the results you get. What do these results suggest about intellectual development beyond the middle years and the factors affecting problem solving?

Suggestions for Further Reading

Anglin, J. M., ed. *Beyond the information given.* New York: W. W. Norton, 1973. A collection of articles by Jerome Bruner, his co-workers and colleagues. Read especially Chapter 12, "The Conditions of Creativity," and Chapter 13, "Going Beyond the Information Given."

Elkind, D. *Children and adolescents.* New York: Oxford University Press, 1970. A slim volume of essays interpreting Piaget's theory of development. Read especially Chapter 4, "Egocentricism in Children and Adolescents," and Chapter 5, "Cognitive Structure and Experience in Children and Adolescents."

Flavell, J. H. *Cognitive development.* Englewood Cliffs, NJ: Prentice-Hall, 1977. Read Chapter 4, "Adolescence."

Inhelder, B., & Piaget, J. *The growth of logical thinking from childhood to adolescence.* New York: Basic Books, 1958. Piaget and Inhelder's own account of the development of formal operational thinking.

National Institutes of Health. *How children grow: Clinical research advances and development.* Bethesda, MD, 1972.

Novak, J. D. *A theory of education.* Ithaca, NY: Cornell University Press, 1977. Read especially Chapter 4, "Crucial Psychological Issues for a Theory of Education," and Chapter 8, "The Evolution of an Educational Program." Chapter 4 provides an extension of Ausubel's theory of learning as it applies to logical thought and a critique of Piaget's theory. Chapter 8 provides some interesting examples of problem solving with references to Piaget's cognitive-structuralist theory and Ausubel's learning theory.

Social and Personality Development

13

I touched all sides, and nobody knew where I belonged. I had no idea of that myself.

You must take your chance on what you are. And you can't sit still. I know this double poser, that if you make a move you may lose but if you sit still you will decay.

We saw in Chapter 12 that dramatic changes in physical and intellectual development occur during adolescence, the period from puberty to about age 18. No less dramatic are the changes in personality and social behavior at this time, and, of course, these various changes are interacting. Elkind explains, "Another structural feature of adolescent thought with repercussions for adolescent experience is the capacity to think about thinking, to introspect . . . the adolescent's self-consciousness about himself is simply a manifestation of this new capacity for introspection" (1970, p. 78). The adolescent becomes intensely aware of many aspects of change and must think these through—seeking a personal identity, becoming independent, adjusting to sexual maturation, establishing relationships with peers and adults that do not deny self-determination, developing a more mature sense of values, and preparing for a vocation. The extent to which a well-balanced personality and social adjustment are achieved depends, in part, on how successfully the adolescent thinks through the introspective searchings and resolves the demands made by the social environment.

My friend Paul sat on a curb, not far from our home. He carried books by André Breton and Franz Fanon. He carried his oboe, too, in a black leather case, neat and tidy, its delicate white stitching holding it together. Musician going on a house call. . . . "I've got to get it together. Then I'll get back to the writing. Maybe poetry, too. I'd like to be back in school. Maybe in a year. I'll pull it together" (Cottle, 1971, p. 100).

As John Conger puts it, adolescence is a time for becoming, a time for many important decisions. Society imposes many developmental tasks on the adolescent. These vary not only among cultures but also within each society. For the youth who is employed, married, and a parent at 19, adolescence is relatively short. For the youth who defers marriage to continue an education, whose job expectations are still future possibilities, and who remains largely dependent on parents into early adulthood, adolescence is a long, drawn-out affair.

Throughout this book we have followed descriptions of social and personality development by such theorists as Freud, Erikson, Bandura, and Kohlberg, and we turn to them once again in considering social and personality development as it occurs during adolescence. After examining the theories of social and personality development, we will look at adolescents' relationships (with parents and with one another), their serious problems, and their values.

Theories of Adolescent Social and Personality Development

Theorists differ in their descriptions of the characteristics of this period. Freud describes the adolescent stage as a time for the development of greater independence from parents. Earlier Oedipal attachments are transferred from parents to new "love objects" (1953). In Erikson's view the adolescent is searching for identity (1963). Anna Freud, daughter of the great psychoanalyst, believes that as the adolescent matures sexually there occurs a "psychological disequilibrium." She states there is a need to come to terms with the emotions of sexuality—and to establish new sets of values and standards. The adolescent may, for example, place great emphasis on introspection and on objective judgment—often to an excessive degree (Anna Freud, 1966). This relationship between intellectual and emotional development is illustrated by the remarks of a woman in early adulthood:

It seems that any new things I picked up took the form of an obsession. . . . I had a very great sense of what I thought was right and became quite upset and confused if I was proven wrong. My personality was characterized by self-righteousness, strivings for perfection, obsessions, compulsions, and emotionality (White & Speisman, 1977, p. 39).

G. Stanley Hall (1904) referred to this period as a time of "storm and stress." Observing that adolescents experienced quite remarkable shifts in emotions, from joy to depression, optimism to hopelessness—even within the space of a single day—he referred to these shifts as "adolescent turmoil." However, it appears adolescence need not be a violently stressful time if the teenager has secure, loving, supportive family relationships.

In comparison to psychoanalysts who emphasize the influence of the psyche on the development of a personal identity, learning theorists believe that personality development and changes in social behavior are the result of adolescents' imitating adult modes. Finally, Kohlberg has suggested that during adolescence there is a move toward "autonomous moral principles which have validity and application apart from authority of the group or persons who hold them and apart from the individual's identification with those persons or groups" (Kohlberg & Gilligan, 1971, pp. 1066–1067). He has called adolescence "the stage of postconventional moral development."

In this section we will take a closer look at each of these viewpoints. Each theorist describes what, in his or her judgment, is most important about the adolescent period of social and personality development. Although in some respects the theorists differ from one another, they also hold ideas in common. As you read through this section, search for these similarities and differences.

Freud: The Genital Stage

The latency period of middle childhood ends with the onset of puberty, the *genital stage of psychosexual/social development.* At this time Freud says that a new sexual energy emerges because of physiological changes and threatens the defenses against Oedipal love feelings that the child established during the Oedipal period. These served the child's will during the five years between 6 and 11. But at puberty the awakening adult sexuality has to be directed toward loved ones other than the parents. Gratification now includes sexual orgasm. The adolescent searches for heterosexual relationships rather than following the young child's interest in same-sex peers. As Thomas has said,

To make the transition from the rejection of sex at the latency phase to the wholehearted pursuit of heterosexual activity is typically a psychologically demanding challenge, particularly in societies that have erected moral barriers against intercourse between unmarried people, especially between adolescents (1979, p. 244).

The most important task for the adolescent, according to Freud (1920), is to become independent from parents. One way of accomplishing this is to look for a partner to fall in love with. In many societies there are still quite severe restrictions on how love can be expressed, especially sexual intercourse. In the normal adolescent the ego operates in a direct fashion to solve problems (the reality principle) and is less likely to fall back on **defense mechanisms,** ways to avoid problems or resist emotions, as was true in earlier stages of development. However, when sexual relationships are restricted, the adolescent uses sublimation as a defense mechanism. *Sublimation* directs sexual energy into a substitute expression and activity. The alternative can be "writing poetry, caring for children, aiding the handicapped, or the like" (Thomas, 1979, p. 244), but whether sublimation acts as a useful substitute for sexual activities remains a controversial issue.

Sigmund Freud did not describe the adolescent genital stage in great detail. It was left to his daughter Anna to provide a more thorough description of this period on the basis of her psychoanalytic study of adolescence.

Anna Freud's View

In her description of personality development during adolescence, Anna Freud (1958) adhered closely to her father's theory. She believed that anxieties adolescents feel about relationships with their parents are the result of physiological changes reawakening Oedipal or Electra feelings. The reaction is to stay away from parents or to ignore them. Many parents do, in fact, find their adolescent children suddenly distant, secretive, and very private. They often leave the house without saying good-bye, are often strangely quiet, and often seem more interested in being out with friends than spending time in the home. According to Anna Freud, this behavior is the result of the adolescent's setting up defense mechanisms to relieve the "sexual" feelings of tension and anxiety in the parents' presence.

One particular defense mechanism is *asceticism,* the adolescent's attempt to forego physical pleasure. Wearing drab clothing, renouncing all kinds of entertainment such as dancing, music, films, and going on strict diets are all examples of adolescent asceticism. Another strategy to safeguard against Oedipal and Electra impulses is *intellectualization.* Perhaps you remember your own adolescent experiences of sitting up half the night putting the world to rights, talking in "grand" abstractions, debating elaborate theories. Anna Freud believed that adolescents substitute abstract intellectualizing for sex and aggression. This example illustrates the search for such sensitivity.

Here is what Thomas Mann says about Tonio Kroger. It could just as easily be James Joyce talking about Stephen Dedalus:
"He surrendered utterly to the power that to him seemed the highest on earth . . . the power of intellect. . . . To this power he surrendered with all the passion of youth."
Tonio Kroger and Stephen Dedalus both underwent a violent oscillation from what they took to be extreme depravity of a physical and sexual kind to the other pole of a spiritual and ascetic kind (Goethals & Klos, 1970, p. 138).

The Freudian view of personality development emphasizes a striving after personal identity that during adolescence involves the final resolution of Oedipal impulses by gaining independence from parents. Since this "struggle" and "turmoil" are believed to be a normal stage of development, all adolescents are expected to be affected by it in much the same way—though not all are expected to resolve the "conflict" to their best advantage.

According to Anna Freud, failure to adequately resolve Oedipal and Electra impulses is manifested in neurotic behavior during late adolescence and adulthood.

Erikson: The Identity Stage

To a large extent Erikson turned away from Freud's emphasis on the inner psyche as the major influence on the development of personality and looked instead toward socializing influences. Erikson has described the adolescent period as a search for ego identity and labeled this *ego identity development* stage as identity versus role confusion (1950).

The sense of ego identity . . . is the accrued confidence that one's ability to maintain inner sameness and continuity is matched by the sameness and continuity of one's meaning for others (1959, p. 89).

The physical changes of puberty, the shift from childhood to adolescence, new social roles to be adopted, and new expectations from adults and peers to deal with can be disturbing. Erikson has described **identity crisis** as the confusion in trying to respond to such questions as, Who am I? How can I find myself? When will I get it all together? However, the search for identity need not result in any extreme form of crisis. Frustrations felt in identity formation are not a new experience for the adolescent. Identity evolves and changes over time from infancy through old age (1968). As Erikson has said, "Identity includes but is more than the sum of all the successive identifications of those earlier years when the child wanted to be, and was often forced to become, like the people he depended on (1956, pp. 91–92).

*Adolescents develop a sense of
identity from physical, social,
and intellectual pursuits. Some
adolescents, uncertain about
their identity, join "in-groups."
(Photos right: John Maher/
EKM-Nepenthe; left: Robert
Eckert/EKM-Nepenthe)*

Personal growth during adolescence is founded on a combination of individual
and group relationships as they help define each other (Erikson, 1968). But it
is also something more than this. The ego is also at work attempting to "synthesize successive identifications into a coherent, consistent, and unique whole"
(Conger, 1978, p. 134). This can be illustrated by the example of the adolescent
girl who had three distinctly different handwriting styles. Asked why she did not
select one particular style, she replied, "How can I only write one way till I know
who I am" (Conger, 1978).

Part of the uncertainty about identity is allayed by joining an "in-group," an
exclusive group. Such groups can vary from ideological political groups to delinquent teenage gangs (Erikson, 1959); but a development of a sense of self can
also grow out of accomplishments—physical and academic pursuits from which
the adolescent creates a picture of being. "One who can do these things" (1959,
pp. 89–90).

For many adolescents, identity formation can be largely an unconscious process. For those teenagers who for some reason feel strongly that they are unable
to make some lasting commitment to an identity, there may be a need for a
psychological moratorium—a "time-out" period to find oneself (Erikson, 1959,
p. 124). Another reason for desiring time-out may be a wish *not* to accept a
particular identity—what Erikson has described as a need to avoid identity
"foreclosure" (1956). Some adolescents drop out of college for a period, take up
various jobs, or just bum around, picking up enough money to satisfy their needs
as best they can.

Other views have been expressed on the extent of identity crisis during adolescence. A longitudinal study of adolescent boys (Offer, 1969; Offer & Offer, 1974, 1975) revealed that normal adolescents did not experience much turmoil and stress. During early adolescence rebellion against parents was over small concerns. "Bickering is the word most characteristic of these disturbances" (Offer, 1969, p. 186). These adolescents were observed over an eight-year period, and it was discovered that about 80 percent of them could be divided into three basic groups.

The "continuous-growth group" did not appear to experience an identity crisis. They had a realistic self-image and did not suffer from any great emotional turmoil. Parents of these adolescents had an understanding of the problems of this age and were supportive and tolerant of growth toward independence. The "surgent-growth group" were quite well adjusted. They were able to resolve most problems of the adolescent years, but they experienced some difficulty during early adolescence in dealing with unexpected problems. Many parents of this group did not share beliefs on how to relate to their teenagers. There were many conflicting values, and mothers had difficulty accepting their children's increasing desire for independence. Only the "tumultuous-growth group" showed the excessive identity crisis and extreme emotional problems that some theorists believe are characteristic of adolescence. They had major problems with parents and society and about one third received some therapy or counseling.

Other studies such as those by Douvan and Adelson (1966) and Elder (1962) have arrived at similar conclusions. Well-adjusted, autonomous adolescents have democratic or authoritative parents, while overly dependent and rebellious teenagers have permissive or authoritarian parents. It appears, then, that family structure and relationships exert an important influence on how teenagers adjust to the personality pressures of the adolescent years.

Bandura's Social-Learning Theory

Another view of the impact of socializing influences on personality development and changes in social behavior is that expressed by social-learning theorists. Bandura is a prominent exponent of this theory (at least one aspect of it).

Both Freud and Erikson make a distinction between identification and imitation. Imitation is considered to be merely the copying of other people's behavior and usually is a short-term reflection of behavior. *Identification* is a process of basing, in socially acceptable ways, long-lasting behavior on those of another person or persons (Bronfenbrenner, 1960). Bandura (1969) has criticized the Freudian view because he is opposed to the distinction made between identification and imitation. For Bandura these two aspects of social learning form a single process. He believes that all social behavior can be explained as a process of learning to imitate the behavior of any model who provides positive reinforcement.

Bandura is also opposed to Freud's claim that adolescence is a stressful period. The results of one study (Bandura, 1964) indicated that adolescents do not suddenly seek independence. In most cases parents had encouraged a degree of independence during childhood. Nor were there any unusual signs of rebellion— no more than one would expect of reasonably independent children. Indeed, the teenagers of this study still looked to their parents for advice and espoused their values. It is true, however, that there are changes in the degree and nature of independence during adolescence. Acceptable forms of a growing autonomy are part-time jobs, having one's own bank account, having a more independent social life, and so on (Gold & Douvan, 1969).

According to Bandura's social learning theory, then, adolescence is part of a continuing process of learning, not a stage in its own right. When special differences occur they are likely to be determined by a particular culture as appropriate behavior. For example, in American society dating is encouraged at puberty, but intimate sexual behavior is discouraged. Samoans encourage sex play in child-hood, and later heterosexual relationships in adolescence are considered a normal progression (Mead, 1939). In other cultures, such as those of the Masai of Africa and aboriginal tribes of Australia, initiation rites mark the onset of adolescence. Most rites include rituals, such as circumcision, to mark sexual identity (Burton & Whiting, 1961). Each of these cultures encourages different types of adolescent behavior, and they treat the onset of adolescence in different ways. So Bandura's theory of social-learning behavior gains some support from cross-cultural studies.

Kohlberg: Stage of Postconventional Morality

Finally, we turn again to Kohlberg's cognitive-structuralist view. Kohlberg associates the third level of postconventional moral judgment with the stage of formal reasoning. In his opinion, many adolescents and adults do not achieve this level but remain at the conventional level. Those adolescents who develop a more abstract form of moral reasoning attempt to identify universal moral values that are, necessarily, tied to an existing social order. At the *postconventional moral reasoning* level there are two stages (see Table 8.2).

Postconventional morality: stage 5, concern for the rights of the individual.   The adolescent at this stage is concerned with the individual's moral rights. These rights may sometimes be above the law. This is not to say that the adolescent believes in social disobedience, but rather he or she sees a need to challenge the law on occasions and hopes to change it by democratic means. Do you remember the story of Heinz? His wife was dying and Heinz could not afford to buy the drug needed to help her recover. After hearing the story, children of different ages were asked if it was right for Heinz to steal the drug. A 16-year-old re-sponded: "In my eyes he'd have just cause to do it, but in the law's eyes he'd be wrong. I can't say more than that as to whether it was right nor not" (Kohlberg, 1963, p. 29).

We see here a desire to express support for Heinz's stealing the drug but, at the same time, no intention of saying that the law against stealing was wrong or that in this situation it did not apply to Heinz.

Postconventional morality: stage 6, concern for ethical principles. Universal ethical principles—**ethics**—are not governed by an existing law. An adolescent at this stage would argue that Heinz was breaking the law in stealing the drug—but he had a moral right to save his wife, which was above the law (Kohlberg, 1970). This would be a universal principle. If asked whether Heinz should do the same for any sick person, the answer would be "yes," since there would be an obligation to save all people. If Heinz were to say that his wife was worth stealing the drug for but that another person unrelated to him was not, this would be an example of a moral judgment at stage 3—value of life is based only on affection for a family member.

Being exposed to different moral points of view in early adolescence appears to result in a breaking down of conventional moral reasoning and an emergence of postconventional judgment (Turiel, 1974). However, while some individuals in late adolescence show an understanding of the value of individual freedom, they can be confused about what is universally moral or what is just social convention (1974).

Kohlberg has said that an adolescent reasons at any of the three levels of moral judgment—preconventional, conventional, or postconventional. The level of reasoning can change from one situation to another. As Gardner (1978) points out, arguing the question, for example, of whether Nixon should have given up the tapes is difficult: If the judgment was not to destroy the tapes, this might be because they were Nixon's and he had the right to do with them as he pleased (low level of moral reasoning). At an intermediate level the adolescent might reason that because Nixon had committed impeachable offenses he should give up the tapes. At a mature level of reasoning, associated with late adolescence, the argument might be put that "It's against the law to destroy government property. Nixon cannot disobey the law—he's a citizen like everyone else and therefore mustn't destroy the tapes" (1978, p. 477).

Kohlberg's theory is not without its critics. Peters (1971) has pointed out that Kohlberg has done little to develop the details of a general ethical theory. "Yet without such a theory the notion of moral development is pretty insubstantial" (1971, p. 264). However, Peters and others agree that this theory is of unquestionable importance. "It remain the most stimulating and potentially fertile model of children's moral growth" (Thomas, 1979, p. 382).

Parent-Adolescent Relationships

As we have already seen, normal development can be helped or hindered depending on the relationships that children at all ages have with their parents. A positive relationship between teenagers and their parents has a special importance for the teenage years, at a time when children are seeking greater independence yet feeling the need for continuing support, at a time when they are making adaptations to the attachment that was created during infancy and childhood, yet not breaking it.

It is a generally held belief among theorists that the rearing of children, and especially adolescents, has become a more challenging task in the past ten to fifteen years (Conger, 1977; Yankelovich, 1974). This can be partly attributed to important changes in American society. There has been increased urbanization, changing patterns of marriage, a remarkable increase in the divorce rate, and an increase in the mobility of families (more than half the families in the United States move about every five years) (Conger, 1977; Elder, 1975; Bronfenbrenner, 1975). Other reasons also contribute to a greater difficulty in child rearing.

Probably no decade in our history included as many shocks to a sense of cultural order (and) continuity . . . as the period between the mid-1960s and the present: the rise and abortive demise of the much heralded war on poverty; the escalation of the peaceful riots; the assassination of the Kennedys and Martin Luther King; increasing awareness that we are destroying at an irreversible rate the water, land, and air of the only planet we have to leave our children . . . (Conger, 1978, p. 143).

It has been claimed that the adolescent period is one of conflict and strained communication between teenagers and their parents (Bigner, 1979, p. 211). An age-old reason given is the **generation gap** of differences in values, life-styles, and what Stone and Church (1973) have called *dual ambivalence,* an ambivalence that both parents and adolescents experience. Parents experience ambivalence because, at the same time that they are seeking the best for their children, they often get the impression that their children are not following the correct course for success. Some parents use very strict controls in an attempt to ensure that their teenagers do all the *right* things (Chand, Crider, & Willits, 1975). Teenagers also get caught in ambivalence. Many accept their parents' values and still feel somewhat dependent on their family. But they are also seeking independence, trying to resolve problems for themselves; and they come to resent parental control (see Inset 13.1). Other writers (Offer, 1969; Weiner, 1977) believe that the generation-gap idea is a myth created by the mass media in reporting on a minority of disturbed adolescents.

Bigner (1979) has remarked that the critical issue relevant to parent-teenage conflict is that of control. Most parents feel a responsibility for their teenagers' behavior. A recurring problem for parents is how to exert control without alienating their children and thereby losing control to some extent. Elkind (1974) has described three types of arrangements that can be negotiated between parents and their teenagers that would help lessen conflict and tension. He calls these the bargain, the agreement, and the contract.

A *bargain* is arranged when parents offer some reward for the teenager's cooperation. The teenager may set up the bargain— "I'll help with the housework if I can use the car later." *Agreements* are long-lasting bargains. "Unless you spend more time making sure you complete homework assignments, you will not be allowed out to meet your friends over the next few weeks." Contracts may be definite agreements or less explicit expectations. According to Elkind a *contract* has three characteristics: (1) parents expect their teenage children to accept certain responsibilities in return for freedom; (2) parents set up expectations regarding levels of achievement and offer emotional support; and (3) parents expect loyalty and commitment to their beliefs and values (Elkind, 1974, pp. 86–87).

It seems to be the case that the adolescent prospers best with democratic or authoritative parents. These parents involve their maturing adolescents in family concerns, they share decision making, they set reasonable and mutually agreed controls, and they encourage the seeking of independence while still accepting responsibility for their children (Baumrind, 1968; Jessor & Jessor, 1974; Kandel & Lesser, 1972; Elder, 1968).

Roger Libby and Gilbert Nass (1971) interviewed 250 parents of varying social class, religion, and age, in Manchester, Connecticut, to find out what they considered to be "appropriate rules and behavior in teenage courtship."

Parents were asked questions such as these:

Who should make up dating rules, and should they differ according to whether the teenager is a boy or girl?

What do you feel a parent should do, if anything, if he or she realizes an 18-year-old daughter/ son is having sexual relations before marriage?

In what ways are you approaching sex education in your family?

Other questions asked about parents' views on their own sex education, whether they believed their attitudes toward teenagers' sexual behavior were different from those of their parents, and whether they believed teenagers should be informed about contraceptives and the dangers of venereal disease and premarital pregnancy. Using the Traditional Family Idealogy Scale, it was also ascertained which parents were *democratic* and which were *autocratic*. How did parents respond to the questions? Were responses different according to sex, social class, religion, and whether parents were democratic or autocratic?

Irrespective of their democratic or autocratic parenting styles parents essentially expressed conservative attitudes regarding courtship behavior. Most parents believed that "parents and teenagers should work out the rules together—50–50." They expressed considerable disapproval of both daughters' and sons' nonmarital sexual involvements and approval of emphasizing sexually transmitted disease and nonmarital pregnancy as a fear technique to deter teenage sexual behavior. Here is a typical parent response:

I try to keep them from knowing too much. . . . My parents did not tell me about it. I don't discuss it either. I think sex education corrupts the minds of 15- and 16-year-olds! I just tell them to behave and keep their eyes open.

An arrangement between parents and a teenage child— for example, to use the family car—may be a bargain, agreement, *or* contract. *(Photo by Rose Stork)*

However, democratic parents, compared to autocratic parents, showed less dissatisfaction with their own sex education and were more willing for their children to have considerable sex education.

Mothers and fathers differed very little in their views on teenage sexual behavior—although mothers were more apt to contend that parents should decide dating rules. Attitudes toward premarital sex differed according to parents' social class. Lower-class parents were rather more restrictive and advocated active restrictions and punishments as a deterent. Parents from the middle and upper-middle class believed that, while showing firm disapproval, it was also necessary to be understanding, to discuss the matter with their children, and, if necessary, to seek outside help from psychiatrists and ministers.

Parents holding different religious views were generally in agreement about courtship norms. All parents who held humanistic, agnostic, atheistic, and Jewish beliefs agreed that teenagers should know about contraceptives. About one third of Catholic and Protestant parents were opposed to this view.

The overall picture showed parents struggling with the determination of the amount of freedom to be entrusted to teenagers in deciding their dating limits and advocating . . . a conservative single standard in regard to courtship rules. . . . Adults preferred to replace the double standard with a conservative single standard, although youth are more prone to adapt a single standard of permissiveness with affection. . . . The fact that nearly all parents took a traditional rather than liberal approach to the sex education of their children is probably typical of many cities and suburban communities. It appeared that parents were seeking an answer to changing sexual standards . . . searching for some way to put the lid back on while maintaining some degree of democratic procedure with their adolescents (Libby & Nass, *Parental Views on Teenage Sexual Behavior,* 1971, pp. 235–236).

Source: Adapted from R. W. Libby and G. D. Nass, "Parental Views on Teenage Sexual Behavior." *The Journal of Sex Research,* 1971.

Peer Relationships

The *peer group* provides a sense of belonging, a contrast with the values and expectations of the family, a chance to engage in behaviors parents do not favor, and confirmation of success as a social adolescent.

Peer relationships that became so important in middle childhood change throughout adolescence. Dunphy (1963) has described three phases of group development. (1) The same-sex groups of middle childhood continue through preadolescence into early adolescence; (2) but as adolescence approaches there is also a move toward relationships with groups of the opposite sex; (3) in early

adolescence heterosexual cliques form. These are usually small groups of dating couples. This is not to say that same-sex peer groups completely disappear. Both types of groups now exist side-by-side and serve rather different socializing functions. One function they share is to influence the development of sexuality and sex-role identity, both of which appear to depend on interactions in both same- and opposite-sex groups.

Dating

Although teenagers spend considerable time in mixed-sex groups, they often join these groups as dating couples. There are different views about dating and how it occurs. When boy meets girl for the first date, usually around age 14 or 15 (though there is an increasing occurrence of dating as early as 11 to 12), this is the beginning of heterosexual relationships (Gold & Douvan, 1969). Gold and Douvan describe dating as being ritualized. Dating partners expect each other to be cheerful and well-mannered. Sorenson (1973) suggested that adolescents are now tending to rush into sexual relationships. He commented that this may be true only for some 17- and 18-year-olds, though more recent evidence notes such relationships occurring as early as ages 11 to 12 years for some adolescents (Hass, 1979). It also appears that many adolescents who begin to *go steady* have low educational and vocational aspirations and feel socially insecure (Larson,

Spreitzer, & Snyder, 1976). Simon, Berger, and Gagnon (1972) have shown that patterns of dating vary widely among peer groups and that there is a strong relationship between dating and frequency of sexual experience. Relationships vary from "just good friends" to very close relationships. As dating frequency increases, it is likely that, for some couples, the pressures, pleasures, demands, and expectations of the dating relationship in terms of frequency of dating, as well as sexual contact and the supportiveness of a close friendship, will overshadow religious, parental, and peer-group influences (Spanier, 1979).

Peer Influence Compared to Parental Influence

Some believe the adolescent peer group is far more influential in setting standards of behavior than is the family or school. This belief rests partly on the fact that American society tends to segregate the high school teenager from parents and other age groups by creating a teenage subculture with its own particular fashions in clothes, music, and entertainment and its own norms of behavior. A major source of influence is the world of advertising and business. Most teenagers find it easy to obtain work, especially staffing many of the nation's fast-food outlets. Earnings go to the purchase of clothes, records, entertainment, and food specially packaged for teenage consumption. In addition, Bronfenbrenner (1970) points out that many parents have abdicated their influence by spending less time with their teenage children. The result, claims Bronfenbrenner, will be the adolescents' greater dependence on peer influences—not all of which can be assumed to be desirable.

While it seems safe to say that peer-group influence has been increasing, it is not necessarily the case that parental influence has been declining (Conger, 1977). For many adolescents peers' and parents' values overlap to some considerable extent, thus serving to reinforce each other (Mussen, Conger, & Kagan, 1979, p. 460). The peer group tends to set standards in music, types of entertainment, fashion fads, and same-age social interactions. Parents usually strongly influence and broaden their teenage children's moral and social values such as acceptance of particular types of social behavior required in the "adult-world" and job aspiration and expectations (Conger, 1977).

However, peer and parental influences vary from one adolescent to another depending on such matters as parental affection and concern, amount and type of attention from parents and adolescents' individual personalities (Condry & Siman, 1974; Elder, 1968; Hirschi, 1969).

Condry and Simon (1974), in comparing peer-oriented adolescents with adult-oriented ones, found that the former had more negative views of themselves. They viewed themselves, as meaner and less obedient and dependable than adult-oriented teenagers. It was also found that parents of peer-oriented adolescents were lacking in attention and affection.

Teenage delinquent gangs are found in slum areas of most cities in the United States. Different gangs frequently fight each other over territorial rights and as an expression of male courage. (Photo by Michael Abramson/Black Star)

Gangs

Juvenile delinquents are young adolescents under the age of 18 who commit crimes ranging from relatively petty acts of running away from home and small thefts to aggravated robbery, rape, and homicide. About three quarters of adolescent delinquents are boys aged between 14 and 16 years (Hauck, 1970). Male delinquency is characterized by aggressive acts. Even theft, the most frequent type of delinquent act, is considered to be a misuse of acceptable male courage and daring. This type of **delinquency** is as common to upper- and middle-class boys as lower-class boys (Vaz, 1969).

Most teenage delinquent acts are commited by gangs. Delinquent gangs have been fast growing since the end of World War II (Federal Bureau of Investigation, 1977). These gangs are predominantly youths found in the slum areas of most of the major United States cities—New York, Philadelphia, Chicago, Detroit, Boston, and so on (see Inset 13.2). Because of the increase in serious acts of crime and a growing death toll, these gangs have stirred up considerable social concern. They are associated with conditions of poverty, broken homes, lack of parental control, lack of educational and vocational models, personality deficiencies, and severe pressures from established delinquent peer groups (Friedman, Mann, & Freidman, 1975). Not all adolescents, even from the most deprived environments, join delinquent gangs. The delinquent gang member is likely to come from a home that is lacking in affection, firm values, and cohesiveness. Parents in these homes are either too lax or consistently use physical punishment

In the slum sections of Chicago, Los Angeles, Boston, and other areas, there has been a recent surge of gang-related violence and death.

Philadelphia, meanwhile, is virtually free of the stabbings and shootings that once earned the city its reputation as the youth-gang capital of America. The gangs still exist, but their constant warfare is over. Police authorities around the country are asking why.

The answer appears to have less to do with effective police tactics or government programs than with citizen action. In fact, the real lesson of Philadelphia begins with a single family. A father and mother and their six sons were primarily responsible for the grass-roots pressure that brought the bloodshed in their city to an end.

The year 1969 had been dubbed "the year of the gun" in Philadelphia. Some forty black teenage males in the city were dying annually in the gang wars, and each year hundreds more were being maimed for life. "We were killing each other off," recalls a former gang member. "There was so much gunfire going on that you'd be out on the streets duckin' bullets. I used to get up each morning and prepare myself for death." The gangs—with names such as Empire, Moon, Valley, Suicide Squad, and Zulu Nation—controlled separate sections of Philadelphia's sprawling slums.

In West Philadelphia, David and Falaka Fattah lived in the midst of the violence with their six sons. Like other parents they were concerned about gang wars; but when they discovered that their oldest son had become a fringe member of the Clymer Street gang, they became so alarmed that they changed not only their career plans but their entire lives. "We felt that the reason for the gangs was the destruction of the family," says Falaka, now known as Sister Fattah. "The kids were substituting the gang for their family."

Most of the gang members did, in fact, come from broken homes where supervision was loose or nonexistent. Within the gangs, they felt a sense of identity, security, and structure for which they were willing to kill and possibly die.

"Our theory was that if the problem was the breakdown of families," Sister Fattah recalls, "then the solution was to rebuild one for them."

And so they responded with one of the boldest, most unorthodox moves ever made by a father and mother. They invited fifteen tough, alienated members of the Clymer Street gang into their small, two-story row house on North Frazier Street and

which leads to mutual hostility. Adolescents from these homes fall easy prey to the pressures of a delinquent gang (Bandura & Walters, 1959).

It appears that one of the most promising ways to treat delinquents is by rehabilitation in group homes (Fixsen, Montrose, & Phillips, in press; Phillips, Phillips, Fixsen, & Wolf, 1973; and see Inset 13.3). The important aspect of this "treatment" is the provision of an alternate home that provides warmth, security, and affectionate surrogate parents. In one home, Achievement Place, a group of about six boys live with their "professional parents." They assume personal and social responsibilities for which they receive special privileges. In the Fattah House in Philadelphia there is a similar arrangement. The Philadelphia house involves the boys in a wide variety of neighborhood programs, with the emphasis on community service. The Fattahs are trying to raise $1 million to be used in renovation of other neighborhood houses. This "settlement" will become the first

renamed the house House of Umoja. If the young men would lay down their weapons and become part of an "extended" family, the Fattahs would supervise and feed them for a year. When the fifteen members of the Clymer Street gang warily moved in, all the furniture in the four-room house was removed to make way for mattresses. David and Falaka began tutoring the young men in English, math, and economics and prepared them for court appearances and job interviews.

"After a year," Sister Fattah recalls, "we were all alive and no one went to jail, nor did any of the kids want to move back home." Moreover, as word spread, members of the other gangs began seeking sanctuary at the house. The Fattah family's impact on the entire city began to be felt. Gang-related deaths dropped to thirty-two in 1974, fifteen in 1975, six in 1976, and only one in the past three-and-a-half years.

With the help of business, church, and civic groups, as well as their own fund-raising efforts, the Fattahs accommodated new arrivals by acquiring and repairing twenty-one rundown houses on the same block of Frazier Street. To maintain their "integrity" as a family unit, David and Falaka never accepted more than 30 boys at a time. Yet to date some 500 needy young men have lived there under their supervision. A point emphasized by Sister Fattah is that the House does not isolate the boys from the community. On the contrary, there is strong guidance toward community service.

Among those studying the House of Umoja is the American Enterprise Institute for Public Policy Research, a conservative-leaning "think tank." Robert L. Woodson, 42, formerly of the Fattahs' West Philadelphia neighborhood and now resident fellow at the Institute, believes the family's success "demonstrates the wisdom of supporting such grass-roots efforts instead of attempting to impose solutions from the outside." Could the House of Umoja be duplicated elsewhere? "It's possible," says Sister Fattah. "There are people like us in cities all over."

Most of the boys who have passed through the House have gone on to live productive lives. Sister Fattah warns, however, that even in Philadelphia the gangs have by no means disappeared. "They're still recruiting," she says, "because there are always new youngsters. The violence in the past was really just a cry for help: 'Look at me—I'm in trouble.' This new generation needs our support in terms of education and jobs."

Source: Adapted from Whittemore, Hank. "One Family Conquers Gang War," *Parade,* May 6, 1980. Reprinted by permission.

Boys Town in an urban setting. It appears necessary for further home-based rehabilitation centers to be established in our cities as speedily as possible, in an attempt to reduce a seriously increasing rate of delinquency.

Disturbances during Adolescence

Searching for identity, coming to terms with an awakening adult sexuality, introspecting about changing personal value systems, dealing with inconsistencies between personal values and those of family and society, reacting to the exacting demands from society are all simultaneously creating problems for the adolescent.

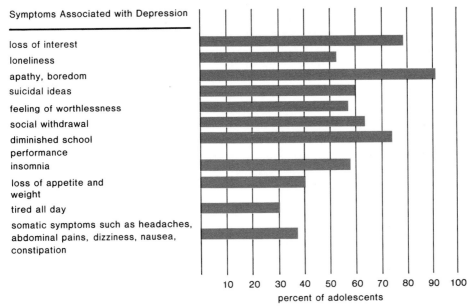

Symptoms Associated with Depression

loss of interest
loneliness
apathy, boredom
suicidal ideas
feeling of worthlessness
social withdrawal
diminished school
performance
insomnia
loss of appetite and
weight
tired all day
somatic symptoms such as headaches,
abdominal pains, dizziness, nausea,
constipation

10 20 30 40 50 60 70 80 90 100
percent of adolescents

Figure 13.1 Symptoms associated with depression during adolescence. In some cases adolescent depression is marked by an incident such as a death in the family, but in other cases depressive moods start gradually. Depressive moods can last for as short a time as a few hours and as long as a day or two. Adolescent depression seems strongly related to loss of interest, apathy-boredom, poor concentration, diminished school performance, and suicidal ideas. (Source: Inamdar, S. C., Siomopoulos, G., Osborn, M., and Bianchi, E. C. "Phenomonology Associated with Depressed Moods in Adolescents." *The American Journal of Psychiatry,* 1979, *136.* 156–159. Copyright 1979, the American Psychiatric Association. Reprinted by permission.)

It is inevitable that some ***adolescent disturbances*** will occur varying from mild forms of rebellion, anxiety, **depression,** (see Figure 13.1) and drug use to serious psychopathic disorders. The severity of disturbance will depend on the type and degree of stress experienced and how well equipped the adolescent is to withstand stress or adjust to it (Chapman, 1974; Conger, 1977).

Anxiety

Anxiety, in a severe form, is an irrational fear of such things as school, being in enclosed or open spaces, heights, animals such as rats and spiders, and so on. Reactions to extreme anxiety or phobias include dizziness, severe headaches, nausea, a fear that one is dying, restlessness and sleeplessness (Anthony, 1970;

Nemiah, 1974). One treatment for severe anxiety is a form of behavior modification called *desensitization*. The person is gradually brought closer to the object that is causing the anxiety while at the same time being provided with something pleasant. Some anxieties are difficult to treat but facing up to an anxiety during treatment helps.

Eating Problems

Two problems associated with eating can occur during adolescence: anorexia nervosa and bulimia. **Anorexia nervosa** is diagnosed as the refusal or inability to eat sufficiently (see Inset 13.3). It is more common in adolescent girls than boys. In some cases dieting is so extreme that it threatens the individual's life (Bruch, 1973). **Bulimia** is the opposite condition of excessive overeating that results in obesity.

Inset 13.3
Anorexia Nervosa

An interesting account of anorexia nervosa has been provided by Hilda Bruch in her book *The Golden Cage: The Enigma of Anorexia Nervosa*. She describes this sickness as the hunger disease:

"It is such a terrible disease because you watch your child deliberately hurting herself, and obviously suffering, and yet you are unable to help her. Another tragedy is that it affects the whole family, for we live in an atmosphere of constant fear and tension." These sentences are taken from the letter of a distressed mother who asked for help for her 20-year-old daughter who had been sick with anorexia nervosa for five years. At 15 Alma had been healthy and well-developed, had menstruated at age 12, was 5 feet 6 inches tall, and weighed 120 pounds. At that time her mother urged her to change to a school with higher academic standing, a change she resisted; her father suggested that she should watch her weight, an idea that she took up with great eagerness, and she began a rigid diet. She lost weight rapidly and her menses ceased. She had been below 70 pounds most of the five years and there had been a marked change in her character and behavior. Formerly sweet, obedient, and considerate she became more and more demanding, obstinate, irritable, and arrogant (1978, pp. 1–2).

This is a fairly typical case of a girl suffering from anorexia nervosa (there are many more girls than boys with this disease), a puzzling disease, full of contradictions and paradoxes. "These youngsters willingly undergo the ordeal of starvation. Whatever their inner feelings, or however inaccurately they interpret or report them, anorexics do not suffer from loss of appetite, but from the panicky fear of gaining weight. Those who experience hunger train themselves to consider it pleasant and desirable" (Bruch, 1978, pp. 3–4).

These are the physical signs of the disease. But what are the causes of this ailment?

Anorexia nervosa is characterized by excessive dieting and resulting severe weight loss. (Photo by Robert Eckert/EKM-Nepenthe)

Behavior during the acute state of starvation, or in long-lasting chronic starvation, reveals little, if anything, about the underlying psychological factors. I have come to the conclusion that the effect on psychological functioning of low food intake is to a large extent responsible for the drawn-out course of the illness, sustaining it and making recognition and resolution of the precipitating psychological issues difficult, if not impossible.

Yet the hunger experience is not sufficient to fully explain the development of anorexia nervosa. It is not a disease that just befalls a girl; she is always a very active participant in the process. Many anorexics express themselves in similar ways, that their whole life has been an ordeal of wanting to live up to the expectations of their families, always fearing they were not good enough in comparison with others and, therefore, disappointing failures. This dramatic dissatisfaction is a core issue in anorexia nervosa and it precedes the concern with weight and dieting (Bruch, 1978, pp. 10–23).

Not all clinicians and therapists are convinced that this disease can be attributed to problematic relationships within the family. Along with differences of opinion about possible factors that might influence the onset and development of this disease, there are different opinions about how to treat it. Those therapists who view anorexia nervosa primarily as one type of maladaptive behavior focus on the form of the behavior itself and attempt to modify it by rewarding alternative, acceptable behaviors and using sanctions against reversals to excessive dieting. Therapists who believe the root cause can be found within the framework of family relationships try to involve the whole family in therapy sessions aimed at identifying underlying psychological causes for a girl's behavior. The girl is then encouraged to attempt to resolve the psychological problems, with the help of the entire family, and in that manner cure herself of the disease.

Source: Bruch, H., *The Golden Cage: The Enigma of Anorexia Nervosa.* Harvard University Press, 1978.

Bruch (1973, 1974) suggests that both conditions may be due to a sense of role diffusion. The young adolescent girl may believe she has been prevented from forming a clear personal identity. This belief and a need to define an identity are reflected in an obsessive attempt to control the body. It has also been suggested that, since excessive dieting produces a slim boyish figure rather than the rounded figure of the young woman, anorexia is an unconscious reaction against growing up. For hospitalized anorexics a behavioristic treatment is to reward weight gain by privileges such as watching television or being allowed out of the hospital for short periods, and to punish weight loss by withdrawing privileges. Another belief is that anorexia nervosa is associated with disturbed families (Minuchin, Rosman, & Baker, 1978). Minuchin treats the anorexic teenager indirectly through psychotherapy with the whole family. He claims successful treatment in about 88 percent of the cases. In most cases bulimia is considered to be an expression of the need for love. This condition usually begins before adolescence and is associated with psychological upsets in early childhood. Yet it reaches a pronounced stage during adolescence. Treatment is usually the same as for anorexia nervosa, differing according to whether the therapist takes a psychoanalytic or behavioristic view.

Suicide

Very few young children (preadolescents) commit suicide. From middle adolescence to early adulthood there is a marked increase in the rate of suicides. Bronfenbrenner (1975) reports that the number of suicides for adolescents aged 15 to 19 has increased from about 3 in every 100,000 in 1951–52 to 7 per 100,000 in 1974. If we include the group age 19 to 24, the figure for males in 1974 increased to 17 in every 10,000 *(U.S. Fact Book, 1977)* for this age group, but only 5 out of 100,000 females committed suicide. The rate increases for older groups, with the highest number of suicides occurring for men 65 and older (37 per 100,000). Only 7 in every 100,000 women in this age group committed suicide in 1974.

Why do teenagers commit or attempt to commit suicide? It is usually because of severe depression or despair and results from events such as school failure, the break up of a romance, an unwanted pregnancy, conflict with parents, loss of a close friend or family member, and so on (Cantor, 1977; Jacobs, 1971; Jacobs & Teicher, 1967). Usually, adolescents who commit suicide have a history of severe family problems (Jacobs, 1971). Adolescents who threaten suicide should be taken seriously—most are serious in their intentions.

When Bill was in the ninth grade, his mother accused him of stealing five dollars from her purse. He told her that he had not taken anything from her purse, but she insisted that he did; upset by her disbelief, he shouted that he was going to go into the bathroom and hang himself. His mother was believed to have said to go ahead. Bill went into the bathroom and approximately one-half hour later, they found him hanging by his belt from the shower rod. He was dead! (Kaluger & Kaluger, 1976, p. 122)

Adolescents who show signs of potential suicide—continued depression, social withdrawal, a breakdown of relations with parents, threats of and attempted suicide—should receive treatment. The most frequent form of treatment is supportive therapy or counseling (Goldberg et al., 1979).

Drug Abuse

The amount of drugs use by some teenagers reached epidemic proportions in the late 1960s and early 1970s. The use of drugs is associated with the need to reduce anxiety; it is a means of "escape" from social pressures or a response to social pressures. Although it is believed that there was a downswing in drug taking during the 1970s, the reasons behind the abuse of drugs remain the same— alienation and peer pressure. For many teenagers it is one of the "things to do" in the peer group, but it is not always a serious problem. Use of such drugs as alcohol, marijuana, and tobacco is widespread. LDS, amphetamines, barbiturates, heroin, cocaine, and the newer drugs like "Angel Dust" and the Quaaludes are not used in anything like the proportions forecast on the basis of drug taking in the 1960s. Only about one in five teenagers use this range of drugs (Conger, 1977; Johnston & Bachman, 1975; Johnston, Bachman, & O'Malley, 1977).

Social and Personality Development **579**

Table 13.1 Adolescent Use of Selected Drugs: Ages 12–18.

Drug	% Use
Marijuana	30
Inhalants	10
Hallucinogens	6
Cocaine	4
Heroin	1
Stimulants	5
Tranquilizers	4
Sedatives	3
Alcohol	60
Tobacco	47

Adapted from National Institute on Drug Abuse. *National Survey on Drug Abuse: 1977. Vol. I: Main Findings*. Washington, D.C.: U.S. Government Printing Office, 1977 and Goldstein, A., & O'Donnell, J. *Handbook of Drug Abuse*. Washington, D.C.: U.S. Government Printing Office, 1979.

The most frequently used drugs in the past decade have been alcohol and tobacco. During this period there has been a dramatic decrease in the use of opiates, such as heroin, and a significant increase in the use of marijuana.

The drug adolescents use most frequently is alcohol, followed by tobacco and marijuana. Although most teenagers are temperate drinkers, about 5 percent of those in grades 7 through 12 drink in excess (see Table 13.1). Teenage drinking can be linked to parental and peer modeling (Jessor, 1977). Results from studies of twins (Coleman, 1976) also suggest that some people may be genetically disposed to become addicted to alcohol.

Marijuana (*cannabis,* also known as pot or grass) is a commonly used drug. Smoked, or eaten as an ingredient in foodstuffs, this drug produces a feeling of being "high." This distortion of the senses is described as a hallucination or delusion, and the drug is therefore classifed as a *hallucinogen.* The study by Johnston, Bachman, and O'Malley (1977) shows an increase in its use by high school seniors (see Figure 13.2). Research has shown that occasional use of marijuana seems to produce no adverse effects (Brecher, 1975). But there is concern that heavy and prolonged use may be harmful. Until further research is conducted, the effects of this drug will remain a question of some concern.

We know that drug use is widespread. Do many adolescents take drugs in serious proportions? Among high school students there appears to be only occasional use (see Table 13.1). Most teenagers who try narcotics do so as an "experiment" and quickly stop. Kandal and Faust (1975) report that the progression from soft drugs such as marijuana to hard drugs such as heroin is directly linked to the intensity of use of the soft drug, not to the soft drug itself.

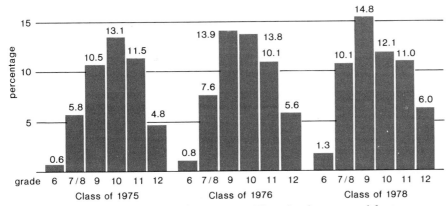

Figure 13.2 First use of marijuana by teenagers. There has been a trend for teenagers to begin first using marijuana at earlier ages. Increases in supply of low-cost marijuana and a relaxation of laws against possession of small amounts of this drug are reasons usually given for the increase in usage. (Source: Johnston, Bachman, and O'Malley, 1977. DHEW Publication No. (ADM) 78–619.)

Serious drug users are a minority, but the "drug scene" is complex. It is important to continue to educate teenagers about drugs and their possible detrimental affects.

Pregnancy

There has been an increasing trend toward sexual activity at earlier ages, and unwed *adolescent pregnancy* has become a very real problem (Sorensen, 1973). In the United States between 1971 and 1976, there was a 30 percent increase in sexual activity by unmarried teenage girls (Zelnick & Kantner, 1977). During the same time the number of pregnancies for unmarried teenage mothers also increased. For unmarried girls between 15 and 19 years of age, one in fifteen became pregnant (Alan Guttmacher Institute, 1976). There are 13,000 births per year to girls aged 15 years or younger (Magrab & Danielson-Murphy, 1979), and one out of every ten girls between the ages of 12 and 17 years in the United States is already a mother (Bartz, 1980). However, adolescent girls who become pregnant are no different in their sexual behavior from those who avoid pregnancy. Furstenberg (1976) was told by young unwed mothers he interviewed that they had become pregnant by accident.

What accounts for this increase? At the top of the list is the fact that many sexually active teenagers simply do not use any birth control methods. Of those

teenage girls questioned by Zelnik and Kantner (1977), 25 percent said they *never* used any form of **contraception,** 45 percent said they sometimes used a contraceptive, and only 30 percent said they always used a contraceptive. Nonuse can be put down mainly to ignorance. Many teenagers do not know enough about "getting pregnant" and about "avoiding pregnancy" by using forms of contraception. Teenagers have claimed that it is difficult to get contraceptives, that they do not know where they can be obtained, or that they fear their parents will find them (Sorensen, 1973). Sorensen also found that 30 percent of the girls questioned actually believed it was impossible to get pregnant "if a girl truly doesn't want to have a baby."

What are the options for the unmarried teenage expectant mother? About 14 percent get married while pregnant. Miscarriage or abortion ends the pregnancy for about 58 percent. Another 28 percent have their babies while remaining unmarried, and most opt to keep and look after them (Alan Guttmacher Institute, 1976).

Problems associated with teenage pregnancies are many. Eight out of ten teenagers who become pregnant at or before age 17 never complete high school. Nine out of ten teenage mothers aged 15 or younger never complete eighth grade (Honig, 1978). Teenagers who marry because of a pregnancy are likely to have marriage problems. For many of these couples there is usually a lack of a loving commitment to each other (Furstenberg, 1976). One fifth of these marriages break up in the first year and three out of five in the first six years (Honig, 1978; Moore & Waite, 1978). Other reasons for these failed marriages are economic problems, a lack of personality and social maturity, and a lack of adjustment in social relationships. In most of these cases help is needed in resolving the various problems that are likely to arise both during pregnancy and after the birth of the baby. Unmarried teenage mothers may benefit from this decision if their families agree to support them and their babies. Many school districts are now offering special programs to help prevent pregnant teenagers from dropping out of school (Furstenberg, 1976).

Adolescents' Values

The fact that this final section on *adolescent values* is presented separately does not mean that we should suppose values develop as an entity apart from other aspects of development. Personality, social-behavior, and value systems that change during adolescence are a complex interacting system—there are no simple cause-and-effect explanations for any of these aspects of development. Adolescence is undoubtedly a time for making important decisions and choices about such things as relationships with one's family and one's peers, attitudes toward school and religion, and the kind of job hoped for. Since we have just been discussing some of the negative characteristics of social and personality development, we will begin with alienation but then move on to consider values that, although they can be reflected in negative behavior, can also be expressed in terms of appropriate social behavior.

Alienation

In working through what Erikson has called the identity crisis, most adolescents achieve a real sense of personal identity. For others identity may become, at least for an extended period of time, an unsurmountable problem. The result is identity or role confusion, also referred to as **alienation.** For Erikson identity crisis refers to a state of alienation from oneself and society. Others have described alienation as the loss or absence of desirable relationships (Keniston, 1960). From Erikson's point of view the conflicts between the adolescent's physical and intellectual development and society's demands are at the root of the problem.

Given the double standards regarding sexual behavior that many adults present to teenagers, it should come as no surprise to find that their judgments about these issues are confused. "Given the sexual hang-ups of our society, much of the crisis of middle adolescence may reflect the attempt of young people to integrate into their identities a sexuality about which they feel considerable ambivalence" (White & Speisman, 1977, p. 93). The intellectual development of this period often results in a deep, introspective evaluation of personal values and those of society. For some adolescents the comparison results in a rejection of society's values.

But there are other cultural reasons for alienation to which youth are most susceptible because of their intense concern with identity. Youths from minority groups and impoverished white communities have alienation thrust upon them by discrimination and poverty. At an extreme level this was demonstrated by the riots in Harlem, New York, 1964, which erupted from a rally to protest the killing of a black youth by a white police officer; the riots in Los Angeles, 1965; in Cleveland, 1966; in Newark and Detroit, 1967; and Washington, 1968. Of the blacks killed in the Miami riots of 1980, most were teenagers and young adults.

The "counter-culture" of the 1960s was a youthful demonstration against United States policies over the war in Vietnam. It also represented intense, abstract philosophical arguments against what was believed to be (and was sometimes demonstrated to be) an unjust, hypocritical, and cruel society (Conger, 1977). Reactions varied from conventional demonstrations to violent revolutionary tactics to the flower children and hippie dropouts.

For others, dealing with cultural alienation is more of an intellectual problem—no less painful for that, as can be illustrated by the thoughts of a black woman at college coming to terms with her minority group status.

Inset 13.4
**Sex Education
in Schools**

Most adolescents become preoccupied with sex. They exchange information about sex, a great deal of which is myth. Ignorance about sex, unfortunately, underlies the rapid increase in recent years of unwanted pregnancies and sexually transmitted diseases. Gordon (1973) has pointed out that such diverse groups as the White House Conference on Children, the National Council of America's Committee on the Family, and the United States Catholic Conference Family Life Bureau have urged the establishment of sensitive sex education programs for adolescents. What form should sex education take in the schools? Gordon suggests the following approach.

Clearly the responsibility for sex education must be shared by parents and social services in the community, as well as the schools. We cannot continue to dump this difficult problem on the schools and expect miracles. . . . Parents must be educated about sexuality so that they can accept much of the responsibility for their children's sex education. Church and social groups for youths must recognize the contribution they can make in this area. Given the context of shared responsibility for sex education, what can we realistically expect the schools to do in making youth more knowledgeable about their own sexuality? . . . The first thing I would suggest including in a sex education course would be basic facts that adolescents need to know—information on sexual maturation, pregnancy, birth control, sexual intercourse. . . .

Another important piece of information that should be taught in schools concerns VD—how it is contracted, its effects, treatment, and how to prevent it (including the use of condoms). But the area of sex education that is most needed, and in the long run will be the most effective in curbing irresponsible sex, disease, and pregnancy, deals with the basic attitudes and orientations to *all* human relationships. It is in this area that the schools, particularly teachers and administrators responsible for social studies, psychology, or human relations courses, must closely examine the limitations and potential. . . .

One obvious limitation on the schools is in the attitudes and values that children bring with them to school. A more "internal" limitation is the factor of student trust and the school's authority. Students are generally suspicious of the school's attempts to control or influence

She was once a freshman. And for a black woman this place was a mass of "never-before-possibilities". . . . [But] this year has been pain. . . . It is too much to be a teacher–educator, confessor to all the white guilt complexes. . . . It is too much sometimes, because you are expected to cope with it all and to integrate it into some cohesion. And you do, somehow. . . . You are marred a little by conflict and you are more than a little sorry that it has been so hard. But you are, and you are black, and you are moving. And that's the wonder of it (Goethals & Klos, 1970, pp. 152–153).

Sexual Relationships

Values placed on sexual relationships change during adolescence. Feinstein and Ardon (1973) describe a sequence of four stages of change. From ages 13 to 15 there is a sexual awakening. Both sexes may feel some insecurity about their sex roles, partly because of differences in physical maturity. During the phase from ages 14 to 17 adolescents depend less on same-sex relationships. There occur more short-term relationships between opposite sex partners (see Inset 13.4).

---

their lives. They are particularly likely to reject anything pushed at them by the establishment, including birth control and VD prevention information. Adolescents will accept information which they can use to their own advantage, but they will not adapt their behavior to the moralizing of teachers, parents, or school board officials. . . . However, if the students enjoy the time spent in school, a great deal can be accomplished. In an environment that is emotionally reinforcing, schools may be able to help adolescents develop a better awareness of their sexuality, along with a greater sensitivity to others. . . .

Since the greatest potential for sex education lies in psychology and human relations courses, let us take a deeper look at what the schools can teach here. A consideration of the question "What is normal?" would be a way of revealing that there is a tremendous range of human behavior that is acceptable. Teenagers have questions about masturbation, homosexuality, pornography, and perversions that must be answered openly and knowledgeably. And no course in human relations would be adequate without considering the implications of women's liberation and the sexism inherent in societal roles, such as the double standard and its implications. Discussing any one of the above issues that adolescents *want* to understand is also what is urgently needed in our sex education efforts.

If the schools are to be even marginally effective in lowering rates of VD and unwanted pregnancy, they must recognize their limitations as well as realize their potential. In psychology, fortunately, there is great potential because adolescents already *want* to know what they *need* to know. Psychology teachers can take advantage of this inherent interest and really *educate* about sexuality, if they foster student trust, communicate honestly and openly, and refrain from moralizing. ("Moralizing," of course, is not the same as presenting one's own opinion as one alternative among many.) The schools cannot handle the job of sex education without help from parents and community services. However, with a realistic assessment of what they can do, the schools can make a real and immediate contribution to educating adolescents for responsible sexual behavior.

Source: Adaptation from *The Sexual Adolescent: Communicating with Teenagers about Sex,* by S. Gordon. Copyright © 1973 by Wadsworth Publishing Co., Inc. Reprinted by permission of the publisher, Brooks/Cole Publishing Company, Monterey, California.

Many young parents now share fathering and mothering roles. (Photo by Jean-Claude Lejeune)

There seems to be a need to *experiment* with relationships rather than to establish long-lasting relationships. Sexual identity and sex role are more surely accepted in the period from ages 16 to 19. Adolescents become more certain about sexual relationships. Finally, between ages 18 and 25, long-term relationships are established. Adolescents are now capable of establishing not merely physical relationships or fleeting friendships but true intimacy.

Traditional sex-stereotypic views of the masculine man and feminine woman are slowly giving way to a belief in an **androgynous** identity (having characteristics of both sexes), at least in certain subcultures (Bem, 1974; Block, 1973; Pleck, 1975). This means that in late adolescence and early adulthood some individuals combine masculine and feminine behavior in many situations (Bem, 1975). One example of this would be young parents who share fathering and mothering roles, as well as a whole range of household chores.

Religious Values

In keeping with changes in values already described, during the adolescent years religious beliefs and attitudes toward religion become less rule oriented and more tolerant (Conger, 1977). Yankelovich (1974) has reported that late adolescents still in high school place a greater importance on religion than young adults do. The fact that more young people than in the past appear disinterested in religion has been attributed to the fact that institutionalized religion has not

Older adolescents become concerned with achievement and success, especially as it applies to vocational interests. (Photo by Allen Ruid)

kept up with the times. Important differences between the values of church and youth have resulted in many teenagers' alienation from religion (Sorenson, 1973).

In the past decade there has been an increasing growth of religious sects that make a direct appeal to youth—for example, the Jesus Movement, Hare Krishna (popularized for a time by George Harrison), and the "Moonies" (members of Sun Myung Moon's Unification Church). The attraction of some of these sects for adolescents is their informality and stated concern for helping others.

There are some sects that use extreme indoctrinating methods to control young people who join. Part of this process involves strengthening alienation from the home. Many young people experiencing role diffusion join these sects. They see them as offering acceptable rules and values as an alternative to those of home and society, which they have rejected (Bengston & Starr, 1975) but not replaced personally.

Achievement Values

Young adolescents often have an idealistic view that "taking part" is just as important as outcome. In later adolescence it is the outcome rather than the effort that becomes more important (Weiner & Peters, 1973). This change in attitude toward achievement value is attributed somewhat to the fact that in American society youths learn that successful achievement pays off, and also they gain a clearer understanding of the relationship between ability and effort (1973).

Social and Personality Development   **587**

In British society from medieval times through the Victorian era and up to the time of World War I, most sons followed in their fathers' jobs or professions. Women worked in mills (predominantly female labor), helped in the home, or took jobs "in service" to other homes. Job aspiration was closely tied to social class. In the United States the relationship between choices of job and social class was clearly pointed out in a study of a midwestern town (*Elmstown's Youth*) by August Hollingshead and his wife in 1949. The lower-class (working-class) adolescents did not value education or believe it would help them to find a worthwhile job. In addition their attitude toward work itself was apathetic. Job opportunities were limited, menial, and poorly paid. The jobs taken by lower-class youths were predominantly those their parents held. Middle-class adolescents believed that obtaining a good job was partly a question of initiative. Their aspirations were higher than those of lower-class youth. Upper- and middle-class parents encouraged education and job training to seek better jobs than they might have held. It is clear that level of education had an important influence on job aspiration and job opportunity.

However, the values of present-day adolescents seem to be working against youth from different social backgrounds. Now it is the middle-class youth who is turned off by the job opportunities education can provide. The working-class youth is more dissatisfied than at any time in the past by unfulfilling and un-demanding jobs. These teenagers now attach greater importance to jobs that provide greater fulfillment. Unfortunately, such jobs are usually difficult to find for young people who have limited educational background.

High schools now offer more vocational guidance. The adolescent from a lower-class home still requires special counseling, as do young girls who aspire to professions that are still very male dominated. However, choosing and obtaining a job remains perhaps the single most difficult problem for many adolescents. For those who choose to go to college it is sometimes difficult to relate education programs to later job expectations. Some youths enter college with no clear vocational interests. Social class, education, sex, ethnic status, and ability all play a part in influencing vocational opportunity—along with the chance effects of knowing the right person or being in the right place at the right time. "Nevertheless, neither college nor noncollege youth have given up. . . . The majority of youth do not currently appear deeply alienated, either with themselves or in their relations with society" (Mussen, Conger, & Kagan, 1979, p. 515).

Summary

Sigmund Freud's psychosexual theory of adolescent development emphasizes the effects of the rise of a new sexual energy at puberty. Love has to be directed away from parents to other "love objects." An important task of adolescence is to accomplish independence from parents. Anna Freud has suggested that adolescents react to the anxieties of relationships with parents (a still present Oedipal or Electra love) by setting up defense mechanisms such as ignoring parents, asceticism, and intellectualism.

Erikson has described adolescence as the search for ego identity, in which an identity crisis results from role diffusion. For most adolescents identity crises are mild and fairly easily resolved. But some adolescents find these years tumultuous. For those unable to make a commitment to a particular identity, there will be the need for a psychological moratorium—an extended "time-out" to find oneself.

Bandura has provided an alternative theory of social development during adolescence. He opposes the Freudian view of adolescence as a stressful period. The indications are that independence begins to emerge during childhood and follows a natural progression through adolescence. Most adolescents receive parental support for their growing autonomy. Social behavior results from the imitation of adult models who provide positive reinforcement. Differences in adolescent behavior can be explained by cultural differences in the reinforcement of appropriate behaviors.

Kohlberg associates postconventional morality with Piaget's stage of formal reasoning. An ability to use abstract reasoning allows the adolescent to consider, ideally, people's moral rights and universal principles of justice. Not all adolescents reach this level of reasoning, and their level of reasoning can change depending on various types of situations.

Changes in the structure and status of American families, as well as in cultural and other areas, have resulted in some of the relationship problems that teenagers and their parents experience. Conflicts have been attributed to a generation gap in values and attitudes. The idea of a generation gap has also been called a myth. The critical issue between adolescents and parents seems to be that of control. The adolescent prospers best with democratic parents (authoritative).

The peer group plays a vital role in influencing adolescent development. During adolescence peer-group relationships change. Although the same-sex peer groups of preadolescence do not entirely disappear, they do make way for opposite-sex groups and dating couples. There have been some reports that peer influence has outweighed parental influence, but, for most adolescents, it appears that peer-group and family values overlap and actually reinforce each other.

Increasing delinquency is causing much social concern. Most teenage delinquents are boys aged 14 to 16 years. Adolescent boys' delinquent acts tend to be more aggressive than those of delinquent girls. Delinquent gangs are composed mostly of adolescent males from minority groups in our large cities. They are associated with poverty, broken homes, and lack of vocational and educational aspirations. Rehabilitation of delinquents has been most successfully achieved in alternate homes with caring surrogate parents in local neighborhoods. Youths in these homes are encouraged to participate in community service and further education.

Severe disturbances in adolescence include anxiety, depression, eating problems, a potential for suicide, drug abuse, and unwanted pregnancies. These disturbances can be associated with extreme identity crises, alienation, and ignorance. Teenagers with severe disturbance problems need special help and care from parents, teachers, social workers, and counselors.

Adolescence is a time for establishing a wide range of values about social behavior, religion, politics, sexual behavior, job aspirations, and so on. To accomplish this task both freedom to experiment and support from parents, teachers, and other social agencies are needed. Crises of identity and confusion over conflicting values can result in alienation, as can economic, cultural and political discrimination and disadvantage. Young adolescents often have idealistic views about achievement, placing as much if not more importance on "taking part" as on the outcome. Older adolescents become more concerned with the outcome of an activity as a job. Middle-class youth have higher job aspirations than lower-class youth and receive more encouragement from parents to seek better jobs than the parents might have held. Choosing a job, especially if there is an intervening period of further higher education, is a difficult problem for many adolescents.

Questions for Review

1. In what respects do psychosocial and social learning theory differ in the description of social and personality development in adolescence?

2. Ask a number of teenagers and young adults to read Kohlberg's story of Heinz and the drug (p. 350) and a story of another real-life moral dilemma such as the Nixon tapes affair or possible responses to a re-established draft. Compare responses to the "contrived" and "real" situations. What was the level of moral reasoning in each case? What do your results suggest about moral reasoning?

3. What are some of the reasons given for the occurrence of disturbances such as extreme anxiety, eating problems such as anorexia nervosa, and suicide during adolescence?

4. What measures can be taken to deal with the problem of teenage unwed pregnancies?

5. Is there any truth in the statement that adolescence is a time of "storm and stress"?

6. What is meant by the term, the "generation gap"?

7. To what extent does the peer-group influence adolescent social development, and how does this influence compare to that of parents?

8. What appears to be a successful method for combating teenage delinquent gangs?

9. What problems face today's teenagers in establishing appropriate values and attitudes? How do we know what an "appropriate" value is? And how can parents and other adults help in this process?

Suggestions for Further Reading

Gordon, S. *The sexual adolescent: Communicating with teenagers about sex.* North Scituate, MA: Duxbury Press, 1973. Written for both professionals and parents, this book describes what adolescents need to know about sex.

Kaluger, G., & Kaluger, M. F. *Profiles in human development.* St. Louis: C.V. Mosby, 1976. A collection of profiles of people's experiences that span the years from early childhood to old age. The section on the adolescent years includes experiences of puberty, relations with parents, on becoming a teenager, the case study of a delinquent, and unwanted pregnancy.

Kanopka, G. *Young girls: A portrait of adolescence.* Englewood Cliffs, NJ: Prentice-Hall, 1976. A far-reaching study of adolescent girls in the United States.

Maccoby, E. E., & Jacklin, C. N. *The psychology of sex differences,* Vol. 1. Palo Alto, CA: Stanford University Press, 1978. Reviews of research on sex differences.

Muuss, E. *Theories of adolescence,* 2nd ed. New York: Random House, 1975. Provides descriptions and comparisons of various theoretical views of development during adolescence.

Schenk, Q. F., & Schenk, E. L. *Pulling up roots.* Englewood Cliffs, NJ: Prentice-Hall, 1978. A book for teenagers and their parents. Suggestions are provided for dealing with problems ranging from parental control and handling finances to conflicting life-styles and career opportunities.

Spanier, G. B. *Human sexuality in a changing society.* Minneapolis: Burgess, 1979. Covers topics such as sexual socialization, consequences of sexual interaction, and changing social attitudes toward sexuality.

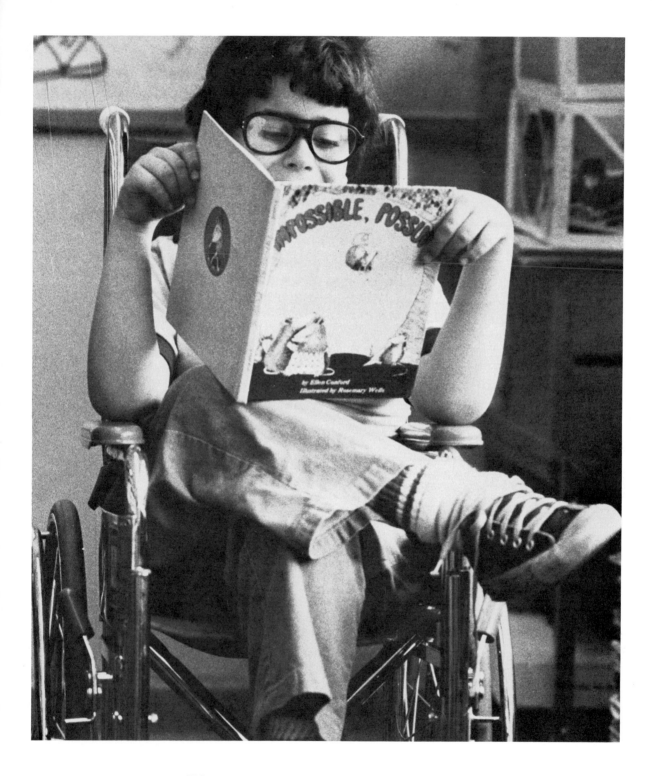

Abnormal Development

Abnormal Development

14

Poor child, you wear your summer dress
And your shoes striped with gold
As the earth wears a variegated cover
Of grass and flowers
Covering caverns of destruction over
Where hollow death are told.

Of what use is my weeping?
It does not carry a surgeon's knife
To cut the wrongly multiplying cells
At the root of your life.

Throughout this text our emphasis has been on normal development. We have made reference, however, to behavior that is not usual, such as excessive temper tantrums of early childhood and severe anxiety problems of adolescence. Western industrial societies, in particular, have established *norms* or standards of measurement for physical, intellectual, and social development. We can say that, on the average, infants begin to walk at age 12 months, adolescent girls achieve menarche at age 12½ years, people with an IQ score of between 90 and 110 are of average intelligence, and most children by middle childhood are relatively mature, seeking mainly reassurance and continuing support from adults. We can measure precisely the average of certain types of development, such as height and weight gains for children of different ages, and establish exact ranges of possible individual differences.

In other words, ***abnormal development*** is measured by the extent to which behavior deviates from the average. For example, pediatricians have pointed out that growth can be stunted by a lack of parents' love. At the Johns Hopkins University children aged 8 with the height of 4-year-olds have been diagnosed as having psychosocial dwarfism. The unusually retarded growth is easily measured. When these children are taken from their homes and placed with loving surrogate parents, many of them grow from five to ten inches. When they are returned to their homes, the children stop growing (Smolensky, 1977, p. 157). In this case, failure to thrive is certainly abnormal because lack of growth is obviously exaggerated and far from being average.

It is not easy to set norms for emotional and social behavior. How would you rate, for example, the behavior of the following case? A young boy developed sudden moodiness, failed at school, did not adapt to his social environment, and, when pressed about his behavior, threw violent fits of temper. To the psychiatrist he explained a fantasy he kept having:

I have my land. It is an island in the middle of a lake–river. . . . The boats that pass my island see high rocks, so they cannot land. Back of two towns and in between them there is a wood. . . . There are big rocks there, and they all look alike but one of them lifts up, and back of it is a door and back of the door is a tunnel, and you can go through that tunnel and under the lake and come out in the middle of the island . . . a little quiet place. That's where I go to think. . . . They don't know about it. They don't know who I am (Wickes, 1966, p. 11).

This fantasy was a retreat from all the proper demands of life. The young boy's behavior might be considered abnormal, and his school achievement was below average—below the norm, but he was helped in working out his problems. When he came to realize that he needed to "leave his island"—his behavior became normal.

What characteristics of behavior must be considered in deciding what is normal and abnormal? Kessler (1966) has described normal behavior as appropriate to the child's age and the time and place in which it occurs. She mentions seven criteria for judging such appropriateness.

1. *Age discrepancy.* Is the child's behavior typical for his or her age? If not, this age discrepancy suggests abnormal development. For example, when a young child's behavior is typical of an older child's, we call this precocity or being gifted. The reverse is referred to as delayed or retarded behavior. When behavior is inappropriate to the chronological or mental age of the child, it may be considered abnormal behavior.

2. *Frequency of occurrence.* How frequent or intense is the behavior in question? Occasional or mild temper tantrums would not be a sign of abnormality, but frequent or violent ones would be. Are frequency and intensity related to positive development as are practice or high level of attention, or are they disruptive as is highly aggressive behavior? It is important to distinguish positive and negative abnormality.

3. *Number of symptoms.* The more problems a child has, the more likely the child will experience abnormal development. For example, a child with a combination of learning disabilities, aggressive behavior, and visual impairment will be more likely to experience abnormal development than a child with only one of these problems.

4. *Degree of social disadvantage.* If the child's environment is severely inhibiting to normal development, abnormal development is likely. Conditions of poverty, broken homes, lack of educational and vocational models, and lack of parental control are social disadvantages that cause the abnormality of severe delinquency.

5. *Degree of suffering.* The more the child suffers—in terms of phobias, depression, crises of identity—as a result of the behavior, the more inappropriate is the behavior. This is also the case when the child causes other people to suffer—by aggression, delinquent acts, and so on.

6. *Intractability of behavior.* Persistent inappropriate behavior that is not easily changed is considered abnormal. For example, the child might be "out of control" in the home and exceptionally difficult to handle. This behavior might have been strongly influenced by parents' excessive physical punishment for a variety of misdemeanors, trivial and serious. The child may, in fact, have no alternatives but to continue to behave in an antisocial way. In such cases, it becomes crucial to seek out and provide the child with alternative, more appropriate behaviors.

7. *General personality appraisal.* It is necessary to evaluate individual behavior in terms of how well the child is coping in general and in various situations—with parents, teachers, peers. The more a behavior interferes with general personality behavior, the greater the problem.

Tavormina (1978) points out the relativity and fluctuation likely to exist in norms of behavior. "Normalcy boils down to what the traffic will bear at a given time. . . . Norms [of behavior] are influenced by culture and society" (1978, pp. 193–194).

Dimensions of Diagnosis

Tavormina (1978, p. 196) has suggested that ***diagnosis*** of abnormal behavior should proceed along four dimensions: (1) **etiology,** the examination of the cause and development of behavior; (2) *symptoms,* the precise description of behavior; (3) **prognosis,** the description of the expected long-term effect or outcome of the behavior; and (4) *therapy,* treatment of the behavior.

Etiology takes into account the child's predisposition toward certain behaviors that may be problematic and caused by some kind of stress. For example, a child might be having serious learning problems. A school psychologist would begin by looking for common situations in which the child experienced the greatest problems in learning, at the same time trying to establish the pressures the child is trying to cope with, which are associated with the learning problems. The next step would be to attempt to isolate the particular type(s) of learning problems the child is having. For example, the child might have serious difficulties with reading. What are the causes? They might be related to early difficulties in learning to read, exacerbated by later embarrassment at not being able to read well, to dyslexia, to some degree of retardation, or to other causes. In the long run, if nothing is done about the problem, the child may be labeled a school failure (for some children, a self-fulfilling prophecy), may become pathologically anxious about school, may turn to antisocial behavior in school, may become delinquent, may become a school "dropout" with all the related socially undesirable cause grievances. How can this problem be treated? There is no single, sure way. The school psychologist, ideally in consultation with parents and teachers, may have to try a variety of treatments, including therapy, to alleviate or cure the problem.

Diagnosis is often a difficult procedure. As we have seen, there are many shades of behavior from normal to abnormal. In deciding the type and degree of abnormal behavior, psychopathologists (specialists who study behavior abnormalities) must often make approximations. Their observation of behavior may be biased by their own points of view or the way in which a case is presented to them.

A teacher told me of a boy whose lack of attention, boredom, and general stupidity had exhausted the patience of several teachers.
One teacher decided to visit the mother and explain the problem. The mother misunderstood and exclaimed— "He's a wonderful boy, isn't he? . . . From morning to night he's busy and when he's not helping me about the house he's doing chores for the neighbors or working for the grocer on the corner and every cent he brings home to me."
The teacher who came to blame remained to praise (Wickes, 1966, p. 126).

Most psychopathologists are aware that diagnoses are often based on limited evaluation of a child. They hesitate to label a child's abnormality in case they establish a self-fulfilling prophecy that may shape the child to actually conform to the label (Tavormina, 1978, pp. 195–196). An initial diagnosis is usually considered as a rough guideline. The problem of diagnosis can be illustrated by the case of a 4-year-old boy labeled by different specialists as brain-damaged, retarded, autistic, and schizophrenic (Clarizio & McCoy, 1976).

Another problem in diagnosis is the considerable research that has been done on methods of diagnosing the infant at risk for abnormal development (e.g., Tjossem, 1976). So that intervention can be made as soon as possible, as in the case of diagnosis of possible handicaps in older children, there are special problems with diagnosis of infants. One particular problem is the reliability of prognosis, which has been clearly identified in research by Parmelee et al. (1976). These researchers used a "cumulative risk-scoring system" to show neonatal factors that might result in later abnormal development with follow-up testing at 3 and 4 months and at 8 and 9 months (see Table 14.1).

Table 14.1 Cumulative Risk-Score Items

Age of Administration	Item
At birth	*Newborn Neurological Examination:* Evaluation of the infant's muscle tone, reflex patterns, and states of arousal.
At birth	*Visual Attention:* Evaluation of the infant's level of visual attention, ability to sustain an optimal level of attention, and the length of time visually attending to objects.
At birth	*Sleep Polygraph:* Assessment of sleep duration following feeding, and body activity, respiration, eye movement, and EEG during sleep as indicators of brain activity.
One week after birth	*Obstetric Complication Scale:* Assessment of the presence or absence of optimal conditions for normal development.
Birth to 1 month	*Postnatal Factors Evaluation:* Examination of the infant's health during the first month after birth with respect to such characteristics as respiration, seizures, and the need for surgery.
3 months	*Sleep Polygraph:* As at birth.
4 months	*Pediatric Evaluation:* Evaluation of neurological problems.
4 months	*Gesell Developmental Evaluation:* Assessment of the infant's developmental level in terms of gross-motor, fine-motor, adaptive, language, and personal–social abilities.
4 months	*Visual Attention:* Evaluation of the infant's preference for looking at particular types of objects (complex, novel, and facelike), ability to remember objects, and ability to differentiate objects.

This study included preterm infants and a control group of full-term infants selected from all socioeconomic groups. Of twenty-two infants considered as high risk on the basis of their newborn score, on the basis of the cumulative risk score at 9 months, only eleven were still at high risk. Parmelee et al. point out that this finding is consistent with previous experiences that infants often improve remarkably during the first year. No single test at a single time of testing reliably predicts long-term handicapping of children. There is merit in using a procedure like the cumulative risk-score process since initial results, certainly with infants, should only be considered tentative and a much clearer picture of the possibility of long-term handicapping should emerge with cumulative testing.

Age of Administration	Item
8 months	*Precision of Hand Manipulation and Sensorimotor Schemas:* Assessment of the types of visual and manipulative schemas the infant uses when interacting with objects. Hand manipulation is assessed in terms of accuracy, speed, and direction of approach, and anticipatory hand movements.
8 months	*Exploratory Behavior and Preference for Novelty:* Evaluation of the infant's ability to explore an object in detail, and then shift attention to a new object and visual and manipulatory responses to familiar and novel objects.
9 months	*Pediatric Evaluation:* As at 4 months.
9 months	*Gesell Evaluation:* As at 4 months.
9 months	*Cognitive Development:* Assessment of the infant's sensorimotor development in areas of object permanence, symbolism, exploration, and combination of objects.

Source: Parmelee, A. H., et al., "A Diagnosis of the Infant at High Risk for Mental, Motor, and Sensory Handicaps." In T. D. Tjossem, Ed, *Intervention Strategies for High Risk Infants and Young Children,* 1976, p. 291. Copyright, 1976, University Park Press, Baltimore. Adapted with permission.

In diagnosing abnormal behavior specialists also consider the etiology, or cause of the disorder. There will be physiological factors, environmental factors, or an interaction between them in the etiology of developmental problems. For example, we know quite precisely the cause of what is known as Down's syndrome; you will remember from Chapter 2 that it is a chromosomal error—the presence of an extra X chromosome. Down's syndrome children are mentally retarded. However, caring parents and teachers can mitigate the effects of this defect as is shown in the following example.

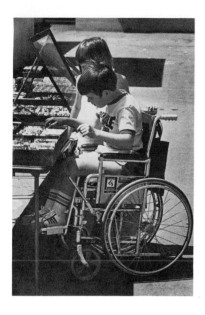

Case history: O.F. was a moderately retarded teenaged Down's syndrome child. He was the middle child in a family of five children, the other four children being normal. His parents accepted him in a manner as much like their nonhandicapped children as possible. He was included in all family social events, and family activity was as full if not more so than most of their neighbors. Because of his lower intellectual functioning and lower mental age, he was typically treated as the younger member of the family. He was, however, accorded all the respect due him within the ability of the family. O.F.'s brothers and sisters routinely invited him to go out with them and their friends. Because his siblings were so at ease with him, their peers were also. Teenage friends of O.F.'s brothers and sisters often invited him out with them for a coke or hamburger on their own, even when his siblings were unable to go. Because O.F.'s parents were so comfortable with him, his siblings were also. Because the siblings demonstrated their positive reaction to their brother with their friends, the friends also began modeling the same behavior (Chinn, Winn, & Walters, 1978, pp. 39–40).

In this case the physiological factor is the genetic disorder, the environment factor is the family, and the lack of stress is a factor produced by interaction of the first two factors. All factors are part of the etiology of this child's condition.

Paul Meehl (1962) has suggested a model of etiology that illustrates the interaction of a number of factors to shape behavior. He calls this a diathesis-stress model and developed it to explain the etiology of schizophrenia. Tavormina (1978, pp. 199–200) has used it as a general model to explain etiology (see Table 14.2). **Diathesis** is an indication of a predisposition toward a particular behavior. Such predispositions may occur because of various combinations of temperament, heredity, physical development, social and cultural experiences, and family and

Table 14.2 Causes of Childhood Behavior Disorders

Explanation of Etiology

Behavior	=	a predisposition toward a certain behavior (diathesis) + stress
Diathesis	=	a function of temperament + heredity + organic factors + sociocultural background + family + environmental factors
Stress	=	the result of situational and developmental crises and pressures the child faces

Many factors contribute to childhood behavior disorders. The more etiology of behavior the clinician can account for the more likely it is that some successful treatment can be used to change disorderly behavior.

Source: Tavormina, J. B., "Behavior Disorders of Childhood."
In W. H. Holtzman, Ed., Introductory Psychology in Depth:
Developmental Topics, 1978, p. 200. Copyright, 1978, Harper
& Row. Reprinted with permission.

environmental influences. *Stress* implies various problem experiences the child must cope with, along with the pressures of physical and emotional tensions they cause. As you can see from Table 14.2, a particular abnormal behavior will be the result of some combination of diathesis and stress factors. The researcher or therapist using this model would attempt to identify what combination of diathesis and stress factors were apparently contributing to the child's abnormal behavior.

Psychoneuroses

Let us now take a look at some of the major types of abnormal behavior. *Psychoneuroses,* or **neuroses,** are psychological, not physical, disorders related to anxiety, fear, or stress. Most young children experience irrational but quite usual fears (Rimm & Somervill, 1977): fear of dark places, loud noises, strange people, and so on. But some fears can be frequent, intensive, and disruptive of normal behavior. Characteristics of children with serious neurotic problems include feelings of inferiority, social withdrawal, extreme shyness, oversensitivity, timidity, and depression (Quay & Werry, 1972).

According to Freud, neuroses spring from intrapsychic (sexual or aggressive) conflict, which results in feelings of anxiety (Kessler, 1966). Learning theorists believe that neuroses are responses to environmental conditions. They are, in fact, learned responses dependent on the child's experiences (Ross, 1974). From both points of view, neuroses interfere with normal behavior and development.

Children may suffer from various types of neuroses. *Anxiety* or overwhelming fright is usually accompanied by feelings of irritability, fatigue, and imagined physical ailments. **Hysteria** may be experienced as a physical sensation such as **functional paralysis** in which the child loses the use of a limb without there being anything physically wrong (conversion type of hysteria). Another type of hysteria is an impairment of awareness such as amnesia or sleep walking (dissociative type of hysteria). **Obsessions** such as the continuous washing of hands (the washing away of guilt, perhaps) and *depressions* such as feelings of inferiority, worthlessness, or helplessness are other types of neurotic behavior (Tavormina, 1978).

However, the most frequent type of neurotic behavior experienced by children is **phobia,** excessive and unfounded fear of a particular object or circumstance. We saw in Chapter 5 that fear of strangers or strange situations is common in infancy. Jersild (1968) has pointed out that 2-year-olds have exaggerated fears of animals, and 3-year-olds fear the dark or being left alone. In late childhood fears about social relationships and school come to the forefront (Bauer, 1976). Because phobias are persistent and frequent, the child has to spend considerable time trying to avoid them. This can significantly affect normal behavior and development. Avoidance of a phobia detracts from normal behavior. More effective ways of dealing with these fears are necessary, and this usually means therapy.

School Phobia

It is not uncommon for children to have a fear of going to school. For the child beginning preschool, or in the early elementary grades, it may be associated with an anxiety of separating from his or her mother (Kennedy, 1965; Yates, 1970). This is more a fear of leaving home than a fear of school. If the child also experiences anxiety-provoking events at school, these can combine with the separation-from-home anxiety. This early type of school phobia can usually be successfully treated. Gradual separation according to some arrangement before the child attends school for the first time usually helps. Setting up a positive relationship between teacher and child, in which the teacher meets the child on arrival at school and the parents immediately depart, usually results in a fairly rapid adaptation to attending school.

Phobias that occur later in the child's school life tend to be more complex and more difficult to treat (Kennedy, 1965; Yates, 1970). Symptoms may result from anxiety-provoking adult–child relationships, negative peer relationships, and unrealistic fears about failing at school. The phobia is maintained by the rewards of avoiding school—a lessening of anxiety and a feeling of safety and security away from school. The usual treatment is to try to make school more attractive by reducing the rewards for avoiding school, by playing up the importance of school and rewarding attendance, or by teaching the child to control the fear of school (Tavormina, 1978).

Death Phobia

Many children experience fears or anxieties about death. It is usually during the preschool years period that children become aware of death. They begin to notice animals that have died—a dead insect, bird, or fish. They may, in a more formal sense, be introduced to the concepts of living and *non*living things. Some children may experience the death of a sibling, a friend, or a relative. Along with questions such as "Where did I come from?" children might ask, "Daddy, when will you die?" "When will I die?" or "Where do you go when you die?"

Very young children have difficulty understanding the concept of death. They may believe that a dead person has merely gone away somewhere for a while but will return. During the years between about 6 and 10 children become more aware that death is final (Koocher, 1975; White, Elsom, & Prawat, 1978). Whereas the child of 6 may believe death is a monster or a ghost that will take you away if it catches you, the older child realizes that death is caused by disease, accidents, or old age.

Many parents are inclined to shield a child from the realities of death (LeShan, 1976), even when it is the child who is dying. Typically, the child is told that the dead person has gone away or is asleep. The young child may become confused by such explanations and associate them with other everyday events such as going to bed or going on vacation (see Inset 14.1). This may lead to a phobia about death. The child becomes obsessed with fears of being taken away or attacked by some "death monster." Kaluger and Kaluger (1976, pp. 83–84) describe how Betsy, a six-year-old, acquired a fear of death. It appears that Betsy's first experience of a "friend" dying was the death of her dog. Her mother told her God had taken away her dog Laddie. Two years later her grandmother died, and Betsy wanted to know where she was. Her aunt told her that God had taken her grandma to join His family in the sky. Betsy, it seems, came to the conclusion that when God took someone away, the person never came back. She began to fear that He might take her away.

Betsy developed a fear of hospitals because that was the place from which God had taken her grandma. A year later Betsy had to go into the hospital to have her tonsils removed. She wondered "Am I going to die" and showed signs of being very much afraid of that possibility. A later ordeal of being thrown into a stream and not being able to swim only reinforced her fear of death. The results, for Betsy, were an exaggerated fear of death and irrational fears of all kinds of situations and circumstances that might result in her dying.

Although some children show little interest in discussing death, for those children who show some concern, ask questions about death, or appear anxious, it seems best to attempt a straightforward and correct explanation (Grollman, 1970; Jackson, 1965; Koch, 1977; LeShan, 1976). The child's understanding of death, ascertained by questioning, should be taken into account when adults give explanations of death. The parent or adult who is explaining about death should do so with as much sensitivity as possible, although this may not always be easily achieved. Parents should be encouraged to talk openly about death when the opportunity presents itself, and the topic of death can be introduced in many different ways from preschool through the elementary grades. Kastenbaum (1972) describes how he explained death to his 18-month-old son. The boy found a dead bird in the yard. He simply explained, yes it is a bird—dead bird. The boy later found another dead bird and wanted his father to bring it back to life by placing it in a tree. The father explained as simply as possible that the bird could not come back to life. Older children and adolescents are able to understand the notion of death and dying at a more complex and abstract level (Kübler-Ross, 1969; Morgan, 1975; Stein, 1974). It is important to alleviate a child's fear of death to prevent its becoming a phobia.

It is also very important to help children who are facing death with their anxieties. Most hospitalized children between the ages of 6 and 10 who have a serious disease or ailment do seem to realize the seriousness of their illness and that it may prove fatal (Spinetta, 1974). It is not a phobia to fear death when it is a visibly real possibility. Many parents find it very difficult to talk about death to a dying child—they may, themselves be refusing to accept the inevitable. Many hospitals now have therapists on staff to help children and parents face the anxieties of illness and related treatment. It is in the dying child's best interest to express emotions about death. It is also important to diagnose a child's fear of death early and to make attempts to alleviate it in order to prevent its becoming a phobia.

Defense Mechanisms

Children usually try to protect themselves from feelings of anxiety by some kind of **defense mechanism.** Defense mechanisms are normal ways or tendencies of coping, but severe stress can convert normal tendencies into abnormal behavior.

Suppose a child develops a severe anxiety about coping with math. The child refuses to cooperate with the teacher, fails to pay attention when math is being taught, and refuses to complete assignments. Another defense mechanism that the child may use is to insist that math is of no value, "It is stupid doing all these problems; I'm never going to use math, so I don't need to learn about it." This type of false justification is termed *rationalization.*

There are other types of defense mechanisms. *Repression* is the refusal to entertain anxiety-provoking thoughts. *Projection* is attributing some despised behavior in oneself to other people. *Regression* is a reversal to an earlier form of behavior (for example, to be excused some misbehavior, an older child might revert to acting in a babyish kind of way). **Sublimation** is diverting sexual energy into behavior that is socially more acceptable.

There appears to be a developmental trend in the form of defense mechanisms (Rappaport, 1972). The type of defense mechanisms that children of different ages use also seems to be related to level of cognitive functioning (Chandler, Piaget, & Koch, 1978). For example, repression is more typical of young children and, in the case of adolescents, projection. A child would—ironically—have to be beyond egocentrism to use projection.

Psychoses

Psychotic disorders are a total breakdown of normal functioning. These disorders are not always easy to diagnose. Diagnoses of psychotic and emotionally disturbed children sometimes overlap. For example, descriptions of behavior supposed to be indicative of childhood psychosis include seclusiveness, irritability, and acute anxiety. These are also sometimes mentioned as symptoms of phobia and depression. A psychotic disorder will, of course, be diagnosed in terms of clusters of behavior all or most of which are of extreme maladaptive proportions. However, disagreement remains about what the necessary and sufficient conditions of behavior are to warrant diagnosis of *psychosis* (Margolies, 1977; Rimm & Somerville, 1977; Rutter & Lockyer, 1967; see also Inset 13.1).

Childhood psychoses are most commonly placed into two categories—**autism** and **schizophrenia.** What are the differences between these two types of psychoses? Autistic children are unable to relate to people. They become preoccupied with objects and engage in compulsive activities with the objects, they cannot tolerate change in their environment, they may sit or stand motionless for long periods or sit rocking, they do not communicate verbally, and indeed they make virtually no attempt to communicate. In the case of schizophrenia, an apparently normal child may become increasingly withdrawn and show symptoms of confusion and disorientation. There may be indications of excessive dependency on parents or other adults and avoidance of autonomy and independence (Rutter, 1975; Yates, 1970).

The most important distinguishing factor between the two conditions is the age at which the symptoms appear. Autism is considered by some psychologists to be present at birth (Rimland, 1964). Behaviors associated with autism certainly appear during early infancy, whereas schizophrenia appears in childhood or later (Rutter, 1975).

Autistic children have difficulties relating to people and spend long periods sitting or standing motionless, preoccupied with some object close by. (Photo by Kirk Kreutzig/Photographics)

What is the cause of these psychoses? Explanations are controversial. Learning theorists such as Eisenberg and Kanner (1956) and Bettelheim (1967) have suggested that childhood psychoses result from a lack of close parental contact and affection. Emotional deprivation is supposed to cause autism, while schizophrenia is said to result from anxious, overprotective parents and from extreme conflicts within the family. However, it has also been proposed that emotional conflicts in the family or withdrawn parents may actually result from, rather than cause, these psychotic disorders (Tavormina, 1978).

An increasing amount of evidence suggests that the underlying cause of autism is likely to be genetic (Knobloch & Pasamanick, 1975; Rosenthal, 1970). The early appearance of autism during infancy suggests that learning experiences may have little to do with this condition. Researchers believe that organic or genetic factors are at the root of schizophrenia also. But since this type of psychosis emerges at least in later childhood, there is a strong suggestion that there are environmental causes as well.

What are the chances of recovery from autism and schizophrenia? The answer is pessimistic. Psychotherapy has not yielded much success in changing psychotic behavior (Margolies, 1977). Training psychotic children in self-help skills by operant conditioning has had some success (Lovaas, Young, & Newsom, 1978; Margolies, 1977). Management of such children and the provision of environmental support through parent training programs has also proved effective

(Schopler & Reichler, 1971). However, it is important to realize that in spite of success in reducing maladaptive behaviors, such as severe tantrums and self-mutilation, and improving self-help and social skills, there is no evidence that a psychotic child can ever become normal. What has become increasingly important in recent years is the avoidance of institutionalizing psychotic children, and improving their living conditions within the family by training parents to more ably cope with these children (Wolman, 1972) or by placing children with severe behavior problems in foster homes (Tavormina et al., 1975).

Learning Disorders

Learning disorders may be the result of genetic, emotional, or environmental factors—or a combination thereof. There are a wide range of learning disorders, but only two of the most common are mentioned here—mental retardation and the general category of learning disability.

Mental Retardation

The American Association on Mental Deficiency (AAMD) has defined *mental retardation* as "subaverage intellectual functioning associated with impairment in adaptive behavior" (1961). Although mental retardation is also defined as an inability to adjust socially, in practice children are classified as retarded on the basis of scores on IQ tests. The AAMD has identified four levels of **retardation.** Children with IQs of between 0 and 24 are classified as *profoundly retarded.* They are usually physically deformed, need constant care and attention, and have relatively short life spans. Children with IQs of between 25 and 39 are classified as *severely retarded.* With considerable training, these children can acquire self-help and simple social skills. *Moderately retarded* children have IQs ranging from 40 to 54. These children can be trained to use language moderately well to communicate, and they function quite well in supervised workshops. Most mentally retarded children fall into the category of *mild retardation,* with IQs of between 55 and 69. It has been estimated that about three quarters of all retardates are mildly retarded (Coleman, 1976). As long ago as 1956, O'Connor and Tizard claimed that most of the people in this category can be trained to live reasonably independent lives.

What are the causes of mental retardation? As we saw in Chapter 2, one of the causes is genetic and includes such symptoms as Down's syndrome. Other causes are birth injuries, certain diseases, and bodily injury. But most retarded individuals have none of these symptoms, and in these cases the main cause appears to be environmental deprivation (Robinson & Robinson, 1965) such as lack of emotional and intellectual stimulation in early childhood.

Learning Disabilities

It is important to realize that children with learning disabilities are *not* retarded. Learning disabilities are such specialized deficiencies in ability that they do not reflect general intellectual deficiency. Some children with learning disabilities have particular problems learning certain types of information or skills. For example, a child may experience a serious difficulty in learning to read, or learning math, or in trying to communicate in speech or writing. Teachers pay more attention to children who have learning problems in these areas since "basic" skills of reading, math, writing, and communication are so important for academic and vocational success in Western cultures. But major learning deficits can occur in general academic performance. Families who have children with learning difficulties are usually referred to a school psychologist (see Inset 14.2).

One of the most frequently referred to causes for reading disabilities is **dyslexia**. Dyslexic children sometimes reverse the order of words or letters and mispronounce words. These children also often have problems telling time and ascertaining direction. Difficulty in learning math concepts and computational skills is called **dyscalcula** (an inability to calculate).

Inset 14.2
"**Family Counseling:
A Case Study**"

The Davis family was referred for family counseling to the psychology service of the school district. The Davises' 11-year-old son John was experiencing difficulties with his schoolwork and episodes of wetting the bed at night. John's school counselor had suggested family counseling because he felt there were relationship difficulties in the family as well as the present problem with John. . . . The Davises were pleasant, outgoing people who seemed to care very deeply about each other. Their presentation of their son's difficulties reflected genuine affection and concern for John and a sincere desire to get at the root of his problems in order to alleviate them.

The family was relatively open and accepted the counselor almost from the first encounter. The picture of the Davis family that became clear to the counselor was what Minuchin (1974) calls an "extruded dyad." The power dyad in the family was not both parents but it was the father–daughter pair. The two exhibited similar personality characteristics: warm, affectionate, outgoing, assertive, strong willed, and outspoken. They shared a favorite sport. The affectional and interactional bond between these two extruded (or pushed out) Mrs. Davis and John, who formed an interactional and affectional bond almost by default—or in self-defense.

The possessiveness Mr. Davis felt toward his daughter Janet involved his reluctance to face and accept her growing up. Their frequent and growing conflicts over her push for independence had involved him more and more deeply in their dyad relationship. The effect (albeit unintentional) was to exclude John—to push him away from the father–son relationship John was desperately seeking. Instead, he was

---

Two other types of learning disability are worth mentioning—aphasia and hyperactivity. Difficulty in either understanding or using speech is referred to as *aphasia*. In some cases children have difficulty in understanding spoken or written communications (receptive aphasia). In other cases children have difficulty in producing language (expressive aphasia) (Mordock, 1975). Some specialists believe that these disorders are the result of a defect in the central nervous system, although other theories have attributed the disorders to a combination of physical and learning factors.

Hyperactivity is behavior characterized by constant, impulsive, and often random movements. This type of behavior is usually disruptive of classroom activities and has recently received considerable attention because of the use of stimulant drugs which, surprisingly, have a calming effect (Gilmore, 1975). It has been suggested that hyperactivity may occur, at least in part, because of brain damage (Gearheart, 1976; Hughes, 1976). Another specialist (Feingold, 1975) attributes the condition to certain food additives and dyes. He has proposed a special diet as a solution to the problem, but there is no convincing evidence as yet that eating certain foodstuffs is a major cause of hyperactivity.

---

almost forced (again unintentionally) into a dyadic relationship with his mother—a not-unwanted relationship, but not the relationship he sought. The plan the counselor developed was to promote a coalition among the three other family members to push out Mr. Davis, thus breaking up the dyad–dyad pattern. Once that was accomplished, the strategy was for the therapist to form a coalition between the two children, thereby promoting a move toward a cohesive parental pair. In this latter move it was expected that the already sound marital bond would be strengthened and that Mrs. Davis could exert a positive influence to help Mr. Davis accept his daughter's maturing development with less anxiety and possessiveness. It was also expected that, as the parental pair became the power or dominant dyad, Mr. Davis would be more equitably accessible to John. When that began to happen, it was anticipated that John's difficulties, or symptoms, would begin to diminish and disappear.

Happily, the anticipated outcomes did, in fact, result from this strategy. About seven months of weekly sessions were involved in accomplishing the objectives. During that time family members learned many of the techniques of Responsive Listening (responding to affective as well as cognitive content) that contribute to "open" communication. Follow-up contact one year later found John and Janet earning excellent marks in school, John spending satisfying time with his father, and Mr. and Mrs. Davis enjoying each other more as marital partners. Janet's dating was reported to be much less of an issue. John's symptoms had been gone for over a year and were not expected to return.

Source: Adapted and quoted in part from Chinn, Philip C.,
Winn, Joyce, and Walters, Robert H.: *Two-way Talking with
Parents of Special Children*, St. Louis, 1978, The C. V. Mosby
Co. Reprinted with permission.

Hyperactive toddlers are described as "children who never walked but ran, jumped up and down holding onto the crib bars wearing a hole in the mattress . . . are into everything but do not play more than seconds with one object" (Weiss & Hechtman, 1979, p. 1349). The hyperactive elementary school child behaves best in one-to-one situations rather than in groups. Social behavior and peer relations are adversely affected because of the hyperactive child's low tolerance of frustration, poor concentration, and often poor self-esteem (Linde et al., 1971). In adolescence hyperactive youths often experience school failure and are frequently antisocial (Mendelson et al., 1971).

The etiology of learning disabilities is unclear. Various theories have been suggested to explain why learning difficulties occur for some children. These include brain dysfunction, neurological damage, and maturational lags. But not all children with learning disabilities seem to have these defects. Even for those children who do, the defects are probably compounded in many cases by school failure and pressure from parents and teachers (Tavormina, 1978).

Remedial programs should be based on the special needs of the individual child. Learning disability problems are so diverse that it is unlikely any single form of treatment—remedial education, psychotherapy, behavior modification, drugs, or counseling—will be effective for all children.

Treatment of Abnormal Behavior

Specialists use various types of intervention and therapy to treat maladaptive behaviors. Whatever technique is used, each child must be treated as a unique case. Tavormina (1978) mentions seven factors that contribute to the outcome of *therapy* (see Table 14.3).

The problems of therapy are threefold. First, the various factors mentioned in Table 14.3 are interactive. It is never a foregone conclusion that a "best fit" between patient and therapy has been achieved since there are so many possible variables to take into account. Second, even when improvement in behavior is achieved as a result of therapy, there is no guarantee this will generalize to all situations or will be long lasting. For example, the prognosis for psychotic children is usually pessimistic. Third, maintaining a change in behavior is often

Table 14.3 Factors that Affect the Outcome of Therapy

Factor	Description
1. Characteristics of child	Level of subjective distress; motivation to work for change; strengths as well as weaknesses in coping ability
2. Characteristics of care givers	Expectations from therapy; real reasons they sought therapy; willingness to see themselves as part of the problem and of the solution; capacity to work to change interaction patterns with the child
3. Characteristics of environment	Level of support in the milieu to reinforce change; capacity to change typical ways others respond to the child
4. The presenting problem	The type and severity of behavioral symptoms
5. Characteristics of the therapist	Capacity for empathy, warmth, and genuineness; acceptance and understanding of the child; awareness of the ways the child's interactive systems affect his behavior; ability to communicate with the child and his care givers; therapist's confidence
6. Therapeutic relationship	Quality of the relationship between therapist and child and therapist and care givers; the psychological climate in which therapy occurs; mutual trust and mutual acceptance
7. Therapeutic technique	Particular methodology used by the therapist to effect change; theoretical framework of the therapist; particular strategies employed to deal with target behaviors

The success of therapy depends on a number of interacting factors. Improvement in a behavior disorder will depend on how good a fit there is among these factors. With so many factors to consider, it is usually difficult for the therapist to bring about a successful change in behavior.

Source: Tavormina, J. B., "Behavior Disorders of Childhood." In W. H. Holtzman, Ed., *Introductory Psychology in Depth: Developmental Topics,* 1978, p. 238. Copyright, 1978, Harper & Row. Reprinted with permission.

difficult. It is one thing to achieve improvement in, say, self-help skills such as toilet training, dressing, and communicating, but it is quite another matter trying to ensure that children continue to use such skills with reasonable efficiency. Without continued training and help, many children regress to previous levels of behavior. Let us take a look at two of the better-known techniques a therapist can choose for treatment: behavior therapy and psychotherapy.

Behavior Therapy

Therapists with a behaviorist view of development first isolate the symptoms of maladaptive behavior and then attempt to *modify* them, that is, to change them into different, more appropriate behavior. For example, Bandura (1968) has suggested a *behavior modeling approach* that trains the child to imitate (or model) a desirable behavior in order to modify undesirable behavior. Other specialists take a different point of view. Yates (1970) believes that, since each case presents a special problem, various types of behavior therapy (for example, modeling, play, psychotherapy) that have previously proved successful should be taken into account when deciding how to treat abnormal behavior.

The behavior therapist must isolate *all* those factors that appear to be affecting or causing the maladaptive behavior. Therapy is then directed toward the various interacting factors. This is important since treating just one apparent source of the problem is unlikely to lead to any permanent change in behavior. For example, training parents to ignore temper tantrums may prove effective, but the child is then likely to use other inappropriate attention-seeking behavior (Tavormina et al., 1975, p. 239). The therapist should teach parents to ignore all inappropriate attention-seeking behavior, while at the same time encouraging and reinforcing appropriate behavior. Combining the parents' need to get rid of inappropriate behavior and the child's need to learn socially acceptable behavior is likely to be more effective than trying to improve either separately.

Psychotherapy

Under this general heading we can refer to a number of traditionally used therapy techniques, probably the best known of which is psychotherapy based on Freud's method of psychoanalysis. Through conversation the therapist and child explore the child's conscious and unconscious thoughts and interpret how they influence behavior. The objective is to extinguish the anxiety that is believed to be causing the neurotic or maladaptive behavior and to suggest alternative forms of behavior.

Another type of psychotherapy used especially with young children is *play therapy*. The therapist begins by observing the child playing.

At 7 years of age Chaim was accepted for treatment at Blueberry, a therapy center. "He became attached to a baby doll and made an attempt to show us what he wanted. He rocked the doll gently, but then stuck a cigarette in her mouth. He kept shoving the doll into the (toy) stove. . . . He guarded the stove. He ate on it. He tried to get in it. Was Chaim guarding the stove of the camp so that no one could put him inside?"

Chaim's parents, Stefan and Channa, both spent time in Nazi extermination camps, Channa for four and a half years, part of that time in the death house. After liberation, they met and married in a displaced persons camp. Chaim was born nine years later in the United States. His mother had seriously maltreated him. To punish him for misbehaving she had scalded his hand, bitten him, and beaten him with a buckled belt.

Chaim's fears, his extreme psychotic behavior can be attributed in large measure to his experiences with his mother. Was there also a genetic disorder that might be associated with his mother's experiences in the extermination camps? It is impossible to say in this case. Stefan and Channa had two other children who appeared to be "normal" (Rothenberg, 1977, pp. 104–108).

Through play the child expresses underlying problems. Play is not necessarily intended to be therapeutic but may serve this purpose. The therapist often uses play situations to observe a child's behavior and then decides on the basis of these observations what types of therapy are necessary. In Chaim's case this included obtaining information from the parents and attempting to change their behavior (such as beating Chaim), as well as trying various types of intervention with the boy. In many cases the therapist may arrange particular play situations to provide clues about a child's underlying problems. Another form of play therapy is *nondirective play therapy* in which the therapist establishes a relationship with the child through play and at the same time guides the child's self-exploration.

Whatever psychotherapeutic technique is used, the therapist's first concern is to establish an accepting and trusting relationship with the child. The child must then be helped to realize why certain behaviors are inappropriate and to try out other more appropriate behaviors. This is usually a long-term task. Many children have to be brought to the point at which they can confront extremely frightening and disturbing thoughts, feelings, and emotions. The natural reactions are to turn away from such experiences, to withdraw, and to grasp at various defense mechanisms. In many cases, especially of psychotic behavior, the rewards for long hours of therapy are small (see Inset 14.3).

"When Anthony came to me he was 10½ years old. He was accompanied by a controversial diagnosis: mental retardation, brain damage, childhood schizophrenia, autism, juvenile delinquency. The most immediate complaint was that Anthony was terribly physically violent against children, against adults, against anything he came in contact with. He consciously identified with Hitler, and was covered from head to toe with swastikas.

"When he came to me, the authorities were ready to throw him out of school and send him to a state hospital. Anthony could not read. His speech was slurred—incoherent. He communicated through his body, mainly through his fists. At times he was beautiful, at other times dull and listless; at times angular and disjointed, and at other times extremely well coordinated. He behaved like a delinquent, and was thus constantly involved with the police. At home, he engineered violent beatings from his father; at school, severe punishments; and in the street, constant warfare. He had made many attempts at suicide. He lived in a jungle of terrors and his life was spent dodging them. But when the terrors became too much for him he walked right into them.

" 'I got nothing to say to you, an' I ain't listenin' to you neither,' he said when he came to see me the first time.

" 'How about a game of checkers?' I said. 'Want to try your luck?' I caught his eye glancing at the checker game.

" 'Okay,' he smirked. 'I'm gonna beat you,' and he looked me up and down.

I got the checkers out; he set them up. The game was strange, for at times winning the game meant losing the battle, and at other times, losing the game meant winning the battle. It depended so much on how it was done.

"He won. 'You see, I beat you,' he said smugly.

" 'Because my opponent is not worth my while,' I said sarcastically.

"He paled. 'I ain't stupid.'

" 'That is exactly the point,' I told him.

"The checker games continued as a means of contact with Anthony. Questions were thrown in as the games progressed. It was discovered that Anthony's parents and teacher considered him stupid, retarded, and a juvenile delinquent. He complained that he was indeed all of these.

"But he began to change. He read books about Washington, Lincoln, Napoleon—looking for a hero. He joined the cadets and proudly displayed his uniform. He brought his school report card to the Center to show how well he was doing.

"I hadn't seen Anthony for two months as I had been in the hospital with a relapse of a back injury. 'Let's have no game now,' he said quietly and firmly. Anthony looked me over carefully. 'No more checkers. Please, no more games. Let's just talk from now on. Okay?' 'It was good and you know so much, and you explain so much to me, and things became okay. Then when you got sick it was as if it was dark all over and then the world stopped and everything stopped.'

"The beginning was ended. Anthony's trust was won. From this point on, we talked, we walked, we did many things together, but never again did we need to or want to play checkers.

"Anthony improved, at school, on the street, at home, a little bit at a time. He continued to beat up kids, slash tires, continued to be involved with the police, continued to disappear from home, continued to hold his head underwater until he lost consciousness, continued to hold back his bowels, and failed some subjects in school, provoked his father, provoked, provoked—but less so.

"His fears were surfacing, and he was able to tie them up with his experiences and tell me about both. . . . The terror of circumcision, the fear of being a nobody, fear of fire, fear of thunder.

"He explained that he held on to his bowels because he was afraid that if he let them go he would explode, and that part of him would be flushed away. He explained how, when he finally moved his bowels, he was able to keep the movement because it would not be flushed out of his pants. He told me of his terror and his shame about it. At eighteen Anthony tried to join the U.S. Army but was turned down. Anthony was crushed by this rejection. In his frustration to be recognized once again he committed his most *public* delinquent act—he set fire to a hundred old buses in the Bronx bus graveyard. This made the front page of *The New York Times*.

"Anthony turned himself in to the police and was apparently shocked by the magnitude of his act. Luckily for Anthony he was not sent to prison, and at last a permanent turning point in his life seemed to have been reached.

"A few months later in my house, Anthony took his news clippings out of his wallet and left them on my table forever.

"Then Anthony came to live with us. He was changed. Now he was a young man, the big brother to my small son. Now he was the big son to me and to my husband, and to his parents. Now at least he was growing up.

"Later, he got himself a job. Then he got an apartment. Then he joined a union and got a better job.

"One day, Anthony brought a girl home for me to meet. She was Polish, Jewish, a musician. They were married in a Polish church. The bride and the groom walked proudly down the aisle. Just as he passed me Anthony stopped. He took hold of my hand, looked at me, and then he walked on.

"Today, Anthony has a good job, a good wife, and a beautiful child. He is a good husband and he is a very warm, understanding father. Anthony has compassion, he has integrity, he is quiet. Anthony is somebody."

Source: Rothenberg, M. Children with Emerald Eyes, 1977, pp. 29-61. Reprinted with permission of the Dial Press.

Handicapped Children and Family Relationships

What is it like to be the parents of a disturbed or handicapped child? How do parents cope with these special children? How can parents be helped when they experience problems of coping?

Children who are retarded as well as emotionally disturbed provide special problems for parents (see Table 14.4). We mentioned in Chapter 7 the effect on parents of a child with Down's syndrome (retarded). Not only does the birth of such a child come as a bitter blow to many parents, but grief, frustration, and denial can be long lasting (Gath, 1979). Autistic children (emotionally disturbed) are usually very destructive of objects in their environment. If parents decide to keep an autistic child at home, they must make special accommodations. It is pointless to have attractive furnishings. Since these children do not acquire appropriate social behaviors, taking them to other peoples' homes or into public places can be an embarrassment (Schreibman & Koegal, 1975). Caring for handicapped children, especially in a poor neighborhood where families are often large, housing crowded, and the environment more physically demanding, is a most important requirement (Dunlap, 1979). When asked what services they believed were most needed, parents of handicapped children listed services such as training in self-care, day-care facilities, special education facilities, financial aid, transportation, health insurance, and medical services (Dunlap, 1976).

Table 14.4 Problems of Rearing Developmentally Disabled Children

Type of Problem	Percentage of Parents Having the Problem
Social stigma	7
Adjustment of brothers and sisters	3
Adjustment of parents	4
Physical demands of caring for child	23
Time demanded	45
Discipline problems	14
Money problems	27
Knowledge of social services	6
Lack of services	8
Other	26

In general, physical care and management are the major problems that interfere with the family without seriously affecting the family. Parents report that a handicapped child affects the family with respect to activities such as trips, vacations, shopping, going to the movies, and going to church and whether the mother can work outside the home.

Source: Dunlap, W. R., & Hollingsworth, S. J., "How does a Handicapped Child Affect the Family? Implications for Practitioners." *Family Coordinator,* July 1977, p. 289. Reprinted with permission.

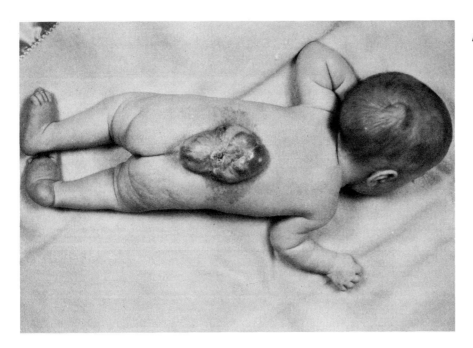

Children with severe handicaps, such as spina bifida provide special problems for parents. (Photo by Glenda Ruggiero; Courtesy of the Alfred I. DuPont Institute.)

It is certainly not an easy job for parents to accommodate to a handicapped child. The more serious the handicap, the greater the problem for parents. Parents pass through different stages of reaction to the realization that they have a child with a serious developmental problem (Baroff, 1974; Keith, 1973; Kessler, 1966; Rosen, 1955). Karnes and Lee (1980, pp. 208–210) have identified seven types of parental reaction.

1. *Denial.* A common reaction is not to believe a problem exists. For the sake of the child, the professional needs to help parents accept the diagnosis so that the child's handicap can be treated as soon as possible.

2. *Anger.* Faced with a handicapped child, and out of initial feelings of help-lessness and frustration toward both the child and themselves, parents may resort to anger (Gardner, 1973). Prolonged anger may result in parents' complete withdrawal of affection (rejection) or physical aggression.

3. *Guilt.* Parents may blame themselves for the child's condition, or one parent may blame the other. Parents must be helped to overcome inappropriate guilt feelings.

4. *Shame.* Often parents feel ashamed at the birth of an impaired child. They become concerned about others' expected disapproval and the belief that their child will be judged inferior.

5. *Blame.* Gardner (1973) has suggested that blame is the parents' attempt to cushion their own feelings by placing the responsibility for their child's condition on others, such as a teacher, a doctor, or perhaps hereditary factors "on the other side of the family."

6. *Overprotection.* Parents may deny their handicapped child the chance to interact with other children. The excuses are several—it's too cold, other children are too rough, other children will ridicule the child. This is actually likely to handicap the child further. Overprotective parents need to be convinced that the handicapped child can be helped by being placed in an education program and extracurricular activities (Karnes, Zehrbach, & Teska, 1972).

7. *Emotional adaptation.* The final stage of adjustment by parents (hopefully) is emotional adaptation. If this occurs, parents will have intellectually and emotionally accepted their child's handicapped condition and be willing to contribute to the child's future.

Programs for Parents

Since nearly all parents of special children experience an initial "transient stress disorder" (an emotional disturbance), it is important to provide parents with the support of a professional (Chinn, Winn, & Walters, 1978). It is not uncommon for parents to be bewildered by such problems, not knowing what to do or who to turn to. Certain organizations have sprung up, mainly in the larger cities, to provide advice and help for families with special children. Parent organizations provide not only information but also emotional support and opportunities for parents with handicapped children to meet, share their experiences, and provide mutual support. To get assistance from local professional organizations or branches of national organizations such as the National Association for Mental Health or the Association for Children with Learning Disabilities, parents need to check for these organizations in their local area and place a phone call (see, for example, Chinn et al., 1978, pp. 168–170).

Follow-up of high-risk infants from the hospital and specific services offered to parents of handicapped children is increasing. However, "planned intervention to optimize the at-risk infant's cognitive and adaptive development is not a function commonly practiced by nurses" (Barnard, 1978, p. 716). A number of programs have been established in the nursing departments at hospitals. Just a few of these are the Eunice Kennedy Shriver Center, Waltham, Massachusetts; the Denver General Hospital; the Child Development and Mental Retardation Center and School of Nursing at the University of Washington. (See also Inset 14.4.)

Barnard (1978) reports that there are too few hospitals and institutes where nurses are involved in specific intervention activities to help at-risk infants. She goes on to say that a number of projects that intervene in the infant's environment in order to improve it are beginning to appear. Racone Zelle, a nursing consultant in Sacramento, California, describes how her center became involved in infant intervention:

Approximately 6 months after our agency opened its door, three infants were referred who had Down's syndrome. The counselors and I acutely sensed the pain which these families were experiencing and the need for intensive support. A counselor and myself conducted an 8-week group counseling session involving these parents. We used a practical, educational-oriented approach versus a therapy-oriented approach because feelings are painful at this stage and can only be expressed over time in a graduated manner. At the end of the 8-week session, we had a potluck group luncheon at one of the parent's homes where I assessed the babies and offered individualized management suggestions. Although the luncheon was held on a weekday, all the fathers attended. Regular follow-up luncheons have been held on an ongoing basis. The parents provided positive feedback to their physicians, and we received more referrals. We conducted two more 8-week sessions for parents with infants with Down's syndrome. The almost perfect attendance reflected the value of the sessions. The parents became very close and supportive, and they continued to keep in touch after the sessions ended. They evolved into a viable group who realized a need for an intensive intervention program. They elicited my help in finding a funding source and in serving as the primary consultant to develop the new program. Our investigation indicated that Title VI-B funds were the most promising, and we contacted the most progressive school district in Sacramento County. The Director of Special Education was responsive, but explained that he had a "bare-bones" administrative staff. He would willingly enter into a joint effort with the parents and Alta California Regional Center if someone could write the proposal. The parents and I assumed this responsibility, and the grant proposal was approved for funding.

A nurse was written in as the key member of the team because I feel that her educational and field experience best prepares her to intervene with infants and families—more so than a member of any other discipline. However, a Master's Degree in Child Development Nursing was specified because she needs specialized theoretical and practical training to relate to the needs of a developmentally disabled child. The program was also family-oriented with interventions focused on developing a positive bond between the parents and the child which accentuates the parents' self-esteem in their roles. When the children reach 18 months of age, they participate in a half-day group program twice a week, which provides respite for the mother and parallel contact with other children.

The staff of the Infant Program consists of a psychologist 2/10-time who is responsible for the evaluation process and Title VI administration, a teacher 3/10-time who is primarily responsible for the half-day group program, a physical therapist 1/4-time who intervenes extensively with the infants with cerebral palsy, a full-time nurse who is primarily responsible for the intervention program in the home, and four infant technicians who provide weekly follow-up support in the home and help with the group program.

The approaches are as natural as possible and lend themselves to the daily routine of the home. I feel that the whole approach has been more family and developmentally oriented because a nurse participated in the developmental stage and is a key member of the team.

Source: Quoted from Barnard, W. E., "Nursing: High-Risk Infants." In T. D. Tjossem, Ed., *Intervention Strategies for High-Risk Infants and Young Children*, 1976, pp. 716–717. Copyright, 1976, University Park Press, Baltimore. Reprinted with permission.

In recent years programs have appeared that have successfully involved parents in helping their handicapped children (Karnes & Lee, 1980, pp. 216–219). Many programs now provide special training for parents with handicapped children. It should be mentioned that many parents do provide suitable care for their handicapped children, and benefits supplied by programs should build on these strengths. This provides a contact with other parents, professionals, and other children. In learning to deal with their own children and having the support of professionals working with them, parents become less frustrated, and their feelings of inadequacy diminish as they gain new competencies and greater confidence (Hayden & Haring, 1978). The following brief descriptions of four such programs provide examples of the wide range of programs now available (see, for further examples, Fine, 1980, and Tjossem, 1978).

The Portage Project is a *home-based* program. Parents are trained in the home by parent educators to use behavior modification techniques with their children. The children range in age from birth to 6 years. Handicaps treated include behavior problems, emotional disturbance, mental retardation, and physical handicaps. The teaching program is based on a checklist of 450 items of behavior in five development areas—cognition, language, self-help, motor skills, and socialization.

The home teaching process goes as follows. The parents first select an activity they would like to use with their child. For example, "_____ (child's name) will grasp a large crayon and holding it correctly will trace over horizontal line— 8 trials each day for one week." The home teacher writes up an activity sheet for the parents that clearly describes the sequence of subtasks for teaching this activity to the child, and only those that can be achieved in one week (see Figure 14.1). The home teacher then models the teaching methods for the parents following directions written up for the activity. Parents then take over and work with the child with the home teacher's offering suggestions and reinforcement. At the next visit in the following week the child's progress is checked. As you can readily see from Figure 14.1, this teaching procedure for training parents and the parents' teaching method is behavioristic. As the parent gains confidence and experience in teaching and recording the child's progress, the parent–teacher increases the number of items to be taught each week (Shearer et al., 1970).

Telstar Project is also a home-based program for children between birth and 6 years who are moderately to severely handicapped. Each handicapped child is placed with a normal child in a day-care home that cares for both. These are called satellite homes and are located near the handicapped child's place of

Child's name _____

Home teacher's name _____

Week of _____

Behavior

Child will grasp a large crayon and holding it correctly will trace over horizontal line—8 trials / day.

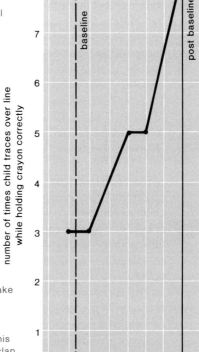

Directions
1. Use a large sheet of paper and with a large crayon make a line across the paper.
2. Tell the child to watch you—using a crayon of another color, trace over the line in one continuous movement.
3. Then give the child the crayon and tell him or her it's his or her turn. Praise the child as he or she traces, and clap your hands when he or she finishes.
4. If the child has difficulty, put your hand over the child's hand to guide him or her. Praise the child, but don't clap.
5. Record success if the child traces over the line without your help.

Figure 14.1 Portage Project activity chart. In this example, it took the child seven days to achieve complete success in tracing eight times correctly over a horizontal line. (Source: Shearer, D. E., and Shearer, M. S., *The Portage Project: A Model for Early Childhood Intervention.* Copyright, 1976, University Park Press, Baltimore. Reprinted with permission.)

residence. The parent in the satellite home agrees to take in one nonhandicapped child with the handicapped child and to participate in in-service training. The intent is to provide the handicapped child with guidance from a trained parent and a normal child of the same age. This program emphasizes self-care, the improvement of motor skills, and language development (Meyer Children's Rehabilitation Institute Teaching Program for Young Children, 1974).

The Read Project is an experimental program that has proved to be highly successful in training parents with handicapped children to use behavior modification techniques. The Read Project trains parents to attend to a range of complex behavior rather than targeting on a specific child behavior (Baker, Heifetz, & Brightman, 1974; Hirsch & Walder, 1969). Parents, in groups of six to twelve families, meet for training in the use of a behavior modification program for retarded children (Baker, 1973; Brightman, 1972). Training methods include lectures, discussions, individual consultation, home visits, hot lines, program exercises, films, videotaped feedback of parent teaching, and the Read Project Series of instructional manuals.

Parents trained only by the manuals improved in their ability to teach their children self-help skills. However, acquiring skill in applying general principles of behavior modification to each individual handicapped child appears to require face-to-face training. For example, modeling and feedback of in-home visits are an essential component of teaching autistic children (Baker & Heifetz, 1978, p. 366).

The Experimental Education Unit operates as one of four units at the University of Washington's Child Development and Retardation Center and is for Down's syndrome children (Hayden & Haring, 1978). The program emphasizes the sequential development of motor, communication, social, cognitive, and self-help skills. An important goal is to prepare Down's syndrome children for placement in special or regular education programs in their home community.

Watching the children's performance over the years has forced our entire staff to raise its expectations about the children's ability. Probably the most obvious example of this is that it was not our intention, when the program began, to teach these children how to read. Yet it became clear . . . that children in the preschool group had acquired the requisite skills to begin a pre-reading and then a reading program (Hayden & Haring, 1978, p. 589).

Parents are trained to use exercises and instructional procedures at home. When their children enter preschool, parents are trained as observers and teaching assistants, and they work in the classroom. Parents also work in the community as counselors. Many make hospital visits to talk to parents of newborn Down's syndrome infants. They lecture to students at the University of Washington. Several parents who moved from the Washington area have set up preschool programs in communities where previously there had been no educational opportunities for Down's syndrome children (Hayden & Dmitriev, 1975).

Many children with physical and mental handicaps are "mainstreamed" with normal children in regular public school classrooms. (Photos: left: Jean-Claude Lejeune; right: Leonard McCombe/Life Magazine © Time, Inc.)

School Programs for the Handicapped

The family usually has the greatest influence on the child's development, followed by the school. Hewett (1972) suggests that the school can provide a therapeutic environment since it is organized to provide for specialized learning and to fulfill emotional and social needs. What is being done to provide educational services for handicapped children?

A number of services are provided through federal legislation—the Handicapped Children's Early Education Program, Head Start, Title I of the Elementary and Secondary Education Act, and Title VI-B of the same act. The emphasis is on providing preschool programs for the handicapped—the reason being obvious, to provide special training as soon as possible (at least within school systems). Although there has been considerable improvement in the provision of programs that are federally funded, only a little over 25 percent of handicapped preschool children get the services they need (Ackerman, Jr., & Moore, 1978).

The term *mainstreaming* in education and special education is well known. It means enabling handicapped children to attend regular schools. Wolfensberger (1972) introduced it as part of the concept of *normalization,* the idea that handicapped children are entitled to as normal an existence as possible, including attendance in a public school program. In schools where mainstreaming occurs handicapped children are provided with a special support teacher and the maximum opportunity to interact with normally developing peers (Bricker & Bricker, 1978, p. 558). It is recognized that there are certain severely handicapped children who cannot be placed in such programs and who need self-contained, special education.

Programs such as the Infant, Toddler, and Preschool Research and Intervention Project (Bricker & Bricker, 1972, 1973) have proved very effective with autistic and Down's syndrome children, as well as with children who have sensory handicaps. In this preschool program each unit has an equal number of handicapped and normal children. As is becoming more and more the case, parents are involved in a related training program that coordinates educational activities in the home and school settings.

The effectiveness of mainstreaming and of the various types of programs for handicapped children is still being evaluated. There is no doubt that many intervention programs should receive continued support. At the same time research efforts should continue to explore, develop, and assess education programs for the handicapped.

Summary

There are various types of abnormal behavior each of which exists on a continuum—the other end of which is normal behavior. The degree of abnormality in development is measured by the extent to which the handicapped behavior deviates from average behavior. Various criteria need to be used in measuring the appropriateness of behavior. These criteria must take into account not only the characteristics of behavior but also their various settings: (1) age discrepancy, (2) frequency of occurrence, (3) number of symptoms, (4) degree of social disadvantage, (5) degree of suffering, (6) intractability of behavior, and (7) general personality appraisal.

Four dimensions of the diagnosis of abnormal behavior have been suggested: etiology (cause and development), symptoms, prognosis (long-term effects, or outcome), and therapy. Diagnosis is a complex task. Specialists tend to be biased in their diagnoses by their own particular view of development and how cases are presented to them.

The *etiology* or causes of abnormal development are physiological, environmental, or a combination of the two. The model of etiology suggested by Meehl (1962), the diathesis–stress model, is based on combinations of predispositions toward particular ways of behaving and degrees of stress the child experiences.

Abnormal behavior falls into three major categories—psychoneuroses, psychoses, and learning disorders. Two common forms of neuroses are school and death phobias. Psychoses are described in terms of autism, which is present from birth and is probably mainly the result of a genetic defect, and schizophrenia, which appears in childhood or later and is usually believed to be caused by an interaction between biological and environmental factors. Learning disorders include learning disabilities such as dyslexia and mental retardation.

Neuroses can be diagnosed relatively easily. Psychoses are not easy to diagnose. In most cases of psychotic disorders the prognosis is pessimistic. However, depending on the seriousness of the abnormality, handicapped children do respond to training in self-help and social skills. Although psychotic children can achieve a degree of competency in these skills, they never achieve normal behavior.

Mental retardation is usually classified on four levels from profound to mild retardation according to the child's score on an IQ test. Children with learning disabilities such as dyslexia, dyscalcula, aphasia, and hyperactivity are *not* retarded.

There are various types of intervention programs and therapy techniques for dealing with abnormal behavior. Each child, however, must be treated as a unique case. Two general forms of treatment are *behavior therapy* and *psychotherapy*. Within each category, various techniques have been identified such as *behavior modification, modeling, psychoanalytic psychotherapy,* and *play therapy.* Parents go through stages of reaction to the birth of a handicapped child; these range from denial and anger to emotional adaptation. In the past two decades many programs have been devised for parents of handicapped children. In many cities there are organizations for assisting parents. There are also training programs, many of which are home based. Most of these programs train parents to use behavior modification techniques to train their children in self-help, social, language, and cognitive skills.

A number of educational services have been provided in public school systems through federal legislation. However, only a little over 25 percent of preschool-age children receive help through these programs. There is obviously room for expansion. A special feature of many educational programs is mainstreaming or normalization. A number of children with abnormal behaviors interact with normal children in usual classroom activities. The handicapped children also have the help and support of a specialist teacher as well as the regular teacher. Most educational programs have a related parent program.

Questions for Review

1. Describe the main dimensions of diagnosis of abnormal behavior. Why is it usually difficult to diagnose abnormal behavior accurately?

2. What signs would suggest a child is suffering from a neurosis? How are neuroses treated?

3. Describe the main characteristic of psychotic disorders. In what ways do autism and schizophrenia differ?

4. List and briefly describe the major etiological factors of child behavior.

5. What types of treatment of abnormal behavior are in most frequent use?

6. Parents of handicapped children face particular problems of child rearing. How do most parents tend to react to the birth of a handicapped child? What programs are available to help parents with a handicapped child?

7. If possible, arrange to visit with a therapist or counselor in the pediatric department of a local hospital. Ask about methods used to diagnose and treat handicapped children.

8. Working in small groups, survey the facilities in your locality that offer services for various types of handicapped children. Contact a number of these facilities personally, by phone, or by letter and obtain descriptions of their screening and treatment procedures. Synthesize your findings in a report.

Suggestions for Further Reading

Brown, S. J., & Lasher, M. G. *Are you ready to mainstream? Helping preschoolers with learning and behavior problems.* Columbus, OH: Charles E. Merrill, 1978. An overview of early childhood intervention programs.

Chinn, P. C., Winn, J., and Walters, R. H. *Two-way talking with parents of special children: A process of positive communication.* St. Louis, MO: C. V. Mosby, 1978. Discusses the impact of a handicapped child on the family and provides a description of a particular process of family interaction aimed at helping communication between parents and their "special" children.

Fine, M. J., ed. *Handbook on parent education.* New York: Academic Press, 1980. See especially Chapter 9, which describes how parents can become involved in the education of their handicapped children.

Rothenberg, M. *Children with emerald eyes.* New York: Pocket Books, 1977. A very moving account of the symptoms and treatment of a number of children with extreme abnormal behavior.

Schifani, J. W., Anderson, R. M., and Odle, S. J. eds. *Implementing learning in the least restrictive environment: Handicapped children in the mainstream.* Baltimore: University Park Press, 1980. A textbook on mainstreaming that focuses on the competencies needed to organize learning for mainstreamed children in public schools.

Trites, R. L. *Hyperactivity in children: Etiology, measurement, and treatment implications.* Baltimore: University Park Press, 1979. A reference text of research and viewpoints of internationally known authorities on hyperactivity with special reference to diagnosis and treatment.

Wolman, B. B., Egan, J., & Ross, A. O., eds. *Handbook of treatment of mental disorders in childhood and adolescence.* Englewood Cliffs, NJ: Prentice-Hall, 1978. See especially the chapter by Lovaas, Young, and Newsom, which describes the behavioral treatment of childhood psychoses.

Glossary

accommodation
The process of adapting already existing knowledge to include new information. For example, a child who pretends that two pieces of wood hammered together are an airplane *accommodates* or changes an already existing concept of an airplane to include the new representation. (*See also* adaptation)

adaptation
The process of selecting and interpreting information to construct knowledge about the environment. Adaptation involves the two complementary processes of assimilation and accommodation.

adolescent growth spurt
Rapid physical growth (particularly in height) that occurs at puberty.

advance organizer
A specially prepared lesson that presents general ideas (superordinate concepts or high-order rules) to be learned before related, more particular information (subordinate concepts, factual information, or particular rules). According to Ausubel, this method of organizing instruction provides the *potential* for meaningful learning. (*See also* meaningful learning)

alienation
The result of identity or role confusion. Erikson refers to an identity crisis as the lack of desirable relationships with oneself and others.

allele
One form of a specific gene at a particular locus on a chromosome.

altruism
Acting in the interest of others; offering help when needed and being concerned about others' welfare.

androgen
A hormone produced by a male's testes that controls sexual changes during puberty.

Apgar scale
A simple technique for assessing a newborn's appearance, pulse rate, reflexes, activity, and respiration.

artificialism
Piaget's term for the preoperational child's belief that all objects are created by people or by a god according to a specific plan. (*See also* finalism)

assimilation
The process of adding new information to already existing knowledge. For example, a child who pretends that two pieces of wood hammered together are an airplane *assimilates* that new object into an already existing concept of an airplane. (*See also* adaptation)

associative learning
Linking one experience with another in the memory.

attachment
The preference an infant develops for adults who provide consistent and predictable care.

authoritarian parenting
A method of parenting in which parents set strict and often restrictive rules of behavior, dissociate themselves from their children's activities, and show little overt affection.

authoritative parenting
A method of parenting in which parents set reasonable rules and expectations for behavior, are usually willing to discuss the restrictions they impose, frequently become involved in their children's activities, and are affectionate.

autism
A childhood psychosis characterized by the child's inability to relate to people; by compulsive behavior; and by long periods spent sitting or standing either motionless or rocking. Autistic children make no attempt to communicate.

autosome
A non-sex chromosome possessed equally by males and females.

babbling
An infant's repetition of combined sounds such as *ma,ma,ma, da,da,da,* or *ba,ba,ba.* This phase in speech development usually begins at about twenty months.

Babinski reflex
An infant's reflex to turn his toes upward when the sole of his foot is touched or stroked. The absence of this reflex suggests a defect in the lower spine.

behavioral objective
A statement of specific, expected changes in a child's behavior following learning.

behavior modification
Shaping behavior through operant conditioning. (*See also* shaping)

behavior therapy
The isolation and treatment of maladaptive behavior using behavior modification techniques.

blastocyst
The mass of cells that forms following cell division in the zygote. The embryo develops from the blastocyst.

bonding or **imprinting**
A term used particularly by ethologists to describe behaviors learned very early in life by animals. These behaviors create a strong bond between the infants and their parents. (*See also* attachment)

bulimia
Compulsive overeating thought to be an expression of a special need for affection. (*See also* obesity)

caregiver
A term describing an infant's parent, surrogate parent, or any other person who provides consistent and reliable care.

centration
Focusing attention on a particular property of an object or situational feature when other objects and features must also be taken into account to correctly solve a problem.

cephalocaudal
Physical development from the head downward.

cervix
The neck of the uterus; the place where the uterus opens into the vagina.

cesarean section
A surgical procedure for delivering a baby through an incision made in the abdomen and uterus. This method is used most frequently when the pelvic opening is too small to allow normal passage of the baby at birth.

chromosome
A stringlike thread on which genes are arranged in a cell. Each body cell has forty-six chromosomes that carry the genetic inheritance passed from parents to their child.

chromosome trisomy abnormalities
The presence of an extra X or Y chromosome, resulting in any of a number of abnormalities such as sterile testes in males or the development of small genitalia in females.

classical conditioning
The process of learning to associate a natural stimulus with a conditioned stimulus. Eventually the response to the conditioned stimulus will be the same as that to the natural stimulus. For example, if an infant, naturally startled by a loud sound, sees an object such as a puppet at the same time, the child will eventually be startled by the sight of the puppet.

classification
The sorting of objects into classes, or the sorting of subclasses (subordinant concepts) into more inclusive classes (superordinate concepts), according to some shared property.

clinical research
Research that combines the observation of children with individualized questioning.

cognitive agency
According to Baumrind, the combination of a well-developed sense of identity and the ability to respond positively to intellectual challenge.

cognitive style
The consistent way an individual perceives, learns, remembers, and uses information.

concept assimilation
Concept assimilation occurs when a child knows the general properties of a class of objects, recognizes members of that class when they occur, and assimilates them to form a concept. For example, a child might know the general properties of sailing ships and include craft such as yachts, tea clippers, and dinghies in the construction of the concept.

concept formation
The recognition that certain objects share a common property and that they can be formed into a class on the basis of that property.

conception
The moment of fertilization, when the male sperm joins with the female ovum to form a zygote.

concrete operations
Piaget's third stage of intellectual development, during which the child develops the ability to think and reason in a logical fashion about objects in the environment.

conditioned response
A response to a conditioned stimulus.

conditioned stimulus
A stimulus (such as a puppet) that has become associated with a natural stimulus (such as a loud noise) and that eventually elicits the same response as the natural stimulus (in this case, a startled reaction).

conservation
According to Piaget, conservation refers to a child's understanding that a particular property of an object remains the same even when other properties change (for example, quantity remains the same even when shape or length changes).

constructive play
Imaginative play involving changes in objects and events. For example, a preschooler is involved in exploratory play while pretending to be a fire truck, a police officer, or a nurse. This type of play is both exploratory and rule governed.

control group
Subjects in a control group are just like those in an experimental group except that they do not receive the experimental treatment. A control group is used to ensure that any changes in the behavior of the experimental group can be attributed to the experimental treatment and not to other factors.

conventional level of moral reasoning
Kohlberg's second level of moral development, during which the child conforms unquestioningly to social rules and regulations.

cooing
The infant's first attempt at speech, beginning at about six weeks of age.

correlation
A statistical term meaning that two factors change together in some predictable way. A *positive correlation* is present when the two factors change in the same direction, while a *negative correlation* occurs when one factor increases and the other decreases in intensity or frequency.

correlational research
Research involving the study of a relationship or correspondence between two factors. Correlations between factors in the child's environment describe relationship *patterns, not* cause-and-effect relationships.

critical period
A fixed time when bonding between the infant animal and parents occurs. (*See also* sensitive period)

cross-over
The joining of chromosome pairs prior to cell division.

cross-sectional research
Research in which groups of children of different ages are tested simultaneously.

cultural amplifier
Some agent in a particular culture that has an important effect on a child's development and learning. Examples might include language, a problem-solving strategy, or a particular teacher or parent.

cumulative learning
A learning process described by behavioral psychologists as the gradual accumulation of abilities and knowledge that form the prerequisites for later learning.

decentering
The ability to focus on more than one property of an object or situational feature, or to take into account more than one point of view.

defense mechanism
A method of behaving or thinking that diverts attention from unbearable inner thoughts and emotions.

delinquency
Acts of aggression against the family and society by adolescents under the age of eighteen. Most delinquent acts are committed by teenage gangs.

dental age
Estimating a child's physical growth and development by observing the primary and secondary teeth.

Deoxyribonucleic acid or **DNA**
Chemical elements combined in thousands of arrangements, causing the reproduction of the genes that determine an individual's traits.

diathesis
An indication of a predisposition towards a particular behavior.

didactic learning materials
Learning materials constructed in such a fashion that they guide the child's use of them. For example, in learning the concept of seriation, (widest to thinnest), the child learns to place a series of wooden cylinders of differing diameters into drilled holes in a wooden block. Many didactic learning materials were developed by Maria Montessori.

digit or **memory span**
A simple measure of memory obtained by counting the number of items a child can remember following a memorization task.

dilation
The first stage of labor, involving the opening or *dilation* of the cervix and vagina (birth canal) to allow passage of the baby.

discovery learning
Spontaneous or self-directed learning. Guided discovery learning results from a balance between directed instruction and self-directed learning.

discrimination learning
Learning to perceive similarities and differences between objects.

disequilibrium
According to Piaget, a state of reasoning in which a child is unable to assimilate and accommodate new information.

dizygotic or **fraternal twins**
Twins who develop from two separate zygotes. Dizygotic twins are no more genetically similar than any other siblings born to the same parents.

dominant allele
An allele that produces some trait or characteristic in the individual. (*See also* phenotype)

Down's syndrome
A genetic abnormality attributed to the presence of a forty-seventh chromosome, making a set of three in the twenty-first chromosome (trisomy 21). Children with this abnormality have distinguishing physical characteristics such as round faces, slanted eyes, and short limbs and are underdeveloped intellectually.

duo sentence
Two-word sentences infants begin to use at the age of about eighteen months. These sentences are believed to indicate the emergence of a grammar.

dyscalcula
The inability to calculate.

dyslexia
A reading disability characterized by the tendency to reverse words or letters and to mispronounce words.

ectoderm
The outer mass of cells in the zygote, from which the nervous system and other parts of the body such as the hair and nails develop.

ego
A Freudian term describing the part of the personality that guides rational action and regulates impulsive and instinctual urges.

egocentrism
A characteristic of preoperational thinking indicated by a young child's preoccupation with herself and lack of concern about the views of others.

embryo
The human organism between two and eight weeks after conception.

embryonic disc
The mass of cells the embryo develops from.

enactive representation
The process of thinking and reasoning about objects and events through sensorimotor actions. (*See also* sensorimotor stage)

endoderm
The inner mass of cells in the zygote, from which inner organs such as the lungs, liver, and pancreas develop.

equilibrium
According to Piaget, the point at which changes are assimilated into cognitive structures. For example, as the infant adapts sensorimotor schemes to preoperations, preoperational thinking eventually reaches equilibrium.

erythroblastosis
The result of Rh blood incompatibility between mother and fetus, causing damage to the red blood corpuscles in the fetal blood supply and reducing the supply of oxygen to the fetus to an inadequate level.

estrogen
A female hormone, produced principally by the ovaries, that regulates sexual development during puberty.

ethics
Standards established to safeguard research subjects from physical or psychological harm.

ethology
The study of animals in their natural habitats.

etiology
The examination of the causes and development of behavior. Etiology is the first step in diagnosing abnormal behavior.

experimental research
A research strategy in which one or more independent variables are manipulated and the effects of the manipulations on other dependent variables are then measured. In this way, cause-and-effect relationships can be inferred. (*See also* variable)

Fallopian tube
One of the tubes through which a female ovum travels to the uterus.

fetoscopy
The insertion into the uterus of an endoscope, containing fiber bundles that transmit light. Fetoscopy allows the physician to inspect the uterus, placenta, and fetus. Samples of tissue or blood can be taken from the fetus, placenta, or amniotic fluid using a hypodermic needle. It is also possible to perform surgery to the fetus by means of this procedure.

fetus
The human organism from about eight weeks after conception to birth.

fontanels
Sections of connective tissue between the bones of the newborn baby's skull. Fontanels allow molding of the skull during birth. They close completely by about one year of age.

formal operations
Piaget's term for the fourth and final stage of intellectual development, which is characterized by hypothetico-deductive reasoning.

functional paralysis
A form of hysteria in which the individual loses the use of a limb with no actual physical disability.

functional play
Play that involves learning about the physical and social environment and exploring cause-and-effect relationships. For example, a child might mix different liquids together to find out what happens. This type of play is considered to be a prerequisite for constructive play.

functional relationship
According to Piaget, the simple association a child makes between one thing and another. For example, the belief that the weather gets colder when leaves begin to fall from the trees is a functional relationship.

fundamental lesson
A method of instruction devised by Maria Montessori. In this method, a teacher introduces a general idea, ensures the child understands the idea by demonstration and questioning, and ascertains the child's level of understanding by observing the extent to which the child can apply the general idea to other objects sharing the properties of the general idea.

gamete
A sex cell. In females, gametes are called ova or eggs, and in males, sperm or spermatozoa.

gene
A segment of DNA carrying genetic information that will determine an individual's traits. Genes are attached to chromosomes.

genital stage
A Freudian term for the stage of psychosexual development that occurs during adolescence. During this stage, gratification includes sexual orgasm, but sexual energy is also channelled toward achieving independence from parents.

genotype
An individual's genetic heritage, including both dominant and recessive alleles.

graphic collections
Arrangements of objects by visual appearance to form a collection that is not a logical class. For example, arranging geometric shapes in the form of a clown.

habituation
A decrease in interest, attention, or responsiveness to a stimulus due to familiarity following repeated presentations. For example, an infant may lose interest in a mobile that is continually suspended over his or her crib.

heterozygous alleles
Two or more alleles at a particular locus on a chromosome that differ with respect to genetic instructions. For example, one allele may "call" for brown eyes and the other for blue eyes.

holophrase
A one-word sentence used by infants at about one year of age.

homozygous alleles
Two or more alleles at a particular locus on a chromosome, each containing the same genetic information.

hormone
A chemical substance that predisposes the body to be either male or female.

hostile aggression
Physical or verbal aggression directed towards another person. This type of aggression is most common among older children.

hybrid vigor
A term used to describe the establishment of dominant genes that determine a high quality of physical development. Hybrid vigor results from a wide variety of people mating and sharing genetic traits.

hyperactive behavior
Constant, impulsive, and random behavior. Hyperactive children find it difficult to concentrate.

iconic representation
A way of thinking about, reasoning about, and representing objects and events as images. For example, a child might represent an airplane as two pieces of wood fastened together at right angles.

id
That part of the personality concerned with biological drives and instinctual urges such as hunger, sex, and aggression. According to Freud, the id needs to be regulated by the ego.

imitative learning
Learning through imitating or modeling another person's behavior.

imprinting
A rapid form of learning that results in the bonding of an infant animal to a parent. (*See also* bonding *and* critical period)

impulsive cognitive style
A learning style characterized by quick, random guessing that usually results in inaccurate answers.

industry versus inferiority
Erikson's fourth stage of psychosocial development, during which the school-age child either accepts intellectual and social challenges and develops new skills or fails to meet these challenges, leading to a sense of inferiority.

initiative versus guilt
Erikson's third stage of psychosocial development, during which the preschool child either begins to initiate activities and to independently explore the environment or feels guilty at daring to do things independently.

innate
A way of acting, thinking, or learning that is inborn; that is, present from the moment of conception. For example, Noam Chomsky has suggested that language is innate and that it "unfolds" as the individual grows older.

instrumental aggression
Mild physical or verbal aggression usually aimed at retrieving an object, territory, or privilege. This type of aggression is most common among younger children.

intelligence quotient
The score an individual obtains on a standardized test of intelligence. IQ is calculated by dividing mental age by chronological age and multiplying by 100 $(IQ = \dfrac{MA}{CA} \times 100)$.

interview research
An indirect observational procedure in which subjects are asked either controlled and structured questions about situations, are allowed to elaborate on questions about situations, or are asked both types of questions.

karyotype
A chart on which photos of an individual's chromosomes are arranged to aid in the diagnosis of chromosomal disorders.

Lamaze
A series of relaxation techniques used to help control pain and anxiety during childbirth.

language acquisition device (LAD)
According to Noam Chomsky, the innate process of developing and using language.

learning hierarchy
A term used by Gagne to describe learning levels ranging from simple signal learning to complex problem-solving strategies. Gagne uses this model to describe the process of cumulative learning (which, from the behaviorist's view, is synonymous with development).

locus of control
An aspect of the self-concept characterized by an awareness of confident control over one's life.

longitudinal research
A method for studying the same group of subjects over a relatively lengthy period of time. In this type of research, repeated observations and measurements of behavior are made to determine the course of development and/or learning.

long-term memory
The retrieval of information over long periods of time.

mainstreaming
Enabling handicapped children to attend regular schools. The objective of mainstreaming is to place handicapped children in a normal learning environment while still providing them with a special education program.

marasmus
A disease of infancy resulting from extreme malnutrition. Marasmus impairs health and physical development and may result in death.

maturation
Physical and behavior changes that occur as a result of the aging process rather than through learning.

meaningful learning
The recognition that new knowledge can be related to or assimilated into previously learned general concepts and high-order rules.

meiosis
The division of a gamete to produce a new sperm or ovum containing twenty-three chromosomes.

memory monitoring
Keeping a check on memory, or on whether a memory strategy is working. Memory monitoring is an aspect of metamemory.

memory strategy
A planned method for remembering information, usually through rehearsal or problem-solving strategies.

menarche
A female's first menstruation, which is usually considered the first sign of puberty. However, menarche does not necessarily indicate fertility.

mental retardation
Subaverage intellectual functioning accompanied by impairment of the ability to adapt to different situations. In practice, level of retardation is measured by IQ tests.

mesoderm
The middle layer of cells in the zygote that become the circulatory and excretory systems, muscles, and skeleton.

metamemory
The individual's understanding of how memory works. For example, many people are aware of the ease or difficulty of remembering different kinds of information, and many use different strategies for memorization.

mitosis
The division of a somatic or body cell to produce two new cells, each containing the same arrangement of *forty-six* chromosomes present in the original cell.

monozygotic or **identical twins**
Two individuals who developed from the same zygote, and who are therefore genetically alike. Monozygotic twins are always the same sex.

Moro reflex
A reflex present during infancy that causes the arms to fling outward in reaction to a sudden noise or movement. The absence of this reflex suggests damage to the central nervous system.

morpheme
The smallest unit of meaningful language, consisting of one-word or sometimes two-word utterances (such as *dada* or *all gone*).

myelination
The development of a fatty, insulating sheath around the nerves. Myelination helps speed up the transmission of nerve impulses.

negative reinforcement
Strengthening a particular behavior by removing an unpleasant stimulus. For example, a child might complete chores to avoid losing her allowance.

neonate
An infant from birth to four weeks of age.

neurosis
An extreme form of anxiety. Characteristics of the neurotic child include feelings of inferiority, social withdrawal, oversensitivity, timidity, and depression.

object permanence
The understanding that objects do not cease to exist when they cannot be seen.

obsession

A neurotic behavior characterized by persistent, often unwanted thoughts and actions that are dominated by the emotions rather than the intellect.

operant conditioning

Providing a consequence to a behavior that is already *operating* or acting upon the environment. For example, giving attention to an infant when he smiles helps condition him to continue to do so.

operation

A Piagetian term describing a logically organized representation of objects and events. According to Piaget, single operations (such as classification or the conservation of length) are always combined with other operations to form a complete structure of knowledge (such as concrete operations).

oral stage

A Freudian term describing the first stage of psychosexual development, which is characterized by gratification through sucking and biting.

organization

That aspect of the intelligence that consistently makes sense out of different experiences. According to Piaget, organization and adaptation are complementary processes of functioning intelligence.

ossification

The hardening of cartilage into bone.

ovary

The female reproductive gland producing ova.

ovum

A female reproductive cell or gamete, sometimes referred to as an egg.

pathology

The study of abnormal behavior.

performance objective

A term used by Gagné to describe a learning objective made up of five elements: situation, learned capability, object (learning materials), action, and tools.

permissive parenting

A parenting method that makes few demands on children and provides little or no enforcement of rules.

phallic stage

A Freudian term describing the stage of psychosexual development that occurs between three and six years of age. During this stage, the child tends to focus attention on and gain pleasure from the genital area.

phenotype

The observable traits or characteristics of an individual, such as brown hair or blue eyes. An individual's phenotype may differ from his or her genotype.

phobia

An excessive and unfounded fear of a particular object, circumstance, or situation.

pivot grammar

The idea that duo sentences are made up from a class of words that always appear in a fixed place (pivot class) and a class of words that have no fixed place (open class). For example, a child might use the duo sentences *coat on, shoe on,* and *hat on,* in which case *on* is the pivot word. The concept of pivot grammar is now considered inadequate to explain the development of duo sentences since it does not include a consideration of semantics, or sentence meaning.

placenta
A layer of cells and blood vessels separating the developing fetus from the mother's blood system. The placenta serves as a screen through which oxygen and nourishment pass from the mother to the fetus and through which waste products pass from the fetus to the mother's system for disposal.

plantar reflex
A reflex present during early infancy that causes the toes to grasp an object placed in the groove between toes and foot. The absence of this reflex may be an indication of a defect in the lower spine.

positive reinforcement
Strengthening a particular behavior by rewarding it with something pleasant.

postconventional morality
The stage of development of moral reasoning that, according to Kohlberg, is achieved by some but not all adolescents. This type of moral reasoning is characterized by a concern for the moral rights of all people and universal, ethical principles governing behavior.

premature baby
A baby born more than three weeks before the due date and weighing less than 5½ pounds. (*See also* small-for-date baby)

preoperations
Piaget's second stage of intellectual development, occurring from about two to seven years of age. During this stage the child begins to understand logical classes, number concepts, conservation, and cause-and-effect relationships. However, thinking is essentially prelogical, limited by egocentrism and centration.

prepared environment
A term used by Montessori to describe a "classroom" where the teacher demonstrates the use of didactic learning materials to promote learning in children.

primary concept
An Ausubelian term describing classes of objects constructed according to concrete properties. For example, a set of wooden blocks may be classified according to size and color.

primary reinforcer
Positive and negative reinforcers of human behavior such as food and warmth, pain, and lack of food related to basic biological functioning.

prognosis
The expected long-term effects or outcome of abnormal behavior.

programmed learning
Learning specific information or skills in a particular sequence usually presented on work sheets, in programmed-learning texts, or by teaching machines. These programs provide immediate positive reinforcement for correct answers.

Project Follow-Through
A long-term compensatory program aimed at sustaining gains made from Head Start programs.

Project Head Start
A preschool program that attempts to improve intellectual development and learning competencies in children from disadvantaged backgrounds and to prepare them for entry into kindergarten.

propositional reasoning
Forming a hypothesis about the relationship between two or more objects or events and providing supporting evidence for that hypothesis. For example, a child using propositional reasoning might say, "*If* John wants a new bike *then* he'll have to get a job *because* that's the only way he can earn enough money to pay for one."

proximodistal development
Physical growth from the center of the body (the spine) toward the extremities.

psycholinguist
A specialist who combines an interest in the relationship between the rules of language and the process of thinking.

psychoneurosis
A psychological disorder related to anxiety, fear, or stress.

psychoprophylactic conditioning
Literally, a psychological preparation to prevent illness and, less precisely, to prevent pain. Psychoprophylactic conditioning was used by Lamaze as a preparation for reducing the pain of childbirth.

psychosis
A total break in normal functioning. The most frequently occurring types of psychoses are autism and schizophrenia.

psychotherapy
Therapy designed to identify and extinguish the anxiety that causes neurotic or maladaptive behavior along with suggesting alternative behavior.

punishment
Either the removal of a positive reinforcer or the presentation of a negative reinforcer as the consequence of a particular response. Punishment is not to be confused with negative reinforcement—while negative reinforcement strengthens behavior, punishment suppresses it.

qualitative change
The reorganization of structures of knowledge, resulting in new and different structures. Cognitive structuralists such as Piaget describe development in terms of qualitative changes.

quantitative change
The continuous and incremental organization of structures of knowledge. According to this concept, development and learning builds and improves continuously over time.

reaction time
The amount of time taken to react to a stimulus. Reaction time is sometimes used to measure the development of motor skills. It is determined to a large extent by maturation (though it can be improved by training).

recall memory
Remembering previously learned information. For example, recall memory is involved in remembering that a certain class of animals is called "mammals." Recall is usually more difficult than recognition, especially when there are no physical clues to prod the memory.

receptive learning
Learning guided by direct instruction.

recessive allele
An allele that does not contribute to the phenotype when in combination with a dominant allele. Recessive alleles can only affect the phenotype when homozygous.

recognition memory
Remembering an actual object or event when seen again. For example, a person might exclaim, "Oh, I've been here before. I remember the unusual design of that building."

referential communication
Communication requiring the description of a referent, or property, of some object (for example, the *black* dog, or the chair *to the right of* the fireplace). Such descriptions differentiate one particular object from other, similar ones.

reflex
An automatic, involuntary response to a stimulus. One example is an infant's startled response to a loud noise.

regression
A defense mechanism that causes a person faced with stress to revert to earlier, more immature behavior.

rehearsal memory strategy
A strategy designed to aid the memory, for example by repeatedly naming objects out loud or in the mind or by forming associations between pieces of information.

retardation
Subaverage intellectual functioning associated with behavioral impairment. Levels of retardation are usually classified on the basis of IQ scores.

reversibility
A Piagetian term describing the reversal of an operation such as classification or conservation. For example, adding three and two to make five can be reversed by subtracting two from five to get three.

Rh factor
An inherited protein substance in the blood. When an expectant mother's blood is Rh negative (the protein is absent) and her fetus's blood is Rh positive, the mother's body may produce antibodies that attack the fetus's blood. This condition may result in abnormalities in the fetus such as anemia and heart defects.

rooting reflex
A reflex of early infancy that causes the infant to search for and suck on a nipple when his cheek is stroked.

rote learning
Learning new knowledge *without* relating it to previously learned structures of knowledge.

rubella or **German measles**
A common virus that, if contracted by a pregnant woman, can cause defects in the newborn such as blindness, deafness, or mental retardation.

rule-governed or **constructive play**
Play that is goal directed. For example, an older preschool child may play by shaking a set of tin cans, each of which contains a different number of beans, and attempting to arrange them in order from the loudest to the softest sound.

sample
A group of research subjects, usually drawn at random from a particular population. For example, observations might be made of a sample of two-year-old infants on the visual-cliff equipment to get an estimate of infant visual perception at age 2 years. This information might be used to draw conclusions about a particular population of two-year-old infants.

schema
A Piagetian term describing cognitive structures formed during the period from birth to about age 6/7 years that the individual uses to assimilate and accommodate new knowledge.

schizophrenia
An emotional disturbance that usually develops during childhood or later. A schizophrenic child becomes increasingly withdrawn and may show symptoms of confusion and disorientation.

secondary concept
New concepts acquired by learning their properties rather than by learning different examples of a concept. For example, children learn that animals that grow hair on their bodies, give birth to young, and are suckled by the mother are called mammals.

secular trend
The tendency for recent generations to achieve physical maturity earlier than previous generations.

self-concept
One's view of oneself as an individual. Taking the views of others into account can help clarify one's self-concept.

self-esteem
The element of the self-concept that involves one's basic attitude of self worth. Children with a great deal of self-esteem have confidence in their own judgments and behavior.

semiotic function
Learning to make one thing represent another. For example, learning to imagine a man as a "daddy."

sensitive period
A term used by some psychologists to refer to the period during which attachment occurs in human infants. (*See also* critical period)

sensorimotor development
A Piagetian term describing the first stage of mental development, which occurs from birth to about age three. During this period, infants represent objects and events in the form of action.

serial ordering
Arranging objects on a continuum according to some dimension such as longest to shortest, widest to thinnest, or loudest to softest.

sex chromosomes
The two chromosomes in every cell that determine the individual's sex characteristics. Each ovum contains two X chromosomes and each sperm either an X or a Y chromosome. When a sperm's X chromosome combines with an X chromosome of the ovum in a female this results in a female baby, while the combination of a Y chromosome and an X chromosome produces a male.

sex stereotype
A strong set of social conventions and expectations about male and female attributes.

sex typing
Encouraging children to identify with a socially defined sex role.

shaping
Reinforcing socially acceptable behavior.

short-term memory
The part of the memory that recalls information over a short period of time.

skeleton or **bone age**
An assessment of physical development made by measuring the rate of development of the bones. These measurements are usually made by examining the bones in the hand and wrist through X rays.

small-for-date baby
A baby weighing less than the average baby of the same gestational age.

social agency
According to Baumrind, the tendency for children to take initiative and show leadership in group activities.

sociolinguistic communication
Communication involving not only referential communication but also features of social interaction such as modifying speech patterns to accommodate a listener, making promises, and understanding indirect requests.

somatic cell
Somatic cells are sometimes referred to as body cells. Each somatic cell contains 46 chromosomes that constantly divide to make new, similar cells throughout the life of an individual.

sperm
The male reproductive cell.

spina bifida
A congenital cleft of the vertebral column involving, in most cases, imperfectly formed meninges.

spiraling curriculum
A term used by Bruner to describe the repeated inclusion of basic concepts in a curriculum at increasing levels of abstraction and complexity. For example, young children may first learn the concept of cooperation in the context of helping parents, peers, and teachers. Later, as adolescents, they may consider cooperation in the context of agreements between major political powers to establish trade agreements or to control the proliferation of nuclear armaments.

sudden infant death syndrome *(SIDS)*
The sudden death of an apparently healthy infant, usually aged two to four months, and most frequently during sleep. This syndrome is also sometimes referred to as "crib death."

super ego
According to Freud, an aspect of the personality that aids the ego in setting standards of right and wrong. The superego develops from the learning of values and standards set by parents and society.

surrogate parent
A person, usually an adult, who takes the place of the natural parents in caring for an infant or child.

symbolic play
Play that is imitative (based on real-life experiences) or fantastic (based on impossible or improbable events) involving changes to or transformations in objects and events.

symbolic representation
The abstract representation of objects and events. Language is an important form of symbolic representation.

telegraphic sentences
Early-appearing forms of sentences containing only essential words, as in a telegram. For example, a young child might say, "I see ball."

teratogens
Drugs, viruses, chemicals, and radiation that can damage the fetus if they cross the placenta. Thalidomide is one example of a teratogen.

testosterone
A male hormone, produced principally by the testes, that regulates sexual development during puberty.

thalidomide
A tranquilizer widely prescribed to pregnant women in England and Australia during the late 1950s. Its use is now banned since it was found to cause serious malformations in a fetus's limbs and defects in sight and hearing.

trust versus mistrust
Erikson's description of the first stage of psychosocial development, which occurs during infancy. Provided with loving and consistent care, the infant develops trust; without such care, an infant develops mistrust and fear of her world.

Turner's syndrome
A sex-chromosome abnormality characterized by the presence of only one X chromosome in each cell. Girls with this syndrome are generally short, have folds of skin around the neck, and develop only small, immature breasts.

umbilical cord
The cord or tube between the fetus and the placenta that carries oxygen and nourishment from the mother to the fetus and waste products from the fetus to the mother's system for disposal.

uterus
The female reproductive organ in which an ovum is deposited approximately once every twenty-eight days during a woman's fertile years. A fertilized ovum develops in the uterus through the embryonic and fetal periods to birth.

variable
Behavior, objects, or situational events that may be treated in research as dependent or independent. A dependent variable is expected to change as a result of an experimental procedure. An independent variable is a characteristic of behavior, objects, or situations changed by the experimenter to assess the effect of the change on behavior. For example, infants might be shown different types of mobiles in different configurations (changes in the independent variable) to assess the effect on the time the infants spend viewing each mobile (the dependent variable).

visual cliff
A sheet of glass placed over two textured surfaces, one "shallow" and close to the glass, the other "deep," or some distance from the glass. Infants usually refuse to move from the shallow to the deep side, which is taken as an indication of the development of depth perception.

zygote
A one-celled organism formed from the union of a sperm with an ovum.

References

Abraham, K. A short study of the development of the libido viewed in light of mental disorders. In *Selected papers of Karl Abraham*. New York: Basic Books, 1927.

Acheson, R. M. Maturation of the skeleton. In F. Faulkner (Ed.), *Human development*. Philadelphia: Saunders, 1966.

Ackerman, P. R., Jr., Moore, M. G. Delivery of educational services to preschool handicapped children. In T. D. Tjossem (Ed.), *Intervention strategies for high-risk infants and young children*. Baltimore: University Park Press, 1976.

Adelson, J., Green, B., & O'Neil, R. Growth of the idea of law in adolescence. *Developmental Psychology*, 1969, *1*, 327–332.

Ahrens, R. Beitrage zur Entwicklung des Physiognomie und Mimikerkennens. *Zeitschrift fur Experimentelle und Angewandte Psychologie*, 1954, *2*, 412–494; 599–633.

Ainsworth, M. D. S. The effects of maternal deprivation: A review of findings and controversy in the context of research strategy. In *Deprivation of maternal care: A reassessment of its effects*. Geneva: WHO, 1962.

Ainsworth, M. D. S. *Infancy in Uganda*. Baltimore: Johns Hopkins University Press, 1967.

Ainsworth, M. D. S. The development of infant-mother attachment. In B. M. Caldwell & H. N. Ricciuti (Eds.), *Review of child development research* (Vol. 3). Chicago: University of Chicago Press, 1973.

Ainsworth, M. D. S., Bell, S. M., & Stayton, D. J. Individual differences in strange-situation behavior of one-year-olds. In H. R. Schaffer (Ed.), *The origins of human social relations*. London: Academic Press, 1971.

Ainsworth, M. D. S., & Wittig, B. A. Attachment and exploratory behavior of one-year-olds in a strange situation. In B. M. Foss (Ed.), *Determinants of infant behavior* (Vol. IV). London: Methuen, 1969.

Alan Guttmacher Institute. *Eleven million teenagers: What can be done about the epidemic of adolescent pregnancies in the United States?* New York: Planned Parenthood, 1976.

Almy, M. *The early childhood educator at work*. New York: McGraw-Hill, 1975.

American Association on Mental Deficiency. *A manual on terminology and classification*. Willimantic, Conn.: American Association on Mental Deficiency, 1961.

American Psychological Association. *Ethical principles in the conduct of research with human participants*. Washington, D.C.: American Psychological Association, 1973.

Anastasi, A. *Psychological testing* (4th ed.). New York: Macmillan, 1976.

Annis, L. F. *The child before birth*. Ithaca, N.Y.: Cornell University Press, 1978.

Anson, B. J. (Ed.). *Morris' human anatomy*. New York: McGraw-Hill, Inc., 1966.

Anthony, E. J. The behavior disorders of children. In P. H. Mussen (Ed.), *Carmichael's manual of child psychology* (Vol. 2; 3rd. ed.). New York: Wiley, 1970.

Apgar, V. A proposal for a new method of evaluation in the newborn infant. *Current Research in Anesthesia and Analgesia*, 1953, *32*, 260.

Apgar, V., & Beck, J. *Is my baby all right?* New York: Simon and Schuster, 1974.

Appel, L. F., Cooper, R. G., McCarrell, N., Sims-Knight, J., Yussen, S. R., & Flavell, J. H. The development of the distinction between perceiving and memorizing. *Child Development*, 1972, *43*, 1365–1381.

Arbeit, S. A. *A study of women during their first pregnancy*. Unpublished doctoral dissertation, Yale University, 1975.

Asher, S. R. Children's peer relations. In M. E. Lamb (Ed.), *Social and personality development*. New York: Holt, Rinehart & Winston, 1978.

Astrand, P. The child in sport and physical activity: Physiology. In J. G. Atkinson & G. M. Andrews (Eds.), *Child in sport and physical activity*. Baltimore: University Park Press, 1976.

Ault, R. L. Problem-solving strategies of reflective, impulsive, fast-accurate, and slow-accurate children. *Child Development*, 1973, *44*, 259–266.

Ausubel, D. P. *The psychology of meaningful verbal learning*. New York: Grune & Stratton, 1963.

Ausubel, D. P., Novak, J. D., & Hanesian, H. *Educational psychology: A cognitive view* (2nd ed.). New York: Holt, Rinehart & Winston, 1978.

Ausubel, D. P., & Robinson, F. G. *School learning: An introduction to educational psychology.* New York: Holt, Rinehart & Winston, 1969.

Ausubel, D. P., & Schwartz, F. C. The effects of a generalizing-particularizing dimension of cognitive style on the retention of prose material. *Journal of General Psychology,* 1972, *87,* 55–58.

Ausubel, D. P., & Sullivan, E. V. *Theory and problems of child development* (2nd ed.). New York: Grune & Stratton, 1970.

Azrin, N. H., & Foxx, R. M. A rapid method of toilet training the institutionalized retarded. *Journal of Applied Behavior Analysis,* 1971, *4,* 89–99.

Baker, B. L. Camp Freedom: Behavior modification for retarded children in a therapeutic camp setting. *American Journal of Orthopsychiatry,* 1973, *43,* 418–427.

Baker, B. L., & Heifetz, L. J. The Read Project: Teaching manuals for parents of retarded children. In T. D. Tjossem (Ed.), *Intervention strategies for high-risk infants and young children.* Baltimore: University Park Press, 1976.

Baker, B. L., Heifetz, L. J., & Brightman, A. J. *Parents as teachers.* Cambridge, Mass.: Education Projects, 1974.

Bakwin, H., & Bakwin, R. M. *Behavior disorders in children.* Philadelphia: Saunders, 1972.

Baldwin, A. L. Socialization and the parent-child relationship. *Child Development,* 1948, *19,* 127–136.

Baldwin, A. L. *Theories of child development.* New York: Wiley, 1968.

Baldwin, A. L., Kalhorn, J., & Breese, F. H. Patterns of parent behavior. *Psychological Monographs,* 1945, *58* (3, Whole No. 268 1–75).

Bandura, A. Vicarious processes: A case of no trial learning. In L. Berkowitz (Ed.), *Advances in experimental social psychology* (Vol. II). New York: Academic Press, 1965.

Bandura, A. A social-learning interpretation of psychological disfunctions. In P. London and D. Rosenhan (Eds.), *Foundations of abnormal psychology.* New York: Holt, Rinehart & Winston, 1968.

Bandura, A. *Principles of behavior modification.* New York: Holt, Rinehart & Winston, 1969.

Bandura, A. Analysis of modeling process. In A. Bandura (Ed.), *Psychological modeling.* Chicago: Atherton, Aldine, 1971.

Bandura, A. *Social learning theory.* Englewood Cliffs, N.J.: Prentice-Hall, 1977.

Bandura, A., & Huston, A. C. Identification as a process of incidental learning. *Journal of Abnormal and Social Psychology,* 1961, *63,* 311–318.

Bandura, A., & McDonald, F. J. Influence of social reinforcement and the behavior of models in shaping children's moral judgments. *Journal of Abnormal and Social Psychology,* 1963, *67,* 274–281.

Bandura, A., Ross, D., & Ross, S. A. Transmission of aggression through imitation of aggressive models. *Journal of Abnormal and Social Psychology,* 1961, *63,* 575–582.

Bandura, A., Ross, D., & Ross, S. A. A comparative test of the status envy, social power, and secondary reinforcement theories of identificatory learning. *Journal of Abnormal and Social Psychology,* 1963, *67,* 527–534.

Bandura, A., & Walters, R. H. *Adolescent aggression.* New York: Ronald, 1959.

Bandura, A., & Walters, R. H. *Social learning and personality development.* New York: Holt, Rinehart and Winston, 1963.

Bane, M. J., & Jencks, C. Five myths about your IQ. *Harper's Magazine,* February 1973, 32–34, 38–40.

Baratz, S. S., & Baratz, J. C. Early childhood intervention: The social science base of institutional racism. *Harvard Educational Review,* 1970, *40,* 29–50.

Barnard, K. E. *A program of stimulation for infants born prematurely.* Paper presented at the meeting of the Society for Research in Child Development, Philadelphia, 1973.

Barnard, K. E. Nursing: High-risk infants. In T. D. Tjossem (Ed.), *Intervention strategies for high-risk infants and young children.* Baltimore: University Park Press, 1976.

Baroff, G. *Mental retardation: Nature, cause and management.* Washington, D.C.: Hemisphere Publishing, 1974.

Bauer, D. H. An exploratory study of developmental changes in children's fears. *Journal of Child Psychology and Psychiatry,* 1976, *17,* 69–74.

Baumrind, D. Effects of authoritative parental control on child behavior. *Child Development,* 1966, *37,* 887–907.

Baumrind, D. Child-care practices anteceding three patterns of preschool behavior. *Genetic Psychology Monographs,* 1967, *75,* 43–88.

Baumrind, D. Authoritarian vs. authoritative control. *Adolescence,* 1968, *3,* 255–272.

Baumrind, D. Current patterns of parental authority. *Developmental Psychology Monographs,* 1971, *4,* (Whole No. 1, Pt. 2).

Baumrind, D. The development of instrumental competence through socialization. In A. D. Pick (Ed.), *Minnesota Symposium on Child Development* (Vol. 7). Minneapolis: University of Minnesota Press, 1973.

Baumrind, D. *Socialization determinants of personal agency.* Paper presented at the biennial meetings of the Society for Research in Child Development, New Orleans, 1977.

Baumrind, D. *Sex-related socialization effects.* Paper presented at the meeting of the Society for Research in Child Development, San Francisco, 1979.

Baumrind, D., & Black, A. E. Socialization practices associated with dimensions of competence in preschool boys and girls. *Child Development*, 1967, *38*, 291–327.

Bayley, N. *Manual for the Bayley scales of infant development*. New York: The Psychological Corporation, 1969.

Beard, R. M. *An outline of Piaget's developmental psychology*. London: Routledge & Kegan Paul, 1969.

Becker, W. G. Consequences of different kinds of parental discipline. In M. Hoffman & L. Hoffman (Eds.), *Review of child development research* (Vol. 1). New York: Russell Sage, 1964.

Becker, W. G., & King, R. S. A circumplex model for social behavior in children. *Child Development*, 1964, *35*, 371–396.

Beilin, H. Learning and operational convergence in logical thought development. *Journal of Experimental Child Psychology*, 1965, *2*, 317–339.

Beilin, H. Training and acquisition of logical operations. In M. F. Rosskopf, L. P. Steffe, & S. Taback (Eds.), *Piagetian cognitive-developmental research and mathematical education*. Washington, D.C.: National Council of Teachers of Mathematics, 1971.

Bell, R. Q. Contributions of human infants to caregiving and social interaction. In M. Lewis & L. A. Rosenblum (Eds.), *The effect of the infant on the caregiver*. New York: Wiley, 1974.

Bell, T. H. *The family, the young child, the schools*. Paper presented at the 10th Annual Conference of South Carolina School Officials, Myrtle Beach, S.C., July, 1974.

Bellow, S. *The adventures of Augie March*. New York: Viking Press, 1953.

Bellugi, V. Learning the language. *Psychology Today*, 1970, *4*, 32–35.

Belsky, J., & Sternberg, L. D. The effects of day care: A critical review. *Child Development*, 1978, *49*, 920–949.

Bem, S. The measurement of psychological androgeny. *Journal of Consulting and Clinical Psychology*, 1974, *42*, 155–162.

Bem, S. Sex role adaptability: One consequence of psychological androgeny. *Journal of Personality and Social Psychology*, 1975, *31*, 634–643.

Bem, S., & Bem, D. Training the woman to know her place. In L. Howe (Ed.), *The future of the family*. New York: Simon and Schuster, 1972.

Bengston, V. L., & Starr, J. M. Contrasts and consensus: A generational analysis of youth in the 1970s. In R. J. Havinghurst & P. H. Dreyer (Eds.), *Youth: The seventy-fourth yearbook of the National Society for the Study of Education, part 1*. Chicago: University of Chicago Press, 1975.

Benjamin, L. S., Serdahely, W., & Geppert, T. V. Night training through parent's implicit use of operant conditioning. *Child Development*, 1971, *42*, 963–966.

Bereiter, C., & Englemann, S. *Teaching the culturally disadvantaged child in the preschool*. Englewood Cliffs, N.J.: Prentice-Hall, 1966.

Berg, F. S., & Fletcher, S. G. *The hard of hearing*. New York: Grune & Stratton, 1970.

Berges, M., Lezine, I., Harrison, A., & Boisselier, F. The "syndrome of the post-premature child": A study of its significance—Part I. *Early Child Development and Care*, 1972, *1*, 239–284.

Berges, M., Lezine, I., Harrison, A., & Boisselier, F. The "syndrome of the post-premature child": A study of its significance—Part II. *Early Child Development and Care*, 1973, *2*, 61–94.

Berkowitz, L. Some determinants of impulsive aggression. *Psychological Review*, 1974, *81*, 165–176.

Berlin, C. M., & Jacobson, C. B. Link between LSD and birth defects reported. *Journal of American Medical Association*, 1970, *212*, 1447–1448.

Bernstein, B. Social class and linguistic development: A theory of social learning. In A. H. Halsey, J. Floud, & C. A. Anderson (Eds.), *Education, economy, and society*. New York: Free Press, 1961.

Bernstein, B. A sociolinguistic approach to socialization, with some references to educability. In F. Williams (Ed.), *Language and poverty: Perspectives on a theme*. Chicago: Markham, 1970.

Berry, J. W., & Dasen, P. R. *Culture and cognition: Readings on cross-cultural psychology*. London: Methuen, 1974.

Bettelheim, B. *The empty fortress*. New York: The Free Press, 1967.

Bettelheim, B. *The uses of enchantment: The meaning and importance of fairy tales*. New York: Alfred A. Knopf, 1976.

Biber, B. A developmental-interaction approach: Bank Street College of Education. In M. C. Day & R. K. Parker (Eds.), *The preschool in action: Exploring early childhood programs* (2nd ed.). Boston: Allyn & Bacon, 1977.

Bigner, J. J. Second-borns' discrimination of sibling's role concepts. *Developmental Psychology*, 1974, *10*, 564–573.

Bigner, J. J. *Parent-child relations*. New York: Macmillan, 1979.

Bijou, S. W. *Child development: The basic stages of early childhood*. Englewood Cliffs, N.J.: Prentice-Hall, 1976.

Bijou, S. W., & Baer, D. M. *Child development* (Vol. 1). Englewood Cliffs, N.J.: Prentice-Hall, 1961.

Bijou, S. W., & Baer, D. M. *Child development: Universal stage of infancy* (Vol. 2). New York: Appleton-Century-Crofts, 1965.

Biller, H. B. *Paternal deprivation: Family, school, sexuality and society*. Lexington, Mass.: Heath, 1974.

Biller, H. B. The father and personality development: Paternal deprivation and sex-role development. In M. E. Lamb (Ed.), *The role of the father in child development*. New York: Wiley, 1976.

Biller, H. B., & Borstelmann, L. J. Masculine development: An integrative review. *Merrill-Palmer Quarterly*, 1967, *13*, 253–294.

Birch, H. G., & Gussow, J. D. *Disadvantaged children: Health, nutrition and school failure*. New York: Grune & Stratton, 1970.

Birch, H. G., & Lefford, A. Intersensory development in children. *Child Development Monographs*, 1963, *28*, 85–95.

Birnbaum, J. A. Life patterns and self-esteem in gifted family-oriented and career-committed women. In M. S. Medrick, S. S. Tangri, & L. W. Hoffman (Eds.), *Women and achievement*. Washington, D.C.: Hemisphere Publishing, 1975.

Blanchard, R. & Biller, H. Father availability and academic performance among third-grade boys. *Developmental Psychology*, 1971, *4*, 301–305.

Blinick, G., Wallach, R. C., & Jeres, U. Pregnancy in narcotics addicts treated by medical withdrawals: The methadone detoxification program. *American Journal of Obstetrics and Gynecology*, 1969, *105*, 997–1003.

Blitsen, D. R. *Human social development*. New Haven, Conn.: College and University Press, 1971.

Block, J. H. *Lives through time*. Berkeley, Calif.: Bancroft Books, 1971.

Block, J. H. Conceptions of sex role: Some cross-cultural and longitudinal perspectives. *American Psychologist*, 1973, *28*, 512–526.

Block, N., & Dworkin, G. (Eds.). *The I.Q. controversy*. New York: Pantheon, 1976.

Bloom, B. L., Asher, S. J., & White, S. W. Marital disruption as a stressor: A review and analysis. *Psychological Bulletin*, 1978, *85*, 867–894.

Bloom, L. *Language development: Form and function in emerging grammars*. Cambridge, Mass.: The MIT Press, 1970.

Bongiovanni, A. *A review of research on the effects of punishment: Implications for corporal punishment in the schools*. Paper presented at the Conference on Child Abuse, Children's Hospital National Medical Center, Washington, D.C., February 19, 1977.

Bossard, J., & Boll, E. *The sociology of child development* (3rd ed.). New York: Harper & Row, 1966.

Bower, T. G. R. The visual world of infants. *Scientific American*, 1966, *215*, 80–92.

Bower, T. G. R. The development of object permanence: Some studies of existence constancy. *Perception & Psychophysics*, 1967, *2*, 411–418.

Bower, T. G. R. The object in the world of the infant. *Scientific American*, 1971, *225*, 30–38.

Bower, T. G. R. *Development in infancy*. San Francisco: W. H. Freeman, 1974. (a)

Bower, T. G. R. The evolution of sensory systems. In R. B. MacLeod & H. L. Picks (Eds.), *Perception: Essays in honor of J. J. Gibson*. Ithaca, N.Y.: Cornell University Press, 1974. (b)

Bower, T. G. R. Repetitive processes in child development. *Scientific American*, 1976, *235*, 38–47.

Bower, T. G. R. *Human development*. San Francisco: W. H. Freeman, 1979.

Bower, T. G. R., Broughton, J. M., & Moore, M. K. Development of the object concept as manifested by changes in the tracking behavior of infants between 7 and 20 weeks of age. *Journal of Experimental Child Psychology*, 1971, *11*, 182–192.

Bower, T. G. R., & Paterson, J. G. Stages in the development of the object concept. *Cognition*, 1972, *1*, 47–55.

Bower, T. G. R., & Paterson, J. G. The separation of place, movement, and the object in the world of the infant. *Journal of Experimental Child Psychology*, 1973, *15*, 161–168.

Bowerman, M. *Early syntactic development: A cross-linguistic study with social reference to finnish*. Cambridge, Mass.: Cambridge University Press, 1973.

Bowlby, J. *Maternal care and mental health*. Geneva: WHO, 1951.

Bowlby, J. *Attachment and loss, vol. 1: Attachment*. New York: Basic Books, 1969.

Bowlby, J. *Attachment and loss, vol. 2: Separation: Anxiety and anger*. New York: Basic Books, 1973.

Braine, M. D. S. The ontogeny of English phrase structure: The first phase. *Language*, 1963, *39*, 1–13.

Braine, M. D. S. Children's first word combinations. *Monographs of the Society for Research in Child Development*, 1976, *41* (1, Whole No. 164).

Braine, M. D. S., Heimer, C. B., Wortis, H., & Freedman, A. M. Factors associated with impairment of the early development of prematures. *Monographs of the Society for Research in Child Development*, 1966, *31*, 1–92.

Brainerd, C. J. Reinforcement and reversibility in quantity conservation. *Psychonomic Science*, 1972, *27*, 114–116. (a)

Brainerd, C. J. The age-stage issue in conservation acquisition. *Psychonomic Science*, 1972, *29*, 115–117. (b)

Brainerd, C. J. Neo-Piagetian training experiments revisited: Is there any support for the cognitive-developmental stage hypothesis? *Cognition*, 1973, *2*, 349–370. (a)

Brainerd, C. J. Order of acquisition of transitivity, conservation and class inclusion of length and weight. *Developmental Psychology*, 1973, *8*, 105–116. (b)

Brainerd, C. J. Training and transfer of transitivity, conservation, and class inclusion of length. *Child Development*, 1974, *45*, 324–334.

Brainerd, C. J. Learning research and Piagetian theory. In L. S. Siegel & C. J. Brainerd (Eds.), *Alternative to Piaget: Critical essays on theory*. New York: Academic Press, 1978. (a)

Brainerd, C. J. *Piaget's theory of intelligence*. Englewood Cliffs, N.J.: Prentice-Hall, 1978. (b)

Brainerd, C. J., & Brainerd, S. H. Order of acquisition of number and liquid quantity conservation. *Child Development*, 1972, *43*, 1401–1405.

Brant, H., & Brant, M. *Dictionary of pregnancy, childbirth, and contraception*. London: Mayflower, 1971.

Brazelton, T. B. Implications of infant development among the Mayan Indians of Mexico. *Human Development*, 1972, *15*, 90–111.

Brazelton, T. B. *The neonatal behavioral assessment scale*. Philadelphia: J. B. Lippincott, 1973.

Brazelton, T. B. Effects of maternal expectations on early infant behavior. In S. Cohen & T. J. Cominskey (Eds.), *Child development: Contemporary perspectives.* Itasca, Ill.: F. E. Peacock Publishers, 1977.

Brazelton, T. B., Tronick, E., Adamson, L., Als, H., & Wise, S. Early mother-infant reciprocity. In *Parent-infant interaction.* Amsterdam: Elsevier, 1975.

Brecher, E. M. *Licit and illicit drugs.* Mount Union, N.Y.: Consumers Union, 1972.

Brecher, E. M. Marijuana: The health questions. *Consumer Reports,* March 1975, pp. 143–149.

Breger, L. *From instinct to identity.* Englewood Cliffs, N.J.: Prentice-Hall, 1973.

Brennan, B., & Heilman, J. R. *The complete book of midwifery.* New York: E. P. Dutton, 1977.

Bresson, F., Maury, L., Pieraut-le Bonniec, G., & de Schonen, S. Organization and lateralization of reaching in infants: An instance of asymmetric function in hand collaboration. *Neuropsychologia,* 1977, *15,* 311–320.

Bricker, D. D., & Bricker, W. A. Toddler research and intervention project report: Year I. *IMRID (Institute on Mental Retardation and Intellectual Development) Behavioral Science Monograph No. 20.* Nashville: George Peabody College, 1971.

Bricker, D. D., & Bricker, W. A. Toddler research and intervention project report: Year II. *IMRID Behavioral Science Monograph No. 21.* Nashville: George Peabody College, 1972.

Bricker, D. D., & Bricker, W. A. Infant, toddler, and preschool research and intervention project report: Year III. *IMRID Behavioral Science Monograph No. 23.* Nashville: George Peabody College, 1973.

Bricker, W. A., & Bricker, D. D. The infant, toddler, and preschool research and intervention project. In T. D. Tjossem (Ed.), *Intervention strategies for high-risk infants and young children.* Baltimore: University Park Press, 1976.

Brightman, A. J. Toward the non-issues of retardation. *Syracuse Law Review, 23,* 1091–1108.

Brody, J. E. Will our baby be normal? *Woman's Day,* August 1969, pp. 47–99.

Bromwich, R. M. Stimulation in the first year of life: A perspective on infant development. *Young Children,* January 1977, pp. 71–82.

Bronfenbrenner, U. Freudian theories of identification and their derivatives. *Child Development,* 1960, *31,* 15–40.

Bronfenbrenner, U. *Two worlds of childhood: U.S. and U.S.S.R.* New York: Basic Books, 1970.

Bronfenbrenner, U. Developmental research, public policy, and the ecology of childhood. *Child Development,* 1974, *45,* 1–5.

Bronfenbrenner, U. *Research on the effects of day care.* Unpublished manuscript, Cornell University, 1975. (a)

Bronfenbrenner, U. *The challenge of social change to public policy and developmental research.* Paper presented at the meeting of the Society for Research in Child Development, Denver, 1975. (b)

Bronfenbrenner, U. Is early intervention effective? In S. Cohen & T. J. Comiskey (Eds.), *Child development: Contemporary perspectives.* Itasca, Ill.: F. E. Peacock, 1977. (a)

Bronfenbrenner, U. *Who needs parent education?* Paper presented at the Working Conference on Parent Education sponsored by the Charles Stewart Mott Foundation, Flint, Mich., 1977. (b)

Bronson, W. C. The role of enduring orientations to the environment in personality development. *Genetic Psychology Monographs,* 1972, *86.*

Bronson, W. C. Developments in behavior with age mates during the second year of life. In M. Lewis & L. A. Rosenblum (Eds.), *The origins of behavior: Friendship and peer relations.* New York: Wiley, 1975.

Brown, A. L. The development of memory: Knowing, knowing about, and knowing how to know. In H. W. Reese (Ed.), *Advances in child development and behavior* (Vol. 10). New York: Academic Press, 1975.

Brown, R. *Psycholinguistics.* New York: Free Press, 1970.

Brown, R. *A first language: The early stages.* Cambridge, Mass.: Harvard University Press, 1973.

Brown, R., & Bellugi, V. Three processes in the child's acquisition of syntax. *Harvard Educational Review,* 1964, *34,* 133–151.

Brown, R., & Berko, J. Word associations and the acquisition of grammar. *Child Development,* 1960, *31,* 1–14.

Brown, R., & Hanlon, C. Derivational complexity and order of acquisition in child speech. In J. R. Hayes (Ed.), *Cognition and the development of language.* New York: Wiley, 1970.

Bruch, H. *Eating disorders: Obesity, anorexia nervosa, and the person within.* New York: Basic Books, 1973.

Bruch, H. Eating disturbances in adolescence. In G. Caplan (Ed.), *American handbook of psychiatry, vol. II: Child and adolescent psychiatry, sociocultural and community psychiatry.* New York: Basic Books, 1974.

Bruch, H. *The golden cage: The enigma of anorexia nervosa.* Cambridge, Mass.: Harvard University Press, 1978.

Bruner, J. S. Going beyond the information given. In H. Gruber (Ed.), *Contemporary approaches to education.* Cambridge, Mass.: Harvard University Press, 1957.

Bruner, J. S. *The process of education.* Cambridge, Mass.: Harvard University Press, 1960.

Bruner, J. S. The act of discovery. *Harvard Educational Review,* 1961, *31,* 21–32.

Bruner, J. S. The course of cognitive growth. *American Psychologist,* 1964, *19,* 1–15.

Bruner, J. S. *Towards a theory of instruction.* Cambridge, Mass.: Harvard University Press, 1966. (a)

Bruner, J. S. *The growth of representational processes in childhood.* Paper presented at the meeting of the 18th International Congress of Psychology in Moscow, August 1966. (b)

Bruner, J. S. Eye, hand, and mind. In D. Elkind & P. J. Flavell (Eds.), *Studies in cognitive development.* New York: Oxford University Press, 1969.

Bruner, J. S. *Poverty and childhood.* Occasional paper, Merrill-Palmer Institute, Detroit, 1970.

Bruner, J. S. *Competence in infants.* Paper presented at the meeting of the Society for Research in Child Development, Minneapolis, 1971.

Bruner, J. S. The nature and uses of immaturity. *American Psychologist,* 1972, *20,* 163–180.

Bruner, J. S. Personality dynamics and the process of perceiving. In J. M. Anglin (Ed.), *Beyond the information given: Studies in the psychology of knowing.* New York: W. W. Norton, 1973.

Bruner, J. S. The organization of early skilled action. In P. M. Richards (Ed.), *The integration of a child into a social world.* New York: Cambridge University Press, 1974.

Bruner, J. S. The ontogenesis of speech acts. *Journal of Child Language,* 1975, *2,* 1–19.

Bruner, J. S., & Kennedy, H. The development of the concepts of order and proportion in children. In J. S. Bruner, R. R. Olver, P. M. Greenfield (Eds.), *Studies in cognitive growth.* New York: Wiley, 1966.

Bruner, J. S., Koslowski, D. Visually preadapted constituents of manipulatory action. *Perception,* 1972, *1,* 3–14.

Bruner, J. S., & May, A. *Cup to lip.* New York: Wiley, 1972. (Film)

Bruner, J. S., Olver, R. R., Greenfield, P. M. (Eds.). *Studies in cognitive growth.* New York: Wiley, 1966.

Bruner, J. S., Wallach, M. A., & Galanter, E. H. The identification of recurrent regularity. *American Journal of Psychology,* 1959, *72,* 200–209.

Bryant, P. E. *Perception and understanding in young children.* London: Methuen, 1974.

Bucher, B., & Schneider, R. E. Acquisition and generalization of conversation by preschoolers using operant training. *Journal of Experimental Child Psychology,* 1973, *16,* 187–204.

Burt, C. The evidence for the concept of intelligence. *British Journal of Educational Psychology,* 1955, *25,* 158–177.

Burton, R. V., & Whiting, J. W. M. The absent father and cross-sex identity. *Merrill-Palmer Quarterly,* 1961, *7,* 85–95.

Bushell, D., Jr. The behavior analysis classroom. In B. Spodek (Ed.), *Early childhood education.* Englewood Cliffs, N.J.: Prentice-Hall, 1973.

Bushell, D., Jr., Wrobel, P., and Michaelis, M. Applying "group" contingencies to the classroom study behavior of preschool children. *Journal of Applied Behavioral Analysis,* 1968, *1,* 55–62.

Buttons, A. Some antecedents of felonies and delinquent behavior. *Journal of Clinical Child Psychology,* 1973, *2,* 35–37.

Buxton, C. L. *A study of psychophysical methods of relief of childbirth pain.* Philadelphia: W. B. Saunders Co., 1962.

Caldwell, B. What does research teach us about day care for children under three? *Children Today,* 1972, *1,* 6–11.

Caldwell, B., & Richmond, J. B. The children's center in Syracuse, New York. In C. Chandler et al. (Eds.), *Early child care.* New York: Atherton, 1968.

Cambell, J. D. Peer relations in childhood. In M. L. Hoffman and L. Hoffman (Eds.), *Review of child development research* (Vol. I). New York: Russell Sage Foundation, 1964.

Campos, J. J., Langer, A., & Krowitz, A. Cardiac responses on the visual cliff in prelocomotor human infants. *Science,* 1970, *170,* 196–197.

Cantor, P. Suicide and attempted suicide among students: Problem, prediction, and prevention. In P. Cantor (Ed.), *Understanding a child's world.* New York: McGraw-Hill, 1977.

Caplan, F., & Caplan, T. *The power of play.* Garden City, N.Y.: Anchor Press/Doubleday, 1974.

Carew, J. V., Chan, I., & Halfar, C. *Observing intelligence in young children: Eight case studies.* Englewood Cliffs, N.J.: Prentice-Hall, 1976.

Carey, S. The child as word learner. In M. Halle, J. Bresnan, and G. A. Miller (Eds.), *Linguistic theory and psychological reality.* Cambridge, Mass.: The MIT Press, 1977.

Carpenter, G. C. Visual regard of moving and stationary faces in early infancy. *Merrill-Palmer Quarterly,* 1974, *20,* 181–194.

Carpenter, G. C. Mother's face and the newborn. In R. Lewin (Ed.), *Child alive.* London: Temple Smith, 1975.

Case, R. Learning and development: A neo-Piagetian interpretation. *Human Development,* 1972, *15,* 339–358. (a)

Case, R. Validation of a neo-Piagetian capacity construct. *Journal of Experimental Child Psychology,* 1972, *14,* 287–302. (b)

Case, R. Structures and strictures: Some functional limitations on the course of cognitive growth. *Cognitive Psychology,* 1974, *6,* 544–573.

Case, R. Gearing the demands of instruction to the developmental capacities of the learner. *Review of Educational Research,* 1975, *45,* 59–87.

Case, R. Responsiveness to conservation training as a function of induced subjective uncertainty, M-space, and cognitive style. *Canadian Journal of Behavioral Science,* 1977, *9,* 12–26.

Case, R. A developmentally based theory and technology of instruction. *Review of Educational Research,* 1978, *48,* 439–463.

Case, R., & Serlin, R. A new model for simulating performance on Pascual-Leone's test of M-space. *Cognitive Psychology,* 1978.

Cattell, P. *The measurement of intelligence of infants and young children* (3rd. ed.). Lancaster, Pa.: The Science Press, 1950.

Cazden, C. *Environmental assistance to the child's acquisition of grammar.* Doctoral dissertation, School of Education, Harvard University, 1965.

Chadwick, B., and Day, R. Systematic reinforcement: Academic performance of underachieving students. *Journal of Applied Behavioral Analysis,* 1971, *4,* 311–319.

Chand, I., Crider, D., & Willits, F. Parent-youth disagreement as perceived by youth: A longitudinal study. *Youth and Society,* 1975, *6,* 365–375.

Chandler, M. J., Paget, K. F., & Koch, D. A. The child's demystification of psychological defense mechanisms: A structural and developmental analysis. *Developmental Psychology,* 1978, *14,* 197–205.

Chapman, A. H. *Management of emotional problems of children and adolescence.* Philadelphia: J. B. Lippincott, 1974.

Chi, M. T. H. Knowledge structures and memory development. In R. Siegler (Ed.), *Children's thinking: What develops?* Hillsdale, N.J.: Lawrence Erlbaum Associates, 1978.

Chinn, P. C., Winn, J., & Walters, R. H. *Two-way talking with parents of special children: A process of positive communication.* St. Louis: The C. V. Mosby Company, 1978.

Chittendon, E. A. *The development of certain logical abilities and the child's concepts of substance and weight: An examination of Piaget's theory.* Doctoral dissertation, Columbia University, 1964.

Chomsky, C. *The acquisition of syntax in children from 5 to 10.* Cambridge, Mass.: The M. I. T. Press, 1969.

Chomsky, N. *Syntactic structures.* The Hague, the Netherlands: Mouton, 1957.

Chomsky, N. *Aspects of a theory of syntax.* Cambridge, Mass.: The MIT Press, 1965.

Chomsky, N. *Reflections on language.* New York. Pantheon, 1975.

Clarizio, H. *Some myths regarding the use of corporal punishment in the schools.* Paper presented at the annual meeting of the American Educational Research Association, April 2, 1975.

Clarizio, H. F., & McCoy, G. F. *Behavior disorders in children* (2nd ed.). New York: Crowell, 1976.

Clarke, E. On the acquisition of antonyms in two semantic fields. *Journal of Verbal Learning and Verbal Behavior,* 1972, *11,* 750–758.

Clarke-Stewart, A. K. Interactions between mothers and their young children: Characteristics and consequences. *Monographs of the Society for Research in Child Development,* 1973, *38,* 6–7.

Clarke-Stewart, A. K. *The father's impact on mother and child.* Paper presented at the Biennial Meeting of the Society for Research in Child Development, New Orleans, 1977.

Clarke-Stewart, A. K. Popular primers for parents. *American Psychologist,* April 1978, pp. 359–369.

Clausen, J. A. Family structure, socialization, and personality. In L. Hoffman and M. L. Hoffman (Eds.), *Review of child development research* (Vol. II). New York: Russell Sage Foundation, 1966.

Clausen, J. A. Perspectives on childhood socialization. In J. Clausen (Ed.), *Socialization and society.* Boston: Little, Brown, 1968.

Clifton, R. K., Graham, F. K., & Hatton, H. M. Newborn heart rate response and response inhibition as a function of stimulus duration. *Journal of Experimental Child Psychology,* 1968, *6,* 265–278.

Cohen, S. E. *Social and personality development in childhood.* New York: Macmillan, 1976.

Cohen, S. E. Maternal employment and mother-child interaction. *Merrill-Palmer Quarterly,* 1978, *24,* 189–197.

Cohen, V. New method of delivering babies cuts down "torture of the innocent." Madison, Wis. *Capital Times,* November 5, 1975.

Colby, A., & Kohlberg, L. *The relationship between logical and moral development.* Unpublished manuscript, 1975. (Available from the Center for Moral Education, Harvard University, Cambridge, Mass., 02138.)

Cole, M., & Bruner, J. S. Preliminaries to a theory of cultural differences. In I. Gordon (Ed.), *Early childhood education.* Chicago: National Society for the Study of Education, 1972.

Coleman, J. C. *Abnormal psychology and modern life* (5th ed.). Glenview, Ill.: Scott Foresman, 1976.

Colletta, N. D. *Divorced mothers at two income levels: Stress, support, and child-rearing practices.* Unpublished manuscript, Cornell University, 1978.

Collins, G. A new look at life with father. *The New York Times Magazine,* June 17, 1979, pp. 31, 49–52, 65–66.

Committee on Nutrition. *Nutrition in maternal health.* American College of Obstetric Gynecology, 1974. (Pamphlet)

Condon, W. D., & Sander, L. W. Neonate movement is synchronized with adult speech: Interactional participation and language acquisition. *Science,* 1974, *183,* 99–101.

Condry, J., & Condry, S. Sex differences: A study of the eye of the beholder. *Child Development,* 1976, *47,* 812–819.

Condry, J., & Siman, M. L. Characteristics of peer- and adult-oriented children. *Journal of Marriage and the Family,* 1974, *36,* 543–554.

Conger, J. J. *Adolescent and youth: Psychological development in a changing world* (2nd ed.). New York: Harper, 1977.

Conger, J. J. Adolescence: A time for becoming. In M. E. Lamb (Ed.), *Social and personality development.* New York: Holt, Rinehart & Winston, 1978.

Connor, J. M., & Serbin, L. A. Behaviorally based masculine- and feminine-activity-preference scales for preschoolers: Correlates with other classroom behaviors and cognitive tests. *Child Development,* 1977, *48,* 1411–1416.

Coopersmith, S. *The antecedents of self-esteem.* San Francisco: W. H. Freeman, 1967.

Copple, C., Sigel, I. E., & Saunders, R. A. *Educating the young thinker: Classroom strategies for cognitive growth.* New York: D. Van Nostrand, 1979.

Corrigan, R. A. Scalogram analysis of the development of the use and comprehension of "because" in children. *Child Development,* 1975, *46,* 195–201.

Cosgrove, J. M., & Patterson, C. J. Plans and the development of listener skills. *Developmental Psychology,* 1977, *13,* 557–564.

Cosgrove, J. M., & Patterson, C. J. Generalization of training for children's listener skills. *Child Development,* 1978, *49,* 513–516.

Costanzo, P. R., & Shaw, M. E. Conformity as a function of age level. *Child Development,* 1966, *37,* 967–975.

Cottle, T. J. *Readings in adolescent psychology: Contemporary perspectives.* New York: Harper & Row, 1977.

Crain, W. C. *Theories of development: Concepts and applications.* Englewood Cliffs, N.J.: Prentice-Hall, 1980.

Cratty, B. J. *Perceptual and motor development in infants and children* (2nd ed.). Englewood Cliffs, N.J.: Prentice-Hall, 1979.

Cratty, B. J., & Martin, Sister Margaret Mary. *Remedial motor activity in children.* Philadelphia: Lea & Febiger, 1975.

Cronenwett, L. R., & Newmark, L. L. Fathers' responses to childbirth. *Nursing Research,* 1974, *23,* 210–217.

Cuffaro, H. K. The developmental interaction approach. In B. D. Boegehold, H. K. Cuffaro, W. H. Hooks, & G. J. Klopf (Eds.), *Education before five.* New York: Bank Street College of Education, 1977.

Cuvo, A. J. Developmental differences in rehearsal and free recall. *Journal of Experimental Child Psychology,* 1975, *19,* 265–278.

Dahlstrom, E., & Ziljestrom, A. (Eds.). *The changing roles of men and women.* London: Duckworth, 1967.

Dale, P. S. *Language development: Structure and function* (2nd ed.). New York: Holt, Rinehart & Winston, 1976.

Damon, A., Damon, S. T., Reed, R. B., & Valadian, I. Age at menarche of mothers and daughters, with a note on accuracy of recall. *Human Biology,* 1969, *41,* 161–175.

Damon, W. *The social world of the child.* San Francisco: Jossey-Bass, 1977.

Danforth, D. N., & Holly, R. G. Other disorders during pregnancy. In O. N. Danforth (Ed.), *Obstetrics and gynecology* (3rd ed.). New York: Harper & Row, 1977.

Dansky, J. Make-believe: A mediator of the relationship between play and associative fluency. *Child Development,* 1980, *51,* 576–579.

Darlington, R. B., Royce, J. H., Snipper, A. S., Murray, H. W., & Lazar, I. Preschool programs and later school competence of children from low-income families. *Science,* 1980, *208,* 202–204.

Darwin, C. A biographical sketch of an infant. *Mind,* 1877, *2,* 286–294.

Dasen, P. R., & Christie, R. D. A regression phenomenon in the conservation of weight. *Archives de Psychologie,* 1972, *41,* 145–152.

Dawe, H. C. An analysis of 200 quarrels of preschool children. *Child Development,* 1934, *5,* 139–157.

Day, R. H., & McKenzie, B. E. Perceptual shape constancy in early infancy. *Perception,* 1973, *2,* 315–321.

DeGuimps, R. *Pestalozzi, his life and work.* New York: Appleton-Century-Crofts, 1906.

Dennis, W. The effects of cradling practices upon the onset of walking in Hopi children. *Journal of Genetic Psychology,* 1940, *56,* 77–86.

Denny & Duffy, Possible environmental causes of stages in moral development. *Journal of Genetic Psychology,* 1974, *125,* 277–283.

Desar, J. A., Maller, O., & Andrew, K. Ingestive responses of human newborns to salty, sour, and bitter stimuli. *Journal of Comparative and Physiological Psychology,* 1975, *89,* 966–970.

Deutsch, F. *The Institute for Developmental Studies annual report and descriptive statement.* New York: New York University, 1962.

Dewey, J. *Experience and education.* New York: Collier Books, 1938.

Dick-Read, G. *Childbirth without fear* (rev. ed.). New York: Harper & Brothers, 1972.

Dickson, W. P. *An instructional device for teaching verbal skills through structured interactions between children in a communication game.* Final Report, NIE Project No. 1–I–101. Stanford, Calif.: Stanford University School of Education, 1974.

Dickson, W. P. *Referential communication between teacher and child: Reliability and validity of measures encoding and decoding effectiveness.* Paper presented at the American Educational Research Association Conference, Toronto, 1978.

Dickson, W. P. Referential communication performance from age four to eight: Effects of referent type, target position, and context. *Developmental Psychology,* 1979, *15,* 470–471.

Dickson, W. P. Accuracy versus style of communication in parent-child interaction. *Interactional Journal of Psycholinguistics,* 1981, *7 1/2* [17/18]: 119–130.

Dickson, W. P., Hess, R. D., Mayake, N., & Azuma, H. Referential communication accuracy between mother and child as a predictor of cognitive development in the United States and Japan. *Child Development,* 1979, *50,* 53–59.

Dishotsky, N. I., Laughman, W. D., Mogar, R. E. & Lipscomb, W. R. LSD and genetic damage. *Science,* 1971, *172,* 431–440.

Dobbing, J. Nutrition and the developing brain. *Lancet,* 1973, *1,* 48.

R–8 References

Dobbing, J. The later development of the brain and its vulnerability. In T. A. Davis & J. Dobbing (Eds.), *Scientific foundations of pediatrics.* Philadelphia: Saunders, 1974.

Dodson, F. *How to parent.* New York: Signet, 1970.

Donaldson, H., & Wales, R. On the acquisition of some relational terms. In J. Hayes (Ed.), *Cognition and the development of language.* New York: Wiley, 1970.

Donaldson, M., & Balfour, G. Less is more: A study of language comprehension in children. *British Journal of Psychology,* 1968, *59,* 461–473.

Douglas, J. W. B. *The home and the school.* Frogmore, St. Albans: Hertfordshire, England. Panther Books, Ltd., 1967.

Douvan, E., & Adelson, J. The self and identity. In E. Douvan & J. Adelson (Eds.), *The adolescent experience.* New York: Wiley, 1966.

Doyle, A. B., & Somers, K. *The effect of group and individual day care on infant development.* Paper presented to the Canadian Psychological Association, Quebec, June 1975.

Drabman, R. S., & Thomas, M. H. Does watching violence on television cause apathy? *Pediatrics,* 1976, *52,* 329–331.

Dreyer, P. H. Changes in the meaning of marriage among youth: The impact of the "revolution" in sex and sex-role behavior. In R. Grinder (Ed.), *Studies in adolescence* (3rd ed.). New York: Macmillan, 1975.

Drillien, C. M., & Ellis, R. W. B. *The growth and development of the prematurely born infant.* Baltimore: Williams and Wilkins, 1964.

Drotar, D., Baskiewicz, A., Irvin, N., Kennel, J., & Klaus, M. The adaptation of parents to the birth of an infant with a congenital malformation: A hypothetical model. *Pediatrics,* 1975, *56,* 710–717.

Dubnoff, S. J., Veroff, J., & Kulka, R. A. *Adjustment to work: 1957–1976.* Paper presented at the meeting of the American Psychological Association, Toronto, 1978.

Duenhoelter, J. H., Grant, N. F., & Jiminez, J. M. Concurrent use of prostaglandin F_2 and laminaria tents for the introduction of midtrimester abortion. *Obstetrics and gynecology,* 1976, *47,* 469–472.

Dunkeld, J., & Bower, T. G. R. *Infant smiling in different situations.* Unpublished manuscript, University of Edinburgh, 1979.

Dunlap, W. R. How do parents of handicapped children view their needs? In L. P. Shapiro (Ed.), *Family interaction and the handicapped child.* Special issue of the Journal of the Division for Early Childhood, 1979, 1.

Dunlap, W. R., & Hollingworth, S. J. How does a handicapped child affect the family? Implications for practitioners. *Family Coordinator,* 1977, *26,* 3.

Dunn, L. M., & Dunn, L. M. *Peabody picture vocabulary test—Revised.* Circle Pines, Minn.: American Guidance Service, 1981.

Dunphy, D. C. The social structure of urban adolescent peer groups. *Sociometry,* 1963, *26,* 230–246.

Durkin, M. C. *Grade three: Four communities around the world. The Taba social studies curriculum* (teachers guide, rev. ed.). San Francisco: San Francisco State College, 1969.

Duvall, E. Conceptions of parenthood. *American Journal of Sociology,* 1946, *52,* 193–203.

Duvall, E. *Marriage and family development* (5th ed.). Philadelphia: J.B. Lippincott, 1977.

Eckerman, C. O., Whatley, J. L., & Kutz, S. L. Growth of social play with peers during the second year of life. *Developmental Psychology,* 1975, *11,* 42–49.

Edlund, C. The effect on the behavior, as reflected in the I.Q. scores, when referred after each correct response. *Journal of Applied Behavioral Analysis,* 1972, *5,* 317–319.

Eimas, P. D., Sequeland, E. R., Jusczyk, P., & Vigorito, J. Speech perception in infants. *Science,* 1971, *171,* 303–306.

Eisenberg, L., & Kanner, L. Early infantile autism, 1943–1955. *American Journal of Orthopsychiatry,* 1956, *26,* 556–566.

Elder, G. H., Jr. Structural variations in the child rearing relationship. *Sociometry,* 1962, *25,* 241–262.

Elder, G. H., Jr. Parent-youth relations in cross-national perspective. *Social Science Quarterly,* 1968, *49,* 216–228. (a)

Elder, G. H., Jr. *Adolescent socialization and personality development.* Chicago: Rand McNally, 1968. (b)

Elder, G. H., Jr. Adolescence in the life cycle: An introduction. In S. E. Dragastin & G. H. Elder, Jr. (Eds.), *Adolescence in the life cycle: Psychological change and social context.* New York: Wiley, 1975.

Eliot, T. S. *Four Quartets.* New York: Harcourt, Brace & World, 1943.

Eliot, T. S. *Collected poems: 1909–1962.* Landar, Faber & Faber, 1963.

Elkind, D. Egocentrism in adolescence. *Child Development,* 1967, *38,* 1025–1034.

Elkind, D. Preschool education: Enrichment or instruction. In B. Spodek (Ed.), *Early childhood education.* Englewood Cliffs, N.J.: Prentice-Hall, 1973.

Elkind, D. *Children and adolescents: Interpretive essays on Jean Piaget.* New York: Oxford University Press, 1974.

Emery, A. E. H. *Heredity, disease and man: Genetics in medicine.* Berkeley, Calif.: University of California Press, 1968.

Emmerich, W. Personality developments and concepts of structure. *Child Development,* 1968, *39,* 671–690.

Engelmann, S., & Osborn, J. *Distar Language I: An instructional system* . Chicago, Ill.: Science Research Associates, Inc., 1976.

Engel, M. *Psychopathology in childhood: Social diagnostic and therapeutic aspects.* New York: Harcourt, Brace, Jovanovich, 1972.

Engen, T., Lipsitt, L. P., & Kaye, H. Olfactory responses and adaptations in the human neonate. *Journal of Comparative and Physiological Psychology,* 1963, *56,* 73–77.

Engen, T., & Lipsitt, L. D. Decrement and recovery of responses to olfactory stimuli. *Journal of Comparative and Physiological Psychology,* 1965, *59,* 312–316.

Enkin, M. W., Smith, S. L., Dermer, S. W., & Emmett, J. L. An adequately controlled study of the effectiveness of PPM training. In N. Morris (Ed.), *Psychosomatic medicine in obstetrics and gynecology.* Basel, Switzerland: Karger, 1972.

Erikson, E. H. *Childhood and society.* New York: Norton, 1950.

Erikson, E. H. The problem of ego identity. *Journal of the American Psychoanalytic Association,* 1956, *4,* 56–121.

Erikson, E. H. Identity and the life cyle. *Psychological Issues* (Vol I, No. 1). New York: International Universities Press, 1959.

Erikson, E. H. *Childhood and society* (2nd ed.). New York: Norton, 1963.

Erikson, E. H. *Identity: Youth and crisis.* New York: Norton, 1968.

Erikson, E. H. Reflections on Dr. Borg's life cycle. *Daedalus,* 1976, *105,* 1–28.

Erikson, M., Catz, C. S., & Yaffe, S. J. Drugs and pregnancy. In H. Osofsky (Ed.), *Clinical obstetrics and gynecology: High-risk pregnancy with emphasis upon maternal and fetal well-being* (Vol. 16). New York: Harper & Row, 1973.

Ershler, J., McAllister, A., & Saunders, R. A. *The Piagetian derived curriculum: Theoretical framework, preschool objects, and program description.* Madison, Wis.: Wisconsin Research and Development Center for Individualized Schooling, 1977. (Working Paper No. 205)

Ervin-Tripp, S. The comprehension and production of requests by children. In E. V. Clark (Ed.), *Papers and reports on child language development* (Vol. 6). Stanford, Calif.: Committee on Linguistics, Stanford University, 1974. (Mimeograph)

Espenschade, A. S. & Eckert, H. M. *Motor development:* Columbus, Ohio: Charles S. Merrill, 1967.

Evans, E. D. *Contemporary influences in early childhood education* (2nd ed.). New York: Holt, Rinehart & Winston, 1975.

Evans, G., & Hall, J. G. The older the sperm. *Ms. Magazine,* January 1976.

Fagot, B. I., & Patterson, G. R. An in vivo analysis of reinforcing contingencies for sex-role behaviors in the preschool. *Developmental Psychology,* 1969, *1,* 563–568.

Fagot, B. I. Sex differences in toddlers' behavior and parental reaction. *Developmental Psychology,* 1974, *10,* 459–465.

Fagot, B. I. Consequences of moderate cross-gender behavior in preschool children. *Child Development,* 1977, *48,* 902–907.

Fagot, B. I. The influence of sex of child on parental reactions to toddler children. *Child Development,* 1978, *49,* 459–465.

Falmagne, R. *Reasoning: Representation and process.* Hillsdale, N.J.: Lawrence Erlbaum Associates, 1976.

Fantz, R. L. Pattern vision in young infants. *Psychological Review,* 1958, *8,* 43–47.

Fantz, R. L. The origin of form perception. *Scientific American,* 1961, *204,* 66–72.

Fantz, R. L. Visual experience in infants: Decreased attention to familiar patterns relative to novel ones. *Science,* 1964, *146,* 668–670.

Fantz, R. L. Visual perception from birth as shown by pattern selectivity. *Annals of the New York Academy of Science,* 1965, *118,* 793–814.

Fantz, R. L., Fagan, J. F., & Miranda, S. B. Early visual selectivity. In L. B. Cohen & P. Salapatek (Eds.), *Infant perception: From sensation to cognition* (Vol. 1). New York: Academic Press, 1975.

Fein, G. Play with actions and objects. In B. Sutton-Smith (Eds.), *Play and learning.* New York: Gardner Press, 1979. (Distributed by Halsted Press, Division of John Wiley & Sons.)

Feinbloom, R. I. (Ed.). *Pregnancy, birth and the newborn baby.* New York: Delta, 1979.

Feingold, R. *Why your child is hyperactive.* New York: Random House, 1975.

Feinstein, S. C., & Ardon, M. S. Trends in dating patterns and adolescent development. *Journal of Youth and Adolescence,* 1973, *2,* 157–166.

Feldman, S. S. *The impact of day care on one aspect of children's social-emotional behavior.* Paper presented at the meeting of the American Association for the Advancement of Science, San Francisco, February 1974.

Feldman, S. S., & Ingham, M. On the interchangeability of attachment objects in two-year-old children. *Child Development,* 1975, *46,* 319–330.

Feldman, S. S., & Nash, S. C. The influence of age and sex on responsiveness to babies. *Developmental Psychology,* 1977, *16,* 675–676.

Ferguson, C. A. Baby talk in six languages. In J. Gumperz and D. Hymes (Eds.), *The Ethnography of Communication,* 1964, *66,* 103–114.

Ferguson, C. A., & Slobin, D. I. (Eds.). *Studies of child language development.* New York: Holt, Rinehart & Winston, 1973.

Feshbach, S. Aggression. In P. H. Mussen (Ed.), *Carmichael's manual of child psychology* (Vol. 2; 3rd ed.). New York: Wiley, 1970.

Feshbach, S., & Feshbach, N. Alternatives to corporal punishment. *Journal of Clinical Child Psychology,* Fall 1973, *2,* 46–49.

Feshbach, S., & Singer, R. *Television and Aggression.* San Francisco: Jossey-Bass, 1971.

Fine, M. J. (Ed.). *Handbook on parent education.* New York: Academic Press, 1980.

Fisher, K. W. A theory of cognitive development: The control and construction of hierarchies of skills. *Psychological Review,* 1980, *87,* 477–531.

Fitzgerald, H. E., & Brockbill, Y. Classical conditioning in infancy: Development and constraints. *Psychological Bulletin,* 1976, *83,* 353–376.

Fixsen, D. L., Montrose, M. W., & Phillips, E. L. Achievement place experiment in self-government with predelinquents. *Journal of Applied Behavior Analysis,* in press.

Flavell, J. H. Developmental studies of mediated memory. In H. W. Reese & L. P. Lipsitt (Eds.), *Advances in child development and behavior* (Vol. 5). New York: Academic Press, 1970.

Flavell, J. H. Stage-related properties of cognitive development. *Cognitive Psychology,* 1971, *2,* 421–453.

Flavell, J. H. *Cognitive development.* Englewood Cliffs, N.J.: Prentice-Hall, 1977.

Flavell, J. H. *Structures, stages and sequences in cognitive development.* Paper presented at the Minnesota Symposium on Child Development, University of Minnesota, Minneapolis, Minnesota, Nov. 1980.

Flavell, J. H., Beach, D. H., & Chinsky, J. M. Spontaneous verbal rehearsal in a memory task as a function of age. *Child Development,* 1966, *37,* 283–299.

Flavell, J. H., Botkin, P. T., Fry, C. L., Wright, J. W., & Jarvis, P. E. *The development of role-taking and communication skills in children.* New York: Wiley, 1968. (Reprinted by Robert E. Krieger Publishing Company, Huntington, New York, 1975.)

Flavell, J. H., & Wellman, H. M. Metamemory. In R. V. Kail & J. W. Hagen (Eds.), *Memory in cognitive development.* Hillsdale, N.J.: Lawrence Erlbaum Associates, 1977.

Fodor, J. A. *The language of thought.* New York: Crowell, 1975.

Forman, G., & Kushner, D. *The child's construction of knowledge: Piaget for teaching children.* Monterey, Calif.: Brooks/Cole, 1977.

Foster, M. A., & Berger, M. Structural family therapy: Applications in programs for preschool handicapped children. In L. P. Shapiro (Ed.), *Family interaction and the handicapped child.* Special issue for early childhood, 1979.

Fowell, N., & Lawton, J. T. *Preschool children's learning of concepts at four levels of abstraction.* (In preparation)

Fowler, W. A developmental approach to infant care in a group setting. *Merrill-Palmer Quarterly,* 1972, *18,* 145–176.

Frank, O. H. *Anne Frank: The diary of a young girl.* New York: Doubleday, 1952.

Frankenberg, W. K., & Dodds, J. B. The Denver Developmental Screening Test. *Journal of Pediatrics,* 1967, *71,* 181–191.

Fraser, I. S., & Brash, J. Comparison of extra- and intraamniotic prostaglandins for therapeutic abortion. *Obstetric Gynecology,* 1974, *43,* 97.

Freud, A. Adolescence. *Psychoanalytic study of the child,* 1958, *13,* 255–278.

Freud, A. *The ego and the mechanisms of defense.* New York: International Universities Press, 1966.

Freud, A. *The writings of Anna Freud* (5 vols.). New York: International Universities Press, 1974.

Freud, S. Three contributions to the theory of sex. [*The basic writings of Sigmund Freud*] (A. A. Brill, trans.). New York: The Modern Library, 1905.

Freud, S. [*An autobiographical study*] (J. Strachey, trans.). London: Hogarth Press, 1935.

Freud, S. [*The problem of anxiety*] (H. A. Bunker, trans.). New York: The Psychoanalytic Press and W. W. Norton, 1936.

Freud, S. *The ego and the id.* London: Hogarth Press, 1950.

Freud, S. *A general introduction to psychoanalysis.* New York: Permabooks, 1953.

Freud, S. Beyond the pleasure principles. In J. Strachey (Ed.), *The standard edition of the complete psychological works of Sigmund Freud* (Vol. 18). London: Hogarth Press, 1957. (Originally published, 1920.)

Freud, S. The relation of the poet to daydreaming. In B. Nelson (Ed.), *On creativity and the unconscious.* New York: Harper Torchbooks, 1958.

Freud, S. [Formulations regarding the two principles of mental functioning] (J. Riviere, trans.). *Collected papers* (Vol. IV). New York: Basic Books, 1959. (Originally published, 1911.)

Freud, S. [Analysis of a phobia in a five-year-old boy] (A. & J. Strachey, trans.). *Collected papers* (Vol. III). New York: Basic Books, 1959. (Originally published, 1909.)

Freud, S. [The passing of the Oedipus complex] (J. Riviere, trans.). *Collected papers* (Vol. II). New York: Basic Books, 1959. (Originally published, 1924.)

Freud, S. [*The ego and the id*] (J. Riviere, trans.). New York: W. W. Norton, 1960. (Originally published, 1923.)

Freud, S. [*New introductory lectures on psychoanalysis*] (J. Strachey, trans.). New York: W. W. Norton, 1965. (Originally published, 1933.)

Friedman, C. J., Mann, F., & Friedman, A. S. A profile of juvenile street gang members. *Adolescence,* 1975, *10,* 563–607.

Friedrich, L. K., & Stein, A. H. Aggressive and prosocial television programs and the natural behaviors of preschool children. *Monographs of the Society for Research in Child Development,* 1973, *38* (Whole No. 151)

Frodi, A. M., & Lamb, M. E. Sex differences in responsiveness to infants: A developmental study of psychophysiological and behavioral responses. *Child Development,* 1978, *49,* 1182–1188.

Frodi, A. M., Lamb, M. E., Leavitt, L. A., & Donovan, W. L. Mothers' and fathers' responses to infants' smiles and cries. *Infant Behavior and Development,* 1978, *1,* 187–198.

Furstenburg, F. F. *Unplanned parenthood.* New York: The Free Press, 1976.

Furth, H., & Wachs, H. *Thinking goes to school: Piaget's theory in practice.* New York: Oxford University Press, 1974.

Gagne, R. M. Contributions of learning to human development. *Psychological Review,* 1968, *75,* 177–191.

Gagne, R. M. *Essentials of learning for instruction.* New York: Holt, Rinehart & Winston, 1974.

Gagne, R. M. *The conditions of learning* (3rd ed.). New York: Holt, Rinehart & Winston, 1977.

Gagne, R. M., & Briggs, L. J. *Principles of instructional design.* New York: Holt, Rinehart & Winston, 1974.

Garbarino, J., & Crouter, A. Defining the community context for parent-child relations: The correlates of child maltreatment. *Child Development,* 1978.

Garber, H., & Heber, F. R. The Milwaukee project: Indications of the effectiveness of early intervention in preventing mental retardation. In P. Mittler (Ed.), *Research to practice in mental retardation: Care and intervention* (Vol. 1). Baltimore: University Park Press, 1972.

Gardner, H. Problem solving in the arts. *Journal of Aesthetic Education,* 1971, *5,* 93–114.

Gardner, H. *The arts of human development.* New York: Wiley, 1973.

Gardner, H. *Developmental psychology: An introduction.* Boston: Little, Brown & Company, 1978.

Garvey, C. *Play.* Cambridge, Mass.: Harvard University Press, 1977.

Gath, A. The mental health of siblings of a congenitally abnormal child. *Journal of Child Psychology and Psychiatry,* 1972, *13,* 211–218.

Gath, A. Siblings' reaction to mental handicap: A comparison of the brothers and sisters of mongol children. *Journal of Child Psychology and Psychiatry,* 1974, *15,* 187–198.

Gath, A. *Down's syndrome and the family: The early years.* London: Academic Press, 1978.

Gath, A. Parents' reactions to Down's syndrome. In L. P. Shapiro (Ed.), *Family interaction and the handicapped child.* Special issue of the *Journal of the Division for Early Childhood,* 1979.

Gearheart, B. R. *Teaching the learning disabled: A combined task-process approach.* St. Louis: The C. V. Mosby Co., 1976.

Gelman, R. Conservation acquisition: A problem of learning to attend to relevant attributes. *Journal of Experimental Child Psychology,* 1969, *7,* 167–187.

Gesell, A. *The first five years of life.* New York: Harper, 1940.

Gesell, A. *Infant development: The embryology of early human behavior.* Westport, Conn.: Greenwood Press, 1972. (Originally published, 1952.)

Gesell, A., & Ilg, F. *The child from five to ten.* New York: Harper and Bros., 1946.

Gesell, A., & Ilg, F. L. Infant and child in the culture of today. In A. Gesell & F. L. Ilg (Eds.), *Child development.* New York: Harper & Row, 1949. (Originally published, 1943.)

Gesell, A., & Thompson, H. *Infant behavior: Its genesis and growth.* New York: McGraw-Hill, 1934.

Getzels, J. W., & Jackson, P. W. *Creativity and intelligence: Explorations with gifted students.* New York: Wiley, 1962.

Gewirtz, J. L. A learning analysis of the effects of normal stimulation, privation, and deprivation on the acquisition of social motivation and attachment. In B. M. Foss (Ed.), *Determinants of infant behavior* (Vol. 1). New York: Wiley, 1961.

Gewirtz, J. L. The course of infant smiling in four child-rearing environments in Israel. In B. M. Foss (Ed.), *Determinants of infant behavior* (Vol. 3). London: Methuen, 1965.

Gewirtz, J. L. Mechanisms of social learning: Some roles of stimulation and behavior in early human development. In D. A. Goslin (Ed.), *Handbook of socialization theory and research.* New York: Rand McNally, 1969.

Gibson, E. J. & Walk, R. R. The "visual cliff." *Scientific American,* 1960, *202,* 80–92.

Gil, D. G. Violence against children. *Journal of Marriage and the Family,* 1971, *33*(4), 637–648.

Gilgoff, A. *Home birth.* New York: Coward, McCann & Geoghegan, 1978.

Gilmore, C. P. The strange malady called learning disability. *The New York Times Magazine,* March 2, 1975, pp. 14–15; 17–21.

Ginott, H. G. *Between parent and child.* New York: Avon Books, 1965.

Ginsberg, H., & Opper, S. *Piaget's theory of intellectual development,* 2nd ed. Englewood Cliffs, New Jersey: Prentice-Hall, 1979.

Glidewell, J. C., Kantor, M. B., Smith, M. L., & Stringer, L. A. Socialization and social structure in the classroom. In M. L. Hoffman & L. Hoffman (Eds.), *Review of child development research* (Vol. II). New York: Russell Sage Foundation, 1966.

Glucksberg, S., & Krauss, R. M. What do people say after they have learned to talk? *Merril-Palmer Quarterly,* 1967, *13,* 307–316.

Glucksberg, S., Krauss, R. M., & Higgins, E. T. The development of referential communication skills. In F. D. Horowitz (Ed.), *Review of child development research* (Vol. 4). Chicago: University of Chicago Press, 1975.

Goethals, G. W., & Klos, D. S. *Experiencing youth: First-person accounts.* Boston: Little, Brown & Company, 1970.

Gold, D., & Andres, D. Developmental comparisons between 10-year-old children with employed and nonemployed mothers. *Child Development,* 1978, *49,* 75–84.

Gold, M., & Douvan, E. (Eds.). *Adolescent development: Readings in research and theory.* Boston: Allyn & Bacon, 1969.

Goldberg, I. D., Regier, D. A., McInery, T. K., Pless, I. B., & Roghmann, K. J. The role of the pediatrician in the delivery of mental health services to children. In S. Chess and A. Thomas (Eds.), *Annual progress in child psychiatry and child development.* New York: Brunner/Mazel, 1980.

Goldberg, R. J. *Maternal time use and preschool performance.* Paper presented at the meeting of the Society for Research in Child Development, New Orleans, 1977.

Goldberg, S. Infant care and growth in urban Zambia. *Human Development*, 1972, *15*, 77–89.

Goldberg, S. R., & Deutsch, F. *Life-span individual and family development*. Monterey, Calif.: Brooks/Cole Publishing, 1977.

Golden, M., & Birns, B. Social class and infant intelligence. In M. Lewis (Ed.), *Origins of intelligence*. New York: Plenum, 1976.

Goldfarb, W. Psychological privation in infancy and subsequent adjustment. *American Journal of Orthopsychiatry*, 1945, *15*, 247–255.

Goodenough, F. L. *Anger in young children*. Minneapolis: University of Minnesota Press, 1931.

Gorbach, A., & Feinbloom, R. I. Diseases and conditions that complicate pregnancy. In R. I. Feinbloom (Ed.), *Pregnancy, birth and the newborn baby*. New York: Delta, 1979.

Gordon, I. J. Developing parent power. In E. Grotberg (Ed.), *Critical issues in research related to disadvantaged children*. Princeton, N. J.: Educational Testing Service, 1969.

Gordon, I. J. *The Florida parent education early intervention projects: A longitudinal look*. Gainesville, Fla.: Institute for Development of Human Resources, University of Florida College of Education, 1973.

Gordon, I. J. Intervention in infant experience. In M. Cohen (Ed.), *Understanding and nurturing infant development*. Washington, D.C.: Association for Childhood Education International, 1976.

Gordon, I. J., Guinagh, B., & Jester, R. E. The Florida parent education infant and toddler programs. In M. C. Day & R. K. Parker (Eds.), *The preschool in action* (2nd ed.), Boston: Allyn & Bacon, 1977.

Gordon, S. *The sexual adolescent: Communicating with teenagers about sex*. North Scituate, Mass.: Duxbury Press, 1973.

Gratch, G., Appel, K. J., Evans, W. F., L Compte, G. K., and Wright, N. A. Piaget's stage N object concept error: Evidence of forgetting or object conception. *Child Development*, 1974, *45*, 71–77.

Gratch, G., and Landers, W. F. Stage N of Piaget's theory of infants' object concepts: A longitudinal study. *Child Development*, 1971, *42*, 359–372.

Gray, S., & Klaus, R. A. An experimental preschool program for culturally deprived children. *Child Development*, 1965, *36*, 887–898.

Green, G. E., & Vore, D. A. Development of conservation in normal and retarded children. *Developmental Psychology*, 1972, *6*, 146–167.

Greenbaum, C. Commentary and discussion. In J. Kagan, R. E. Klein, G. E. Finley, B. Rogoff, & E. Nolan (Eds.), A cross-cultural study of cognitive development. *Monographs of the Society for Research in Child Development*, 1979, *44* (No. 5, Serial No. 180), 67–73.

Greenbaum, C., & Landau, R. Mothers' speech and the early development of vocal behavior: Findings from a cross-cultural study in Israel. In P. H. Leiderman, S. R. Tellkin, & A. Rosenfeld (Eds.), *Culture and infancy: Variations on the human experience*. New York: Academic Press, 1977.

Greenfield, P. M., & Smith, J. H. *The structure of communication in early language development*. New York: Academic Press, 1976.

Greif, E. B. Peer interaction in preschool children. In R. A. Webb (Ed.), *Social development in childhood: Day-care programs and research*. Baltimore: The Johns Hopkins University Press, 1977.

Grollman, E. A. *Talking about death: A dialogue between parent and child*. Boston: Beacon Press, 1970.

Gruen, G. E. & Vore, D. A. Development of conservation in normal and retarded children. *Developmental Psychology*, 1972, *6*, 146–157.

Guilford, J. P. *The nature of human intelligence*. New York: McGraw-Hill, 1967.

Guilford, J. P., & Merrifield, P. R. *The structure of the intellect model: Its uses and implications* (Psychological Laboratory Report No. 24). Los Angeles: University of Southern California, 1960.

Hagen, J. W., Jongeward, R. H., & Kail, R. V. Cognitive perspectives on the development of memory. In H. W. Reese (Ed.), *Advances in child development and behavior* (Vol. 10) New York: Academic Press, 1975.

Haith, M. M. *Day care and intervention programs for infants*. Atlanta: Avatar, 1972.

Haith, M. M. *Organization of visual behavior at birth*. Paper presented at the International Congress of Psychology, Paris, July 1976.

Hall, G. S. *Adolescence: Its psychology and its relations to physiology, anthropology, sociology, sex, crime, religion, and education*. New York: Appleton, 1916. (Originally published, 1904.)

Halliday, M. A. K. *Explorations in the function of language*. London: Arnold, 1973.

Halliday, M. A. K. *Learning how to mean: Explorations in the development of language*. London: Arnold, 1975.

Hamilton, W. J., & Mossman, H. W. *Hamilton, Boyd and Mossman's human embryology: Prenatal development—Form and function* (4th ed.). Cambridge, England: Heffer, 1972.

Harlow, H. The formation of learning sets. *Psychological Review*, 1949, *56*, 51–65.

Harlow, H. The nature of love. *American Psychologist*, 1958, *13*, 673–685.

Harlow, H. F. *Learning to love*. San Francisco: Albion, 1971.

Harlow, H., & Harlow, M. K. Effects of various mother-infant relationships on rhesus monkeys' behaviors. In B. M. Foss (Ed.), *Determinants of infant behavior* (Vol. 4). New York: Barnes and Noble, 1969.

Harlow, H., & Zimmerman, R. R. Affectual responses in the infant monkey. *Science*, 1959, *130*, 421–432.

Harris, P. L. Perseverative errors in search by young children. *Child Development*, 1973, *44*, 28–33.

Harris, P. L. Perseverative search at a visibly empty place by young children. *Journal of Experimental Child Psychology*, 1974, *18*, 535–542.

Harris, P. L. Development of search and object permanence during infancy. *Psychological Bulletin,* 1975, *82,* 175–195.

Hartup, W. W. Friendship states and the effectiveness of peers as reinforcing agents. *Journal of Experimental Child Psychology,* 1964, *1,* 154–162.

Hartup, W. W. Peer interactions and social organization. In P. H. Mussen (Ed.), *Carmichael's manual of child psychology* (Vol. 2). New York: Wiley, 1970.

Hartup, W. W. Aggression in childhood: Developmental perspectives. *American Psychologist,* 1974, *29,* 336–341.

Hartup, W. W. Towards a social psychology of childhood, from *Patterns of child-rearing to 1984.* Paper delivered at the American Psychological Association Conference, Washington, D.C., 1976.

Hartup, W. W. Peer interaction and the process of socialization. In M. J. Guralnick (Ed.), *Early intervention and the integration of handicapped and nonhandicapped children.* Baltimore: University Park Press, 1977.

Hartup, W. W. Children and their friends. In H. McGurk (Ed.), *Issues in childhood social development.* London: Methuen, 1978.

Hartup, W. W. The social worlds of childhood, *American Psychologist,* 1979, *34,* 944–950.

Hass, A. *Teenage sexuality: A survey of teenage sexual behavior.* New York: Macmillan, 1979.

Hauck, B. B. Differences between the sexes at puberty. In E. D. Evans (Ed.), *Adolescents: Readings in behavior and development.* Hinsdale, Ill.: Dryden Press, 1970.

Hayden, A. H., & Dmitriev, V. Multidisciplinary preschool program for Down's Syndrome children at the University of Washington Model Preschool Center. In B. Z. Friedlander, G. Kirk, & G. Sterritt (Eds.), *The exceptional infant* (Vol. III). New York: Brunner/Mazel, 1975.

Hayden, A. H., & Haring, N. G. Early intervention for high-risk infants and young children: Programs for Down's syndrome children. Hayden & Haring 1970–6, In T. D. Tjossem (Ed.), *Intervention strategies for high-risk infants and young children.* Baltimore: University Park Press, 1976.

Haynes, H., White, B., & Held, R. Visual accommodation in human infants. *Science,* 1965, *148,* 528–530.

Heathers, G. Emotional dependence and independence in nursery school play. *Journal of Genetic Psychology,* 1955, *77,* 37–58.

Heimler, A., & Lieber, E. Detecting defects before birth. *Journal of Nursing Care,* 1978, *11,* 20–24.

Hein, K., Cohen, M. I., & Litt, I. Illicit drug use among urban adolescents: A decade in retrospect. In S. Chess and A. Thomas (Eds.), *Annual progress in child psychiatry and child development.* New York: Brunner/Mazel, 1980.

Heinstein, M. *Child rearing in California.* Berkeley, Calif.: Bureau of Maternal and Child Health, Department of Public Health, 1966.

Hendrick, J. *The whole child: New trends in early education* (2nd ed.). St. Louis: The C. V. Mosby Co., 1980.

Henly, W. L., & Fitch, B. R. Newborn narcotic withdrawal associated with regional enteritis in pregnancy. *New York Journal of Medicine,* 1966, *66,* 2565–2567.

Herrnstein, R. J. *IQ in the meritocracy.* Boston: Little, Brown & Company, 1973.

Hess, E. H. "Imprinting" in animals. *Scientific American,* March, 1958, 81–90.

Hess, R. D., Block, M., Costello, J., Knowles, R. T., & Largay, D. Parent involvement in early education. In E. H. Grotberg (Ed.), *Day care: Resources for decisions* (Pamphlet 6106–1). Washington, D.C.: Office of Economic Opportunity, June 1971.

Hess, R. D., Dickson, W. P., Price, G. G., & Leong, D. J. Some contrasts between mothers and child care staff in interaction with four-year-old children. *American Educational Research Journal,* 1979, *16,* 307–316.

Hess, R. D., & Shipman, V. C. Early experience and the socialization of cognitive modes in children. *Child Development,* 1965, *34,* 869–886.

Hess, R. D., & Shipman, V. C. Cognitive elements in maternal behavior. In J. P. Hill (Ed.), *Minnesota Symposium on Child Psychology* (Vol. 1). Minneapolis: University of Minnesota Press, 1967.

Hetherington, E. M. The effects of familial variables on sex-typing, on parent-child similarity and on imitation in children. In J. P. Hill (Ed.), *Minnesota Symposium on Child Psychology* (Vol. 1). Minneapolis: University of Minnesota Press, 1967.

Hetherington, E. M. Effects of father absence on personality development in adolescent daughters. *Developmental Psychology,* 1972, *7,* 303–326.

Hetherington, E. M. Divorce: A child's perspective. *American Psychologist,* 1979, *34,* 851–858.

Hetherington, E. M., Cox, M., & Cox, R. Divorced fathers. *The Family Coordinator,* 1976, *25,* 417–428.

Hetherington, E. M., Cox, M., & Cox, R. *Play and social interaction in children following divorce. Journal of Social Issues* (in press).

Hetherington, E. M., Cox, M., & Cox, R. Stress and coping in divorce: A focus on women. In J. E. Guallahorn (Ed.), *Psychology and women: In transition.* Washington, D.C.: V. H. Winston & Sons, 1979.

Hetherington, E. M., & Deur, J. L. The effects of father absence on child development. *Young Children,* 1971, *26,* 233–248.

Hetherington, E. M., & McIntyre, C. W. Developmental Psychology. M. R. Rosenzweig & L. W. Porter (Eds.), *Annual review of psychology* (Vol. 26). Palo Alto, Calif.: Annual Reviews, Inc., 1975.

Hewett, F. *The emotionally disturbed child in the classroom: A developmental strategy for educating children with maladaptive behavior.* Boston: Allyn & Bacon, 1968.

Hiernaux, J. Ethnic differences in growth and development. *Eugenics Quarterly,* 1968, *15,* 12–21.

Hilgard, E. R., & Bower, G. H. *Theories of learning* (4th ed.). Englewood Cliffs, N.J.: Prentice-Hall, 1975.

Hinde, R. A. *The origins of human social behavior.* New York: McGraw-Hill, 1974.

Hirsh, I., & Walder, L. Training mothers in groups as reinforcement therapists for their own children. *Proceedings of the 77th Annual Convention of the American Psychological Association,* 1969, *4,* 561–562.

Hirschi, T. *Causes of delinquency.* Berkeley, Calif.: University of California Press, 1969.

Hock, E. Working and nonworking mothers and their infants: A comparative study of maternal caregiving characteristics and infant social behavior. *Merrill-Palmer Quarterly,.*

Hoffman, L. W. The father's role and the child's peer group adjustment. *Merrill-Palmer Quarterly,* 1961, *7,* 97–105.

Hoffman, L. W. Effects of maternal employment on the child—A review of the research. *Developmental Psychology,* 1974, *10,* 204–228.

Hoffman, L. W. Maternal employment. *American Psychologist,* 1979, *34,* 859–865.

Hoffman, M. L., & Saltzstein, H. D. Parent discipline and the child's moral development. *Journal of Personality and Social Psychology,* 1967, *5,* 45–47.

Hollingshead, A. B. *Elmtown's youth.* New York: Wiley, 1949.

Honig, A. S. *Parent involvement in early childhood education* (Rev. ed.). Washington, D.C.: National Association for the Education of Young Children, 1977.

Honig, A. S. What we need to know to help the teenage parent. *The Family Coordinator,* 1978, *27,* 113–119.

Hopkins, J. R. Sexual behavior in adolescence. *Journal of Social Issues,* 1977, *33,* 67–85.

Hoving, K. I., Hamm, M., & Galvin, P. Social influence as a function of stimulus ambiguity at three age levels. *Developmental Psychology,* 1969, *1,* 631–636.

Hughes, J. R. Biochemical and electroencephalographic correlates of learning disabilities. In R. M. Knights and D. J. Bakker (Eds.), *The neuropsychology of learning disorders: Theoretical approaches.* Baltimore: University Park Press, 1976.

Hunt, J. McV., & Uzgiris, I. C. *Cathexis from recognitive familiarity: An exploratory study.* Paper presented at the Convention of the American Psychological Association, Los Angeles, September 1964.

Huttenlocher, J. The growth of conceptual strategies. In J. S. Bruner, R. R. Olver, & P. M. Greenfield (Eds.), *Studies in cognitive growth.* New York: Wiley, 1966.

Hyman, I. A. *Some effects of teaching style on pupil behavior.* Unpublished doctoral dissertation, Rutgers University, 1964.

Hyman, I. A., McDowell, E., & Raines, B. Corporal punishment and alternatives in the schools: An overview of theoretical and practical issues. In *Inequality in education: Center for law and education* (No. 23). Cambridge, Mass.: Gutman Library, 1978.

Ilg, F. L., & Ames, L. B. *The Gesell Institute's child behavior.* New York: Dell, 1955.

Illich, I. *Deschooling society.* New York: Harper & Row, 1971.

Inamdar, S. C., Siomopoulos, G., Osborn, M., & Bianchi, E. C. Phenomenology associated with depressed moods in adolescents. *American Journal of Psychiatry,* 1979, *136,* 156–159.

Inhelder, B. Information-processing tendencies in recent experiments in cognitive learning: Empirical studies. In S. Farnham-Diggory (Ed.), *Information processing in children.* New York: Academic Press, 1972.

Inhelder, B., & Piaget, J. *The growth of logical thinking from childhood to adolescence.* New York: Basic Books, 1958.

Inhelder, B., & Piaget, J. *The early growth of logic in the child.* London: Routledge & Kegan Paul, 1964.

Inhelder, B., & Sinclair, H. Learning cognitive structures. In P. H. Mussen, J. Langer, & M. Covington (Eds.), *Trends and issues in developmental psychology.* New York: Holt, Rinehart & Winston, 1969.

Inhelder, B., Sinclair, H., & Bovet, M. *Learning and the development of cognition.* Cambridge, Mass.: Harvard University Press, 1974.

Jackson, D., & Angelino, H. Play as learning. *Theory into practice,* 1974, *13,* 317–323.

Jackson, E. N. *Telling a child about death.* New York: Hawthorn Books, 1965.

Jacobs, J. *Adolescent suicide.* New York: Wiley, 1971.

Jacobs, J., & Teicher, J. D. Broken homes and social isolation in attempted suicides of adolescence. *International Journal of Social Psychiatry,* 1967, *13,* 139–149.

Jaffe, J., Stern, D. N., & Perry, J. C. 'Conversational' coupling of behavior in prelinguistic human development. *Journal of Psycholinguistic Research,* 1973, *2,* 321–329.

James, W. *Principles of psychology.* New York: Harry Holt, 1980.

Janerich, D. T., Piper, J. M., & Glebatis, D. H. Oral contraceptives and congenital limb-reduction defects. *New England Journal of Medicine,* 1974, *291,* 597–700.

Jelliffe, D. B., & Jelliffe, E. F. P. *Fat babies: Prevalence, perils and prevention.* London: Incentive Press, 1974.

Jensen, A. R. How much can we boost IQ and scholastic achievement? *Harvard Educational Review,* 1969, *39,* 1–123.

Jensen, A. R. *Genetic, educability and subpopulation differences.* London: Methuen, 1973.

Jensen, A. R. Cumulative deficit in IQ of blacks in the rural south. *Developmental Psychology,* 1977, *13,* 184–191.

Jersild, A. T. *Child psychology* (6th ed.). Englewood Cliffs, N.J.: Prentice-Hall, 1968.

Jessor, R., & Jessor, S. L. *Problem behavior and psychosocial development: A longitudinal study of youth.* New York: Academic Press, 1977.

Jessor, S. L., & Jessor, R. Maternal ideology and adolescent problem solving. *Developmental psychology,* 1974, *10,* 246–254.

Johnson, B., & Morse, H. A. Injured children and their parents. *Children,* 1968, *15,* 147–152.

Johnson, H. *School begins at two.* New York: Agathon Press, 1970. (Originally published, 1934.)

Johnson, J. E. Relations of divergent thinking and intelligence test scores with social and nonsocial make-believe play of preschool children. *Child Development,* 1976, *47,* 1200–1203.

Johnson, J. E., Ershler, J. A., & Bell, C. Play behavior in a discovery-based and a formal-educational preschool program. *Child Development,* 1980, *51,* 271–274.

Johnson, J. E., Ershler, J. A., & Lawton, J. T. Intellective correlates of preschoolers' spontaneous play. *Journal of Genetic Psychology* (in press).

Johnston, L., & Bachman, J. *Monitoring the future: A continuing study of the life styles and values of youth.* Ann Arbor, Mich.: Institute for Social Research, 1975.

Johnston, L., Bachman, J., & O'Malley, P. *Drug use among American high school students 1975–1977* (DHEW Publication No. (ADM) 79–619). Rockville, Md.: National Institute on Drug Abuse, 1977.

Jones, J. W. *The visually handicapped child at home and school* (Rev. ed.). Washington, D.C.: U.S. Department of Health, Education and Welfare, 1969.

Jones, K. L., Smith, D. W., Ulleland, C., & Streissguth, A. P. Pattern of malformation in offspring of chronic alcoholic mothers. *Lancet,* 1973, *1*(7815), 1267–1271.

Jones, M. C. Psychological correlates of somatic development. *Child Development,* 1965, *36,* 899–911.

Kagan, J. The concept of identification. *Psychological Review,* 1958, *65,* 296–305.

Kagan, J. Acquisition and significance of sex typing and sex-role identity. In M. L. Hoffman & L. W. Hoffman (Eds.), *Review of child development* (Vol. 1). New York: Russell Sage Foundation, 1964.

Kagan, J. Generality and dynamics of conceptual tempo. *Journal of Abnormal Psychology,* 1966, *71,* 17–24.

Kagan, J. Attention and psychological change in the young child. *Science,* 1970, *170,* 826–832.

Kagan, J. *Understanding children, behavior, motives and thought.* New York: Harcourt, Brace, Jovanovich, 1971.

Kagan, J. Do infants think? *Scientific American,* March 1972, pp. 78–82.

Kagan, J. Emergent themes in human development. *American Scientist,* 1976, *64,* 186–196.

Kagan, J., Kearsley, R. B., & Zelazo, P. R. *Infancy: Its place in human development.* Cambridge, Mass.: Harvard University Press, 1978.

Kagan, J., & Klein, R. E. Cross-cultural perspectives on early development. *American Psychologist,* 1973, *28,* 947–961.

Kagan, J., Klein, R. E., Finley, G. E., Rogoff, B., & Nolan, E. A cross-cultural study of cognitive development. *Monographs of the Society for Research in Child Development.* 1979, *44* (5, Serial No. 180).

Kagan, J., & Moss, H. *Birth to maturity: A study in child development.* New York: Wiley, 1962.

Kagan, J., Rosman, B. L., Day, D., Albert, J., & Phillips, W. Information processing in the child: Significance of analytic and reflective attitudes. *Psychological Monographs,* 1964, *78,* (1, Whole No. 578).

Kail, R. V. *The development of memory in children.* San Francisco: W. H. Freeman, 1979.

Kail, R. V., & Hagen, J. W. (Eds.). *Memory in cognitive development.* Hillsdale, N.J.: Lawrence Erlbaum Associates, 1976.

Kaiser, I. H. Fertilization and the physiology of fetus and placenta. In D. N. Danforth (Ed.), *Obstetrics and gynecology* (3rd ed.). New York: Harper & Row, 1977.

Kalnins, I., & Bruner, J. S. Control of visual focus by sucking. *Journal of Child Psychology,* 1974.

Kaluger, G., & Kaluger, M. F. *Profiles in human development.* Saint Louis: The C. V. Mosby Co., 1976.

Kamii, C., & DeVries, R. Piaget for early education. In M. C. Day & R. K. Parker (Eds.), *The preschool in action: Exploring early childhood programs* (2nd ed.). Boston: Allyn & Bacon, 1977.

Kamii, C., & DeVries, R. *Physical knowledge in preschool education: Implications of Piaget's theory.* Englewood Cliffs, N.J.: Prentice-Hall, 1978.

Kamii, C. K., & Radin, N. L. Class differences in the socialization practices of Negro mothers. *Journal of Marriage and the Family,* 1977, *49,* 302–310.

Kamin, L. J. *The science and politics of IQ.* Potomac, Md.: Lawrence Erlbaum Associates, 1974.

Kandel, D. B., & Faust, R. Sequences and stages in patterns of adolescent drug use. *Archives of General Psychiatry,* 1975, *32,* 923–932.

Kandel, D. B., & Lesser, G. S. *Youth in two worlds.* San Francisco: Jossey-Bass, 1972.

Karmel, M. *Painless childbirth: Thank you, Dr. Lamaze.* Philadelphia: Lippincott, 1959.

Karnes, M. B., & Lee, R. C. Involving parents in the education of their handicapped children: An essential component of an exemplary program. In M. J. Fine (Ed.), *Handbook on parent education.* New York: Academic Press, 1980.

Karnes, M. B., Zehrbach, R. R., & Teska, J. A. Involving families of handicapped children. *Theory into Practice,* 1972, *11,* 150–156.

Kastenbaum, R. The kingdom where nobody dies. *Saturday Review,* December 23, 1972, pp. 33–38.

Katz, E. W., & Brent, S. B. Understanding connectives. *Journal of Verbal Learning and Verbal Behavior,* 1968, *7,* 501–509.

Kazdin, A. Role of instruction and reinforcement in behavior changes and token reinforcement. *Journal of Educational Psychology,* 1973, *64,* 63–71.

Keeney, T. J., Cannizzo, S. R., & Flavell, J. H. Spontaneous and introduced verbal rehearsal in a recall task. *Child Development,* 1967, *38,* 953–966.

Keith, R. The feelings and behavior of parents of handicapped children. *Developmental Medicine and Child Nemology,* 1973, *15,* 524–527.

Keller, F. S. Goodbye teacher. *Journal of Applied Behavioral Analysis,* 1968, *1,* 69–89.

Keller, F. S., & Schoenfeld, W. N. *Principles of psychology.* New York: Appleton-Century-Crofts, 1950.

Kelley, H. H. The process of causal attribution. *American Psychologist,* 1973, *28,* 107–128.

Kellogg, R. Understanding children's art. *Psychology Today,* May 1967, pp. 16–25.

Kellogg, R., & O'Dell, S. *Analyzing children's art.* Palo Alto, Calif.: National Press Books, 1969.

Kelly, J., & Wallerstein, J. The effects of parental divorce: Experiences of the child in early latency. *American Journal of Orthopsychiatry,* 1976, *46.*

Kempe, C. H. Child abuse and neglect. In N. B. Talbot (Ed.), *Raising children in modern America: Problems and prospective solutions.* Boston: Little, Brown & Company, 1976.

Kempe, R. S., & Kempe, C. H. *Child abuse.* Cambridge, Mass.: Harvard University Press, 1978.

Keniston, K., & The Carnegie Council on Children. *All our children: The American family under pressure.* New York: Harcourt, Brace, Jovanovich, 1977.

Kennedy, W. A. School phobia: Rapid treatment of fifty cases. *Journal of Abnormal Psychology,* 1965, *70,* 285–289.

Kennell, J. H., Jerauld, R., Wolfe, H., Chesler, D., Kreger, N. C., McAlpine, W., Steffa, M., & Klaus, M. H. Maternal behavior one year after early and extended postpartum contact. *Developmental Medicine and Child Neurology,* 1974, *16,* 172–179.

Kerlinger, F. N. *Foundations of behavioral research.* New York: Holt, Rinehart & Winston, 1964.

Kessen, W. Sucking and looking: Two organized congenital patterns of behavior in the human newborn. In E. H. Stevenson, E. H. Hess, & H. L. Rheingold (Eds.), *Early behavior: Comparative and developmental approaches.* New York: Wiley, 1967.

Kessen, W., Haith, M. M., & Salapatek, B. H. Human infancy: A bibliography and guide. In P. H. Mussen (Ed.), *Carmichael's manual of child psychology* (Vol. 1; 3rd ed.). New York: Wiley, 1970.

Kessler, J. W. *Psychopathology of childhood.* Englewood Cliffs, N.J.: Prentice-Hall, 1966.

Kirkendall, L. A., & Rubin, I. Sexuality and the life cycle. In G. B. Spanier (Ed.), *Human sexuality in a changing society.* Minneapolis: Burgess Publishing, 1979.

Klaus, M. H., & Kennell, J. H. *Maternal-infant bonding: The impact of early separation or loss on family development.* St. Louis: The C. V. Mosby Co., 1976.

Klaus, M. H., Kennell, J. H., Plumb, N., & Zuehlke, S. Human maternal behavior at the first contact with her young. *Pediatrics,* 1970, *46,* 187–192.

Knight, M., Hasazi, S., and McNeil, M. A home based program for the development of reading skills for preschoolers. In E. Ramp and B. Hopkins (Eds.), *A New Direction for Education: Behavior Analysis.* Lawrence, Ks.: University of Kansas, Department of Human Development, 1971, 223–234.

Knobloch, H., & Pasamanick, B. Some etiologic and prognostic factors in early infantile autism and psychosis. *Pediatrics,* 1975, *55,* 182–191.

Koch, H. The relation of certain formal abilities of siblings to attitudes held toward each other and toward their parents. *Monographs of the Society for Research in Child Development,* 1960, *25* (Whole No. 76).

Koch, J. When children meet death. *Psychology Today,* August 1977, pp. 64–66; 79–80.

Kohlberg, L. *Global rating guide with new materials.* Cambridge, Mass.: Harvard University School of Education, 1958.

Kohlberg, L. The development of children's orientations towards a moral order: I. Sequence in the development of moral thought. *Vita Humana,* 1963, *6,* 11–33.

Kohlberg, L. A cognitive-developmental analysis of children's sex-role concepts and attitudes. In E. Maccoby (Ed.), *The development of sex differences.* Stanford, Calif.: Stanford University Press, 1966.

Kohlberg, L. Stage and sequence: A cognitive-developmental approach to socialization. In D. A. Goslin (Ed.), *Handbook of socialization theory and research.* Chicago: Rand McNally, 1969.

Kohlberg, L. The child as a moral philosopher. *Readings in developmental psychology today.* Del Mar, Calif.: CRM Books, 1970.

Kohlberg, L. From is to ought: How to commit the naturalistic fallacy and get away with it in the study of moral development. In T. Mischel (Ed.), *Cognitive development and genetic epistemology.* New York: Academic Press, 1971.

Kohlberg, L. Continuities in childhood and adult moral development revisited. In P. B. Baltes & K. W. Schaie (Eds.), *Life-span developmental psychology: Personality and socialization.* New York: Academic Press, 1973.

Kohlberg, L. Moral stages and moralization: The cognitive-development approach. In T. Lickona (Ed.), *Moral development and behavior.* New York: Holt, Rinehart & Winston, 1976.

Kohlberg, L., Colby, A., Gibbs, J., Speicher-Dubin, B., & Power, C. *Assessing moral stages: A manual.* Unpublished manuscript, 1977. (Available from the Center for Moral Education, Graduate School of Education, Harvard University, Cambridge, Mass. 02138.)

Kohlberg, L., & Elfenbein, D. The development of moral judgments concerning capital punishment. *American Journal of Orthopsychiatry,* 1975, *45,* 614–640.

Kohlberg, L., & Gilligan, C. The adolescent as philosopher: The discovery of the self in a postconventional world. *Daedalus,* Fall, 1971, 1051–1086.

Konopka, G. *Young girls: A portrait of adolescence.* Englewood Cliffs, N.J.: Prentice-Hall, 1976.

Koocher, G. Why isn't the gerbil moving anymore? *Children Today,* 1975, *4,* 181.

Korner, A. Neonatal startles, smiles, erections and reflexes as related to state, sex and individuality. *Child Development,* 1969, *40,* 1039–1053.

Kotelchuck, M. *The nature of a child's tie to his father.* Unpublished doctoral dissertation, Harvard University, 1972.

Kotelchuck, M. *The nature of the child's ties to his father.* Paper presented at the meeting of the Society for Research in Child Development, Philadelphia, 1973.

Kotelchuck, M. The infant's relationship to the father: Experimental evidence. In M. E. Lamb (Ed.), *The role of the father in child development.* New York: Wiley, 1976.

Kotelchuck, M., Zelano, P. R., Kagan, J., & Spelke, E. Infant reaction to parental separations when left with familiar and unfamiliar adults. *Journal of Genetic Psychology,* 1975, *126,* 255–262.

Kounin, J. S. *Discipline and group management in classrooms.* New York: Holt, Rinehart & Winston, 1970.

Kounin, J. S., Gump, P. V., & Ryan, J. J. Explorations in classroom management. *Journal of Teacher Education,* 1961, *12,* 235–246.

Krauss, R. M., & Glucksberg, S. The development of communication: Competence as a function of age. *Child Development,* 1969, *40,* 255–266.

Kreutzer, M. A., Leonard, C., & Flavell, J. H. An interview study of children's knowledge about memory. *Monographs of the Society for Research in Child Development,* 1975, *40* (1, Serial No. 159).

Krogman, W. M. *Child growth.* Ann Arbor, Mich.: The University of Michigan Press, 1972.

Kübler-Ross, E. *On death and dying.* New York: Macmillan, 1969.

Kuhn, D. The application of Piaget's theory of cognitive development to education. *Harvard Educational Review,* 1979, *49,* 340–360.

Kuhn, D., Langer, J., Kohlberg, L., & Haan, N. S. The development of formal operations in logical and moral judgement. *Genetic Psychology Monographs,* 1977, *95,* 97–188.

Kuhn, D., Langer, J., Kohlberg, L., & Haan, N. S. The development of formal operations in logical and moral judgement. *Genetic Psychology Monographs,* 1978, *95,* 97–188.

Kurtines, W., & Greif, E. B. The development of moral thought: Review and evaluation of Kohlberg's approach. *Psychological Bulletin,* 1974, *81,* 453–470.

Labinowitcz, E. *The Piaget primer: Thinking, learning and behavior: Proceedings.* Cambridge, Mass.: The MIT Press, 1968.

Labouvie-Vief, G. Personality and socialization in later life. In M. E. Lamb (Ed.), *Social and personality development.* New York: Holt, Rinehart & Winston, 1978.

Labov, W. The logic of nonstandard English. In F. Williams (Ed.), *Language and poverty: Perspectives on a theme.* Chicago: Markham, 1970.

Lamb, M. E. Interactions between eight-month-old children and their fathers and mothers. In M. E. Lamb (Ed.), *The role of the father in child development.* New York: Wiley, 1976.

Lamb, M. E. The development of mother-infant and father-infant attachments in the second year of life. *Developmental Psychology,* 1977, *13,* 637–648. (a)

Lamb, M. E. The development of parental preferences in the first two years of life. *Sex Roles,* 1977, *3,* 495–497. (b)

Lamb, M. E. The effects of divorce on children's personality development. *Journal of Divorce,* 1977, *1,* 163–164. (c)

Lamb, M. E. (Ed.), *Social and personality development.* New York: Holt, Rinehart & Winston, 1978. (a)

Lamb, M. E. Social interaction in infancy and the development of personality. In M. E. Lamb (Ed.), *Social and personality development.* New York: Holt, Rinehart & Winston, 1978. (b)

Lamb, M. E. Influence of the child on marital quality and family interactions during the prenatal, perinatal and infancy periods. In R. M. Lerner & G. D. Spanier (Eds.), *Contributions of the child to marital and family interaction through the life-span.* New York: Academic Press, 1979.

Lamb, M. E., and Baumrind, D. Socialization and personality development in the preschool years. In M. E. Lamb (Ed.), *Social and personality development.* New York: Holt, Rinehart & Winston, 1978.

Lamb, M. E., Easterbrook, M. A., & Holden, G. W. Reinforcement and punishment among preschoolers: Characteristics, effects and correlates. *Child Development,* 1980, *51,* 1230–1236.

Lamb, M. E., Owen, M. T., & Chase-Lansdale, L. The father-daughter relationship: Past, present and future. In C. B. Kopp & M. Kirkpatrick (Eds.), *Becoming female.* New York: Plenum, 1979.

Lamb, M. E., & Roopnarine, J. L. Peer influences on sex-role development in preschoolers. *Child Development,* 1979, *50,* 1219–1222.

Lamb, M. E., & Stevenson, M. B. Father-infant relationships: Their nature and importance. *Youth and Society,* 1978, *9,* 277–298.

Lamb, M. E., & Urberg, K. A. The development of gender role and gender identity. In M. E. Lamb (Ed.), *Social and personality development.* New York: Holt, Rinehart & Winston, 1978.

Lambert, B. G., Rothschild, B. F., Altland, R., & Green, J. B. *Adolescence: Transition from childhood to maturity.* Monterey, Calif.: Brooks/Cole, 1972.

Lambie, D. Z., Bond, J. T., & Weikert, D. P. *Home teaching with mothers and infants.* Ypsilanti, Mich.: High/Scope Educational Research Foundation, 1974.

Landau, R. Extent that the mother represents the social stimulation to which the infant is exposed: Findings from a cross-cultural study. *Developmental Psychology,* 1976, *12,* 399–405.

Langer, J. *Theories of development.* New York: Holt, Rinehart & Winston, 1969.

Larson, D. L., Spreitzer, E. A., & Snyder, E. E. Social factors in the frequency of romantic involvement among adolescents. *Adolescence,* 1976, *11,* 7–12.

Lasko, J. K. Parent behavior toward first- and second-born children. *Genetic Psychology Monographs,* 1954, *49,* 96–137.

Lavatelli, C. S. *Early childhood curriculum: A Piagetian program.* Boston: American Science & Engineering, 1970.

Lavatelli, C. S. *Piaget's theory applied to an early childhood curriculum.* Boston: American Science & Engineering, 1973.

Lawson, A. E., Nordlund, F. H., & DeVito, A. Piagetian formal operational tasks: A crossover study of learning effect and reliability. *Science Education,* 1974, *58,* 569–575.

Lawton, J. T. The use of advance organizers in the training and retention of logical operations and social studies concepts. *American Educational Research Journal,* 1977, *14,* 25–43. (a)

Lawton, J. T. The development of causal and logical connectives in children. *British Journal of Educational Psychology,* 1977, *47,* 81–84. (b)

Lawton, J. T. Success in preschool learning related to formal and open-framework programs: A preliminary report. *Home Economics Research Journal,* 1978, *7,* 34–43.

Lawton, J. T., & Ershler, J. *Effects of preschool programs on children's learning of logical concepts.* (In preparation)

Lawton, J. T., & Fowell, N. Effects of advance organizers on preschool children's learning of math concepts. *Journal of Experimental Education,* 1978, *47,* 76–81.

Lawton, J. T., Hooper, F. H., Saunders, R. H., & Roth, P. *A comparison of three early childhood instructional programs.* Madison, Wis.: Wisconsin Research and Development Center for Individualized Instruction, 1978. (Technical Report No. 462)

Lawton, J. T., Lewis, R. A., & Deibert, J. *The contributions of Ausubelian theory to early childhood education.* Madison, Wis.: Wisconsin Research and Development Center for Individualized Instruction, 1976. (Working Paper No. 154)

Lawton, J. T., & Wanska, S. K. The effects of different types of advance organizers on classification learning. *American Educational Research Journal,* 1979, *16,* 223–239.

Laxova, R. Prenatal diagnosis of genetic effects. *Postgraduate Medicine,* 1979, *65,* 247–252.

Lazar, I., & Darlington, R. *Lasting effects after preschool* (Final Report, HEW Grant 90C-1311). United States Department of Health, Education and Welfare, 1979. (DHEW Publication No. (OHDS) 79-30179)

Leboyer, F. *Birth without violence.* New York: Alfred A. Knopf, 1975.

Lenneberg, E. H. *Biological foundations of language.* New York: Wiley, 1967.

Lenz, W. Malformation caused by drugs in pregnancy. *American Journal of Diseases of Children,* 1966, *112,* 99–106.

LeShan, E. *Learning to say goodbye: When a parent dies.* New York: Macmillan, 1976.

Leventhal, A. S., & Lipsitt, L. P. Adaptation, pitch discrimination and sound localization in the neonate. *Child Development,* 1964, *35,* 759–767.

Levine, J. *And who will raise the children?* Philadelphia: J. B. Lippincott, 1976.

Lewin, L., Lippitt, R., & White, R. K. Patterns of aggressive behavior in experimentally created "social climates." *Journal of Social Psychology,* 1939, *10,* 271–299.

Lewis, M., & Brooks-Gunn, J. *Social cognition and the acquisition of self.* New York: Plenum, (in press).

Lewis, M., & Weinraub, M. Sex of parent × sex of child: Socioemotional development. In R. Richart, R. Friedman, and R. Vande Wiele (Eds.), *Sex differences in behavior.* New York: Wiley, 1974.

Lewis, M., & Weinraub, M. Origins of early sex-role development. *Sex Roles,* 1979, *5,* 135–153.

Libby, R. W., & Nass, G. D. Parental views on teenage sexual behavior. *The Journal of Sex Research,* 1971, 235–236.

Lickona, T. Research on Piaget's theory of moral development. In T. Lickona (Ed.), *Moral development and behavior.* New York: Holt, Rinehart & Winston, 1976.

Liebert, R. M., Neale, J. M., & Davidson, E. S. *The early window: Effects of television on children and youth.* New York: Pergamon Press, 1973.

Lightfoot, S. L. Families and schools: Creative conflict or negative dissonance. *Journal of Research and Development in Education,* 1975, *9,* 34–44.

Lillard, P. P. *Montessori: A modern approach.* New York: Shocken Books, 1972.

Lippitt, R. Improving the socialization process. In J. Clausen (Ed.), *Socialization and society.* Boston: Little, Brown & Company, 1968.

Lipsitt, L. P. The study of sensory and learning processes of the newborn. *Symposium on Neonatal Neurology, Clinics in Perinatology,* 1977, *48,* 772–785.

Lockwood, A. L. The effects of values clarification and moral development curricula on school-aged subjects: A critical review of current research. *Review of Educational Research,* 1978, *48,* 325–364.

Loeb, R. Content—Concomitants of boys' locus of control examined in parent-child interactions. *Developmental Psychology*, 1975, *11*, 353–359.

Lonergan, B. J. F. *Insight: A study of human understanding.* New York: Longmans, 1968.

Lorenz, K. King Solomon's ring. London: Methuen, 1952.

Lorenz, K. Companionship in bird life. In C. Schiller (Ed.), *Instinctive behavior.* New York: International University Press, 1957.

Lorenz, K. *On aggression.* New York: Harcourt, Brace, and World, 1966.

Lovaas, O. I., Young, D. B., & Newsom, C. D. Childhood psychosis: Behavioral treatment. In B. B. Wolman, J. Egan, & A. O. Ross (Eds.), *Handbook of treatment of mental disorders in childhood and adolescence.* Englewood Cliffs, N.J.: Prentice-Hall, 1978.

Lowenfeld, M. *Play in childhood.* New York: Wiley, 1967.

Lowenstein, B. E., & Preger, P. D., Jr. *Diabetes: New look at an old problem.* New York: Harper & Row, 1976.

Lubs, H. A., & Riddle, F. H. Chromosomal abnormalities in the human population: Estimation of rates based on New Haven newborn study. *Science*, 1970, *169*, 495–498.

Lunzer, E. A. Formal reasoning. In E. A. Lunzer and J. F. Morris (Eds.), *Development in human learning.* New York: American Elsevier Publishing Company, 1968.

Lunzer, E. A. *Formal reasoning: A reappraisal.* Keynote paper presented to the second Conference of the Jean Piaget Society, Philadelphia, June, 1973.

Lunzer, E. A. The development of advanced reasoning abilities. *Italian Journal of Psychology*, 1975, *2*, 369–390.

Lunzer, E. A., & Morris, J. F. (Eds.). *Development in human learning.* New York: American Elsevier Publishing Company, 1968.

Luria, Z., & Rubin, J. Z. The neonate's gender and the eye of the beholder. *Scientific American*, (in press)

Lurie, N. O. (Ed.). *Mountain Wolf Woman: The autobiography of a Winnebago Indian.* Ann Arbor, Mich.: The University of Michigan Press, 1973.

Lynn, D. *The father: His role in child development.* Monterey, Calif.: Brooks/Cole, 1974.

McCall, R. B. *Infants.* Cambridge, Mass.: Harvard University Press, 1979.

Maccoby, E. E. The development of moral values and behavior in childhood. In J. A. Clausen (Ed.), *Socialization and society.* Boston: Little, Brown & Company, 1968.

Maccoby, E. E. *Sex differences revisited: Myth and reality.* Paper delivered at the annual meeting of the American Educational Research Association, Chicago, 1974.

Maccoby, E. E. *Social development: Psychological growth and the parent-child relationship.* New York: Harcourt, Brace, Jovanovich, 1980.

Maccoby, E. E., & Jacklin, C. N. *The psychology of sex differences.* Stanford, Calif.: Stanford University Press, 1974.

Maccoby, E. E., & Zellner, H. *Experiments in primary education: Aspects of Project Follow-Through.* New York: Harcourt, Brace, Jovanovich, 1970.

Macfarlane, J. A. Olfaction in the development of social preferences in the human neonate. In M. A. Hofer (Ed.), *Parent-infant interaction.* Amsterdam: Elsevier, 1975.

Macfarlane, J. A. *The psychology of childbirth.* Cambridge, Mass.: Harvard University Press, 1977.

McGhee, P. E. Development of children's ability to create the joking relationship. *Child Development*, 1974, *45*, 552–556.

McGhee, P. E. Children's appreciation of humor: A test of the cognitive congruency principle. *Child Development*, 1976, *47*, 420–426.

McGloltein, W. H., Sparkes, R. S., & Arnold, D. O. Effects of LSD on human pregnancy. *Journal of American Medical Association*, 1970, *212*, 1483–1487.

McNeill, D. *The acquisition of language: The study of developmental psycholinguistics.* New York: Harper & Row, 1970. (a)

McNeill, D. The development of language. In P. Mussen (Ed.), *Carmichael's manual of child psychology* (Vol. 1; 3rd ed.). New York: Wiley, 1970. (b)

Maddock, J. W. Sex in adolescence: Its meaning and its future. *Adolescence*, 1973, *8*, 325–342.

Magrab, P. R., & Danielson-Murphy, J. Adolescent pregnancy: A review. *Journal of Clinical Child Psychology*, 1979, 121–125.

Mahler, M. S., Pine, F., & Bergman, A. *The psychological birth of the human infant.* New York: Basic Books, 1975.

Maier, H. W. *Three theories of child development.* New York: Harper & Row, 1969.

Man, a course of study. Washington, D.C.: Curriculum Development Associates, 1976.

Manning, J. Discipline in the good old days. *Phi Delta Kappan*, December 1959, p. 114.

Maratsos, M. P. Nonegocentric communication abilities in preschool children. *Child Development*, 1973, *44*, 697–700.

Margolies, P. J. Behavior approaches to the treatment of early infantile autism: A review. *Psychological Bulletin*, 1977, *84*, 249–264.

Margolin, G., & Patterson, G. R. Differential consequences provided by mothers and fathers for their sons and daughters. *Developmental Psychology*, 1975, *11*, 537–538.

Martin, B. Parent-child relations. In F. D. Horowitz (Ed.), *Review of child development research* (Vol. 4). Chicago: University of Chicago Press, 1975.

Martin, H. *The abused child.* Cambridge, Mass.: Ballinger, 1976.

Martorano, S. *Formal operations thinking: Now you see it, now you don't.* Paper presented at the Society for Research in Child Development Conference, Denver, April, 1975.

Masur, E. F., McIntyre, C. W., & Flavell, J. H. Developmental changes in apportionment of study time among items in a multitrial free recall task. *Journal of Experimental Child Psychology,* 1973, *15,* 237–246.

Maurer, A. All in the name of the "last resort": The abuse of children in American schools. In *Inequality in education: Center for law and education* (No. 23). Cambridge, Mass.: Gutman Library, 1978.

Maurer, D., & Salapatek, P. Developmental changes in the scanning of faces by young infants. *Child Development,* 1976, *47,* 523–527.

Mead, M. *Sex and temperament in three primitive societies.* New York: Morrow, 1935.

Mead, M. *From the South Seas: Studies of adolescence and sex in primitive societies.* New York: Morrow, 1939.

Mead, M. *Coming of age in Samoa.* New York: Morrow, 1961.

Mead, M. Childbirth in a changing world. In R. I. Feinbloom (Ed.), *Pregnancy, birth, and the newborn baby.* New York: Delta, 1979.

Meehl, P. E. Schizotaxia, schizotypy, schizophrenia. *American Psychologist,* 1962, *17,* 827–838.

Meeway, F. B. The generation of educational practice from developmental theory. *Educational Psychologist,* 1979, *14,* 30–43.

Mendelson, W., Johnson, N., & Stewart, M. A. Hyperactive children as teenagers: A follow-up study. *Journal of Nervous and Mental Disease,* 1971, *153,* 273–279.

Menyuk, P. *The acquisition and development of language.* New York: Prentice-Hall, 1971.

Meredith, H. V. Research between 1960 and 1970 on the standing height of young children in different parts of the world. In H. W. Reese & L. P. Lipsitt (Eds.), *Advances in child development and behavior* (Vol. 12). New York: Academic Press, 1978.

Messer, S. B. The effect of anxiety over intellectual performance on reflection-impulsivity in children. *Child Development,* 1970, *41,* 723–735.

Messer, S. B. Reflection-impulsivity: A review. *Psychological Bulletin,* 1976, *83,* 1026–1052.

Midlarsky, E., & Bryan, J. H. Training charity in children. *Journal of Personality and Social Psychology,* 1967, *5,* 405–415.

Miller, G. A. Language and psychology. In E. H. Lenneberg (Ed.), *New directions in the study of language.* Cambridge, Mass.: The MIT Press, 1964.

Miller, J. F., & Chapman, R. S. Collecting and recording speech samples. In J. F. Miller (Ed.), *Assessing language production in children: Experimental procedures.* Baltimore: University Park Press, 1981.

Miller, N. E., & Dollard, J. *Social learning and imitation.* New Haven, Conn.: Yale University Press, 1941.

Miller, W. R., & Lief, H. I. Masturbatory attitudes, knowledge and experience: Data from the Sex Knowledge and Attitude Test (SKAT). *Archives of Sexual Behavior,* 1976, *5,* 447–467.

Minde, K., Lewin, D., Weiss, G., Lavingueur, H., Douglas, V., & Sykes, E. The hyperactive child in elementary school: A five year controlled follow up. *Exceptional Child,* 1971, *39,* 215–221.

Minerva, A. N. Psychomotor education and general development of preschool children: Experiments with twin controls. *Journal of Genetic Psychology,* 1935, *46,* 433–454.

Minuchin, S. *Families and family therapy.* Cambridge, Mass.: Harvard University Press, 1974.

Minuchin, S., Rosman, B. L., & Baker, L. *Psychosomatic families.* Cambridge, Mass.: Harvard University Press, 1978.

Mischel, W. Sex typing and socialization. In P. H. Mussen (Ed.), *Carmichael's manual of child psychology* (Vol. 2; 3rd. ed.). New York: Wiley, 1970.

Mischel, W. Toward a cognitive social-learning reconceptualization of personality. *Psychological Review,* 1973, *80,* 252–283.

Moffit, A. R. Consonant cue perception by twenty- to twenty-four-week-old infants. *Child Development,* 1971, *42,* 717–731.

Money, J., & Ehrhardt, A. *Man and woman, boy and girl.* Baltimore: Johns Hopkins University Press, 1972.

Money, J., Hampson, J. G., & Hampson, J. L. Imprinting and the establishment of gender role. *A.M.A. Archives of Neurology and Psychiatry,* 1957, *77,* 333–336.

Monroe, R. *Schools of psychoanalytic thought.* New York: Henry Holt, 1955.

Montessori, M. *Education for a new world.* Wheaton, Ill.: Theosophical Press, 1963.

Montessori, M. *The absorbent mind.* Wheaton, Ill.: Theosophical Press, 1964.

Moore, K. A., & Waite, L. J. Early childbearing and educational attainment. *Family Planning Perspective,* 1978, *9,* 220.

Moore, T. W. Exclusive early mothering and its alternatives. *Scandinavian Journal of Psychology,* 1975, *16,* 256–272.

Mordock, J. B. *The other children: An introduction to exceptionality.* New York: Harper & Row, 1975.

Morgan, E. (Ed.) *A manual of death education and simple burial.* Burnsville, N.C.: The Celo Press, 1975.

Morgan, S., & Ricciuli, H. N. Infant's responses to strangers during the first year. In B. M. Foss (Ed.), *Determinants of infant behavior* (Vol. 4). New York: Wiley, 1969.

Moss, H. A. Sex, age, and state as determinants of mother-infant interaction. *Merrill-Palmer Quarterly,* 1967, *13,* 19–36.

Munn, N. L., Fernald, L. D., & Fernald, P. S. *Introduction to psychology* (3rd ed.). Boston: Houghton Mifflin, 1974.

Munroe, R. *Schools of psychoanalytic thought.* New York: Henry Holt & Company, 1955.

Murphy, L. B. Children under three: Finding ways to stimulate development. In R. Smart & M. Smart (Eds.), *Readings in child development and relationships.* New York: Macmillan, 1972.

Murray, F. B. The generation of educational practice from developmental theory. *Educational Psychologist,* 1979, *14,* 30–43.

Murray, F. B., & Armstrong, S. L. Adult nonconservation of numerical equivalence. *Merrill-Palmer Quarterly,* 1978, *24,* 255–263.

Mussen, P. H. Early socialization: Learning and identification. In T. M. Newcomb (Ed.), *New directions in psychology* (Vol. 3). New York: Holt, Rinehart & Winston, 1967.

Mussen, P. H. *The psychological development of the child.* Englewood Cliffs, N.J.: Prentice-Hall, 1973.

Mussen, P. H., Conger, J. J., & Kagan, J. *Child development and personality* (5th ed.). New York: Harper & Row, 1979.

Mussen, P. H., & Eisenberg-Berg, N. *Roots of caring, sharing, and helping.* San Francisco: W. H. Freeman, 1977.

Mussen, P. H., & Rutherford, E. Parent-child relations and parental personality in relation to young children's sex-role preferences. *Child Development,* 1963, *34,* 589–607.

Muuss, R. E. Adolescent development and the secular trend. *Adolescence,* 1970, *5,* 267–284.

Muuss, R. E. *Theories of adolescence* (3rd ed.). New York: Random House, 1975.

Mynatt, C. R., Doherty, M. E., & Tweney, R. D. Confirmation bias in a simulated research environment: An experimental study of scientific inference. *Quarterly Journal of Experimental Psychology,* 1977, *29,* 85–95.

Nelson, K. Structure and strategy in learning to talk. *Monograph of the Society for Research in Child Development,* 1973, *38* (102, Serial No. 149).

Nelson, T. F. *The effects of training in attention deployment on observing behavior in reflective and impulsive children.* Unpublished doctoral dissertation, University of Minnesota, 1968.

Nemiah, J. C. Anxiety: Signal, symptom, and syndrome. In S. Ariety & E. B. Brody (Eds.), *American handbook of psychiatry, vol. III: Adult clinical psychiatry* (2nd ed.). New York: Basic Books, 1974.

Nesbitt, R. E. L. Coincidental medical disorders. In D. N. Danforth (Ed.), *Obstetrics and Gynecology* (3rd ed.). New York: Harper & Row, 1977.

Newson, J., & Newson, E. *Infant care in an urban community.* London: Allen and Unwin, 1963.

Niemark, E. D. Intellectual development during adolescence. In F. D. Horowitz (Ed.), *Review of child development research* (Vol. 1). Chicago: University of Chicago Press, 1975. (a)

Niemark, E. D. Longitudinal development of formal operations and thought. *Genetic Psychology Monographs,* 1975, *91,* 171–225. (b)

Nilsson, L., Furuhjelm, M., Ingelman-Sundberg, A., & Wirsen, C. *A child is born* (2nd ed.). New York: Delacorte Press/Seymour Lawrence, 1977.

Noelting, R. *Stages and mechanisms in the development of the concept of proportion in the child and adolescent.* Paper presented at the Fifth Interdisciplinary Seminar on Piagetian Theory and its Implications for the Helping Profession, Los Angeles, February 1975.

Novak, J. D. *A theory of education.* Ithaca, N.Y.: Cornell University Press, 1977.

Nowicki, S., & Strickland, B. A locus of control scale for children. *Journal of Consulting and Clinical Psychology,* 1973, *40,* 148–154.

O'Connor, N., & Tizard, J. *The social problem of mental deficiency.* Elmsford, N.Y.: Pergamon Press, 1956.

Odom, R., Astor, E., & Cunningham, J. Adults thinking the way we think children think but children don't think that way: A study of perceptual salience and problem solving. *Bulletin of the Psychodynamic Society,* 1975, *6,* 545–548.

Offer, D. *The psychological world of the teenager: A study of normal adolescent boys.* New York: Basic Books, 1969.

Offer, D., & Offer, J. B. Normal adolescent males: The high school and college years. *Journal of the American College Health Association,* 1974, *22,* 917–924.

Offer, D., & Offer, J. B. *From teenage to young manhood.* New York: Basic Books, 1975.

Olson, D. R. On conceptual strategies. In J. S. Bruner, R. R. Olver, P. M. Greenfield et al (Eds.), *Studies in cognitive growth.* New York: Wiley, 1966.

Olver, R. R. *A developmental study of cognitive equivalence.* Unpublished doctoral dissertation, Radcliffe College, 1961.

Oppel, W. C., Harper, P. A., & Rider, R. V. The age of attaining bladder control. *Pediatrics,* 1968, *42,* 614–626.

Ornstein, P. A., Naus, M. J., & Liberty, C. Rehearsal and organizational processes in children's memory. *Child Development,* 1975, *46,* 818–830.

Ornstein, P. A., Naus, M. J., & Stone, B. P. Rehearsal training and developmental differences in memory. *Developmental Psychology,* 1977, *13,* 15–24.

Orwell, G. *The road to Wigan Pier.* New York: Penguin Books, 1976. (Originally published, 1937.)

Oshman, H. P., & Manosevitz, M. Father absence: The effects of stepfathers upon psychological development in males. *Developmental Psychology,* 1976, *12,* 479–480.

Palermo, D. S. More about less: A study of language comprehension. *Journal of Verbal Learning and Verbal Behavior,* 1973, *12,* 211–221.

Palermo, D. S. Still more about the comprehension of 'less'. *Developmental Psychology*, 1974, *10*, 827–829.

Parfitt, R. R. *The birth primer*. Philadelphia: Running Press, 1977.

Paris, S. G. Integration and inference in children's comprehension and memory. In F. Restle, R. Shiffrin, J. Castellan, H. Lindman, & D. Pisoni (Eds.), *Cognitive theory* (Vol. 1). Hillsdale, N.J.: Lawrence Erlbaum Associates, 1975.

Paris, S. G., and Lindauer, B. K. The role of inference in children's comprehension and memory for sentences. *Cognitive Psychology*, 1976, 217–227.

Paris, S. G., Lindauer, B. K., and Cox, G. L. The development of inferential comprehension. *Child Development*, 1977, *48*, 1728–1733.

Paris, S. G., & Upton, L. R. Children's memory for inferential relationships in prose. *Child Development*, 1976, *47*, 660–668.

Parke, R. D. The father of the child. *The Sciences*, 1979, *19*, 12–15. (a)

Parke, R. D. Perspectives on father-infant interaction. In J. D. Osofsky (Ed.), *Handbook of infant development*. New York: Wiley, 1979. (b)

Parke, R. D., & Collmer, W. C. Child abuse: An interdisciplinary analysis. In E. M. Hetherington (Ed.), *Review of child development research*. (Vol. 5). Chicago: University of Chicago Press, 1975.

Parke, R. D., & Duer, J. L. Schedule of punishment and inhibition of aggression. *Developmental Psychology*, 1972, *7*, 266–269.

Parke, R. D., & O'Leary, S. E. Father-infant interaction in the newborn period: Some findings, some observations, and some unresolved issues. In K. Riegel & J. Meacham (Eds.), *The developing individual in a changing world*. The Hague, Netherlands: Mouton, 1976.

Parke, R. D., O'Leary, S. E., & West, S. *Mother-father-newborn interaction: Effects of maternal medication, labor, and sex of infant*. Proceedings of the 80th Annual Convention of the American Psychological Association, 1972.

Parke, R. D., & Sawin, D. B. Fathering: It's a major role. *Psychology Today*, November 1977, pp. 108–112.

Parmelee, A. H., Sigman, M., Kopp, C. B., & Haber, A. Diagnosis of the infant at high risk for mental, motor and sensory handicaps. In T. D. Tjossem (Ed.), *Intervention strategies for high-risk infants and young children*. Baltimore: University Park Press, 1976.

Parsons, T. Family structure and the socialization of the child. In T. Parsons & R. F. Boles (Eds.), *Family socialization and interaction process*. New York: Free Press, 1955.

Parsons, T. Social structure and the development of personality: Freud's contribution to the integration of psychology and sociology. *Psychiatry*, 1958, *21*, 321–340.

Pascual-Leone, J. A. A mathematical model for the transition rule in Piaget's developmental stages. *Aeta Psychologia*, 1970, *63*, 301–345.

Pascual-Leone, J. A. *Cognitive development and cognitive style*. Lexington, Mass.: Heath, 1973.

Pascual-Leone, J. A. Compounds, confounds, and models in developmental psychology: A reply to confused critics. *Journal of Experimental Child Psychology*, 1978.

Patterson, C. J., & Kister, M. C. The development of listener skills for referential communication. In W. P. Dickson (Ed.), *Children's oral communication skills*. New York: Academic Press, 1981.

Patterson, C. J., & Massad, C. M. Facilitating referential communication among children: The listener as teacher. *Journal of Experimental Psychology*, 1980, *29*, 357–370.

Patterson, G. R., Littman, R. A., & Bricker, W. Assertive behavior in children: A step toward a theory of aggression. *Monographs of the Society for Research in Child Development*, 1967, *32*(5), 1–43.

Patterson, J. How popular is the paddle? *Phi Delta Kappan*, 1974, *56*, 707.

Pavlov, I. *Conditioned reflexes*. New York: Dover, 1927.

Penick, S. B., & Stunkard, A. J. Newer concepts of obesity. In N. Kiell (Ed.), *The psychology of obesity*. Springfield, Ill.: Charles C Thomas, 1973.

Peters, R. S. Moral development: A plea for pluralism. In T. Mischel (Ed.), *Cognitive development and epistemology*. New York: Academic Press, 1971.

Peterson, D. R. Behavior problems of middle childhood. *Journal of Consulting Psychology*, 1961, *25*, 205–209.

Phillips, E. L., Phillips, E. A., Fixsen, D. L., & Wolf, M. M. Achievement place: Behavior-shaping works for delinquents. *Psychology Today*, June 1973, pp. 75–79.

Piaget, J. *The child's conception of the world*. New York: Harcourt & Brace, 1929.

Piaget, J. *The moral judgment of the child*. London: Kegan Paul, 1932.

Piaget, J. *Play, dreams and imitation in childhood*. London: Heinemann, 1951. (a)

Piaget, J. The right to education in the modern world. In UNESCO (Ed.), *Freedom and culture*. New York: Columbia University Press, 1951. (b)

Piaget, J. *The origins of intelligence in children*. New York: International University Press, 1952. (a)

Piaget, J. *The child's conception of number*. New York: Humanities, 1952. (b)

Piaget, J. *The child's construction of reality*. London: Routledge & Kegan Paul, 1955.

Piaget, J. Logique et equilibre dans le comportements du sujet. In L. Apostel, B. Mandelbrot, & J. Piaget (Eds.), *Etudes d'epistemologie genetique, II: Logique et equilibre*. Paris: Presses Universitaires de France, 1957.

Piaget, J. Development and learning. In R. Ripple & R. Rockcastle (Eds.), *Piaget rediscovered*. Ithaca, N.Y.: Cornell University Press, 1964.

Piaget, J. *Six psychological studies*. New York: Random House, 1967. (a)

Piaget, J. *Biology and knowledge*. Chicago: University of Chicago Press, 1967. (b)

Piaget, J. *On the development of memory and identity.* Worcester, Mass.: Clark University Press, 1968.

Piaget, J. *The mechanisms of perception.* London: Routledge & Kegan Paul, 1969.

Piaget, J. Piaget's theory. In P. H. Mussen (Ed.), *Carmichael's manual of child psychology* (Vol. 1). New York: Wiley, 1970. (a)

Piaget, J. *The science of education and the psychology of the child.* New York: Viking Press, 1970. (b)

Piaget, J. A conversation with Jean Piaget. *Psychology Today,* 1970, *3*(12), 25–33. (c)

Piaget, J. Intellectual evolution from adolescence to adulthood. *Human Development,* 1972, *15*, 1–12.

Piaget, J. *The child and reality.* New York: Grossman, 1973. (a)

Piaget, J. *To understand is to invent: The future of education.* New York: Viking Press, 1973. (b)

Piaget, J., Grize, J. B., Szeminska, A., & Vinh Bang. *Epistemologie et psychologie de la fonction.* Paris: Presses Universitaires de France, 1968. (Vol. 23 of the Etudes d'Epistemologie Genetique series)

Piaget, J., & Inhelder, B. *Le development des quantites chez l'enfant.* Neuchatel, Switzerland: Delachaux et Niestle, 1941.

Piaget, J., & Inhelder, B. *The child's conception of space.* London: Routledge & Kegan Paul, 1956.

Piaget, J., & Inhelder, B. *Memory and intelligence.* New York: Basic Books, 1973.

Piaget, J., Inhelder, B., & Szeminska, A. *The child's conception of geometry.* New York: Harper, 1960.

Piaget, J., Sinclair, H., & Vinh Bang. *Epistemologie et psychologie de l'identite.* Paris: Presses Universitaires de France, 1968. (Vol. 24 of the Etudes d'Epistemologie Genetique series)

Pickler, E. Data on gross motor development of the infant. *Child Development and Care,* 1972, *3*, 297–310.

Pirsig, R. *Zen and the art of motorcycle maintenance.* New York: Bantam Books, 1975.

Pleck, J. H. Masculinity-femininity: Current and alternate paradigms. *Sex Roles,* 1975, *1*, 161–178.

Potter, M. C. On perceptual recognition. In J. S. Bruner, R. R. Olver, & P. M. Greenfield (Eds.), *Studies in cognitive growth.* New York: Wiley, 1966.

Powell, D. R. The interpersonal relationship between parents and caregivers in day-care settings. *American Journal of Orthopsychiatry,* 1978, *48*, 680–689.

Preyer, W. *Die Seele des Kindes.* Leipzig, Germany: T. Grieben, 1882.

Pritchard, J. A., & Macdonald, P. C. *Williams obstetrics* (15th ed.). New York: Appleton-Century-Crofts, 1976.

Provence, S., & Lipton, R. C. *Infants in institutions.* New York: International Universities Press, 1962.

Quay, H. C. Patterns of aggression, withdrawal, and immaturity. In H. C. Quay & J. S. Werry (Eds.), *Psychopathological disorders of childhood.* New York: Wiley, 1972.

Radin, N. Three degrees of maternal involvement in a preschool program: Impact on mothers and children. *Child Development,* 1972, *43*, 1355–1364.

Radin, N. The role of the father in cognitive, academic and intellectual development. In M. E. Lamb (Ed.), *The role of the father in child development.* New York: Wiley, 1976.

Rappaport, L. *Personality development: The chronology of experience.* Glenview, Ill.: Scott Foresman, 1972.

Raven, J. C. *Coloured progressive matrices: Sets A, A_b and B.* London: H. K. Lewis & Co., 1962.

Resnick, L. B. *Design of an early learning curriculum.* Pittsburgh: University of Pittsburgh Learning Research and Development Center, 1973. (LRDC Publication 1973/20) (a)

Resnick, L. B. (Ed.). Hierarchies in children's learning: A symposium. *Instructional Science,* 1973, *2*, 311–362. (b)

Resnick, L. B. Wang M. C., & Rosner, J. Adaptive education for young children: The primary education project. In M. C. Day & R. W. Parker (Eds.), *The preschool in action: Exploring early education programs* (2nd ed.). Boston: Allyn & Bacon, 1977.

Rheingold, H. L., & Cook, K. V. The contents of boys' and girl' rooms as an index of parents' behavior. *Child Development,* 1975, *46*, 459–463.

Rheingold, H. L., Gewirtz, J. L., & Ross, H. W. Social conditioning of vocalization in the infant. *Journal of Comparative and Physiological Psychology,* 1959, *52*, 68–73.

Ribble, M. A. *The rights of infants.* New York: Columbia University Press, 1943.

Rice, R. D. Neurophysiological development in premature infants following stimulation. *Developmental Psychology,* 1977, *13*, 69–76.

Rigney, J. C. *A developmental study of cognitive equivalence transformations and their use in the acquisition and processing of information.* Unpublished honors thesis, Radcliffe College Department of Social Relations, 1962.

Riles, W. *Administration of corporal punishment in the California public schools.* A report to the California legislature as requested by ACR–69. Sacramento: California State Department of Education, 1974.

Rimland, B. *Infantile autism.* Englewood Cliffs, N.J.: Prentice-Hall, 1964.

Rimm, D. C., & Somervill, J. W. *Abnormal psychology.* New York: Academic Press, 1979.

Robinson, H. B., & Robinson, N. M. *The mentally retarded child: A psychological approach.* New York: McGraw-Hill, 1965.

Robinson, W. P. The elaborated code in working-class language. *Language and Speech,* 1965, *8*, 243–252.

Rohwer, W. D., Jr., Amman, P. R., & Cramer, P. *Understanding intellectual development: Three approaches to theory and practice.* Hinsdale, Ill.: The Dryden Press, 1974.

Rosen, L. Selected aspects in the development of the mother's understanding of her mentally retarded child. *American Journal of Mental Deficiency,* 1955, *59,* 522.

Rosenberg, B. G., & Sutton-Smith, B. *Sex and identity.* New York: Holt, Rinehart & Winston, 1972.

Rosenfeld, A. H. *Parent education in a pediatric clinic* (United States Department of Health, Education and Welfare.) Washington, D.C.: U.S. Government Printing Office, 1979.

Rosenhan, D. Prosocial behavior of children. In W. W. Hartup (Ed.), *The young child: Reviews of research* (Vol. 2). Washington, D.C.: NAEYC, 1972.

Rosenthal, D. *Genetic theory and abnormal behavior.* New York: McGraw-Hill, 1970.

Ross, A. O. *Psychological disorders of children.* New York: McGraw-Hill, 1974.

Ross, H. L., & Sawhill, I. V. *Time of transition: The growth of families headed by women.* Washington, D.C.: The Urban Institute, 1975.

Rothbart, M. K. Birth order and mother-child interaction in an achievement situation. *Journal of Personality and Social Psychology,* 1971, *17,* 113–120.

Rothenberg, M. *Children with emerald eyes.* New York: Pocket Books, 1977.

Rousseau, J. J. *Emile: On education.* London: J. M. Dent & Sons, 1948.

Rousseau, J. J. *The Emile of Jean Jacques Rousseau.* (W. Boyd, Ed.). New York: Columbia Teacher's College, 1962. (Originally published, 1762.)

Rubenstein, J. L., & Hawes, C. Caregiving and infant behavior in day care and in homes. *Developmental Psychology,* 1979, *15,* 1–24.

Rubin, K., & Maioni, T. Play preference and its relationship to egocentrism, popularity, and classification skills in preschoolers. *Merrill-Palmer Quarterly,* 1975, *21,* 171–179.

Rubin, R. A., Rosenblatt, C., & Balow, B. Psychological and educational sequelae of prematurity. *Pediatrics,* 1973, *52,* 352–363.

Ruff, H. A., & Birch, H. G. Infant visual fixation: The effect of concentricity, curvilinearity, and number of directions. *Journal of Experimental Child Psychology,* 1974, *17,* 460–473.

Rugh, R., & Shettles, L. B. *From conception to birth: The drama of life's beginnings.* New York: Harper & Row, 1971.

Rutherford, E., & Mussen, P. Generosity in nursery school boys. *Child Development,* 1968, *39,* 755–765.

Rutter, M. Sex differences in children's responses to family stress. In E. J. Anthony & C. Koupernik (Eds.), *The child in his family.* New York: Wiley, 1970.

Rutter, M. *Helping troubled children.* New York: Plenum, 1975.

Rutter, M., & Lockyer, L. A five to fifteen year follow-up of infantile psychosis: 1. Description of sample. *British Journal of Psychiatry,* 1967, *113,* 1169–1182.

Sachs, J. S. Development of speech. In E. C. Cartevette & M. P. Friedman (Eds.), *Handbook of reception* (Vol. VII). New York: Academic Press, 1976.

Salapatek, P. *Visual investigation of geometric patterns in the human newborn.* Paper presented at the Society for Research in Child Development, Philadelphia, March 1973.

Salapatek, P. Stimulus determinants of attention in infants. In B. B. Wolman (Ed.), *International encyclopedia of psychiatry, psychology, psychoanalysis, and neurology* (Vol. 10). New York: Aesculepius Publishers, 1977.

Salapatek P., & Kessen, W. Visual scanning of triangles by the human newborn. *Journal of Experimental Child Psychology,* 1966, *3,* 155–167.

Salter, A. Birth without violence: A medical controversy. *Nursing Research,* 1978, *27,* 84–88.

Saltz, R. Effects of part-time "mothering" on IQ and SQ of young institutionalized children. *Child Development,* 1973, *44,* 166–170.

Saltz, E., & Johnson, J. Training for thematic fantasy play in culturally disadvantaged children: Preliminary results. *Journal of Educational Psychology,* 1974, *66,* 623–630.

Sameroff, A. J. The components of sucking in the human newborn. *Journal of Experimental Child Psychology,* 1968, *6,* 607–623.

Sameroff, A. J. Learning and adaptation in infancy. In H. W. Reese (Ed.), *Advances in child development and behavior* (Vol. 7). New York: Academic Press, 1972.

Sameroff, A. J., & Chandler, M. J. Reproductive risk and the continuum of caretaking casualty. In F. Horowitz (Ed.), *Review of child development research* (Vol. 4). Chicago: University of Chicago Press, 1975.

San Francisco Examiner and Chronicle, March 14, 1976.

Santrock, J. W. Maternal absence, sex-typing, and identification. *Developmental Psychology,* 1970, *2,* 262–274.

Sapon, S. Contingency management and programmed instruction in the preschool. *Audiovisual Instruction,* 1968, *13,* 980–982.

Sayegh, Y., & Dennis, W. The effects of supplementary experiences upon the behavioral development of infants in institutions. *Child Development,* 1965, *36,* 81–90.

Scardamalia, M. Information-processing capacity and the problem of horizontal decolage: A demonstration using combinatorial reasoning tasks. *Child Development,* 1977, *48,* 28–37.

Scarr, S., & Salapatek, P. Patterns of fear development during infancy. *Merrill-Palmer Quarterly,* 1970, *16,* 53–90.

Scarr, S., & Weinberg, R. A. IQ test performance of black children adopted by white families. *American Psychologist,* 1976, *31,* 726–739.

Scarr-Salapatek, S. B. Race, social class, and IQ. *Science,* 1971, *174,* 1285–1292.

Scarr-Salapatek, S. B. IQ: Methodology and other issues. *Science,* 1972, *178,* 229–240.

Scarr-Salapatek, S. B., & Williams, M. L. The effects of early stimulation on low-birth-weight infants. *Child Development,* 1973, *44,* 94–101.

Schaffer, H. R. *The growth of sociability.* Baltimore: Penguin Books, 1971.

Schaffer, H. R. *Mothering.* Cambridge, Mass.: Harvard University Press, 1977.

Schardein, J. L. *Drugs as teratogens.* Cleveland: CRC Press, 1976.

Scheinfeld, A. *Heredity in humans* (rev. ed.). Philadelphia: J. B. Lippincott, 1972.

Schenk, Q. F., & Schenk, E. L. *Pulling up roots.* Englewood Cliffs, N.J.: Prentice-Hall, 1978.

Schlesinger, B. *The one-parent family: Perspectives and annotated bibliography* (3rd ed.). Toronto: University of Toronto Press, 1975.

Schopler, E., & Reichler, R. J. Parents as cotherapists in the treatment of psychotic children. *Journal of Autism and Childhood Schizophrenia,* 1971, *1,* 87–102.

Schreibman, L., & Koegal, R. L. Autism: A defeatable horror. *Psychology Today,* March 1975, pp. 61–67.

Schulman, C. A. *Sleep patterns in newborn infants as a function of suspected neurological impairment of maternal heroin addiction.* Paper presented to the Meeting of the Society for Research in Child Development, April 1969.

Schuster, D., & Schuster, L. Speculative mechanisms affecting sex ratio. *Journal of Genetic Psychology,* 1972, *12,* 245–254.

Schvaneveldt, J., Freyer, M., & Ostler, R. Concepts of "goodness" and "badness" of parents as perceived by nursery school children. *Family Coordinator,* 1970, *19,* 98–103.

Scott, J. P., Stewart, J. M., & DeGhelt, V. J. Critical periods in the organization of systems. *Developmental Psychology,* 1974, *7,* 489–513.

Scrimshaw, N. S., & Gordon, J. E. (Eds.). *Malnutrition, learning and behavior: Proceedings.* Cambridge, Mass.: The MIT Press, 1968.

Sears, R. R. Relation of early socialization experiences on self-concepts and gender role in middle childhood. *Child Development,* 1970, *41,* 267–289.

Sears, R. R., Maccoby, E. E., & Levin, H. *Patterns of child rearing.* New York: Harper & Row, 1957.

Sears, R. R., Rau, L., & Alpert, R. *Identification and child rearing.* Stanford, Calif.: Stanford University Press, 1965.

Seligman, M. E. P. *Helplessness.* San Francisco: W. H. Freeman, 1975.

Selman, R. Social-cognitive understanding: A guide to educational and clinical practices. In T. Lickona (Ed.), *Moral development and behavior: Theory, research and social issues.* New York: Holt, Rinehart & Winston, 1976.

Selman, R., & Byrne, D. A structural-developmental analysis of levels of role taking in middle childhood. *Child Development,* 1974, *45,* 803–806.

Seltzer, C. C., & Mayer, J. Body build and obesity: Who are the obese? *Journal of American Medical Association,* 1964, *189,* 677–684.

Seraficca, F. C. The development of attachment behaviors: An organismic-developmental perspective. *Human Development,* 1978, *21,* 119–140.

Shantz, C. V. The development of social cognition. In E. M. Hetherington (Ed.), *Review of child development research* (Vol. V). Chicago: University of Chicago Press, 1975.

Shapiro, A. G. Extraovular prostaglandin F_{2a} for early mid-trimester abortion. *American Journal of Obstetric Gynecology,* 1975, *121,* 333.

Shapiro, E., & Biber, B. The education of young children: A developmental-interaction approach. *Teachers College Record,* 1972, *74,* (No. 1).

Shapiro, L. P. (Ed.). Family interaction and the handicapped child. Special issue of the *Journal of the Division for Early Childhood,* 1979, *1.*

Shatz, M., & Gelman, R. The development of communication skills: Modifications in the speech of young children as a function of listener. *Monographs of the Society for Research in Child Development,* 1973, *38* (5, Serial No. 152).

Shearer, D. E., & Shearer, M. S. The Portage Project: A model for early childhood intervention. In T. D. Tjossem (Ed.), *Intervention strategies for high-risk infants and young children.* Baltimore: University Park Press, 1976.

Sheppard, J. L. Conservation of part and whole in the acquisition of class inclusion. *Child Development,* 1973, *44,* 380–383.

Sheppard, J. L. Compensation and combinatorial systems in the acquisition and generalization of conservation. *Child Development,* 1974, *45,* 717–730.

Shirley, M. M. *The first two years.* Minneapolis: University of Minnesota Press, 1933.

Shotwell, J. M., Wolf, D., & Gardner, H. Exploring early symbolization: styles of achievement. In B. Sutton-Smith (Ed.), *Play and learning.* New York: Gardner Press, 1979. (Distributed by Halsted Press, Division of John Wiley & Sons.)

Shultz, T. R. Development of the appreciation of riddles. *Child Development,* 1974, *45,* 100–105.

Shultz, T. R. A cognitive-developmental analysis of humor. In A. J. Chapman & H. C. Foot (Eds.), *Humor and laughter: Theory research and applications.* London: Wiley, 1976.

Shultz, T. R., & Horibe, F. Development of the appreciation of verbal jokes. *Developmental Psychology,* 1974, *10,* 13–20.

Siegel, L. S. The cognitive basis of the comprehension and production of relational terminology. *Journal of Experimental Child Psychology,* 1977, *24,* 40–52.

Siegel, L. S. The relationship of language and thought in the preoperational child. A reconsideration of nonverbal alternatives to Piagetian tasks. In L. S. Siegel and C. J. Brainerd (Eds.), *Alternatives to Piaget: Critical essays on the theory.* New York: Academic Press, 1978.

Siegel, L. S., McCabe, A. E., Brand, J., & Mathews, J. Evidence for the understanding of class inclusion in preschool children: Linguistic factors and training effects. *Child Development,* 1978, *49,* 589–603.

Siegler, R. S. Three aspects of cognitive development. *Cognitive Psychology,* 1976, *8,* 481–520.

Siegler, R. S., & Liebert, R. M. Effects of presenting relevant rules and complete feedback on the conservation of liquid quantity. *Developmental Psychology,* 1972, *7,* 133–138.

Siegler, R. S., & Liebert, R. M. Acquisition of formal scientific reasoning by 10- and 13-year-olds: Designing a factorial experiment. *Developmental Psychology,* 1975, *11,* 401–402.

Sigel, I. E. The distancing hypothesis: A causal hypothesis for the acquisition of representational thought. In M. J. Jones (Ed.), *The effects of early experience.* Miami, Fla.: University of Miami Press, 1970.

Sigel, I. E., & Cocking, R. R. *Cognitive development from childhood to adolescence: A constructive perspective.* New York: Holt, Rinehart & Winston, 1977.

Silvian, L. *Understanding diabetes.* New York: Monarch Press, 1977.

Simon, W., Berger, A. S., & Gagnon, J. H. Beyond anxiety and fantasy: The coital experiences of college youth. *Journal of Youth and Adolescence,* 1972, *1,* 203–222.

Sinclair, D. *Human growth after birth* (3rd ed.). London: Oxford University Press, 1978.

Sinclair, H. Recent Piagetian research in learning studies. In M. Schwebel & J. Raph (Eds.), *Piaget in the classroom.* New York: Basic Books, 1973.

Sinclair-de Zwart, H. Recent developments in genetic epistemology. *Genetic Epistemologist,* 1977, *VI*(4), 1–4.

Singer, J. L. *The child's world of make-believe: Experimental studies of imaginative play.* New York: Academic Press, 1973.

Skeels, H. M. Adult status of children with contrasting early life experiences. *Monographs of the Society for Research in Child Development,* 1966, *31*(3, Whole No. 105).

Skinner, B. F. *Walden two.* New York: Macmillan, 1948.

Skinner, B. F. *Science and human behavior.* New York: Macmillan, 1953.

Skinner, B. F. *Verbal behavior.* New York: Appleton-Century-Crofts, 1957.

Skinner, B. F. *The technology of teaching.* Englewood Cliffs, N.J.: Prentice-Hall, 1968.

Skinner, B. F. *Contingencies of reinforcement.* Englewood Cliffs, N.J.: Prentice-Hall, 1969.

Slobin, D. I. Children and language: They learn the same way all around the world. In E. M. Hetherington & R. D. Parke (Eds.), *Contemporary readings in child psychology.* New York: McGraw-Hill, 1977.

Smart, M. S., & Smart, R. C. *Adolescents: Developments and relationships.* New York: Macmillan, 1973.

Smedslund, J. The acquisition of substance and weight in children: II. External reinforcement of conservation of weight and the operations of addition and subtraction. *Scandinavian Journal of Psychology,* 1961, *2,* 71–84.

Smilanski, S. *The effects of sociodramatic play on disadvantaged children: Preschool children.* New York: Wiley, 1968.

Smolensky, J. *A guide to child growth and development* (2nd ed.). Dubuque, Iowa: Kendall/Hunt Publishing Company, 1977.

Solnit, A. J., & Stark, M. H. *Mourning and the birth of a defective child.* In R. S. Essler, A. Freud, H. Hartmann, & M. Kris (Eds.), *The psychoanalytic study of the child* (Vol. XVI). New York: International Universities Press, 1961.

Sorensen, R. C. *Adolescent sexuality in contemporary America.* New York: World, 1973.

Spanier, G. B. *Human sexuality in a changing society.* Minneapolis, Minn.: Burgess Publishing, 1979.

Spelke, E., Zelazo, P., Kagan, J., & Kotelchuck, M. Father interaction and separation protest. *Developmental Psychology,* 1973, *9,* 83–90.

Spinetta, J. J. The dying child's awareness of death. *Psychological Bulletin,* 1974, *81,* 256–260.

Spitz, R. A. Hospitalism: An inquiry into the genesis of psychiatric conditioning in early childhood. In D. Fenschel et al. (Eds.), *Psychoanalytic studies of the child* (Vol. 1). New York: International Universities Press, 1946.

Spock, B. *Baby and child care.* New York: Pocket Books, 1946.

Spock, B. A. Common-sense book of baby and child care (rev. ed.). New York: Hawthorne, 1968.

Spock, B. A. Common-sense book of baby and child care (rev. ed.). New York: Pocket Books, 1976.

Sroufe, L. A. Attachment and the roots of competence. *Human Nature,* 1978, *1,* 50–57.

Staats, A. W., & Staats, C. K. *Complex human behavior.* New York: Holt, Rinehart & Winston, 1963.

Stein, A. H., & Friedrich, L. K. Impact of television on children and youth. In E. M. Hetherington (Ed.), *Review of child development research* (Vol. V). Chicago: University of Chicago Press, 1975.

Stein, S. B. *About dying: An open family book for parents and children together.* New York: Walker and Company, 1974.

Stein, Z. A., & Susser, M. Mutability of intelligence and epidemiology of mild mental transitions. *Review of Educational Research,* 1970, *40,* 29–67.

Stein, Z. A., Susser, M. W., Saenger, G., & Marolla, F. *Famine and human development: The dutch hunger winter 1944–1945.* New York: Oxford University Press, 1975.

Steinglanz, S., & Serkin, L. Sex-role stereotyping in children's television programs. *Developmental Psychology,* 1974, *10,* 710–715.

Stern, D. *The first relationship: Infant and mother.* Cambridge, Mass.: Harvard University Press, 1977.

Stone, L. *The family, sex and marriage in England, 1500–1800.* New York: Harper & Row, 1977.

Stone, L. J., & Church, J. *Childhood and adolescence: A psychology of the growing person* (4th ed.). New York: Random House, 1979.

Stott, D. H. The child's hazards in utero. In J. G. Howells (Ed.), *Modern perspectives in international child psychiatry.* New York: Brunner/Mazel, 1971.

Stott, L. H., & Ball, R. S. Consistency and change in ascendance-submission in the social interaction of children. *Child Development,* 1957, *28,* 259–272.

Strauss, M., Lessen-Firestone, J., Starr, R., & Ostrea, E. Behavior of narcotics-addicted newborns. *Child Development,* 1975, *46,* 887–893.

Sullivan, W. Boys and girls are now maturing earlier. *The New York Times,* January 24, 1971, pp. 1; 36.

Suomi, S. J., & Harlow, H. F. The role of reason in peer relationships in rhesus monkeys. In M. Lewis & L. A. Rosenblum (Eds.), *Friendship and peer relations.* New York: Wiley, 1975.

Surwillo, W. W. Speed of movement in relation to period of electroencephalogram in normal children. *Parapsychology,* 1974, *11,* 491–496.

Sutton-Smith, B. A developmental structural account of riddles. In B. Kirschenblatt—Gimblett (Ed.), *Speech play: Research and resources for studying linguistic creativity.* Philadelphia: University of Pennsylvania Press, 1976.

Sutton-Smith, B. *Piaget, play and cognition, revisited.* Paper presented at the Annual Meeting of the Jean Piaget Society, Philadelphia, 1979. (a)

Sutton-Smith, B. (Ed.). *Play and learning.* New York: Gardner Press, 1979. (Distributed by Halsted Press, division of John Wiley & Sons.) (b)

Sutton-Smith, B., & Rosenberg, B. G. Age changes in the effects of ordinal position on sex-role identification. *Journal of Genetic Psychology,* 1965, *107,* 61–73.

Sutton-Smith, B., & Rosenberg, B. G. Sibling consensus on power tactics. *Journal of Genetic Psychology,* 1968, *112,* 63–72.

Sutton-Smith, B., & Rosenberg, B. G. *The sibling.* New York: Holt, Rinehart & Winston, 1970.

Swanson, H. D. *Human reproduction: Biology and social change.* New York: Oxford University Press, 1977.

Swanson, H. D. *Human reproduction: Biology and social change* (2nd ed.). New York: Oxford University Press, 1977.

Swift, J. W. Effects of early group experience: The nursery, school and day nursery. In M. L. Hoffman & L. Hoffman (Eds.), *Review of child development research* (Vol. 1). New York: Russell Sage Foundation, 1964.

Tanner, J. M. *Growth at adolescence* (2nd ed.). Philadelphia: Davis, 1962.

Tanner, J. M. The adolescent growth spurt and developmental age. In G. A. Harrison, J. S. Werner, J. M. Tanner, & N. A. Barnicot (Eds.), *Human biology: An introduction to human evolution, variation, and growth.* Oxford: Clarendon, 1964.

Tanner, J. M. Early maturation in man. *Scientific American,* 1968, *218,* 21–27.

Tanner, J. M. Physical growth. In P. H. Mussen (Ed.), *Carmichael's manual of child psychology* (Vol. 1; 3rd ed.). New York: Wiley, 1970.

Tanner, J. M. Sequence, tempo, and individual variation in the growth and development of boys and girls aged twelve to sixteen. *Daedelus,* 1971, *100,* 907–930.

Tanner, J. M. Growing up. *Scientific American,* 1973, *229,* 35–43.

Tanner, J. M., Whitehouse, R. M., & Marshall, W. A. *Assessment of skeletal maturity and prediction of adult height, TW2 method.* London: Oxford University Press, 1975.

Tanzer, D., & Block, J. L. *Why natural childbirth: A psychologist's report on the benefits to mothers, fathers and babies.* New York: Schocken Books, 1976.

Tapp, J., & Kohlberg, L. Developing senses of law and legal justice. *Journal of Social Issues,* 1971, *27,* 65–91.

Taub, H. B., Goldstein, K. M., & Caputo, D. V. Indices of neonatal prematurity as discriminators of development in middle childhood. *Child Development,* 1977, *48,* 797–805.

Tavormina, J. B. Behavior disorders of childhood. In W. H. Holtzman (Ed.), *Introductory psychology in depth: Developmental topics.* New York: Harper's College Press, 1978.

Tavormina, J. B., Luscomb, R., & Walker, J. *Parents of physically handicapped children assess the quality of their family functioning.* Paper presented at the meeting of the Southeastern Psychological Association, Atlanta, 1975.

Taylor, R. G. Personality traits and discrepant achievement: A review. *Journal of Counseling Psychology,* 1964, *11,,* 76–81.

Terman, L. M., & Merrill, M. A. *Measuring intelligence: A guide to the administration of the new revised Stanford-Binet tests of intelligence.* Cambridge, Mass.: Houghton Mifflin, 1973.

Terman, L. M. & Merrill, M. A. *Stanford-Binet intelligence scale.* Boston: Houghton Mifflin, 1973.

Thomas, A., Chess, S., & Birch, H. G. The origin of personality. *Scientific American,* 1970, *223,* 102–109.

Thomas, E. B., Becker, P. T., & Freese, M. P. Individual patterns of mother-infant interaction. In G. P. Beckett (Ed.), *Observing behavior.* Baltimore: University Park Press, 1978.

Thomas, R. M. *Comparing theories of child development.* Belmont, Calif.: Wordsworth, 1979.

Thompson, H. Physical growth. In L. Carmichael (Ed.), *Manual of child psychology* (2nd ed.). New York: Wiley, 1954.

Tinbergen, N. *The study of instinct.* London: Oxford University Press, 1951.

Tjossem, T. D. (Ed.), *Intervention strategies for high-risk infants and young children.* Baltimore: University Park Press, 1976.

Torrance, E. P. *Rewarding creative behavior.* Englewood Cliffs, N.J.: Prentice-Hall, 1965.

Torrance, E. P., & Myers, R. E. *Creative learning and teaching.* New York: Dodd, Mead, 1972.

Torrance, E. P., & Torrance, J. P. *Is creativity teachable?* Bloomington, Ind.: Phi Delta Kappan, 1973.

Trabasso, T., & Foellinger, D. B. Seeing, hearing, and doing: A developmental study of memory for actions. *Journal of Experimental Child Psychology,* 1978.

Tschirgi, J. E. Sensible reasoning: A hypothesis about hypotheses. *Child Development,* 1980, *51,* 1–10.

Turiel, E. Conflict and transition in adolescent moral development. *Child Development,* 1974, *45,* 14–29.

Turnbull, C. M. *The mountain people.* New York: Wiley, 1965.

Turnbull, C. M. *The mountain people.* New York: Simon and Schuster, 1972.

Turner, R. K., & Taylor, P. D. Conditioning treatment of nocturnal enuresis in adults: Preliminary findings. *Behavioral Research and Therapy,* 1974, *12,* 41–52.

United Nations Education, Scientific and Cultural Organization. Final report from the meeting on Preschool Education as the First Phase of Life-Long Education, Paris, March 1976.

United States Bureau of the Census. *Population profile of the United States: 1979* (Current population reports, Series P–20, No. 350). Washington, D.C.: U.S. Government Printing Office, 1980.

United States Department of Commerce, Bureau of the Census. *Population profile of the United States: 1978, population characteristics* (Current population reports, Series P–20, No. 336). Washington, D.C.: U.S. Government Printing Office, 1979.

United States Department of Health, Education and Welfare. *The health consequences of smoking.* Washington, D.C.: U.S. Government Printing Office, 1973.

United States Department of Health, Education and Welfare. *Smoking and health.* Washington, D.C.: U.S. Government Printing Office, 1979.

U.S. Department of Labor, Women's Bureau. *Working mothers and their children.* Washington, D.C.: U.S. Government Printing Office, 1977.

The U.S. fact book. New York: Grosset and Dunlop, 1977.

Utech, D. A., & Having, K. L. Parents and peers as competing influences in the decisions of children at different ages. *Journal of Social Psychology,* 1969, *78,* 267–274.

Uzgiris, I. C. Situational generality of conservation. *Child Development,* 1964, *35,* 831–841.

Vandell, D. L., Wilson, K. S., & Buchanon, N. R. *Peer interaction in the first year of life: An examination of its structure, content, and sensitivity to toys.* Unpublished manuscript, 1979.

Van Wagenen, R. K., Meyerson, L., Kerr, N. J., & Mahoney, K. Field trials of a new procedure for toilet training. *Journal of Experimental Child Psychology,* 1969, *8,* 147–159.

Vasta, R. *Studying children: An introduction to research methods.* San Francisco: W. H. Freeman, 1979.

Vaz, E. W. Delinquency and the youth culture: Upper- and middle-class boys. *Journal of Criminal Law, Criminology, and Police Science,* 1969, *60,* 33–46.

Vygotsky, L. *Thought and language.* Cambridge, Mass.: The MIT Press, 1962.

Wachs, T., Uzgiris, I. C., & Hunt, J. McV. Cognitive development in infants of different age levels and from different environmental backgrounds: An exploratory investigation. *Merrill-Palmer Quarterly,* 1971, 17: 283–317.

Walker, L. J. Cognitive and perspective-taking prerequisites for moral development. *Child Development,* 1980, *51,* 131–139.

Wallach, M. A., & Kogan, N. *Modes of thinking in young children.* New York: Holt, Rinehart & Winston, 1965.

Wason, P. C., & Johnson-Laird, P. N. *Psychology of reasoning: Structure and content.* Cambridge, Mass.: Harvard University Press, 1972.

Watson, E. H., & Lawrey, G. H. *Growth and development of children* (5th ed.). Chicago: Yearbook Medical Publishers, 1967.

Watson, J. B. . *Psychological care of infant and child.* New York: Norton, 1928.

Watson, J. D. *The double helix.* New York: Atheneum, 1968.

Watson, J. S. Smiling, cooing and "the game." *Merrill-Palmer Quarterly,* 1973, *18,* 323–339.

Weatherley, D. Self-perceived rate of physical maturation and personality in late adolescence. *Child Development,* 1964, *35,* 1197–1210.

Wechsler, D. Intelligence defined and undefined: A relativistic appraisal. *American Psychologist,* 1975, *30,* 135–139.

Weikert, D. P. *Preschool intervention: Preliminary results of the Perry Preschool Project.* Ann Arbor, Mich.: Campus Publishers, 1967.

Weikert, D. P. *Development of effective preschool programs: A report on the results of the High/Scope-Ypsilanti Preschool Projects.* Paper presented at the High/Scope Educational Research Foundation Conference: Using the High/Scope Cognitive Approach to Learning in Infant, Preschool and Early Elementary Education, Ann Arbor, Mich., May 1973.

Weil, W. B. Infantile obesity. In M. Winick (Ed.), *Childhood obesity.* New York: Wiley, 1975.

Weiner, B., & Peters, N. A cognitive-developmental analysis of achievement and moral judgments. *Developmental Psychology,* 1973, *9,* 290–309.

Weiner, I. The generation gap: Fact and fancy. *Adolescence,* 1977, *12,* 155–166.

Weisler, A., & McCall, R. B. Exploration and play. *American Psychologist,* 1976, *31,* 492–508.

Weiss, G., & Hechtman, L. The hyperactive child syndrome. *Science,* 1979, *205,* 1348–1354.

Weiss, R. The contribution of an organization of single parents to the well-being of its members. *Family Coordinator,* 1973, *22,* 321–326.

Wellman, H. M. Tip-of-the-tongue and feeling-of-knowing experiences: A developmental study of memory-monitoring. *Child Development,* 1977, *48,* 13–21.

Welsh, R. S. Severe parental punishment and delinquency. *Journal of Clinical Child Psychology,* 1974, *3.*

Welsh, R. S. Severe parental punishment and delinquency: A developmental theory. *Journal of Clinical Child Psychology,* 1976, *5,* 17–21.

Werner, P. Education of selected movement patterns of preschool children. *Perceptual Motor Skills,* 1974, *39,* 795–798.

Wertheimer, M. Psychomotor coordination of auditory-visual space at birth. *Science,* 1961, *134,* 1962.

Wetherford, M. J., & Cohen, L. B. Developmental changes in infant visual preferences for novelty and familiarity. *Child Development,* 1973, *44,* 416–424.

White, B. L. An experimental approach to the effects of environment on early human behavior. In J. P. Hill (Ed.), *Minnesota Symposium on Child Psychology* (Vol. 1). Minneapolis: University of Minnesota Press, 1967.

White, B. L. *Human infants: Experience and psychological development.* Englewood Cliffs, N.J.: Prentice-Hall, 1971.

White, B. L. *The first three years of life.* Englewood Cliffs, N.J.: Prentice-Hall, 1975.

White, B. L. *Experience and environment: Major influences on the development of the young child.* Englewood Cliffs, N.J.: Prentice-Hall, 1978.

White, B. L., Castle, P., & Held, R. M. Observations on the development of visually directed reading. *Child Development,* 1964, *35,* 349–364.

White, B. L., & Held, R. M. Plasticity of sensorimotor development in the human infant. In J. Rosenblith & W. Allensmith (Eds.), *The causes of behavior: Readings in child development and educational psychology.* Boston: Allyn & Bacon, 1966.

White, B. L. & Watts, J. C. *Experience and environment: Major influences on the development of the young child.* Vol. 1. Englewood Cliffs, N.J.: Prentice-Hall, 1973.

White, E., Elsom, B., & Prawat, R. Children's conception of death. *Child Development,* 1978, *49,* 307–310.

White, K. M., & Speisman, J. C. *Adolescence.* Monterey, Calif.: Brooks/Cole, 1977.

Whiting, B. B., & Whiting, J. W. M. *Children of six cultures: A psycho-cultural analysis.* Cambridge, Mass.: Harvard University Press, 1975.

Whitt, J. U., & Prentice, N. M. Cognitive processes in the development of children's enjoyment and comprehension of joking riddles. *Developmental Psychology,* 1977, *13,* 129–136.

Whittemore, F. One family conquers gang war. *Parade,* May 6, 1981.

Wichware, D. S. (Ed.), Amniocentesis: For whom by whom? *Patient Care,* 1977, *11*(20), 16–61.

Wickes, F. G. *The inner world of childhood.* Englewood Cliffs, N.J.: Prentice-Hall, 1966.

Williams, F., Hopper, R., & Natalicio, D. S. *The sounds of children.* Englewood Cliffs, N.J.: Prentice-Hall, 1977.

Williams, J., Bennett, S., & Best, D. Awareness and expression of sex stereotypes in young children. *Developmental Psychology,* 1972, *6,* 14–25.

Williams, J., & Stith, M. *Middle childhood: Behavior and development.* New York: Macmillan, 1974.

Wilson, R. S. Twins: Early mental development. *Science,* 1972, *175,* 914–917.

Winick, M. *Malnutrition and brain development.* New York: Oxford University Press, 1976.

Wishart, J. G., & Bower, T. G. R. *The comprehension of spatial relations in infancy.* Unpublished manuscript, University of Edinburgh, 1977.

Wittes, G., & Radin, N. *Ypsilanti home and school handbooks: Helping your child to learn—The reinforcement approach.* San Rafael, Calif.: Dimensions Publishing, 1969.

Wolfensberger, W. *The principle of normalization in human services.* Toronto: National Institute on Mental Retardation, 1972.

Wolff, P. H. Observations on the early development of smiling. In B. M. Foss (Ed.), *Determinants of infant behavior.* New York: Wiley, 1963.

Wolff, P. H. The causes, controls and organization of behavior in the neonate. *Psychological Issues,* 1966, *5*(1, Whole No. 17).

Wolff, P. H. The natural history of crying and other vocalizations in early infancy. In B. M. Foss (Ed.), *Determinants of infant behavior* (Vol. 4). London: Methuen, 1969.

Wolff, P. H. Heredity or environment? In R. I. Feinbloom (Ed.), *Pregnancy, birth and the newborn baby.* New York: Delta, 1979.

Wolman, B. W. (Ed.). *Manual of child psychopathology.* New York: McGraw-Hill, 1972.

Wood, B. S. *Children and communication: Verbal and nonverbal language development.* Englewood Cliffs, N.J.: Prentice-Hall, 1976.

Woodward, K. L., & Malamud, P. The parent gap. *Newsweek,* September 22, 1975, p. 50.

Wright, H. F. *Recording and analyzing child behavior.* New York: Harper & Row, 1960.

Yankelovich, D. *The new morality: A profile of American youth in the 70s.* New York: McGraw-Hill, 1974.

Yarrow, L. J. Attachment and dependency: A developmental perspective. In J. L. Gewirtz (Ed.), *Attachment and dependency.* Washington, D.C.: Winston, 1972.

Yates, A. J. *Behavior therapy.* New York: Wiley, 1970.

Yogman, M. J., Dixon, S., Tronick, E., Als, H., & Brazelton, T. B. *The goals and structure of face-to-face interaction between infants and fathers.* Paper presented at the biennial meeting of the Society for Research in Child Development, New Orleans, April 1977.

Youniss, J. Classification schemes in relation to class inclusion before and after training. *Human Development,* 1971, *14,* 171–183.

Youniss, J. Another perspective on social cognition. In A. Pick (Ed.), *Minnesota Symposium on Child Psychology* (Vol. 9). Minneapolis: University of Minnesota Press, 1975.

Zahn-Waxler C., Radke-Yarrow M., & King, R. A. Child-rearing and children's prosocial initiations toward victims of distress. *Child Development* 1979, *50,* 319–330.

Zelazo, N. A., Zelazo P. R., & Kolb S. Walking in the newborn. *Science,* 1972, *176,* 314–315.

Zelnick, M., & Kantner, J. F. The probability of premarital intercourse. *Social Science Research,* 1972, *1,* 335–341.

Zelnick, M., & Kantner, J. F. Sexual and contraceptive experiences of young unmarried women in the United States, 1976 and 1971. *Family Planning Perspectives,* 1977, *9,* 55–73.

Zelniker, T., & Jeffrey, W. Reflective and impulsive children: Strategies of information processing underlying differences in problem solving. *Monographs of the Society for Research in Child Development,* 1976, *41,* 1–59.

Zelniker, T., & Oppenheimer, L. Effects of different training methods on perceptual learning in impulsive children. *Child Development,* 1976, *47,* 492–497.

Zilbach, J. I. Family development. In J. Marmor (Ed.), *Modern psychoanalysis.* New York: Basic Books, 1968.

Zimmerman, D. R. Your family's health. *Ladies' Home Journal,* October 1976.

Zussman, J. S. U. *Situational determinants of parental behavior.* Dissertation submitted to the Department of Psychology, Stanford University, 1977.

Name Index

Subject Index